RPG:
REPORT PROGRAM GENERATOR

JOYCE CURRIE LITTLE

Community College of Baltimore

PRENTICE-HALL, INC.

Englewood Cliffs, New Jersey

To John

Current printing (last digit):

10 9 8 7 6 5 4 3 2 1

13-783365-2

Library of Congress Catalog Card No. 72-137987

Printed in the United States of America

PREFACE

This book is intended to serve as an introduction to RPG, the Report Program Generator computer programming system. Although RPG was used as early as 1961 on the IBM 1401 computer, it made its greatest gains in popularity after revision for its 1964 release on the IBM SYSTEM/360. RPG II was announced in 1969 as the major programming language for the IBM SYSTEM/3.

Small computers have begun to replace unit record data processing equipment all over the country. In most of these small job shops, RPG is the language being used, not only because it is designed to duplicate the logic of unit record equipment, but also because the only alternative programming system on some of the machinery being used is the assembler language, which requires much more time to learn. RPG can be learned in a short time, and can be used on relatively inexpensive equipment, to produce quick and easy business reports. Systems originally designed for unit record equipment can be easily transformed, in RPG, to third generation computer usage. RPG is therefore especially popular on the IBM SYSTEM/360, Model 20, and the UNIVAC 9200, both of which have replaced unit record equipment in many small job shops. The IBM SYSTEM/3, although using a completely different, 96-column, *mini-card* for program and data entry, offers RPG II, an extension of the basic RPG language. The IBM 1130, usually found in engineering or scientific environments, has RPG; this enables such equipment to be used for business reports without the need to learn FORTRAN, APL, or the assembler language. In larger job shops, where the IBM SYSTEM/360, Models 25, 30, and up are used, RPG is perhaps less well known, but is being used for many programming tasks in spite of the fact that COBOL is also available on that equipment. People who are moving from small installations to large ones are taking their RPG skills with them; it is therefore beginning to be used more and more as a supplement to COBOL as knowledge about its value spreads. IBM-compatible RPG is also available on the larger UNIVAC 9000-series computers, on the RCA Spectra-70, and has recently been announced for the GE-120. Report generator languages using different forms and coding are available on other equipment, but are not discussed in this book.

I have attempted to use an old-fashioned method of teaching in organizing this material into a text: *Tell them what you are going to teach them, teach them, then tell them what you taught them.* The questions usually asked as review at the end of a lesson, are, in this book, at the beginning. The questions point out what is important so that the student will know what to look for in the lesson; they serve as an aid to independent study by helping the student decide what he may skip and when. Only the material needed for a report of the lesson's difficulty is presented in the lesson. Extraneous matter not vital to that type of report is omitted until a problem arises which needs it. There is therefore a lot of repetition; some lessons build upon a topic barely mentioned in a former lesson. There are 30 lessons; exercises are at the back of most lessons and answers may be written in the book. Each set of 3 lessons is a section; at the end of each section, there are either projects to do or programs to write. Several programs from each section should be written, punched, tested on a computer, and completely debugged. Some of them in later sections offer additional challenge for those who have more background in mathematics or accounting.

This book should serve to guide the student through the necessary steps in using a computer to prepare business reports. Enough introductory material is presented in Section 1 through Section 7 to get him familiar with the punch card and its design, the report form, the type of lines on the form, the control of the printer, and the preparation of data in making various types of reports. The student should progress from designing the card to punching it, from designing the report to writing the program to produce it. He learns the steps to follow in using the computer to solve a problem, and is guided step-by-step and line-by-line in writing the first few programs. The reports done in the book progress in difficulty—from a simple list, to one with a heading, to one with a total line, to one with many calculations, to one with a control break, . . . etc. Table design, storage, and retrieval is covered in Section 8. The use of data files on magnetic tape, including file updating and maintenance, is discussed in Section 9. The more advanced techniques of branching, looping, exception lines, and subroutines are covered in Section 10.

The book is suitable for the data processing curriculum in many of the two-year community and junior colleges. Business schools, computer institutes, and vocational and technical schools may also find that it suits their curriculum needs. The unit record operator or wiring technician should find the book helpful as a semi-programmed guide to the language; it may be used in an on-the-job or evening training program to enable him to convert his knowledge to computer concepts. The computer programmer who already knows another programming language, such as **COBOL**, may use it as a quick way to orient himself to the potential of RPG as a supplementary computer aid.

In the data processing department of a two-year college, the book should be used with a teacher in a lecture and laboratory/conference environment, with computer equipment available. Reference manuals from the computer manufacturer should be available, as should flow charting templates and RPG specifications forms. The book could be used in a first programming course, sometimes called INTRODUCTION TO COMPUTER PROGRAMMING, taken either concurrently with, or after, INTRODUCTION TO DATA PROCESSING. It is designed for a one-semester course, although there is more material in the 30 lessons than can comfortably be covered in a 15-week semester. Its use could be continued into a second semester, with the sections on magnetic tape, tables, and branching and logic change given then, leading to the introduction of the assembler language through RPG subroutines. When used in this manner, the book could be supplemented in the second semester with a book such as Cashman and Shelly's *Introduction to Computer Programming, IBM SYSTEM/360, Assembler Language,* Anaheim Publishing Co. or Saxon, Englander, and Englander's *SYSTEM/360 Programming, a Self-Instructional Manual*, Prentice-Hall, Inc.

Other data processing schools are blending RPG into a course called PUNCH CARD DATA PROCESSING, which was, formerly, all unit record equipment operation and wiring. This book could be used to replace the report-producing activity of the electric accounting machines, the IBM 402, 403, and 407. When used in this manner, this book should be supplemented by a workbook or projects manual, such as Feingold's *Fundamentals of Punch Card Data Processing,* Wm. C. Brown and Co., or Cashman and Keys' *Practical Projects in Data Processing,* Anaheim Publishing Co.

Students using this book need not have previous academic backgrounds in data processing, mathematics, or accounting. They should be able to add, subtract, multiply and divide *easily,* and have a strong motivation to learn. The student need not be young and brilliant; he may be mature, patient, methodical. In some cases, the methodical slower student produces computer programs, completely debugged, in less time than the over-zealous young "brain" who is often careless in his haste to get his problem onto the computer. RPG is within the grasp of the eighteen-year-old with persistence as well as the forty-five-year-old with practical experience, both of whom wish to advance themselves. After mastering most of the programs in this book, the student should be skilled enough to begin to handle reasonably difficult data processing tasks. He should be comfortable with the RPG language, and should be able to use reference manuals in order to continue learning about data processing.

All programs presented in this text were tested on an IBM SYSTEM/360 computer—some on the TOS, tape operating system, and some on the DOS, disk operating system. Both of these RPG implementations run on the Model 25 and 30, depending on what hardware is available. These implementations of RPG are therefore emphasized throughout the book. Differences known on certain other computer configurations are given in some instances in the text and in others in the Appendix.

I am indebted to the International Business Machines Corporation for photographs and materials, and for their permission to reprint certain sketches from reference manuals. Thanks must also go to the administration of Chamberlayne Junior College in Boston for support in doing curriculum revision and for permission to use their IBM SYSTEM/360 even after my stay there was complete. Without Gerd Bond, formerly of Chamberlayne Junior College, and John McSorley, Jr., of Prentice-Hall, Inc. in Boston, I might never have had the nerve to begin this book; without being able to share RPG concepts with programmers Ed Cowman, of the Community College of Baltimore, and Priscilla Caira, of Decatur Hopkins Bigelow Dowse Co., in Needham Heights, I might not have had the enthusiam to keep going; without Bob Mori, of the IBM Corporation in Baltimore, I might not have had access to much necessary information. I am also grateful to David Knellinger, a former student and now my colleague at the Community College of Baltimore, not only for his continual support, but for an admiration of RPG that almost equals mine. Finally, I would like to thank the twenty-six freshmen at Chamberlayne Junior College with whom I learned what RPG *will* and *will not,* do.

Joyce Currie Little

Baltimore, Maryland

CONTENTS

Section 9

REPORTS WITH MAGNETIC TAPE   341

Section 10

REPORTS WITH BRANCHING   381

SECTION 1

FUNDAMENTALS OF
DATA PROCESSING

Lesson 1

DATA PROCESSING CONCEPTS

You will become acquainted with the field of data processing, computers, and programming.

The questions given here are answered on the back of this page. They summarize the lesson and serve to emphasize the vocabulary of the profession. If you are already familiar with data processing, and answer all the questions correctly, go on to Lesson 2.

1. Why is *data processing* considered a relatively new field?
2. What are the basic parts of a digital computer?
3. Name some types of input/output media.
4. What is a *bit*? a *byte*?
5. What is the difference between *hardware* and *software*?
6. How are most unit-record machines controlled? most computers?
7. What is a *programming system*?
8. How does an *operating system* assist with computer operations?
9. What is the difference between a *systems flow chart* and a *program flow chart?*
10. What types of employment are possible in the data processing field?

ANSWERS

1. Because the computer has only recently become a part of it. Data processing itself was going on long before the computer was used; the term data processing has now come to mean the *use of computers* in doing the work.
2. Internal storage, input and output device, an arithmetic unit for calculations, and a means of control.
3. Magnetic tape, magnetic disk, punch cards, paper tape, and a magnetic drum.
4. The smallest unit of recorded information in the computer, physically a magnetized ring of core, or a magnetized spot, but logically represented by $\emptyset$ as one state and 1 as the other; a collection of bits, usually handled together, with 8 bits in each byte on the IBM SYSTEM/36$\emptyset$.
5. Hardware refers to the machines and equipment; software refers to the programming support packages, usually available from the manufacturer as well as from other companies.
6. By external wires placed into a removable panel, and plugged into the machine when the job is to be run; by a programmed set of instructions placed into storage in the computer.
7. A programming aid—usually called an assembler, compiler, or generator—designed to be used on a particular computer. It accepts information coded in symbolic form and converts it into the machine code of the computer.
8. The operating system maintains a constant job stream, guided by control cards, calling in programming systems or utility programs as needed, handling the input/output routines, and serving to increase the effectiveness of the computer system.
9. A systems chart gives an overall view of the complete job to be done, including preparation of input, definition of equipment and programs to be used, and all necessary handling until presentation of output. A program flow chart describes in detail the task of one individual program.
10. Programmer, systems analyst, systems designer, keypuncher, technical writer, electronic maintenance worker, salesman, systems programmer, computer operator, data processing technician, and program librarian.

Lesson 1   Data Processing Concepts

Data processing began a long time ago when people first started to keep records. Early man probably counted his sheep by cutting notches on a fence post. Eventually the abacus came to be used in the Orient for calculations, and in ancient Egypt paper was developed that could be written on with red dye. Record-keeping as we know it was first practiced by Italian merchants in dealing with the world's first banks. Data processing, loosely defined as the recording, calculating, and handling of information to produce meaningful results, had begun.

Over the years, improvements in data processing methods were slow. Modern techniques of bookkeeping were introduced in the late 1400's, yet it was in the late 1600's that an adding machine was developed. In the 1800's, mechanical desk calculators were in use in the United States, and near the turn of that century, Dr. Herman Hollerith, working with the Bureau of the Census, developed counting machinery, which was powered by electricity and would accept information coded in punch cards. Since the record of all information about one person, event, or activity was coded into one card, it became known as a *unit record*; machines using these cards came to be known as *unit-record equipment*. These machines were the business tools of the early 1900's. Almost all data processing for business during the period 1900-1950 was done on machinery descended from those early devices.

Machines and equipment have become known as *hardware*. The development of computer hardware in the 1930's and 40's led to the UNIVAC I, the first large business data processing computer, used in the Bureau of the Census early in the 1950's. The IBM 7Ø1 was released soon after, and a whole new industry of competitive equipment manufacturing was begun. From this fairly recent beginning, the digital computer has become the most important and valuable piece of hardware in the data processing installation. The IBM SYSTEM/36Ø computer system was announced in 1964, in a variety of models to fit almost any data processing need. Model 25 of the IBM SYSTEM/36Ø line, shown in Figure 1-1, is a more recent release. On some computer configurations, unit-record machines may serve as peripheral equipment to be used along with the computer system. With a full array of associated devices, however, a computer can do alone all tasks formerly done by its predecessors, faster, and with less handling of data by operating personnel.

Of great importance to the management of a data processing installation is the method used to operate and control the machinery to get the work done. The IBM 4Ø7 electric accounting machine, shown in Figure 1-2, which produced most of the reports of its time, was controlled by circuitry wired into removable panels, which set up the machine for a particular job. Data processing technicians, after preparing a diagram of where the wires should go, would place the wires into the panel, then test the panel until it was ready to do the job. An operator would insert the panel into the machine, feed the punch cards into the hopper, and do the report required. Although panels used in production work could be reserved and used repeatedly, the wiring diagram was often kept instead so that the panel could be released to be wired for some other task. There was a great need during this time for experienced wiring technicians. Since digital computers are controlled by an internally stored program, and not by wires, the need for wiring technicians has become a need for *programmers*. To understand how a computer is controlled by a program, it is helpful to know something about its basic structure.

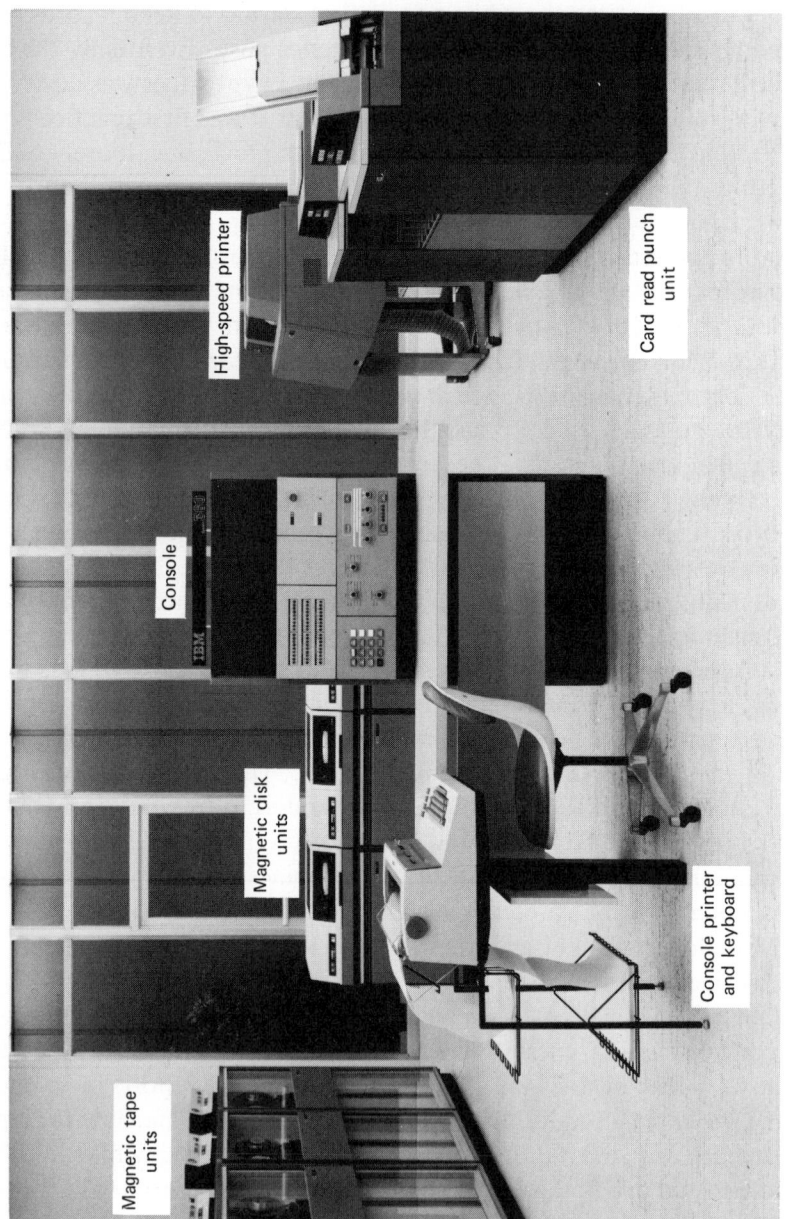

FIG. 1-1 IBM SYSTEM/360, Model 25. (Courtesy of International Business Machines Corporation.)

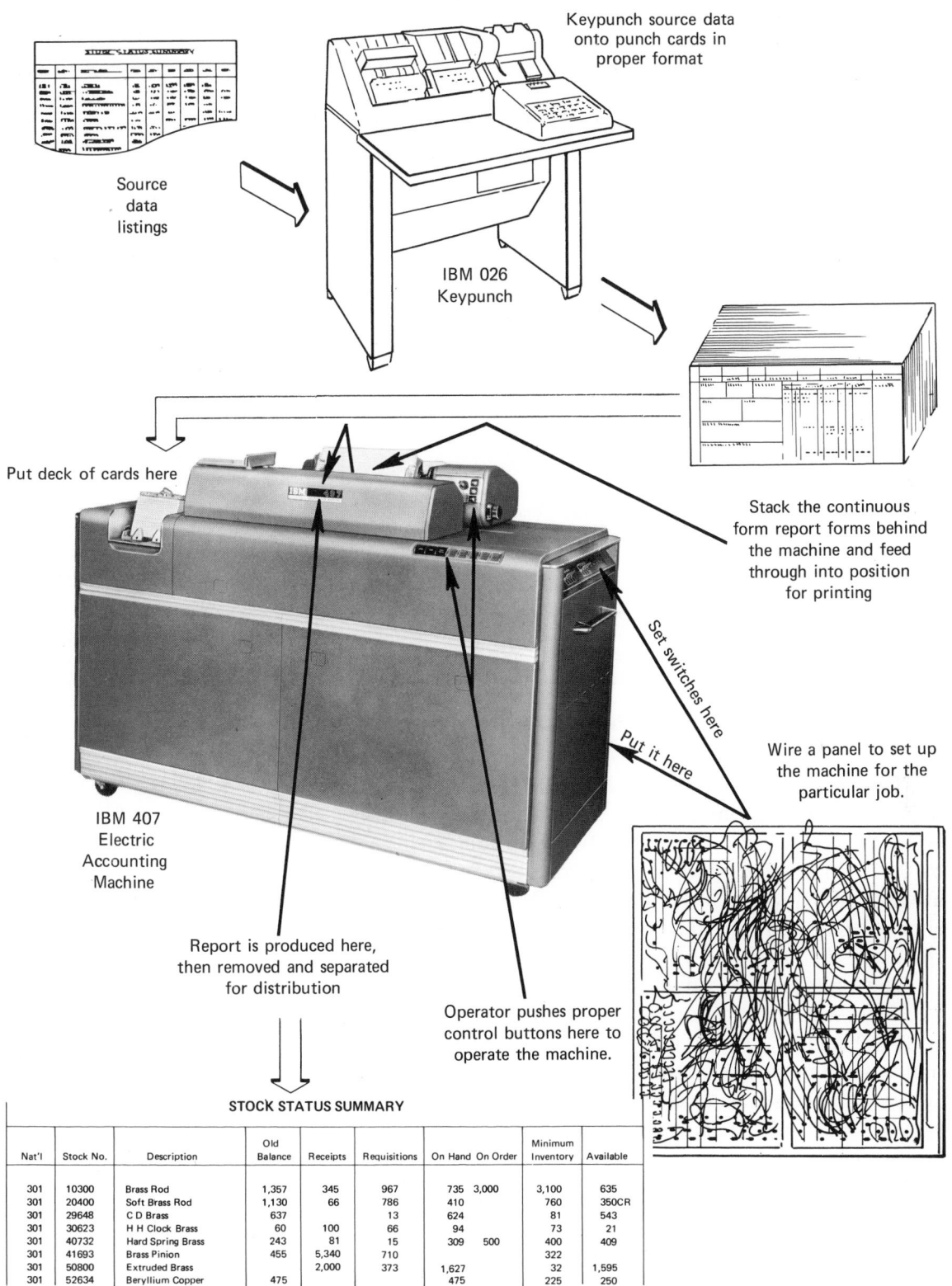

Source
data
listings

Keypunch source data
onto punch cards in
proper format

IBM 026
Keypunch

Put deck of cards here

Stack the continuous
form report forms behind
the machine and feed
through into position
for printing

IBM 407
Electric
Accounting
Machine

Set switches here

Put it here

Wire a panel to set up
the machine for the
particular job.

Report is produced here,
then removed and separated
for distribution

Operator pushes proper
control buttons here to
operate the machine.

STOCK STATUS SUMMARY

Nat'l	Stock No.	Description	Old Balance	Receipts	Requisitions	On Hand	On Order	Minimum Inventory	Available
301	10300	Brass Rod	1,357	345	967	735	3,000	3,100	635
301	20400	Soft Brass Rod	1,130	66	786	410		760	350CR
301	29648	C D Brass	637		13	624		81	543
301	30623	H H Clock Brass	60	100	66	94		73	21
301	40732	Hard Spring Brass	243	81	15	309	500	400	409
301	41693	Brass Pinion	455	5,340	710			322	
301	50800	Extruded Brass		2,000	373	1,627		32	1,595
301	52634	Beryllium Copper	475			475		225	250

FIG. 1-2 Reports with unit-record equipment IBM Ø26 and 4Ø7. (Courtesy of International Business Machines Corporation.)

The computer has a place to hold information—internal storage; a way to calculate using the stored information—the arithmetic unit; a way to get data in and out of storage—the input/output units; and a way to determine what to do—the control unit. The interrelation of these units is illustrated in Figure 1-3. The control unit is guided by a set of instructions called a *computer program.* This program is placed in the storage in coded form. The arithmetic unit can do calculations with information that is placed in storage, and can also put the results of the calculation in storage. The input unit can bring information into storage, and the output unit can bring it out again.

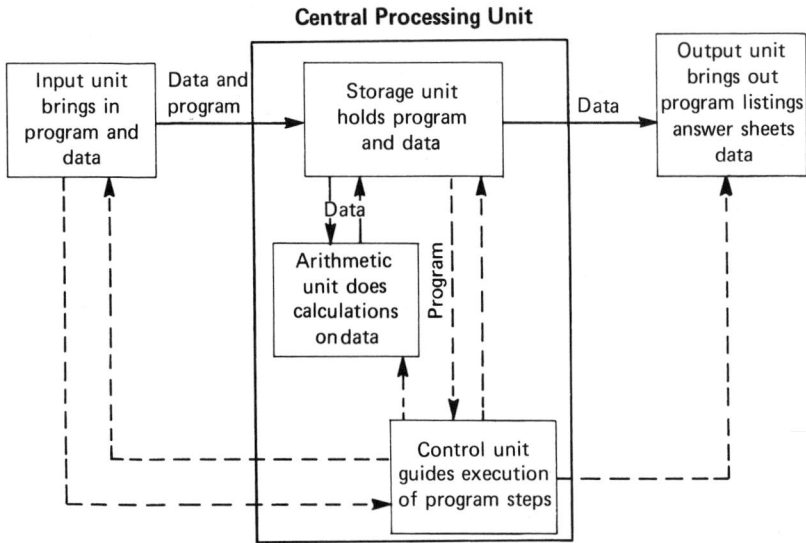

FIG. 1-3 Major parts of a digital computer.

The storage, also known as the memory, holds information, some of which is data, and some of which is the program. One common type of storage, called core, is made of tiny rings, which can be magnetized in one of two directions, giving a binary condition easily represented by ∅ or 1. The representation on one ring is called a binary digit, or *bit*; a group of these bits is usually called a *byte.* In the IBM SYSTEM/36∅, 8 of these bits make 1 byte; 1 byte can hold either 1 alphameric character, or 2 numeric decimal digits. Perhaps because the word "byte" rhymes with "bite," half a byte, 4 bits, has become known as a *nibble*!

The 8 bits are grouped into two sets of 4 bits each, with the left-most set being called a *zone*, and the right-most one a *digit* portion. Each set is read in binary, with bits identified as 8, 4, 2, and 1, as shown in Figure 1-4. Decimal numbers from ∅ to 15 are possible in each nibble, making the hexadecimal number system, with its base of 16, useful to represent them. Decimal numbers from ∅ to 9 are the same in hexadecimal and are used to represent numeric values from ∅ to 9; decimal numbers from 1∅ to 15, however, must be represented by 1 character, not 2 digits, so the letters A through F are used, respectively. Each byte, consisting of 2 nibbles or 8 bits, may therefore be read as 2 hexadecimal digits, as shown in Figure 1-4. Coding patterns for characters, letters, and numbers for the IBM SYSTEM/36∅ are said to be in EBCDIC code, pronounced by some as e⁻ by- dick and by others as eb⁻ sy- dick, which stands for *Extended Binary Coded Decimal Interchange Code.* The EBCDIC coding for all assigned characters is given in the Appendix; it is not yet necessary to worry about it.

Internal storage, or memory, is obtained for a computer system in sizes chosen according to customer need. The letter K, for kilo, is used to represent the memory size closest to

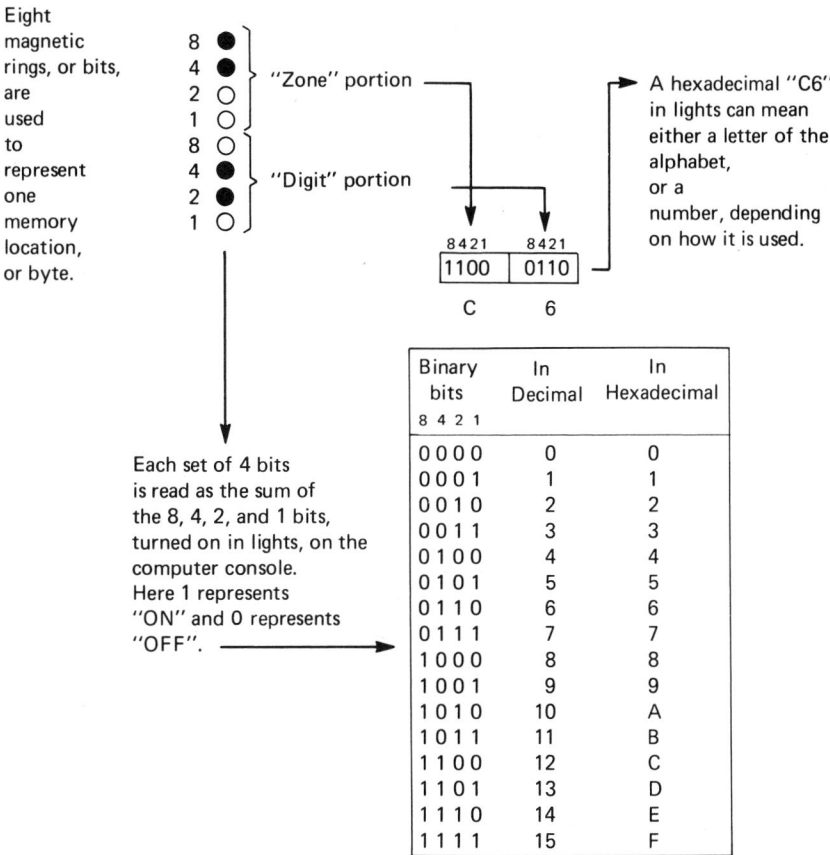

FIG. 1-4 Binary to decimal to hexadecimal number systems.

thousands—an 8K memory, in an 8-bit byte machine, is actually 8192 bytes, not 8000. Sizes of 16K, 24K, 32K, etc., are available. On the IBM SYSTEM/360, letters are used to represent memory size, with C being used for 8K, D for 16K, E for 32K, etc., with memory size doubling for each letter. D25 therefore means a Model 25, IBM SYSTEM/360 with 16K storage. Each byte of memory has a memory location or *address*. Memory locations begin with byte 00000, and using the hexadecimal numbering system, run by ones until the largest memory location on the system has been numbered.

Internal storage can be accessed either by an input unit, which brings information in, or by an output unit, which brings it out again. Input is *destructive*: information brought into a memory location destroys the previous contents stored there. Output, on the other hand, is *nondestructive*: information can be brought out without damaging its status in storage. It can be used repeatedly and will still be there! *Access time* is the time necessary to bring information from storage to be used. It is usually measured in *microseconds*, millionths of a second, or in *nanoseconds*, billionths of a second; when used alone, it is not an effective means of comparing computer speeds, since many models retrieve 8 bits with one access time, and others get 64!

Input devices include card readers, magnetic tape units, and magnetic disks or drums. Output devices include card punches, magnetic tapes, disks, and drums, but also include high-speed printers. The recording media on these input/output devices allow many of them to be used as *external storage*. Data that have been output from the computer to external storage devices can be used later as input.

The computer system shown in Figure 1-1 is the IBM SYSTEM/36Ø, Model 25, with the IBM 14Ø3 printer, the IBM 254Ø card read punch unit, the IBM 24Ø 1 magnetic tape units, and the IBM 2311 magnetic disk units. It is a medium-size computer, which would rent for $5000-$10,000 per month, perhaps more, depending on the particular configuration. The Models 3Ø, 4Ø, and larger usually rent for progressively more, depending on input/output devices and memory size.

Programming for early *first*-generation vacuum-tube computers was tedious and time consuming. Programmers were required to use a *machine language*, sometimes called the *absolute* language, which was a coded instruction set, with each set being different for each particular type of machine. The programmer had to assign exact memory addresses to the data and program and write out, in code, the operations to be done. Training people to become programmers took a very long time. Even when a person became an experienced programmer, it took him a long time to get a program written and working. Since machine languages vary from one machine to another, programming in that manner is a highly specialized and detailed skill. It was, in some cases, not worth the time and expense to train programmers to convert many of the jobs already on unit-record equipment to computer use. Output was often displayed on the screen of a cathode-ray tube, punched into a continuous roll of paper tape, or placed onto a reel of magnetic tape. Many early computers were predominantly calculation devices, with emphasis on scientific, not business, jobs. Reports were printed, off-line, from reels of magnetic tape or from punch cards.

Since coding of programs in machine language was very exacting and slow, the computer itself was put to use to help with the programming. An *assembly language programming system* was developed to allow the programmer to write *symbolic* instructions and memory addresses in the program instead of *absolute* instructions and *actual* memory addresses. The computer was programmed to convert this *source program* into its equivalent machine language code, which was still required by the computer to actually do the job. The machine language program written by a computer is called an *object program*. Although, like machine languages, assembly languages vary greatly for each type of computer and require much training time, they make it possible for programs to be written in much less time than originally required.

Programming systems, such as an assembly language, designed to help the computer user make better use of the equipment, are called *software packages*. *Utility programs,* used for routine jobs, may also be considered software. They are usually stored in the computer system library, either on tape or disk. One type of utility program is used to sort records on a tape, putting them into sequence according to some key. Others convert tape input to printed output, list decks of cards, merge the records from two tapes together into one, and so on.

Second-generation computers, introduced about 1960 and characterized by transistors and diodes, offered faster computing speeds, high-speed magnetic tape and disk, and advanced software capabilities. Problem-oriented software became more prevalent; new programming systems became known as *languages* as they grew more like English than machine code. In the late 1950's, the computer language FORTRAN, named for *formula translation*, was released by IBM especially for use in scientific work. It allows the programmer to write instructions in a manner very like algebra. A translator, or *compiler*, uses the computer to convert these source program instructions into the machine code required. Efforts at standardization among computer manufacturers and users resulted in FORTRAN compilers for several different computers, so that a programmer had to worry only a little about which hardware he was going to use. FORTRAN was one of the first successful machine-independent problem-oriented languages. Later, standards for a similar language for business were established, and COBOL, for *CO*mmon *B*usiness *O*riented *L*anguage, was ready for use in the early 1960's. FORTRAN and COBOL are generally considered the most used computer languages today.

Representative of a different type of development in programming systems is the generator type, of which RPG, Report Program Generator, is one. It is not considered, by some authorities, to be a programming language since the programmer writes specifications on a fixed form and does not have the same type of control as with other high-level languages. The RPG programmer specifies what data are to be used, what type of action the computer should take, and what each type of report line should look like; instructions are generated by the computer to do the job. RPG was released in January, 1961, for the IBM 1401 computer. It was used by many installations as an aid in converting unit-record work to computer usage. The improved RPG, which was released with the IBM SYSTEM/360, has found much success, since it is efficient, quick, and easy to use. An even more recent release, for the IBM SYSTEM/3, is called RPG II. RPG is designed specifically for doing business reports, and in a manner similar to the logic of unit-record equipment. For that reason, it is very easy for experienced unit-record personnel to learn. It may be used even on small, relatively inexpensive computers, at much less cost than for comparable FORTRAN or COBOL systems. Even on larger, more expensive computer configurations, where FORTRAN and COBOL are also available, it serves a particular need— that of producing quick and easy reports from data files. Several computer manufacturers have RPG software available; it is relatively machine independent. Most required changes between machines are caused by the different input/output units that are often on different systems. Many of these changes are given in the text and others, in the Appendix.

The IBM SYSTEM/360 is a *third*-generation computer, characterized by integrated circuits and microminiature components. The third generation offers many features—faster computing speeds; really high-speed printers; magnetic disks, tapes, drums, and data cells; optical scanners; graphing devices; audio response; time sharing of computer via remote terminals; multiprogramming; multiprocessing; and more advanced computer languages. The larger and faster the computer system, however, the more essential it is to get more efficient use of its time. To save time between jobs and get more use of the computer, some second-generation machines, and almost all third-generation ones, have an *operating system*—a supervisory control program that resides in storage. Jobs are stacked into a *job stream* and processing continues from one job to another, guided by instructions given on *control cards* to the *job control* portion of the operating system. An operating system is made up of several highly complex programs, which not only handle job control but perform other services as well. It prepares all input/output, maintains storage of programs in its library, controls the calling of utility programs, performs accounting record-keeping for each user, and guides the operator, by appropriate messages, in control of the computer system. A major part of learning how to use a computer is spent in learning how to prepare control cards to make it do what *you* want done!

Before a given job is programmed, much planning is necessary. The analysis of a job establishes what equipment is needed, how data records should be formed, what programs are necessary, and sometimes what programming system should be used. Several types of charts may be used to visualize the logical steps in the job. The *system's flow chart* is used to show data preparation, requested input and output, and all processing steps or handling that should occur. Figure 1-5 shows a systems chart for a payroll job. Symbols used on systems charts are made with a special template, which is shown in the Appendix. A *program flow chart* gives the logic of what is to be done by *one* particular program. Figure 1-5 also shows a program flow chart, which could be used to write the program for doing the payroll job. Other charts used are *process charts*, designed to show the flow of paper, forms, and information from one place to another within a business; and *decision tables*, prepared during analysis to show the logic of decision making and the procedures used. *Object program logic charts*, which explain the sequence of logical steps performed by a programming system during execution of an object

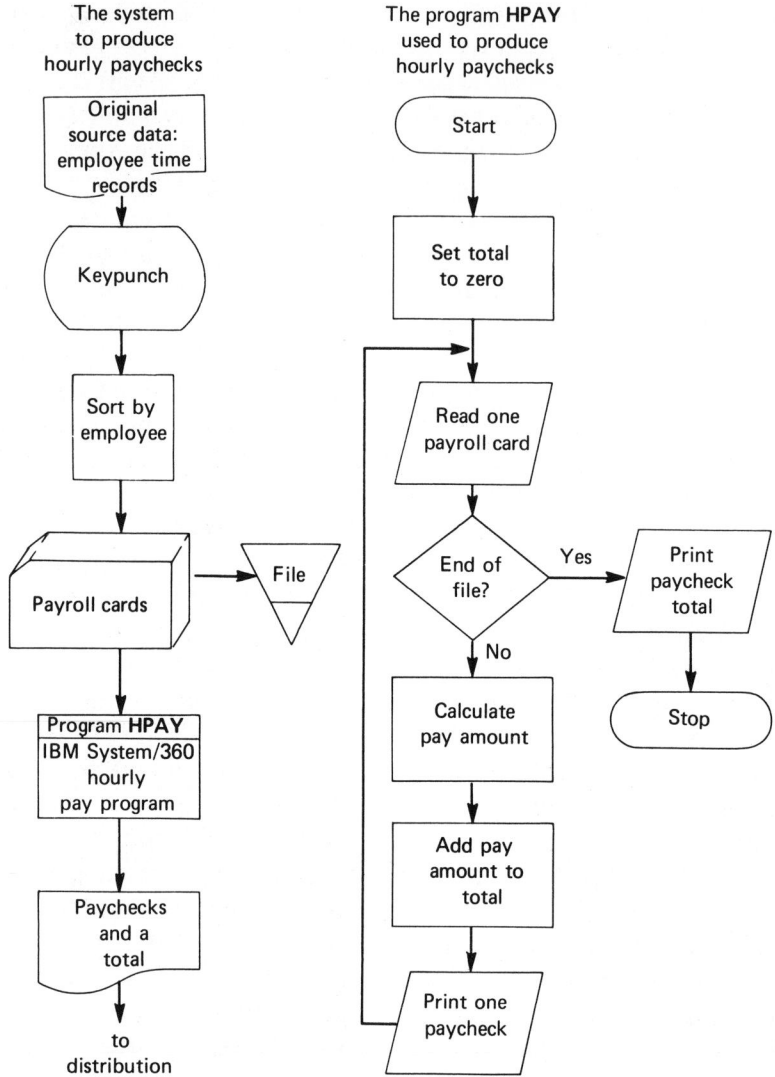

FIG. 1-5 Systems flow chart compared to program flow chart.

program, are not used during job analysis, but in understanding the programming language being used.

Although data processing has been going on for a long time, it has only recently come to imply *the use of computers*. Data processing is concerned with the storing and handling of information to maintain records, to present accurate and meaningful reports, and to make information usable for many special purposes. The digital computer has caused data processing to become a rapidly growing new industry. The computer has been instrumental in the development of the advanced technological age we now live in, creating many new employment positions. A *systems analyst* may, for example, determine whether or not a problem is feasible, and if so, on what equipment, with what personnel, and on what schedule. A *systems designer* may, for example, draw systems charts for the programs and determine data arrangement; several *programmers* may work on writing programs for the project. *Systems programmers* keep the programming languages and operating system in good working order, in some cases writing new ones. *Keypunch personnel* punch programs and data from source records. *Verifier operators* check to be sure that the prepared data are accurate. *Computer operators* assist in testing programs, and do the production runs when tests are complete. *Technical writers* assist with much of the documentation of programs and write systems and procedures manuals for data processing technicians to follow in working with the new system. And then there are the *managers*, the *salesmen*, the *repairmen*, the *data analysts*, the *librarians*, and so on. There is no doubt that data processing is here to stay.

Lesson 2

PUNCH CARDS

You will learn how to prepare data for use with RPG programs.

The questions given here are answered on the back of this page. If you already have experience in data processing or another computer language, and can correctly answer the questions, go on to Lesson 3.

1. How many columns of information can be put onto the standard IBM punch card?
2. How are the holes in punch cards read by a computer system?
3. Give the Hollerith punch card code for the letters of the alphabet.
4. How can you quickly determine the length of a field when given its assigned card columns?
5. What are the two possible modes for RPG data fields? How is mode determined?
6. Compare the rules for punching information into numeric and alphameric fields in RPG.
7. How are keypunched cards usually proof-checked before the computer uses them?
8. Define the relationship between a *field,* a *record*, and a *file.*
9. What is a *record identification code*?
10. What is meant by a *master* record as compared to a *detail* record?

ANSWERS

1. 8∅.
2. By a photocell, which detects light shining through the holes, causing electrical impulses to be stored.
3. A-I uses the 12 zone, with 1 through 9 punches, respectively.
   J-R uses the 11 zone, with 1 through 9 punches, respectively.
   S-Z uses the ∅ zone, with 2 through 9 punches, respectively.
4. Take the right-end column number, subtract the left-end column number, and then add 1.
5. Numeric and alphameric. A decimal indication, even though ∅, causes the numeric mode to be used; otherwise the alphameric mode is assumed.
6. For numeric, you must punch them right-justified, usually with left-zero-fill, but never blank; no letters or special characters are allowed, except for an 11 punch over the low-order digit to represent a negative number, or possibly a 12 punch over it for a positive one. Alphameric mode fields should be left-justified, with the unused portion of them blank, and may contain any valid character.
7. By a procedure very like keypunching, which checks that the correct hole is there, done on a machine similar to the keypunch called a *verifier*.
8. A file is a set of records, a record is a set of fields, and a field is a group of adjacent columns on the card handled as a unit.
9. A special character placed somewhere on the card to identify it by record type from all other record types in the file.
10. A record that contains fairly constant information to be kept for some period of time, rather than transactions that are only of temporary or current interest.

Lesson 2   Punch Cards

The most common way to get information from the printed page into a computer system is to use punch cards for input. These cards are fairly inexpensive and easy to handle, re-arrange, and punch. They are manufactured by several different companies and can be pur-chased in quantities of 2000 per box, or 10,000 per carton, in almost any color. They can be ordered either in standard preprinted format, special-order format, or no printed format at all. They usually have rectangular corners, but often have rounded ones; most of them have an upper-corner cut, either on the right or left, but all cut the same way so that it is easy to tell when a card is upside down or backwards in the deck. They are sensitive to humidity and temperature, and should be stored in a cool, dry place. They can become damaged by rough handling or by excessive usage. The trite slogan of today's age, "Do not staple, bend, or fold," should really be followed, since mutilated cards will not feed properly into a computer system.

Information collected for computer use is sometimes marked directly onto the card with a pencil. These marks are later detected on a machine with a mark-sensing device and a corre-sponding hole is cut into the card for that mark. Source information in typewritten form can now be read by a machine called an *optical reader*, which then either punches holes onto cards, places data onto magnetic tape, or transfers information directly into the storage of a computer system. You may be familiar with punch card sets, such as those used by many credit card companies. Handwritten information is put on when the form is used; it is keypunched later onto the same card by a keypunch operator who reads the source data directly from the card. The IBM Porta-punch card, however, already has perforations at cutting positions, which can easily be pushed out with a stylus or the point of a pencil; later keypunching is not needed on many jobs using this type of card. Mark-sense or Porta-punch cards are often used for data collection in jobs such as meter reading, transformer inspection, test scoring, or inventory. A variety of preprinted cards is shown in Figure 2-1.

When punch cards are ready for computer processing, they are placed into a card reader, which is connected to the computer system. The IBM 2501 card reader, shown in Figure 2-2, reads, column by column, at a speed of 600 cards per minute. Light is used to detect holes on the card; that which passes through each hole is converted by a photocell into electrical impul-ses. Information is transferred directly to the memory of the computer system.

Punch cards are used not only for input, but for output as well. One commonly used out-put device is the IBM 1442 card punch, also shown in Figure 2-2. Blank cards, placed into the hopper, can be punched at speeds up to 90 cards per minute under the guidance of the com-puter program, and are automatically stacked for removal from the machine.

The IBM 1442 can also be obtained as a card read punch. This term is used to indicate a device that can either read or punch, either in the same hopper or in separate hoppers. When only a single hopper is available, cards going into the machine are usually only partially filled with input data so that the card can also be used to receive output information. This type of file, in RPG, is called a *combined* file, since both input and output operations may be done on it.

The most common machine used for input/output on the IBM SYSTEM/360 computer, Model 30 and up, is the IBM 2540 card read punch. It has one hopper for reading cards and another for punching; the two hoppers are independent of each other, and can operate at the same time. Both hoppers have a buffer capability, which is used for temporary storage of infor-mation until it is accessed by the computer for transfer to or from memory. An optional

Pre-printed all alike but in different
colors, or banded; to be punched by
keypunch or computer.

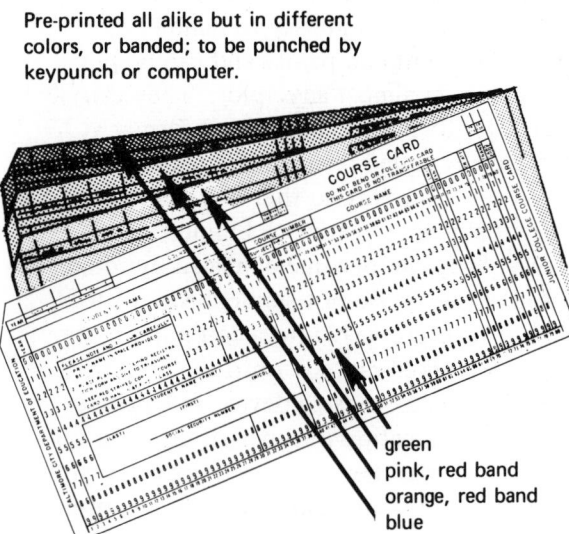

green
pink, red band
orange, red band
blue

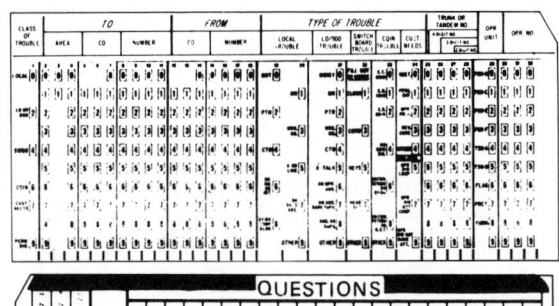

Pre-printed, with blocks or bubbles
for pencil markings; for punching by a
mark-sense reader.

Pre-printed tissue over a card, with
carbon; written on; card later
keypunched.

Pre-printed, with space for
handwritten information; keypunched
from handwriting.

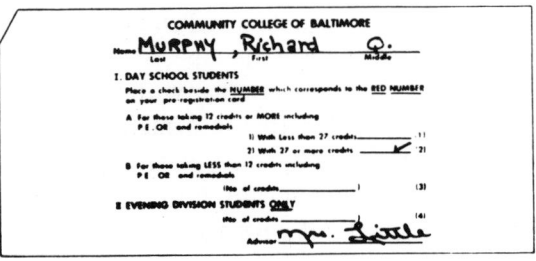

Pre-printed to YOUR special need
with perforations to push out to
make holes; no keypunching needed.

(Form courtesy of IBM.)

FIG. 2-1 Punch cards in preprinted formats.

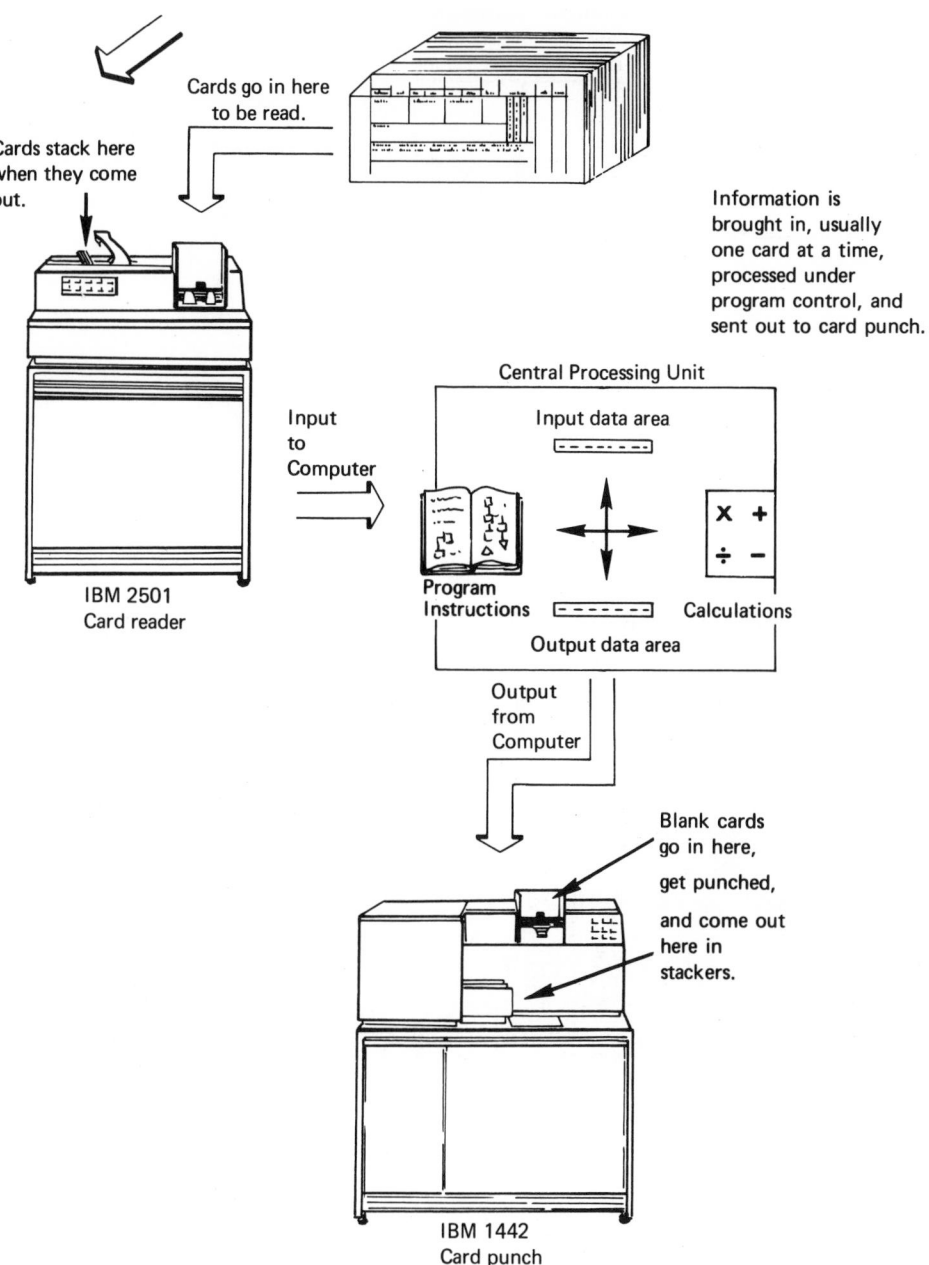

FIG. 2-2 Card input and output to computer.

feature on this punch unit allows it to be used as a combined file as well, but generally the machine is used as two separate ones—one for reading cards, and one for punching them. It can read at speeds up to $1\emptyset\emptyset\emptyset$ cards per minute, and can punch at speeds up to $3\emptyset\emptyset$ cards per minute.

Information from a printed source is usually put onto punch cards by use of a keypunch machine. When a key on that machine is struck, the pattern of corresponding holes for that character is automatically cut into the card. The IBM $\emptyset$29 card punch machine, shown in Figure 2-3, is recommended for use with the IBM SYSTEM/36$\emptyset$. Its keyboard is very like that

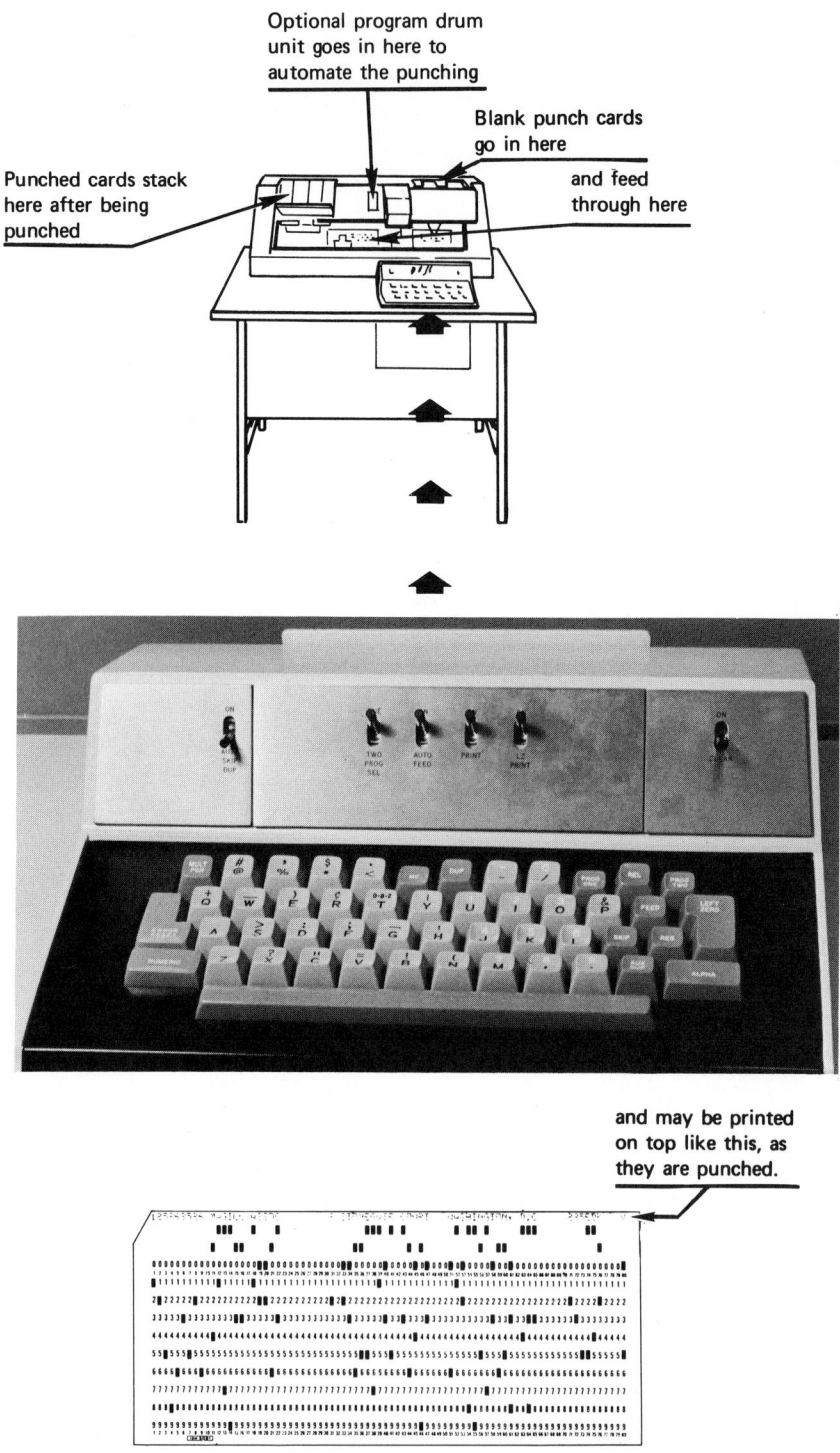

Optional program drum
unit goes in here to
automate the punching

Blank punch cards
go in here

Punched cards stack
here after being
punched

and feed
through here

and may be printed
on top like this, as
they are punched.

FIG. 2-3 IBM ∅29 keypunch machine.

of a typewriter, and has two characters given on most keys. Holding down the NUMERIC
shift key during punching causes the upper character to be cut; keyboard use without holding
it down causes the lower one to be cut. A space bar at the bottom is used to make blank
columns. A switch may be turned on so that printing of each character will be done directly
above the column it occupies on the card.

To increase efficiency on the keypunch machine, a program card may be used. When properly coded and placed onto the drum unit of the machine, it will automate the punching by assigning alphabetic and numeric keyboard modes, so that the operator need not continue to use the NUMERIC shift key. The program card can also be used to cause skipping over columns not to be punched, can permit entrance of left-most zeros into numeric fields automatically, and can cause duplication of information from one card to another. Two different program arrangements can be placed on one program card on the IBM Ø29 keypunch.

Most production keypunching is checked by using the IBM Ø59 verifier, which looks much like the IBM Ø29. Almost everyone associated with data processing has had the experience of sitting down at one of these machines, mistakenly thinking that it was a keypunch! An operator places the punched deck into the machine and, rereading the same source data, goes through the punching motions again. Rather than cut a hole, this machine *reads* the hole already cut, and compares it to the one on the key pressed by the operator. When it is certain that a difference exists, a notch is placed above that column, so that corrections can be made before the records reach the computer system. When the entire card is through the verifier without any errors detected, a verification notch is cut at the right end of the card.

Each data card has a format with a specified arrangement of columns; each column can contain either a numeric digit, an alphabetic letter, a special character, or a blank space. Figure 2-4 shows a standard 8Ø-column IBM 5Ø81 punch card, as used by the IBM 36Ø computer, with characters on it punched and printed by an IBM Ø29 card punch machine. It also shows the smaller IBM 37ØØ punch card used on the IBM SYSTEM/3, made by a special keypunch machine designed for that system. It contains space for three tiers of 32 characters each, giving 96 characters on each card. The smaller card also has additional space at the top so that information may be printed by the keypunch machine as the card is made.

The standard 8Ø-column card has a layout that assigns a position to each of 12 different rows. Not all combinations of holes are valid characters; if you use an invalid pattern, the accuracy of information stored in the computer system will be in doubt, and in some cases, will cause the computer system to halt. The 12 possible punch positions within a given column are identified by a *row number*. Since the row at the bottom of the card is the 9 row, the bottom of the card is called the *9-edge* of the card. Above the Ø row is the position for an 11 punch, known also as a minus. Above that, at the very top of the face of the card, is the position for a 12 punch, known as the symbol & in EBCDIC. This punch is often called a plus punch, but note that it is *not* the same as the pattern of holes made when the character + is struck. Since the 12 row is the closest to the top of the card, the top edge is known as the *12-edge*.

The coding structure of the holes placed into the card for each character was developed from that used by Hollerith at the turn of the century, and is known as the *Hollerith code*. It is important that you know the code for letters and numbers. For numeric digits a single hole is punched at the corresponding row. A numeric 9, for example, is a hole at row 9, and the numeric 3 has a hole in row 3. Letters are double-punched combinations, with a zone punch and a digit punch placed in the same column. The coding for letters of the alphabet divides the alphabet into three sets—A-I, J-R, and S-Z, which use zone positions 12, 11, and Ø, respectively. The digit punches for the first two sets are 1-9, in order, with A using 1, B using 2, and so on, through the letters of the set. Since there are only eight letters in the last set, however, digits 2-9 are used, rather than 1-8, so that the S is a Ø-2 punch, the T a Ø-3 punch, and so on, to the Z, which is a Ø-9 punch. Punch card patterns for letters, numbers, and IBM 36Ø special characters are given in Figure 2-5. Recall that on the IBM Ø29 keypunch, the 12 row is the & key and the 11 row is the minus, or – , key. The Ø row serves in two ways: when used alone it is a numeric zero; when used as part of a letter or special character, it is a zone.

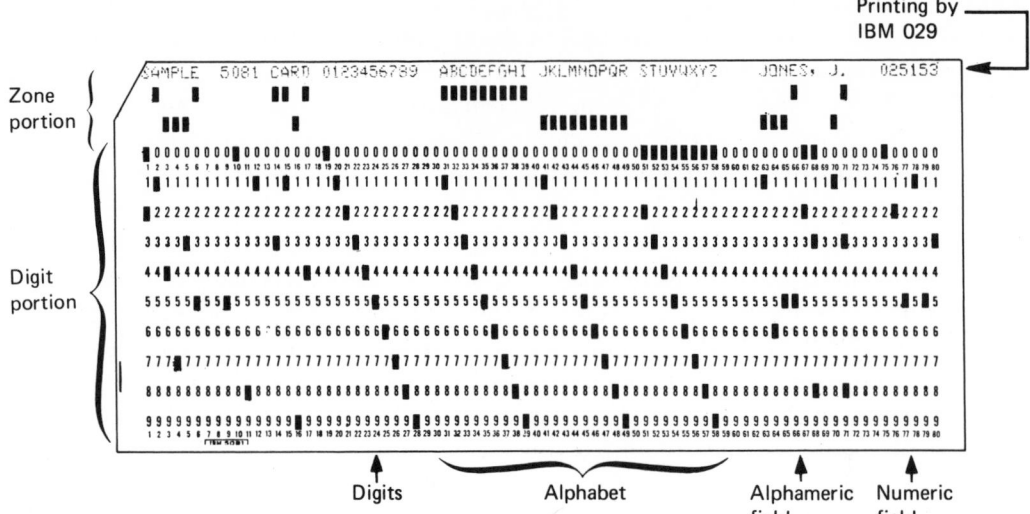

1 tier of 80 columns for 80 characters, using Hollerith code.

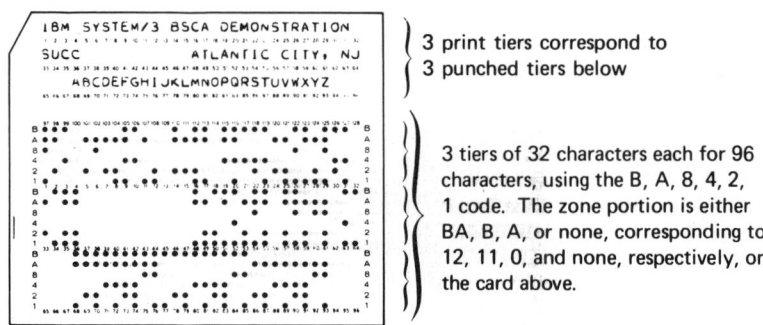

3 print tiers correspond to
3 punched tiers below

3 tiers of 32 characters each for 96
characters, using the B, A, 8, 4, 2,
1 code. The zone portion is either
BA, B, A, or none, corresponding to
12, 11, 0, and none, respectively, on
the card above.

FIG. 2-4   IBM 5081 80-column standard punch card and IBM 3700 96-column
SYSTEM/3 mini-card punch card.

Special characters which have double or triple punches in each column have patterns of holes that vary widely among different computer systems. On most IBM SYSTEM/360 systems, it is necessary that they be punched with the holes given on the IBM 029 keypunch, as shown in Figure 2-5. Should a different keypunch machine be used, or should the 029 be converted for the character set of another computer, proper holes may be made by multipunching one column to get correct patterns as specified. A chart giving all meaningful EBCDIC patterns for holes is given in the Appendix.

Meaningful information is placed on the card in groups of adjacent columns, called *fields*. The right-most end of the field, the units position, is called the *low-order digit*. The digit at the left end of the number is worth much more, such as hundreds, thousands, etc., and is called the *high-order* digit. All the fields on one card make a *record*, and all the records of a given deck make a *file*.

Each field is given a name and assigned to certain columns on the card. A field named **ACCT**, for example, may be used for an account number, and may perhaps be assigned to columns 11-15. Field names are used for reference in the program. The name **STREET**, for example, may be used when referring to the field that contains a street address. It is important for you to know the difference between the *name* of the field and the *contents* of it. The

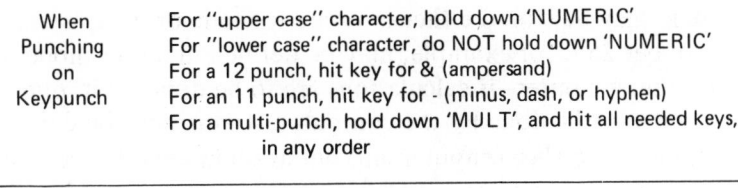

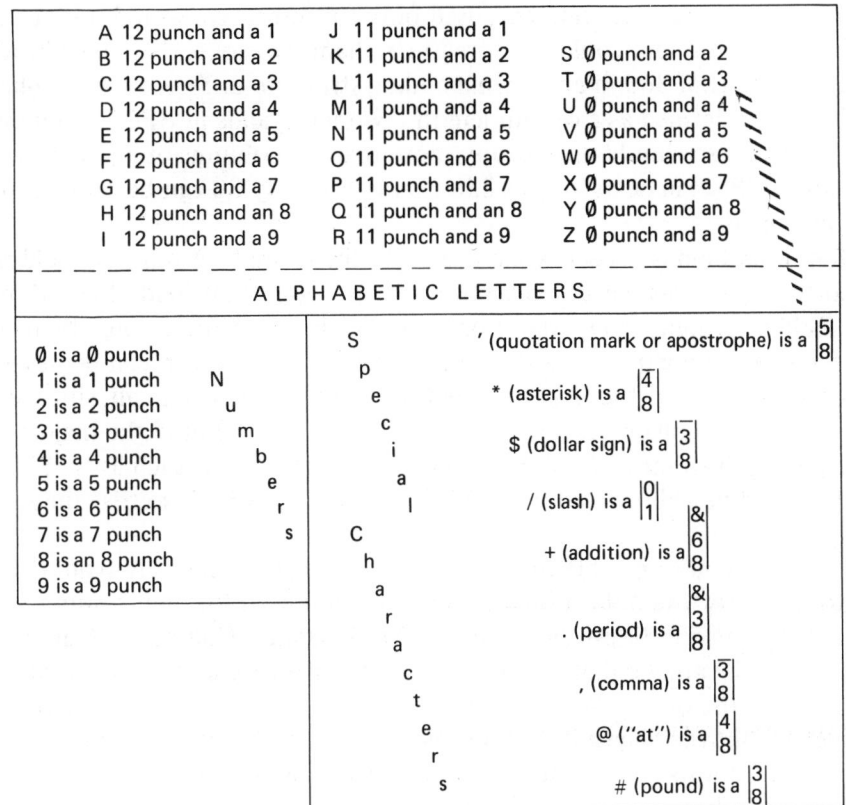

FIG. 2-5 Codes for punch cards as used by IBM SYSTEM/36Ø.

field named **STREET** could have contents '24Ø NEWBURY STREET' for one record and '29Ø1 LIBERTY HEIGHTS AVENUE' for another.

The names of fields must follow the rules for the computer language being used. For RPG, names must begin with a letter, may be continued with either letters or numbers but ordinarily *not* special characters, and must be from 1 to 6 characters long. They must *not* be one of the few reserved names, such as **PAGE**, which is used for a special purpose. Some implementations of RPG, however, consider the dollar sign, $, the pound sign, #, and the "at" sign, @, to be *alphabetic*, and would permit them in a field name; it is much better, however, not to become accustomed to that peculiarity, since some implementations may not permit it on their equipment.

In RPG, each field must be specified as one of two modes: *numeric*, or *alphameric*. (Alphameric is also called alpha*nu*meric.) Fields in numeric mode may contain any of the digits Ø, 1, 2, ..., 9. Alphameric fields may contain any valid character used on your particular computer system, whether alphabetic, blank, numeric, or special characters. The street address '321 BEECHFIELD RD., APT. 1A' *must* be defined as alphameric because letters, special characters, and numbers are all present in it. The name 'CHAMBERLAYNE' is also alphameric, since it is composed of alphabetic letters. Since the numeric digits are a subset of the alphameric ones, a completely numeric field may be stored either in numeric mode or in alphameric mode. The field containing the number 257, for example, may be defined in either mode, depending on how it is to be used by the computer—if calculations are to be done on it, *numeric* mode must be used; if special editing must be done by the computer, it must also be defined as numeric; if however, it is to be brought into the computer and out again in exactly the same form, it is permitted to be alphameric. An item number, used only for reference, would not need any calculation or editing done on it and could be stored in alphameric mode. Numbers in RPG numeric mode are stored in the IBM 36∅ in an internal coding structure different from alphameric ones.

Each field must be defined as a certain length. Numeric fields in RPG should be not more than 15 digits long, and so should not occupy more than 15 columns of a punch card. Although alphameric fields in RPG can be as long as 256 characters, only 8∅ can be brought in at one time from a punch card.

The length of each field is chosen when designing the format. A numeric field must be long enough to hold the largest value ever expected to be needed in that field. Should most of the numbers for a field be 3 digits long, even if only one of them is 5 digits long, then the field must be defined as 5 columns long on the card. Alphameric fields, however, can be designed by selecting a length that *most* of the field information will fit, rather than all, since abbreviations are usually permitted on alphameric information. For example, should the majority of street addresses for a given job fit into 2∅ columns, those few that do not, such as '1357 HUNTING HILLS PLACE', could be abbreviated to '1357 HUNTG HILLS PL.', so that they would fit into 2∅ columns.

It is important for you to be able to determine field length accurately from the column numbers assigned to it. If, for example, a field uses from column 26 through column 59, your first impression is that the field is 33 positions long. *That is wrong!* Columns 1-6 are 6 characters long, and columns 11-19 are 9 columns long, but note that the length is *not* obtained by subtracting one end from the other! When you do that the length obtained is 1 character short: 9 – 1 is 8 characters, but the length is 9. Likewise, 59 – 26 is 33, but the length is 34! To get the length of a field from its column numbers, do the subtraction, then *add 1*. A handy rule to remember: length = last column – first column + 1.

Data punched into fields must be correctly aligned within the assigned columns. For an established numeric field of length 5, the number 125, for example, should be punched as ∅∅125. Although leading blanks are permitted in RPG fields, a blank in the units position should *not* be used in numeric mode in RPG because it will, in most implementations, cause the machine to stop. Leading blanks, other than the units position, in numeric fields are stored as zeros, so even though they were blank when brought in they will be zeros coming out unless you zero-suppress or edit them. For compatibility with COBOL the field should have all leading zeros punched. The field ƀƀ125, where ƀ means a blank column, although acceptable on most RPG systems, is not recommended since it may lead you into leaving the entire field blank when you mean zero; it should be punched as ∅∅125. The number in the field must be aligned on the right side of the field, called *right-justified*, and should be filled in with zeros on the left, called *left-zero-fill*. The values for alphameric fields, however, must be lined up on the left side of the field, called *left-justified*, and should be filled out with blank spaces, not zeros, on the right! Some alphameric information does not need all the space provided for it, so blank columns remain in the unused portion. Before you worry about memorizing how to punch data properly, think of the way you write information. When you write a name or street address on a form supplied for that purpose, you begin at the *left* side and move toward the right, leaving blank all unused spaces. When you fill in numeric information, such as an amount of money, it is filled in, and calculated with, from the *right* side and aligned properly so that dollars and cents are underneath each other. RPG follows the natural way of alignment with numeric and alphameric information. The only additional thing to remember is how to indicate the sign, when needed, and to left-zero-fill all numeric fields.

Numeric fields used in calculations may be either positive or negative. The zone portion of the right-most digit of the field is used for the *sign* of that field. If no zone position is punched, or if a 12 punch zone is present, the sign of the field is considered *positive*. If an 11 punch is placed over the right-most position of the field, the sign of the field is considered *negative*. The 11 punch will be denoted by a dash, or minus. The zone portion of the right-most position of the field is often called an *overpunch*, since it is punched over the numeric value of the field. Negative numbers represent, in business work, an *overdrawn* condition, or a *credit*. If 25 items of stock are on hand for a particular item, the 25 is a positive number; if the stock is overdrawn by 25 items, then the 25 should be a negative number. The negative 25 will be punched, in a 5-digit field, as $\emptyset\emptyset\emptyset2\overline{5}$, with the dash indicating an 11 punch over the right-most digit. If the field is to be used alphamerically, that column will be given as its equivalent alphabetic character, causing it to appear as $\emptyset\emptyset\emptyset2N$, since a $\overline{5}$ is the character N when used alphabetically. The value $\emptyset\emptyset\emptyset2\overset{\&}{A}$ will be 21; $134\overset{\&}{D}$ will be 1344; and the value $\emptyset\emptyset23\overline{0}$ will be printed as $\emptyset\emptyset23\not{b}$, since the $\overline{\emptyset}$ is not a valid letter! The $\emptyset$ zone in combination with 2 through 9 does become a letter; a zero with either an & or a – zone, however, is a nonprintable character, and will print as a blank position unless you edit or zero-suppress it!

A field in RPG is considered *numeric* mode if, and only if, decimal location specification is marked for it in the program. The decimal point, however, is *not punched into the data field on the data card*. Numeric fields on data cards are not allowed to contain commas, decimal points, dollar signs, or any other special characters; they must be composed only of the digits $\emptyset$, 1, ..., 9, with sign indication permitted over the low-order right-most digit, with leading blanks permitted but not recommended! Since the decimal point is not punched, its location must be specified in the program so that the computer system, and people involved with the job, will know that it does have decimal places, and how many. The decimal position for numeric fields, unless otherwise stated on the card description, is assumed to be at the right end, making the field a whole number. The number of decimal places for that case must be stated as $\emptyset$.

Field format is specified by using X's for each unknown digit and giving a caret symbol, $_\wedge$, to indicate where the decimal point is implied. The example $XXX_\wedge XX$ indicates length 5, 2 decimal places. Up to 9 decimal places may be specified in a maximum numeric field length of 15 digits.

To punch the value 125.46 in a field of length 6, you would punch $\emptyset12546$. Notice that the decimal point is not punched; notice that left-zero-fill is used. In the program, you would specify that 2 decimal places are present. In the example $\emptyset12_\wedge453$, the length is 6, with 3 decimals; the number will be used as 12.453 by the computer. The value -257.25, meaning perhaps a "credit" of $257.25, should be punched in a 6-digit field as $\emptyset2572\overline{5}$, using 2 implied decimal places and an 11 overpunch for the sign. The sign is given over the low-order position of the field regardless of how many decimal places are specified.

PROBLEM DEFINITION: *Design a card record for a payroll application. The card should contain fields for employee name, social security number, number of hours worked, and rate per hour to be paid.*

When designing a card record, it is helpful to use the information from the source document in somewhat the same order as it appears. It is then possible for keypunching to be done directly from the document without expensive transfer of the information to coding sheets. In this case, the social security number will be placed first on the record, since it is the "key" field, and will probably be used for sequencing the deck. It is 9 digits long, but has the definite pattern given by XXX-XX-XXXX; make it numeric mode so that editing can be used to put in the dashes for easy reading of the report. Assign it to columns 1-9. The employee name should be handled next. It will need about 2∅ columns, and since alphabetizing by last name may be used occasionally, the last name should be given *first* within the field. Assign it to columns 11-3∅. The field for number of hours worked is assumed to be a whole number, and will for this job be assumed to be 4∅ hours or less. Give it two columns. Since it will be used in calculations, it must be in numeric mode; you must give it ∅ decimals. The rate of pay for this job shall be assumed not more than $9.99 per hour, so three positions are adequate, with 2 decimal places. A possible card layout and sample data for it are given in Figure 2-6.

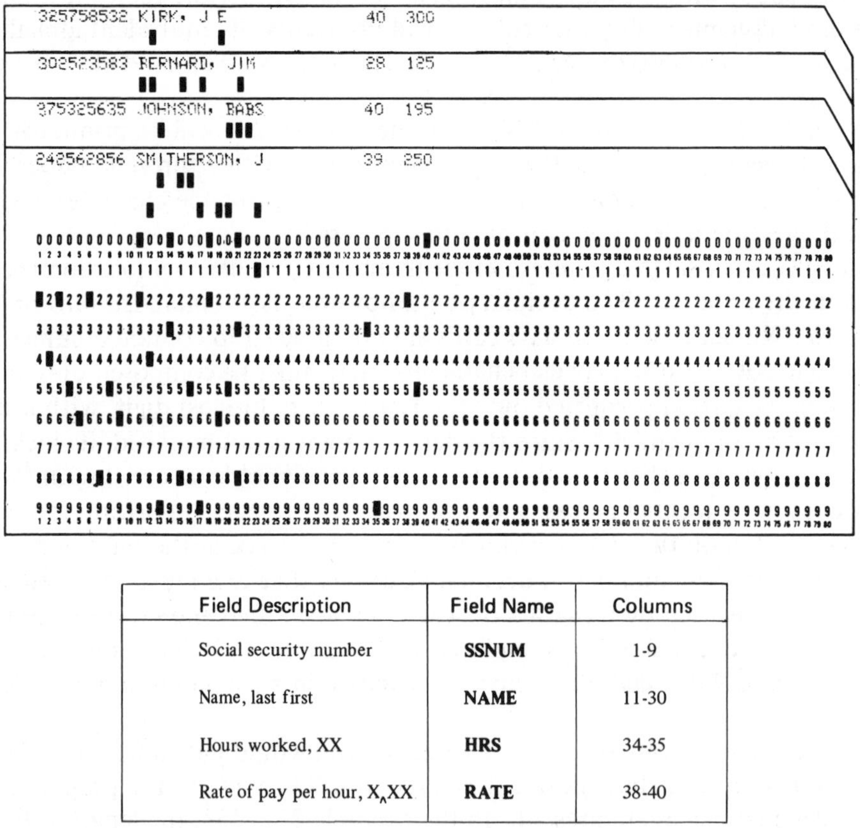

Field Description	Field Name	Columns
Social security number	SSNUM	1-9
Name, last first	NAME	11-30
Hours worked, XX	HRS	34-35
Rate of pay per hour, X∧XX	RATE	38-40

FIG. 2-6 Possible card design for hourly payroll.

It is often necessary to store information that is long and bulky, not fitting a standard format. Information of this type can sometimes be *coded* so that it will not be necessary to store explanatory phrases in the computer system. Suppose, for example, that a real estate dealer wishes to put information about all his apartment houses into a computer system. It would be very lengthy to put in phrases such as *"floors are hardwood, in top condition," "wall-to-wall carpeting,"* or *"vinyl tile."* Instead of putting these phrases into the computer, you can assign a code number to each phrase to be used instead. Code number 12 may, for example, mean *"vinyl tile, worn in spots,"* whereas 13 may mean *"no tile at all."* The name for this coded field of information could be **FLOOR** since it gives information about floors in the apartment.

Other information can be coded with a number that means *how many*. Information about fireplaces could use code Ø to mean none, code 1 to mean one, etc., with code 5 perhaps meaning *not* just 5, but 5 or more! The number of dependents, for example, can be coded as the exact number you have, not requiring further coding.

It is important to make the code into *one* field, and not several. In coding multiple-choice responses on test questions, each response can be assigned to letters A, B, and C, or to digits 1, 2, and 3, as needed. The answer selected to question 1 should be assigned to *one* column; for question 2, use a different column. It is not necessary to use three columns for each question, such as column 15 for an A response, column 16 for a B response, and column 17 for a C response! When one column is used instead of several, *one* operation with a punch card unit-record sorter machine can separate the cards *by question,* whereas it would require much more time should 3 columns be used.

It is possible to have several record types within a single deck of cards. A deck of payment cards, for example, can be merged with a deck of charge cards to form a single deck. One record type can be used for inventory receipts and another record type for inventory issues. The MULTIPLE-CARD LAYOUT FORM, shown in Figure 2-7, is used for designing card layouts, especially when more than one card format is needed. Note that fields in common are aligned, using the same card columns on each type of card. Column 5Ø contains an identifying punch, called a *record identification code.* It is usually one column, but sometimes several columns, of information punched into the card to identify the type of record it represents. The code B in Figure 2-7 means a balance card; R and I stand for receipts and issues,

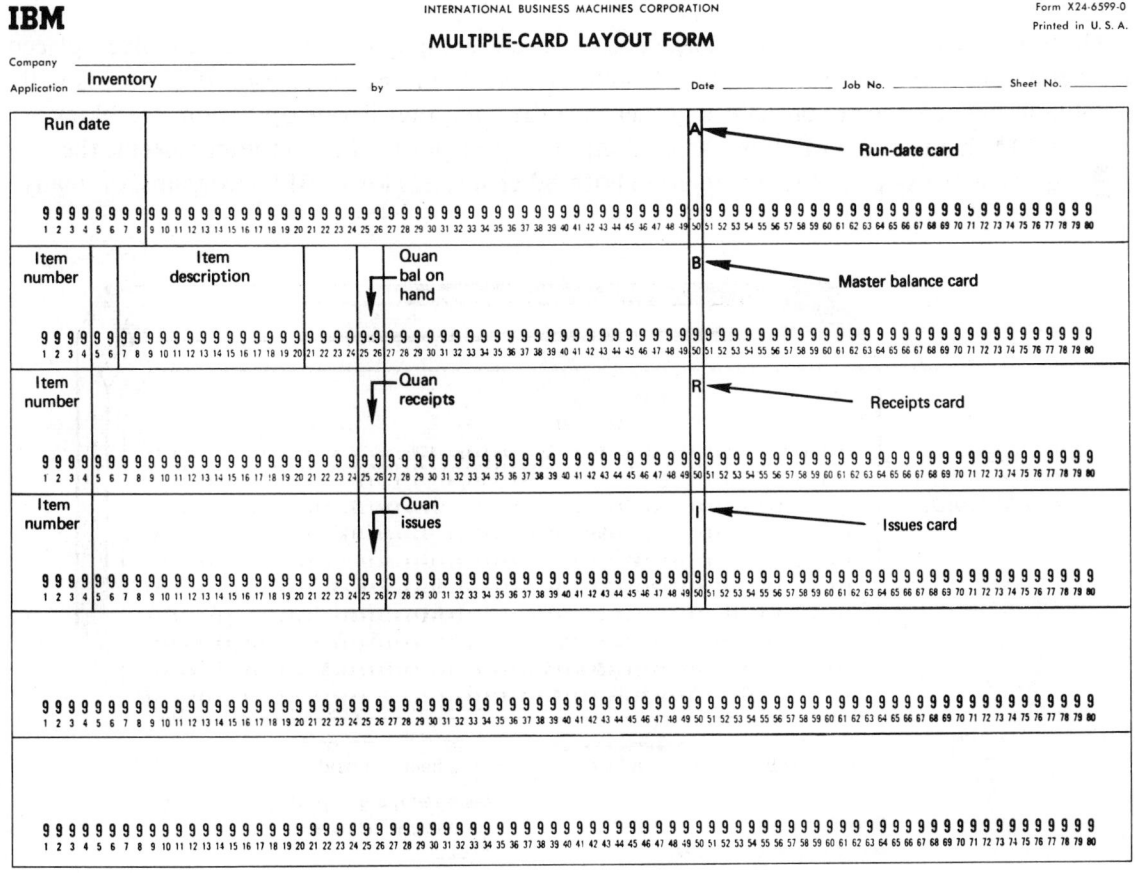

FIG. 2-7 MULTIPLE-CARD LAYOUT FORM for an inventory job.

respectively. The card giving the date the run is to be made contains an A for record identification. The code could be a numeric digit punch or even a zone punch. In the layout of most records, one column is reserved for the record identification, even though, at the time of design, a need for one is not anticipated because you think only one type of card is needed. Record identification codes are used only to identify the record types. They are therefore not considered fields, and do not require field names. They can be punched when the other fields on the card are punched, or can be put into the deck in one operation later by using the unit-record IBM 519 machine, the keypunch, or a computer.

Data that are prepared and placed onto punch cards usually record one daily activity about a particular account, such as the purchase of a pair of shoes on a charge account at a department store. It is, in this case, a record of a transaction that is of interest for a short period of time, perhaps only until the billing is done. It then becomes a matter of history and is put away. Data of this nature are called *detail* transactions. Another type of record, called *master* record, is relatively unchanging with portions being the same from month to month. A record containing your name and address, your account number, and your balance from the previous billing period is an example. When punch cards are used for master information, it is necessary to create a new deck each time the information is changed or updated.

Punch cards for input to the computer system are 8Ø-column records. Each record is made up of several fields. Since the fields have names, it is also appropriate for the entire record to have one. A record for a payroll job may be called **PAYREC**; one for course cards for classes may be called **CLASSCD**. Record names are for the use of the programmer, and although an abbreviation of the record name is permitted to be used in one place in an RPG program, record names are not required.

On input media that are continuous, such as magnetic tape, several records are often placed together and brought into the computer system as a block, in one operation. If 5 records with 8Ø columns in each one are brought together into the computer in one operation, the block length is 4ØØ characters. For all punch card input and output to the computer system, the blocking size is the same as the record size—both 8Ø characters long. RPG programs, on many

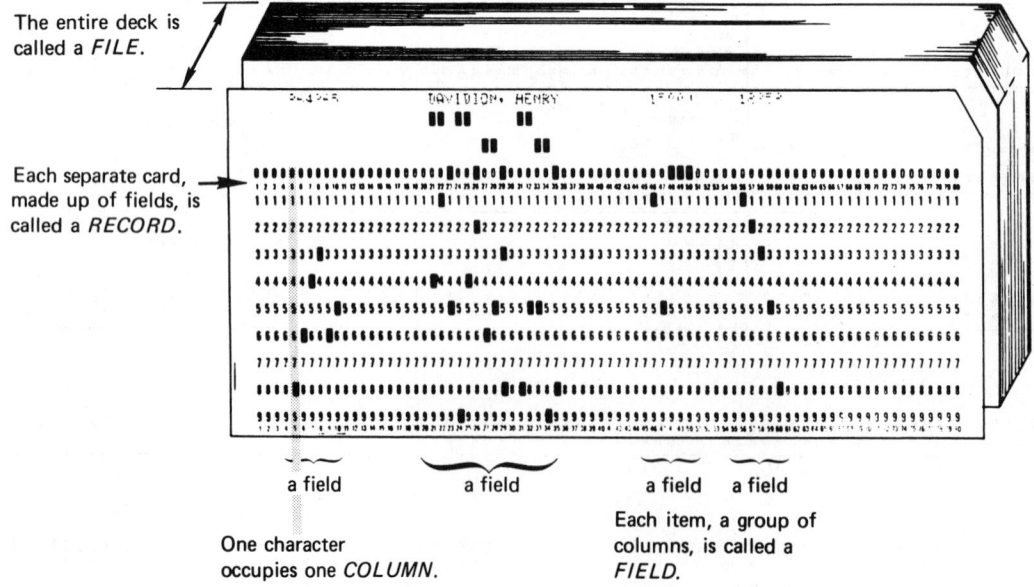

FIG. 2-8 Punch cards: columns, fields, records, files.

implementations, require that both record and block length be specified: on some, only record length is required; on others, both may be omitted.

Each deck of cards concerning one particular application is considered a file. For a given job, there may be a file of cards going in as input, and another coming out as output. Each file is identified by a name. Common names for input and output files are **INPUT** and **OUTPUT**! File names can be much more imaginative than that, however, since a name such as **PAYFILE** may be assigned to a file of payroll records just as easily as a name such as **LEMONS**. Keep in mind that a *file* is a whole deck of cards, a *record* is a single card, and a *field* is a usable piece of data on the card, made up of several columns, as shown in Figure 2-8.

EXERCISES

1. Give the punch card pattern of holes made by the keypunch machine for each of the following:

EXAMPLE: DMV ≡ & - ∅
                  4 4 5

(a) Your own last name   _____   (d) The period, .   _____

(b) Your favorite author   _____   (e) The asterisk, *   _____

(c) A telephone number: SA23157 _____

2. Give requested information for each of the following numeric values:

	High-order Digit	Low-order Digit	Algebraic Sign
EXAMPLE 3∅14	3	4	Positive
(a) 2∅2314$\overline{6}$			
(b) 1∅1346			
(c) ∅129			
(d) 7			
(e) 21764			
(f) ∅21∅$\overline{∅}$			

(note: (e) has a "&" above the 21764)

3. Show how the following information should be aligned and punched into a 12-position alphameric field to be used by RPG:

	1	2	3	4	5	6	7	8	9	1∅	11	12
EXAMPLE: 5.∅%ᵇFEE	5	.	∅	%	ᵇ	F	E	E	ᵇ	ᵇ	ᵇ	ᵇ
(a) JONES, ᵇJ.												
(b) 234-96-∅192												
(c) K2738.1D												
(d) SUSYᵇSMITH												
(e) .276CR												
(f) CCB.ᵇCORP.												

4. Give the numeric equivalent of each of the following fields, and its algebraic sign:

   EXAMPLE: ∅245J is ∅245$\overline{1}$, meaning *negative* ∅2451

   (a) ∅∅∅3N   _____

   (b) 23576K   _____

   (c) ∅∅147   _____

   (d) 2358C   _____

   (e) 27397I   _____

5. Show how the following values given should be aligned and punched into a numeric 8-digit field to be used by RPG:

   EXAMPLE: $2,341.92CR

∅	∅	2	3	4	1	9	$\overline{2}$

   (a) $1.26

   (b) –2154.326

   (c) 32,674

   (d) 27.62CR

   (e) 19.

   (f) ∅

6. Choose a field name for each of the fields shown on the card below, then specify the length and number of decimal places for each:

∅∅∅1345	PLASTIC SOFA	13752	27
Reference Number	Name of item	Price of each	Number on hand
1-7	8-27	44-48	54,55

	Name	Length	Number of Decimal Places
(a)			
(b)			
(c)			
(d)			

7. Design a card record:

(a) Social security number

(b) Last name

(c) First name

(d) Date of hire

(e) Code for type of employee: hourly or salaried

(f) Amount of pay

(g) Amount of income tax deducted

(h) Amount of bonds deducted

(i) Record ID code

Card Columns	RPG Field Name	Length	Number of Decimal Places

Lesson 3

PRINTED REPORTS

You will learn how the printer is controlled and how reports are made.

The questions given here are answered on the back of this page. If you have had experience in working with reports produced on unit-record tabulating equipment or other programming systems, and if you can answer the questions accurately, go on to the Projects at the end of this section.

1. What is meant by a *preprinted* form?
2. What is a *multiple-part* form?
3. What is meant by overflow pages?
4. Why is it necessary on some implementations to use a *printer control tape*?
5. Name the three most common types of lines possible on a report.
6. Which channel on the printer control tape is aligned with the first printing line on the form?
7. Which channel on the printer control tape refers to the last detail line of printing on the body of the form?
8. Compare *spacing* and *skipping* functions.
9. How is the **PRINTER SPACING CHART** used in writing a program?
10. What is meant by *zero suppression*?

ANSWERS

1. Report forms that contain certain constant information already printed on the form, with specified places reserved for the detailed, variable information.

2. A form that has several copies produced at the same time by use of carbon, so that the information prints through onto the pages behind. By use of carbon stripping, selected information on one form can be printed through to another form without the entire report printing through. Several copies of a report may be made by having two or more images of the report, side by side, rather than one behind the other with carbon; these reports, however, are not considered multiple-part.

3. Pages containing information that was not printed on the first form of that group because it became full.

4. To control the vertical skipping of the form, causing it to move down to specified positions.

5. Heading lines, detail lines, and total lines.

6. Channel Ø1.

7. Channel 12.

8. Spacing is used to move the form either one, two, or three rolls forward, whereas skipping is done for any distances greater than that.

9. The mock-up of the report provides information about print positions, editing and zero suppression, spacing and skipping, and constant information that should be printed on the report.

10. Changing the left-zero-fill digits of numeric fields to blanks so that they will not print.

Lesson 3   Printed Reports

Reports are usually made on a printer, connected on-line to the computer system by a cable. As each data card is fed into the card reader, it is processed by the CPU, and a corresponding line of print then comes out on the on-line printer. Totals needed for the bottom of the page or for the end of the report are accumulated, but remain in storage, while the detail lines for a given page are coming out. The IBM 36Ø computer system can have, depending on the model, any of the several printers attached. The IBM 14Ø3, a line printer of the "chain" type, is one. An image of the line to be printed is set up in a "print buffer." A movable chain contains several multiples of the character set. As the correct character "flies by," the paper is struck by a magnet-driven hammer, which causes it to be pressed against an ink-filled ribbon and to print the character on the paper. Although the characters on the line do not all get struck at exactly the same instant, they are all struck within a very short time, which makes it appear that the line is produced all at once. The IBM 14Ø3, shown in Figure 3-1, can print from 6ØØ to 11ØØ lines per minute, depending on the model, with either 12Ø or 132 positions per line. It prints 1Ø characters to an inch, with operator control for either 6 or 8 lines per

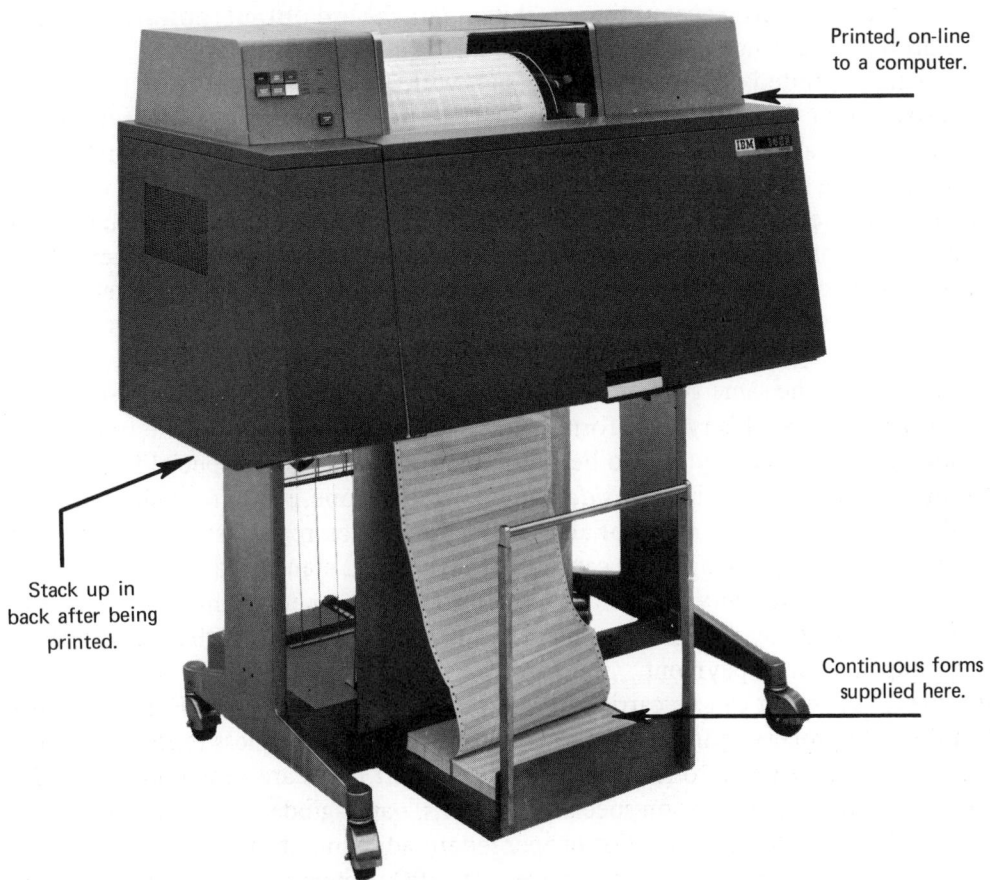

Printed, on-line to a computer.

Stack up in back after being printed.

Continuous forms supplied here.

FIG. 3-1 IBM 14Ø3 printer using continuous form stock paper. (Courtesy of International Business Machines Corporation.)

inch. Other printers that are often on the IBM 36Ø computer are the IBM 1443, which uses a type bar instead of a chain, and is slower and less expensive; the IBM 1445, which can produce magnetic ink characters for character recognition machines, such as those used by many banks; the IBM 14Ø4, which can not only print on continuous forms, but can also print up to 25 lines onto the face of a punch card.

The printing pressure on the ribbon is sufficiently great to allow several copies of a report to be made at the same time with multiple-part paper. By proper placement of carbon stripping within the several parts of the form, printing can be done on one part of the form copy and be suppressed on others, producing a variety of reports at one time. Pressure of the platen can be adjusted to allow for the extra thickness so that feeding of the forms will not be restricted. A *forms switch*, when properly set, causes a halt, to signal the operator when the forms are almost all used, so that more may be inserted before processing continues.

On almost any computing system, input and output speeds are much slower than computing speeds. For that reason, some installations with a large, expensive computer do not allow reports to be printed on-line, but require that information be placed temporarily onto magnetic tape or disk, which are much faster output devices. The report is usually recorded on the tape, line by line, exactly as it should appear on a printed report. In a separate operation, a smaller, less expensive computer can be used to print the report, or it may be printed by the same computer system at a more leisurely time. Before high-speed printers were readily available, punch cards were often used as output instead of a report. The decks of cards prepared were usually printed on an off-line electric accounting machine. Punch card output, however, is slower than high-speed printers and is not often used now in this manner.

Reports can be printed onto plain stock paper, with all headings and titles put on by the computer program, or they can be printed on special-order forms already preprinted with headings and titles. Standard stock paper for a printer, as shown in Figure 3-1, is usually 11 in. long by 14 in. across, with shaded bands on it to make the printing easier to read. It can easily hold 132 characters on one line, and from 66 to 88 lines on each page. Forms are usually a continuous-feed type, with pin-feed holes down each side so that the printer can pull them through. A variety of forms are commercially available—they can be made in almost any size, color, or design, and can range from cardboard weight to tissue paper. Additional copies are often made at the same time, some by using carbon, and others by having several forms side by side. When two forms of exactly the same type are side by side, the form is said to be "two-up"; the programmer must know that this type of form is to be used since two sets of the information on that line must be placed side by side to be printed at one time. Some special forms allow privileged information to be printed *inside* a presealed envelope, ready to mail. Other types include adhesive mailing labels; cards of almost any size; check registers; file folders; coupon envelopes made of clear plastic so you can see through them; stencil masters attached to reports, so that the printer cuts a stencil as the report is made, permitting more copies of that portion to be made by stencil later; and accounts receivable forms that include envelopes for prompt return of payment. One form, an envelope made for the steel industry, is made of asbestos so that it can be carried into hot areas inside the plant! Forms are very important in the data processing industry; they serve to make the business report even more usable to the person who is going to read it. Several different types are shown in Figure 3-2.

For proper *width* adjustment on special-size forms, paper guides on the printer are manually moved to fit the width needed. For proper *length* adjustment, however, *spacing* is used to roll the carriage either one, two, or three spaces. In RPG, spacing can be done both *before* and *after* the line is printed, so that it is possible to have as many as six spaces specified, three before and three after, which would leave five blank lines between the two printed lines. For positioning the form for longer distances, or for moving the printer to the top of a new form or

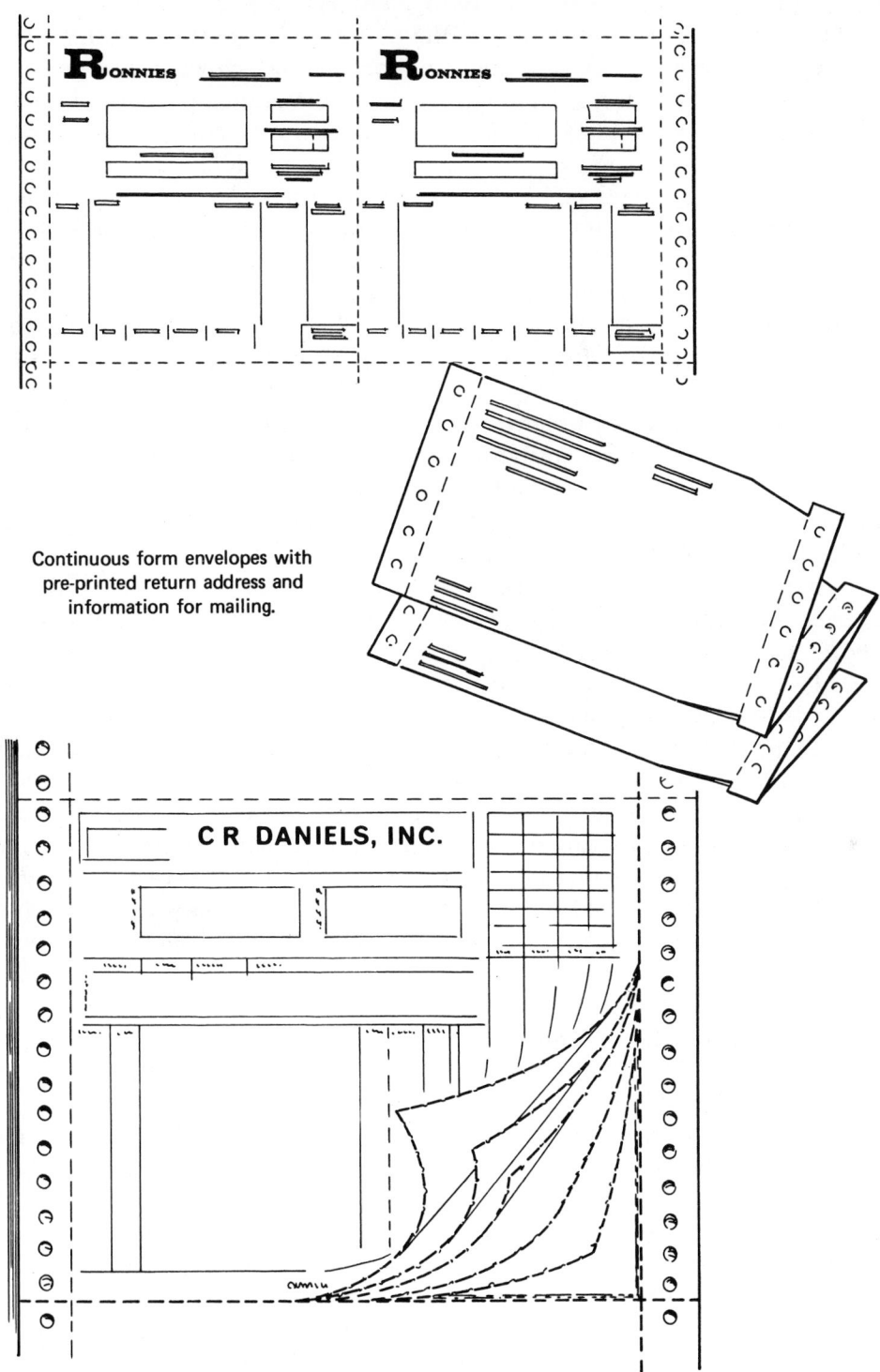

Two copies made side by side,
sometimes with more copies made
with carbon.

Continuous form envelopes with
pre-printed return address and
information for mailing.

Ten copies produced all at one time . . . salesman
copy, work order, shipping notice, packing lists,
shipping master, etc.—uses carbon stripping to put
information on some forms but not on others.

FIG. 3-2 Other preprinted business forms. (Courtesy of Moore Business Forms
and Baltimore Business Forms.)

to a specific printing line position within the form, an operation known as *skipping* is used. On all implementations of RPG except the one on IBM SYSTEM/3, a carriage control tape is used to correspond to these specific print positions. The control tape, shown in Figure 3-3, is prepared on a special punching device; it is then inserted into the printer and aligned to the top of the form being used. The control tape may have holes at any of several different positions, permitting the printer to be stopped for printing onto the form. Holes punched into the carriage control tape may be at any of 12 punch positions, called *channels*. Channel $\emptyset$1 is used to correspond to the *first* printing line of the form. Channel 12, called the *overflow channel*, is used to signal the *last* printing line, so that when the body of the form is full, overflow onto another form may occur. Channel holes $\emptyset$2-11 are used to indicate places on the form where other special stops for printing are anticipated. Channel $\emptyset$9 is usually used for marking the place for a total or summary line, often near the bottom of the form, possibly even after the channel 12 punch.

The program directs the printer to move to one of these punched channels by *skipping*. To cause the printer to roll up the form until it reaches the first printing line of the next form, an instruction is given to "skip to channel $\emptyset$1"; to cause it to move to the summary line at the bottom of a form, the instruction would be "skip to channel $\emptyset$9." Channel 12, not usually used for a printing line, detects when the body of the form is full, and internal indicators are turned on, so that the program can cause skipping to another form.

The paper control tape shown in Figure 3-3 has channel $\emptyset$1 punched to correspond to line 5 of the report; channel 12 will correspond to line 59, allowing 55 lines of printing per form, single-spaced. It is customary to prepare a control tape for more than one length of the form being used. At six lines per inch, on 11-in. paper, there are 66 lines that may be used—the carriage control tape could have enough lines for 132 lines, equivalent to two images of the paper. Line 5 on the second form would correspond to line 71 on the control tape, which should be punched at channel $\emptyset$1; line 59 of the second form would correspond to line 125 of the control tape, which should be punched at channel 12. The paper control tape is cut at the line corresponding to the total length of the two forms, which is, in this case, line 132. It is then glued to the other end to form a loop. When completely dry, it is placed onto the printer and mechanically aligned with the top of the form. Figure 3-4 shows a preprinted form that has a heading—channel $\emptyset$1 is cut at line 4 for the first heading line. The body starts at line 12—it has a channel $\emptyset$2 hole; the last printing line on the form should be at line 62—it has a channel 12 hole. In both Figures 3-3 and 3-4, the carriage control tape lines are used in a one-to-one correspondence with the stock paper or form, measured in six lines to the inch down the page. Should eight lines to the inch be used instead, an adjustment must be made before cutting the carriage control tape. Figure 3-5 shows how it can be done; remember that a lever on the printer must also be set to eight lines per inch rather than six in order to have that type of report properly printed.

The IBM SYSTEM/3 computer does not use a carriage control tape, but instead uses the skipping function to refer to specific line numbers on the form. Specifications within the program are used to adjust to different-size forms.

To ensure a well-balanced report, a PRINTER SPACING CHART form is prepared as a mock-up of the real thing. Lines of the report are categorized into one of these four classes: *heading lines, detail lines, exception lines, and total lines*. Your report may have several lines of each of these classes, and within each class, there may be different types of line formats. There may be, for example, several different lines of heading. Each line is copied onto the spacing chart in the exact print position it will occupy on the report. There may be more than one type of detail line—perhaps one format for a $9\emptyset$-day account line, and another for a $3\emptyset$-day

Tape Punch

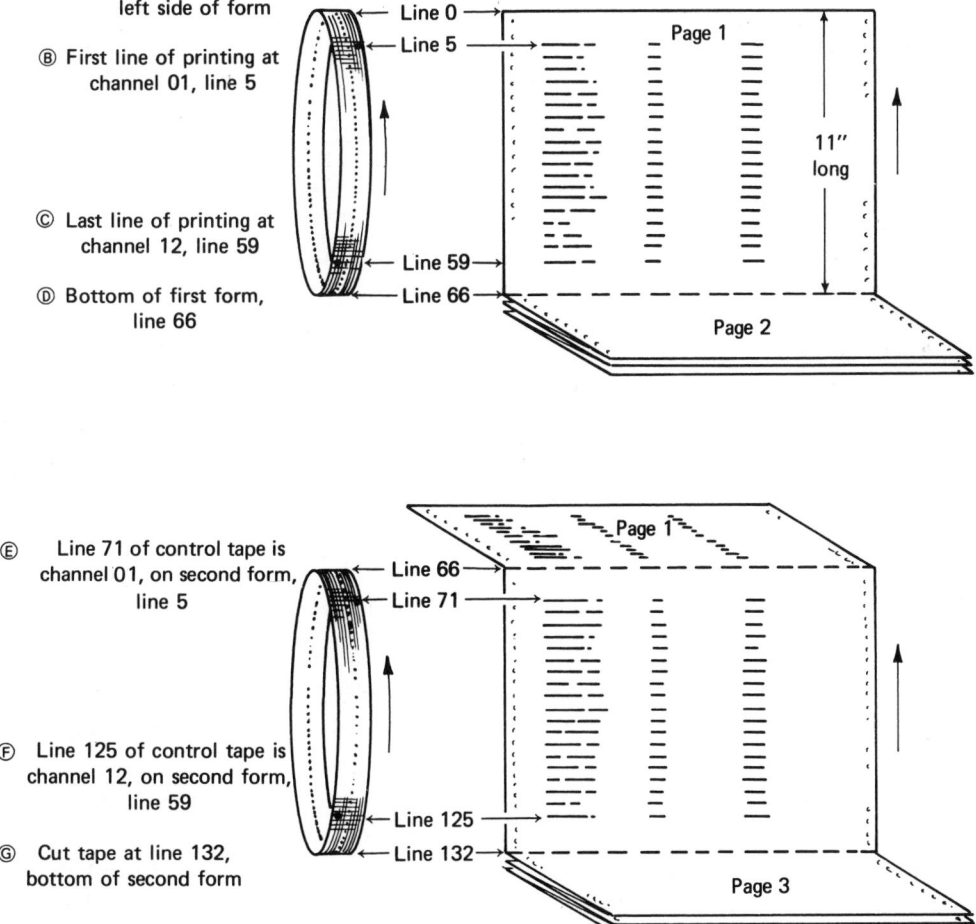

Ⓐ Align control tape alongside left side of form

Ⓑ First line of printing at channel 01, line 5

Ⓒ Last line of printing at channel 12, line 59

Ⓓ Bottom of first form, line 66

— Line 0
— Line 5
Page 1
11" long
— Line 59
— Line 66
Page 2

Ⓔ Line 71 of control tape is channel 01, on second form, line 5

Ⓕ Line 125 of control tape is channel 12, on second form, line 59

Ⓖ Cut tape at line 132, bottom of second form

Page 1
— Line 66
— Line 71
— Line 125
— Line 132
Page 3

FIG. 3-3 Planning, punching, and gluing a control tape for stock paper for six-lines-per-inch printing, using two form images on the tape.

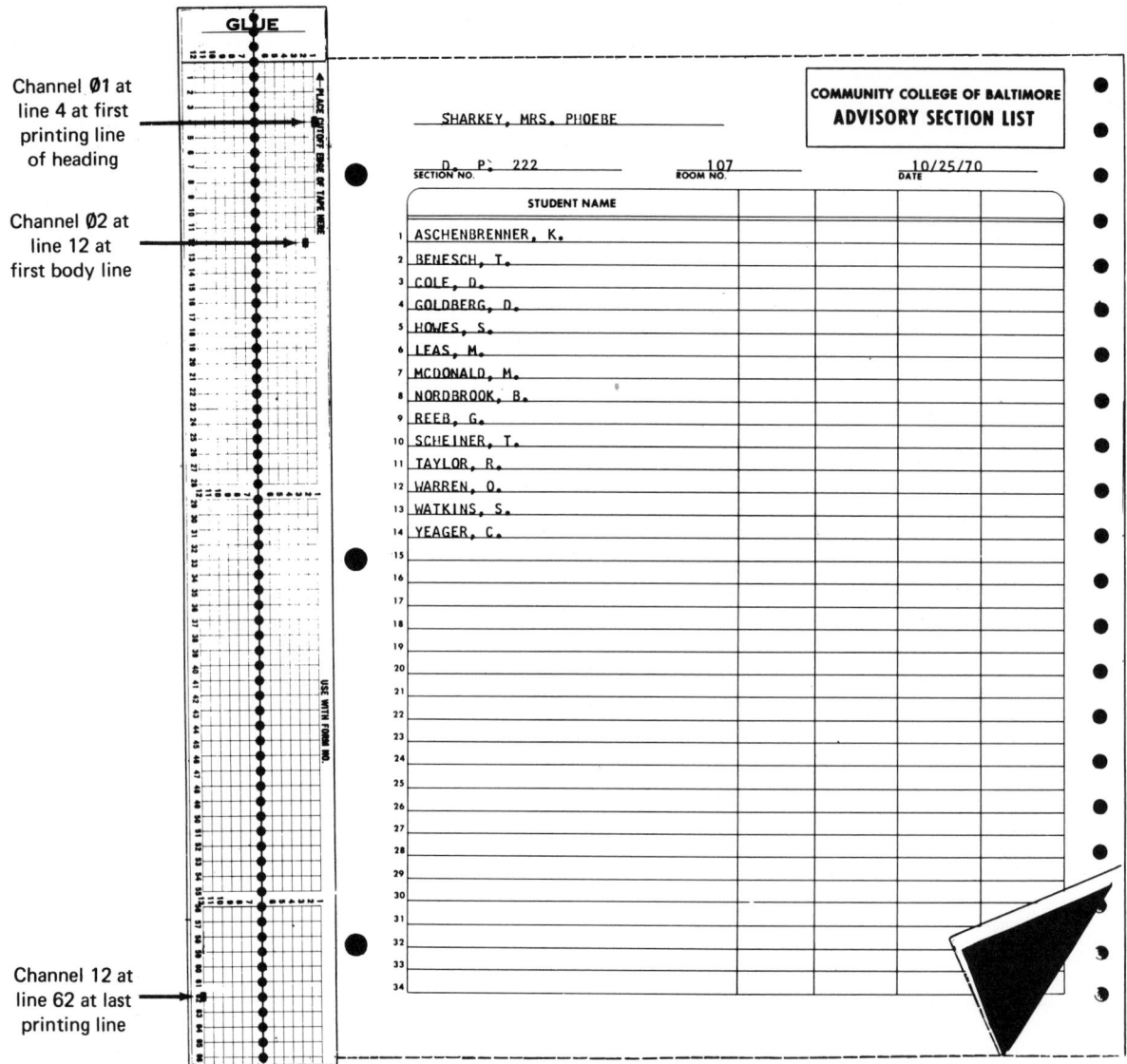

FIG. 3-4 A control tape for preprinted form. (Courtesy of Owens Forms, Baltimore, Md.)

type. The spacing chart shows what type of lines the report will contain, what information will be on what line, in what order, in what form, and in which print positions. The chart is generally made after consultation with the people who will be using the report.

On a spacing chart, heading lines, detail lines, exception lines, and total lines are identified by an **H**, **D**, **E**, or **T**, respectively. Heading lines generally contain constant information, which is the same each time the report is run, but could also give variable information, such as the date of the run, the page number, or the name of the group to which the particular page applies. Detail lines, coded **D**, are usually those lines that are found in the body of the report, but could also be those that identify the name of a group to which a particular page applies. Heading and detail lines are handled in RPG at the same time, so that the programmer is not rigidly held to a definition distinguishing them. Some installations prefer that **H** coding be reserved for constant headings that are printed only on the first page and overflow pages, and

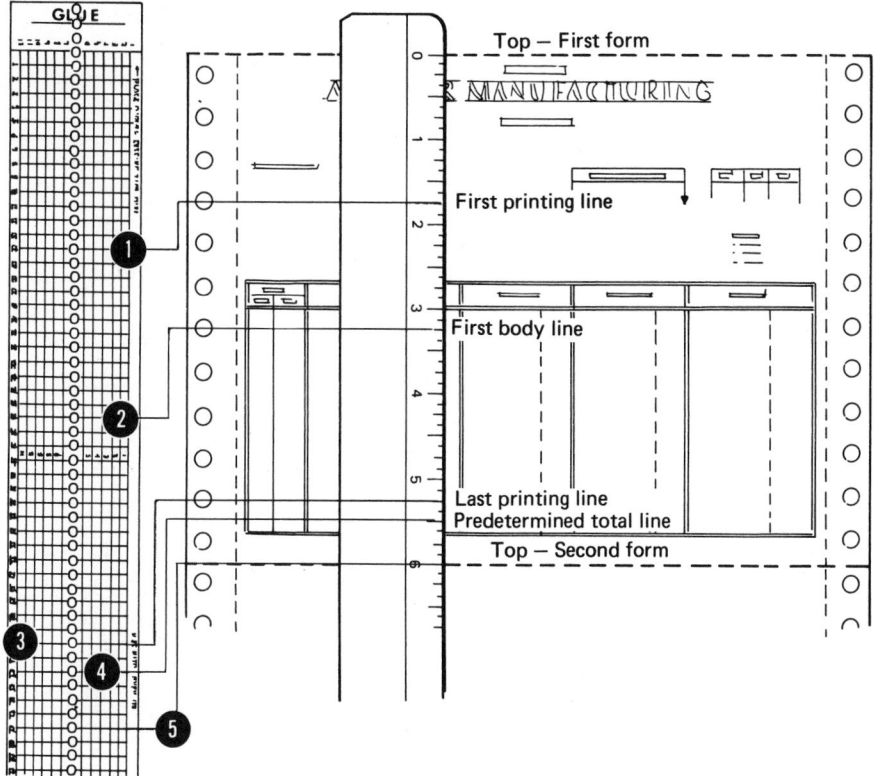

1   14 lines from the top
2   26 lines from the top
3   42 lines from the top
4   44 lines from the top
5   48 lines from the top

FIG. 3-5 Control tape for heading, body, and total lines, adjusted for eight-lines-per-inch printing. (Courtesy of International Business Machines Corporation.)

that other types of headings be considered detail lines. In general, however, the coding **H** is used to indicate any kind of line that is printed only once near the top of a particular page, whether or not variable information is on the line.

Exception lines, with an **E** code on the spacing chart, are those that are printed *during*, rather than *after*, calculations. One card of information could, for example, specify that an entire table should be printed—where each line of the table, except the first, depends on the previous line rather than on the original input card. Some implementations do not permit the use of **E**, but rather require that this type of line be done by an internal looping process, with printing done as a total line. This class of line need not concern you at this time.

Total lines, denoted by **T** on the spacing chart, are usually printed either just below the body portion of the report, or at a special position at the bottom of the page. The spacing chart need not show them on the exact line at which they are to be printed, but may instead show them at any of the next available lines; a comment should appear to state which actual line is to be used, and whether or not a channel punch corresponds to that line.

Comments about spacing, skipping, and calculations may be given anywhere on the chart. You will notice in the spacing charts shown in Figure 3-6 that an image of the carriage control tape is on the left side of the chart and the channel Ø1 hole is shown on it, but other channel holes are sometimes specified by comments. Notice also that the names of the fields being

Indicates headings and
one type of detail line

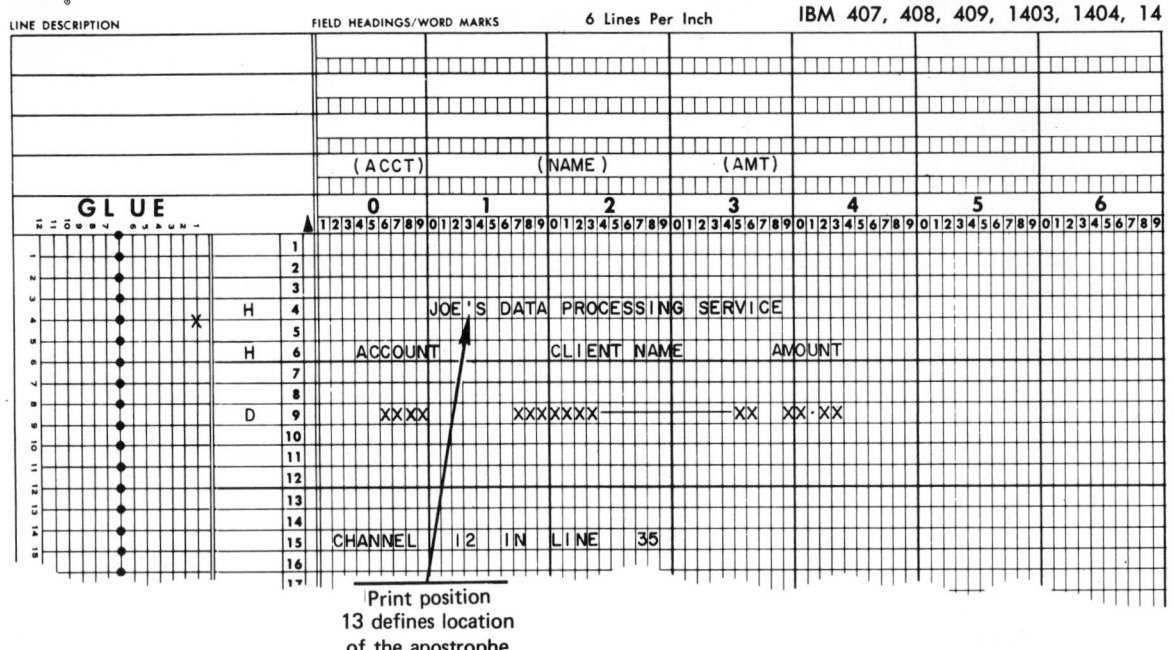

Print position
13 defines location
of the apostrophe

Indicates headings, one type of detail
line, and two types of total lines

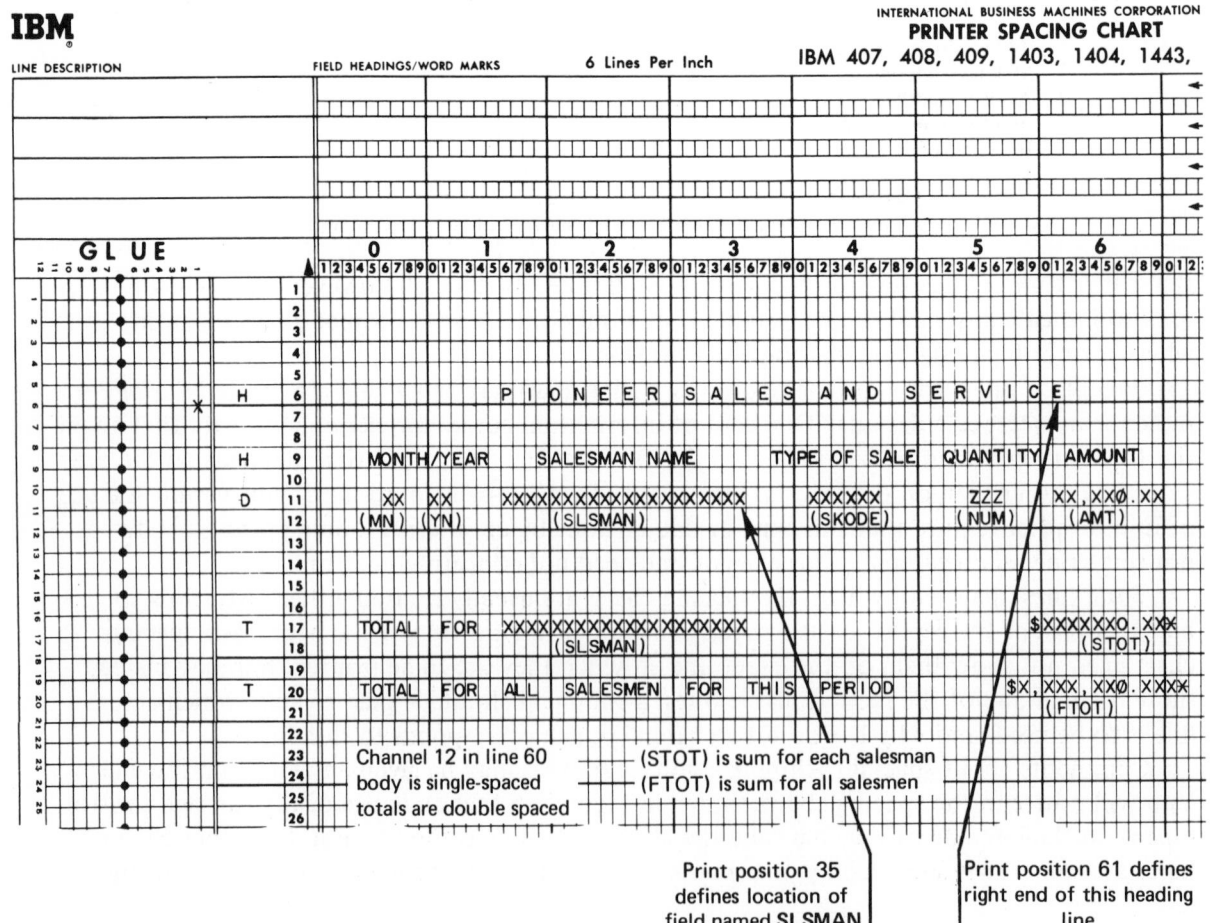

Channel 12 in line 60
body is single-spaced
totals are double spaced

(STOT) is sum for each salesman
(FTOT) is sum for all salesmen

Print position 35
defines location of
field named SLSMAN

Print position 61 defines
right end of this heading
line

FIG. 3-6 Examples of PRINTER SPACING CHARTS.

printed are given in parentheses, either in capital letters near where they are to be printed, or at the top of the chart. These assigned field names are used for reference by the programmer.

Although the contents of the fields are unknown at the time the spacing chart is made, the characteristics, such as length and mode, must be known. Both the X and Z codes indicate variable information, which will be taken from input punch cards or generated by calculations within the computer. Those fields coded Z are used to indicate *numeric* fields that are whole numbers, to be zero suppressed when printed. The X code indicates alphameric characters in some cases, and numeric digits in others. The special characters $, commas, decimal points, etc., are to be inserted, by *editing*, for readability. The Ø in a position instead of an X indicates that the left-zero-fill digits should be changed to blanks before being printed, but only up to that position and no further. On fields that represent dollars and cents, zero suppression of this type is usually done, in this manner, up to the decimal point. The mock-up for the field given by $XX,XXØ.XX*, for example, specifies that data for that field should be printed as $b̸1,426.75*, $b̸b̸b̸275.59*, $b̸b̸b̸b̸b̸b̸.98*, or $b̸b̸b̸b̸b̸b̸.Ø3*, where the b̸ represents a blank print position on the report. Recall that fields to be edited in this manner must be stored in numeric mode by giving the field a decimal indication anywhere from Ø to 9.

In using RPG to print a report, it is important to know how to read print positions from the spacing chart in order to put them into the program. In Figure 3-6, on the chart for PIONEER SALES AND SERVICE, you can see the print positions that appear at the top of the form, given in sets of 1Ø positions each: Ø for print positions 1-9, 1 for 1Ø-19, 2 for 2Ø-29, etc. The first heading line here ends at print position 61, as shown in the figure. The field giving the salesman's name **SLSMAN**, which is to be printed on the detail line of the report, is 2Ø positions long, ending in print position 35, as shown in the figure. Extreme care must be taken in reading these print positions from the chart.

An important part of data processing is the handling of the report when the computer has completed it. Reports are usually stacked at the back of the printer in a continuous-fold pile. They must be separated by part, then each single part must be split into individual pages. The pin-feed margins must be removed before the reports are distributed. When the number of reports is large, or if several carbon copies have been made, certain machines should be available to assist in this work. A separator machine, called a *detacher,* or *deleaver,* can separate different parts of the report and remove the carbon between, piling each continuous form in a separate stacker. It may be used on-line to the printer, or off-line at a later time. The perforated pin-feed strips may also be removed, and center perforations on two-up forms broken. The continuous-fold stack of a single part may then be put through a *burster* machine, as shown in Figure 3-7, to split the individual pages apart from each other and stack them for distribution

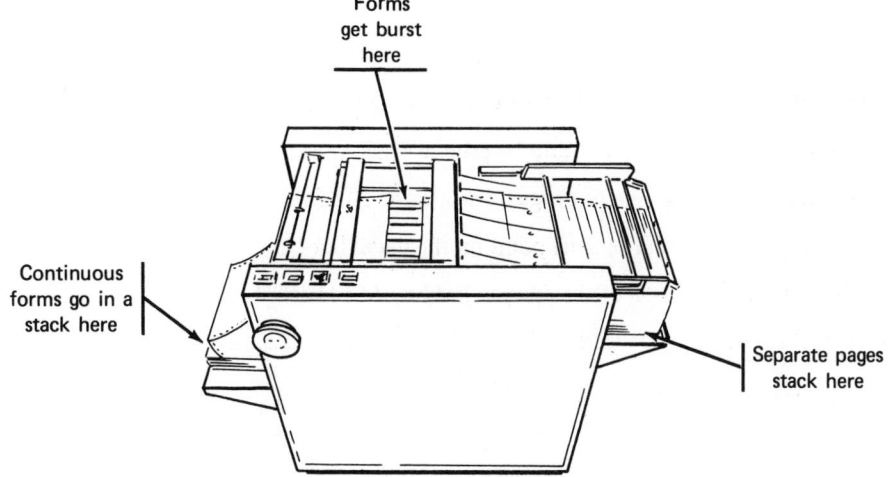

Forms get burst here

Continuous forms go in a stack here

Separate pages stack here

FIG. 3-7 Forms burster-stacker. (Courtesy of UARCO, Inc.)

EXERCISES

1. For each of the following field formats, give the requested information:

	Number of Required Print Positions	Number of Digits of Data It Uses	Number of Decimal Places
EXAMPLE: XX,XXX.XX	9	7	2
(a) XX.XX			
(b) $XXX,XXX.XX			
(c) ZZZZZ			
(d) XXØ.XXX			
(e) XX,XXØ.XXXX*			
(f) $XX,XXØ.XX			

2. The continuous-form envelope in Figure 3-2 is exactly 21 lines long. Only 3 lines are to be printed on it. A channel Ø1 hole is needed to locate the first printing line, at line 13. In making a carriage control tape containing four images of this form, answer each of these:

   (a) At what lines should the channel Ø1 holes be punched on the tape?_____

   (b) Where should the control tape be cut? _____

   (c) How will the printer be controlled in printing the *first* line of each form? _____

   (d) What kind of control will be used in printing the second and third line on each form? _____

3. A carriage control tape is to be made for the two-up form shown in Figure 3-2. The form is 42 lines long, with the first printing line to be on line 1Ø, the address change line on line 16, the body line on line 23, the overflow at line 37, and the total line at line 4Ø. To make 3 images of this form on a carriage control tape, channel holes must be made at what line numbers?

   (a) at channel Ø1 _____   (c) at channel 12 _____

   (b) at channel Ø2 _____   (d) at channel Ø9 _____

4. Answer these questions about the printer spacing chart for **JOE'S DATA PROCESSING SERVICE** in Figure 3-6:

   (a) How many heading lines are defined? _____

   (b) What kind of spacing is indicated between the heading lines? _____

   (c) Where should the first line on the form be printed? _____

   (d) Where should the last line on a full page be printed? _____

   (e) At what print position is the decimal point on the detail line? _____

   (f) What is the right-end position of the column heading ACCOUNT? _____

   (g) How many characters may be in the client's name? _____

Section 1

PROJECTS TO DO

A. PROBLEM NAME: **KP**:   keypunching data card

Make a list of possible values for the fields specified. Use a keypunch machine to punch them; save for later use.

Field Information	Columns	Example
Social security number	1-9	434560188
Student last name	11-20	JONES
Student first name	21-30	JANE
Class department	31-35	D.P.
Class number	36-38	105
Class section	39-40	AX
Class description	41-54	COMP. PGMMG.
Name of teacher	55-67	PRITZ
Number of teacher	68-70	061
Semester code: 1 or 2	71	1
School year	72-75	7172
Credits	79-80	04

B. PROBLEM NAME: **MOCKUP**:   spacing chart and control tape

Make a spacing chart to use when listing class cards from Problem A. Indicate where channels 01 and 12 should be placed when using stock paper. Make a control tape and glue it; save it for later use.

C. PROBLEM NAME: **MAKEUP**:   card layout

Use one section of a **MULTIPLE CARD LAYOUT** form to show your design for the following information, giving field names and assigned columns.

Field information: account name and number, street address, city/state, zip code, and balance from preceding month.

SECTION 2

INTRODUCTION TO RPG

Lesson 4

THE RPG LANGUAGE

You will become familiar with RPG *as a computer language.*

The questions given here are answered on the back of this page. They represent the kind of material taught in this lesson. If you are doing independent study, and answer all of them correctly, go on to Lesson 5.

1. What is a computer language?
2. What do the letters **RPG** stand for?
3. Why is **RPG** called a *problem-oriented* language?
4. What advantages does **RPG** have when compared to other languages?
5. What are the four commonly required forms?
6. What is the purpose of each of the four forms?
7. What are **RPG** *differences due to implementation*?
8. Who is responsible for the accuracy of a computer program?
9. What is the basic data processing cycle?
10. What is the difference between the *source* program and the *object* program?

ANSWERS

1. A programming system to allow communication of information between people and computers. The language consists of certain characters, symbols, and operations with rules for arranging them into a program to achieve certain meanings. For each language, there must be a *processor*, which is written in the code of the machine, used to convert the user's program into machine code.
2. Report Program Generator.
3. Because it is more closely related to the problem being solved than to the characteristics of the machine. It is designed so that people who are familiar with the problem can use it without knowing the internal characteristics of the machine.
4. It is quicker to learn, quicker to use for simple reports, very machine independent, and runs on less expensive equipment than some other languages.
5. FILE DESCRIPTION, INPUT, CALCULATION, and OUTPUT-FORMAT.
6. FILE DESCRIPTION, to describe the input and output files; INPUT, to describe the records within the input files by fields; CALCULATION, to specify the arithmetic and logical decisions; and OUTPUT-FORMAT, to describe the records for output.
7. Variations in the language as required by the programming system for different computers, or variations in the output produced by identical source statements when used on different computers.
8. The programmer.
9. Input of a data record, processing of that record, output of results, then repeat of the cycle with the next input record, and so on, until all records are completed.
10. The source program is written by the programmer in the computer language; the object program is produced by the computer by conversion of the source program into machine code.

Lesson 4   The RPG Language

RPG, Report Program Generator, is a computer programming system through which the programmer tells the computer what to do. It is a very simple language to learn and to use, since the programmer writes only the specifications: what information is to come in, what should be done with it, and what information should come out. The RPG programming system uses these specifications to generate the object program. The program that you write is called the *source* program; it is translated by the RPG programming system *processor* into machine language coding called the *object* program. The computer uses the object program to accept the data and do the job requested.

In writing a program, the machine does more tedious and detailed work than the programmer does. It writes the actual machine-coded program—the set of instructions that will cause the computer to operate in a predetermined way. You, the programmer, are telling the machine what coding to do. If your program logic is correct, but the specifications you give the machine are wrong, then the program it produces must also be wrong. If the program specifications and logic are *both* correct, then the program it generates should also be correct. However, even when the program is correct, the input data that you give the machine may be wrong, which will cause the answers to be wrong. Therefore, it is the programmer's responsibility not only to write the program, but to be sure that all the output produced is proper for the input provided.

Many small data processing installations use RPG as their main programming language. With it, many business applications can be done quickly, easily, and on relatively inexpensive equipment. Since it can be learned in a minimal amount of time, RPG is a very practical computer language to use. If you have had some experience in wiring or using unit-record equipment, you can learn RPG even more rapidly, because the logic of the language is closely patterned after the logic of the tabulating machine. Some of the large installations use RPG as one of many other programming languages because of its ease of application to the simple business report—unequaled even among the more complicated computer languages.

When compared to COBOL, Common Business Oriented Language, RPG is simpler to use, punch, and run when used on simple jobs. It has easier programming techniques for carriage control, field definitions, record identification codes, and control breaks between groups. It cannot, however, match the ease with which COBOL can perform complex calculations. In RPG, each addition, subtraction, multiplication, or division is done with a separate instruction; in COBOL, one sentence can be used to do all these, as well as exponentiation, in a single formula. Some installations are able to use the COBOL Report Writer, which is a set of instructions within the set of COBOL statements, very similar to RPG in nature. However, it is currently not as commonly available for use on the same relatively inexpensive equipment for which RPG is available.

Although you cannot, in RPG, do the intricate manipulations that the Basic Assembler Language can do, it gives you a way to write programs without your learning the complexities of hardware characteristics that the assembler language would require. Since RPG is a more *problem-oriented* than *machine-oriented* language, it is easy to use on a variety of computers from several different manufacturers.

RPG programming systems are currently available for most of the models within the IBM SYSTEM/36Ø computer family. They are also available on the IBM 113Ø and the IBM

SYSTEM/3. The UNIVAC 9000 computer series and the RCA SPECTRA-70 computer both have RPG capability; since they use specification forms and instructions of the same type as those used by the IBM computers, they are said to be *IBM-compatible*. The General Electric Company has recently announced that an IBM-compatible RPG will be available for their GE-120 computer.

There are often differences in the RPG programming system for different computers. When the memory characteristics of the machines differ, then the language almost certainly does—perhaps by having different data forms of storage, and therefore different rules about instructions or limitations on the size of answers. Certain *extensions* to the language have been developed; these are perhaps a result of better support, by the manufacturer, for some configurations of equipment than for others, with certain additions to the language available on some machine types but not on others. Differences are also caused by the various arrangements of storage devices that may be used. For example, some portions of the language may be available only on a magnetic disk system, and others, only on a card system. Differences of all these types are generally said to be *differences in implementation*, caused by the design of language for one particular machine configuration. When learning a new programming language of this nature, it is often better to study first those features that are most compatible when transferring from one machine type to another. Differences for several of the IBM SYSTEM/360 computer models are referred to, not by the models that are used to run them, such as Models 20, 25, 30, and so on, but by the operating systems under which they run. The programs shown in this text, for example, specify the machine configuration under which they were run, as either *TOS*, tape operating system, or *DOS*, disk operating system; whether they were run on a Model 25 or any other model is not stated, since they could run on any model that has the *TOS* RPG or the *DOS* RPG, respectively. The IBM SYSTEM/360, Model 20, has available several different versions of RPG—among them are *CPS* RPG, card programming support RPG, and *DPS* RPG, disk programming support RPG. Reference to RPG for the IBM 1130, however, is usually by machine name. Differences for certain IBM systems and for the UNIVAC 9300 and RCA SPECTRA-70 are given in the Appendix.

It has been found that very few changes must be made in basic RPG programs that are written for use of data on similar input/output devices. RPG is very machine independent, making it a practical programming system to use for a computer installation if changes in equipment are anticipated.

Detailed information about a particular implementation of RPG will be found in the RPG reference manual, obtained for a particular system by an order number, such as C26-3570 for the DOS/TOS system. Although manuals should be available for reference when you are *learning* RPG, they are even more necessary after you become experienced and try to do more complicated programs. The RPG programming system is constantly under revision by the manufacturer. Documentation of necessary changes is sent to the director of each installation so that they can be put onto each RPG system, whether on cards, disk, or tape. Just as the software is kept up to date, so the reference manuals must be, also. Replacement pages are periodically received by users; they represent changes caused by the revision of the programming system, as well as by corrections of errors or clarification of explanations. When the number of changes to a manual becomes great, an entirely new manual will be published; it will usually be given a revision number following the original number, such as C26-3570-1. A limited number of copies of reference manuals are supplied with the rental or purchase of equipment; they are also available for purchase from the equipment manufacturer.

The RPG language on several of the implementations will permit the use of subroutines previously written in the assembler language. The experienced programmer can use the two programming systems together to do problems that require more intricate manipulation of data than RPG alone will allow. With this combination of languages, full potential of the computer can be attained with minimal programming time.

RPG programs, no matter how simple or complex, basically consist of input, processing, and output. *Input* refers to data being brought into the computer system to be stored, commonly from punch cards, magnetic tapes, or magnetic disks. *Processing* refers to what happens to the data within the CPU, the central processing unit. Some fields are simply used for output; others may be used in calculations; still others may be used in making logical decisions. If, for example, the number of hours worked in a week is more than 4∅, an additional calculation for overtime pay must be done. The processing is done under the control of specifications in your program. *Output* refers to bringing out answers, which have been either calculated or moved to appropriate output areas. Output is most often a printed report, but may also be punch cards, magnetic tapes, or magnetic disks.

The execution of an RPG object program works with one input data record at a time. The CPU will get a record, process it, then output the results. Then it will go back and get another record, process it, and output those results. One record at a time is processed, with answers for that record brought out of the computer before the next record is brought in. This basic data processing cycle, shown in Figure 4-1, is indicated by using a line to form a loop, which shows that the steps are repeated until the input data cards have all been read into the computer, processed, and the appropriate output released. Variations of this basic cycle are possible. Sometimes a heading will be given at the beginning of a job, but never again. Other times a group of cards are brought in together to be used as a group, producing one or more lines of the report. Or only one record may be brought in, resulting, however, in several lines of a report. For some of the simplest RPG programs, the basic data processing cycle—input, calculation, and output—is followed exactly.

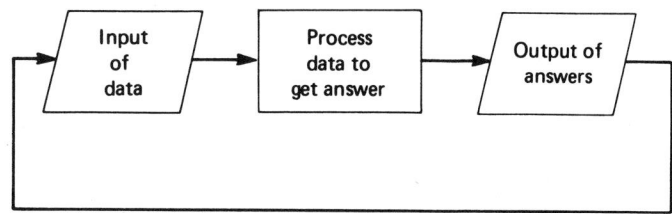

FIG. 4-1 Basic data processing cycle.

The RPG language uses specification forms such as those shown in Figure 4-2. The first two forms shown have provision for two types of specifications and are numbered separately here:

1. RPG CONTROL CARD specification establishes parameters for the RPG generation process.
2. FILE DESCRIPTION specifications tell the computer what equipment the program uses and whether it is for input or output.
3. FILE EXTENSION specifications give information about data tables, if any.
4. LINE COUNTER specifications give carriage control information either for reports that are to be printed at a later time, or for nonstandard reports being printed on a printer that does not have a carriage control tape.
5. INPUT specifications tell the specific record format and style of the input data deck, tape, or disk.

IBM

International Business Machines Corporation

Form X21-9094-0
Printed in U.S.A.

RPG INPUT SPECIFICATIONS

Date _____
Program _____
Programmer _____

Punching Instruction — Graphic / Punch

Page | 1 2

Program Identification | 75 76 77 78 79 80

Record Identification Codes — 1, 2, 3

Field Location

Line — Form Type — Filename — Sequence — Number (1-N) — Option (O) — Record Identifying Indicator — Position — Not (N) — C/Z/D — Character — Position — Not (N) — C/Z/D — Character — Position — Not (N) — C/Z/D — Character — Stacker Select (P) — Packed (P) — From — To — Decimal Positions — Field Name — Control Level (L1-L9) — Matching Fields or Chaining Fields — Field Record Relation — Field Indicators (Plus, Minus, Zero or Blank) — Sterling Sign Position

3 4 5 6 7 8 9 10 11 12 13 14 15 16 17 18 19 20 21 22 23 24 25 26 27 28 29 30 31 32 33 34 35 36 37 38 39 40 41 42 43 44 45 46 47 48 49 50 51 52 53 54 55 56 57 58 59 60 61 62 63 64 65 66 67 68 69 70 71 72 73 74

IBM

International Business Machines Corporation

Form X21-9091-1
Printed in U.S.A.

RPG EXTENSION AND LINE COUNTER SPECIFICATIONS

Date _____
Program _____
Programmer _____

Punching Instruction — Graphic / Punch

Page | 1 2

Program Identification | 75 76 77 78 79 80

Extension Specifications

Line — Form Type — Record Sequence of the Chaining File — Number of the Chaining Field — From Filename — To Filename — Table or Array Name — Number of Entries Per Record — Number of Entries Per Table or Array — Length of Entry — P = Packed/B = Binary — Decimal Positions — Sequence (A/D) — Table or Array Name (Alternating Format) — Length of Entry — P = Packed/B = Binary — Decimal Positions — Sequence (A/D) — Comments

0 1 E
0 9 E
1 0 E

Line Counter Specifications

Line	Form Type	Filename	1		2		3		4		5		6		7		8		9		10		11		12	
			Line Number	FL or Channel Number	Line Number	OL or Channel Number	Line Number	Channel Number	Line Number	Channel Number	Line Number	Channel Number	Line Number	Channel Number	Line Number	Channel Number	Line Number	Channel Number	Line Number	Channel Number	Line Number	Channel Number	Line Number	Channel Number

3 4 5 6 7 8 9 10 11 12 13 14 15 16 17 18 19 20 21 22 23 24 25 26 27 28 29 30 31 32 33 34 35 36 37 38 39 40 41 42 43 44 45 46 47 48 49 50 51 52 53 54 55 56 57 58 59 60 61 62 63 64 65 66 67 68 69 70 71 72 73 74

IBM

International Business Machines Corporation

Form X21-9092-0
Printed in U.S.A.

RPG CONTROL CARD AND FILE DESCRIPTION SPECIFICATIONS

Date _____
Program _____
Programmer _____

Punching Instruction — Graphic / Punch

Page | 1 2

Program Identification | 75 76 77 78 79 80

Control Card Specifications

Line — Form Type — Core Size to Compile — Object Output — Listing Options — Core Size to Execute — MFCM Stacking Sequence — Sterling (Input-Shillings, Input-Pence, Output-Shillings, Output-Pence) — Inverted Print — 360/20 2501 Buffer — Number Of Print Positions — Alternate Collating Sequence — Refer to the specific System Reference Library manual for actual entries.

0 1 H

File Description Specifications

Line — Form Type — Filename — File Type — File Designation — End of File — Sequence — File Format — I/O/U/C — P/S/C/R/T — E — A/D — F/V — Block Length — Record Length — Mode of Processing — Length of Key Field or of Record Address Field — Record Address Type — Type of File Organization or Additional Area — Overflow Indicator — Key Field Starting Location — L/R — K/I — I/D/T or 1-9 — Extension Code E/L — Device — Symbolic Device — Name of Label Exit — Labels (S, N, or E) — Extent Exit for DAM — File Addition — Number of Tracks for Cylinder Overflow — Number of Extents — Tape Rewind — A — N/U

0 2 F
F
F

3 4 5 6 7 8 9 10 11 12 13 14 15 16 17 18 19 20 21 22 23 24 25 26 27 28 29 30 31 32 33 34 35 36 37 38 39 40 41 42 43 44 45 46 47 48 49 50 51 52 53 54 55 56 57 58 59 60 61 62 63 64 65 66 67 68 69 70 71 72 73 74

FIG. 4-2 RPG specification forms.

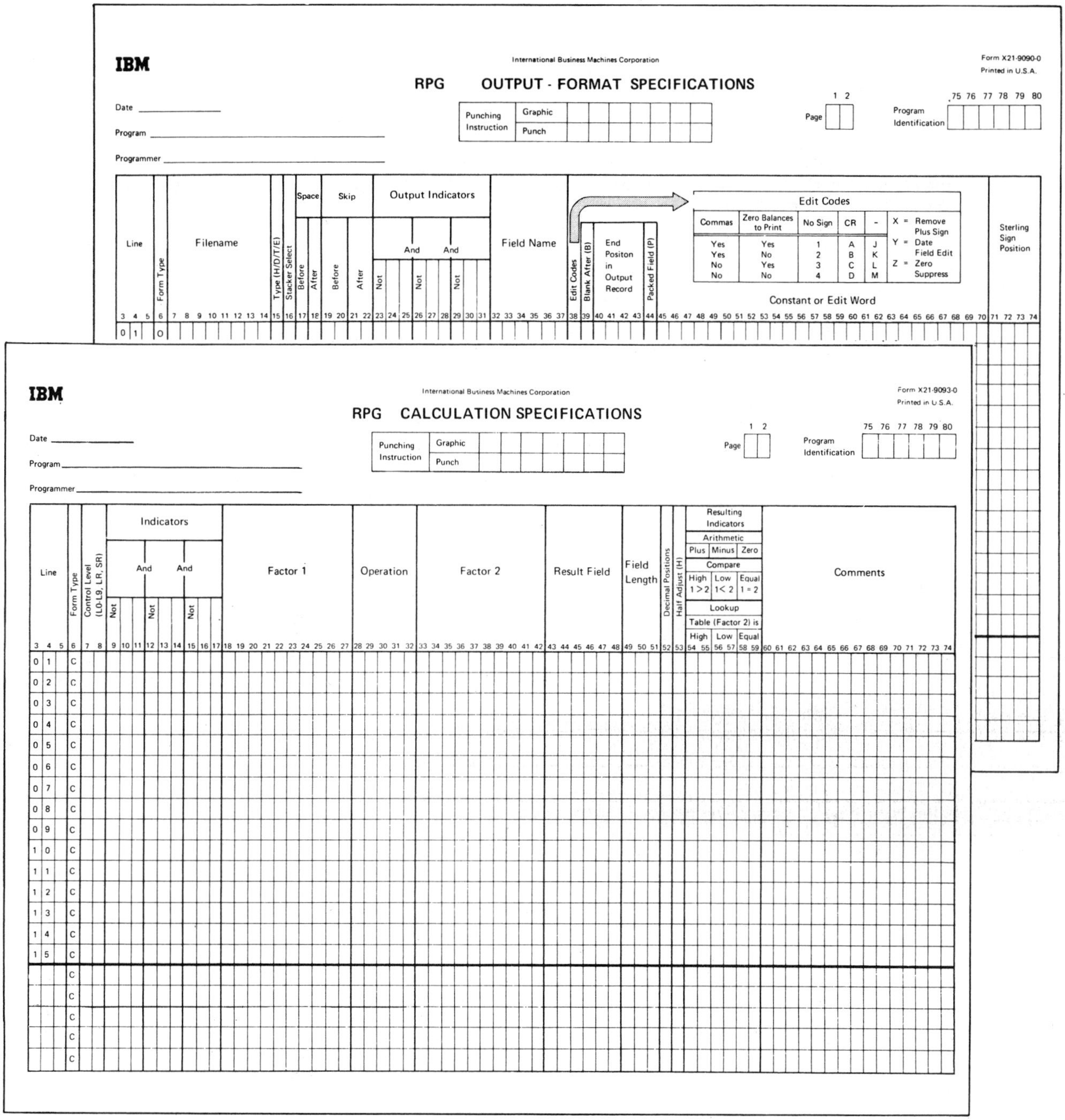

IBM

International Business Machines Corporation

RPG   OUTPUT - FORMAT SPECIFICATIONS

Form X21-9090-0
Printed in U.S.A.

Date _____

Program _____

Programmer _____

Punching Instruction — Graphic | Punch

Page [1 2]

Program Identification [75 76 77 78 79 80]

Line	Form Type	Filename	Type (H/D/T/E)	Stacker Select	Space Before	Space After	Skip Before	Skip After	Output Indicators And / And — Not / Not / Not	Field Name	Edit Codes	Blank After (B)	End Positon in Output Record	Packed Field (P)	Edit Codes	Sterling Sign Position

Edit Codes

Commas	Zero Balances to Print	No Sign	CR	-	X = Remove Plus Sign
Yes	Yes	1	A	J	Y = Date Field Edit
Yes	No	2	B	K	
No	Yes	3	C	L	Z = Zero Suppress
No	No	4	D	M	

Constant or Edit Word

3 4 5 6 | 7 8 9 10 11 12 13 14 15 | 16 | 17 18 | 19 20 | 21 22 | 23 24 | 25 26 27 | 28 29 30 | 31 | 32 33 34 35 36 37 | 38 | 39 | 40 41 42 43 | 44 | 45 46 47 48 49 50 51 52 53 54 55 56 57 58 59 60 61 62 63 64 65 66 67 68 69 70 | 71 72 73 74

0 1 0

IBM

International Business Machines Corporation

RPG   CALCULATION SPECIFICATIONS

Form X21-9093-0
Printed in U.S.A.

Date _____

Program _____

Programmer _____

Punching Instruction — Graphic | Punch

Page [1 2]

Program Identification [75 76 77 78 79 80]

Line	Form Type	Control Level (L0-L9, LR, SR)	Indicators And / And — Not / Not / Not	Factor 1	Operation	Factor 2	Result Field	Field Length	Decimal Positions	Half Adjust (H)	Resulting Indicators	Comments

Resulting Indicators

Arithmetic — Plus / Minus / Zero

Compare — High 1>2 / Low 1<2 / Equal 1=2

Lookup — Table (Factor 2) is — High / Low / Equal

3 4 5 6 | 7 8 | 9 10 11 12 13 14 15 16 17 | 18 19 20 21 22 23 24 25 26 27 | 28 29 30 31 32 | 33 34 35 36 37 38 39 40 41 42 | 43 44 45 46 47 48 | 49 50 51 52 | 53 | 54 55 56 57 58 59 | 60 61 62 63 64 65 66 67 68 69 70 71 72 73 74

0 1 C
0 2 C
0 3 C
0 4 C
0 5 C
0 6 C
0 7 C
0 8 C
0 9 C
1 0 C
1 1 C
1 2 C
1 3 C
1 4 C
1 5 C
C
C
C
C
C

FIG. 4-2—Cont.

6. CALCULATION specifications describe the arithmetic, decisions, or data movements, if the job requires any.

7. OUTPUT-FORMAT specifications tell the specific arrangement and style of the printed report, or output tape, card, or disk.

Although simple problems may use the RPG CONTROL CARD, the FILE DESCRIPTION, the INPUT, and the OUTPUT-FORMAT specifications, most problems also require the CALCULATION form. The FILE EXTENSION form is used when tables or arrays of data are to be stored for retrieval. The LINE COUNTER is very seldom used on the IBM 36Ø if reports are to be printed at the same time that the job is run; it is used on the IBM SYSTEM/3 to obviate the need for a carriage control tape, and is not used at all on the IBM 113Ø.

These **RPG** Specifications Forms, identified by the numbers X21-9090, X21-9091, X21-9092, X21-9093, and X21-9094, are recent releases by IBM for use with **RPG** and **RPG II**. Other versions of these forms, in which each specification is on a different sheet, have slightly different headings, but are still in use. These forms are used interchangeably throughout this text. It is important that forms are available for learning and using **RPG**. Still another form, X21-9095, the **RPG INDICATOR SUMMARY**, is optional and need not concern you yet.

When the specifications are completed on these forms, each line is punched onto one card, using the columns indicated on the form headings. Each card will contain, in column 6, a letter that tells the **RPG** programming system which form it represents. An F in column 6 means **FILE DESCRIPTION** and an O, **OUTPUT-FORMAT**. The first card of each program deck therefore has an H in column 6, meaning the **RPG CONTROL CARD**. In many cases, this card contains nothing else! It is used to affect the object program generation and execution, to define certain input/output limitations, establish certain options, and define core storage capacities. In many cases, that information is provided to the computer at system generation time, when the entire set of programming languages and support is initially custom prepared for each installation. For instructions on how to prepare the **RPG CONTROL CARD** in any other way, see the **RPG** operating procedures manual for your machine configuration.

When the source program cards are punched from these specification forms, they are properly stacked for entry to the computer for program generation. For the IBM SYSTEM/360, Models 25, 30, and up, these program cards are stacked in the same order as they are listed: H, F, E, L, I, C, and O. Several other implementations, however, require that they be stacked in a different order; you will also find this information in the **RPG** operating procedures manual for your equipment.

Recall that this source program deck is used to produce the object program, which is then used with data to produce the answers you are hoping to get. The procedures followed in using **RPG** to write computer programs are very similar to those used with other computer languages, such as **COBOL** and **FORTRAN**. The familiarity you have with **RPG** will serve you well if you should ever wish to transfer your programming knowledge to another language.

Lesson 5

PROCEDURES IN WRITING A PROGRAM

You will learn what steps to follow in using a computer to solve a problem by means of the RPG *language.*

The questions given here are answered on the back of this page. They represent the kind of material taught in this lesson. If you are doing independent study, and get all of them correct, go on to Lesson 6.

1. What is meant by job *analysis* and who is likely to do it?
2. What are the *source program*, the *source deck*, and their purpose?
3. How are *diagnostic* errors discovered and what is done about them?
4. Why is it necessary to use *control cards*?
5. What are the *object program*, the *object deck*, and their purpose?
6. How are *logic* errors usually discovered and what is done about them?
7. What does it mean to *debug* a program?
8. What is *turnaround* time and why does it matter?
9. Name some types of information that should be included in the *documentation* of a program.
10. What is the difference between *open-* and *closed*-shop management of a data processing installation?

ANSWERS

1. Study of the problem to be solved to determine what equipment and what programs are needed, what each program should do, what its input format will be, contents and form of output, and how other programs are related to it. Usually done by a systems analyst or someone in systems design, but sometimes by the programmer.

2. The set of instructions that are written in a computer language to do the job; the key-punched deck of these instructions; to be used in generation to obtain an object deck.

3. Errors discovered by the programming system during generation; they are corrected by the programmer in the source deck and another attempt at generation is made.

4. To direct the actions of the control program, which not only handles the stream of jobs as they enter the computer but also maintains supervision over all activities inside the computer.

5. The set of machine language instructions produced by the generation process; the deck into which these instructions are punched by the computer; they are used with your data to make the computer prepare your report.

6. Discovered by observing incorrect results on the printed report or by having your execution run terminated by the control program. Changes in logic are made in the source deck; you must repeat the generation process to get another object program.

7. To clear it of all diagnostic and logic errors, ensuring that it works correctly with properly prepared data.

8. The amount of time it takes to receive back a computer run after it has been submitted to be run. It matters because it greatly affects the schedule of completion of the debugging of your program. If you get only one turnaround every three days, it may take weeks to debug the program.

9. Systems chart, operating instructions, data preparation instructions, program flow chart, copy of source program, copy of test data, copy of sample output produced by the test data, calculations to prove accuracy of the test results, and work procedures by which the job is used in production. Decks of the source program, the object program, and the test run should be stored.

10. *Open* shop generally allows everyone access to the data processing equipment, even the computer, so that the programmer may run his own programs. *Closed* shop usually requires that the programmer stay out, with his programs being run by an operator.

Lesson 5 Procedures in Writing a Program

In the preparation of any job by a computer, the programmer must go through a series of steps in planning the job, writing the program, testing it to ensure its accuracy, and documenting it so that it can be used for production. The systems chart given in Figure 5-1 shows the steps in using the RPG language and the IBM SYSTEM/360 computer to do this job preparation. Generation of the object program and execution of the program is shown in two separate passes through the computer, each called a run, although on some configurations, one pass can accomplish both without the need for the object deck to be punched. The steps in Figure 5-1 are discussed in this lesson at length, using in many places the slang of the computer profession so that you will be able to communicate with other programmers. The shapes of the symbols used in Figure 5-1 have specific meanings. A sketch of the template used and an explanation of each symbol used is given in the Appendix.

The first step is to evaluate the problem to see what is required for the report. The programmer must know exactly what is needed and how he is to achieve that result. In most of the large computer installations, this analysis is done by a *systems analyst* or a *systems designer*, who gives the programmer a flow chart and the input and output specifications. In smaller installations, the programmer does his own analysis and systems design. This analysis is, in some instances, the most difficult and crucial part of the job. Decisions must be made on what equipment to use, how data are to be obtained and prepared, what is needed on each report, how the report form should look, whether or not preprinted forms are to be used, and if so, what their design should be and how long it takes to get them made. It is vital that systems design be done with care so that any other programs using data files in common with this program may easily be integrated into the total system.

Once the requirements for the report have been determined, a PRINTER SPACING CHART is made showing the format of the report to be produced. Using the program flow chart, specification forms are written. All input and output files to be used during the execution of the job must be named and defined on the FILE DESCRIPTION form. Entries on the INPUT form describe the record layout of the input data files. The CALCULATION form will contain programming instructions—add, subtract, etc.—which make up the required processing. On the OUTPUT-FORMAT specification form, entries are made that give the end printing positions, carriage control, constants, and field names that are to be used in printing the report.

After the specification forms are completed, a card is punched for each line used. These program cards, punched either by a keypunch operator or the programmer himself, should be proofread so that most keypunch errors will be caught. If keypunch mistakes were made, the card must be discarded and another one made and inserted in its proper place. The deck of program cards is called the *source deck*.

Most computers use an internal job control and supervisor program to guide the operations of the computer system. Since a variety of jobs can be done by the computer, the task you want to be done must be specified so that the computer can be made ready to do it. Remember that a computer may have at its disposal several programming systems—you must tell it which of them you are using. Instructions are given to this internal control program on special punch cards, called *control cards*, prepared ahead of time in a certain way. Figure 5-2 shows the necessary control cards for the IBM SYSTEM/360, Model 25, for separate generation and execution, with TOS. Figure 5-3 shows control cards for doing both, in one pass, as permitted with DOS. Detailed instructions on how you are to make these control cards may be found in the RPG reference manual for your equipment.

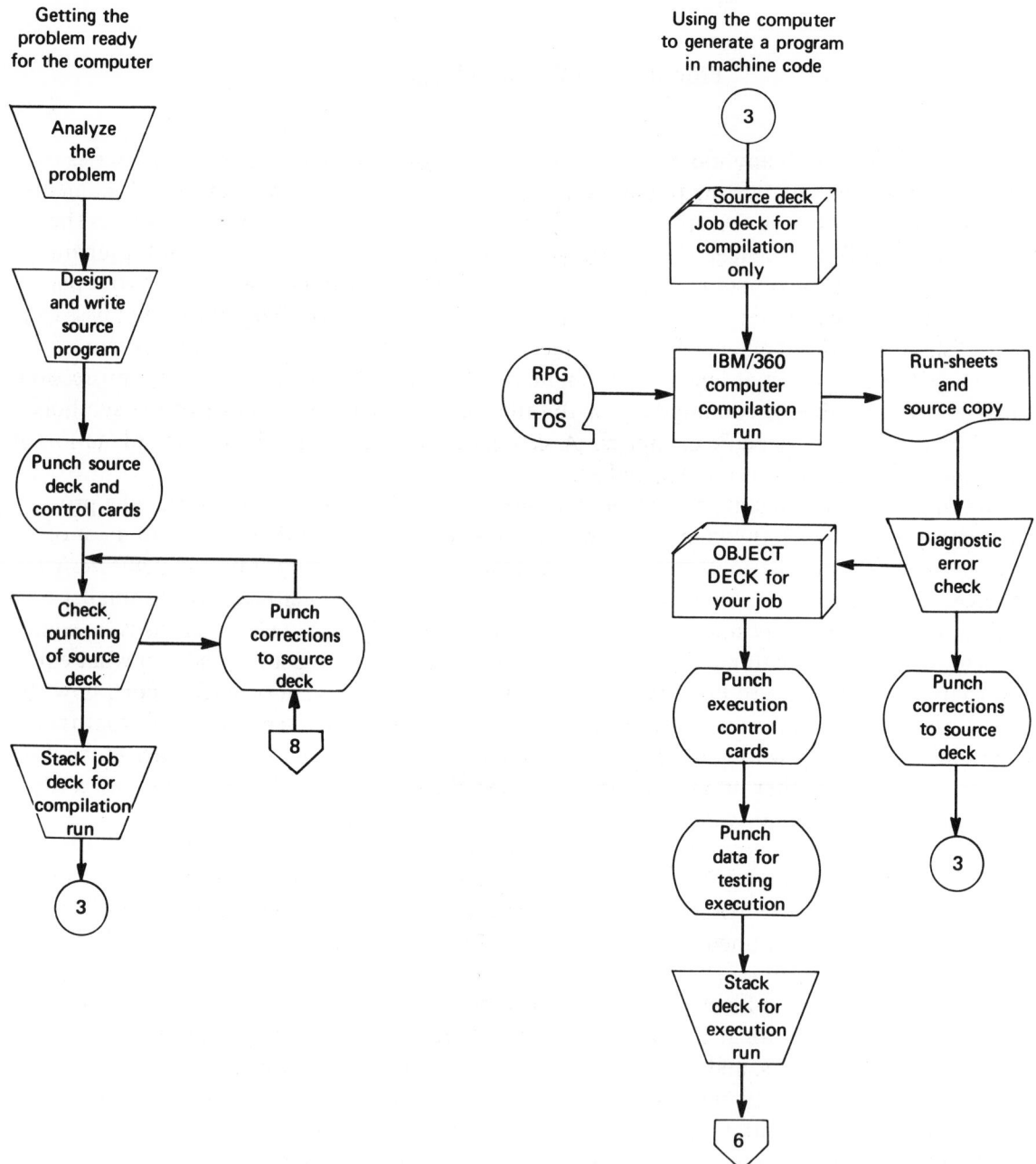

FIG. 5-1 Programmer procedure—IBM SYSTEM/36Ø, TOS.

The control cards will inform the control program inside the computer that a source deck, in the RPG language, is to be brought into the machine for conversion to an object program. This conversion, called *translation*, or *compilation* with most languages, is called *generation* when RPG is the language used. Your source deck with the proper control cards, as shown in Figure 5-2, is ready for a generation run. The deck is placed into an input device and loaded into the computer along with the RPG programming system, which, in TOS, the tape operating system, is on a magnetic tape unit.

During the generation of the object deck, *diagnostic errors* that are found by the system

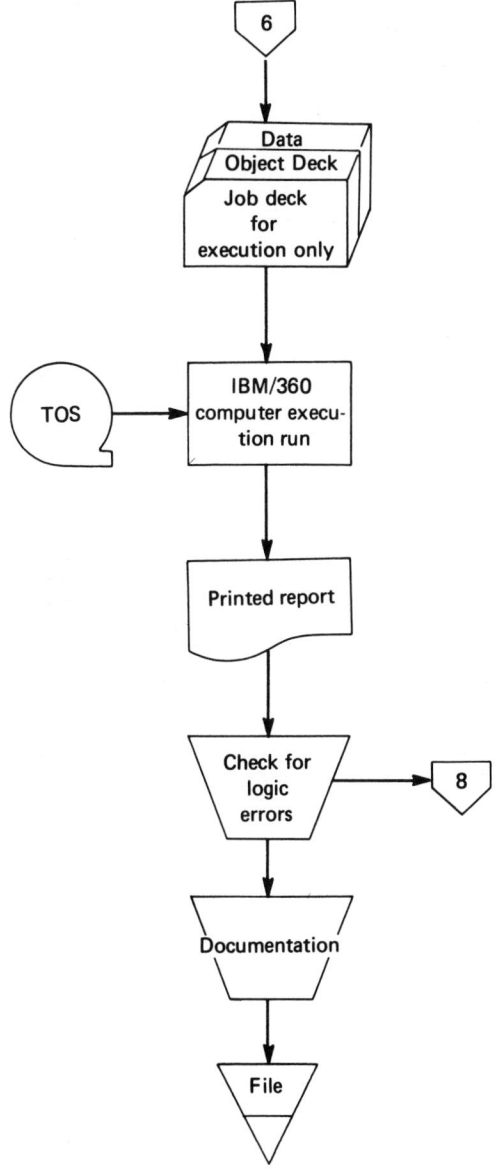

Using the computer
again, with the
machine code program,
to solve the problem.

FIG. 5-1—*Cont.*

will be written on the printer along with a copy of the source program. These errors may be caused by incorrect keypunching or, more likely, by programmer oversight. These diagnostic messages will be printed as numbered notes along the side of the line of the source program to which they apply. Farther down an explanation of the type of mistake will be given. The programmer must make corrections in the source deck, then resubmit it for another generation attempt. Expect to make several generation runs before a *clean source copy* is obtained!

Some of the diagnostic error messages may tell you that the programming system has itself made some assumption about what you intended. If, for example, you forget to specify spacing

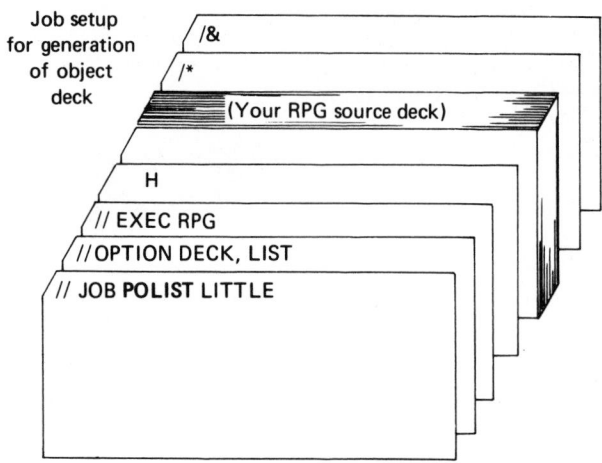

Job setup
for generation
of object
deck

/&
/*
(Your RPG source deck)
H
// EXEC RPG
//OPTION DECK, LIST
// JOB **POLIST** LITTLE

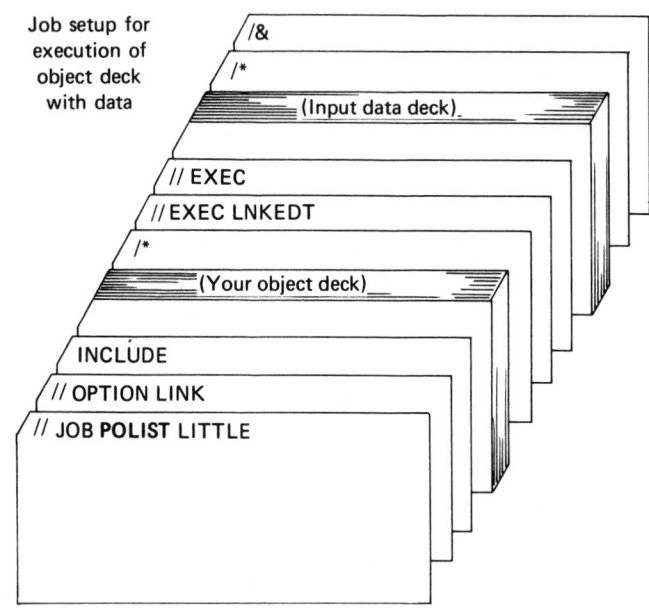

Job setup for
execution of
object deck
with data

/&
/*
(Input data deck)
// EXEC
//EXEC LNKEDT
/*
(Your object deck)
INCLUDE
// OPTION LINK
// JOB **POLIST** LITTLE

FIG. 5-2 Generation and execution in two passes–IBM SYSTEM/36∅, TOS job setup.

on the printing of a detail line, the diagnostic message will indicate that you must specify spacing, but since you did not do so, it is going to assume that you mean single spacing. These assumptions on the part of the programming system are called *default* conditions; the object program produced can be used if you accept the default it chose to use. These types of diagnostics are also called *warnings* to the programmer; use of the object deck may be attempted but proper execution of your job depends on the type of warning received.

The object program produced after a clean source listing has been obtained is often capable of preparing the report specified by the program. It must now be thoroughly tested in an execution run. Test data are prepared and placed with the object deck, together with the necessary control cards to do an execution run, as shown in Figure 5-2. More times than most

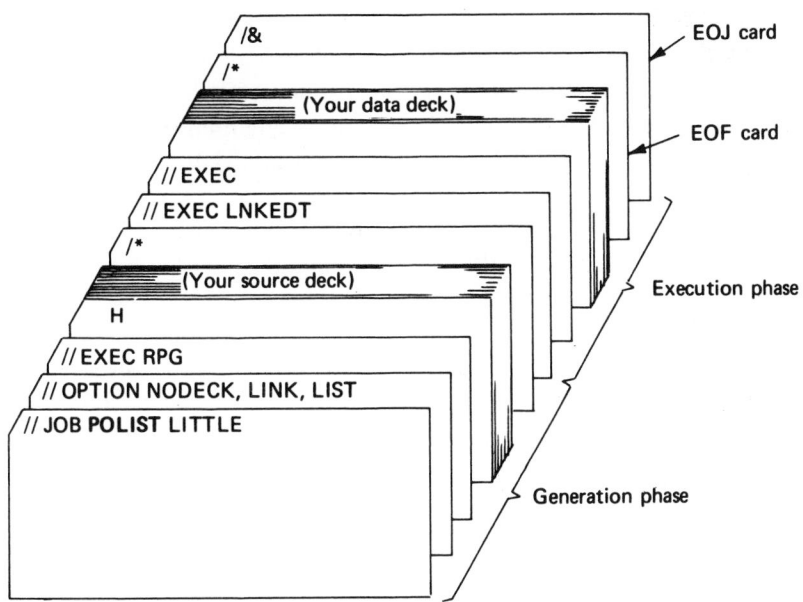

FIG. 5-3 Generation and execution in one pass—IBM SYSTEM/36Ø, DOS job setup.

experienced programmers would care to admit, the first execution attempt *bombs out* and is not successful. Even though all diagnostic error messages were corrected, other errors may be detected during execution.

Your execution run may be terminated by the control program, with a coded message printed on the run sheets. This may be caused by invalid input data, such as an entire field of blanks in a numeric field instead of zeros. If that is the cause, the data may be corrected and another execution attempted with the same object deck. However, termination is often caused by an error in your *program logic*; you may have, for example, inadvertently called for a division in which the divisor was zero, or perhaps given a multiplication instruction instead of an addition as you intended.

Your execution run may instead be completed and produce a report, but with wrong answers! These are usually detected only by careful examination of the printed report, armed with hand calculations for comparison. Many of these errors are also called *logic errors* because they are caused by your giving wrong instructions or wrong problem definitions to the machine. Errors in alignment that are noticed during this inspection should be corrected on the source copy for a better appearance on the report.

Changes to repair errors in logic must be made in the source program deck. A new object program must be generated, after which testing with data begins once again. Enough appropriate test data must be selected to enable you to assert *with great certainty* that all the answers from this program will be valid.

This process of clearing errors from a program, whether they are diagnostic or logical in nature, is called *debugging*. It is one of the most frustrating parts of the job of the programmer. Remember that the accuracy of all output is your responsibility. Persistence and endurance under stress are therefore cherished traits in the profession.

The debugging process may take several hours or several weeks, depending on the computer facilities and services offered at your installation. If you are allowed to do your own operation of the computer system, you might finish the program check-out in a few hours, although if you are paying for computer time by the hour, this can be quite expensive for your employer. In many installations the computer system is under the control of an *operator* who has instructions to keep all programmers out! This management procedure in a computer installation is called *closed shop*, in contrast to *open shop*, which lets each programmer run his own work. In the closed-shop environment, you usually submit your program to a dispatcher at a sign-in desk, filling in a job submittal card, as shown in Figure 5-4. It is assigned a number and entered into the job stream. When its turn comes, the run is made. You are usually allowed to watch, although sometimes from outside a glass window! Run-sheets from the printer will be returned to a shelf or file, along with your card deck. You call for your program at the sign-in desk by number, or get it from a shelf. The time it takes to get your computer run completed and ready for pick-up is called the *turnaround time*. It can greatly affect the amount of time it takes you to debug the program.

Once it is certain that the program will execute properly, documentation is done. A program is of little use if no one knows what it is supposed to do. This part of the job of the programmer is the most unrewarding and is usually postponed to be done later when there is more time! It should eventually be done on all jobs to be put into production by operator personnel in the data processing department.

Documentation differs greatly from one installation to another. Some installations require explicit details on what the program does; others require only a test run with formulas given. It is good programming practice to document your programs completely and soon—with a systems flow chart, operating instructions on how to run the job, instructions for preparing data files, a copy of the source program, a detailed program flow chart, a test run with sample input and report, and examples of calculations done by hand or by desk calculator to show that the answers are correct. If modifications should be needed for an undocumented program several months after it was written, as much time might be required to modify it as to write a new program! A fully documented program, however, can usually be better understood and more easily modified.

After documentation, the source program and sometimes the object program as well are stored along with the test data cards. Some data processing installations have program libraries with a clerk to catalog and store programs; others keep one master deck of source and object program, with test run, in a locked file, and keep a production copy of the object program near the computer so that it is easily accessible. Programs usually are stored by a *program name*, which is often punched into the program cards for reference.

The most important concept in the procedures taught in this lesson and shown in Figure 5-1 is that of distinguishing between *generation* and *execution*. Much of the coding put into your source program is to assist the computer in doing the translation into machine code; the *length* of each field, for example, is established during generation, but the *contents* of the fields are used during execution. The calculation instructions, for example, are *designed* during generation but are actually *performed* on data during execution. During generation, the computer is merely helping you to write your own program. The correct *execution* of the job you are trying to do is your primary goal.

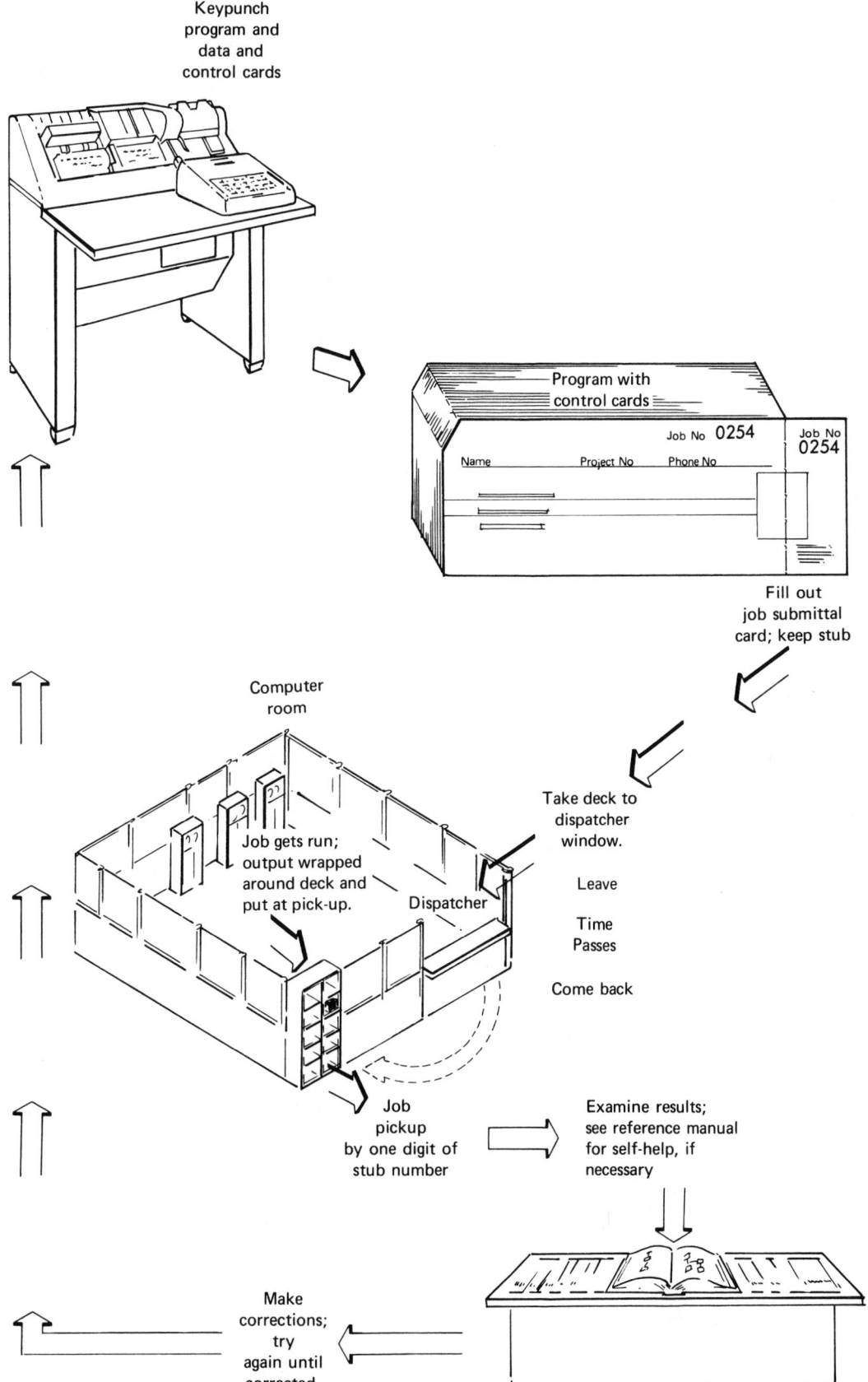

FIG. 5-4 Job submittal and turnaround in a closed-shop computer service department.

Lesson 6

A PRINTED REPORT TO LIST CARDS

You will learn how to make printed lists using data from punch cards.

The questions given here are answered on the back of this page. They represent the fundamentals of report listing as taught in this lesson. If you are doing independent study, but have never written an RPG program, read over the lesson quickly, and then attempt to answer the questions. If you get all of them correct, then write the Programs at the end of the section.

1. What is an *8∅/8∅* list?
2. Where is PROGRAM IDENTIFICATION given in the source program? Is it required? Why is it used?
3. How are *comment* lines coded in the source program?
4. Where are page and line numbers given in the source program? Are they required? Why are they used?
5. Which column of the source program card identifies the type of form the card was punched from? What happens during generation if this column is left blank or is invalid?
6. What are the required forms, other than the RPG CONTROL CARD form, used in writing a *listing* program?
7. What are the rules for the selection of a file name?
8. What does it mean to say you have a *clean source copy*?
9. What are the rules for the selection of field names?
10. What is the difference between *primary* and *secondary* input?
11. How are input data fields defined on the INPUT form?
12. What is the purpose of alphabetic letters, such as NS, in the SEQUENCE field on the INPUT form record description?
13. What is *editing* and why is it necessary?
14. What are the two modes of data storage in RPG?
15. What does it mean to say that a field is in the wrong mode?
16. How does the programmer control spacing of the printer?
17. What does it mean to get a diagnostic message about an *undefined* field?
18. What does it mean to say that a field is *unreferenced*?
19. How does the computer know that the data deck is to be placed into the IBM 25∅1 card reader?

ANSWERS

1. An alphameric listing of 8∅ columns from an input card onto 8∅ print positions of the printer, with no editing.
2. Columns 75-8∅; no; to give the program an identification for use in cataloging and storage.
3. By using an asterisk in column 7 of any of the valid format types. Column 6 giving format type must also be valid.
4. Page numbers are in columns 1 and 2; line numbers are in columns 3-5; no; so that the source deck can be reassembled if dropped, and so that cards are easier to locate for corrections.
5. Column 6; the card is, in some implementations, bypassed and not included in the object program; in others, it terminates generation.
6. FILE DESCRIPTION, INPUT, and OUTPUT-FORMAT.
7. Up to eight characters, of which the first seven must be unique when compared to other file names; the first character must be a letter; the other characters may be letters or numbers, but may not be special characters or embedded blanks.
8. The generation run did not give any diagnostic errors.
9. Up to six characters, of which the first must be a letter, and the others letters or numbers. On some implementations, a few characters are considered alphabetic, and would therefore be permitted.
10. The *primary* file would feed first if both primary and secondary input files were in the program. If only one input file is used, it must be labeled **P** for primary.
11. By giving the column number of the left end of the field, the column number of the right end of the field, the field names, and decimal indication if necessary. The information about the fields must follow a line of information about the record to which they belong.
12. To tell the RPG programming system that no sequenced groups of data cards are used. Each record within the file is handled separately.
13. The insertion of dollar signs, decimal points, commas, and other symbols to make the output look better. Editing also includes a type of zero suppression, which can be stopped at any position by the zero-suppress stop digit.
14. *Numeric*, which is stored with a sign position, and is used for all editing, all zero suppression, and all calculations; *alphameric*, which permits any valid character, whether it be a letter, number, or special character.
15. You have tried to edit or zero-suppress a field that is not in numeric mode, or have tried to calculate with a field that is not in numeric mode.
16. By allowing you to space up to three lines either before or after printing a line.
17. It means that the field is referred to in the program without ever being brought into the computer as an input field.
18. It means that a field was brought into the computer as an input field, but you never used it elsewhere in the program.
19. Because the FILE DESCRIPTION form would have the name **READ∅1** listed under DEVICE NAME.

The simplest program to write in RPG is one that lists a deck of cards. It requires only RPG CONTROL CARD, FILE DESCRIPTION, INPUT, and OUTPUT-FORMAT. Lists may be of several varieties: they may be an 8∅/8∅ list, with all 8∅ of the card columns printed exactly as they are punched; they may rearrange the fields from the data card in some manner on the report; or they may list *some* of the punched fields from the card but not others. Reports of this type are often used so that visual checking can be done for better control of data accuracy. Most printed reports, however, do have the information presented in a more readable form than was used for input. A program to list purchase order cards will be written to illustrate programming to make lists.

PROBLEM DEFINITION: *A list is needed of all the fields on the purchase order cards. Edit fields where necessary; place the date field between the department number and purchase order number on the report. The input format is given:*

Field Description	Field Name	Columns
Department number	DEPT	1-2
Purchase order number	PONUM	3-10
Vendor number, from whom purchased	VENDOR	11-15
Description of item ordered	DESCR	16-35
Quantity of item ordered	QUAN	36-40
Price of each item, 2 decimals	PRICE	46-50
Date order was placed: month, day, year	DATE	61-66

A systems flow chart and a program flow chart are shown in Figure 6-1. Since every input data card has only 8∅ columns of punched information, it is often filled completely, which would not permit blank columns between all the fields. Although you can get more on the card by filling it, the fields are very difficult to read when printed as close together as actually punched. The purchase order card has several fields that are adjacent to others, as can be seen in Figure 6-2; they would, as seen in Figure 6-3, be difficult to read on an 8∅/8∅ list. And, since the date field is to be arranged in an order *different* from that appearing on the input data card, this report cannot be done with an 8∅/8∅ listing. A program will be written to print the 8∅ columns of input data conveniently placed for easy reading, rearranged as requested. Printers attached on-line to the computer have either 12∅, 132, or 144 print positions, so the information on the report can be placed anywhere between the first and last printing positions for your particular printer size.

Recall that values in numeric fields on input data cards may be positive or negative, but that they are punched without commas, dollar signs, or decimal points. Only the necessary numeric information is punched, with minus signs, if needed, placed over the right-end position of the field. Numeric data to be printed onto a readable report can be prepared either by editing or zero-suppressing into some better format for output. After examining the sample data sketched in Figure 6-2, the need for some type of preparation is apparent.

Editing is used to insert necessary decimal points, dollar signs, commas, and the letters CR for sign indication, or to prevent the printing of leading zeros in a field. If, for example, the

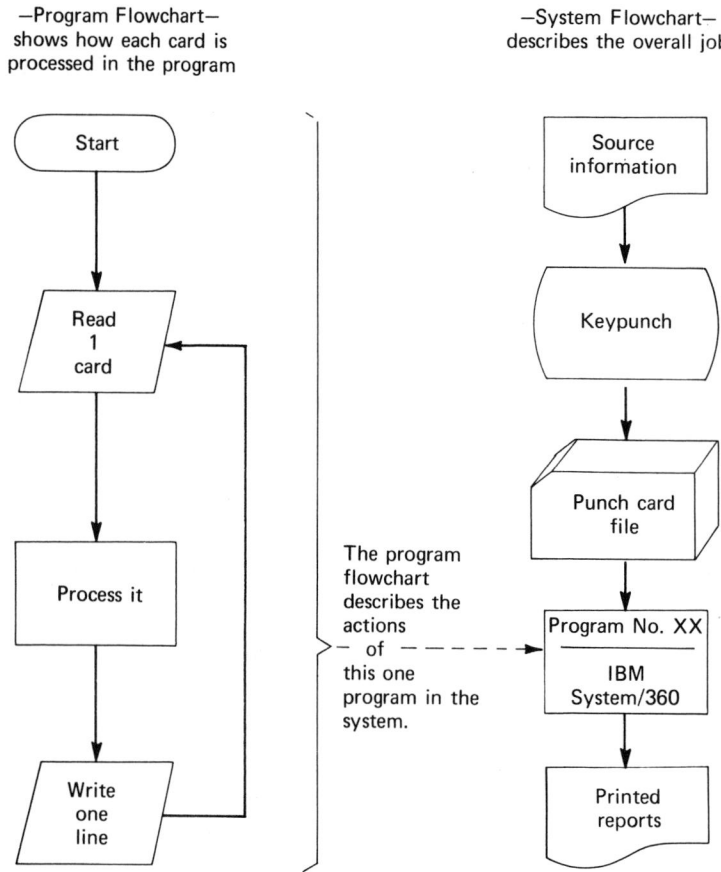

—Program Flowchart—
shows how each card is
processed in the program

—System Flowchart—
describes the overall job

The program
flowchart
describes the
actions
— of — — —▶
this one
program in the
system.

FIG. 6-1 System chart and program chart methods.

number to be printed is brought into the computer as ∅∅75, it can be considered money and printed out as $∅∅.75. Editing includes a type of zero suppression that causes leading zeros in the field to be replaced by blanks, denoted here by the symbol ∅. Zero suppression *alone* can be used to print whole numbers in numeric mode that do not need inserted characters or decimal points. **PRICE** in the Purchase Order List program will be edited; **QUAN** will be zero suppressed.

Alphameric fields do not usually require any special preparation for output but are printed just the same as they appear on the input data card. Certain fields, even though numeric, may be used as alphameric since they require no zero suppression and no editing. **DEPT**, **PONUM**, and **VENDOR** in the Purchase Order List program will be considered alphameric. The sample report given in Figure 6-3 will show how the listing should look.

There is only one type of line to be printed—a detail line. There will be no heading and no total line. To determine which of the 12∅ print positions to use for the report, a printer spacing chart is made. Recall that it is a *layout* of the printed report, giving the programmer a guide to follow in spacing fields for proper balance. Figure 6-3 shows a PRINTER SPACING CHART for the Purchase Order List program and the report that it will be used to produce. The letter X is used on the spacing chart to show where information from the input data card should be placed for printing. On long fields, such as **DESCR**, a line may be drawn to show the continuation of X's—every one of them need not be written. Each one of them must be counted, however, for proper fit. The letter Z is used on whole numbers instead of X to show, for that field, that all of the numeric digits are to be blanked out if they are zero. The slash symbol, / , is

Purchase Order Card Layout

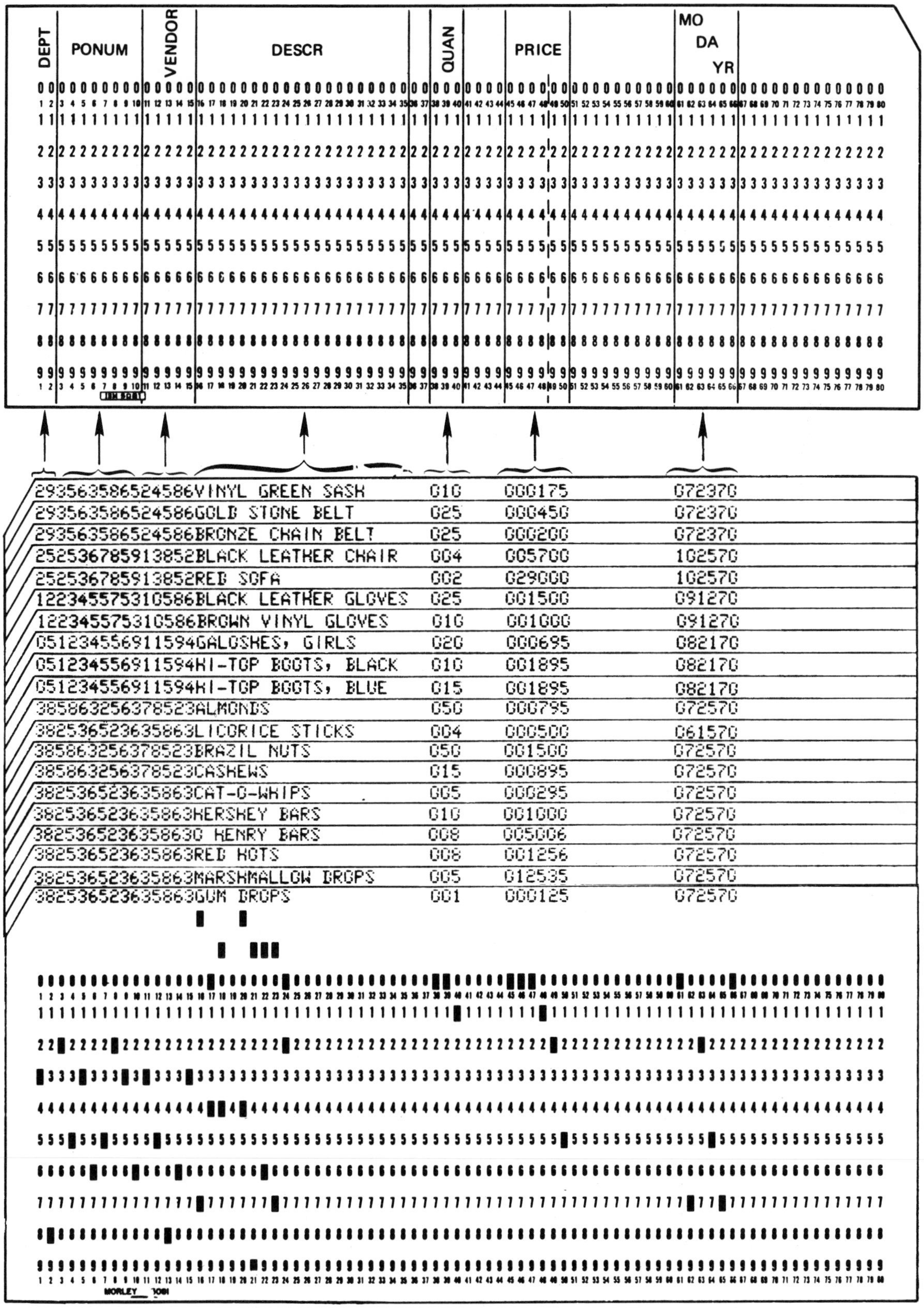

DEPT | PONUM | VENDOR | DESCR | QUAN | PRICE | MO DA YR

Punched Data on Cards

```
293563586524586VINYL GREEN SASH        010    000175    072370
293563586524586GOLD STONE BELT         025    000450    072370
293563586524586BRONZE CHAIN BELT       025    000200    072370
252536785913852BLACK LEATHER CHAIR     004    005700    102570
252536785913852RED SOFA                002    029000    102570
122345575310586BLACK LEATHER GLOVES    025    000150    091270
122345575310586BROWN VINYL GLOVES      010    001000    091270
051234556911594GALOSHES, GIRLS         020    000695    082170
051234556911594HI-TOP BOOTS, BLACK     010    001895    082170
051234556911594HI-TOP BOOTS, BLUE      015    001895    082170
385863256378523ALMONDS                 050    000795    072570
382536523635863LICORICE STICKS         004    000500    061570
385863256378523BRAZIL NUTS             050    001500    072570
385863256378523CASHEWS                 015    000895    072570
382536523635863CAT-O-WHIPS             005    000295    072570
382536523635863HERSHEY BARS            010    001000    072570
382536523635863O HENRY BARS            008    005006    072570
382536523635863RED HOTS                008    001256    072570
382536523635863MARSHMALLOW DROPS       005    012535    072570
382536523635863GUM DROPS               001    000125    072570
```

MORLEY 1061

FIG. 6-2 Data for program POLIST.

71

The data cards
may be printed
80/80 on forms;
proofed by people;
corrections written
in just below where
needed

80/80 List of Data Deck

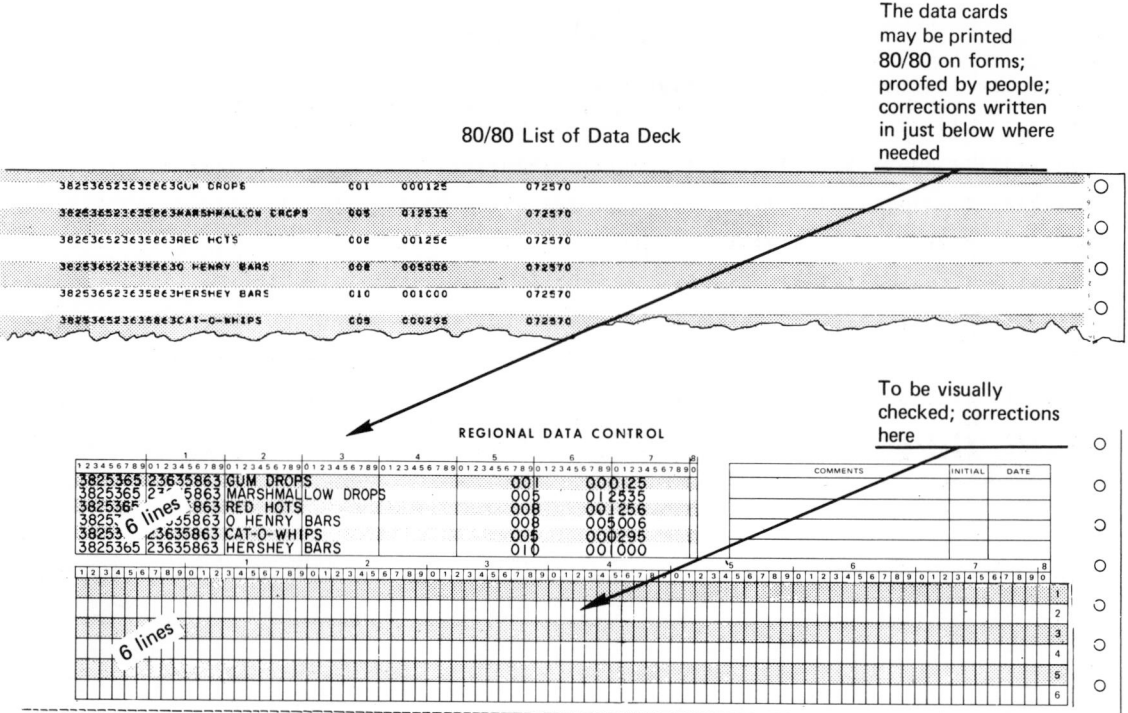

To be visually
checked; corrections
here

REGIONAL DATA CONTROL

Or
may be printed
by this format
to look like this

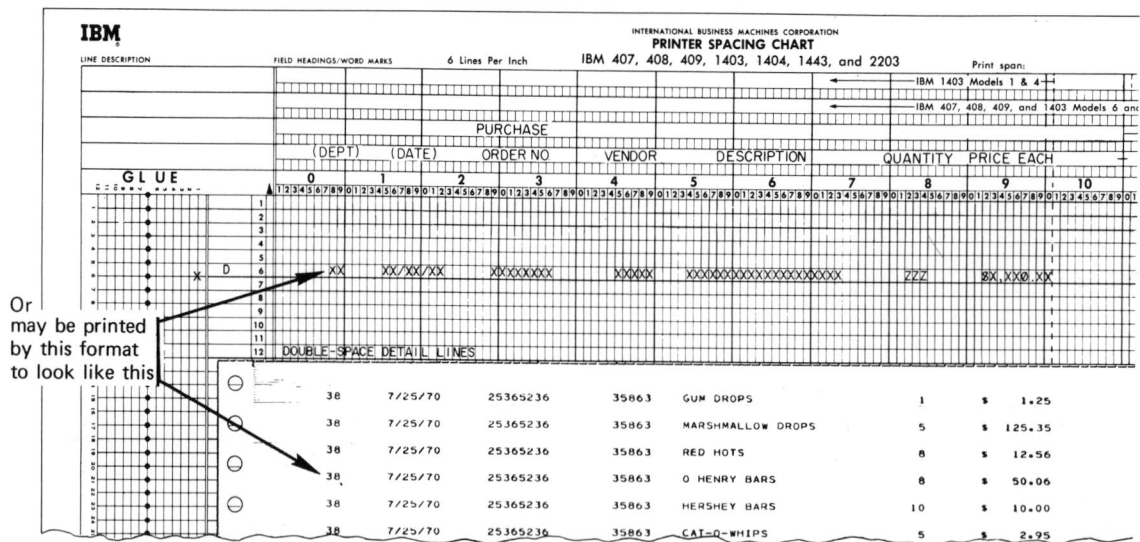

Or could become a
part of a larger
purchase order report,
to be printed on forms
like this

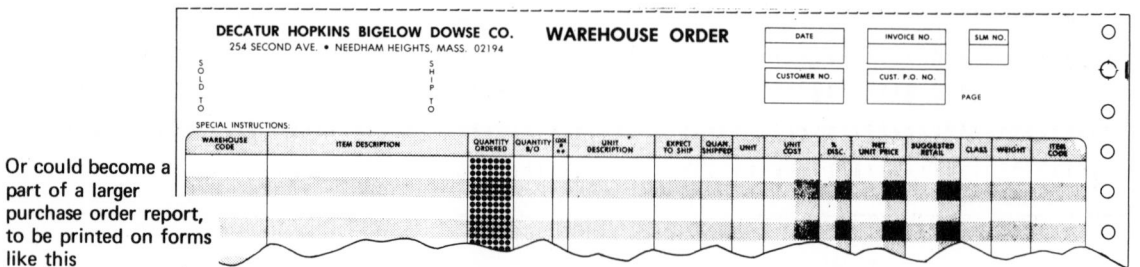

FIG. 6-3 Some possible reports with purchase order cards. (Courtesy of Warren
Business Forms.)

shown where it will be inserted to separate the month, day, and year of **DATE**, the date of the order. The dollar sign, decimal point, and comma are shown where they will be needed to indicate money. The Ø in the field for **PRICE** shows the position at which zero suppression is to stop. The names of the fields will not be printed on the list; they are given on the upper portion of the spacing chart so that it will be easier to read.

After examining the input data cards and preparing the PRINTER SPACING CHART, specification forms are prepared. Recall that each line of the specifications will be punched onto a card and that these program cards are the source program deck.

There are several items that are common to all the forms: programmer identification on the top of each form, page number, line number, and program identification. The *programmer* identification written on the left side of the top of each form should not be punched. The *program* identification, which may be punched into columns 75-8Ø of each program card, can be any name, such as **PGM1**, for program 1, or **JOE7**, for Joe's seventh program, or **INVCRD**, for an inventory card list. This name is *not* required; the field may instead be left blank or used for numbering the cards. It usually is given, however, for purposes of cataloging and maintaining libraries of programs. The Purchase Order List program will be named **POLIST**.

The page number will be punched in columns 1 and 2 of each form. A program may have any number of pages and therefore may have any number of cards. It is *not* necessary for the FILE DESCRIPTION specifications to be completely contained on page Ø1, although they usually will be. Any of the forms may run for several pages; they are numbered in sequence as they occur. Line numbers, punched in columns 3-5, are usually assigned in increments of 1Ø, rather than by ones. As given by

IBM

INTERNATIONAL BUSINESS MACHINES CORPORATION

REPORT PROGRAM GENERATOR FILE DESCRIPTION SPECIFICATIONS

IBM System/360

Date **Fall, 1970**

Program **Purchase Order List**

Programmer **Little**

Punching Instruction — Graphic / Punch

Page Ø1

line 1 will be Ø1Ø, line 2 will be Ø2Ø, etc. Most programmers will find that they occasionally overlook necessary steps and must go back to insert them into their proper places. The inserted lines may be given numbers between any 2 lines already written. The bottom of the page provides a special place for inserted lines. These may be numbered by ones there, punched, and then moved to their proper sequence.

Page and line numbers are not required, and therefore may be left blank. However, when they are used, the RPG programming system will sequence check them during generation and print a warning S along the side of each one that is out of sequence.

Column 6 of each form contains either the letters H, F, E, L, I, C, or O, which will indicate during the generation process whether the card is an RPG CONTROL CARD, a FILE DESCRIP-

TION, a FILE EXTENSION, a LINE COUNTER, an INPUT, a CALCULATION, or an OUT-PUT-FORMAT specification. If column 6 is left blank, some implementations cause a diagnostic message to be printed and the card to be bypassed. Others may cause termination of the generation there!

Comment lines may be placed on any of the form types by putting an asterisk, * , in column 7. These comments are listed, along with the rest of the source program, during the generation of the object program; they do not, in any way, affect the programming job. They do, however, help in documenting the program and in recalling details that are easily forgotten. Always put 1 comment line at the beginning of a job, giving the programmer's name and the name of the job. Comment lines are usually used to explain what that part of the program is supposed to do.

The older version of the forms will be used, with the RPG CONTROL CARD to be added later. A *comment* statement will be the first line on the FILE DESCRIPTION form:

```
           Form                    I/O        A/D    Block    Record    L/R   K/I   -/ Field      Ext
                                   P/S         F/V    Length   Length         I/D   Starting
  3  4  5   6   7  8  9 10 ...15 16 17  18 19 20 21 22 23 24 25 26 27 28 29 30 31 32 33 34  Location 39 40 ... 52 53 54 ... 57
 0 1  Ø  F  *  RPG  PROGRAM  TO  LIST  PURCHASE  ORDER  CARDS  -  LITTLE
 0 2  Ø  F
 0 3     F
```

After that, 1 line will be given for each of the files to be used. In doing a list from a deck of data cards, there are two files—the input data deck, and the printed report. Therefore, the FILE DESCRIPTION form consists of three lines—one comment, one line describing the input file, and one line describing the output file.

In describing files, a name is selected for each one. The name must be eight characters or less in length; it must begin with a letter of the alphabet, but may have either letters or numeric digits in it. It should not ordinarily have special characters, such as periods or asterisks in its name, although certain implementations do permit certain characters that are considered alphabetic to be used. It may not have embedded blanks because that would make it appear as two names and not as one. The name selected should be unique within the first seven of its characters, because, on at least one implementation, only the first seven of the eight characters are compared to other file names within the program. Although there is much liberty in *choosing* the name of the file, once you *select* it, it must be used in *exactly* the same way everywhere it occurs. The name may be **SCARDS** for summary cards, or **JUDY**, for a friend, or **P575**, for personnel file number 575, or almost anything. If, however, a file is named **JUDY**, it is not allowed to be called by any other name, not even a misspelling of the first, such as **JUDI**. Although it is a good idea to name files something appropriate and easy to remember, some programmers pride themselves on the colorful humor of their file names. For the Purchase Order List program, the input file name **CARDS** and the output file name **LIST**, as given by

```
           F                      P    W              Length   ength    L    K/I         ting       Ext              Lab
                                                                              I/C         Location
  3  4  5   6   7  8  9 10 ...15 16 17  18 19 20 21 22 23 24 25 26 27 28 29 30 31 32 33 34 35 36 37 38 39 40 ... 52 53 54 55 56 57 58
 0 1  Ø  F  *  RPG  PROGRAM  TO  LIST  PURCHASE  ORDER  CARDS  -  LITTLE
 0 2  Ø  F  CARDS
 0 3  Ø  F  LIST
 0 4     F
```

are used.

FILE TYPE, in column 15, designates whether a file is input or output. For the file **CARDS**, an **I** is used to indicate input; for the file **LIST**, an **O** is used to indicate output. FILE DESIGNATION, column 16, should be **P**, for primary file, on the input line, but should be left blank on the output file, as given by:

Line	Form Type	Filename	I/O/U/C P/S/C/R/T	E	A/D	F/V	Block Length	Record Length	L/R	K/I I/D/	Field Starting Location	Ext			Lab	
0 1 Ø	F	✱ RPG PROGRAM TO														
0 2 Ø	F	CARDS	I P													
0 3 Ø	F	LIST	O													
0 4	F															

When more than one file is being used, whichever file should be read into the computer *first* is designated **P** for primary; all others are designated **S**, for secondary.

FILE FORMAT, BLOCK LENGTH, and RECORD LENGTH should be given next. FILE FORMAT, in column 19, should be an **F**, which stands for *fixed*-length. This means that all records in the file are the same length, which is to be given. The other possibility is a **V**, for *variable*-length records, which is mostly used for magnetic tape. BLOCK LENGTH, in columns 20-23, and RECORD LENGTH, in columns 24-27, are both given on the IBM SYSTEM/36Ø, but only the record length is needed on the IBM SYSTEM/3 and IBM 113Ø. Block length and record length for a punch card is **8Ø**, since there are 8Ø characters on the card. Printers, however, may have block length and record length equal up to whatever number of print positions they have. Throughout the text it is assumed that the printer has 12Ø positions. Block and record length for input and output for the IBM SYSTEM/36Ø for this program is given:

Line	Form Type	Filename	I/O/U/C P/S/C/R/T	E	A/D	F/V	Block Length	Record Length	L/R	K/I I/D/T	Type Organization / Overflow Indicator / Key Field Starting Location	Extension Code	Device	Symbolic Device	Labels (S, N,	Label Exit
0 1 Ø	F	✱ RPG PROGRAM TO LIST PURCHASE														
0 2 Ø	F	CARDS	I P			F	8Ø	8Ø								
0 3 Ø	F	LIST	O			F	12Ø	12Ø								
0 4	F															

Notice that numeric fields are aligned on the forms in the right-most positions, while the names of fields are aligned on the left. This is consistent with the use of left and right justification on input data fields—numeric fields are right-justified and alphameric ones are left-justified.

Each piece of hardware being used for either input or output must have DEVICE NAME in columns 4Ø-46. Some implementations, such as the IBM SYSTEM/36Ø, TOS/DOS, also require SYMBOLIC DEVICE NAME, given in columns 47-52. Symbolic device names are usually **SYSRDR**, which stands for system reader, the card input device, and **SYSLST**, the system lister, the printing device. The IBM SYSTEM/3 and IBM 113Ø do not require symbolic device names. Device names for several different IBM card readers and printers are given in Figure 6-4. The device name for any of several different printers is **PRINTER**. The completed FILE DESCRIPTION form, on an older type of form that does not show the RPG CONTROL CARD specification, is given by:

	Form Type						I/O/U/C	P/S/C/R/	E	A/D	F/V	File Format Block Length			Record Length				L/R			K/I	I/D/T	Organ... Overflow indicator	Key Field Starting Location			Extension C.							vice					Labels (S,				
3	4	5	6	7	8	9	10	11	12	13	14	15	16	17	18	19	20	21	22	23	24	25	26	27	28	29	30	31	32	33	34	35	36	37	38	39	40	41	42	43	44	45	46	47	48	49	50	51	52	53	54	55	56	57	58
0	1	Ø	F	✱ RPG PROGRAM TO LIST PURCHASE ORDER CARDS – LITTLE
0	2	Ø	F	CARDS IP F 80 80 READ01 SYSRDR
0	3	Ø	F	LIST O F 120 120 PRINTERSYSLST
0	4		F	

RPG Device Name	Refers to This Hardware
READ01	IBM 2501 Card Reader
READ42	IBM 1442 Card Read Punch
READ20	IBM 2520 Card Read Punch
READ40	IBM 2540 Card Read Punch
MFCU1	IBM SYSTEM/3 Primary Read Hopper
MFCU2	IBM SYSTEM/3 Secondary Read Hopper
MFCM1	IBM 2560 MFCM, Primary Read Hopper
MFCM2	IBM 2560 MFCM, Secondary Read Hopper
PRINTER	IBM 1403, 1443, 2203, on IBM 360 IBM SYSTEM/3 Printer IBM 1132 on IBM 1130
PRINT03	IBM 1403 on IBM 1130

FIG. 6-4 Some RPG device names.

The INPUT form should next be prepared. It describes the fields to be brought into the computer from the input data card. Several lines of coding are necessary to name and describe one complete record, giving the style of each field. The first line of the INPUT form describes things concerning the record as a whole, and gives, in columns 7-14, the name of the file from which the record is to come. This name must be the same as the one selected on the FILE DE-SCRIPTION form. The name **CARDS** was used for the **POLIST** program; it is used again here:

		Form Type	Filename							Sequence	Number (1-N)	Option (O)	Resulting Indicator	Record Identification Codes 1 Position	Not (N)	C/Z/D	Character	2 Position	Not (N)	C/Z/D	Character	3 Position	Not (N)	C/Z/D	Character	Stacker Select	Packed (P)	Field Location From			To			Decimal Positions	Field Name					Control Level (L1-L9)
3	4	5	6	7	8	9	10	11	12	13	14	15	16	17	18	19	20	21	22	23	24	25	26	27	28	29	30	31	32	33	34	35	36	37	38	39	40	41	42	43	44	45	46	47	48	49	50	51	52	53	54	55	56	57	58	59	
0	1	Ø	I	CARDS	NS		99																														
0	2	Ø	I																																			
0	3	Ø	I																																			
0	4		I	
0	5		I	

On the same line with the file name, the sequence of the record type, within a group of different records in the input data deck, must be given. Since the Purchase Order List program has only one type of input data card, it does not have any sequencing within a group, so **NS**, which stands for nonsequenced, may be entered in columns 15 and 16. Any two letters, such as **AA**, **BB**, or **AZ**, or an abbreviation of a record name, such as **PO** for purchase order card, could be used instead, but **NS** is often used because it does seem to remind everyone of nonsequenced groups.

A resulting indicator, columns 19 and 2∅, must be given for each record type coming into the computer from the input data file. Since only one type of record is used on this program, only one indicator is needed. Any indicator from number ∅1 to number 99 may be used; this program will use indicator 99. It is chosen for your first program because if you forget to select one, it is the one assigned by the default conditions of at least one of the **RPG** implementations. Indicator ∅1, 57, or 92, however, could be used, or any of the others. The indicator that is chosen will be turned on internally when the input card is read, and will tell the program that this type of card is now available for processing.

All lines following the record description line will be used to describe fields from that record. Each line gives the column locations and name of the field on the data card. Since the Purchase Order List program uses an input data card with seven fields, seven lines follow the record description line—one line for each field being specified. In columns 44-47, the column number of the *left* end of the data field should be placed; in columns 48-51, the column number of the *right* end of the data field should be placed. The *name* of the field goes in columns 53-58, left-justified, as shown:

Number (1-N) 17	Option (O) 18	Resulting Indicator 19 20	Position 21 22 23 24	Not (N) 25	C/Z/D 26	Character 27	Position 28 29 30 31	Not (N) 32	C/Z/D 33	Character 34	Position 35 36 37 38	Not (N) 39	C/Z/D 40	Character 41	Stacker Select 42	Packed (P) 43	From 44 45 46 47	To 48 49 50 51	Decimal Positions 52	Field Name 53 54 55 56 57 58	Control Level (L1-L9) 59 60	Matching Fields or Chaining Fields 61 62	Field-Record Relation 63 64	Plus 65 66	Minus 67 68	Zero or Blank 69 70	Sterling Sign Position 71 72 73 74
		99																										
																	1	2		DEPT							
																	3	1∅		PONUM							
																	11	15		VENDOR							
																	16	35		DESCR							
																	38	40		QUAN							
																	45	50		PRICE							
																	61	66		DATE							

The field name may be six characters or less, must start with an alphabetic character, but may have either alphabetic letters or numbers thereafter. The names given in the Problem Definition are used for this program. Each of these names will be put in storage by the **RPG** processor into a *symbol table*. In the table each name will have an assigned memory address, which will be reserved to hold the actual value of the data during execution. The field name, **DEPT**, for example, may be assigned to memory address ∅∅∅123, a place where enough space will be reserved to hold the two columns of information to be brought in as **DEPT**. Names, therefore, must be used in *exactly* the same way anywhere else that they appear in the program. If a field is named **SALE** on the **INPUT** form, but later called **SALES**, the computer will *not* identify them as the same field, but will instead assume that you mean a different one. In these cases, a diagnostic message will inform you that **SALE** is *unreferenced*, meaning that it was brought in, but never used for anything, not even output, and that **SALES** is *undefined,* meaning that it was used in the program somewhere, but was not brought in from an input data card, nor defined elsewhere in the program. An undefined field is almost certain to cause an error in an answer, and should be corrected before you proceed. An unreferenced field, however, may sometimes be caused by defining a field of data that is actually not needed for the job. It should be investigated, however, since you may instead have forgotten to use it as you intended.

Decimal places should now be given in column 52 to all fields for which calculations are to be done, for which editing is needed, or for which zero suppression has been requested. If any field represents alphameric information, it should have the decimal indication in column 52 left blank, causing the field to be stored in alphameric mode. If a field is to represent an account number or a department number, for example, it may be used as alphameric information even though it is completely formed with numeric digits! If decimal places *are* specified, the number in that field will be stored in numeric mode, with a sign position. Amounts of money are usually given 2 decimal places; counted quantities usually need zero suppression and should be given Ø decimal places to put them into numeric mode.

In the **POLIST** program, **DATE** will have editing done to cause it to print with the slashes inserted between month, day, and year; put Ø decimals on the INPUT specifications for **DATE**. **QUAN** is to be zero-suppressed; put Ø decimals on **QUAN**. **PRICE** should be given 2 decimals because it represents money and is to be edited. **DEPT, PONUM, VENDOR,** and **DESCR** are not given any decimal indication:

The OUTPUT-FORMAT specifications may now be prepared. The first line of programming for each printed line of an output file gives information about the whole line; successive lines then describe the fields of printed matter that are to be placed onto that line. The first line of coding is the *record* description; lines following give *field* descriptions for that record.

The file name used for the OUTPUT-FORMAT form must be the same as the one given on the FILE DESCRIPTION form. For the **POLIST** program, the output file name is **LIST**. The type of line, given in column 15, is a **D**, for detail line, as indicated on the spacing chart given in Figure 6-3. The carriage on the printer should be rolled forward between lines so that overprinting on top of a previously printed line does not occur. This rolling up of the carriage is called *spacing*. Columns 17 and 18 are used to specify spacing for the detail line, either before or after the printing occurs, or both. Up to three spaces can be specified on most implementations; if the specification for spacing *after* is omitted, however, some implementations have a default condition that causes it to occur. On those systems, Ø spaces *after* must be specified if no spacing after is desired. The **POLIST** program will be double spaced, done after the printing of each line:

Line	Form Type	Filename	Type (H/D/T/E)	Stacker Select	Before	After	Before	After	Not	And / Not	And / Not	Field Name	Edit Codes	Blank After (B)	End Position in Output Record	Packed Field (P)	Commas	Zero Balances to Print	No Sign
																	Yes	Yes	1
																	Yes	No	2
																	No	Yes	3
																	No	No	4
																			Constant or E
010	O	LIST	D				2				99								
02	O																		
03	O																		

An output indicator must be given to tell the computer *when* to print the line. It should be the same as the indicator you selected to be turned on when the detail card was brought in. That indicator, which appears in columns 19 and 2Ø of the INPUT form, should therefore be used again for the output indicator; place a 99 in columns 24 and 25, the first of the three places where indicators may be given. The line that describes the output record is complete, and should now be followed by description of the individual fields within that record.

On each of the lines following the record description just given, a field is named in columns 32-37. The field names must be spelled *exactly* as they were when defined to the computer on the INPUT form. By referring to the PRINTER SPACING CHART given in Figure 6-2, the right-end positions may be obtained; place them, right-justified, in columns 4Ø-43. Fields need not be listed in the order that they occur on the printed report; they are printed in place on the line according to the right-end print position given in columns 4Ø-43, and not by the order given on the OUTPUT-FORMAT form. Care must be taken, however, to be sure that enough space is allowed for the contents of each field to be printed; some implementations will allow one field to overlap another inadvertently and destroy it without warning.

For each of the fields defined as numeric mode on the INPUT form, editing or zero suppression is given:

Filename	Type (H/D/T)	Stacker Select	Before	After	Before	After	Not	And / Not	And / Not	Field Name	Zero Suppress (Z)	Blank After (B)	End Position in Output Record	Packed Field (P)	Constant or Edit Word
LIST	D						2				99				
										DEPT			9		
										DATE			22		'ƀƀ/ƀƀ/ƀƀ'
										PONUM			36		
										VENDOR			49		
										DESCR			73		
										QUAN	Z		84		
										PRICE			100		'$ƀ,ƀƀ0.ƀƀ'

For QUAN, put a Z in column 38 along the side of the field name. This will cause the leading zeros in the field to be changed to blanks; it will also cause the sign position to be removed from the field before printing. For PRICE and DATE, edit words are given. The value of the date, for example, should be printed as 12/15/7Ø, rather than 12157Ø. The edit word to do that is placed in columns 45-7Ø. It should be preceded by a quotation symbol; it should have blanks where digits are to print; it should give the two slash marks; and it should end with another quotation symbol. The edit word for DATE is 'ƀƀ/ƀƀ/ƀƀ', where each ƀ indicates a blank column. For the field **PRICE**, the edit word must include several editing features. After the beginning quotation symbol, there will be a dollar sign; a blank followed by a comma, two blanks, and a $\emptyset$ digit; then two more blanks for the decimal positions, with a closing quotation symbol. The digit $\emptyset$, given in the units position for the value of money, will cause zero suppression to be stopped at that point; amounts of money contained in memory, such as the digits $\emptyset\emptyset\emptyset\emptyset\emptyset7$, should be printed as \$bbbbb.07, with blanks only up to the decimal point and no farther, rather than \$bbbbbbb7. The edit word for **PRICE** is '\$b,bb0.bb'.

Note that a type of zero suppression is *implied* by the use of the edit word. The suppression is prevented from its continuation throughout the whole field by placing a *zero-suppress stop digit* in the field. Zero suppression of whole numbers, which is done by putting a **Z** in column 38 along the side of the field name, is used only on fields for which no other editing is required. If **Z** is given in column 38, the number is assumed to be a whole number; other editing on it is not allowed.

The complete program for the Purchase Order List is shown in Figure 6-5 on RPG coding forms, with sample input and the output it produced. The source program can now be punched into cards. When finished and checked, the source program deck is placed in the proper sequence with the proper control cards. Figure 5-2 gives the sequence of the deck for operation on the IBM SYSTEM/36$\emptyset$, TOS. A generation run is made on the computer, producing an object deck. Figure 6-6 shows run-sheets that were prepared by the computer during the generation and execution runs of the program **POLIST**. Note that on the source program listing, produced during generation, a sequence number is placed on each line, except for comments. Information about the *symbol table*, which gives memory addresses for all field names, literals, and indicators, and about the *memory map*, which gives memory addresses of major portions of the object program, is printed during the generation run. The source program does not contain any **NOTE**, either on the right side of the source listing, or below the symbol tables, so it is considered a *clean* source copy; execution with the object deck may be attempted.

Run-sheets from the successful execution are also given in Figure 6-6. They are illustrative of all execution runs; you will get, from most computer systems, a list of certain control cards on the first page, then two pages of linkage information used in getting your program ready for execution, and then a line printed from the control card, which gives control over to *your* program. On the same page as the control card mentioned, the list is produced. The next page denotes the end of your job.

A different program to list purchase order cards, renamed **POERRS**, is used to illustrate how diagnostic errors are produced during generation. Run-sheets are given in Figure 6-7; they may be studied to learn how to read diagnostic messages and how to correct them. The object deck from the generation run must be discarded since several serious errors were found.

A sequence number is assigned to each program line that was acceptable to the RPG programming system. This number, shown at the left side of the source program listing, allows easy reference to individual lines of the program. Notice that some of the lines did not receive a sequence number. Those program lines were either comments, or contained errors of such a serious nature that the RPG programming system could not determine what the programmer intended; these lines were not used in making the object program. Other lines showing diagnostic messages, however, did contribute to the object program and have a sequence number. The assumptions that the RPG programming system makes upon detection of certain errors in the source deck are called *default* conditions; for example, if you forget to give printer spacing, most implementations assume that single spacing is intended. If that is *really* what you intended, the object deck may be used.

Page number and line number are given if the source program card contains them. Any page

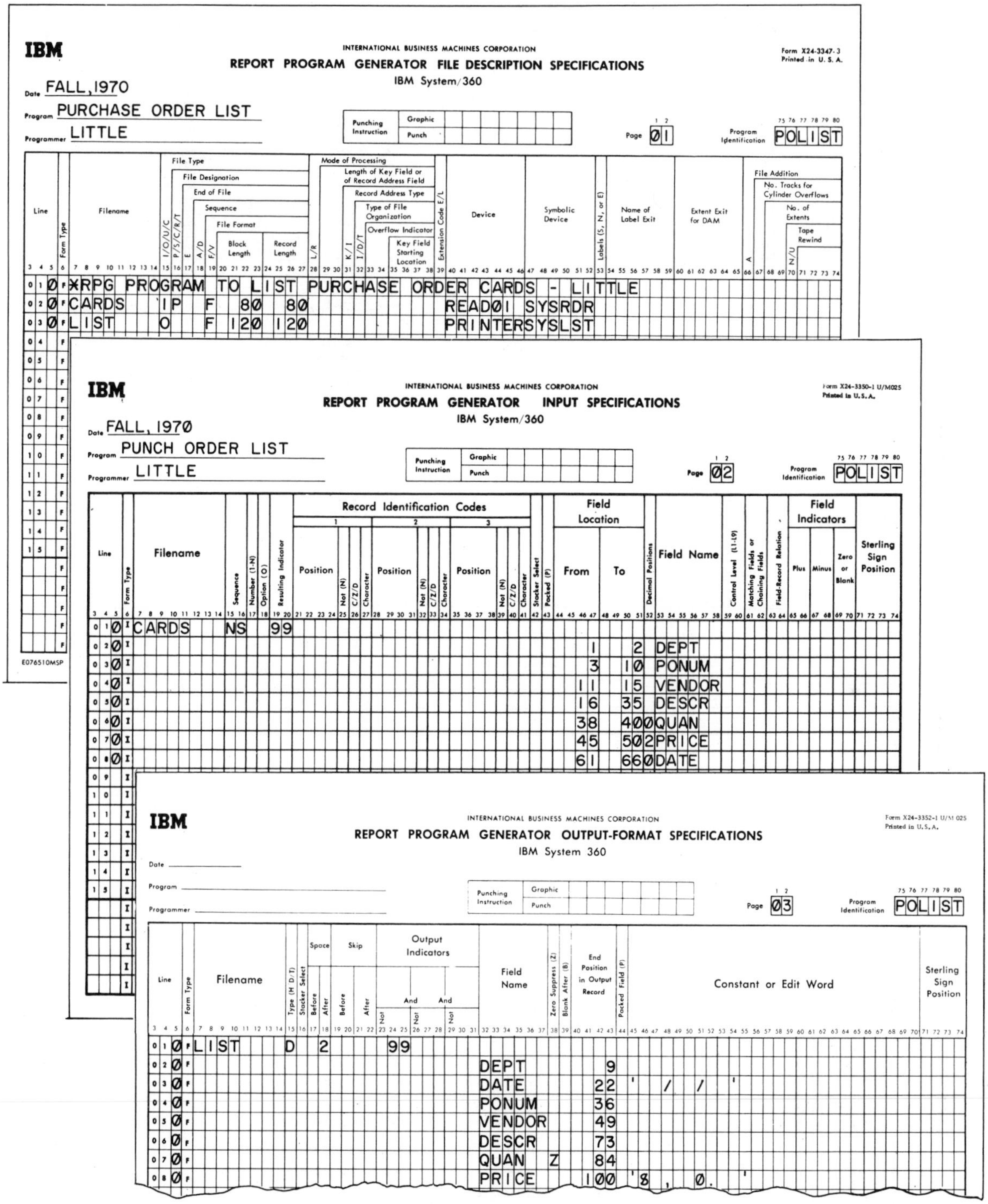

FIG. 6-5 Source program specification forms—program **POLIST**.

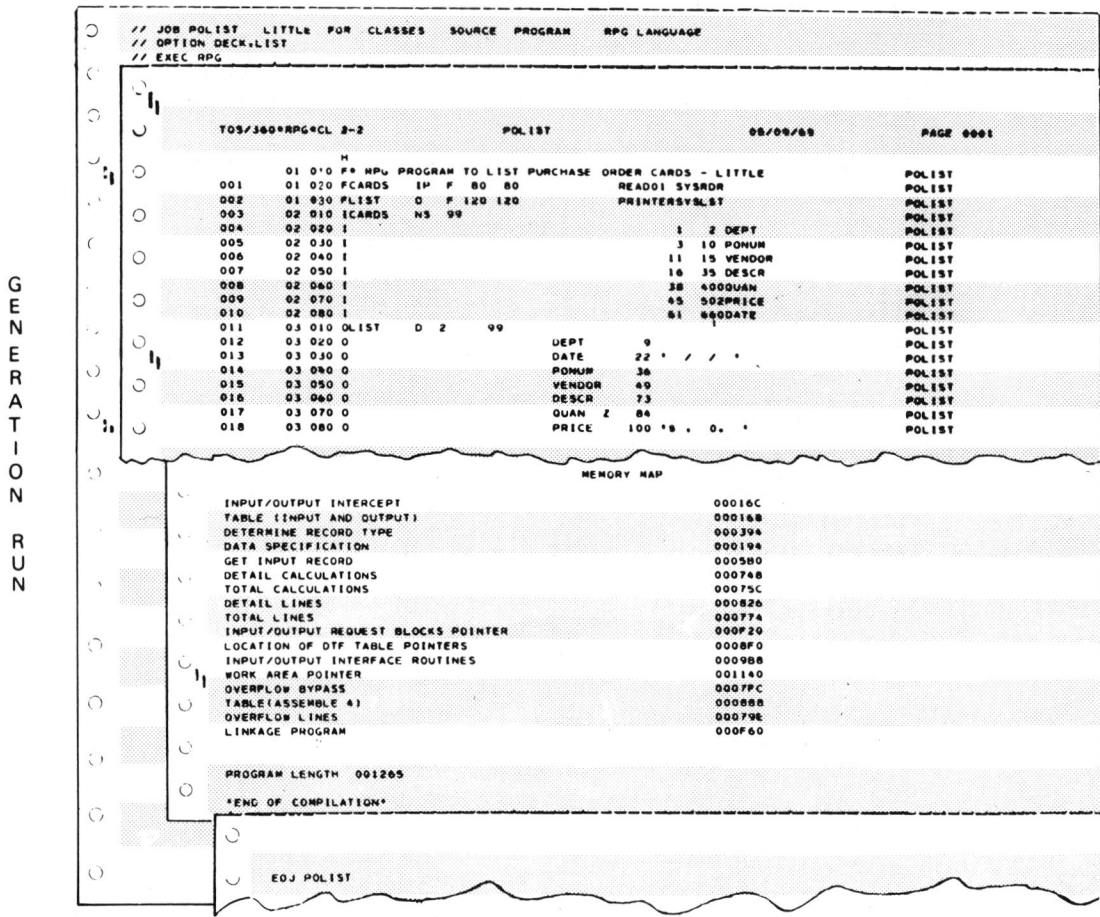

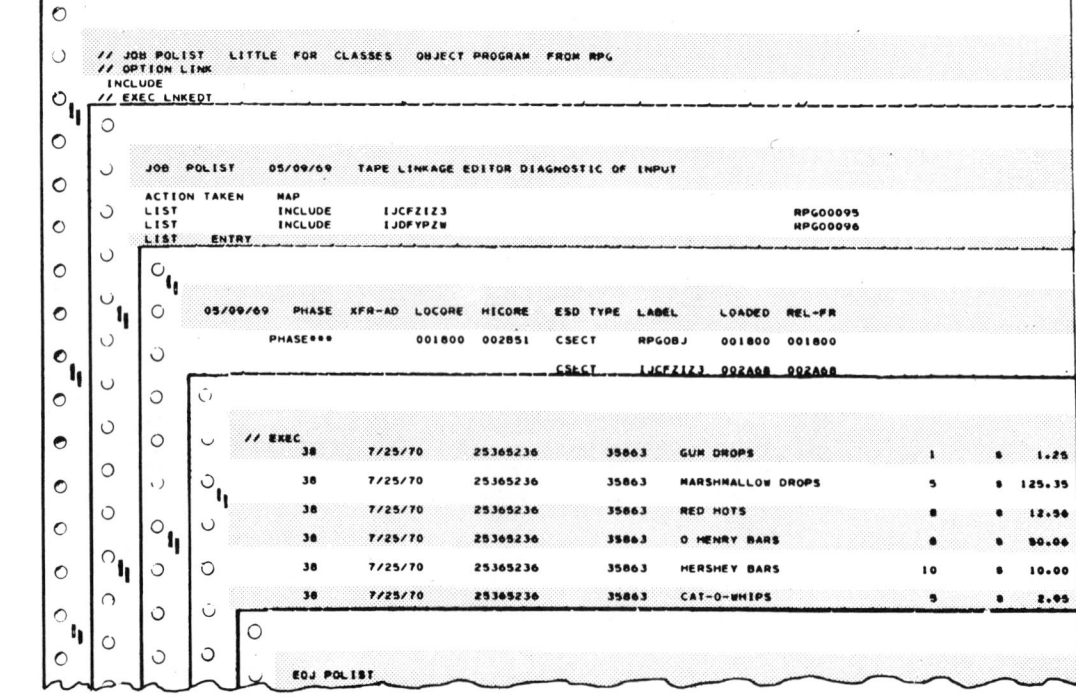

FIG. 6-6 Run-sheets for program **POLIST**–IBM SYSTEM/36∅, TOS.

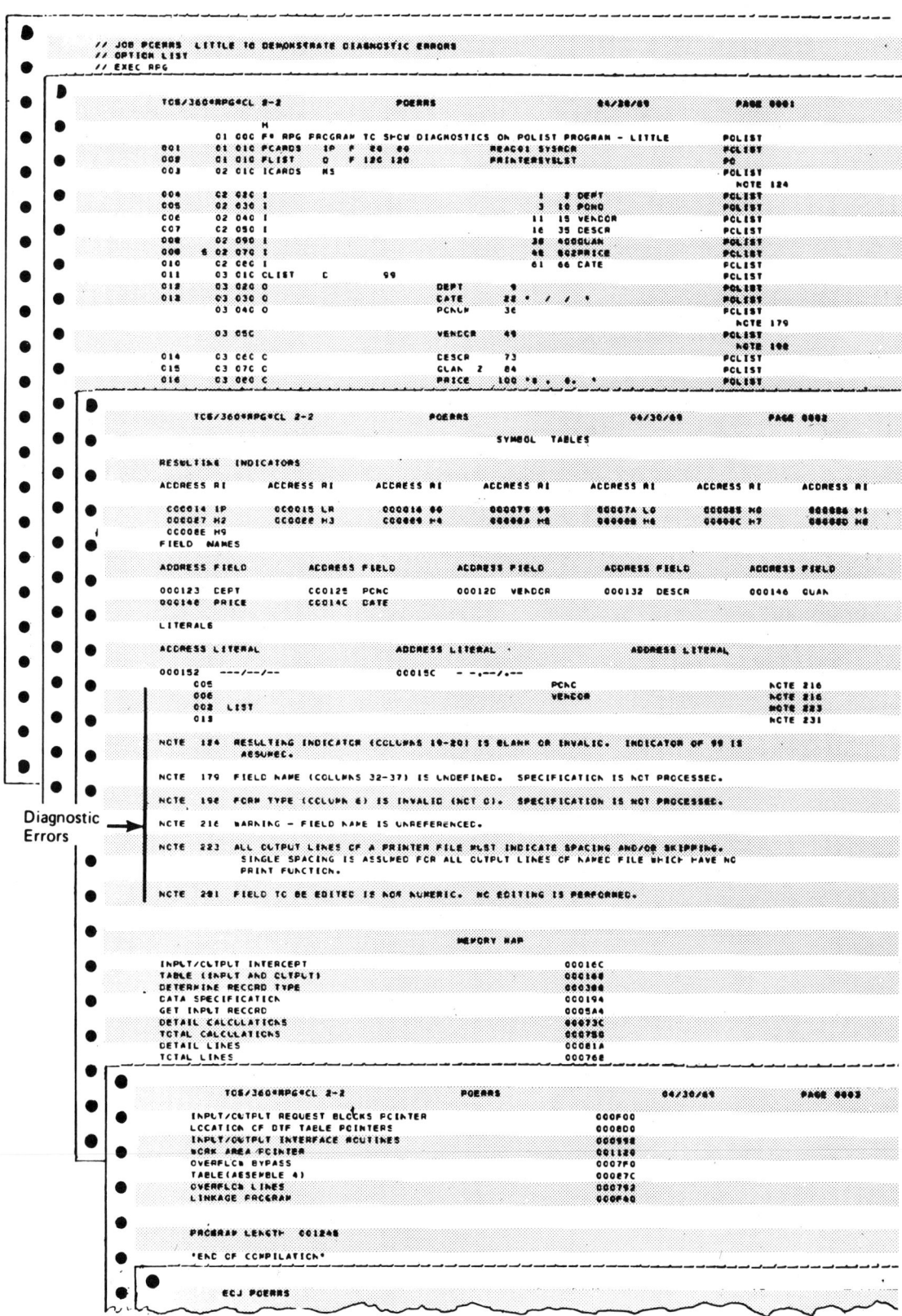

FIG. 6-7 Compilation with diagnostic errors–IBM SYSTEM/36Ø, TOS.

and line numbers that are out of sequence will be flagged with a warning S along the side. See line ∅∅9 of the run-sheet in Figure 6-6.

Notice that the job name, given in columns 75-8∅, may be present or not, whatever you desire. No messages are printed even though line ∅∅2 has only the **PO** and not the complete name.

NOTE 124 refers to line ∅∅3, page number ∅2, line number ∅1∅. It is a warning that the indicator was omitted; an indicator, number 99, was assigned to the input record by default. Be sure to notice the explanation for **NOTE 124** farther down on the run-sheets.

NOTE 179 says that the field name of the card given by page ∅3, line ∅4∅, is *undefined*. It should have been defined on the **INPUT** form, so look there to see what is the matter. Upon scanning the field names given there, the name **PONO** is discovered. It was mistakenly used instead of **PONUM**. Keep whichever name you like best and change the other one to be the same.

NOTE 198 says that the column 6 indication of form type is wrong on the line given by page number ∅3, line number ∅5∅. The line is bypassed; it does not become a part of the object program. Correct it by putting an O in column 6.

Other **NOTE** messages are given farther down on the run-sheet. **NOTE**'s **124**, **179**, and **198** have already been justified. **NOTE 216** tells you that a field name is unreferenced; to find out which one, look for a list of **NOTE**'s, field names, and sequence line reference numbers given above the messages. **NOTE 216** refers to **PONUM** on sequence line ∅∅5. It has already been taken care of by the changing of **PONO** to **PONUM**. It was unreferenced because it was not brought into the computer by the correct name. **NOTE 216** also refers to the field named **VENDOR** on sequence line ∅∅6. By referring to the source program listing, the field **VENDOR** is brought in but after searching for where it is printed out, you discover that an error, on the line to print out **VENDOR**, caused it to be bypassed; hence **VENDOR** is unreferenced. Correcting column 6 will allow **VENDOR** to be used for output, and then it *will* be referenced.

NOTE 223 is a warning that every file using the printer should have spacing given, but this program did not. The default condition, single spacing, was provided by the system so that the line could be included in the generation of the object deck.

NOTE 231 states that a field to be edited is not a numeric field as it should be. Find out why. The field name is not given, but the sequence reference number of the line is ∅13, which is the edit line for the field **DATE**. **DATE** should be in numeric mode—and it is not—which means that it was *not* given decimal indication when it was brought into the computer. Put ∅ into decimal indication for **DATE** on sequence number line ∅1∅.

To avoid getting a multitude of diagnostic errors on the first generation attempt, prepare an 8∅/8∅ listing of your source program deck, made either on a computer or on an electric accounting machine. Carefully proofread it, checking alignment of fields, edit words, decimal indication, accuracy of names, etc. A few minutes of extra care can save a lot of time later.

EXERCISES

1. Write **FILE DESCRIPTION** specifications for **IBM SYSTEM/36∅, DOS,** for each of the following. Use the form provided.
   (a) Card file input on the 254∅ card reader, printer file output on the 14∅3 printer.
   (b) Card file input on the 25∅1 card reader, printer file output on the 1443 printer.
   (c) Card file input on the 252∅ card reader, printer file output on the 22∅3 printer.

Line	Form Type	Filename	I/O/U/C	P/S/C/R/T	E	A/D	F/V	Block Length	Record Length	L/R	Mode of Processing	K/I	I/D/T	Key Field Starting Location	Extension Code E/L	Device	Symbolic Device
3 4 5	6	7 8 9 10 11 12 13 14	15	16	17	18	19	20 21 22 23	24 25 26 27	28	29 30	31	32	33 34 35 36 37 38	39	40 41 42 43 44 45 46	47 48 49 50 51 52
0 1 (a)	F																
0 2	F																
0 3	F																
0 4 (b)	F																
0 5	F																
0 6	F																
0 7 (c)	F																
0 8	F																
0 9	F																
1 0	F																
1 1	F																

Header labels above the columns: File Type, File Designation, End of File, Sequence, File Format (covering E, A/D, F/V, Block Length, Record Length); Mode of Processing, Length of Key Field or of Record Address Field, Record Address Type, Type of File Organization, Overflow Indicator, Key Field Starting Location.

2. Write INPUT specifications for each of the card records given. Use the space provided on page 86.

   (a) Address cards from the file named **ADDRCD** should be read, using indicator 98, and the following fields obtained from the card:

Field Information	Columns	
Name, last first	1-12	
Street address	13-25	
City, state	26-4∅	
Zip code	61-65	
Social security number	71-79	to be edited

   (b) Inventory cards from a file named **INVCD** should be read, using indicator 92, and the following fields obtained from the card:

Field Information	Columns	
Description of the item	1-2∅	
Branch plant name	35-5∅	
Quantity of item on hand	51-54	to be zero suppressed
Reorder level of the item	55-6∅	to be zero suppressed
Wholesale price, per item	65-7∅	to be edited
Retail price, per item	75-8∅	to be edited

Line			Form Type	Filename							Sequence	Number (1-N)	Option (O)	Resulting Indicator		Field Location				Decimal Positions	Field Name						Control Level (L1-L9)
																From		To									
3	4	5	6	7	8	9	10	11	12 13 14		15	16	17	18	19 20	44 45 46 47		48 49 50 51		52	53 54	55	56	57	58	59 6	
0	1	(a) I																									
0	2	I																									
0	3	I																									
0	4	I																									
0	5	I																									
0	6	I																									
0	7	I																									
0	8	(b) I																									
0	9	I																									
1	0	I																									
1	1	I																									
1	2	I																									
1	3	I																									
1	4	I																									
1	5	I																									

3. Write OUTPUT-FORMAT specifications for printing detail lines on a report. Use the form provided.
   (a) Information has been brought in, with the following field names, modes, and lengths. Print the detail line using indicator 95, in the order given. Edit money with $ and . , rate with decimal point.

Field Name	Length	Mode
REFNUM: reference number	5	alpha
PRIN: principal, money	6	2 decimals
RATE: rate of interest	4	3 decimals
YEARS: number of years	2	0 decimals
INT: interest, money	5	2 decimals
AMT: amount of return, money	6	2 decimals

(b) Sales record cards are used in a program from a file named **SCARDS**. The following fields have been brought in with names, modes, and lengths as given. Print the detail line on the printer file **LIST**, using indicator 91, in the order given. Edit money with $ and decimal point.

Field Name	Length	Mode
DEPT: department name	2∅	alpha
SNAME: salesman's name	15	alpha
AMT: amount of sale	6	2 decimals
BCODE: buyer code: M male, F female	1	alpha
CCODE: sale code: C cash, B bill later		
DAY weekday number, 1-7, for day of sale B bill later	1	alpha
DAY: weekday number, 1-7, for day of sale	1	alpha

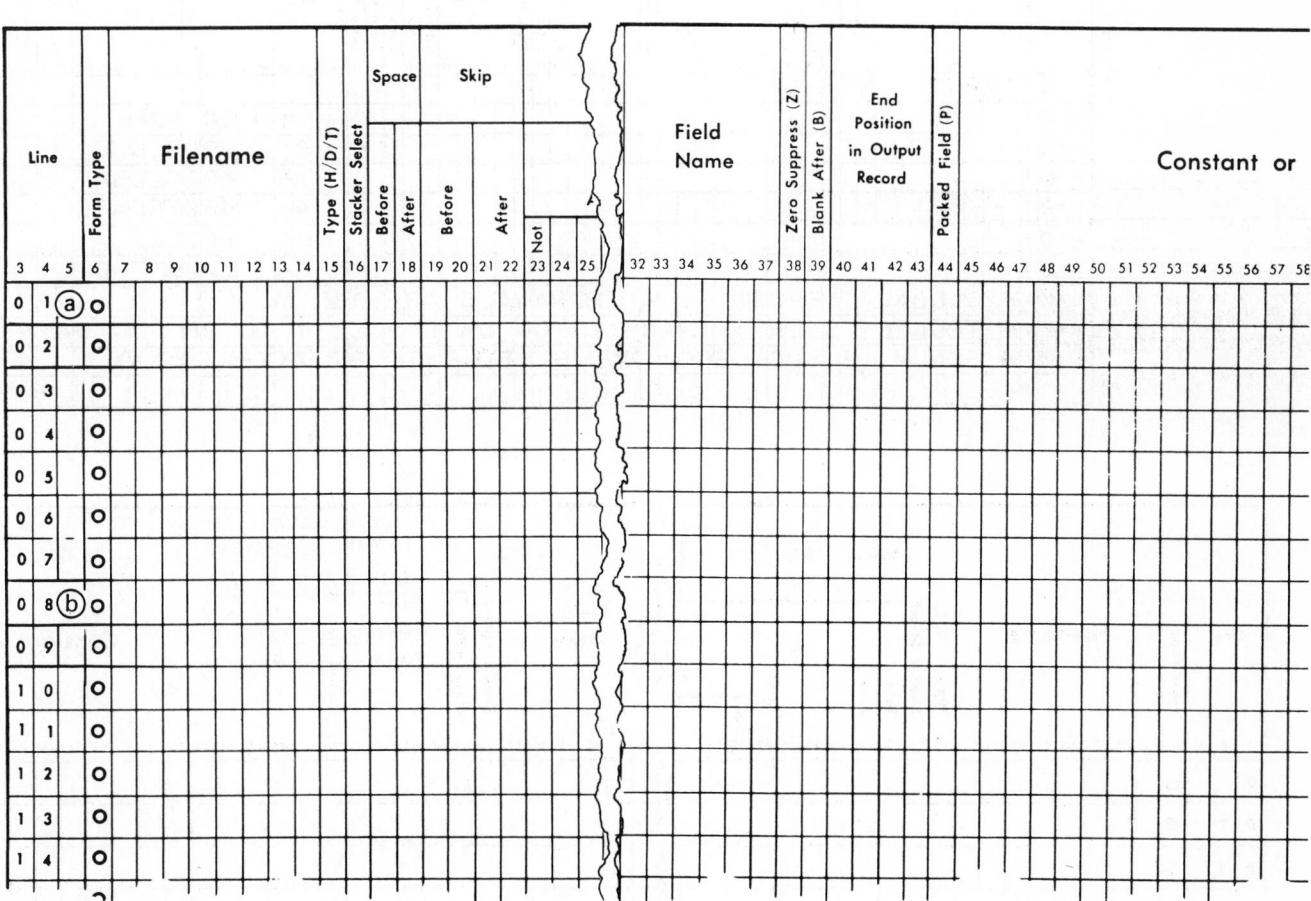

4. Using the **FILE DESCRIPTION** and **INPUT** specifications given, write **OUTPUT-FORMAT** lines to print the fields into one detail line.

File Description Specifications

Line	Form Type	Filename	I/O/U/C P/S/C/R/T	E	A/D	F/V	Block Length	Record Length	L/R	K/I	I/D/T	Overflow Indicator	Key Field Starting Location	Extension Code E/L	Device	Symbolic Device	Labels	Name of Label Exit	Extent Ex for DAM
0 1 0	F	* RPG PROGRAM TO LIST BANK ACCOUNT SUMMARY CARDS - LITTLE																	
0 2 0	F	INPUT	IP			F	80	80							READ01	SYSRDR			
0 3 0	F	OUTPUT	O			F	120	120							PRINTER	SYSLST			
0 4	F																		

Input Specifications

Line	Form Type	Filename	Sequence	Number (1-N)	Option (O)	Resulting Indicator	Position	Not (N)	C/Z/D	Character	Position	Not (N)	C/Z/D	Character	Position	Not (N)	C/Z/D	Character	Stacker Select	Packed (P)	From	To	Decimal Positions	Field Name	Control Level (L1-L9)	Matching Fields or Chaining Fields	Field-Record Relation
0 1 0	I	INPUT	NS			99																					
0 2 0	I																				1	20		NAME			
0 3 0	I																				21	29	0	SSNUM			
0 4 0	I																				36	40	2	OLDBAL			
0 5 0	I																				41	46	0	TRDATE			
0 6 0	I																				56	60	2	DEP			
0 7 0	I																				66	70	2	WITHD			
0 8 0	I	* OLDBAL, DEPOSITS, WITHDRAWALS ARE ALL MONEY																									
0 9 0	I	* TRDATE IS LAST TRANSACTION DATE - EDIT TO BE MO/DAY/YR																									
1 0 0	I	* SSNUM IS SOC. SEC. NUM - EDIT TO BE XXX-XX-XXXX																									
1 1	I																										

Output-Format Specifications

Line	Form Type	Filename	Type (H/D/T)	Stacker Select	Space Before	Space After	Skip Before	Skip After	Not		Field Name	Zero Suppress (Z)	Blank After (B)	End Position in Output Record	Packed Field (P)	Constant or
0 1	O															
0 2	O															
0 3	O															
0 4	O															
0 5	O															
0 6	O															
0 7	O															
0 8	O															
9	O															

5. Using the OUTPUT-FORMAT specifications given, select the correct answer from those given within the braces in each of the following:

Line	Form Type	Filename	Type (H/D/T)	Stacker Select	Space Before	Space After	Skip Before	Skip After	Output Indicators Not	And Not	And Not	Field Name	Zero Suppress (Z)	Blank After (B)	End Position in Output Record	Packed Field (P)	Constant or Ec
0 1	O	SALES	D	2					95								
0 2	O											NAME			20		
0 3	O											REF			30		
0 4	O											ITEM			40		
0 5	O											DESCR			60		
0 6	O											QUAN	Z		66		
0 7	O											AMTBAL			75		'Ƀ,ƀƀØ.ƀƀ'
0 8	O																

(a) The field **AMTBAL** should have been given $\begin{Bmatrix} \emptyset \\ 2 \\ no \end{Bmatrix}$ decimal positions on the INPUT specifications form.

(b) There will be $\begin{Bmatrix} 5 \\ 3 \\ 8 \end{Bmatrix}$ blank print positions between the field named **REF** and the field named **ITEM**, if

   ITEM is five digits long.

(c) The detail line will be printed when indicator $\begin{Bmatrix} 99 \\ \emptyset 2 \\ 95 \end{Bmatrix}$ is on.

(d) The detail line will be brought out of the computer on the file named $\begin{Bmatrix} \text{LIST} \\ \text{SALES} \end{Bmatrix}$

(e) The spacing of the carriage for the detail line calls for $\begin{Bmatrix} \text{two spaces before printing} \\ \text{two spaces after printing} \\ \text{neither of these} \end{Bmatrix}$

Section 2

PROGRAMS TO WRITE

A. PROBLEM NAME: **LIST8Ø**: listing 8Ø/8Ø alphameric
   The program should prepare an 8Ø/8Ø listing of a deck of cards that contain alphameric information. Use indicator 99, card file name **DECK**, and printer file name **REPORT**. You may use the cards prepared in Section 1, Problem A, as data for this program.

B. PROBLEM NAME: **LISTCC**: listing class cards
   The program should prepare a listing of the class cards, as given in Section 1, Problems A and B. Use indicator 99; edit all fields that need it.

C. PROBLEM NAME: **ACCTLIST**: listing account status cards

The program should prepare a listing of the account cards described below, editing where necessary. Use indicator 95 and your own choice of field and file names.

Field Information	Columns
Account number	1-6
Old balance, 2 decimals	15-2∅
Amount of payments, 2 decimals	26-3∅
Amount of charges, 2 decimals	36-4∅
Date of last charges: month, day, year	75-8∅

D. PROBLEM NAME: **ADDRENV**: to address envelopes

The program should read cards containing name, address, city, state, and zip code and prepare an envelope for mailing. A 3-line single-spaced address should be made for each input data card, with triple spacing between addresses.

Field Information	Field Name	Columns
Name of addressee	**NAME**	1-3∅
Street address	**STREET**	31-5∅
City, state	**CITYST**	51-7∅
Zip code	**ZIP**	71-75

SECTION 3

REPORTS WITH CALCULATIONS AND HEADINGS

Lesson 7

BASIC CALCULATIONS

You will learn to use the instructions for addition, subtraction, multiplication, and division, with rounding.

The questions given here are answered on the back of this page. They represent the topics taught in this lesson. If you are doing independent study, read the lesson, then be sure you get all the questions correct before going on to Lesson 8.

1. What part of the instruction tells the computer what to do?
2. What part of the instruction tells the computer what to do it *with*?
3. What are the four basic calculations in RPG?
4. In what mode must data be stored for calculations?
5. Can the RESULT FIELD ever be a numeric literal?
6. Why is temporary storage sometimes needed?
7. What is it called to determine proper lengths of results?
8. What is *truncation*?
9. What is rounding off called? How is it done? What coding tells the computer to do it?
10. Which of the four basic calculations can have FACTOR 1 and FACTOR 2 interchanged and produce the same result?

ANSWERS

1. The operation.
2. The operands: FACTOR 1, FACTOR 2, and RESULT FIELD.
3. **ADD, SUB, MULT**, and **DIV**.
4. Numeric.
5. No.
6. To hold a partial result to be used in a later step.
7. Scaling.
8. Loss of either high-order or low-order digits because of length or decimal place error.
9. Half-adjusting; by adding a 5 into the position next to the one being saved, then truncating; an **H** in column 53.
10. **ADD**, and **MULT**.

Lesson 7   Basic Calculations

The computer does many data processing jobs that consist of little more than bringing in data from cards, temporarily storing it, and printing it out into a report. It can do this swiftly, and much more accurately than humans can copy the same information from one form to another. The computer's greatest accomplishment, however, is not just in storing and printing information, but in doing repetitive calculations at speeds impossible to attain by manual methods. Its accuracy, too, is impossible to match by humans, whose errors tend to increase as they get tired or bored! The computer does calculations by following its instructions exactly as they are specified by the programmer. They must be carefully planned and must be coded exactly right to get correct answers.

Instructions for doing calculations with **RPG** are coded on the form designed for that purpose—the **CALCULATION** form. Each line of this form will be punched into a card, which will, in turn, be a part of the source program deck. Calculation cards, identified by the **C** in column 6, are, on the **IBM SYSTEM/36Ø**, **DOS**, placed between the **INPUT** program cards and the **OUTPUT-FORMAT** ones. Comment lines may be included in the **CALCULATION** specifications at any time by putting an asterisk in column 7 as shown by:

RPG   CALCULATION SPECIFICATIONS

Date **Fall, 1970**
Program **No. 25**
Programmer **J. Little**

Page **Ø3**
Program Identification **JMLØ25**

Line	Form Type	Control Level (LØ-L9, LR, SR)	Indicators And Not	And Not	And Not	Factor 1	Operation	Factor 2	Result Field	Field Length	Decimal Positions	Half Adjust (H)	Resulting Indicators Arithmetic Plus High 1>2	Minus Low 1<2	Zero Equal 1-2	Comments
Ø1	Ø	C	✳			MAKE A HABIT OF EXPLAINING AS YOU GO . . .				SAVES TIME LATER . . .						
Ø2	Ø	C	✳													
Ø3	Ø	C	✳			NOW GET A GOOD START ✳ ✳										
Ø4		C														

Note, too, that the page number, line number, and program identification are used in the same way as on the other forms. There is, however, an *additional* place for comments on the **CALCULATION** form. Columns 6Ø-74 on each instruction line may contain remarks to help explain what is being done. These additional comments are helpful in that they allow the programmer to document the calculations line by line, giving field lengths, decimal places, etc., for later reference.

Each instruction consists of two parts: the *operation* and the *operands*. The operation tells *what* is to be done—for example, **ADD** means do an addition, **MULT** means do a multiplication, **SUB** is the operation for subtract, and **DIV** means divide. The operation is placed in the OPERATION field in columns 28-32. The operands tell what the operation should be done *with*—a field named **PAY** can be added to the field named **BONUS**, with the answer being placed in a field named **GROSS**. The operands are **PAY**, **BONUS**, and **GROSS**; the instruction is written as shown:

95

Line	Form Type	Control L		And		And			Factor 1	Operation	Factor 2	Result rield	Field Length	Decimal P
3 4 5	6	7 8	9	10	11	12	13	14	15	16	17	18 19 20 21 22 23 24 25 26 27	28 29 30 31 32	33 34 35 36 37 38 39 40 41 42	43 44 45 46 47 48	49 50 51	52
0 1 0	C								PAY	ADD	BONUS	GROSS		
0 2	C													

The first two operands are used to *do* the operation and are written on the sheet under FACTOR 1, columns 18-27, and under FACTOR 2, columns 33-42. The third operand, which tells what the result is to be called and where it is to be placed, is given under RESULT FIELD in columns 43-48. All operands must be numeric fields; they must have had decimal places specified on the INPUT form or on the CALCULATION form. The values of the fields named in FACTOR 1 and FACTOR 2 are used in doing the calculation, but are left unchanged. The answer is placed in the field named by the RESULT FIELD, which destroys any value previously stored there. Examples for each of the basic instructions for addition, subtraction, multiplication, and division will be given.

On any of the basic calculations, FACTOR 1 or FACTOR 2 may either be field names or numeric literals. Numeric literals are constants, which will never change in a given program. If everyone on a particular job should be paid a $50.00 bonus, for example, then the calculation given by

	Form 1	Control		And		And			Factor 1	Operation	Factor 2	Result Field	Field Length	Decimal
3 4 5	6	7 8	9	10	11	12	13	14	15	16	17	18 19 20 21 22 23 24 25 26 27	28 29 30 31 32	33 34 35 36 37 38 39 40 41 42	43 44 45 46 47 48	49 50 51	52
0 1	C								NETPAY	ADD	50.00	PAY		
0 2	C													

would serve to calculate **NETPAY** + fifty dollars. The literal **5Ø.ØØ**, used in FACTOR 2 of the instruction, may be written as 5Ø., as +5Ø, as 5Ø, or as 5Ø.Ø. If a numeric literal is a signed value, such as −15.25, it is written with the sign punched *immediately in front* of the value. A positive sign may be omitted; positive will be assumed if no minus sign is given. Constants may be up to 1Ø characters in length, including the sign and decimal point, when used. Numeric literals and field names are left-justified within their fields on the CALCULATION form.

Field names used in FACTOR 1 or FACTOR 2 must be *defined*, either by being listed as one of the incoming data fields on the INPUT specifications, or by a previous calculation. The RESULT FIELD must be a field name, not a literal, since it defines the place where the answer is to be stored. Fields defined on the CALCULATION form as a RESULT FIELD may be referenced later, either by a calculation, or by use on the OUTPUT-FORMAT form to bring out an answer.

Each field must have length and number of decimal places assigned, usually done at the time of its first use in the source program. The RPG programming system establishes storage lengths and mode for each field during the generation of the object program. Fields that have decimal places indicated, even though Ø, are considered numeric fields; they are stored in the memory of the computer with a sign position. Only numeric fields are permitted in arithmetic calculations. Fields that are defined on the INPUT form are given length and decimal places at that time. New field names that are first used on the CALCULATION form should have length and decimal places specified on that form. Even though the field is used in several calculations, its length and decimal indication need be given only once. Columns 49-51 are used to designate the total length of the numeric field; column 52 is used to state how many of that total length are decimal places. On the IBM SYSTEM/36Ø and SYSTEM/3, fields may be up to 15 digits long, with as many as 9 of the 15 used as decimal places. On the IBM 113Ø, the length is restricted to 14 digits or less. When a field is needed in both alphameric and numeric mode, it may be defined twice, with two different names on the INPUT form. When a field is one column long, that column number is placed both in the FROM field and in the TO field. A field may be defined within another field, such as **SSNUM** from 1-9, and **CARD** from 1-8Ø. Fields may even be defined that overlap, such as **COURSE**, from 1-1Ø, with **ID** from 1-3, then with **DESCR** from 8-14.

Care must be taken to define an adequate length to hold the calculated result. If an answer is generated that is too long for the RESULT FIELD to hold, *truncation*, the dropping of excess digits, will occur. If these excess digits are on the left-end *high-order* part of the number, serious errors may result. If they are on the right-end *low-order* part, decimal places could be lost. *Scaling*, a method of analyzing an arithmetic problem to determine how large the answer will be, is usually done to ensure selection of proper lengths for results. In the example,

Line	Form Type	Control Lev	Not	And Not	And Not	Factor 1	Operation	Factor 2	Result Field	Field Length	Decimal Pl
0 1	C					RATE	MULT	TIME	PAY	7	2
0 2	C										

it is important to determine how *long* to make the field named **PAY** so that no high-order digits are lost; It is also important to know when and how to *round off* so that **PAY** will be accurate to the penny. You need not worry about length or rounding until the basic instructions are understood, even though FIELD LENGTH and DECIMAL POSITIONS are given in these examples.

The **ADD** instruction performs the algebraic addition of two values and places the result of that addition into a third field. FACTOR 1 and FACTOR 2 on the CALCULATION form may either give the names of the two fields that are to be added together, one constant value and a field, or two constants. FACTOR 1 and FACTOR 2 themselves are unchanged by the execution of the instruction. The order of the two fields does not matter, because the same answer will be obtained in either case. In the two different **ADD** lines specified,

	Form	Cont	Not	And Not	And Not	Factor 1	Operation	Factor 2	Result Field	Field Length	Decimal Pos	Half Adjust	Minus/blank Compare High 1>2	Low 1<2	Equal 1=2
1	C					NETPAY	ADD	BONUS	PAY	5	2				VALID
2	C	*													
3	C	*	IS THE SAME AS												
4	C	*													
5	C					BONUS	ADD	NETPAY	PAY	5	2				VALID
6	C														
7	C														

the same result will be accomplished—**PAY** will contain the sum of **NETPAY** and **BONUS**. If **BONUS** were 15.ØØ and **NETPAY** were 15Ø.ØØ, **PAY** would be 165.ØØ. Figure 7-1 gives examples.

The subtract instruction **SUB** causes algebraic subtraction of one field from another, of one constant value from a field, or a field from a constant; the result is placed into another field. FACTOR 1 is the name of the minuend—that number which is to have something taken away. FACTOR 2 gives the name of the subtrahend—that number which is to *be* taken away. The order of these two factors *does* matter; their order may not be changed without getting a different result! The RESULT FIELD gives the name of the field that will hold the answer, and

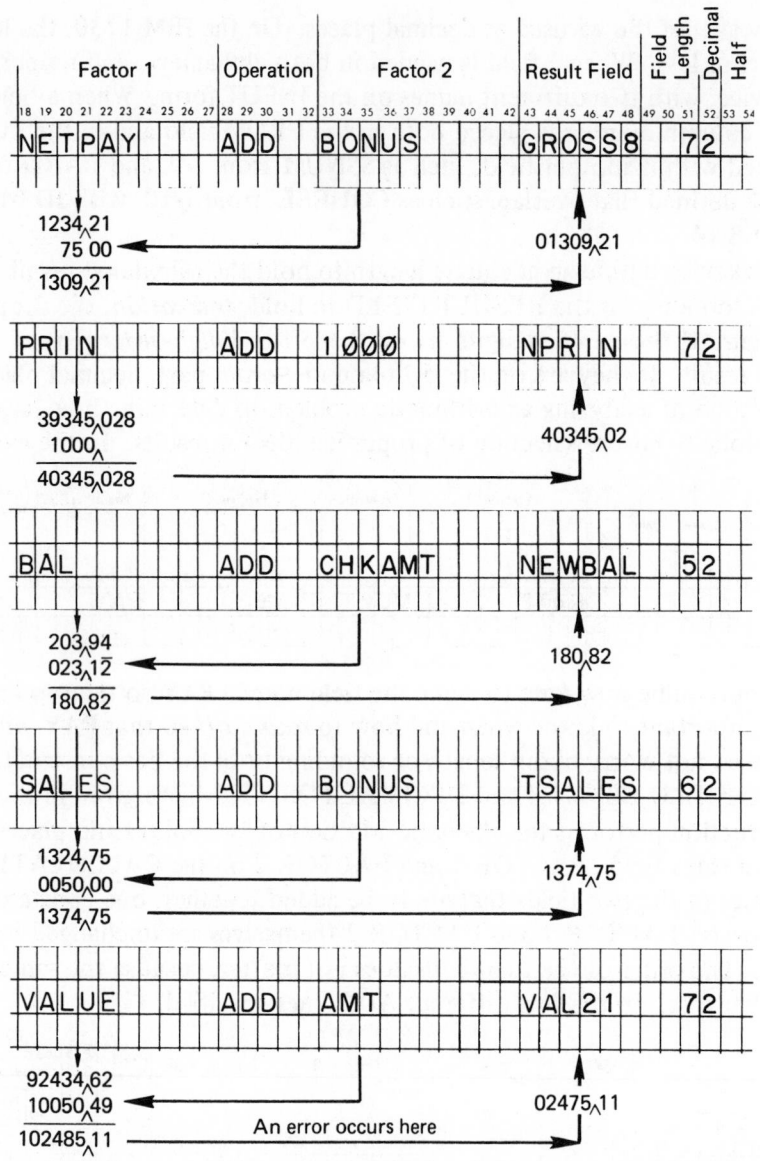

FIG. 7-1 Addition.

if it has not been previously defined, length and number of decimal places must be given. In the example,

the value of **GROSS** will have the value of **BONDS** subtracted from it; the result will be placed into **NET**. In the example,

			For	Cr		And		And		Factor 1	Operation	Factor 2	Result Field	Field Length	Decimal Posi
0	1	C								NUMBER	SUB	1	NEWNUM	5 0	
0	2	C													

the constant 1 will be subtracted from **NUMBER**, placing the result into **NEWNUM**. The value of **NUMBER** will be unchanged in memory. It is possible to store a result so that it *does* change one of the values used in doing the operation. In the example,

			For	Cr		And		And		Factor 1	Operation	Factor 2	Result Field	Field Length	Decimal Position
0	1	C								NUMBER	SUB	1	NUMBER	5 0	
0	2	C													

the value of **NUMBER** has 1 subtracted from it, and the result *is placed back into* **NUMBER**, destroying its original value! Other examples of the subtract instruction are given in Figure 7-2.

Calculations may be done not only on fields that have been defined on input data cards, but on fields that result from previous calculations. In the example,

			Fc	C		And		And		Factor 1	Operation	Factor 2	Result Field	Field Length	Decimal Position
0	1	C								NET	ADD	BONUS	FLD1	8 2	
0	2	C								FLD1	SUB	BONDS	TAKE	8 2	
0	3	C													

the result of **NET + BONUS – BONDS** is placed into **TAKE**. The field named **FLD1** is used to hold the temporary result of **NET + BONUS**; it need not be printed out or ever referred to again in the program. The example

			For	Cor		And		And		Factor 1	Operation	Factor 2	Result Field	Field Length	Decimal Position
0	1	C								X	ADD	A	TEMP	5 2	
0	2	C								TEMP	SUB	7.4	Y	5 2	
0	3	C													

shows the use of the temporary field **TEMP** to hold the calculation of **X + A** until it can be used in a further calculation. The final result **X + A – 7.4** is placed into **Y**. Both **TEMP** and **Y** are available for output if the programmer wishes.

A field name may be used for temporary storage, then used to hold the final result as well. Each time that a field is used as a RESULT FIELD its new value destroys the previous contents of the field. In the example,

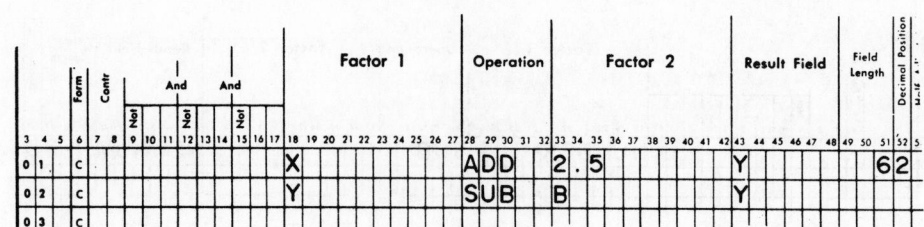

the value of **X + 2.5** will be placed into **Y**, which is then used again in the next calculation when **B** is subtracted from it; the final result is placed into **Y**, destroying the previous and temporary

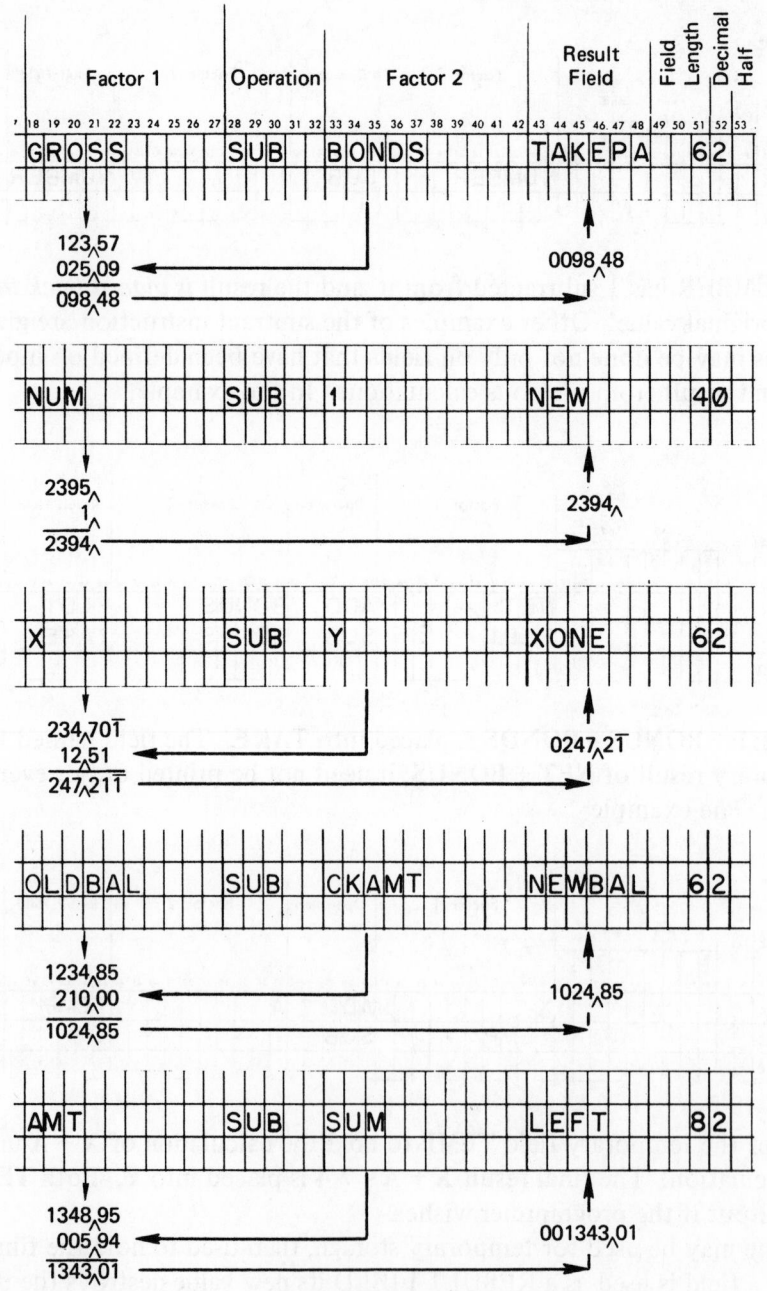

FIG. 7-2 Subtraction.

value stored there. This technique can be used to conserve memory space, since each different field name used in a program requires additional storage.

The operation for a multiply instruction is **MULT**. The field names or literals given in FACTOR 1 and FACTOR 2 are those fields being multiplied; the RESULT FIELD specifies where the answer will be placed. In the example,

		Factor 1	Operation	Factor 2	Result Field	Field Length	Decimal Position
0 1	C	HOURS	MULT	RATE	PAY	6	2
0 2	C						

the amount of **PAY** is obtained by multiplying the hours worked, **HOURS**, by the rate of pay per hour, **RATE**. Multiplication is algebraic; the product of two like signs is positive, while that of two unlike signs is negative. Since multiplication gives the same result regardless of the order, FACTOR 1 and FACTOR 2 may be interchanged without changing the answer. The values of **HOURS** and **RATE** are unchanged by the execution of the instruction.

The length of the RESULT FIELD is usually determined by a method known as *scaling*. Assuming that the length of the field **HOURS** is 2, with $\emptyset$ decimals, and the length of the field **RATE** is 4, with 2 decimal places, the size of the product can be estimated by using the largest anticipated values in the calculations, as shown:

$$99.99$$
$$\underline{99.}$$
done by the method $99.99\,(1\emptyset\emptyset - 1)$

which is equivalent and which gives 9999. –99.99, or $9899.\emptyset 1$. The result will be at most 6 digits long, with 2 decimal places. A 4-digit number multiplied by a 2-digit number can produce a 6-digit number. The field length of the result of a multiplication will be, at most, the sum of the lengths of the two contributing fields. If the contents of the fields have some reasonable upper limit lower than all nines, then a smaller-scaled length may sometimes be found. In the example,

		Factor 1	Operation	Factor 2	Result Field	Field Length	Decimal Position
0 1	C	PRIN	MULT	TIME	AMT	9	2
0 2	C						

PRIN could have length 6, 2 decimals and **TIME** could have length 3, $\emptyset$ decimals, which would cause the result to be, at most, length 9, with 2 decimals.

When enough space is not given to hold the answer, truncation may cause an answer of $1,\emptyset\emptyset 5.95$ to be 5.95! If the value of **DEP** were $85\emptyset.$ and **RATE** were $1.5\emptyset$, the example

		Factor 1	Operation	Factor 2	Result Field	Field Length	Decimal Position
0 1	C	DEP	MULT	RATE	BOOK	5	2
0 2	C						
0 3	C						

would not produce the correct answer 1275.∅∅, but would give 275.∅∅! The length of **BOOK** is not long enough to hold the answer. No error message will be given by the execution of this instruction! It is the programmer's responsibility to assign proper lengths to hold the high-order digits of every result.

If more decimal places are generated in a calculation than are specified to be saved in the RESULT FIELD, excess decimal places on the right are truncated. In the example

	Factor 1	Operation	Factor 2	Result Field	Field Length	Dec Half	High 1>2	Low 1<2	Equal 1=2
	SALES	MULT	.∅15	COMM	6 2				

an error could arise in **COMM**; if **SALES** were length 5, 2 decimals, the result could be length 7, 5 decimals. Since only 2 decimals were saved in **COMM**, the right-most 3 were dropped. The last one saved may even be wrong since rounding was not done. A calculated result of 35.78953 would be stored as 35.78, without proper rounding to get 35.79.

Rounding on any calculation can be accomplished by placing an **H** in column 53 of the line. The H stands for *half-adjusting* and is done by the computer by adding 5 into the position to right of the last decimal place being kept. If an answer were calculated as 145.6787 and placed into storage with length 5, 2 decimals, the answer would ordinarily be stored as 145.67, since truncation would occur to make it the length specified. However, with half-adjusting, the answer would be found by:

$$\begin{array}{r} 145.6787 \\ \underline{.∅∅5} \\ 145.6837 \end{array}$$

after which truncation occurs to give the result of 145.68. Rounding of this type should be done on all business reports that have calculations resulting in more than 2 decimal places. Figure 7-3 gives several examples.

Formula evaluation may be done by using combinations of the add, subtract, and multiply instructions. To calculate the value of the equation $3x^2 + 5x - 7$:

	C	Factor 1	Operation	Factor 2	Result Field	Field Length	Decimal Posit
0 1	C	X	MULT	X	TEMP	6	2
0 2	C	TEMP	MULT	3	TERM1	6	2
0 3	C	X	MULT	5	TERM2	6	2
0 4	C	TERM1	ADD	TERM2	TEMP		
0 5	C	TEMP	ADD	-7	Y	7	2

By rewriting the formula as $x \cdot (3x + 5) - 7$, it is shorter:

Factor 1	Operation	Factor 2	Result Field	Field Length	Decimal Posit	Half Adjust	Plus	Minus	Zero or Blank	High 1>2	Low 1<2	Equal 1=2
X	MULT	3	TEMP	6	2							
TEMP	ADD	5	PAREN	6	2							
PAREN	MULT	X	TERM1	7	2							
TERM1	ADD	-7	Y	8	2							

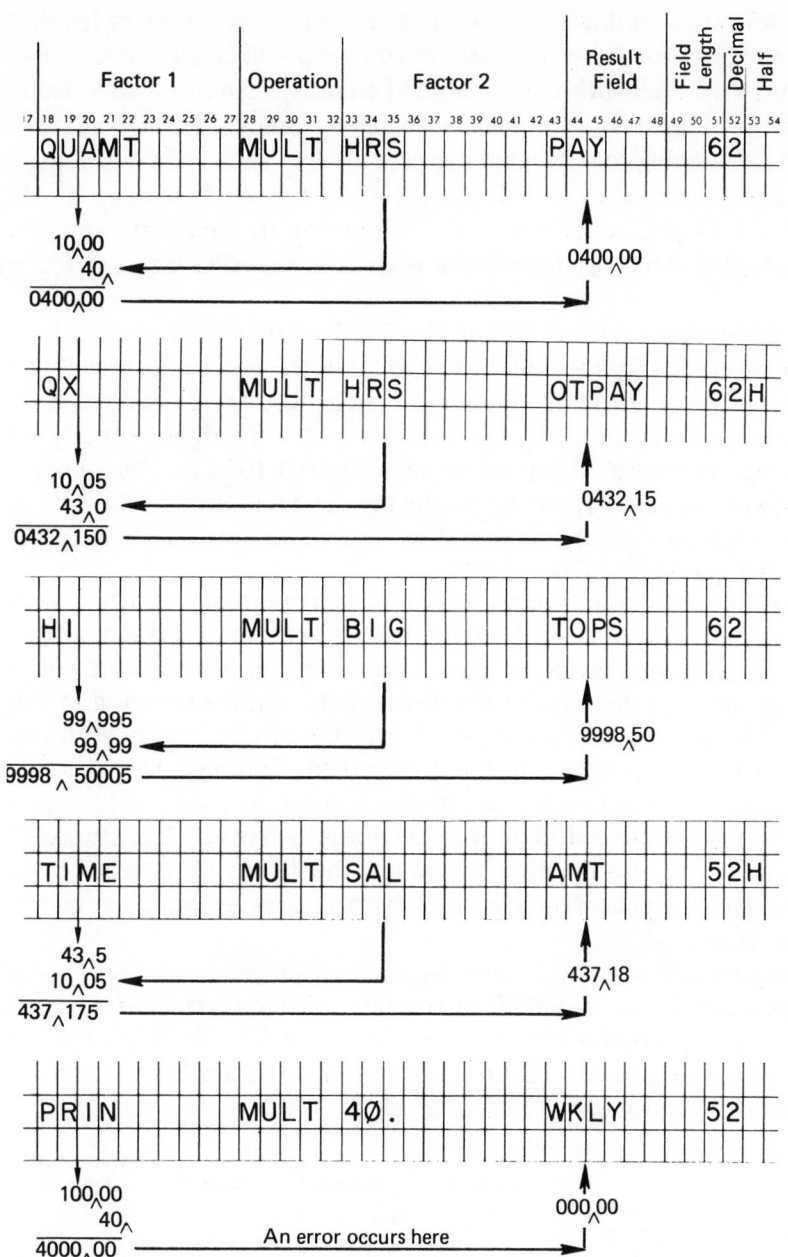

FIG. 7-3 Multiplication.

A value may be raised to an integer power by successive multiplication. To find compound interest by the formula **AMOUNT = P · (1.∅5)⁴**, the calculations are

			And	Not	Not			Factor 1	Operation	Factor 2	Result Field	Field Length	Decimal Posi	Half Adjust
3 4 5	6	7 8	9 10 11	12 13 14	15 16	17		18 19 20 21 22 23 24 25 26 27	28 29 30 31 32	33 34 35 36 37 38 39 40 41 42	43 44 45 46 47 48	49 50 51	52	53
0 1 ∅	C							1.∅5	MULT	1.∅5	TEMP	6 4		
0 2 ∅	C							TEMP	MULT	1.∅5	TEMP			H
0 3 ∅	C							TEMP	MULT	1.∅5	TEMP			H
0 4 ∅	C							TEMP	MULT	P	AMOUNT	6 2		H
0 5	C													

The number **1.Ø5**, when multiplied by itself as in line Ø1Ø, produces length 6, with 4 decimal places, so no half-adjusting is necessary if you keep 4 decimal places. The next calculation, however, produces length 9 with 6 decimals and truncates the result to 4 decimals; half-adjusting may be done by putting an **H** in column 53, to cause rounding to 4 decimal places rather than truncation to 4. Rounding to 4 decimal places is done in each later multiplication until the last, at which time the rounding to 2 decimals is done for the final result in **AMOUNT**. If higher powers are needed, looping techniques and a subroutine are necessary; you need not be concerned with that now. No single instruction is given in the RPG language for calculations with exponents.

The divide instruction, given as **DIV** in the OPERATION field, causes the dividend, in FACTOR 1, to be divided by the divisor, in FACTOR 2. The quotient will be placed in the RESULT FIELD. The dividend and divisor are unchanged by the execution of the instruction. Decimal places are automatically aligned so that the answer will be properly calculated; the length and decimal places stored depend on the RESULT FIELD. The quotient will be algebraically positive or negative depending on the dividend and divisor. If their signs are algebraically the same—both positive or both negative—the quotient will be positive; if they have opposite signs, the quotient will be negative.

There is one very common error that often occurs on programs that have division in them. You must be aware of it in order to guard against its occurrence. It is simply this: you must never allow the computer to divide by zero, since the result is mathematically undefined. Since this error is dependent on the value of the divisor field during execution, it may not show up until the program is already in production. It may have run correctly with your test data, since you naturally avoid putting zeros into the divisor field. During a production run, however, invalid data could accidentally be used, permitting division by a zero field to happen, and causing your program to have an error stop during execution. After you learn more RPG, you will be able to build a safeguard into the program, to test the divisor for a value of zero before the division is done, and to bypass the division. An error message may then be printed, saying that invalid data has been used.

Answers may be half-adjusted in division, or, instead, the remainder may be saved and moved to a temporary field. The **MVR** instruction, for *move remainder*, may be used to move the remainder of a division into whatever field is specified by RESULT FIELD. If the **MVR** is used, it must immediately follow the **DIV** instruction. The algebraic sign on the remainder is the same as that of the quotient. In the example,

an **AMOUNT** of 129.623, and a **K** of 4, will cause **QUO** to be 32.4Ø5, with the value of **REM** .ØØ3. The remainder can be verified by multiplying back **QUO** by **K**, then adding **REM** to get **AMOUNT**. If, instead of saving the remainder, rounding were to be done, the instruction would be

The value of **QUO** for the numbers given would be 32.41. Other examples of the divide instruction are given in Figure 7-4.

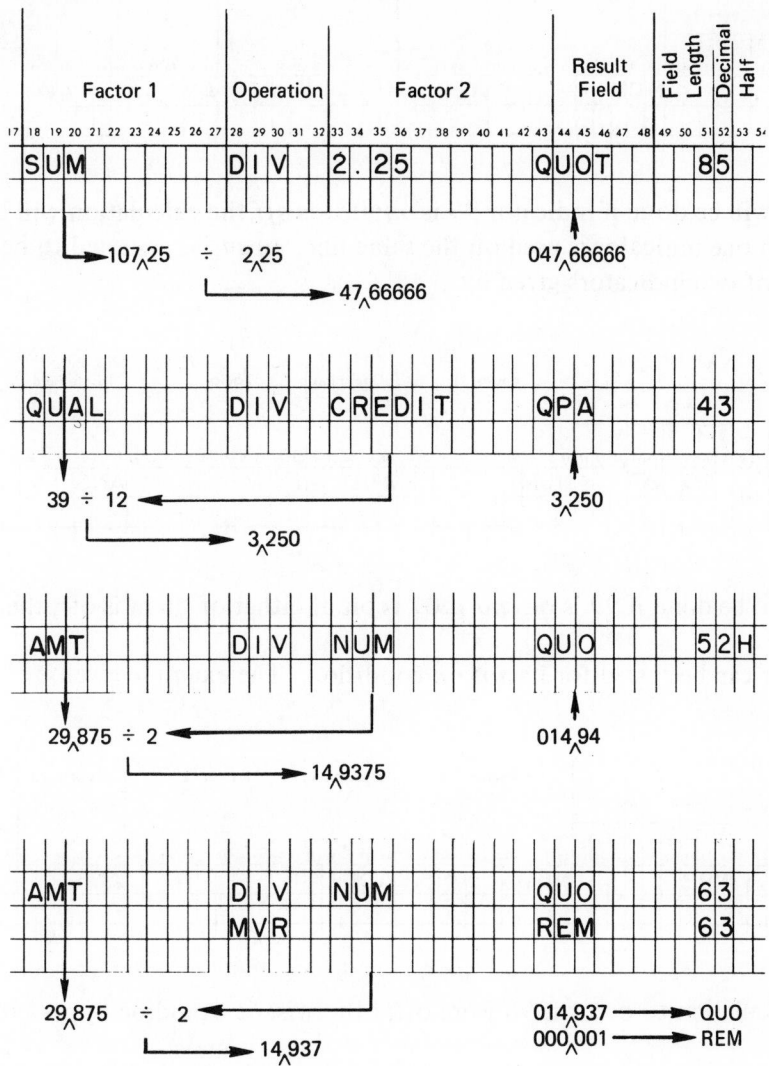

FIG. 7-4 Division.

It is possible to have certain calculations done on some records in the input data deck and different calculations done on others. Indicators are used to tell the computer *when* to do calculations. Up to three indicator settings can be given in columns 9-17 on each instruction. An indicator can be used when *on* or when *not on*. A column is reserved on each of the three indicator setting locations so that an **N** can be inserted as a test for *not on*; without the **N** in that column, the indicator is tested for an *on* condition. Indicators are not required on the CALCULATION form at all; if they are omitted, that line of the CALCULATION form will be done on every detail card of the input data deck. On simple jobs where only one type of card is used for input, it may be easier to omit mention of indicators on the CALCULATION form; on larger jobs involving several data card types, they are given so that the proper arithmetic gets done to the proper card type. It is recommended that indicators be used on all CALCULATION form lines.

In the example,

Indicators (And / And)	Factor 1	Operation	Factor 2	Result Field	Field Length	Decimal Positions / Half Adjust (H) / High 1>2
99	NUM	ADD	1	ANS	40	

the calculation will be done if indicator 99 is *on*; if it is *off* the calculation will be bypassed. When more than one indicator is used on the same line, an *and* is assumed to be between them. The use of two indicators given by

And / And	Factor 1	Operation	Factor 2	Result Field	Field Length	Decimal Pos
99 07	NUM	ADD	1	ANS	40	

causes the line to be done if 99 is on *and* if Ø7 is on; if either of them is off, the calculation is bypassed.

An indicator can be tested for its *not on* condition. The example given by

And / And	Factor 1	Operation	Factor 2	Result Field	Field Length	Decimal Pos
N98	NUM	ADD	1	ANS	40	

would cause calculation to occur if 98 were off; otherwise it would be bypassed. The example

And / And	Factor 1	Operation	Factor 2	Result Field	Field Length	Decimal Position
98 NØ3	NUM	ADD	1	ANS	40	

would be done if indicator 98 were *on* and Ø3 were *off*; any other combination of settings of 98 and Ø3 would cause execution of the instruction to be bypassed.

If you should wish a calculation to be done either on indicator 98 *or* 99, note that you may not specify them on the same line, as that would be an *and* condition. It is necessary to write the calculation twice:

		Form	Cont	Not	And	Not	And	Not		Factor 1	Operation	Factor 2	Result Field	Field Length	Decimal Position
0	1		c		98					AMT	ADD	BONUS	PAY	52	
0	2		c		99					AMT	ADD	BONUS	PAY		
0	3		c												

Of course, if indicators 98 and 99 were *both on*, the calculation would be done twice! One way to prevent that is to make each one *exclusive* of the other, as shown by

		Form	Con	Not	And	Not	And	Not		Factor 1	Operation	Factor 2	Result Field	Field Length	Decimal Posi
0	1		c		98	N	99			AMT	ADD	BONUS	PAY	52	
0	2		c		99	N	98			AMT	ADD	BONUS	PAY		
0	3		c												

which would cause the calculation to be done when 98 is *on,* but 99 *off,* or when 99 is *on,* but 98 is *off.*

These basic instructions for add, subtract, multiply, and divide can be used in all kinds of problems. This lesson concerns itself with calculations on individual *detail cards* and not any group of cards; neither does it attempt to teach totals for a group. On every detail card, the list of calculations is run through by the computer, with execution occurring as determined by indicator; then output is done for that detail card. This describes *detail-time* calculations. When calculations are to be done for values resulting from a group of data cards, it is said to be a *total-time* calculation, which need not be of concern yet.

Totals can, however, be calculated from information which is given on fields *across* a detail card. These totals are programmed by successive additions to be done when the detail card indicator 99 is on:

		For	Cr	Not	And	Not	And	Not		Factor 1	Operation	Factor 2	Result Field	Field Length	Decimal Posi
0	1		c		99					AMT1	ADD	AMT2	CRTOT	62	
0	2		c		99					CRTOT	ADD	AMT3	CRTOT		
0	3		c		99					CRTOT	ADD	AMT4	CRTOT		

The value of **AMT1 + AMT2 + AMT3 + AMT4** would be placed in the sum field, **CRTOT**.

EXERCISES

1. Write a calculation in the place provided for each:
   (a) Interest = principal $\times$ rate $\times$ time.
   (b) The bond code multiplied by $18.75 gives the bond amount.
   (c) The sales value equals the quantity times the price of each.
   (d) The balance is equal to the old balance minus the adjustment.

(e) Add 17 to **K** and put it back into **K**.

(f) Divide the quality points by the number of credits and put the result into **QPA**.

(g) Multiply the percent discount by the price to get the reduction amount.

	Factor 1	Operation	Factor 2	Result Field	Field Length	Decimal Position	Half Adjust (H)	Plus	Minus
								Compa	
								High 1 > 2	Low 1 < 2
	5 16 17 18 19 20 21 22 23 24 25 26 27	28 29 30 31 32	33 34 35 36 37 38 39 40 41 42	43 44 45 46 47 48	49 50 51	52	53	54 55	56 57
(a)									
(b)									
(c)									
(d)									
(e)									
(f)									
(g)									

2. Determine by scaling the length necessary to do each of the following calculations:

(a) **P** × **R**, lengths 4,2 and 4,3, respectively, round to 2. _____

(b) **BAL** added to **CHGS**, lengths 6,2 and 5,2, respectively. _____

(c) 25ØØ divided by .Ø5, 2 decimals needed _____

(d) **BILL** divided by **K**, lengths 6, 2 and 3, 2, respectively with 2 decimals needed, rounded. _____

3. Give the equation that calculates **Y** in each of these:

(a)

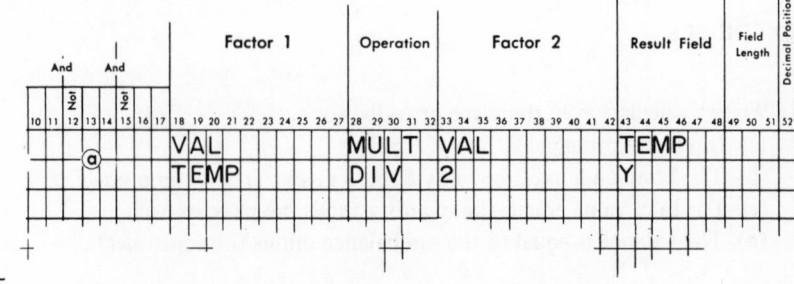

_____

(b)

10 11 12	... 18 19 20 21 22 23 24 ... 27	28 29 30 31 32	33 34 35 36 37 38 39 40 41 42	43 44 45 46 47 48 49 50 51 52
	AMT	DIV	2	T
ⓑ	T	ADD	75.2	K
	K	MULT	2	Y

(c)

10 11 12 13 14 15 16 17	18 19 20 21 22 23 24 25 26 27	28 29 30 31 32	33 34 35 36 37 38 39 40 41 42	43 44 45 46 47 48 49 50 51 52
	BAL	SUB	PAY	BILL
ⓒ	BILL	ADD	CHG	BILL
	BILL	ADD	SERCHG	Y

(d)

10 11 12 13 14 15 16 17	18 19 20 21 22 23 24 25 26 27	28 29 30 31 32	33 34 35 36 37 38 39 40 41 42	43 44 45 46 47 48 49 50 51 52
	SALES	MULT	RATE	COMM
ⓓ	COMM	ADD	SAL	Y

4. Write calculations for the equation given:

   (a) $y = 2x - 5$

   (b) **AMOUNT** equals the difference between the sales price and the original price, multiplied by .1∅.

   (c) The take home pay equals hours multiplied by rate plus the overtime hours times 1.5 times the rate, minus the deductions.

   (d) The number of items in inventory can be found by taking the balance, adding in the receipts, and subtracting off the issues.

And		Not			Factor 1	Operation	Factor 2	Result Field	Field Length	Decimal Pc
13	14	15	16	17	18 19 20 21 22 23 24 25 26 27	28 29 30 31 32	33 34 35 36 37 38 39 40 41 42	43 44 45 46 47 48	49 50 51	52
ⓐ										
ⓑ										
ⓒ										
ⓓ										

5. Show what the result will be in each of these:

	Data in Factor 1	Operation	Data in Factor 2	Result Data	Length	Decimals	Rounding
(a)	234.47	ADD	182.91		5	2	
(b)	312.ØØ	ADD	15.7$\overline{2}$		5	2	
(c)	19	ADD	17.328		5	2	H
(d)	1$\overline{7}$	ADD	43$\overline{2}$		3	2	
(e)	32173	ADD	Ø23415		8	6	H
(f)	27.9324	SUB	27.9324		6	2	
(g)	1.9324	SUB	Ø.3621		5	3	H
(h)	193.5$\overline{4}$	SUB	192.4$\overline{7}$		5	2	
(i)	321.76	MULT	2Ø		7	2	
(j)	892.ØØ	MULT	1ØØ		7	2	
(k)	347.9	MULT	Ø1.$\overline{5}$		5	2	
(l)	849.31	MULT	2		5	2	
(m)	31.465	MULT	2.ØØØ		5	2	H
(n)	.1932	MULT	25		4	3	H
(o)	1937	MULT	51.2		6	Ø	H
(p)	3.425	MULT	256.Ø		5	3	H
(q)	193.24	DIV	2.1		5	2	H
(r)	135.2	DIV	4.		6	3	
(s)	Ø2345	DIV	.Ø2		7	3	
(t)	81.563	DIV	2		6	2	H

Lesson 8

EDIT WORDS AND CONSTANTS

You will learn to edit data to print dollar signs, decimal points, commas, and other special characters and constants to make the report look better.

The questions given here are answered on the back of this page. They represent the topics taught in this lesson. If you are doing independent study, but have done editing in some other computer language, look over the examples in the lesson, then attempt the exercises at the back of the lesson before going on to Lesson 9.

1. Why is editing necessary?
2. What is an *edit word* and how is it used?
3. In what mode must a field be stored to be edited?
4. Give two ways to accomplish zero suppression.
5. What is *check protection*?
6. What two ways can you use to indicate the sign of a field?
7. What is an *alphameric literal*?
8. How can you get the zero suppression to allow some zeros to print but others at the left to be suppressed or replaced by asterisks?
9. What happens if an edit word is too long or too short?
10. How can you cause an *apostrophe* to print on the report?

ANSWERS

1. To make numeric fields readable by inserting commas, decimal points, dollar signs, asterisks, etc., and to give sign indication.

2. A *mask*, formed with certain digit positions for the actual value from the field to be inserted, and with other character positions to print exactly as given on the report. The values of the field being edited are brought into the mask into position before printing occurs.

3. Numeric.

4. By using **Z** in column 38 if zero suppression and sign removal are all that need to be done; by using an edit word if other editing is also needed.

5. The insertion of asterisks into the leading positions of the field up to the first significant digit. It serves as a protection against alteration of the amount field.

6. By using **CR** or by using a minus sign.

7. A constant, enclosed in quote marks. It may contain numbers, letters, or special characters.

8. By using the zero-suppress stop digit, ∅, in an edit word, or by using the check protection asterisk in an edit word.

9. On some implementations, you get diagnostic warning messages, and possibly wrong answers. On others, if it is too long, extra zeros are inserted on the left to make the field length fit and only when it is too short is a diagnostic warning message given.

10. By putting *two* quotation marks in an edit word, *one* will print.

Reports are read by people who are not programmers. Since the information contained in a report must be understood by the people who have to use it, all fields on the report should be easy to read and well identified. Coded information should be written out with descriptive remarks so that programmer codes will not have to be memorized by the user. Headings should be given when preprinted forms are not being used, and contents of fields should have appropriate characters inserted to make them more readable. The RPG language uses *edit words* to make data fields more legible by insertion of characters, *zero suppression* to allow leading zeros to be changed to blanks and the sign to be removed, and *constants* to insert headings or explanatory remarks.

If an input data field is merely to be printed onto the report, without any type of calculations, insertion of editing characters, or suppression of zeros, then it should be considered an alphameric field and no decimal entry given for it. If a field is given a decimal entry, it is considered to be in *numeric* mode. On the IBM SYSTEM/36Ø, it can be as long as 15 digits, of which there may be from Ø to 9 decimal places. Only fields in numeric mode can be edited, zero suppressed, or used in calculation.

Leading zeros are those zeros in a field at the left of the first nonzero digit. The first nonzero digit and all digits that follow are considered *significant* digits by RPG. In the number ØØØ123Ø3Ø14Ø, three leading zeros appear. The first significant digit is therefore a 1; all the digits 123Ø3Ø14Ø are significant. The process of changing the leading zeros to blanks before printing them is called *zero suppression*. A *small b with a slash* through it (ƀ) is used to indicate where a blank position or column occurs; you should be able to justify each one when it appears.

A **Z** may be placed in column 38 of the OUTPUT-FORMAT form along the side of a field name. This automatically prevents the leading zeros in the field from printing and prevents the internal sign position from printing. Any digits *following* the first significant digit, however, *will* print, even though they are zeros. If by some chance the whole field should be zeros, then there would be no printing at all! In some instances a field that is completely blanked out might be confusing to the user of the report; if so, editing should be used instead, so that the final zero can be forced to print. Editing may also be used to insert dollar signs and punctuation marks into the number. If editing is used, the **Z** should *not* be given in column 38.

To *edit* a field means to prepare it for printing. The programmer may choose to use commas, decimal points, or any of several other special characters to make the data look more presentable. Editing provides for automatic zero suppression and the removal of the sign position from the field. For each field to be edited, an *edit word* must be formed. It will be used as a *mask* or *overlay* into which the digits from the field will be placed. The edit word is written into columns 45-7Ø of the OUTPUT-FORMAT form on the same line as the field name. The quotation mark, a multipunched 5 and 8 in one column, must enclose each edit word; column 45, for that reason is always the beginning quotation mark. Since numeric fields, on most implementations, have a maximum length of 15 digits, edit words that accommodate up to 15 digits may be formed.

The edit word consists of three parts: the *body*, the *status*, and the *expansion*. The body begins at the left-most character of the edit word, after the beginning quotation mark, and usually contains a combination of inserted characters, blanks, asterisks, dollar signs, or zeros to satisfy the printing requirements of the number of digits in the field being printed. The status portion of the edit word may be used to display an algebraic sign—either in the form of a CR for credit, or a minus sign. It extends from the body portion to the appearance of either the CR symbol or a minus symbol. Edit words that do not have either of these two symbols do not have a status portion. The expansion portion is that part at the right of the status portion, until the closing quotation mark. It may contain alphameric characters that are to be inserted on the line along with the contents of the field.

The edit word is designed by referring to the PRINTER SPACING CHART. For every X or Z on the chart, there should be a digit position in the edit word. These digit positions will be filled with the actual values from that field during execution. For each X or Z, leave a blank position in the edit word. When forming an edit word on the proper OUTPUT-FORMAT form, the grid markings make it possible to count blank positions, so that the use of a small b with a slash through it is permitted, but not necessary; when forming edit words on plain paper, be sure to denote each blank with ƀ. Punctuation symbols from the spacing chart are placed exactly as they appear. The edit word given by

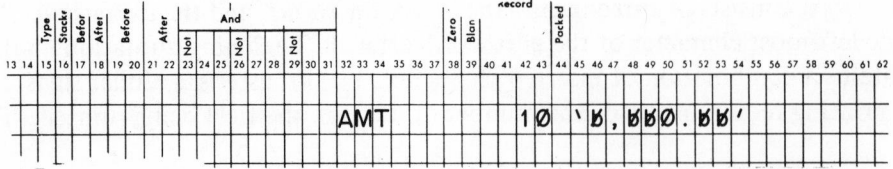

is used for a field that was coded as X,XXX.XX. Note that the beginning quotation mark is in column 45 and that an ending one encloses the edit word. **AMT** could be a numeric field with length 6, of which 2 are decimal places. A value of 23Ø174 would be printed as 2,3Ø1.74, with the comma and decimal point inserted. The printed value, shown in Figure 8-1, occupies eight print positions—two more than were required to store the number in memory. If the value were ØØØ125, the report would read ƀƀƀ1.25 with the three leading zeros and the comma changed to blanks. Zero suppression, *implied on all edit words*, causes commas and decimal points to be suppressed when only blanks precede them. If the value of **AMT** were ØØØØØ7, representing seven cents, the edit word given would cause it to print as ƀƀƀƀƀƀ7! On the report this would appear as   7, with 5 blanks where the zeros were, and 2 where the comma and decimal were, rather than   .Ø7, which would be more desirable. It is by far more indicative of money to have the decimal point *printed*, and there *is* a way to do it. The implied zero suppression may be *stopped* at some predetermined point. The edit word will be modified to include a *stop* on zero suppression.

A *zero* in an edit word causes the suppression to stop. The value of the data for that position will itself be suppressed if zero, but be printed if not zero. The *zero-suppress stop digit* can be used only once in an edit word, and should be placed in the position where the *last* suppression is to occur. The edit word given by

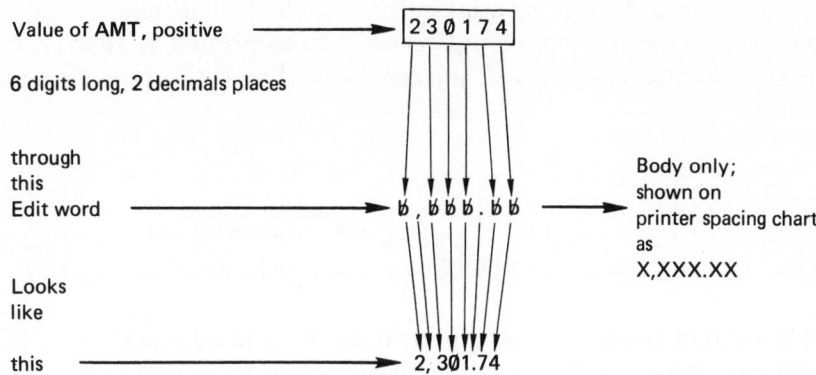

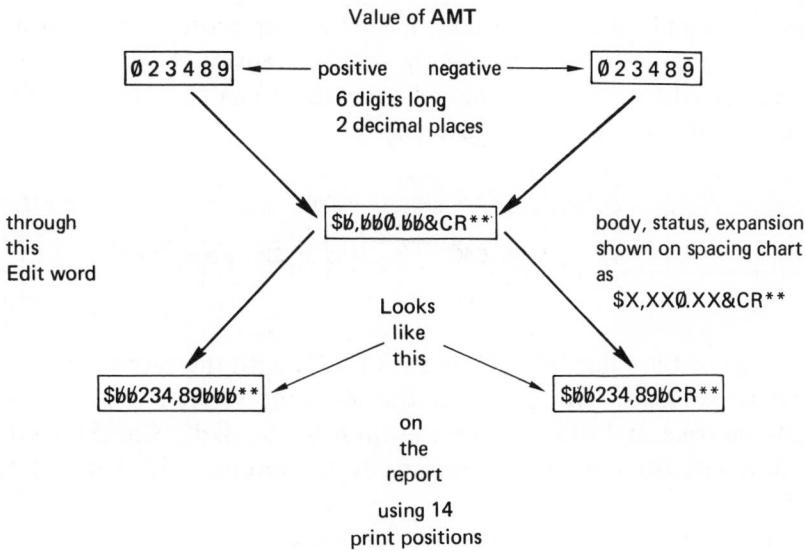

FIG. 8-1 Edit word usage.

will permit the printing of a field with length 6, 2 decimal places. It will suppress leading zeros and commas but will always print the decimal point and the two decimal digits. If the value of **AMT** were Ø00007, it would be printed as ⊄⊄⊄⊄.Ø7, which is preferable to ⊄⊄⊄⊄⊄⊄7. The zero-suppress stop digit should always be used for fields where a completely blanked-out field is undersirable on a field of zero, and for all fields representing money so that the decimal point and decimal positions will print.

Fields that contain amounts representing money are usually printed with a dollar sign. It may, on most implementations, either be *fixed*—printed in position *in front of* the field—or *floating*—printed immediately at the left of the first significant digit. The single dollar sign, placed where shown in the edit word given, will cause a fixed-position dollar sign to print in front of the 6-digit field. If the value of **AMT** in memory were ∅∅1295, the edit word would cause it to be printed as $ɓɓɓ12.95. If the single dollar sign is given in the floating position, adjacent to, and on the left of, the zero-suppress stop digit, as shown,

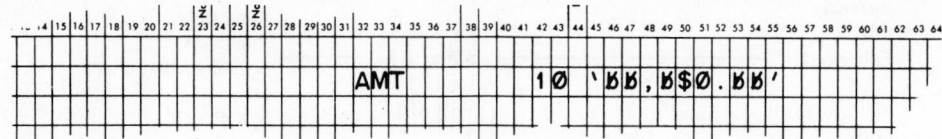

the value would be printed as ɓɓɓ$12.95, appearing on the printed report as $12.95 with three preceding blanks. When the floating dollar sign is used, there should be an extra blank on the left end of the edit word to allow the dollar sign a place to print if all the digits are significant! The dollar sign is never suppressed; when used, it must be given some position in which to print. Examples of the use of the dollar sign are given in Figure 8-2.

The floating dollar sign is often used as one means to help protect checks from being altered. Most checks, however, are produced with an even better means of check protection than the floating dollar sign. Asterisks can be inserted *between* the dollar sign and the first significant digit of the check amount. The edit word given by

will cause the printing of the value ∅∅1275 as $***12.75, with the zero-suppressed positions being replaced by the asterisks. The asterisk in the edit word serves two purposes: to replace leading zeros with asterisks, and to serve as zero-suppress stop digit. Checks printed in this manner are relatively safe from numeric insertions in the amount field. Further examples are given in Figure 8-2.

The portion of the edit word used for dollar sign indication, commas, decimal points, and the digit positions of the value of the field is the *body* of the edit word. Since numeric values may be either positive or negative, there must also be a way to indicate the algebraic *sign* on the report. The usual way is to print either a minus sign or the letters CR, which stand for *credit*. Sign indication, when needed, is given on the right side of the edit word in the *status* portion. If no sign indication is given in an edit word, the sign is suppressed and does not print. The edit word given by

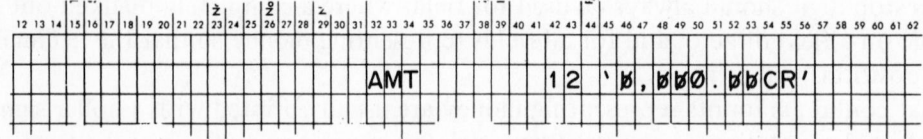

shows both the body and status. The status will cause the printing of the letters CR if the number is negative, but will place blanks instead of the CR if the number is positive. If the value of **AMT** were ∅∅129\overline{5}, the edit word would cause ɓɓɓ12.95CR to print; if it were 1∅62∅5, the value 1,∅62.∅5ɓɓ would print. Recall that the eleven punch over the units position in the rightmost digit of the input data field serves as a negative sign.

Field Contents	Edit Word	Result Printed
001234	ƀ,ƀƀƀ.ƀƀ	ƀƀƀ12.34
000012	ƀ,ƀƀƀ.ƀƀ	ƀƀƀƀƀ12
000012	ƀ,ƀƀ0.ƀƀ	ƀƀƀƀ.12
000027	$ƀ,ƀƀ0.ƀƀ	$ƀƀƀƀ.27
000027	ƀƀ,ƀ$0.ƀƀ	ƀƀƀƀ$.27
000000	ƀ,ƀƀƀ.ƀƀ	ƀƀƀƀƀƀƀ
023069	ƀƀ/ƀƀ/ƀƀ	ƀ2/30/69
238765	ƀƀ&ƀƀ&ƀƀ	23ƀ87ƀ65
002387	ƀ,ƀƀ*.ƀƀ	***23.87
001349	$ƀ,ƀƀ*.ƀƀ	$***13.49
000250	$ƀ,ƀƀ*.ƀƀCR	$****2.50ƀƀ
001595	ƀ,ƀƀ0.ƀƀCR	ƀƀƀ15.95CR
0123	ƀ0ƀƀ	ƀ123
0007	ƀ0ƀƀ	ƀƀ07
0000	ƀ0ƀƀ	ƀƀ00
23456	ƀƀƀ.ƀƀ&-	234.56ƀƀ
01342$\bar{9}$	ƀƀƀ.ƀƀƀ&-	ƀ13.429ƀ-
3458	ƀƀ.ƀƀ&**	34.58ƀ**
23000	ƀƀ.ƀƀƀ***	23.000***
00000	ƀƀ.ƀƀƀ***	********
00000	ƀ0.ƀƀƀ***	ƀƀ.000***
2347895	ƀƀ0-ƀƀƀƀ	234-7895
135759	ƀƀƀ,ƀƀƀ.ƀƀ	ƀƀ1,357.59
097834	ƀƀ$0/ƀƀƀ	ƀ$97.834
00134$\bar{5}$	$ƀ,ƀƀ0.ƀƀ&CR	$ƀƀƀ13.45ƀCR
00134$\bar{5}$	ƀƀ,ƀ$0.ƀƀ&-	ƀƀƀ$13.45ƀ-
00004$\bar{7}$	$ƀ,0ƀƀ.ƀƀCR	$ƀƀƀ00.47CR

FIG. 8-2 Edit word examples.

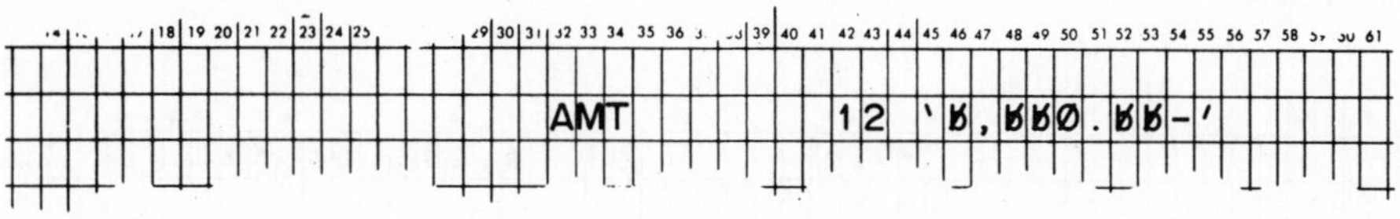

If the meaning of the job being done is not best served by the letters CR, the actual minus sign, or *hyphen*, may be printed. The edit word given by

will cause the value $\emptyset 12398$ to be printed as $\emptyset\emptyset 123.98-$ with the minus sign following the last digit of the number.

The *ampersand*, &, a single punch, is used in an edit word to create a blank position on the report. The edit word given by

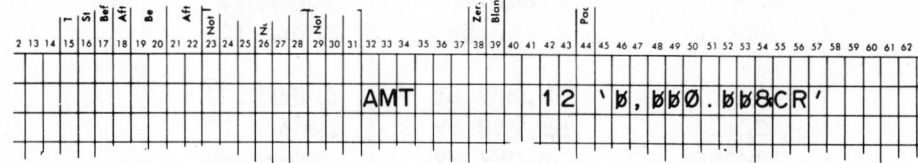

shows the ampersand placed after the body in the status portions of the edit word. It will cause one blank to be placed on the report *between* the number and the sign indication. The value of $\emptyset 12398$ would be printed as $\emptyset\emptyset 123.98\emptyset CR$, where the $\emptyset$ represents a blank print position. The ampersand may be used to cause blanks to appear in front of the minus sign indication in the same manner.

Other special insert characters are, on some implementations, allowed in the body of the edit word: the *slash* symbol, / , and the minus sign, –, also called a dash or hyphen. The edit word given by

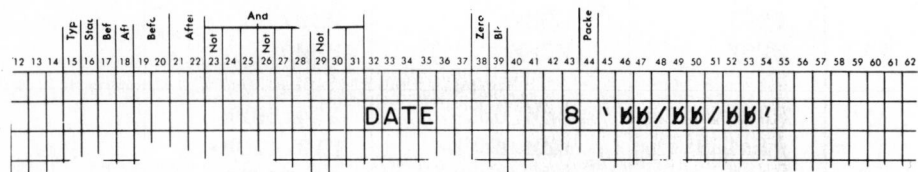

will cause the value of **DATE** to be printed as a month, day, and year, with slash marks separating them. The value of **DATE** given by 121649, for example, would be printed as 12/16/49. On some implementations, the edit word given by

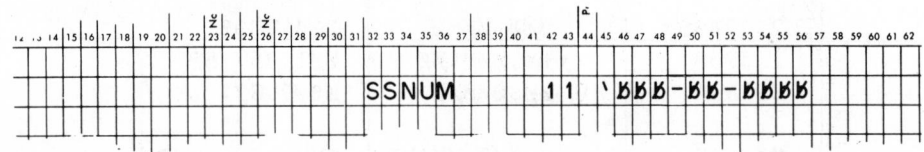

will cause a social security number of $43489\emptyset 138$ to be printed as $434\text{-}89\text{-}\emptyset 138$. Recall that fields to be edited must be in numeric mode; **DATE** and **SSNUM** must have had decimal places assigned to cause them to be stored in numeric mode; $\emptyset$ would ordinarily be used.

Asterisks may be used in a way other than for check protection—that of giving special attention to certain fields on the report. One or more asterisks can be specified in the status portion of the edit word to cause asterisks to print *to the right of* the value of the number. One asterisk is usually used on a total for a group or department; several may be used for the total over all departments. The edit word

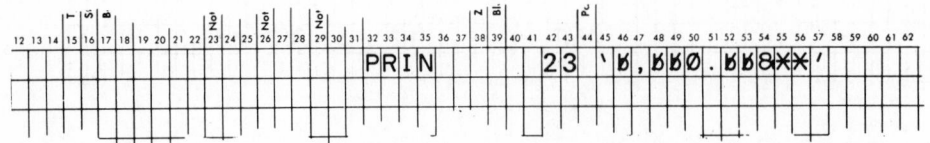

would cause the value Ø0Ø1259 to print as ØØØ12.59Ø**. An ampersand has been used to cause
a blank position to separate the actual value from the highlighting asterisks. When using asterisks in this manner, a zero-suppress stop digit *must* be given in the digit portion of the edit word,
to prevent the highlighting asterisks from being considered check protection asterisks. They
may also be used in combination with sign indication, as shown in the examples in Figure 8-2.

On many implementations, the edit word must *exactly* fit the length specified for the field.
On others, however, if an edit word is given that has more digit positions than the field it represents, leading zeros are inserted during execution to make the field fit the edit word. If an edit
word is too short, a diagnostic error message is given during compilation as a warning so that
you will know that low-order digits may be lost due to truncation. The programmer must be
certain that the edit word contains a correctly positioned decimal point, because decimal alignment is *not* done by the use of an edit word. A field of length 6 may have 2 decimal places but
be printed by an incorrect edit word as length 6 with 3 decimal places!

Occasionally, programmers are surprised to find that certain numeric fields are printing
with a letter in their low-order position, such as ØØ12C, or Ø134K. Once a field is made numeric
mode, a sign position is stored for it. This sign is equivalent to an overpunch—a 12 punch for
positive numbers, and an 11 punch for negative ones. When a field stored as numeric is printed
alphamerically, without any editing or zero suppression, the letter equivalent to its units position
and sign may be printed. The value Ø134K is in reality the value Ø134$\overline{2}$, printing without
properly being prepared for output on the printer. Either zero-suppress or edit those fields to
eliminate the letter; use a status portion in the edit word when the sign of the field needs to be
indicated.

The edit word used on numeric fields greatly improves the appearance of the printed report.
Portions of the edit word are *inserted characters,* such as the dollar sign, which are merely put
into place on the report. It is also possible to insert *whole words*, names, numbers, or special
characters and put them into the report. These inserted characters, called *constants*, do not
change from one processing of the program to the next—they print exactly the same way every
time the program is run.

Constants, also called *literals*, are of two types: *numeric*, such as those used in doing calculations; and *alphameric*, which are used for output of words, names, or special characters. A
literal means that an actual value is being used, rather than the field name that *refers* to that
value. For example, the name **DEPT** is a field name that refers to the memory address in
storage where the actual value of the department number is stored, while the literal,
'**DEPARTMENT**', is a constant that you might wish to print as a heading above the value of
the department number. The most common use of constants is to make heading lines.

Alphameric literals are easily distinguished from field names by the single quotation mark
at the beginning and end of each one. Within them may be letters, numbers, or special characters. Even though numeric digits alone may be used as a constant heading, quotation marks
must enclose them. The literal is written with beginning and ending quotation marks, left-
justified, in columns 45-7Ø on the OUTPUT-FORMAT specification form. The line given by

could be used to print a heading for some used-car dealer. Note that no field name is given. A field name used on the same line with a constant will cause a diagnostic error message.

The single quotation mark should not be placed *within* the beginning and ending ones, since it would cause termination of the literal at that point. A special method is used to tell the computer that a quotation mark should actually be printed. At the place where one is needed, put two. The literal 'O''HARA' would be used to cause the printing of the name O'HARA on the report. The symbol is often used to print the apostrophe on possessive headings, such as

which would print JOE'S CAR COMPANY onto the top of the report.

Headings are formed in the computer by the consecutive placement of literals. If column headings are needed for **DEPT, PRICE,** and **QUAN,** for example, the literals might be 'DEPART-MENT NUMBER', 'PRICE EACH', and 'QUANTITY ORDERED'. The heading words are not required to be the same as the exact name of the field they represent! The heading for the field named **PRICE** could not only be 'PRICE', but could also be 'UNIT PRICE', 'PRICE EACH', or 'SELLING PRICE'. Heading words are usually completely written out, since they are for the report user and do not have to follow the rules for field names.

Explanatory words may be printed along the side of values on the detail lines. The constant and editing given by

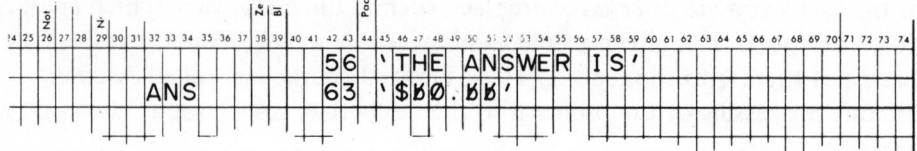

would, if **ANS** were 2792, print as

THE ANSWER IS $27.92

ending in print position 63. If heading constants are longer than 24 characters, they must be broken into several separate ones. The heading 'GOVERNMENT OF THE UNITED STATES OF AMERICA', for example, will not fit into one constant, but must be broken into two:

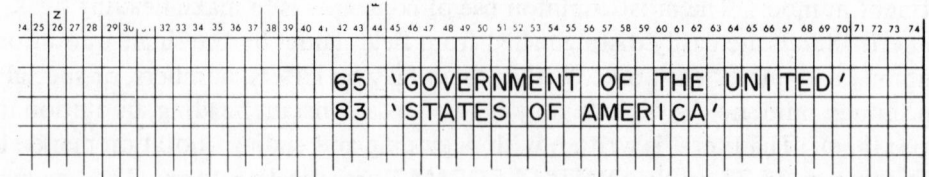

When printed, it will be placed onto one line of the report. The right-end positions given align the constants properly so that they appear as one heading. Care must be taken in assigning right-end positions, as shown by the example in error here:

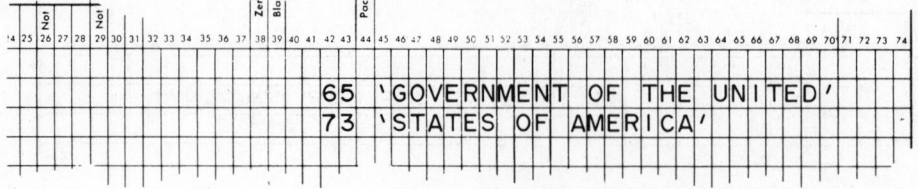

which will, on at least one implementation, cause no diagnostic error message, but will print as

GOVERNMENT OF TSTATES OF AMERICA

since the second constant overlays, and thus destroys, part of the first.

　　Combinations of fields and constants may be used to make readable report lines.　The example

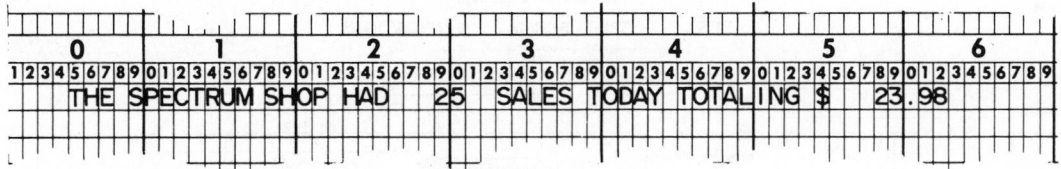

will produce, assuming that **NUM** is $\emptyset\emptyset\emptyset25$ and **SUM** is $\emptyset\emptyset2398$, the line given by

```
          0         1         2         3         4         5         6
 1234567890123456789012345678901234567890123456789012345678901234567890123456789
 THE SPECTRUM SHOP HAD    25 SALES TODAY TOTALING $    23.98
```

　　Certain extensions provided on some implementations of **RPG** permit other *edit codes*, such as the **Z** in column 38 of the **OUTPUT-FORMAT** form to be placed in that column to represent certain standard types of edit words.　This feature reduces programming and debugging time since it eliminates much of the tedious detail of counting field lengths and punching the characters to be inserted into the exact position where needed.　These edit codes are currently available only on certain implementations, such as the IBM SYSTEM/36$\emptyset$, Model 2$\emptyset$, DPS, the IBM 113$\emptyset$, and the IBM SYSTEM/3.

　　Edit codes may be used instead of edit words to place decimal point and commas or not, to print zero balances or not, to cause zero suppression, to remove sign position or indicate its status, or to edit a date field.　In the example given by

Filename	Type (H/D/T/E)	Stacker Select	Space Before	Space After	Skip Before	Skip After	Not	Output Indicators And	Not	And	Not	Field Name	Edit Codes	Blank After (B)	End Positon in Output Record	Packed Field (P)	Commas	Zero Balances to Print	No Sign	CR	−		Constant or Edit Word
																	Yes	Yes	1	A	J	X = Remove Plus Sign	
																	Yes	No	2	B	K	Y = Date Field Edit	
																	No	Yes	3	C	L	Z = Zero Suppress	
																	No	No	4	D	M		
REPORT	D		1					$\emptyset$1															
												AMT	A		2$\emptyset$								
												AMT	C		4$\emptyset$								
												AMT	M		6$\emptyset$								
	D		1					$\emptyset$1															
												NUM	X		2$\emptyset$								
												NUM	Z		4$\emptyset$								
												NUM	1		6$\emptyset$								

the edit codes would, for a value of **AMT** given by –Ø2347.92, and **NUM** equal to + Ø1.325, in memory, produce

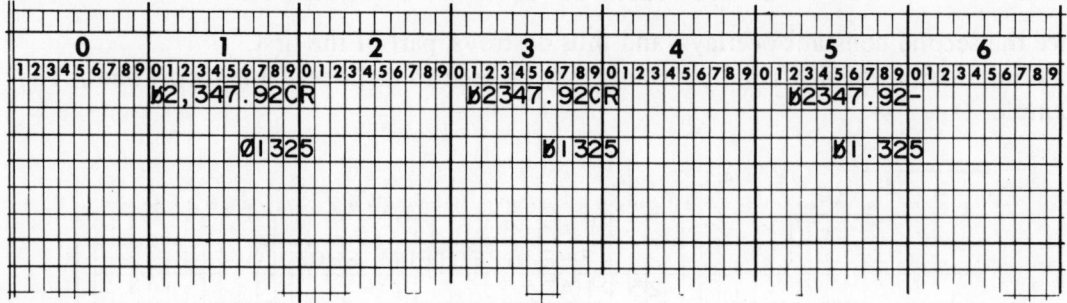

without the use of edit words at all. A table of edit codes that are permitted in column 38 is given in Figure 8-3, shown on the **OUTPUT-FORMAT** form, which lists them in the heading above where they are to be used.

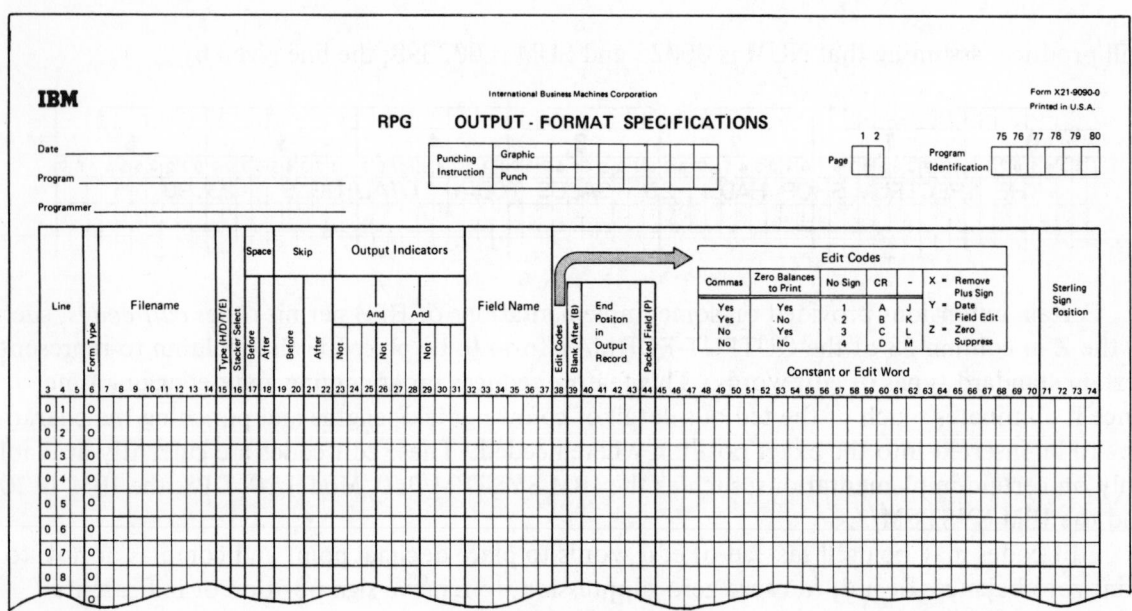

FIG. 8-3 Edit codes.

EXERCISES

1. Show results of each of the edit words given, using the data given. Work from the right side of the field, using the character ∅ to show any blank positions specified. Then tell how many print positions are used to hold the result.

	Data in Field	Edit Word to Use	How Results Print	Number of Print Positions Needed
a.	23‸46	$∅∅.∅∅		
b.	∅∅‸64	$∅∅.∅∅		

Data in Field	Edit Word to Use	How Results Print	Number of Print Positions Needed
c. 4232.14	ƀ,ƀƀ∅.ƀƀ		
d. 4325.27	ƀƀƀ∅.ƀƀ		
e. 16.42	$ƀƀ.ƀƀCR		
f. 18.1̄9̄	$ƀƀ.ƀƀCR		
g. 1214.65	ƀƀƀƀ*.ƀƀ		
h. ∅∅∅1.19	ƀƀƀƀ*.ƀƀ		
i. 1298.	$ƀ∅.ƀƀ		
j. ∅∅26.54	ƀƀƀ$∅.ƀƀ**		
k. 1.26̄4̄	ƀƀƀƀƀ∅.ƀƀƀ-		
l. ∅1.23	ƀƀ,ƀƀ∅.ƀƀƀ**		
m. ∅123.89	∅.ƀƀ		
n. 7893.7̄5̄	ƀƀ,ƀ$.ƀ*.ƀƀ&**		
o. .∅35	∅.ƀƀƀ		
p. ∅52∅7∅.	∅ƀ/ƀƀ/ƀƀ		
q. ∅14459.	ƀƀ-ƀƀƀƀ		
r. 23467.	ƀƀƀ/ƀƀ		
s. 12.666888777	$ƀƀƀ,ƀƀ∅.ƀƀƀƀƀƀƀƀƀ		
t. ∅∅∅∅.∅∅	$ƀ,ƀƀƀ.ƀƀ		

2. Show the printed result line as it would appear if the following combination of constants and data were printed:

(a) Assume that **NUM** is ∅∅19, and that OUTPUT-FORMAT form contains:

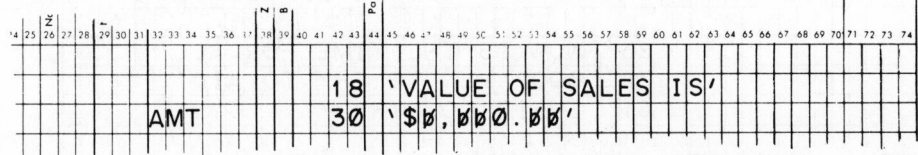

(b) Assume that **AMT** is ∅12394, and that OUTPUT-FORMAT form contains:

(c) Assume that **DESCR** is alphameric, and is '**HAZEL**'.

And	And			Zero Blank	Pack		
				22		'SUBJECT EYE COLOR WAS'
		DESCR		28		

(d) Assume that **NUMBER** is ∅∅25.

Not				Zero Blank	Pack	
				22		'COMMUNITY COLLEGE IN'
				32		'BALTIMORE'
				42		'PAGE NUM.'
		NUMBER	Z	47		

(e) Assume that **OLDBAL** is ∅12395̄.

Nc				Z E	Pa	
				13		'OLD BALANCE'
		OLDBAL		25		'∅∅,∅$∅.∅∅CR'

(f) Assume that **BILL** is ∅5∅∅∅∅, **DAY** is 12, **MONTH** is '**FEBRUARY**'.

Not				Ze R	Pac	
		BILL		10		'$∅,∅∅∅.∅∅'
				28		'IS TO BE PAID BY'
		MONTH		38		
		DAY	Z	41		
				47		',∅1970'

(g) Assume that **NUM** is ∅1, **YEAR** is 69.

And	∧			Zero Blank	Packed	
Not		Not				
				20		'CHAMBERLAYNE GRADES'
		NUM	Z	24		
				36		'SEMESTER,19'
		YEAR	Z	38		

(h) No field names are used on the **OUTPUT-FORMAT** form given:

Not	Z			Z.	Pa	
				23		'NOW IS THE TIME FOR ALL'
				36		'GOOD MEN TO TRY TO AID'
				61		'THEIR COUNTRY.'

(i) What must you do to correct what is probably *intended* to print in part (h)? _____

A PRINTED REPORT WITH HEADINGS

You will learn how to put heading lines on reports to identify the installation, the job, and the information presented.

The questions given here are answered on the back of this page. They serve as a summary of the techniques taught in this lesson. If you are doing independent study, but have never written heading lines before, read over the lesson and then attempt to answer the questions. If you miss any, study the program given in Figure 9-3 and try the questions again. When you can complete all of them correctly, write the programs at the end of this section.

1. Why are preprinted forms used only when necessary?
2. What are the two indicators commonly used to print constant headings?
3. What indicator is turned on to signal the bottom of the page?
4. How is coding specified for an *or* condition?
5. How many print lines are usually used on an 11 X 14-in. computer sheet?
6. Does the order in which alphameric literals are given on the OUTPUT-FORMAT form affect the order in which they are printed?
7. What is a *connector*?
8. What is the purpose of the record-description line on the OUTPUT-FORMAT form?
9. What will happen if your program says to skip to channel Ø2 and you forget to put your carriage control tape on during execution and use the standard tape instead?
10. What coding must you change in a program to make the major heading print only on the first page and never again?

ANSWERS

1. Because they are expensive, and they require more run time for changing the paper and control tape.
2. **1P** and **OF**, for first page and overflow, respectively.
3. **OF**, for overflow.
4. By a line immediately following the record-description line, with an **OR** in columns 14 and 15, and the indicator in 24 and 25.
5. 66 printing lines at six lines per inch are available; usually 55-6∅ are used.
6. No, they are printed at the position given as their right-end print position.
7. A circle, used on a flow chart, to indicate the lines of flow. Reference numbers are used so that the flow can be determined.
8. To establish a type of line for output. Each new record-description line on the OUTPUT-FORMAT form means another printed line on the report.
9. It will search for channel ∅2, spewing paper out as it goes. Some systems have *run-away prevention*, causing it to stop after a certain number of forms have been bypassed.
10. Remove the **OR OF** coding line, leaving only the **1P** coding.

Many reports are printed by the computer directly onto preprinted forms which are put on the printer during execution of the job. These forms, which are designed specifically for the size and style of report the job demands, usually give the name of the company and the column headings for the job. They may be done with colored ink, set in unusual type, or have special places for certain fields to be printed. Special carriage control tapes must usually be made to use with the form. These forms, however, are expensive. Installations avoid using them when they can; others use them only for reports that will be sent outside the company. It is important to know how to print headings onto reports so that preprinted forms will not always be required to identify information on the report.

The program **POLIST** from Lesson 6 will be modified for calculations and headings. It will be called **POLEDG**.

PROBLEM DEFINITION: *Prepare a detail listing of a ledger for the purchase order cards, giving all fields, with* **DATE** *placed between department number and purchase order number. Calculate the cost of items ordered from each purchase order card, by multiplying* **QUAN** *by* **PRICE**. *This cost should be on the ledger, occupying the last field position on the printed report. A major heading and column headings should be given on all pages of the report. Input information is given:*

Field	Field Name	Columns
Department number	**DEPT**	1-2
Purchase order number	**PONUM**	3-1∅
Vendor number, from whom purchased	**VENDOR**	11-15
Description of item ordered	**DESCR**	16-35
Quantity of item ordered	**QUAN**	38-4∅
Price of item, each, 2 decimals	**PRICE**	45-5∅
Date order was placed: month, day, year	**DATE**	61-66

The spacing chart in Figure 9-1 shows the two required headings: the name of the job, and the column headings for all fields. An H along the side of the format for each of the headings distinguishes them from the detail line, which has a D. The heading should be written on the report exactly as shown. The chart has an X to mark where the paper control tape should contain the channel ∅1 punch indicating the top of the page. The major heading is to start on line 5. A channel 12 punch should be made at line 6∅ to indicate the last line on which printing will be allowed. Figure 9-1 shows the relationship between the paper control tape, the spacing chart, and the actual report.

Headings that are printed at the top of the first page of a report are called *first-page* headings; those at the top of additional pages, printed because the first was filled, are called *overflow* headings. The programmer must distinguish between these two types of headings, because some jobs will require major headings on the first page only, while others will require headings on all pages. The RPG programming system has two special indicators to use for specifying these situations: the overflow indicator, **OF**, and the first-page indicator, **1P**.

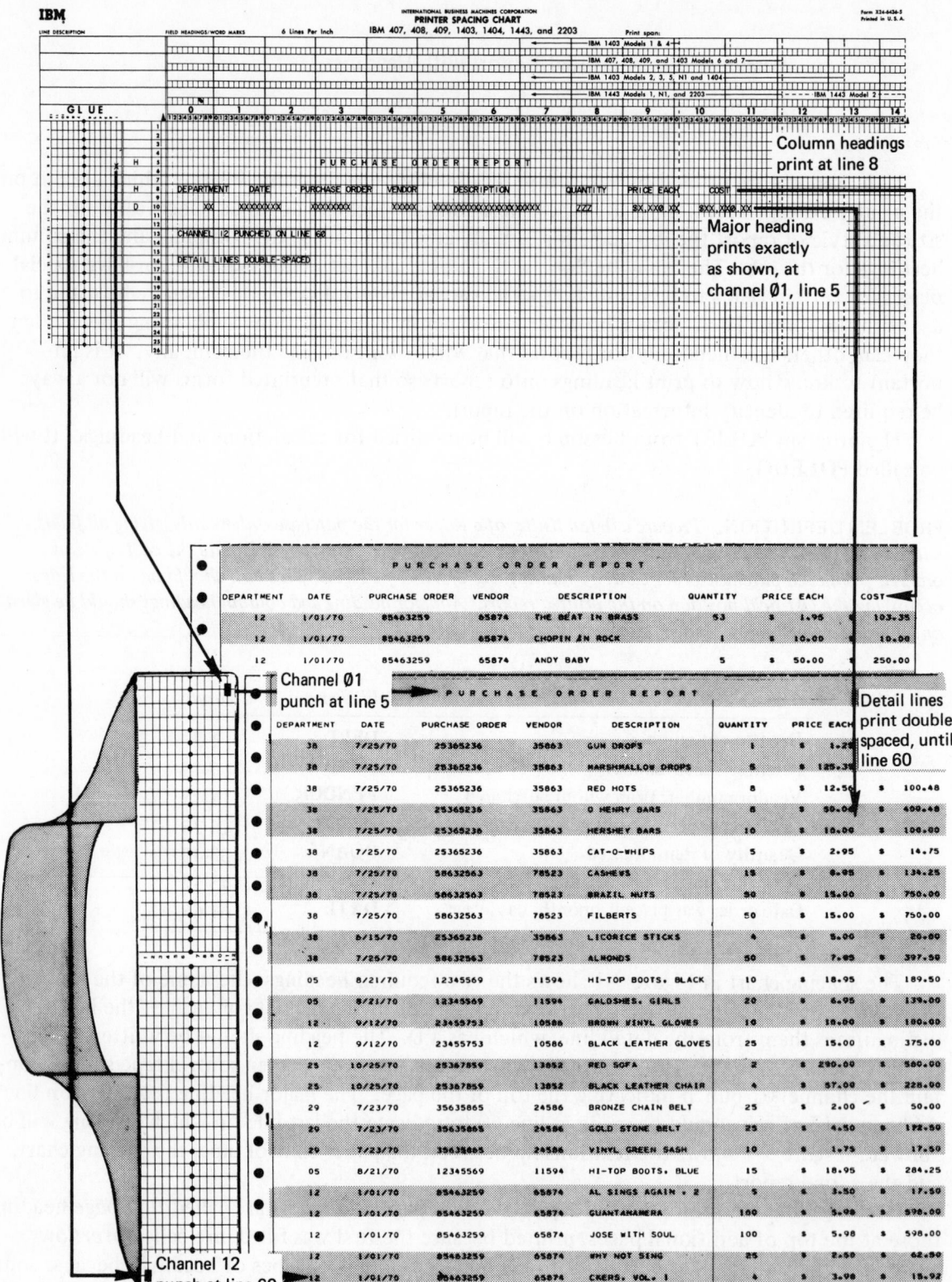

FIG. 9-1 Relation between PRINTER SPACING CHART and the report **POLEDG** program.

The overflow indicator, **OF**, goes on during the execution of the program after a channel 12 punch has been detected in the control tape. In most implementations, it causes the printer to skip over the crease in the paper and the next printing of detail lines is on the next page. Headings, however, are not repeated just because the carriage rolled up to the top of the next page! The programmer must instruct the computer to do that. First of all, most implementations require the **OF** indicator be specified on the **FILE DESCRIPTION** form by writing **OF** in columns 33 and 34 of the line that describes the printer. Once that is done, the **OF** indicator may be used in the program. It will be used in **POLEDG** as an indicator on the **OUTPUT-FORMAT** form to print the headings on the report. When the **OF** indicator goes on during the execution of the program, it remains on long enough to print any detail or heading lines that are using it, then turns off. It is not, however, turned on at the beginning of the job, so it *cannot* be used to put headings on the first page of the report.

For first-page headings, the **1P** indicator is used. It is automatically turned on at the beginning of the execution of every job, and can be used as an **OUTPUT-FORMAT** indicator to print constant information before any data cards are read. Immediately after it is used to print all the headings that refer to it, it is turned off. By the time the first data card is read, **1P** is already *off*, so it cannot be used to print information from input data cards. It has only one purpose: to control printing of constant headings on the first page of a report.

Positioning the printer to a particular line on a report form is done by programming a *skip* to the line. On all implementations except IBM SYSTEM/3, this skip corresponds to a punch in a channel on the carriage control tape. Skipping to a channel is done by putting the channel number to be used in the program either under SKIP BEFORE, in columns 19 and 2∅, or SKIP AFTER, in columns 21 and 22. First-page headings are usually printed at the top of a new page, in a position corresponding to channel ∅1, by placing the channel number, ∅1, under SKIP BEFORE, and by using a carriage control tape with the proper channel ∅1 punch. To be able to move the carriage to line 31 of a report, for example, *before* printing on line 31, you must prepare a carriage control tape with a channel cut corresponding to line 31. Assuming that channel ∅2 is punched there, you would then, in your program, put ∅2 under SKIP BEFORE on the specifications describing the line. Before skipping can be executed, however, the carriage control tape must be put on the printer—even during the test runs you make for debugging purposes. You can, on some implementations, cause a lot of blank forms to come through the printer, usually very fast, by skipping to a channel that has either not been punched, or has not yet been placed onto the printer! On other equipment, a built-in runaway prevention will terminate the runaway after two forms have gone through.

On the IBM SYSTEM/3, SKIP refers to a line number on the report rather than to a channel on a carriage control tape. Lines 6 and 60 are ordinarily used for the top of a new page and overflow, respectively, unless changed by use of the **LINE COUNTER** specifications form. An indication of ∅6 placed under SKIP BEFORE would therefore cause the line to be printed at the top of a new page. If you wanted a line to be printed at line 58 of the form, you would put the line number, 58, under SKIP BEFORE on the **OUTPUT-FORMAT** specifications for that line.

As each report line is printed, the carriage should ordinarily be rolled up so that a line does not overprint on the previous line. This is usually done by *spacing*; from one to three lines can be spaced, either before or after the printing occurs. Column 17 is used to specify how many spacing lines are to be rolled up *before* printing; column 18 is used to tell how many to roll up *after* printing. Either spacing before, after, or both, may be used on a given line. On some implementations, if you should omit spacing indication, one space after printing is done anyway. On those systems, *no* spacing after printing is obtained by specifying a ∅ in column 18.

On most reports, major headings are set off from the column headings by using three spacing lines after printing. For column headings, either two or three are customary. In the example,

Line	Form Type	Filename	Type (H/D/T)	Stacker Select	Space Before	Space After	Skip Before	Skip After	Output Indicators (Not)		(And) (Not)		(And) (Not)		Field Name	Zero Suppress (Z)	Blank After (B)	End Position in Output Record	Packed Field (P)
3 4 5	6	7 8 9 10 11 12 13 14	15	16	17	18	19 20	21 22	23	24 25	26	27 28	29	30 31	32 33 34 35 36 37	38	39	40 41 42 43	44	45 46 47 48 49 50
0 1	O		H				3Ø1												
0 2	O																		
0 3	O																		

a skip to channel Ø1 has been specified, after which the detail line will be printed, then 3 spaces will be rolled up on the carriage of the printer.

The flow chart given in Figure 9-2 illustrates the job done by RPG on first-page and over-flow headings. Notice that the printing of the headings is done, by indicator, before input, at the top of the loop, after which the 1P indicator goes off. The overflow headings are done later, only after the channel 12 punch has been detected and the OF indicator has turned *on*. Notice on the flow chart that a decision is shown by using a diamond-shaped figure, with alternatives leaving the figure. Circles are used for connectors, allowing the flow to be indicated with a minimum number of lines. The numbers in the connectors are for reference only and do not follow any particular order.

The FILE DESCRIPTION and INPUT forms from POLIST, Lesson 6, may be reused; add OF to the former to allow that indicator in the program. POLEDG should have calculations, and a different output form. On the CALCULATION form,

Line	Form Type	Control Le	(Not)	(And) (Not)	(And) (Not)	Factor 1	Operation	Factor 2	Result Field	Field Length	Decimal Pos
3 4 5	6	7 8	9 10	11 12 13	14 15 16 17	18 19 20 21 22 23 24 25 26 27	28 29 30 31 32	33 34 35 36 37 38 39 40 41 42	43 44 45 46 47 48	49 50 51 52	
0 1	C		99			QUAN	MULT	PRICE	COST	7 2	
0 2	C										

indicator 99 is used. It could be omitted because there is only one type of detail card in this job, and the calculation is to be done on every detail card anyway. The operation needed is MULT for multiplication. The operands being used in the multiplication are QUAN and PRICE. Note that they are both in numeric mode as they must be for calculation. The answer will be placed into COST, which is to be 7 digits long, with 2 decimal places. Since QUAN is 3 digits long, with Ø decimal places, and PRICE is 6 digits long, with 2 decimal places, it is possible for COST to be 9 digits long, with 2 decimals. However, assuming that the largest value of QUAN will be somewhat less than 15Ø, and the largest anticipated value for PRICE will be in the range of $500.00, then COST may safely be given only 7 digits.

In preparing the OUTPUT-FORMAT form, the heading lines should precede the detail line. One line of coding, with an H or D, is given for each type of line to be printed on the report, followed by field descriptions for that line. There are three types of lines on the POLEDG program: the major heading line will be coded first, then the column heading line, then the detail line. Coding for the major heading line begins with:

Line	Form Type	Filename	Type (H/D/T)	Stacker Select	Space Before	Space After	Skip Before	Skip After	Output Indicators And Not	And Not	And Not	Field Name	Zero Suppress (Z)	Blank After (B)	End Position in Output Record	Packed Field (P)	
3 4 5	6	7 8 9 10 11 12 13 14	15	16	17	18	19 20	21 22	23 24 25	26 27 28	29 30 31	32 33 34 35 36 37	38	39	40 41 42 43	44	45 46 47 48 49 50 5
0 1	Ø	o LIST				H	3Ø1		1P								
0 2		o															

The file name for the printer, **LIST**, is given on the record-description line; this name *must* be the same as the one given on the FILE DESCRIPTION form. An **H** in column 15 defines the line as a heading. The 3 in column 18 causes three lines to be rolled up on the carriage after printing the major heading. The Ø1 in columns 19 and 20 causes the major heading to go onto the top of a new page, when the proper carriage control tape is used. The indicator **1P**, given in columns 24 and 25, makes the heading print onto the first page of the report. Since the heading is to be printed on all other pages of the report, **OF** must be used. It cannot, however, be *on* at the same time as **1P**, so it is not placed on the same line of RPG coding. It is instead given as an **OR** condition line, as given by:

	Form		Type (H.	Stacker	Before	After	Before	After	And Not	And Not	Not		Zero	Blank		Packer	
3 4 5	6	7 8 9 10 11 12 13 14	15	16	17	18	19 20	21 22	23 24 25	26 27	28 29 30 31	32 33 34 35 36 37	38	39	40 41 42 43	44	45 46 47 48 49 50
0 1	Ø	o LIST				H	3Ø1		1P								
0 2		o	OR						OF								
3																	

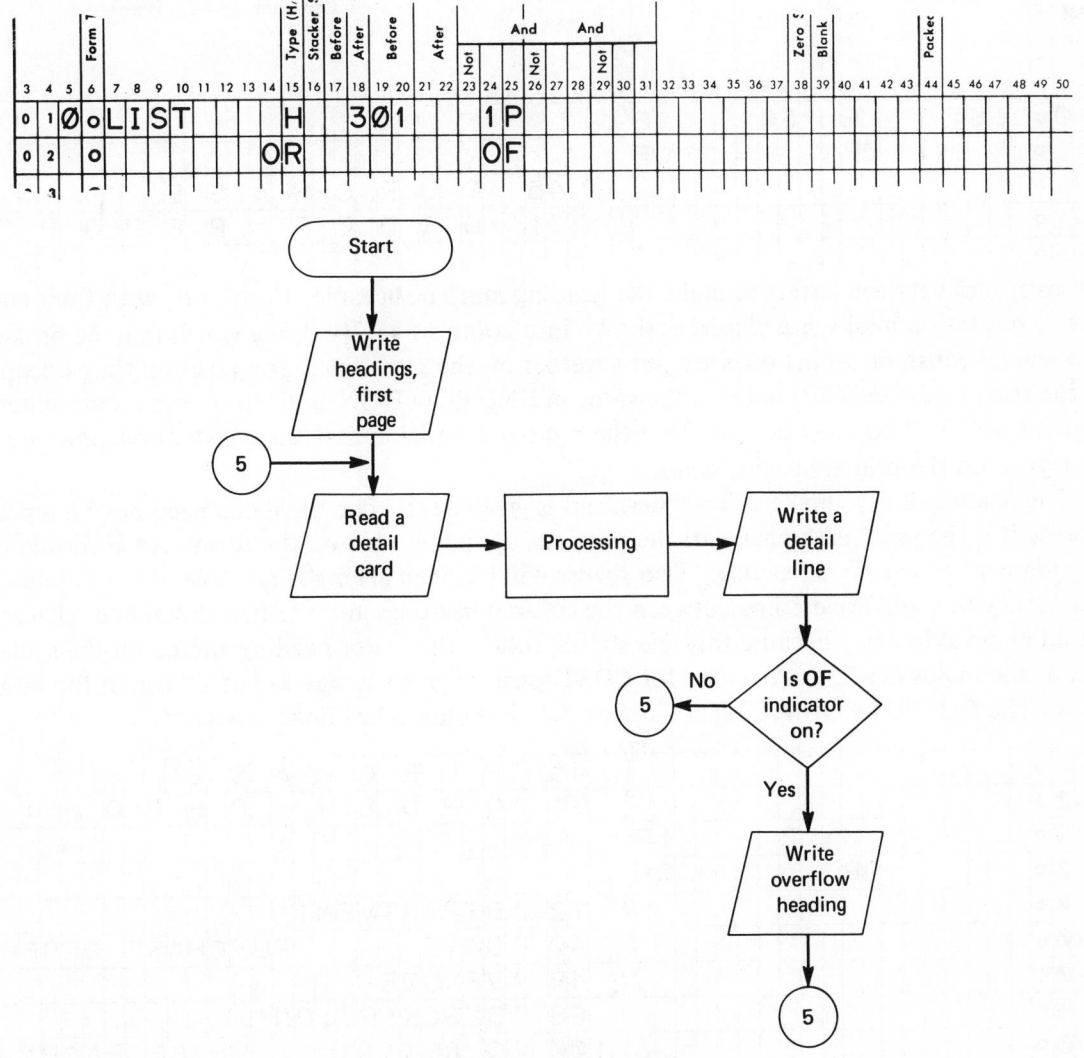

FIG. 9-2 Flow chart for **POLEDG.**

The **OR** goes in columns 14 and 15 of the next coding line, with **OF** given as the indicator to be used. When spacing and skipping specifications are both omitted on an **OR** line, spacing and skipping from the line above it is used. The two coding lines *define* the major heading of the report, tell it *when* to print, and give carriage control for it. The lines following it define the actual constants to be placed in the heading.

Constant alphameric information, such as that put into headings, is called an alphameric literal, and is written inside single quotation marks and placed underneath CONSTANT OR EDIT WORD on the OUTPUT-FORMAT form, left-justified. Heading constants are selected so that they will be meaningful to the people who *use* the report. Major headings sometimes give company name or department name. The alphameric literal 'DEPARTMENT' could be placed over a field named **DEPT**, which holds the number for that department, for example. Words that are too long to be used as field names may be printed over the field to make the information easier to read. The alphameric literal 'DESCRIPTION' could be part of am a major heading or a column heading, but could not be a field name because it is too long; **DESCR** could be used as the field name. The completed coding for a major heading is given:

Line	Form Type	Filename	Type (H/D/T)	Stacker Select	Space Before	Space After	Skip Before	Skip After	Ind Not 23 24 25	Not 26	End Position in Output Record 41 42 43	Packed Field (P) 44	Constant or Edit Word
0 1	O	LIST	H			3	0 1		1	P			
0 2	O		OR							OF			
0 3	O										4 5		'P U R C H A S E'
0 4	O										7 1		'O R D E R R E P O R T'
0 5	O												

It uses spaces between letters to make the heading more noticeable. Constants, with their enclosing quotation marks, are placed as shown into columns 45-7Ø. Long words may be broken into several constants; short ones are put together on the same line. The position they occupy on the final report depends only on the value in END POSITION as given by the programmer in columns 4Ø-43. This must be read from the right-end position that the constant occupies on the layout on the printer spacing chart.

The heading line to make column headings is given next. The file name need not be repeated because it is the same as the name of the previous file name used on the form. An **H** should be in column 15 to specify a heading. Two spaces will be given after the printing of the column headings, which will leave 1 line between the column headings and the first detail line. There should be no skip entry because this line should follow the major heading and be on the same page as the major heading. An entry for **COST** must be given as well as entries for all the input fields. The OUTPUT-FORMAT specification for the column headings is given:

Line	Form Type		Type	Space		Ind	End Position	Constant or Edit Word
0 3	O						4 5	'P U R C H A S E'
0 4	O						7 1	'O R D E R R E P O R T'
0 5	O		H	2		1 P		
0 6	O		OR			OF		
0 7	O						1 2	'DEPARTMENT'
0 8	O						4 0	'DATE PURCHASE ORDER'
0 9	O						4 9	'VENDOR'
1 0	O						6 8	'DESCRIPTION'
1 1	O						1 0 0	'QUANTITY PRICE EACH'
1 2	O						1 1 0	'COST'

Detail specifications for the **POLEDG** program are the same as for the program **POLIST** in Lesson 6, except that the field **COST** must also be printed. Editing is given for its length of 7 digits, with 2 decimal places. The complete program is given in Figure 9-3. Run-sheets are in Figure 9-4.

It is by programmer choice that the major heading appears on all pages of the report. It is possible to use the skip entry on the OUTPUT-FORMAT form to print both a major heading and column headings on the first page, then put column headings only on all the following pages. When preprinted major headings are used, giving company name, for example, the program need not provide them. Column headings are often supplied on preprinted forms as well. When column headings are not provided on the form, however, they may be put on by the RPG program. Recall, that an entire line comes out of the printer at one time—so the top portions of the two-line column heading must all be put on one line, then the bottom portion on the next line, as given by:

Line	Form Type	Filename	Type (H/D/T)	Stacker Select	Space Before	Space After	Skip Before	Skip After	Not	And	Not	End Position Output Record	Packed Field (P)	Constant or Edit Word
010	o	LIST	H				30	1		1 P				
020	o											45		'PURCHASE'
030	o											71		'ORDER REPORT'
040	o		H				1			1 P				
050	o		OR				1	01		OF				
060	o											12		'DEPARTMENT'
070	o											40		'DATE PURCHASE ORDER'
080	o											49		'VENDOR'
090	o											68		'DESCRIPTION'
100	o											100		'QUANTITY PRICE EACH'
110	o											110		'COST'
120	o		H		2					1 P				
130	o				2					OF		9		'NAME'
140	o											35		'OF SALE NUMBER'
150	o											49		'NUMBER'
160	o											67		'OF ITEM'
170	o											86		'ON HAND'
180	o											98		'ITEM'

Card Electro Numbe

The major heading and the two-line column heading will be printed on the first page; on the overflow pages, only the column headings will print. Notice that a skip to channel Ø1 is given on line Ø5Ø of the OUTPUT-FORMAT form; since it is an **OR** line, unspecified spacing or skipping would cause those from the previous line to be used, and since the line above has none specified, spacing and skipping are given here as it applies to the overflow pages, where the major heading will not be printed.

Another useful variation of a listing program has each card of input data printed not just on one line of output, but on several, with some fields on each line. Each coding line on the

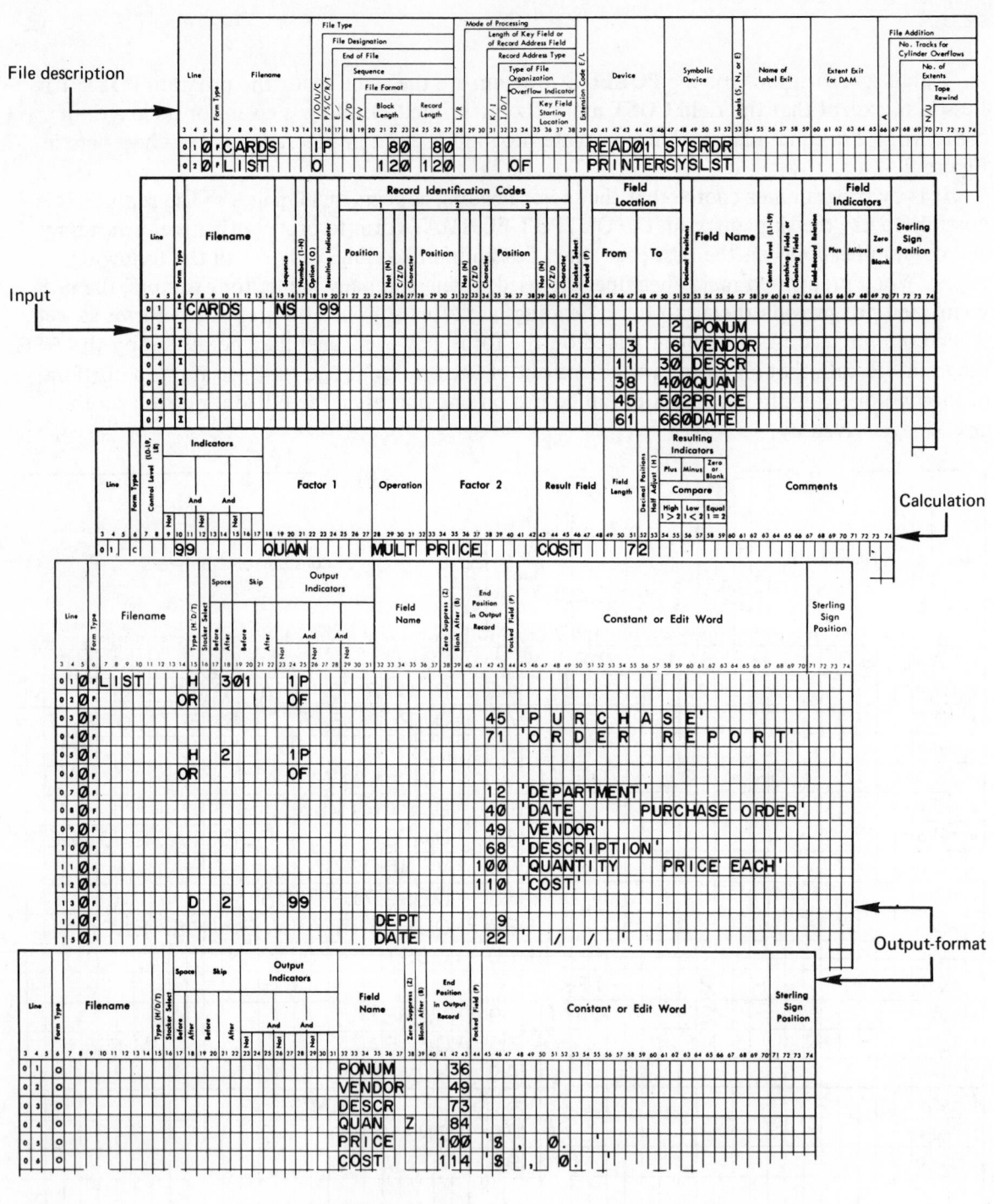

File description

Input

Calculation

Output-format

Field Information for Purchase Order Cards	Columns
Department number	1-2
Purchase Order number	3-10
Vendor number	11-15
Description of item	16-35
Quantity ordered	38-40
Price, 2 decimals	45-50
Date of order, month, day, year	61-66

COST is calculated by multiplying Quantity times Price.

FIG. 9-3 Source program **POLEDG** and data format.

136

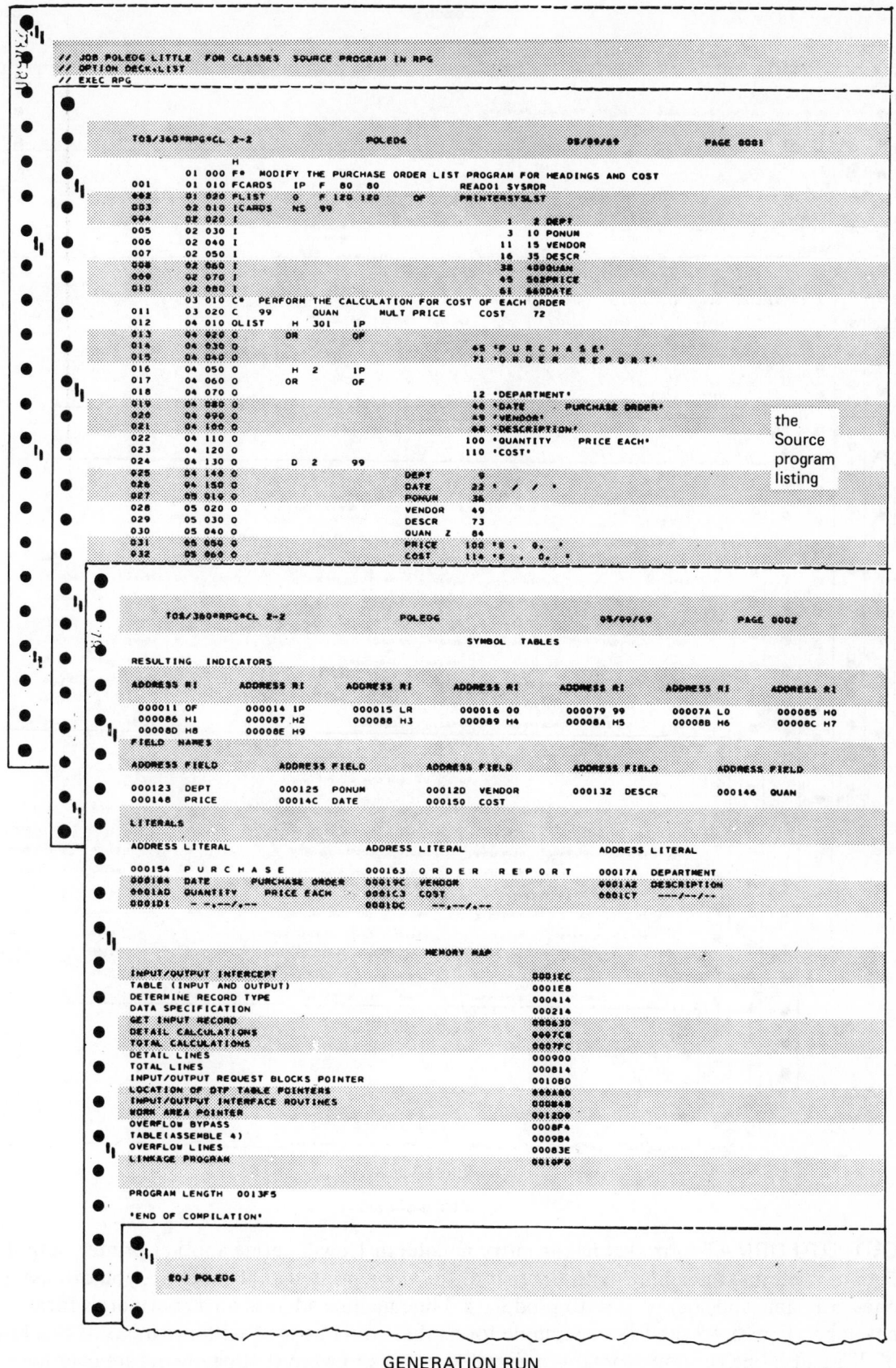

the
Source
program
listing

GENERATION RUN

FIG. 9-4 Run-sheets for program **POLEDG**–IBM SYSTEM/36Ø, TOS.

137

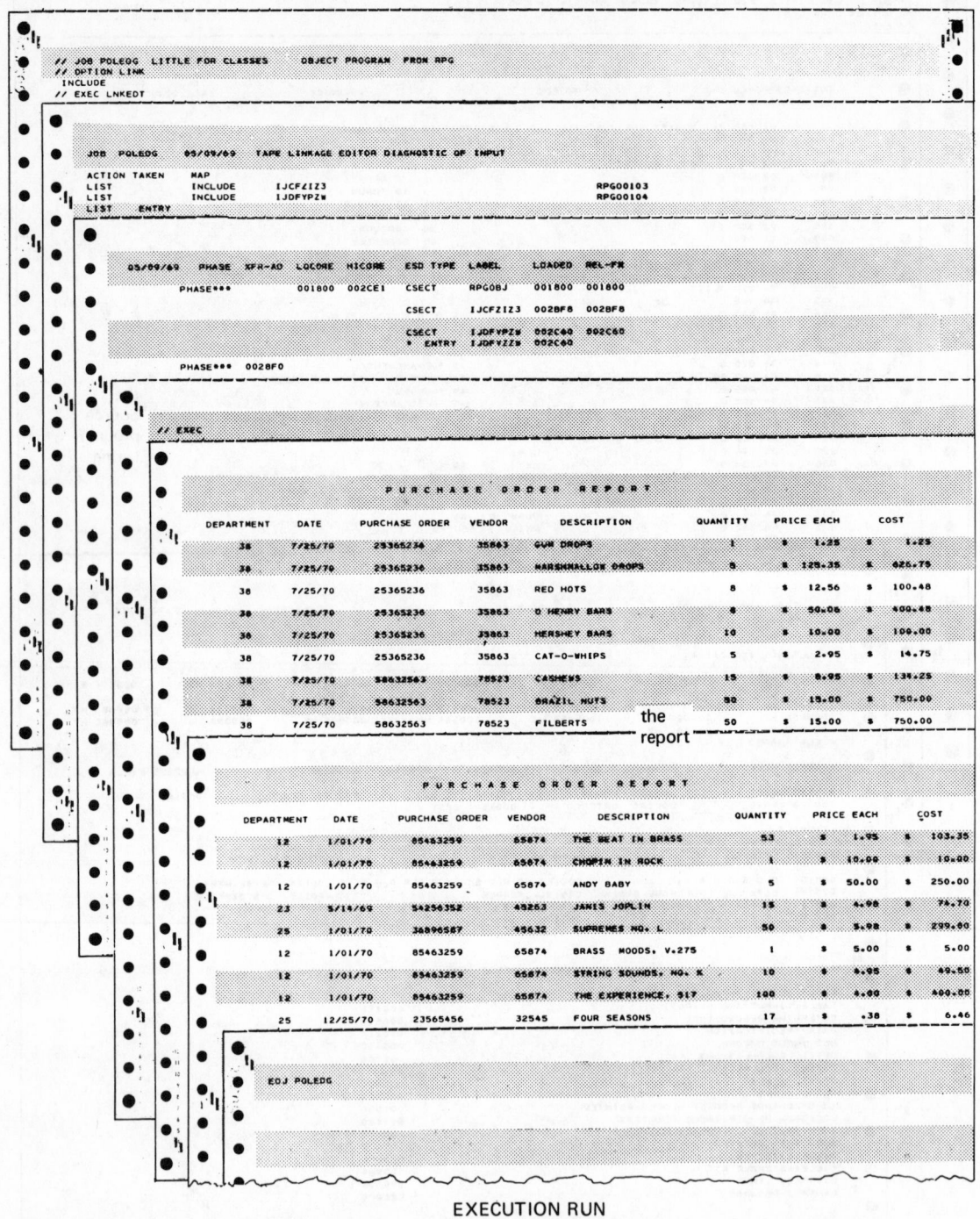

EXECUTION RUN

FIG. 9-4—*Cont.*

OUTPUT-FORMAT form that has an entry in column 15 will define another printer output line. By defining three lines, with the first of the three printed at channel Ø1, you can use a one-card name and address card to produce a 3-line mailing address on a continuous-form envelope. Figure 9-5 shows some sample forms that could be used with programs of this level of difficulty; one envelope contains preprinted notices to warn that payments are overdue; another produces library identification cards. There are an almost unlimited number of applications for this type of RPG program.

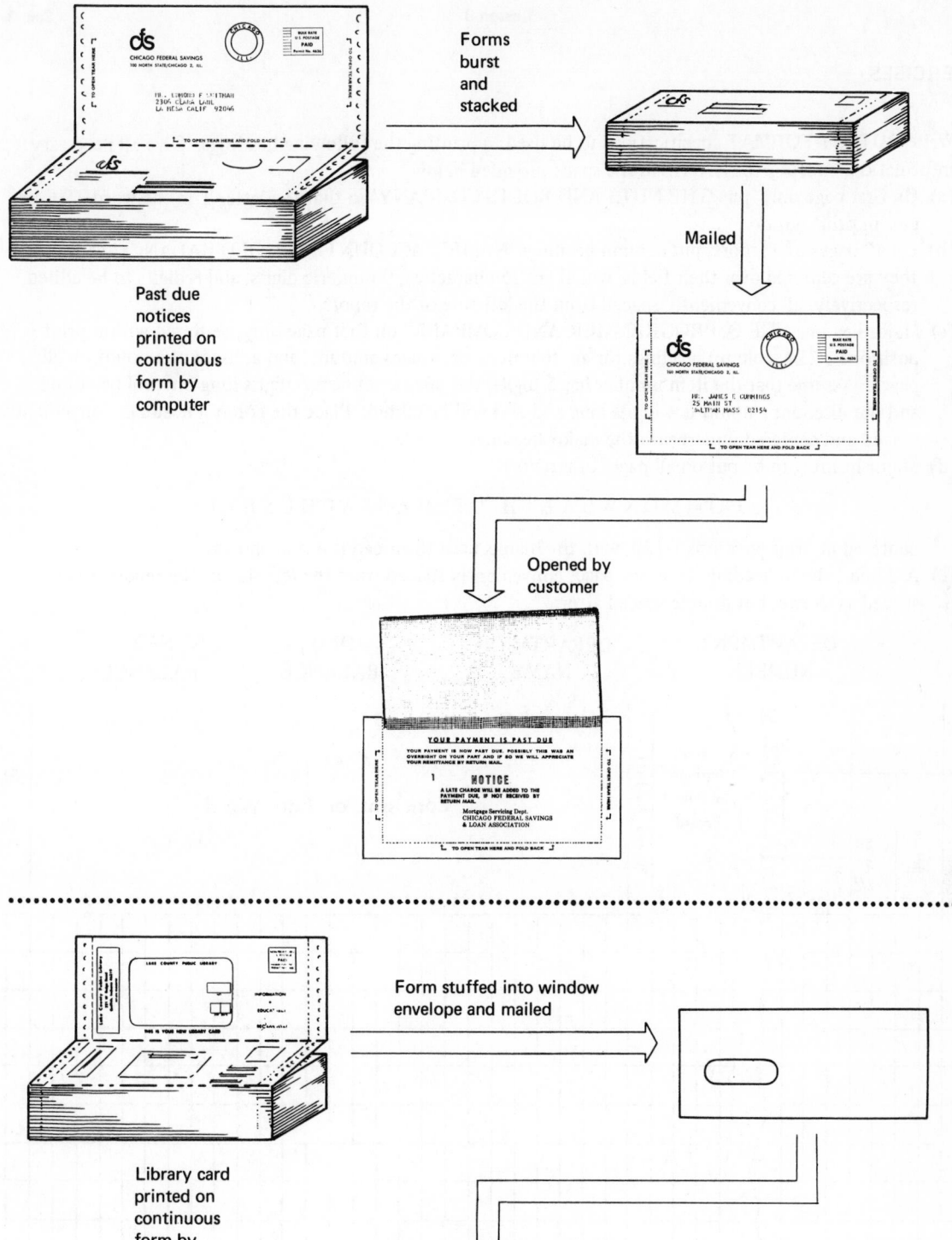

Forms
burst
and
stacked

Past due
notices
printed on
continuous
form by
computer

Mailed

Opened by
customer

Form stuffed into window
envelope and mailed

Library card
printed on
continuous
form by
computer

LAKE COUNTY PUBLIC LIBRARY

James Johnson
127 Oak Ave.
Griffith, Ind. 46319

1732
NO.

Ø7 75
EXP. DATE

IND.

Library user
tears out,
signs new library
card from form

FIG. 9-5 Name and address printing for mailing. (Courtesy of UARCO, Inc., and
Moore Business Forms.)

EXERCISES

1. Write OUTPUT-FORMAT specifications to be used in printing the following headings. Give all necessary information, except FILENAME, in the space provided below.

   (a) On first page only, put 'THE NUTS AND BOLTS COMPANY' so that the letter T in the word THE begins in print position 7.

   (b) On all pages of a report, put column headings 'NAME', 'ACCOUNT', and 'OLD BALANCE' so that they are centered over their fields, which are 25 characters, 9 numeric digits, and 8 digits to be edited, respectively, all conveniently spaced from the left side of the report.

   (c) Major heading 'JOE Q. PROGRAMMER AND COMPANY' on first page only, centered within print positions 1-12∅; column headings for an item number, a sales amount, and a discount amount on all pages. Assume that the item number has 5 digits, the sales amount is 6 digits long but will be edited, and the discount amount is 4 digits long and also will be edited. Place the column headings conveniently spaced and centered underneath the major heading.

   (d) Major heading to be put on all pages of a report:

COMMONWEALTH OF MASSACHUSETTS

centered in print positions 1-12∅, with the blanks used to spread it out as shown.

   (e) A 2-line column heading, on every page, conveniently spaced from the left side of the report, single-spaced as shown, but double-spaced after:

DEPARTMENT   DEPARTMENT   OLD   NEW
NUMBER   NAME   BALANCE   BALANCE

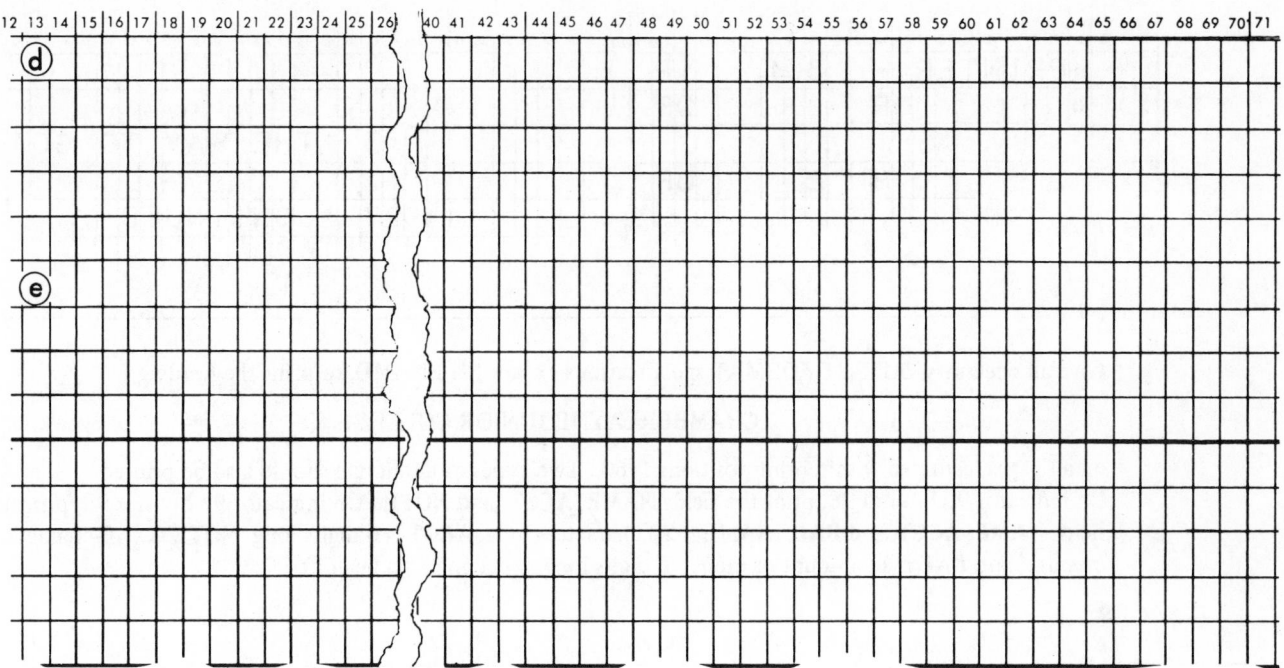

2. What headings do each of the following produce and when and where?

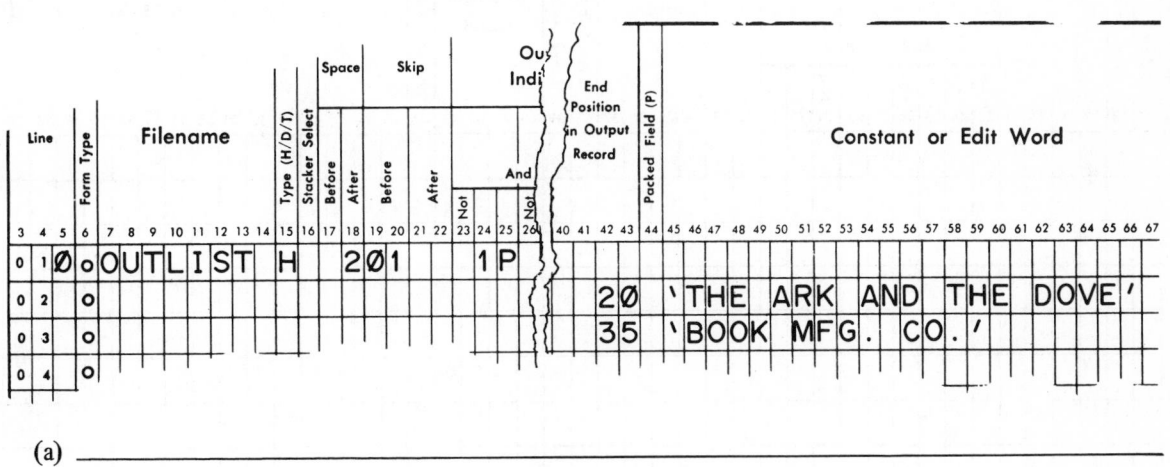

(a) _____

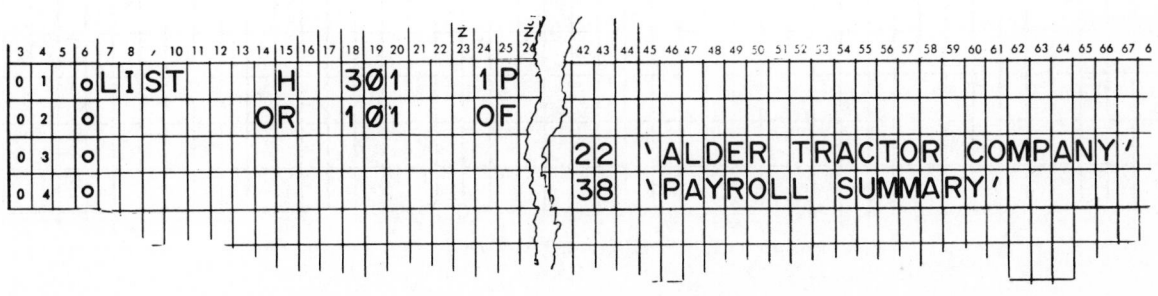

(b) _____

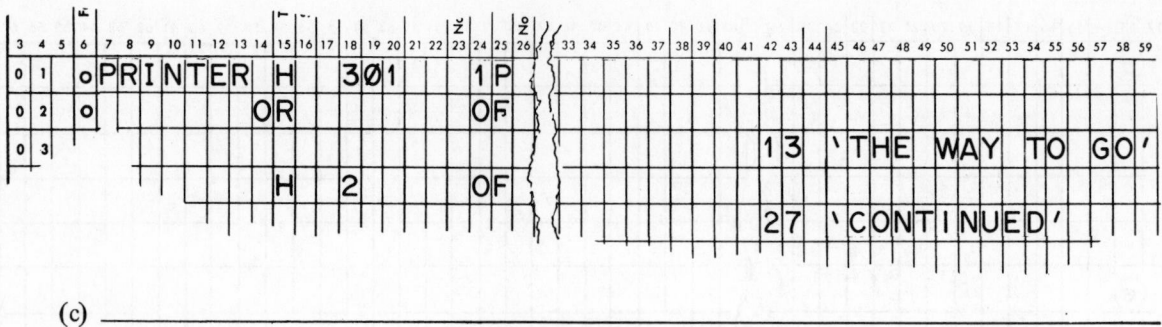

			3 4 5 6	7 8 9 10 11 12 13 14	15 16 17	18 19 20 21 22 23	24 25 26	33 34 35 36 37 38 39 40 41 42 43 44	45 46 47 48 49 50 51 52 53 54 55 56 57 58 59
0	1		o PRINTER	H	301	1P			
0	2		o	OR		OF			
0	3					OF		13 'THE WAY TO GO'	
				H	2	OF		27 'CONTINUED'	

(c) ————————————————————————————————————

3. Give all necessary OUTPUT-FORMAT specifications except FILENAME, to print the heading

CHAMBERLAYNE JUNIOR COLLEGE

on all pages, centered within print positions 1–60. Two types of detail line should also be printed. On indicator 99 but not 98, print the fields **NAME, ACCT**, and **NOTE**. On indicator 98 but not 99, print the fields **NAME, ACCT**, and **BAL**. **NAME** is 20 characters long, **ACCT** is 6 digits long, **NOTE** is a 10-character message, and **BAL** is an amount of money 6 digits long, 2 decimals, to be edited.

Type (H/D/T)	Stacker Select	Space Before	Space After	Skip Before	Skip After	Output Indicators Not	And	Not	And	Not	Field Name	Zero Suppress (Z)	Blank After (B)	End Position in Output Record	Packed Field (P)	Constant or Edit
13 14	15 16	17	18	19 20	21 22	23	24 25	26	27 28	29	30 31 32 33 34 35 36 37	38	39	40 41 42 43	44	45 46 47 48 49 50 51 52 53 54 55 56 57 58 59 60

PROGRAMS TO WRITE

A. PROBLEM NAME: **EQUA:**   substituting into an equation

The program should be written to do the calculation $y = 5x + 4$ for each value of x brought into the computer on a data card. A report heading should appear on the first page: 'FORMULA EVALUATION', column headings should contain 'X' and 'Y'. Sign indication should be given as minus for any values of x or y that are negative.

Field Information	Columns
Value of x, 2 decimals	1-4

B. PROBLEM NAME: **SIMINT:**   calculation of simple interest

Write a program to calculate simple interest by multiplying principal by annual interest rate by time in years. Print the principal, rate, time, interest, name and reference number for each data card. Column headings appropriate to the problem should be printed at the top of all pages of the report.

Field Information	Field Name	Columns
Reference number	**REFNUM**	1-6
Name	**NAME**	11-3∅
Principal, 2 decimals	**PRIN**	35-4∅
Annual interest rate, 3 decimals	**RATE**	47-5∅
Time, in years	**TIME**	58-6∅

C. PROBLEM NAME: **DONLST:**   to determine donation differences

The program should prepare a list of donations made by alumni, giving the difference in donations between this year and last year as calculated by amount this year minus amount last year. If the difference is negative, sign indication should print a minus. All input fields and the difference should be printed underneath appropriate column headings.

Field Information	Columns
Year of graduation	1-4
Name of graduate	11-3∅
Zip code of residence	36-4∅
Amount donated last year, 2 decimals	65-7∅
Amount donated this year, 2 decimals	75-8∅

D. PROBLEM NAME: ACCTBAL: calculation of amounts of new balances
Write a program to list accounts information, giving old balance, amount of payments, amount of charges, and new balance. The amount of new balance will be old balance minus payments plus charges. Account number and date of last charges should also be printed. Negative amounts should be printed with CR.

Field Information	Columns
Account number	1-6
Old balance, 2 decimals	15-2∅
Amount of payments, 2 decimals	26-3∅
Amount of charges, 2 decimals	36-4∅
Date of last charges: month, day, year	75-8∅

SECTION 4

REPORTS WITH RUN-DATES, PAGE NUMBERS, AND TOTALS

Lesson 10

CALCULATION OF SUMS

You will learn how to accumulate sums both across rows and down columns of tabulated data, and to do calculations and printing at the end of the job.

The questions below summarize the calculation of totals and the printing of them at the end of the job, and are answered on the back of this page. Should you already have experience in getting and using job totals, after correctly answering the questions below, go on to Lesson 11.

1. How is a total of different fields across one data card obtained?
2. How is the total of the same field accumulated over many data cards?
3. How can you tell that an RPG calculation instruction is intended to *accumulate*?
4. What changes must be made to print out totals in *several* lines, rather than in one line?
5. What is meant by *initialize*?
6. To what value are all numeric fields initialized by RPG?
7. How can you determine what field length to use for a sum?
8. How can you tell whether an RPG instruction for calculation is programmed for detail-time or total-time?
9. What causes the LR indicator to be turned on?
10. What additional parts of the RPG program cycle can be called into action by the LR indicator?

ANSWERS

1. By doing a series of additions with the different fields contributing to the sum. The additions are done by use of the detail card indicator, and the total acquired may be printed out on the appropriate detail line.
2. By using the same addition instruction on each detail card, with each card contributing one more value to the sum. The sum is not available for printing until all the cards that contribute to that sum are processed.
3. The RESULT FACTOR field name will be the *same* field name as either FACTOR 1 or FACTOR 2, since its previous value is replaced after being changed by a current amount from the card in use.
4. Each line description must have a **T** in column 15, spacing or skipping, if any, and an appropriate indicator, such as **LR**, in columns 24 and 25. The file name need not be repeated. Fields belonging to a given line description follow it.
5. To set a field to its proper starting values. This is usually to zero, for sums, but could be to other values in certain cases.
6. Zero.
7. By scaling. You should have an estimate of the largest value ever expected to be in the field being summed, and the maximum number of cards over which the sum is to be taken. Based on this information, you can find the length required by doing a multiplication and looking at the result length.
8. If columns 7 and 8 have L-indicators given, it is a total-time calculation; if those two columns are blank, it is a detail-time calculation.
9. The detection by RPG of the end-of-file condition, the /* card in the job stream, which should be directly behind your last data card.
10. Total-time calculations, total-time output, and end of the job. Should any instructions contain **LR** in columns 7 and 8 on the **CALCULATIONS** specifications form, it will be executed if other conditions on it are also satisfied. Should there be output lines with a **T** in column 15, they will be executed if indicator conditions are satisfied. Afterwards, the LR indicator will cause termination of the job.

Reports generally require totals. A report may need a total of the number of records used in doing the job, a total of an amount of money received in payments, or a sum of the several different charges attributed to one person. A total or a sum, often called an *accumulation*, is generally either a counted number, a sum of amounts across a row, or a sum of amounts down a column.

A sum of amounts across a row is calculated by adding *different* fields, from the same record, as shown in the row totals in Figure 10-1. Since it is taken from fields across a given card record, it is often called a *cross-total*. The result is usually printed on the report in a position at the right of the fields being added together. Since all the fields being added have different field names, calculations to do the sum are written in a series of instructions, to be done when the indicator for that card is on. The calculations given by

Line	Form Type	Control Level (L0-L9 LR)	Indicators Not	And	Not	And	Not	Factor 1	Operation	Factor 2	Result Field	Field Length	Decimal Positions	Half Adjust (H)
0 1 ,	C	*						DO ADDITION TO GET TOTAL						
0 2	C	Ø7						AMT1	ADD	AMT2	TOTAL	82		
0 3	C	Ø7						AMT3	ADD	TOTAL	TOTAL			
0 4	C	Ø7						AMT4	ADD	TOTAL	TOTAL			
0 5	C													

would cause the fields **AMT1**, **AMT2**, **AMT3**, **AMT4** from a card to be added and put into **TOTAL**. The result of the addition, stored in **TOTAL**, may be printed on the same line as **AMT1**, **AMT2**, **AMT3**, and **AMT4**.

A column total, however, is not calculated in the same manner. It represents a sum of the *same* field, not different ones, and is accumulated over a whole file or over a particular group of records in the file. It must be calculated gradually, with each card contributing one value to the accumulation. The final result is therefore not available for printing until *all* the cards in the file are processed. This type of column total, as shown in Figure 10-1, is usually aligned for printing directly underneath the column whose total it represents. The instruction given by

0 1	C	Ø1		AMT		ADD	TOTAL		TOTAL	82
0 2	C									
0 3	C									

will cause, for each card using indicator Ø1, the value of the field **AMT** to be added to the previous value of **TOTAL**. You will notice that either FACTOR 1 or FACTOR 2 must have the same name as the RESULT FACTOR to cause the accumulation. The previous value of the RESULT FACTOR field **TOTAL** will have the value of the field **AMT** from each detail card added to it; it is stored, after each addition, back in **TOTAL**. In the example

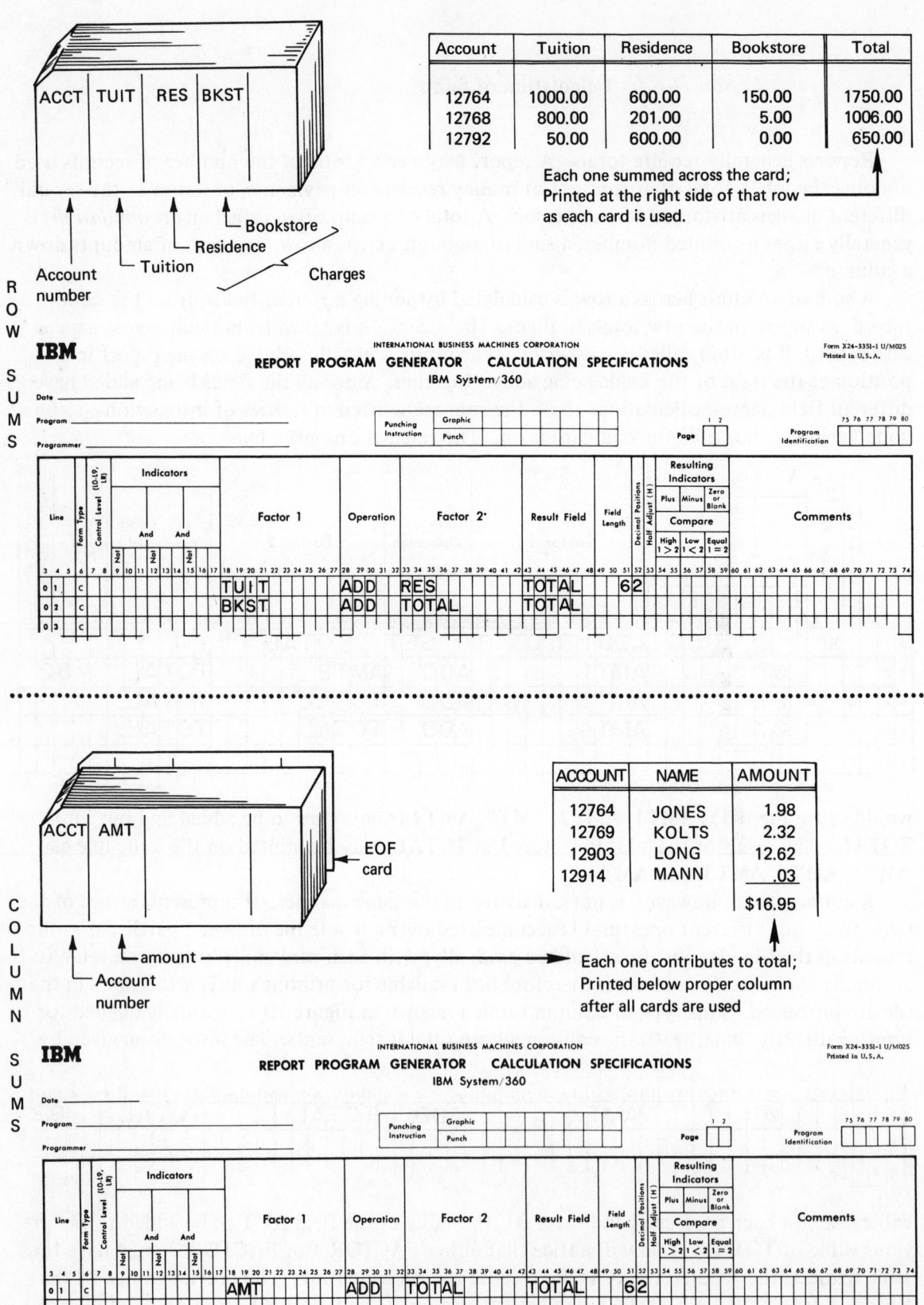

FIG. 10-1 Row and column sums.

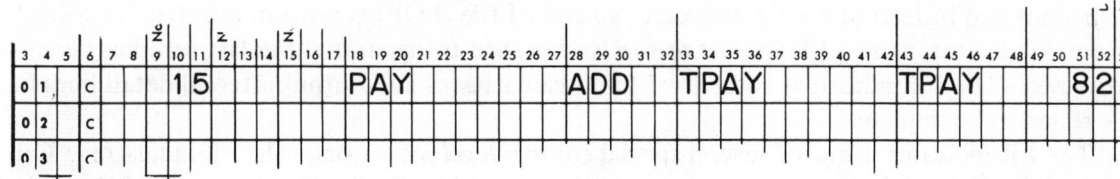

the field **PAY** is accumulated into a field named **TPAY**, for all detail cards in the deck that use indicator 15. **TPAY** has 8 digits, with 2 decimal places. Although the field **TPAY** could be printed on each detail line to give the partial sum up to that time, the *final* result is not available for printing until all the cards are processed, and is usually printed only at the end of the job.

Another type of total that is not usually printed except at the end of a job is called a "*card-count*" total. As each card comes in, 1 is added to the total field; when five cards are in, the field will then contain 5. A total of this type is often needed, not only for a card count of a whole deck, but for certain types of cards within the deck, for example, a total number of payments, or a total of all students who are seniors. Its partial value can be printed on any detail line, but the final card count is not available until all the cards are processed. In the example,

the field named **CTOT** is the accumulation field; 1 is added to it for every card that uses indicator 98. **CTOT** has length 5 digits, with Ø decimals.

A field used for a total should have an appropriate name, an adequate length, and decimal places. Fields may be named anything you like that follows the rules of RPG, but preferably should be named something appropriate to what is being added. The name **DOT**, although amusing to see in a program, does not necessarily remind people of a total amount of gross pay! The field name **GPAY** is surely more mnemonic! All numeric fields are automatically set to zero at the beginning of the execution of RPG program. This serves to *initialize* the field—set it to a proper starting value. Totals are obtained by calculation, requiring that numeric mode be used for them, so decimal indication must be given. For money, 2 decimal places are usual; for a card count, Ø.

Each field must have a specific length. If a field is not specified as an input field, it must be given a length in at least one place on the **CALCULATION** form when it is used there. The length specified must be carefully chosen by examining the expected size of the result. If you sum a field that is 6 digits long, with 2 decimal places, over a deck of 1Ø,ØØØ cards, the result will most probably be much larger than 6 digits! Scaling should be done to find the largest possible result size needed for the job. One good way to do that is to estimate the *largest* field possible, then multiply that value by the number of cards being used. For example, if the largest value were 9999.99, 6 digits long, the biggest value the sum could become over 1ØØØ cards is 99,999,9ØØ.ØØ, or 1Ø digits long. This length estimate may safely be reduced if more accurate data are available concerning the *usual size* of the result. Be sure to use 1 or 2 digits more than you think necessary. Digits lost from the left end of a field that is too short are the programmer's responsibility, even though errors causing checks for $1.00, rather than for $1001.00, are usually reported as being the computer's fault!

For the RPG program to know when all the data cards are processed, an *end-of-file card*, as shown in Figure 10-1, is placed in the control card setup for each computer run. When this card is encountered instead of a valid data card, an end-of-file (EOF) condition is noted. A special internal indicator, named **LR** for *last record*, is designed to signal that the last card has been processed. The LR indicator can be used to do calculations and output after all detail lines in the report are complete.

The LR indicator is one of several special *control level* indicators, called L-indicators. Calculations or output that are done at a change in a control level or at the detection of the end-of-file condition are considered *total-time* operations, in contrast to detail calculations and output of headings and detail lines, called *detail-time* operations. The output of a total field at the end of the job is a *total-time* output operation, triggered by LR being on. It is programmed on the **RPG OUTPUT-FORMAT** form by using **T** in column 15 and **LR** in columns 24 and 25. Program lines following that line give the fields and constants that are to appear.

A program that counts cards in a deck is given in Figure 10-2. Indicator 98 goes on when the card comes in. Since indicator 98 is on, 1 is added to **COUNT**, which is 5 digits long, with $\emptyset$ decimals. The detail line specification causes the contents of the card to print, after which another card is read. This looping continues, until the EOF is detected. The LR indicator goes on, which puts the program into *total-time* operations. There are no total-time calculations to be done, so the total-time output occurs, producing the total line giving the value of **COUNT**, zero suppressed. Figure 10-2 also gives a program flow chart for the card count program. Recall that the value of **COUNT** is automatically set to zero at the beginning of the job

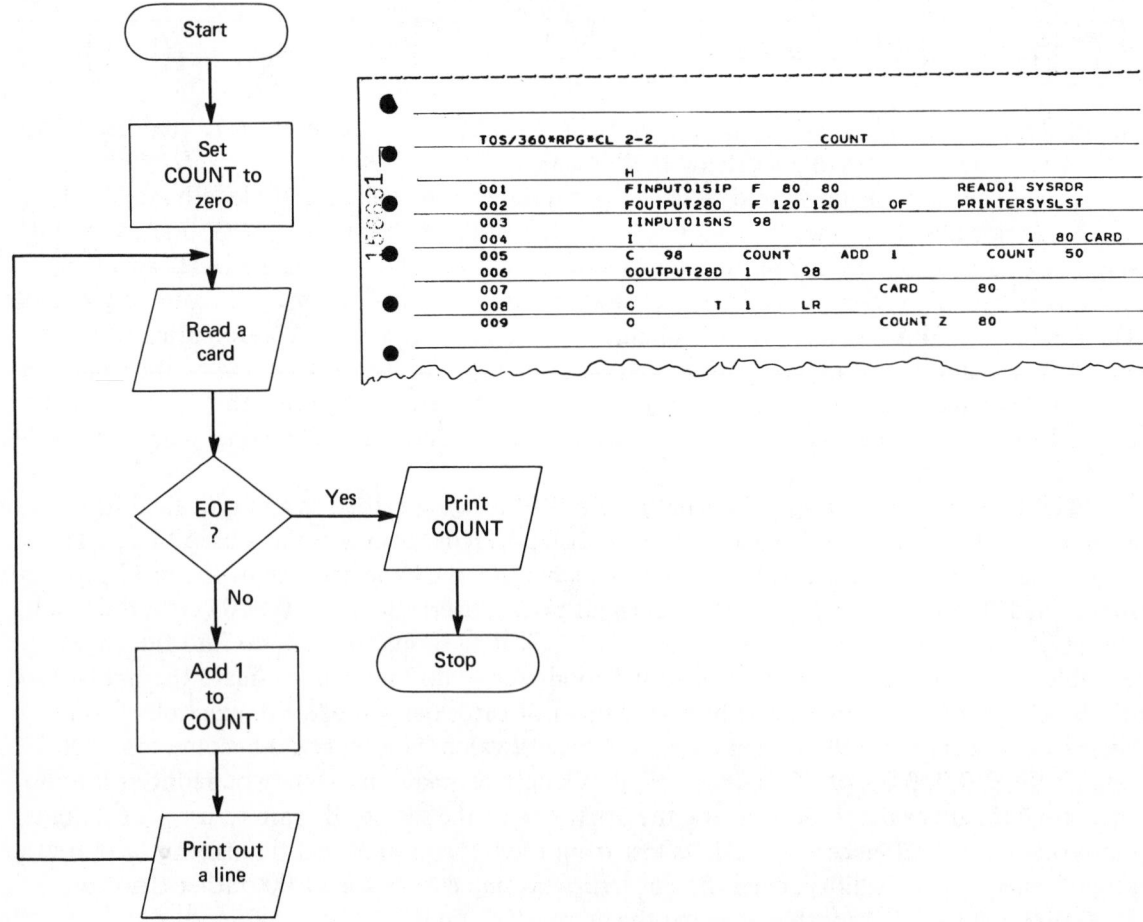

FIG. 10-2　80/80 list program with card count–IBM SYSTEM/360, TOS.

by RPG; that is shown on the flow chart. This program could be modified by removing the detail lines, resulting in a counting program with no printing until the end-of-file condition is detected, at which time the final value of **COUNT** would be printed.

PROBLEM DEFINITION: *A program to list alumni donation cards and give the sum and average of the amount donated is called* **ALUMNI**. *The input is given by*

Field Name	Field Description	Columns	Example
YEAR	Year of graduation	1-4	1957
NAME	Present name of graduate	11-3Ø	JONES, JOHN
AMOUNT	Amount of donation	67-7Ø	Ø1584Ø

Indicator Ø7 is used for the donation card. A job heading and column headings are printed on the first page. The detail cards are printed line by line, giving the graduation year, the name of the person, and the amount the person donated. At the end-of-file condition, the sum of all the donations is printed. Figure 10-3 gives a flow chart for this job, illustrating total-time calculation and output at LR. The two necessary sums for the average of all donations are calculated during the processing of the detail cards: the total number of cards, and the total of the donations. When the end-of-file condition occurs, the LR indicator is turned on, and total-time calculations perform the division. The average donation **AVE** is then available for total-time output.

To do total-time calculations at the end-of-file condition, columns 7 and 8, CONTROL LEVEL (LØ-L9, LR) on the **CALCULATIONS** form is used. Place **LR** in those columns, and give the necessary instruction in the usual manner. Length and decimal places must be given to the new field, **AVE**. Total-time calculations must be given after all detail-time calculations have been listed. Notice that 3 total lines are specified at LR, bringing out the sum, the card count, and the average on separate lines. Each **T** in column 15 indicates another output line. Notice that the file name need not be repeated on lines that belong to the file already given. The coding given in the example

would cause two total lines to be printed, with the card count and sum of the donations on one line, and the average of the donations given on the next line.

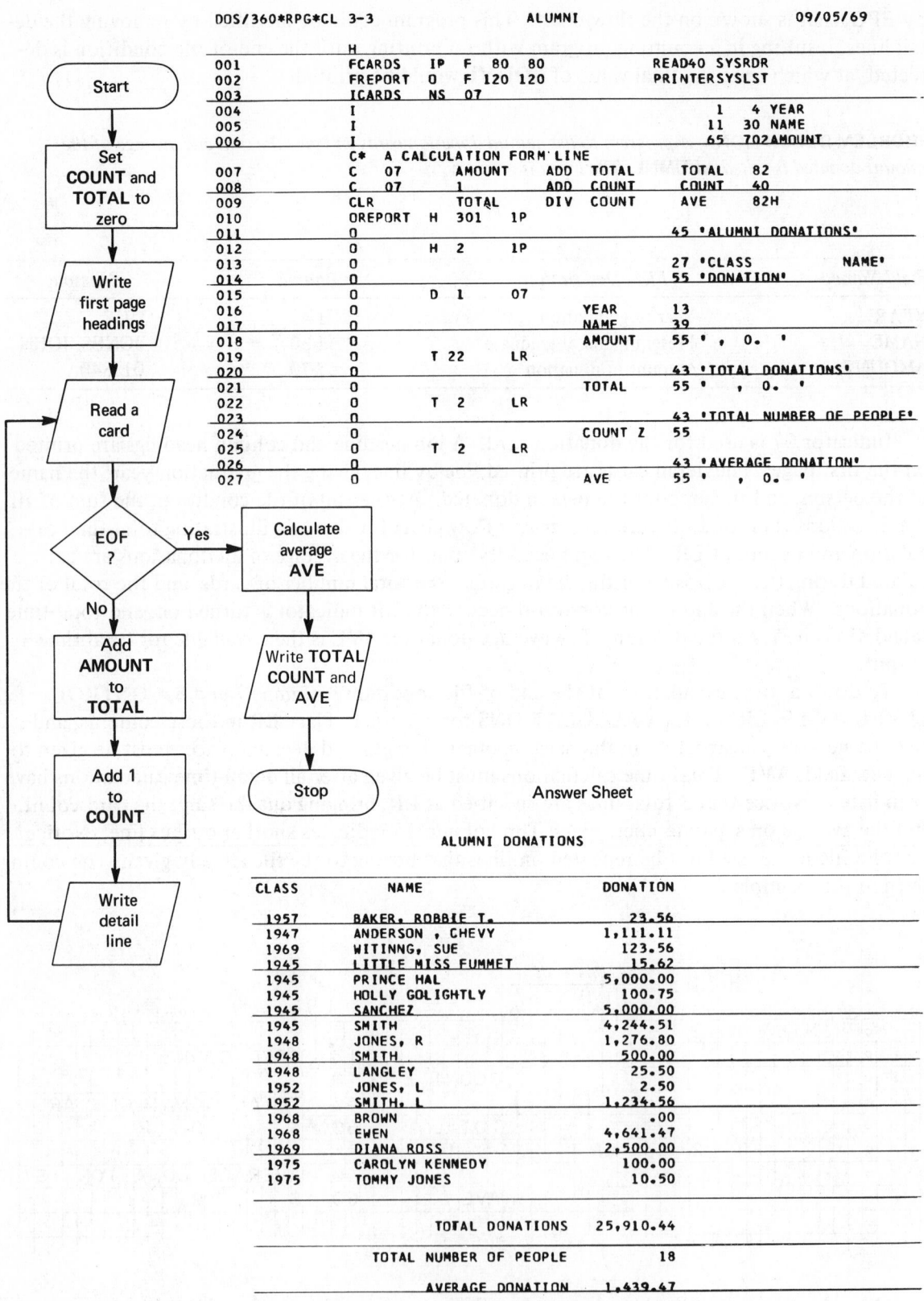

DOS/360*RPG*CL 3-3   ALUMNI   09/05/69

```
         H
001      FCARDS   IP  F  80  80          READ40 SYSRDR
002      FREPORT  O   F 120 120          PRINTERSYSLST
003      ICARDS   NS  07
004      I                                1    4 YEAR
005      I                               11   30 NAME
006      I                               65  702AMOUNT
         C*    A CALCULATION FORM LINE
007      C    07         AMOUNT   ADD  TOTAL    TOTAL  82
008      C    07         1        ADD  COUNT    COUNT  40
009      CLR            TOTAL    DIV  COUNT    AVE    82H
010      OREPORT  H  301    1P
011      O                                45 'ALUMNI DONATIONS'
012      O        H  2     1P
013      O                                27 'CLASS         NAME'
014      O                                55 'DONATION'
015      O        D  1     07
016      O                      YEAR      13
017      O                      NAME      39
018      O                      AMOUNT    55 ' ,  0. '
019      O        T  22    LR
020      O                                43 'TOTAL DONATIONS'
021      O                      TOTAL     55 '  ,  0. '
022      O        T  2     LR
023      O                                43 'TOTAL NUMBER OF PEOPLE'
024      O                      COUNT Z   55
025      O        T  2     LR
026      O                                43 'AVERAGE DONATION'
027      O                      AVE       55 '  ,  0. '
```

Start

Set COUNT and TOTAL to zero

Write first page headings

Read a card

EOF ? — Yes → Calculate average AVE

No

Add AMOUNT to TOTAL

Add 1 to COUNT

Write detail line

Calculate average AVE

Write TOTAL COUNT and AVE

Stop

Answer Sheet

ALUMNI DONATIONS

CLASS	NAME	DONATION
1957	BAKER, ROBBIE T.	23.56
1947	ANDERSON , CHEVY	1,111.11
1969	WITINNG, SUE	123.56
1945	LITTLE MISS FUMMET	15.62
1945	PRINCE HAL	5,000.00
1945	HOLLY GOLIGHTLY	100.75
1945	SANCHEZ	5,000.00
1945	SMITH	4,244.51
1948	JONES, R	1,276.80
1948	SMITH	500.00
1948	LANGLEY	25.50
1952	JONES, L	2.50
1952	SMITH, L	1,234.56
1968	BROWN	.00
1968	EWEN	4,641.47
1969	DIANA ROSS	2,500.00
1975	CAROLYN KENNEDY	100.00
1975	TOMMY JONES	10.50

TOTAL DONATIONS   25,910.44

TOTAL NUMBER OF PEOPLE   18

AVERAGE DONATION   1,439.47

FIG. 10-3 Program **ALUMNI** to calculate total and average—IBM SYSTEM/360, TOS.

EXERCISES

1. Give calculations for
   (a) The sum over all records of the field **NET**, to be put into **TNET**.
   (b) The sum over all records of the field **K**, to be put into **TOTAL**.
   (c) The sum of the fields named **AMT1**, **AMT2**, and **AMT3**, from the same record.
   (d) The sum of the field named **CHG**, to be put into **TCHG**, over all records.
   (e) Increment the counter **K** by 2.
   (f) Increment the value of **TOTAL** by the field named **QAMT**.

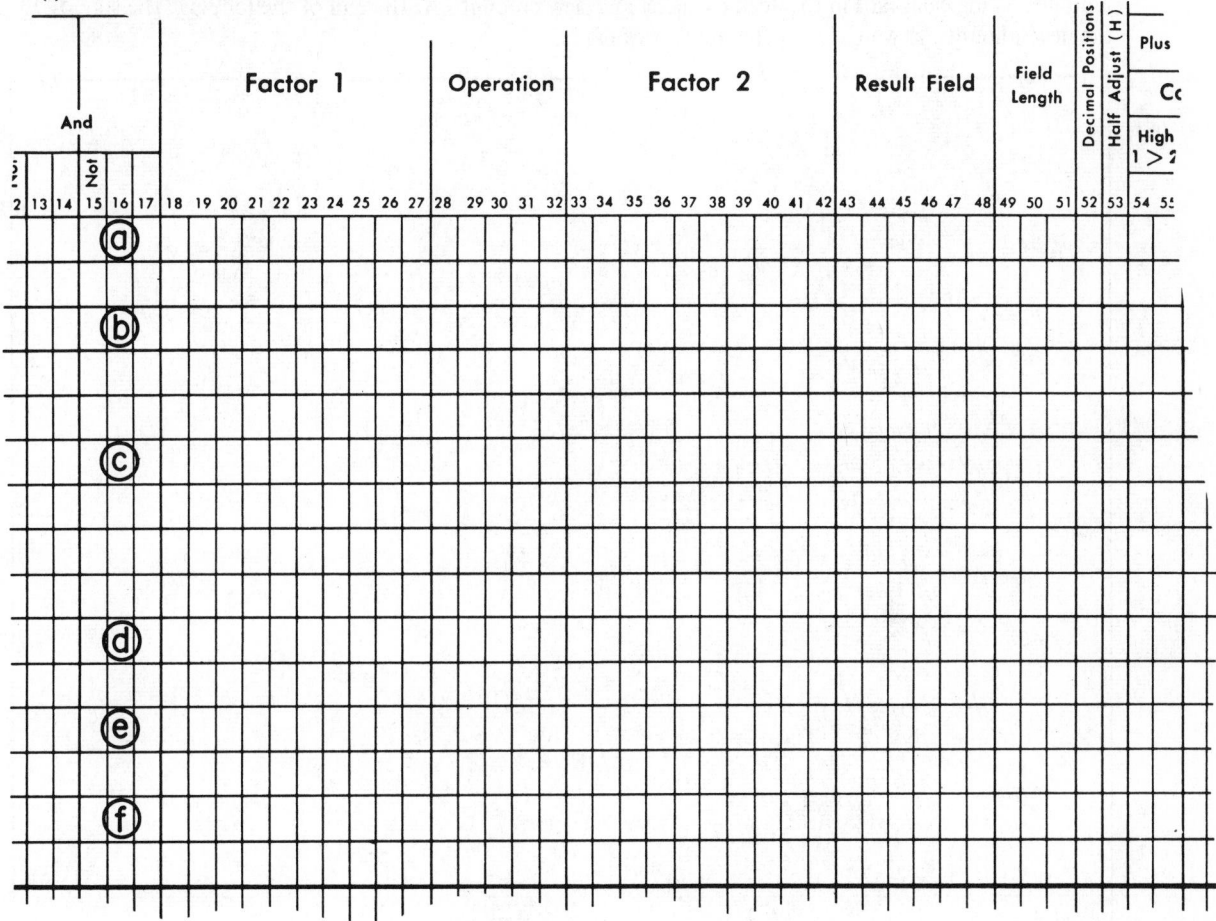

2. Write calculations to get a total of the 5 digit, 2 decimals field named **SALES**, over all records, putting it into **TSALES**. At the end of the job, calculate **SPRICE** by calculating 5% of **TSALES** and subtracting it from **TSALES** to get **DSALES**. Define field length and decimal positions for all fields.

3. In calculating a sum, what length should the result field be assigned?
   (a) Over 1ØØØ cards, field length is 5 columns each. _____
   (b) Over 15,ØØØ cards, field length is 7, with 2 decimals. _____
   (c) Over 5ØØ cards, field length is 3, maximum value in the field is 8ØØ. _____
   (d) Over 5ØØ cards, field length is 3, maximum value in the field is 1ØØ. _____

4. Draw a flow chart. A card deck contains fields for name, number, and amount. Add $25.00 to each amount, listing each card in the deck by name and new amount. At the end of the job, give the sum of all the new amounts, as well as the total number of cards.

Lesson 11

VARIABLE HEADINGS

You will learn how header cards are used to provide a run-date or heading information, and how to do consecutive numbering on the report.

The following questions are answered on the back of this page. If you have had experience with heading cards on unit-record equipment, read the lesson in order to answer the questions correctly before proceeding to Lesson 12.

1. What built-in field does RPG have for consecutive numbering?
2. How can you cause **PAGE** to number detail lines instead of pages?
3. How can a page number be initialized to something *other than* zero?
4. What is the purpose of record identification codes?
5. What kinds of tests for the record identification code can the programmer specify to be done?
6. In what order are record identification codes tested to identify a record?
7. If no record identification code is given for an input record, how does RPG handle the record types that reach that point to be tested?
8. What is the purpose of a header card? Give an example of its use.
9. Why should the 1P indicator *not* be used to print information from header cards?
10. When header cards are not printed by the indicator that was turned on when they came in, what precaution must be taken for data storage of their contents?

ANSWERS

1. **PAGE**, and in some implementations, **PAGE1** through **PAGE7**.
2. By using it as a field name to be printed on a detail line, rather than just at the top of the page.
3. By reading in a header card with a 4-digit value to be stored in the field named **PAGE**. The value should be one less than the first required page number.
4. To allow the computer to identify which record type it is processing at the time and to set indicators for control in other parts of the program for that record type.
5. **C** for character test, which tests the entire column; **D** for digit test, which tests the numeric punches only; and **Z** for zone test, which tests the zone punches only.
6. *In order* as they are listed on the INPUT specifications form. If a record does not satisfy the requirements for the first type, it is tested against the second, and so on.
7. Every card that is tested for that record type automatically passes the requirements, and is assumed to be that type.
8. To get information into the computer at the beginning of the run, to be used throughout the program. It may be for such purposes as a run-date, a heading, a return address for envelopes, or a slogan to be printed on every report.
9. Because by the time the header card comes into the computer, the 1P indicator has already been turned *off*. It is *on* only for output at run-in time, *before* the first data card has been read.
10. The names of fields must be different from those used on other records, so that the entire message or heading is uniquely stored. It will remain in memory by those names throughout the processing of that program unless these field names are changed or are used again for input of more information.

Headings that do not ever change may be printed by use of the 1P and OF indicators. When programmed in that manner, the heading 'JONES MOTOR CO.' will be exactly the same every time the program is run. Constant headings of that nature could even be preprinted on the form rather than by the computer. Some information on headings, however, is not constant, but changes either on every page or every time the job is run. For example, it is often helpful for each page of a report to be numbered, as shown in Figure 11-1. It is sometimes necessary to give the date the run was made, called a *run-date*, and print it either on every page, or possibly on just the first page, of the report. Even the name of the company for whom the report is produced can be put in at the time of the running of the report rather than at the time the program is written.

The RPG generator can build an automatic consecutive numbering field into every program. This field, called **PAGE**, is designed to be used for either page numbering or line numbering. It is automatically initialized to Ø at the beginning of the job; 1 is added to it immediately before it is printed. **PAGE** is a 4-digit field in numeric mode, with Ø decimals, and therefore must be either zero suppressed or edited when printed.

Sequential numbering of almost any type can be done by using **PAGE** as a field on the **CALCULATION** form. For example, adding 1 to it *before* printing will cause 2, 4, 6, 8, to print rather than 1, 2, 3, 4. Since adding 1 is done automatically, your addition of 1 causes it to increment by twos. The field name **PAGE** may be used to print page numbers on headings both on the first page of a report and on overflow pages, as shown in Figure 11-1. Alphameric

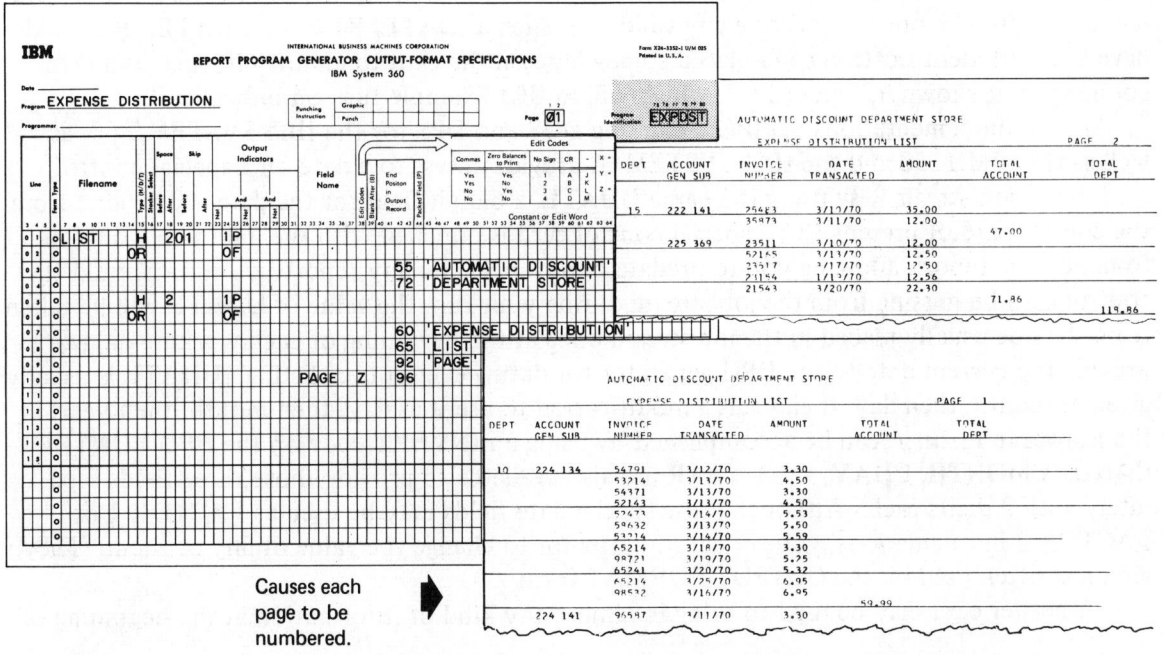

FIG. 11-1 Numbering pages with **PAGE** at 1P or OF.

constants, such as 'PAGE NO.' or 'P.', or even 'PAGE', may be printed alongside the page number. **PAGE** should *not*, however, be used for *page* numbering in more than one place on the page. Its automatic incrementing by 1 before each printing would cause it to be changed, between its two occurrences, giving two different page numbers on the same page! This automatic incrementing, however, makes it possible to use **PAGE** for consecutive numbering on each line of a page or a report, or to count the number of cards in a deck as they are used. Some implementations of RPG provide several different page numbering fields: **PAGE, PAGE1, PAGE2, . . ., PAGE7**. These are available so that consecutive numbering on different output devices can be done, each with a different page numbering field. See the IBM reference manual to determine how many your implementation can use.

Consecutive numbering of pages need not always start with $\emptyset\emptyset\emptyset1$. A sales report, run *this* week, might perhaps need to begin with the page number where the pages of the *last* report stopped. An initial value of **PAGE** can be brought in on a header card, with a special record identification code punched on it to allow it to be distinguished from a detail card. The initial value may be either positive or negative, but it must be named **PAGE, PAGE1, . . ., PAGE7**, etc., on the INPUT form, and given length 4 with $\emptyset$ decimals. The starting value should always be *one less than* the one you want first to be printed, since 1 is added to it before printing. In Figure 11-2, the record identification code is an H in column 8$\emptyset$; the value of **PAGE** is being initialized to 1874, punched in columns 1-4, which will cause the first page of the report to be numbered 1875.

A header card may also be used to bring in a current date: month, day, and year. It is often printed onto a heading line to be used as a *run-date*, giving the date the report was produced. For example, when statements are sent to the customers of a department store, there is usually a date of billing somewhere on the statement. The run-date header card is placed in front of the regular data cards for the report, read by the computer, and stored. It can be printed out anytime it is needed throughout the remainder of the program. The card may be designed to contain the month, day, and year, with slashes between, such as 12/21/7$\emptyset$ for December 21, 1970. When the slashes are included in the field, it must be read as eight alphameric characters. When the date is, instead, punched in six columns, without slashes, it should be in numeric mode so that editing can be done to get slashes printed on the output sheet. The field name used for the run-date may be any valid one, such as **DATE, RUN**, or **RDATE**. It should have a record identification code placed somewhere on the card to identify it, such as a D in column 80, as shown in Figure 11-3, which will in that example turn on indicator 99.

Several implementations of RPG, including DOS and DPS for the IBM SYSTEM/36$\emptyset$, as well as the IBM 113$\emptyset$ and the IBM SYSTEM/3, provide access to a date on a special control card in the job stream. By using the name **UDATE**, a 6-digit field for the date is provided from the control card, if present. This special control card is punched with the date you would like to use on the report, allowing you to predate or advance-date any report you run. Should the control card be missing from the job stream during your run, the value of **UDATE** will be taken from the one usually placed in the job stream once at the beginning of each working day, to provide the current date to the RPG generator for dating each source listing. **UDATE** is usually given as month, then day, then year; a modification to use it as day, then month, then year, in the European manner, can be accomplished by using an INVERT code on the **RPG CONTROL CARD. UMONTH, UDAY**, and **UYEAR** are also available to provide those three fields separately with 2 digits each. Although these special date fields may be used as FACTOR 1 or FACTOR 2 in calculations, you should not attempt to change the value of any of them. They are most often used on the OUTPUT-FORMAT form.

A header card may be used to bring in almost any kind of information at the beginning of

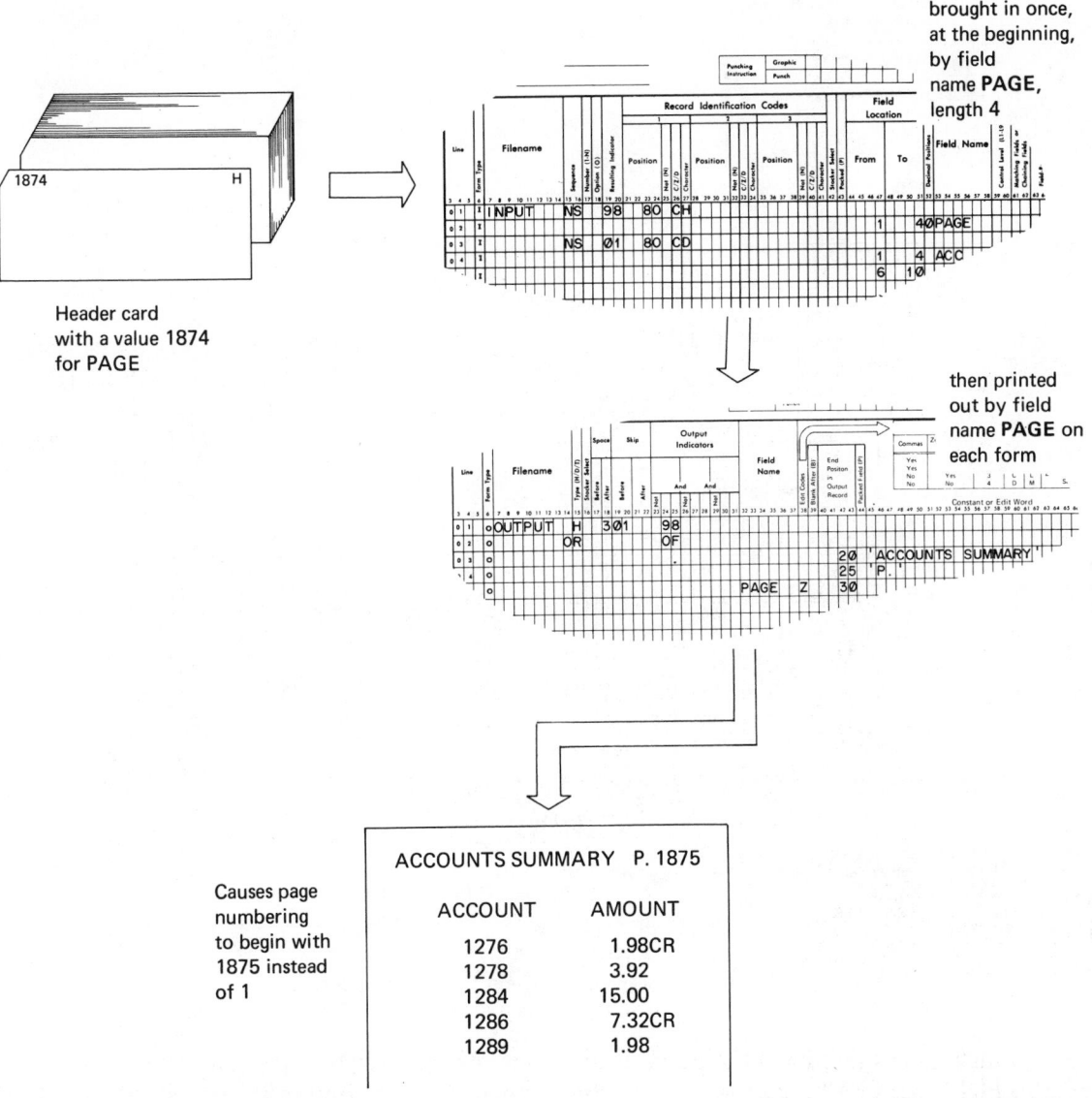

FIG. 11-2 Initialize **PAGE** by use of header card.

the job. The design of a header card can be different for each job; it may have one large field or several smaller ones, either alphameric or numeric mode. The information is stored—once— but may be used throughout the program, and so need not be brought in again. Paychecks produced by several large companies have a slogan for each week's payroll, read from a header card and printed on the face of each check stub; some large department stores advertise a monthly special in this way on the statement you get from them. A personalized report can be made by using a heading from a header card, so that a name can be changed each time the job is run. The heading given by 'PASS PATTERNS FOR ROMAN GABRIEL' can be changed to one for 'JOHN UNITAS' or 'JOE NAMATH' at the time the job is run. Continuous-form envelopes, often used for addressing mailings to every name in a data deck, can have a return address read from a header card placed in front of the deck.

Testing of record identification codes is done in the order that they are given on the INPUT form. The method of testing, however, is specified by the programmer. Tests may be *character*

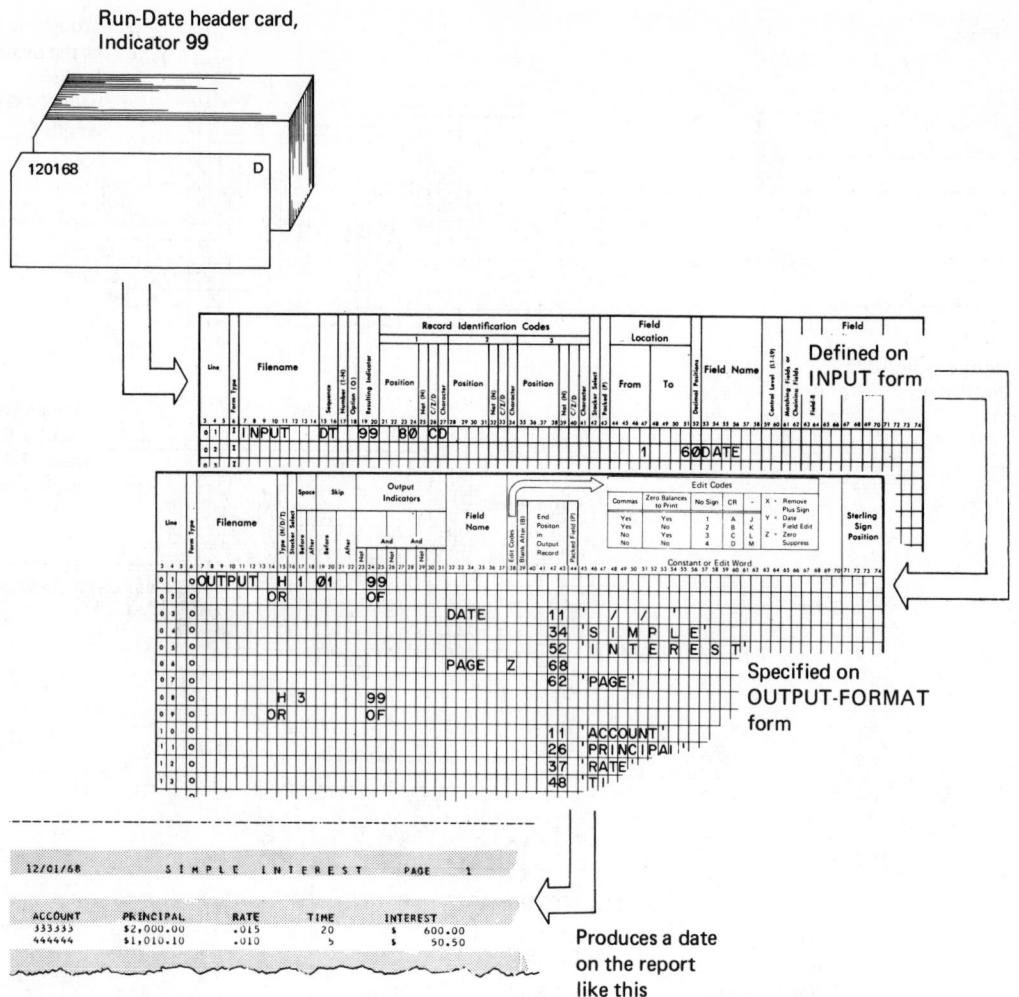

FIG. 11-3 Run-date on report by use of header card.

tests, which means that both the numeric and zone punches for that column are tested; digit tests, which means that only the numeric digit punches of the column are tested; or *zone* tests, which means that only the zone punches of the column are tested. These tests are coded by RPG as **C**, **D**, and **Z**, respectively. The use of a character test is recommended at this time since it is much simpler to use and more efficient for RPG to handle. Testing can be done *for* a particular character, such as a D in column 80, or for *anything except* a particular character, such as *not* a D in column 80.

Not all cards are required to have a record ID code. If record identification for a card is not given in an RPG program, however, *every* record is assumed to be of that type! Usually, record ID codes are assigned to each type of card, with the header card having perhaps an H in column 1, and the detail card having a different letter there. A T could be used to mean time cards; an I could mean cards for inventory. It is important that you select a column for this ID code with a unique character that will *never* appear in that column on any of the other card types. For example, if column 1 were chosen and a D there used for ID code for the date header card, a name field in columns 1-2Ø of the other cards could cause errors to occur. A card for a Mr. Davis or a Mr. Donaldson, for example, anywhere in the deck, would be taken as another date card, with strange consequences!

Record ID codes are used in RPG as a means to determine card type and set appropriate indicators. Whichever indicator is turned on usually controls the printing of lines on the OUT-PUT-FORMAT form. Remember that the 1P indicator will *not* print information from a header card. It is turned *on* at the beginning of the job, used for first-page headings, and then turned *off* before any cards are read. To print information from a header card at the top of each page, the header card indicator is *itself* usually used to print it onto the first page. The OF indicator, however, may be used to put it onto overflow lines. Since the information on the header card is, in some cases, not to be printed at the time it is brought in, it is stored, by field name. The indicator, which is turned on at the time the header card comes in, will be, in this case, listed as *unreferenced*. This source program diagnostic error is a warning that the indicator is not again used; it will not prevent execution, and may therefore be ignored. Field names, used for storage of several different header cards to be stored at the same time, must, however, be unique; should the same name be used, the value from each header card would destroy that stored from the previous one. For example, if **LINE1**, specified as an 8∅-character message, were used for another header card as well, the contents of the first message would be destroyed when the second one was entered, since only one storage area was reserved by that name in the memory of the computer.

Some installations prefer that heading lines containing variable information be coded as detail lines, by using **D** in column 15 of the OUTPUT-FORMAT form, rather than **H**. Since RPG handles both heading and detail type lines during the same detail-time cycle, it may be done either way. Some managers feel that better documentation results if the use of H is reserved for constant headings that are printed only on the first page or on overflow pages.

EXERCISES

1. (a) Design a header card that can be used to bring in a value of **PAGE** to start page numbering at 1∅∅1, as well as a run-date card of the form XX/XX/XX, with column 8∅ an H for record identification code.

INTERNATIONAL BUSINESS MACHINES CORPORATION

MULTIPLE-CARD LAYOUT FORM

Company _____

Application _____ by _____ Date _____ Job No. _____ Sheet No. _____

```
9 9 9 9 9 9 9 9 9 9 9 9 9 9 9 9 9 9 9 9 9 9 9 9 9 9 9 9 9 9 9 9 9 9 9 9 9 9 9 9 9 9 9 9 9 9 9 9 9 9 9 9 9 9 9 9 9 9 9 9 9 9 9 9 9 9 9 9 9 9 9 9 9 9 9 9 9 9 9 9
1 2 3 4 5 6 7 8 9 10 11 12 13 14 15 16 17 18 19 20 21 22 23 24 25 26 27 28 29 30 31 32 33 34 35 36 37 38 39 40 41 42 43 44 45 46 47 48 49 50 51 52 53 54 55 56 57 58 59 60 61 62 63 64 65 66 67 68 69 70 71 72 73 74 75 76 77 78 79 80
```

```
9 9 9 9 9 9 9 9 9 9 9 9 9 9 9 9 9 9 9 9 9 9 9 9 9 9 9 9 9 9 9 9 9 9 9 9 9 9 9 9 9 9 9 9 9 9 9 9 9 9 9 9 9 9 9 9 9 9 9 9 9 9 9 9 9 9 9 9 9 9 9 9 9 9 9 9 9 9 9 9
1 2 3 4 5 6 7 8 9 10 11 12 13 14 15 16 17 18 19 20 21 22 23 24 25 26 27 28 29 30 31 32 33 34 35 36 37 38 39 40 41 42 43 44 45 46 47 48 49 50 51 52 53 54 55 56 57 58 59 60 61 62 63 64 65 66 67 68 69 70 71 72 73 74 75 76 77 78 79 80
```

   (b) What would you enter on the data card for the value of **PAGE**? _____

   (c) What mode would you use for reading in the date field? _____

2. Write OUTPUT-FORMAT specifications for each of these, omitting FILENAME information.
   (a) A heading line, to be printed on the first page and on overflow pages, giving the heading 'KRAMER KATS INVENTORY', the word 'PAGE', and the actual page number by using **PAGE**.

(b) A detail line, giving the value of **NUM** and **NAME**, with consecutive numbering on each line.

(c) A total line, to be printed at the end-of-file condition, giving the value of the field **TOTAL** and the run-date **RUN** for the report, both on a separate page following the report.

ne	Type (H/D/T)	Stacker Select	Space Before	Space After	Skip Before	Skip After	Output Indicators Not		And Not		And Not		Field Name	Zero Suppress (Z)	Blank After (B)	End Position in Output Record	Packed Field (P)	Constant or Edit Word
12 13 14	15	16	17	18	19 20	21 22	23	24 25	26	27 28	29	30 31	32 33 34 35 36 37	38	39	40 41 42 43	44	45 46 47 48 49 50 51 52 53 54 55 56 57 58 59 60 61 62 63 64
(a)																		
(b)																		
(c)																		

Lesson 12

A PRINTED REPORT WITH HEADINGS AND TOTALS

You will be able to combine the features of a run-date, a page number, and detail lines with final total into one report.

The questions below are answered on the back of this page. If you can answer them correctly from your knowledge of data processing and the lessons up to this point, go on to the programs to write at the end of this section.

1. Why are both header and detail cards given record identification codes?
2. Why should the header card specification be written *second* rather than *first* on the INPUT specifications form?
3. Why is it better to use the *character* test for record identification code, rather than the zone test or the digit test?
4. What is the purpose of using **N**, for *not*, on a record identification test?
5. Why is a counter usually necessary on a job requiring an average based on totals over the whole job?
6. In doing a detail list with totals *only* at the end of a job, when are the total-time operations executed?
7. What is the difference between a run-date and the date of the transaction?
8. What indicators are usually used to print report and column headings that contain information from the header card?
9. What would result if the end-of-file card were placed prematurely in the data deck *in front of* some of the data cards?
10. Under what condition would you use page numbers in a first page heading line?

ANSWERS

1. Although only one of them is *required* to have an ID code, allowing the other to be assigned to all cards without that code, it is far better that each have one, since the first one written on the form, usually the detail card, *must* have one, and the header card *should* have one to prevent invalid cards from changing header information.

2. Since the detail card is the most frequently encountered one in the deck, and since the tests are administered in order from top to bottom on the list, the most frequent ones should be listed first to minimize execution time of the record identification tests.

3. It is easier for RPG to handle, easier for you to understand, and since, on most of your beginning programs, data columns are plentiful and one entire column can be used.

4. To cause everything *except* the particular character, digit, or zone specified to be acceptable as a record ID code.

5. Because an average that is based on a column sum requires a division, usually by the total number of cards in the deck.

6. Only at the detection of the end-of-file condition. They are always bypassed at the first card, and also at other times if there is nothing specified on an indicator that is satisfied.

7. A run-date is the one brought in by a header card, usually to place the current date of the production of the report onto the report somewhere. The date of transaction, usually on the detail card, gives the date of its occurrence, such as when the item was purchased or ordered, or when the sale was made.

8. The indicator set *on* by the header card, as well as the OF indicator for getting it onto overflow pages. However, heading information can also be placed into the detail lines of the report, in which case the detail indicator would be used.

9. The job would be prematurely terminated and totals for the data up to that point would be given. The data cards *following* the end-of-file card would cause errors in the job control stream following the termination of the program.

10. When you want them to begin with page 0001.

In doing a report with a current run-date on each page, a header card is often used. Recall that a header card is placed in front of the deck of data cards to be used in the job, it is read once and identified, and the information on it is stored. It is then available for printing throughout the program.

The code that distinguishes the card as being a header card is given under record identification code on the INPUT form. Although three codes or fewer may be used on each specification line, only one is needed for most simple jobs. Columns 21-27, underneath the specifications for record ID 1, will be used. The column number that is to contain the ID code is written under POSITION in columns 21-24. C in column 26 of the INPUT form indicates that a character test, for a specific alphanumeric character, is to be made. The character given in column 27 specifies exactly what character the test is to use. If column 25 contains N, the test is made for any character *other than* the one specified. In the example,

Form Type	Filename	Sequence	Number (1-N)	Option (O)	Resulting Indicator	Record Identification Codes 1 Position	Not (N)	C/Z/D	Character	2 Position	Not (N)	C/Z/D	Character	3 Position	Not (N)	C/Z/D	Character	Stacker Select	Packed (P)	Field Location From	To	Decimal Positions	Field Nan
I	INPUT	NS			75	12		C	D														
I																				1	8		DATE
I																							
I																							

a character test is made on column 12, to determine whether a D is present, and, if it is, indicator 75 will be turned on, and the alphanumeric field **DATE** will be brought in from columns 1-8 of the card. In the example,

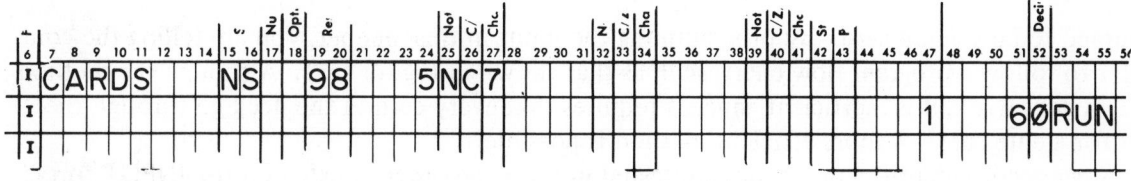

column 5 will be tested, and should it contain anything other than a 7, indicator 98 will be turned on, and the numeric value of the field **RUN** will be brought from columns 1-6.

Since it is necessary to specify every record type that is to be permitted in the file, both types of cards, the header card and the detail card, must be described. One way to do it is given in Figure 12-1. Each time a card is read, a test is made for a D in column 8Ø. If the test is successful, indicator 75 will be turned on and the card will be used as a run-date card. If there is anything other than a D in column 8Ø, indicator 75 stays off, and the card is considered for the next record type. Since the next record type does not have a record ID code given, no further test is made; it "falls through," indicator 99 is turned on, and the card is

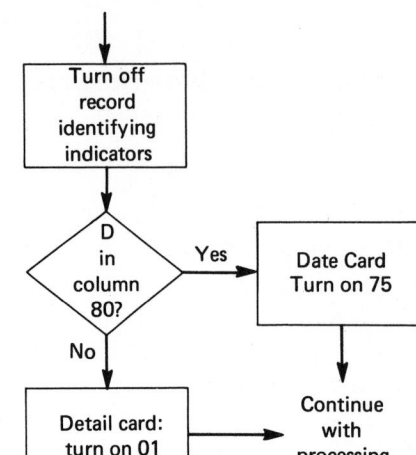

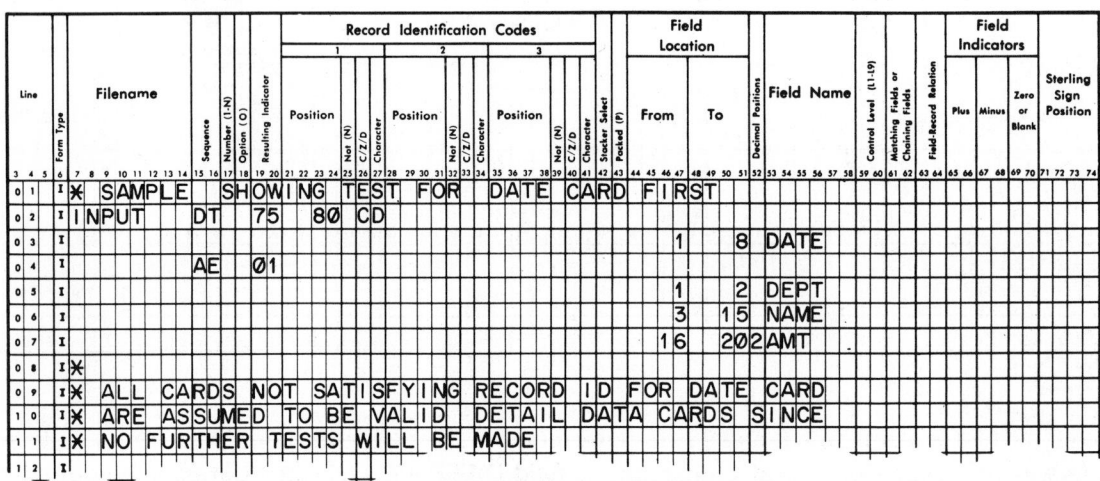

FIG. 12-1 Record identification test with one ID code tested.

assumed to be a detail card. By programming the input in this manner, you are telling the computer to follow a program flow chart, such as that shown in Figure 12-1. Although the method shown does work, it is inefficient, since it requires that every card in the deck go through the test for a date card! A more efficient method is possible.

Since record identification codes are tested in the same order as listed on the INPUT form, the record that occurs most often in the deck should be listed *first* in order to minimize execution time. Since the detail card type occurs most often, it should be specified first, with the run-date card next. However, in order to be listed first, the detail card must *itself* be given a record identification code. Figure 12-2 shows that when the date card comes in, it will be tested to determine whether it is a detail card. Since there is *not* an A in column 8Ø, indicator 99 remains off and it is sent on to the next test; and since a D is in column 8Ø, indicator 75 will be turned *on*, and the card will be used as a run-date card. A detail card that has an A in column 8Ø will make its proper identification with one test.

For a given record, up to three record ID codes may be specified in one coding line. These

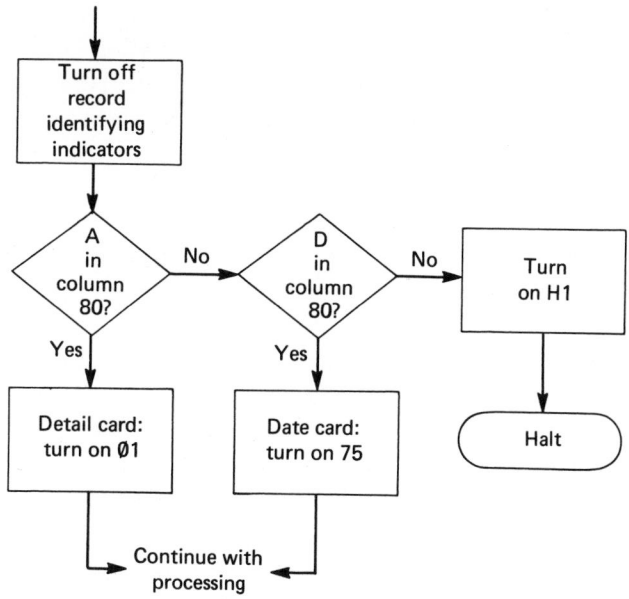

Line	Form Type	Filename	Sequence	Number (1-N)	Option (O)	Resulting Indicator	Record Identification Codes												Field Location			Decimal Positions	Field Name	Control Level (L1-L9)	Matching Fields or Chaining Fields	Field-Record Relation	Field Indicators			Sterling Sign Position
							1			2			3			Stacker Select	Packed (P)	From	To						Plus	Minus	Zero or Blank	
							Position	Not (N)	C/Z/D	Character	Position	Not (N)	C/Z/D	Character	Position	Not (N)	C/Z/D	Character													
3 4	5 6	7 8 9 10 11 12 13 14	15 16	17	18	19 20	21 22 23 24	25	26	27	28 29 30 31	32	33	34	35 36 37 38	39	40	41	42	43	44 45 46 47	48 49 50	51 52	53 54 55 56 57	58	59 60	61 62	63 64	65 66	67 68	69 70	71 72 73 74
0 1	I✳	SAMPLE SHOWING TEST FOR DETAIL CARD FIRST, THEN FOR DATE																														
0 2	I✳																															
0 3	I	INPUT	NS	01			80		C	A																						
0 4	I																			1	2		DEPT								
0 5	I																			3	15		NAME								
0 6	I																			16	20	2	AMT								
0 7	I		DT	75			80		C	D																						
0 8	I																			1	8		DATE								
0 9	I✳																															
1 0	I✳	CARDS WITH A IN COL. 80 ARE VALID DETAILS																														
1 1	I✳																															
1 2	I✳	CARDS WITH D IN COL. 80 ARE DATE CARDS																														
1 3	I✳																															
1 4	I✳	ALL OTHER CARDS CAUSE THE COMPUTER SYSTEM TO STOP																														
	I																															

FIG. 12-2 Record identification test with two ID codes tested.

codes are related in an *and* condition by the computer—they must all be satisfied by the data card for the record to be identified as that record type. In the example,

	Form Type	Filename	Sequence	Number (1-N)	Option (O)	Resulting Indicator	Position	Not (N)	C/Z/D	Character	Position	Not (N)	C/Z/D	Character	Position	Not (N)	C/Z/D	Character	Stacker Select	Packed (P)	From	To	Decimal Positions	Field N
5	6	7 8 9 10 11 12 13 14	15 16	17	18	19 20	21 22 23 24	25	26	27	28 29 30 31	32	33	34	35 36 37 38	39	40	41	42	43	44 45 46 47	48 49 50 51	52	53 54 55
	I						53		01	C1			02	C7										
	I																							

the number 17 must be punched in columns 1 and 2 of the data card to cause indicator 53 to go on. If more than three codes should be needed, an **AND** coding line must be used, with the **A** in column 14, and the **ND** in columns 15 and 16 under SEQUENCE. All record ID codes specified on an **AND** line are assumed to be in an *and* relationship with the codes on the previous line.

Instead of using several required codes on the same record, *one* of several possible codes may identify a record. If, for example, a payment card is punched either with a P in column 8∅ or an R in column 79, an *or* condition is used to specify that *one or* the *other* is present. The letters **OR** are placed with the **O** in column 14 and the **R** in column 15; column 16 must be blank.

Generally only one record-type indicator will be on at a given time. Any cards that do not fit the record identification codes listed will cause the computer system to stop. On some configurations, the offending card may be *stacker selected*, that is, put into a different stacker when it comes out of the machine. Note that, on the INPUT form, the file name need not be repeated on every record type, as long as it refers to the same file as that used previously. The field SEQUENCE, however, in columns 15 and 16, must contain valid alphabetic characters on every record indication line when no sequencing within a group is required. Any two alphabetic characters, other than **ND** and **R∅**, which are part of **AND** and **OR**, respectively, can be used, not necessarily the same ones in successive record types. Many programmers use meaningful abbreviations of the record type, such as **DT** for a date record type and **PO** for a purchase order record type.

Record ID codes specified for a character test may contain any letter of the alphabet, any numeric digit, or any special character. This requires that one column, or part of one, of the 8∅ possible card columns be devoted to record identification. Occasionally there may not be enough space left on a card to permit a whole column to be used for this purpose, so tests for zone or for digit, which use only the zone portion or the digit portion, respectively, are permitted. Since on simple jobs the necessary card column is readily available, and since the character test is much more efficient for the RPG generator to produce, the zone and digit tests are not yet of concern.

PROBLEM DEFINITION: *Write a program, named* **POTOTAL**, *to produce a report listing of the purchase order cards, with totals, as shown in Figure 12-3. The value of* **COST** *is obtained by multiplying the quantity by the price. Give the total number of cards processed, and the total* **COST**. *Give a run-date and page numbering as shown.*

In the program, the detail purchase order card should be described before the run-date card. The heading lines are printed by indicator 75, set by the run-date header card, and *not* with the 1P indicator, since it is already off by the time the header card has come in. A two-line total is given; total cost is aligned underneath **COST**, edited; the total number of cards processed is given on a separate line. The two total lines are printed by use of the LR indicator, which is turned on at the detection of the end-of-file card, located behind the data deck. The source listing produced by the IBM SYSTEM/36∅, DOS is given in Figure 12-4.

Notice that the field name **DATE** was used on the purchase order card to mean the date that the item was ordered. The field name **DRUN** was selected for the run-date header card and used to indicate the date that the computer run was made, or perhaps the date that the report is to be released. Should the same two names have been used for both those dates, the value of the run-date would *not* have been preserved, but would have been replaced by the date from each detail card, causing the run-date to be wrong on every page except the first. To guard against heading errors of this type, you must test the program with a data deck large

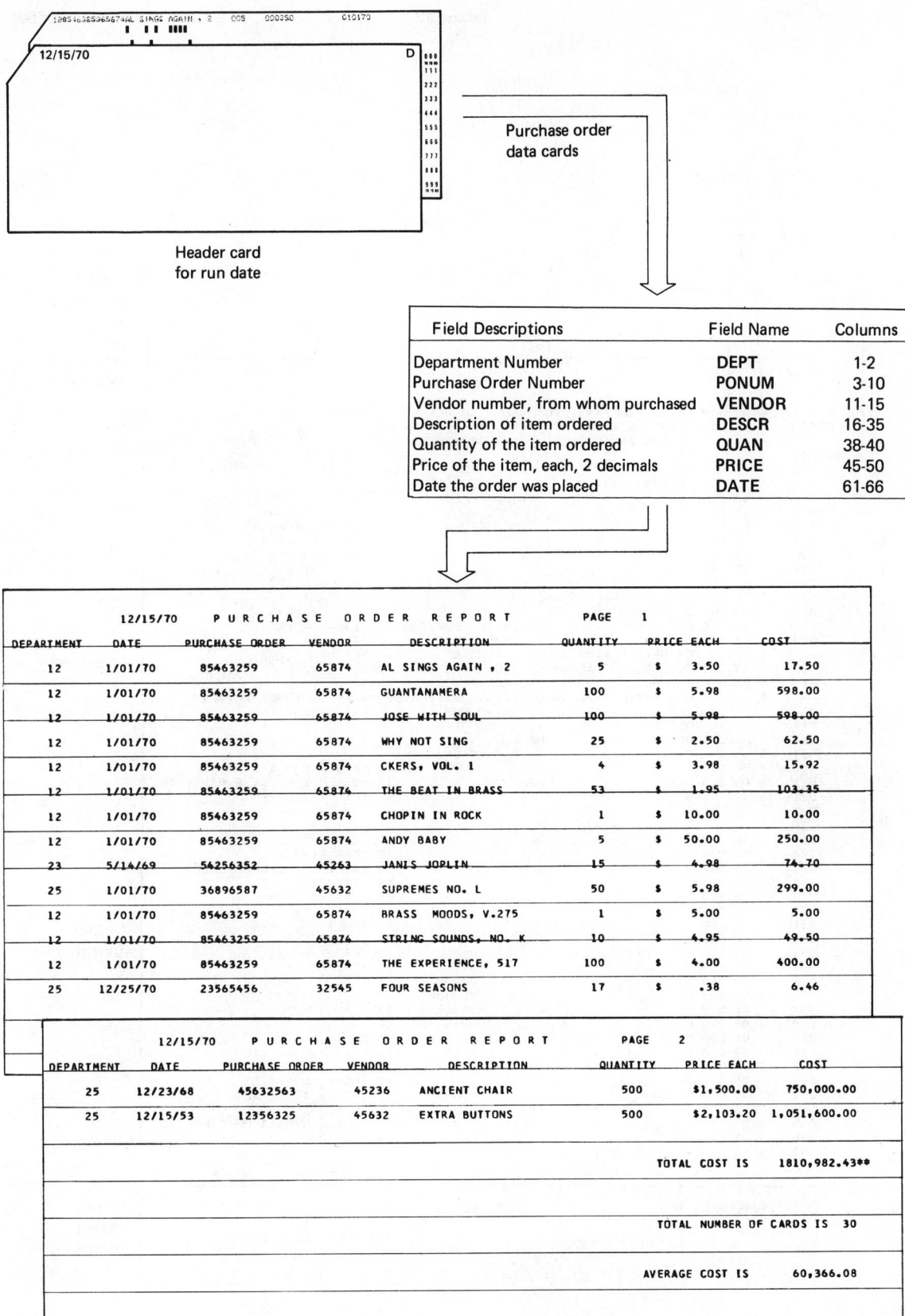

The card image at the top reads:

```
12854632596574AL SINGS AGAIN , 2    005    000250         010170
```

```
12/15/70                                                    D
```

Header card
for run date

Purchase order
data cards

Field Descriptions	Field Name	Columns
Department Number	DEPT	1-2
Purchase Order Number	PONUM	3-10
Vendor number, from whom purchased	VENDOR	11-15
Description of item ordered	DESCR	16-35
Quantity of the item ordered	QUAN	38-40
Price of the item, each, 2 decimals	PRICE	45-50
Date the order was placed	DATE	61-66

```
        12/15/70      P U R C H A S E   O R D E R   R E P O R T      PAGE    1
DEPARTMENT    DATE      PURCHASE ORDER    VENDOR      DESCRIPTION        QUANTITY    PRICE EACH      COST
```

DEPARTMENT	DATE	PURCHASE ORDER	VENDOR	DESCRIPTION	QUANTITY	PRICE EACH	COST
12	1/01/70	85463259	65874	AL SINGS AGAIN , 2	5	$ 3.50	17.50
12	1/01/70	85463259	65874	GUANTANAMERA	100	$ 5.98	598.00
12	1/01/70	85463259	65874	JOSE WITH SOUL	100	$ 5.98	598.00
12	1/01/70	85463259	65874	WHY NOT SING	25	$ 2.50	62.50
12	1/01/70	85463259	65874	CKERS, VOL. 1	4	$ 3.98	15.92
12	1/01/70	85463259	65874	THE BEAT IN BRASS	53	$ 1.95	103.35
12	1/01/70	85463259	65874	CHOPIN IN ROCK	1	$ 10.00	10.00
12	1/01/70	85463259	65874	ANDY BABY	5	$ 50.00	250.00
23	5/14/69	54256352	45263	JANIS JOPLIN	15	$ 4.98	74.70
25	1/01/70	36896587	45632	SUPREMES NO. L	50	$ 5.98	299.00
12	1/01/70	85463259	65874	BRASS MOODS, V.275	1	$ 5.00	5.00
12	1/01/70	85463259	65874	STRING SOUNDS, NO. K	10	$ 4.95	49.50
12	1/01/70	85463259	65874	THE EXPERIENCE, 517	100	$ 4.00	400.00
25	12/25/70	23565456	32545	FOUR SEASONS	17	$ .38	6.46

```
        12/15/70      P U R C H A S E   O R D E R   R E P O R T      PAGE    2
DEPARTMENT    DATE      PURCHASE ORDER    VENDOR      DESCRIPTION        QUANTITY    PRICE EACH      COST
```

DEPARTMENT	DATE	PURCHASE ORDER	VENDOR	DESCRIPTION	QUANTITY	PRICE EACH	COST
25	12/23/68	45632563	45236	ANCIENT CHAIR	500	$1,500.00	750,000.00
25	12/15/53	12356325	45632	EXTRA BUTTONS	500	$2,103.20	1,051,600.00

```
                                              TOTAL COST IS      1810,982.43**

                                              TOTAL NUMBER OF CARDS IS   30

                                              AVERAGE COST IS      60,366.08
```

FIG. 12-3 Input and output for program **POTOTAL**.

171

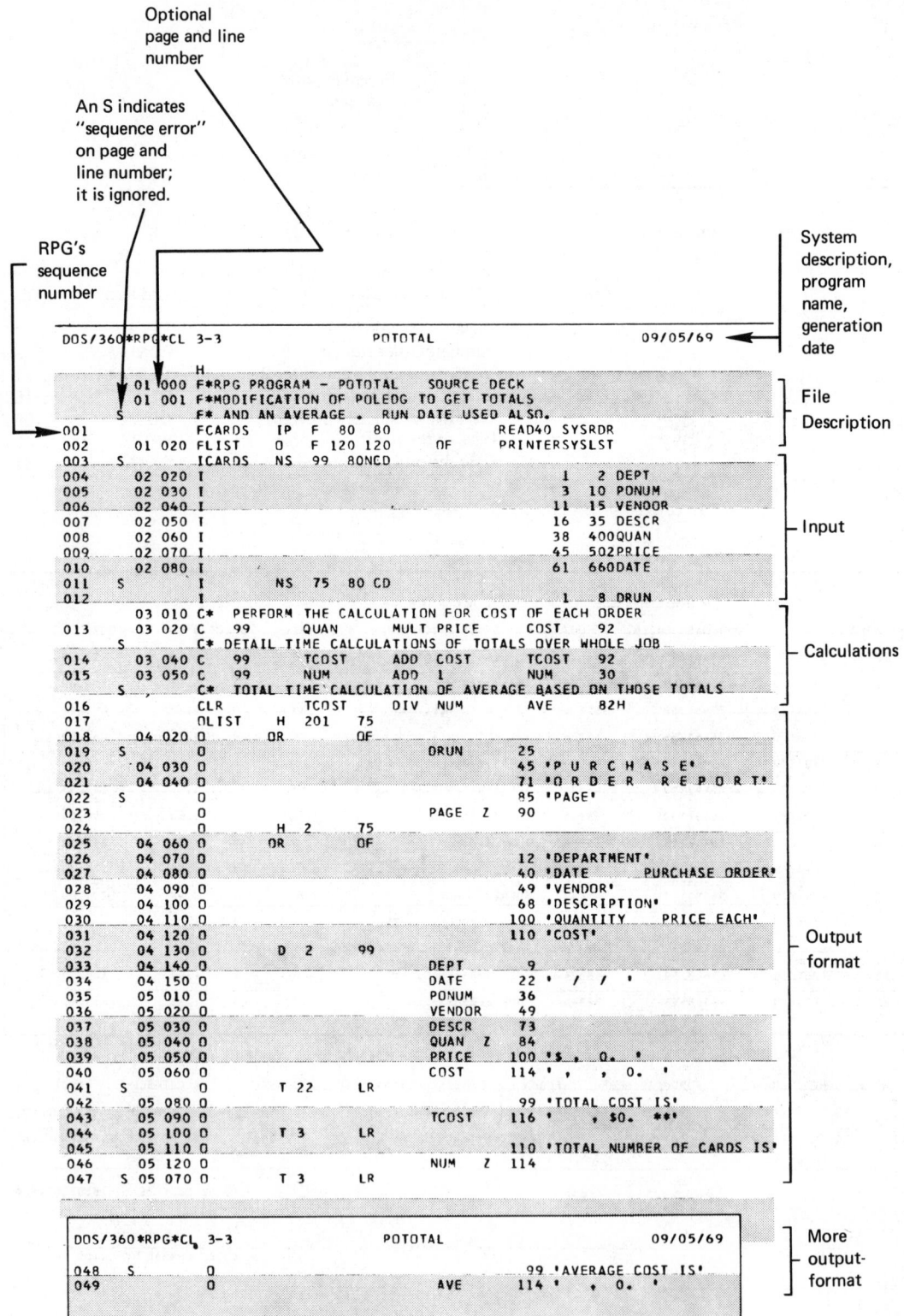

Optional
page and line
number

An S indicates
"sequence error"
on page and
line number;
it is ignored.

RPG's
sequence
number

System
description,
program
name,
generation
date

```
DOS/360*RPG*CL 3-3                 POTOTAL                      09/05/69  ◄──

                     H
        01 000 F*RPG PROGRAM - POTOTAL    SOURCE DECK
        01 001 F*MODIFICATION OF POLEOG TO GET TOTALS
     S         F* AND AN AVERAGE . RUN DATE USED ALSO.
001            FCARDS    IP  F  80  80           READ40 SYSRDR
002     01 020 FLIST     O   F 120 120      OF   PRINTERSYSLST
003  S         ICARDS    NS  99  80NCD
004     02 020 I                                     1   2 DEPT
005     02 030 I                                     3  10 PONUM
006     02 040 I                                    11  15 VENDOR
007     02 050 I                                    16  35 DESCR
008     02 060 I                                    38  400QUAN
009     02 070 I                                    45  502PRICE
010     02 080 I                                    61  660DATE
011  S         I         NS  75  80 CD
012            I                                     1   8 DRUN
        03 010 C*  PERFORM THE CALCULATION FOR COST OF EACH ORDER
013     03 020 C    99    QUAN      MULT PRICE      COST    92
     S         C* DETAIL TIME CALCULATIONS OF TOTALS OVER WHOLE JOB
014     03 040 C    99    TCOST     ADD  COST       TCOST   92
015     03 050 C    99    NUM       ADD  1          NUM     30
        C*  TOTAL TIME CALCULATION OF AVERAGE BASED ON THOSE TOTALS
016            CLR       TCOST     DIV  NUM         AVE     82H
017            OLIST     H 201  75
018     04 020 O         OR        OF
019  S         O                            DRUN      25
020     04 030 O                                      45 'P U R C H A S E'
021     04 040 O                                      71 'O R D E R  R E P O R T'
022  S         O                                      85 'PAGE'
023            O                            PAGE  Z   90
024            O         H 2   75
025     04 060 O         OR        OF
026     04 070 O                                      12 'DEPARTMENT'
027     04 080 O                                      40 'DATE      PURCHASE ORDER'
028     04 090 O                                      49 'VENDOR'
029     04 100 O                                      68 'DESCRIPTION'
030     04 110 O                                     100 'QUANTITY    PRICE EACH'
031     04 120 O                                     110 'COST'
032     04 130 O         D 2   99
033     04 140 O                            DEPT       9
034     04 150 O                            DATE      22 ' / / '
035     05 010 O                            PONUM     36
036     05 020 O                            VENDOR    49
037     05 030 O                            DESCR     73
038     05 040 O                            QUAN  Z   84
039     05 050 O                            PRICE    100 '$ , 0. '
040     05 060 O                            COST     114 ' ,  , 0. '
041  S         O         T 22      LR
042     05 080 O                                      99 'TOTAL COST IS'
043     05 090 O                            TCOST    116 '  , $0. **'
044     05 100 O         T 3       LR
045     05 110 O                                     110 'TOTAL NUMBER OF CARDS IS'
046     05 120 O                            NUM   Z  114
047  S  05 070 O         T 3       LR
```

File
Description

Input

Calculations

Output
format

```
DOS/360*RPG*CL 3-3                 POTOTAL                      09/05/69

048  S         O                                      99 'AVERAGE COST IS'
049            O                            AVE      114 '  , 0. '
```

More
output-
format

FIG. 12-4 Program **POTOTAL**–IBM SYSTEM/36Ø, DOS.

enough to produce an overflow page, so that page number and date on it can be verified. Observe also that the output is not in any particular order—sorting the data by department, date, or vendor is possible and would help make the report more readable.

A flow chart is given in Figure 12-5 to illustrate what is accomplished by the program **POTOTAL**. After automatic initialization of fields, a card is read. The record identification code is used to recognize the type of card. If it is a date card, the heading line will be printed, after which another card is read. The detail card turns on the appropriate indicator to accomplish calculations and detail output, after which another card is read. This forms the basic loop for the handling of all detail cards. When the end-of-file card is detected, the totals are printed and the job halted.

The flow chart given in Figure 12-5 serves to show what happens in the problem **POTOTAL**, but does not serve as a true picture of what actually is going on inside the RPG object program. The RPG object program logic chart, given in the Appendix, illustrates the execution in a more accurate manner, but it need not concern you at this time.

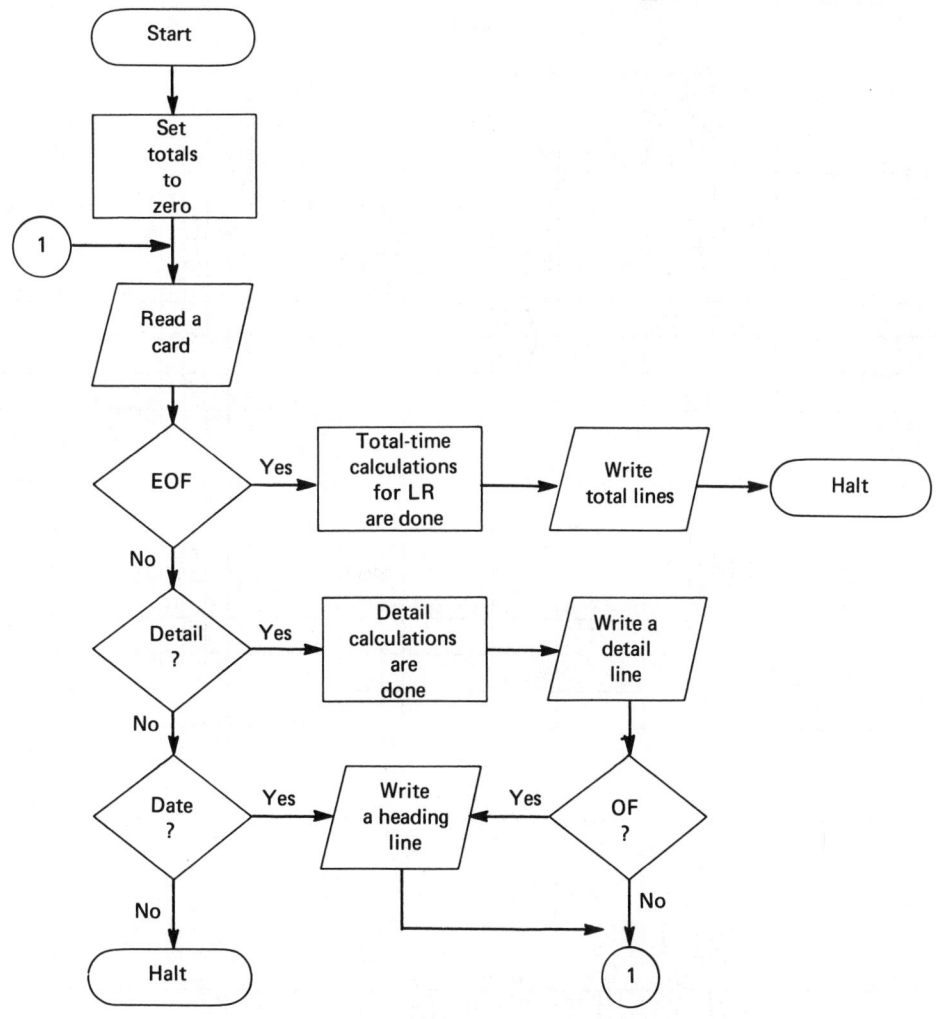

FIG. 12-5 Job flowchart for program **POTOTAL**.

EXERCISES

1. State the record ID code tests for each:

(a)

Line		Form Type	Filename	Sequence	Number (1-N) Option (O)	Resulting Indicator	Record Identification Codes																Field Location			
							1				2				3				Stacker Select Packed (P)						
							Position	Not (N)	C/Z/D	Character	Position	Not (N)	C/Z/D	Character	Position	Not (N)	C/Z/D	Character		From	To					Decimal Positions
3 4 5	6	7 8 9 10 11 12 13 14	15 16	17	18	19 20	21 22 23 24	25	26	27	28 29 30 31	32	33	34	35 36 37 38	39	40	41	42	43	44 45 46 47	48 49 50 51	52			
0 1	I	CARDS	NS				75		80	CH																
0 2	I																									
0 3	I																									

(b)

Line		Form Type	Filename	Sequence	Number (1-N) Option (O)	Resulting Indicator	Position	Not (N)	C/Z/D	Character	Position	Not (N)	C/Z/D	Character	Position	Not (N)	C/Z/D	Character	Stacker Select Packed (P)	From	To	Decimal Positions
3 4 5	6	7 8 9 10 11 12 13 14	15 16	17	18	19 20	21 22 23 24	25	26	27	28 29 30 31	32	33	34	35 36 37 38	39	40	41	42 43	44 45 46 47	48 49 50 51	52
0 1	I		DT				07		21	CA												
0 2	I		OR						22	CA												
0 3	I																					

(c)

Line		Form Type		Sequence	Number (1) Option (O)	Resulting	Position	Not (N)	C/Z/D	Character	Position	Not (N)	C/Z/D	Character	Position	Not (N)	C/Z/D	Charact	Stacke	Packe	Decimal
3 4 5	6		7 8 9 10 11 12 13 14	15 16	17	18	19 20	21 22 23 24	25	26	27	28 29 30 31	32	33	34	35 36 37	38 39	40	41	42 43	44 45 46 47	48 49 50 51 52
0 1	I			NS			35		12	CZ												
0 2	I			OR					12	NCZ												
0 3	I																					
	I																					

(d)

Line		Form Type	Filename	Sequence	Number (1-N) Option (O)	Resulting Indic	Position	Not (N)	C/Z/D	Character	Position	Not (N)	C/Z/D	Character	Position	Not (N)	C/Z/D	Character	Stacker Select Packed (P)	From	To	Decimal Posi
3 4 5	6	7 8 9 10 11 12 13 14	15 16	17	18	19 20	21 22 23 24	25	26	27	28 29 30 31	32	33	34	35 36 37	38 39	40	41	42 43	44 45 46 47	48 49 50 51	52
0 1	I		PC				71		78	C1			79	C2			80	C3				
0 2	I		AND						50	NC												
0 3	I																					
0 4																						

2. Write INPUT specifications for each of the following, omitting FILENAME information.
  (a) Define a header card, containing a value of PAGE in columns 1-4, with record ID code being a P in column 8∅, and using indicator 13.
  (b) Define a run-date header card, using indicator 13, with a D in column 3 and date in columns 1-6, numeric.
  (c) Specify a three-card header card, each one punched in columns 1-6∅ of each card, containing HD1, HD2, and HD3 headings, respectively, with record ID codes 7, 8, and 9, respectively, in column 8∅, turning on indicators 13, 14, and 15.

	Record Identification Codes			Field Location			Field Name	
	1	2	3	From	To			

(a)

(b)

(c)

Section 4

PROGRAMS TO WRITE

A. PROBLEM NAME: **DONTOT:** to get totals of donations

Write a program to prepare a list of alumni donations, for this year and last year, with a major heading, and column headings over all fields. At the end of the job, print the word 'TOTALS' and the total of donations for both this year and last year, aligned underneath the proper columns. Input records are the same as those defined for Problem C, Section 3:

Field Information	Columns
Year of graduation	1-4
Name of graduate	11-3∅
Zip code of residence	36-4∅
Amount donated last year, 2 decimals	65-7∅
Amount donated this year, 2 decimals	75-8∅

B. PROBLEM NAME: **PAYTOT**: to calculate net pay, with totals
Write a program to calculate hourly gross pay by multiplying hours worked by rate of pay per hour, then subtract deductions to give net pay. At the end of the job, give the total gross pay, total deductions, and total net pay, each aligned under the appropriate columns. Print both a major heading line and column headings.

Field Information	Columns
Record identification: P or	1
F	7∅
Employee number	5-8
Employee name	13-32
Rate of pay, per hour, 2 decimals	35-38
Hours worked	4∅-41
Deductions, 2 decimals	54-58

C. PROBLEM NAME: **AVE**: calculate the average of a set of numbers
The program should read an entire deck of data cards, counting them as they come in, printing the value of **X** brought in on each one, and adding it to **SUMX**. At the end of the job, print the card count, the value of **SUMX**, and the average. Give sign indication for all values of **X**, for **SUMX**, and for the average. Design your own headings.

Field Information	Columns
X, 2 decimals	5-1∅

D. PROBLEM NAME: **INTSUM**: calculate sum of interest and amount of return
Write a program to calculate simple interest by multiplying *principal* by *annual rate* by *time*, then add it to *principal* to get *amount of the return*. The total of calculated interest should be printed at the end of the job. The report should have a major heading on all pages giving the run-date, which comes from a header card; the page number; and the words 'SIMPLE INTEREST'. Column headings should identify each field printed: account number and name, principal, interest rate, time, interest, and amount. Input records are the same as Problem B, Section 3.

	Field Information	*Columns*
Run-date header card	Record ID code: D	7
	Date of run: month, day, year	1-6
Detail cards	Record ID code: A	7
	Account number	1-6
	Account name	11-3∅
	Principal, 2 decimals	35-4∅
	Annual rate of interest, 3 decimals	47-5∅
	Time in years	58-6∅

SECTION 5

REPORTS WITH CONTROL GROUPS

Lesson 13

SORTING FOR CONTROL GROUPS

You will learn how to group data in sequential order by control fields, assign control level indicators, and reset control group totals.

The questions below summarize the lesson. If you have had experience with control groups on unit-record equipment, after a brief survey of the lesson, answer the questions and go on to Lesson 14.

1. Why is the sorting of information into sequential order necessary?
2. How can you get a deck of cards sorted by some numeric field?
3. What differences are apparent when sorting with some recording medium other than cards?
4. What is a *control field*?
5. What is meant by a *control break*?
6. What control level indicators are available in **RPG** to detect changes in control fields?
7. When three control levels are used, such as L1, L2, and L3, in what order should the control fields in the data deck be sorted?
8. What is the difference in the use of an L-indicator at *total-time* from that used at *detail-time*?
9. Why do control group totals need to be reset?
10. Give several different ways to reset a control group total to zero.

ANSWERS

1. So that the computer can process all the records for a given report by bringing them into memory as needed, line by line, rather than all at one time, or at random.
2. By using the IBM Ø82 or Ø83 sorter, which is the usual method in a punch card installation; by using the computer for reading the entire deck, rearranging the cards in memory, and punching out a new deck, which is not often done because of memory limitations; or by hand, when needed for only a small volume of cards. When magnetic tape or disk is available, card data may be temporarily stored on that medium, then sorted by a utility program and placed onto another tape or disk, to be used in its rearranged condition without punching a new deck.
3. Large volumes of data can be sorted and used without the original deck becoming shuffled; it is usually much faster and much less prone to operator error.
4. A key field on the data record, used for control group identification and for arranging the records into sequential order.
5. A change in the control field, indicating the end of one group and the beginning of another.
6. L-indicators: L1, L2, . . ., L9.
7. By sublevel under L1 first, if any, then by L1 field, L2 field, and L3 field.
8. During total-time operations, data fields available are from the previous group, and the L-indicator is usually used to produce totals for that group. During detail-time operations, the L-indicator is *on* only for the first card following the control break, and is usually used to select fields for group indication or for resetting control totals.
9. Because otherwise the totals for one group will be added to those from previous groups.
10. By using "blank-after" on the OUTPUT-FORMAT form; by a MOVE or a MOVEL of the exact number of zeros to the total field; by a Z-ADD or Z-SUB of a zero to the total field; by a SUB operation, which causes the field to be subtracted from itself.

Lesson 13   Sorting for Control Groups

The method of handling punch card information on a computer is to get all the records you need for the lines of the report into the memory, one behind the other, in sequential order as they are needed. When preparing a bill to send to Mr. Jones, for example, you need to have all the transaction cards for him together so that his statement is completed before you go on to do Mr. Jordan's. It would be difficult to back up to find Mr. Jones' printed report to add something to it later! All of one group of information should be *together* before the report is made. *Sorting* is done to get the records into these groups.

Sorting is the process of grouping records into numeric or alphameric sequence, according to some key classification field on the record, called a *control field*. In some cases, this may be an account number, or, in others, an alphabetic name. Sorting may be done in either ascending or descending order, on either numeric or alphameric fields. Sorting not only puts records into sequential order by these key fields, but forms *control groups*, all the records located together that have the same control field value. A control field may be the account number, for example, with each control *group* having a variable number of transactions in it for that account number.

Sorting with punch cards is often done using the IBM Ø83 sorter, shown in Figure 13-1, or the older IBM Ø82. Cards are sorted 1 column at a time, at a speed of either 1ØØØ or 600 cards per minute on those machines, respectively. Numeric sorting is usually done by the *reverse-digit method*, which uses the field, one column per pass, from the right-most low-order position, to the left-most high-order position. After each pass through the machine, the cards are collected from the many pockets in order and are placed back into the feed hopper for the next pass. Control fields of length 9 require nine passes before being in numeric sequence. When alphabetic sorting is done, the same method is used, but *two* passes are usually required for each column of the field—one for the numeric portion and one for the zone portion—so that more time is needed to sort alphameric fields than numeric ones.

Since card sorting on the mechanical unit-record sorters requires much card handling and time, and full operator attention, sorting with large data files is usually done by using magnetic tape or disk, when available, instead of cards. When tape is used, the cards themselves are not rearranged. The information is recorded on tape in the order in which the cards occur, and the sorting, usually done by a *utility program*, produces another tape, with the records in sequence. When a sorted card deck is needed, it is punched at the end of the tape sort, since the input deck remains in its original order.

Control level indicators, called L1, L2, . . ., L9, are available in RPG for assignment to control fields. Up to nine control fields can be specified on any given program. Columns 59-6Ø of the INPUT form are used to make the assignment, giving the L-indicator alongside the name of the control field. In the example given by

				Record Identification Codes																Field Location				Field Name		Control Level (L1-L9)	Matching Fields or Chaining Fields	Field-Record Relation
					1				2				3															
Sequence	Number (1-N)	Option (O)	Resulting Indicator	Position	Not (N)	C/Z/D	Character	Position	Not (N)	C/Z/D	Character	Position	Not (N)	C/Z/D	Character	Stacker Select	Packed (P)	From	To	Decimal Positions								
																	1	9Ø		SSNUM		L1		
																	11	3Ø		NAME				
																	35	4Ø	2	AMT				

183

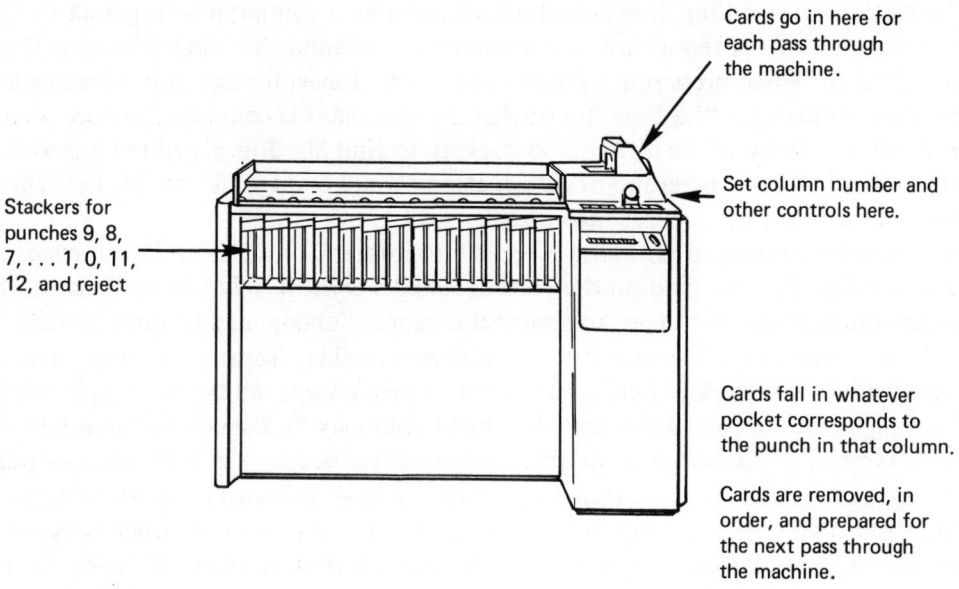

Cards go in here for
each pass through
the machine.

Stackers for
punches 9, 8,
7, . . . 1, 0, 11,
12, and reject

Set column number and
other controls here.

Cards fall in whatever
pocket corresponds to
the punch in that column.

Cards are removed, in
order, and prepared for
the next pass through
the machine.

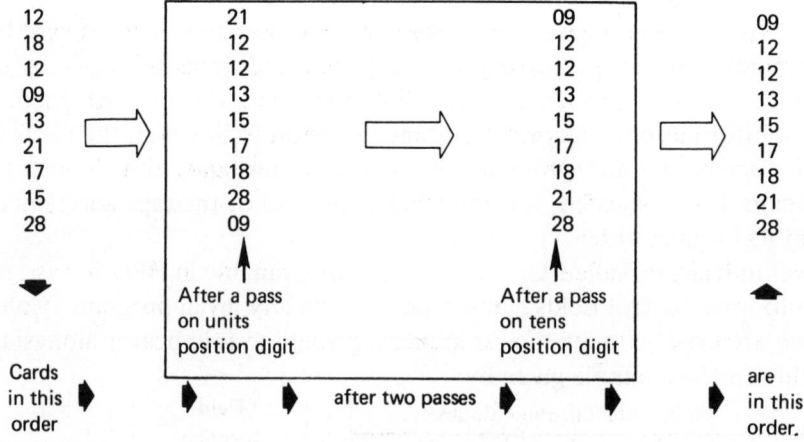

	12		21		09		09
	18		12		12		12
	12		12		12		12
	09		13		13		13
	13		15		15		15
	21		17		17		17
	17		18		18		18
	15		28		21		21
	28		09		28		28

After a pass
on units
position digit

After a pass
on tens
position digit

Cards
in this
order

after two passes

are
in this
order.

FIG. 13-1   The IBM Ø83 sorter. (Courtesy of International Business Machines
Corporation.)

L1 is assigned to the field **SSNUM**, causing the information from that field to be saved during processing so that it can be compared from one card to the next. This is done for the purpose of detecting a change in the contents of the field, meaning the *end* of one control group and the *beginning* of the next. A *control break* is said to occur when this change is detected. It causes the assigned L-indicator, and all lower L-indicators, to go *on* at the detection of the change, so that special action may be taken by the program. At a control break, a discount rate or interest charge, for example, may be applied to the total from the previous group, then printed out before going on to the next group.

More than one field may be used for the same level of control, by using what is called a *split-control field*. If a control field should be needed on an area location, for example, that is defined by the fields **CTY** and **STATE**, the coding given by

Position	Position	Position	From	To	Decimal Positions	Field Name	Control Level (L1-L9)
			1	20		NAME	
			21	40		ADDR	
			41	50		CTY	L1
			51	60		STATE	L1
			61	65		ZIP	
			66	70	2	BAL	

will assign control level indicator L1 to the two fields; it then performs as though both of these fields were actually one field, and will detect a change in either of them. All the fields to be used in a split manner must be of the same mode, and must not be listed with other intervening control levels given on the **INPUT** form. See your reference manual for several other rules concerning split-control levels if you intend to use them in any way other than what is shown here. It is more common to see two *different* control levels assigned to different fields, such as an L1 to a department number field, and an L2 to a branch number field, so that separate group totals may be obtained, one by department only, then one by branch. You need not be concerned with more than one control level at this time.

In doing comparisons for a control break, each value in the control field is compared to the one on the card in front of it, except for the first card in the data deck. The first card has its control field value compared to zeros, if the control field is defined as numeric, or to blanks, if the control field is defined as alphameric. If the control field on the first card is not itself zero or blank, L1 is turned *on*—even on the *first* card of the *first* control group. The L1 indicator remains on through one detail-time cycle, and is usually used to print the group heading material as well as the first detail line for that group. It is turned *off*, however, after one pass through detail-time operations, making it effective only once for each control group—on the *first* card of the group.

PROBLEM DEFINITION: *Class lists should be printed, with each class on a different page. Records are sorted by course number, which consists of three fields, named* **ID**, **NUM**, *and* **SEC**. *Input fields for the program are shown in Figure 13-2.*

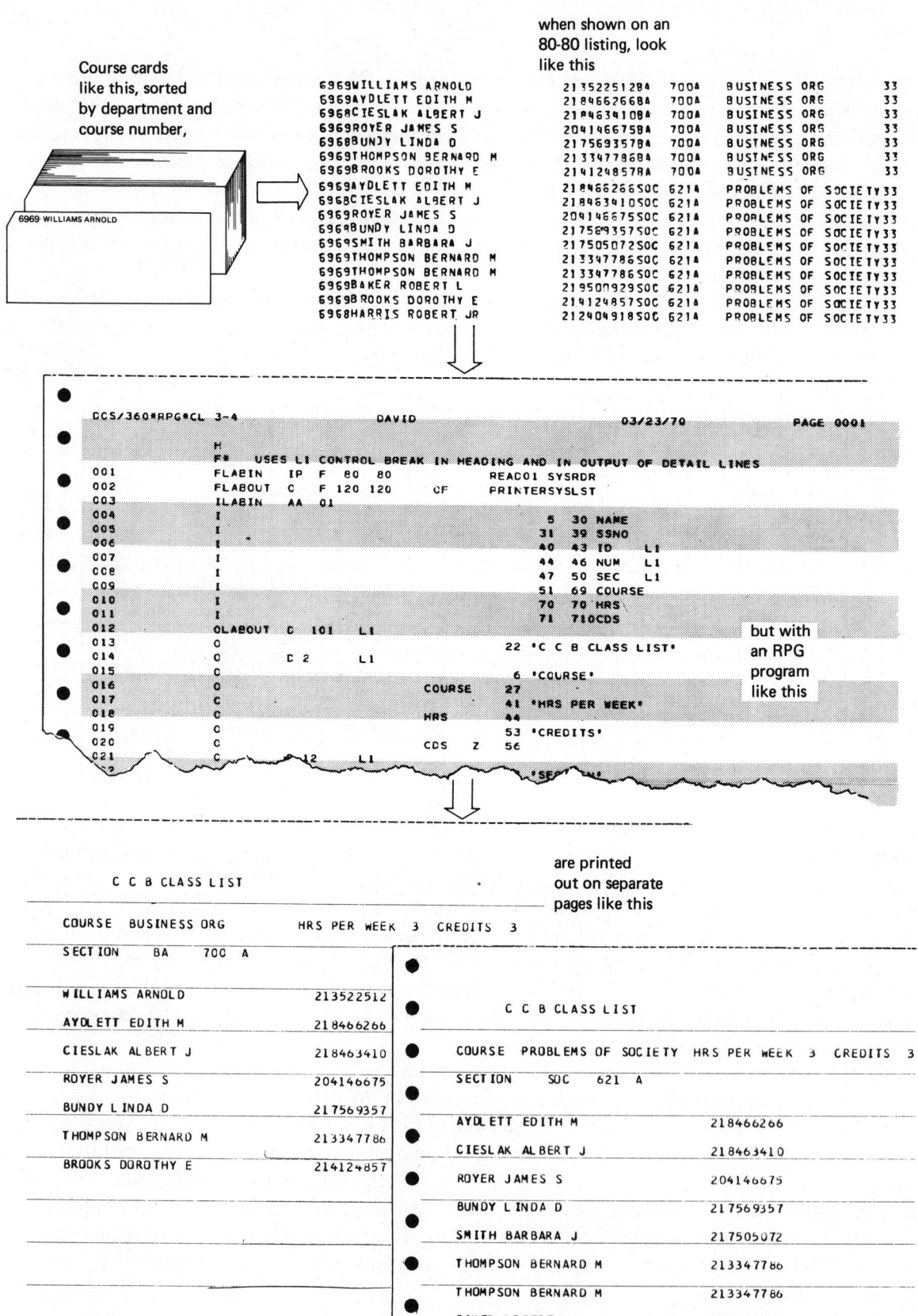

FIG. 13-2 Class list program DAVID—IBM SYSTEM/360, DOS.

Since the program should produce each class list on a separate page, a control level indicator must be used to cause a control break at a change in any of the three fields named. Indicator L1 will be assigned to all three fields, in what is called a split-control field, as given by:

Sequence	Number (1-N)	Option (O)	Resulting Indic	Position	Not (N)	C/Z/D	Character	Position	Not (N)	C/Z/D	Character	Position	Not (N)	C/Z/D	Character	Stacker Select	Packed (P)	From	To	Decimal Positions	Field Name	Control Level (L1-L9)	Matching Fields or Chaining Fields	Field-Record Relation	P
																		5	30		NAME				
																		31	39		SSNO				
																		40	43		ID	L1			
																		44	46		NUM	L1			
																		47	50		SEC	L1			
																		51	69		COURSE				
																		70	70		HRS				
																		71	71	0	CDS				

Notice that some information on the data card is not used in this program, and is not defined on the INPUT form.

Recall that both heading lines, coded by an **H** in column 15 of the OUTPUT-FORMAT form, and detail lines, coded by a **D**, are both performed by RPG during detail-time operations. When heading lines are printed for a control group, they often contain variable information from that group, and are usually *not* considered the same as heading lines produced by **1P OR OF**. On the program, named **DAVID** and given in Figure 13-2, you will notice that group heading lines are coded with a **D**, not an **H**, on the OUTPUT-FORMAT form. Although either **D** or **H** would be acceptable to the RPG programming system, better documentation is accomplished by using a **D**, since the lines contain variable information brought in from a card at the detail-time input cycle. Your particular installation may have a specific standard or custom concerning this that you may wish to follow.

Program output is shown in Figure 13-2. You may notice that one student inadvertently has two course cards for the same course! If a course card is in the deck twice, the program will list it twice. A certain amount of checking on the validity of the data deck can be done by a computer program, but this program does no checking of that nature. You can see how important it is to have good control over the validity of input data at all times. You may also notice that the list would be easier to read if student names were in alphabetic order within each class, rather than by social security number. When a large number of students are enrolled in each class, some kind of order within the page is a necessity. A presorting of the data deck could accomplish that. If the deck were first sorted alphabetically by student name, next by class section, number, and ID, then order within each class list would result. When a level and sublevel of sortings are needed, they should be done in order from the inner level up through the outer level, just as the parentheses in an equation are resolved in an algebra problem.

One data file is often used for many different types of lists. The deck of course cards, for example, could be sorted in many different ways, to put the same information into many different forms. For the student, a list should contain his courses, preferably by department, but for the teacher, who perhaps has many different course responsibilities, another type of list would perhaps be better. Each course should be contained on a different page, and for each course, the names of students should be in alphabetic order. A variety of reports can be obtained by changing the arrangement of the data in one data file.

Totals are often needed for each control group. On a class list, for example, totals for the number of students in each class or for the number of courses for each teacher may be needed. This brings up a need for totals *other* than those required at the end of the job. Totals may often be needed at control breaks, which occur throughout the program. The RPG object program logic chart, in the Appendix, shows that the total-time operations can be done at certain times throughout the program other than at the last record, by having the proper L-indicator condition satisfied. In programs without any control groups, there is often no need for total-time operations at this point, but when control groups are used, total-time output is often used to print totals at the end of each group. The appropriate control level indicators are specified as a condition on the total line.

When an L-indicator is used on a detail-time operation, it refers to the first detail card of a given control group. This is *not* so for total-time operations! They refer, instead, to the previous control group, since at the detection of a control break, data fields for the next card have not yet been stored. When the L1 indicator goes on because of a change being detected in the control field, all data cards for the previous group are processed. Even though the indicator for the *next* card, which caused the control break, is already *on*, the L-indicators can be used to do the total-time operations for the *previous* group. To accomplish this, the programmer writes a total line on the OUTPUT-FORMAT form, with the appropriate L-indicator governing its printing. In some cases, he must also specify that the total is to be *cleared* after printing. In the example,

Line	Form Type	Filename	Type (H/D/T)	Stacker Select	Space Before	Space After	Skip Before	Skip After	Output Indicators And	And Not	Field Name	Zero Suppress (Z)	Blank After (B)	End Position in Output Record	Packed Field (P)	Con
0 1	o	REPORT	T		2				L1							
0 2	o										TOTAL		B	32		` , Ø . '
0 3	o															

an appropriate total for the previous group will be printed. The B, given in column 39 alongside the field name TOTAL, stands for "blank-after" and causes the total from the previous group to be cleared to zero immediately after its printing is finished.

Indicator L1 is used to control printing of the total for the *previous* group, before that field is again used as a total for the *next* group. Even though L1 is *on* for the detail-time heading printed for the first group, it does *not* cause total lines for the group *in front of the first group*—since there is not one there! The total-time operations are *bypassed* at the start of the job to avoid that, and are also bypassed in the event that a control group is specified for a given data record but never brought in! It is possible for even the LR output to be bypassed in that case.

In doing a job with totals for each control group, remember that the total must be reset, after use with one group, before being used for another. If you do not do this, the group 1 total may be accurate, but totals for group 2 and all those thereafter will contain *accumulated sums* for all groups up to that point, which is wrong! One way to reset the field is to use the "blank-after" option, by putting a B in column 39 of the OUTPUT-FORMAT form for that field. When used on alphameric fields, resetting is to blanks; on numeric fields, resetting is to zero. Since the printing for control totals is done at the bottom of each group, with resetting afterwards, the field is cleared for use by the next group. "Blank-after" can also be used to remove constants from certain lines of the report, after their first printing. Care must be taken, however, in using the "blank-after" feature. If the total should be output more than once in one program cycle, it must *not* be blanked on any except the last.

One disadvantage of the "blank-after" method of resetting is that it can be used only on fields that are to be output in some manner. Often a sum is obtained only for use in a further calculation, and is never itself output in any way. This total cannot be reset by "blank-after" since it is never listed on the OUTPUT-FORMAT form.

One way to reset a total, whether it is to be printed or not, is to use a MOVE or a MOVEL instruction. These instructions can be used to put the contents of any field into another, or to move a given constant into a field. The MOVE does its transfer by starting from the right-most position of the field; the MOVEL does its moving from the left. Decimal alignment is not done on either of these instructions. Fields up to 10 digits long may be cleared with either the MOVE or the MOVEL. The instruction

Line	Form Type	Control Lev.		And		And			Factor 1	Operation	Factor 2	Result Field	Field Length	Decimal Positio	Half Adjust (+
0 1	C									MOVE	00	TOTAL	2 0		
0 2	C														
0 3	C														

puts zeros into a field named TOTAL, length 2, 0 decimals. The MOVE instruction and its associated MOVEL do not use FACTOR 1 at all. Use FACTOR 2 to specify what is to be moved, and RESULT FACTOR to give the name of the receiving field. FACTOR 2 may either be a constant or the name of a field. The RESULT FACTOR must have a length specified, if not already defined, and must have decimal indication given if it is numeric and not yet specified.

You must be extremely careful in the use of MOVE and MOVEL when resetting a field, in order to be sure that the entire length of the RESULT FACTOR field is cleared. The exact number of zeros needed to fill the field must be given, since the MOVE and MOVEL instructions are terminated when the end of either one of the fields is detected. If the receiving field is shorter, then not all the sending field is transferred; if the sending field is shorter, not all the receiving field is cleared. In the example,

Line	Form T.	Contro		And		And			Factor 1	Operation	Factor 2	Result Field	Field Length	Decimal Position	Half Adjust (+
0 1	C									MOVEL	000	TOTAL	5 0		
0 2	C														
0 3	C														

the field **TOTAL** will have its 3 left-most digits set to zeros, but its right-most digits remain unchanged. *The instruction should give a 5-digit zero under FACTOR 2 to clear the entire 5-digit field to zeros.*

The **Z-ADD** instruction is a better instruction to use to clear numeric fields, since it can do even those that are longer than 10 digits, and since you need not worry about field length at all. The **Z-ADD** causes the entire RESULT FIELD to be cleared to zero, after which the information specified by FACTOR 2 is added to it. By using a FACTOR 2 of zero, the necessary zero result is obtained. Since the **Z-ADD** instruction is an arithmetic one, it also aligns decimals before addition occurs, which the **MOVE** and **MOVEL** do *not* do. The instruction

Line	Form Type	Control Level	Not	And Not	And Not	Factor 1	Operation	Factor 2	Result Field	Field Length	Decimal Pos	Half Adjust
0 1	C						Z-ADD	Ø	TAMT	15	9	
0 2	C											
0 3	C											

will completely clear the 15-digit, 9-decimal-place field named **TAMT**. The instruction **Z-SUB** can be used in the same manner, the only difference being that FACTOR 2 is subtracted from the cleared RESULT FACTOR instead of being added. Another method to use to reset totals is to use the **SUB** instruction to subtract the field *from itself*, which places zero in the RESULT FIELD.

Instructions for resetting totals should be given in the program at the proper time. The resetting must not be done on every detail card, or the total will never be accumulated at all! The appropriate L-indicator can be used at detail-time calculation, as given by

Line	Form Type	Control Level	Not	And Not	And Not	Factor 1	Operation	Factor 2	Result Field	Field Length	Decimal Pos	Half Adjust
0 1	C		L1	Ø1			MOVE	000	TOT	3	0	
0 2	C		Ø1		1		ADD	TOT	TOT			
0 3	C											
0 4	C											

to cause resetting to be done *only* on the first card of each group, just before the **ADD** instruction is done. For all remaining cards in the control group, the L1 indicator is *off*, and the **MOVE** does not get executed again until the beginning of the *next* group.

PROBLEM DEFINITION: *Write a program to prepare a list of insurance premium amounts, giving the number in each group. The input data file is sorted in ascending order on the control field named* **PREM**. *For each premium group, the name, department, amount, and premium value for each person should be given. A total of the number of cards in each group is needed. Field descriptions are given in Figure 13-3.*

Since the list is to contain all premium types, separate pages are not needed for each type. Spacing, rather than skipping, will therefore be done at each control break. The total field, **CNTR**, will be reset by a **MOVE** instruction, using exactly the same number of zeros as the

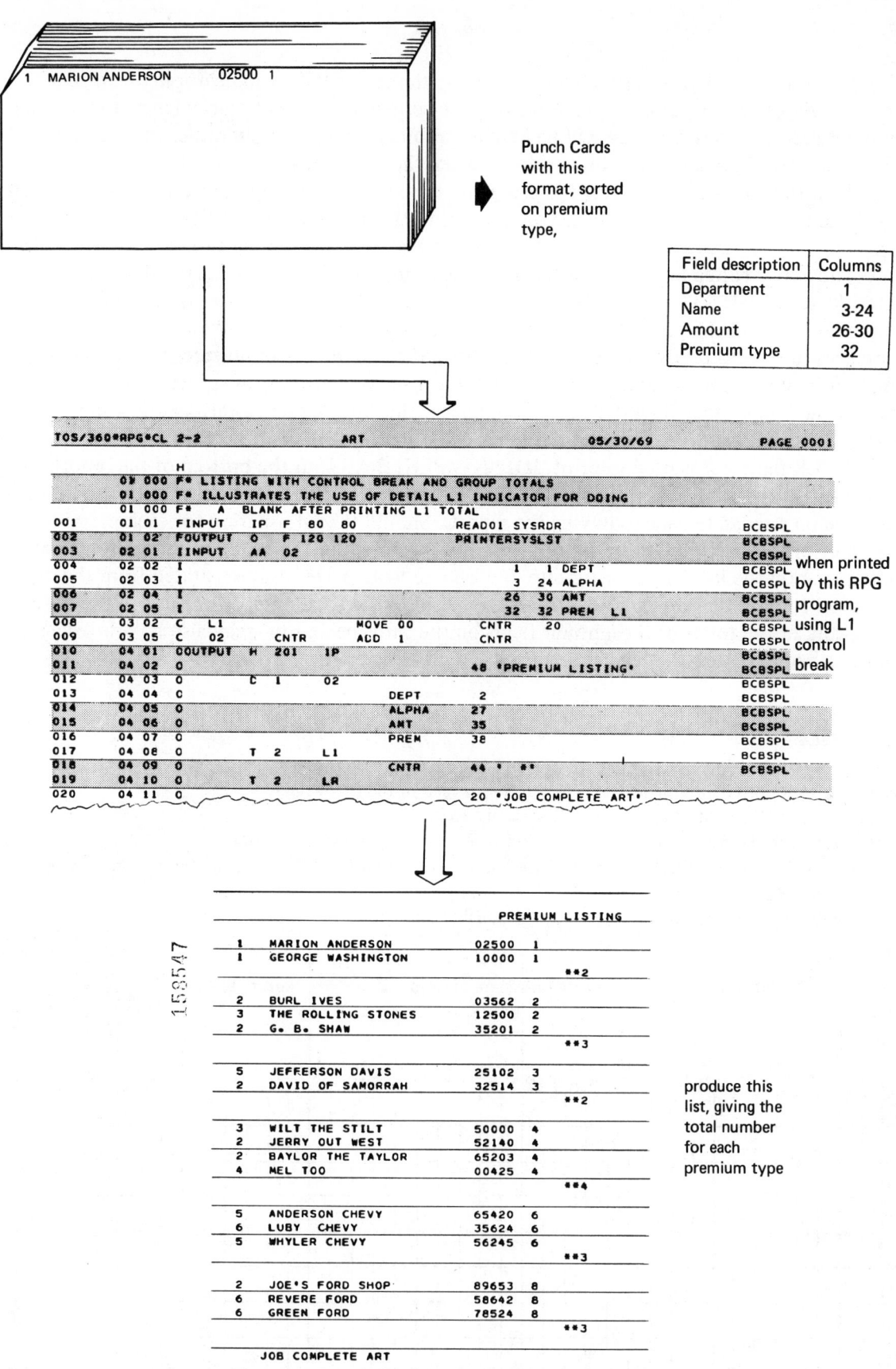

FIG. 13-3 Premium listing program ART with group totals—IBM SYSTEM/36∅, TOS.

191

length of the field. This resetting will be done by the use of the L1 indicator at *detail-time*, when it will be *on* for the first card following the control break. For convenience, the information between columns 3 and 24 will be handled as one alphameric field rather than separate ones. An end-of-job message will be printed when the data cards are all used.

The program, named **ART** for the programmer's name, is given in Figure 13-3. Calculation is done on indicator $\emptyset2$. You can see on the output sheet, also shown in Figure 13-3, that the total number of cards for each **PREM** group is slightly offset to the right for easy reading. Its value, however, edited to print an asterisk beside it on the right for emphasis, instead has asterisks to the left! This illustrates the two different purposes of the asterisk in an edit word— in the *body*, for check protection, and in the *expansion*, for emphasis. What was intended for emphasis turns out to be check protection! Since the edit word had no zero-suppress-stop digit in the body, and no status portion at all, the asterisk in the edit word was considered a part of the body rather than the expansion; hence, check-protecting asterisks fill in all unused positions to the left of the value of the field.

The LR indicator is used to print 'JOB COMPLETE ART' at the bottom of the report. In this case, the message is on the same page as the report. In some cases, however, it should instead be on a separate page following the report. Should the information for each premium group be on a separate page for distribution, for example, the end-of-job message should surely not appear on the list for the last group, but on a separate page easily separated from the distribution copies. Certain *batch-control-totals*—such as the total number of cards in the batch being run, or the totals of the amount fields on the cards being run—may also be printed at the end of a run to ensure that all cards for that batch are present.

EXERCISES

1. Give instructions on the **CALCULATION** form for each of the following:
   (a) Initialize the field **AMT**, length 7, 2 decimals, to $\emptyset$.
   (b) Initialize the field **BAL**, length 12, 4 decimals, to zero by using the **Z-ADD**.
   (c) Initialize the field **SUM**, length 10, 2 decimals, to zero by using a **MOVE** to do the right-most 6 digits and a **MOVEL** to do the left-most 6.
   (d) Initialize the field **PROD**, length 15, 9 decimals, to 1.

2. Give specifications on the INPUT form to do each of the following:

    (a) Specify the field **ACCT**, columns 1-6, alphameric mode, as an L1 control field.

    (b) Specify the fields **SUB** and **MAIN** as split-control field, level L1, columns 1-5 and 15-2∅, respectively.

    (c) Specify the fields **BRANCH**, **DEPT**, and **SNUM**, respectively, as L3, L2, and L1 control fields, with columns 1-8, 9-12, and 78-8∅, respectively.

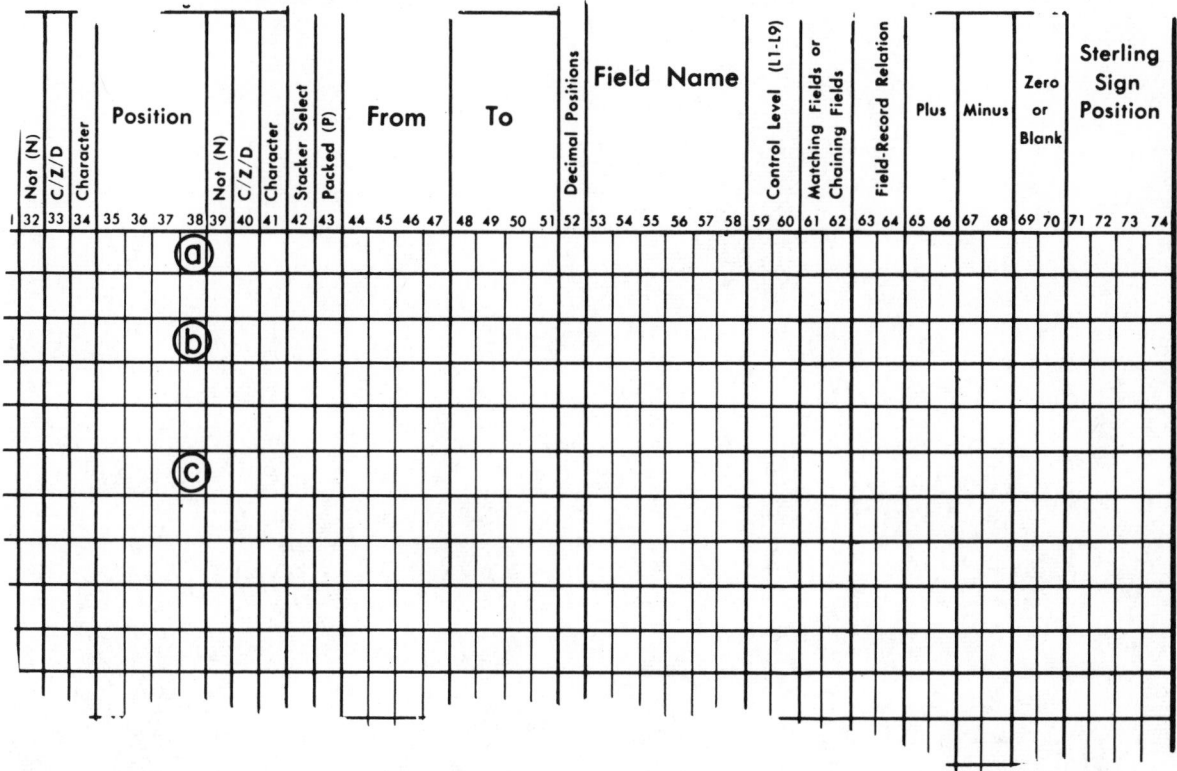

3. Give sorting instructions to get a deck of course cards into order for a room assignment list. The cards should be ready to use for a list that would give, for each room number, the names of the courses, by department, that meet in that room, with the students listed alphabetically within each course.

_____

_____

_____

Lesson 14

CONTROL LEVEL CALCULATIONS

You will learn the logic of control level calculations, and how to use the LØ indicator and the **SETON, SETOF** *instructions.*

The following questions summarize the lesson. After you study the logic of the RPG fixed-program cycle as discussed in this lesson, and can answer the following questions correctly, go on to Lesson 15.

1. What is the purpose of the LØ indicator?
2. What happens to a record for which no control levels are specified if it occurs in the middle of a control field group?
3. What are meant by minor, intermediate, major, and final totals, and to what do they correspond in RPG?
4. How is *total-transfer* used to reduce execution time in a program when several control levels are in use?
5. Under what conditions should you use an *L-indicator* for headings rather than the *header card indicator* or the *1P indicator*?
6. How are skipping and spacing an **OR** line executed?
7. Explain how overflow lines are handled in RPG.
8. What is meant by *run-in time*?
9. Why is it necessary to have the **SETON** and **SETOF** instructions in RPG?
10. How can an indicator be used to prevent a job from running if its header card is missing?

ANSWERS

1. To allow control level calculations at a time when no control breaks have occurred. The use of L∅ can put an instruction with total-time calculations rather than with detail-time ones.
2. It will be processed immediately, without affecting the setting of the control level indicator from the previous card type.
3. *Minor* is the "lower"-level total, *intermediate* the next level, and *major* a still higher level, in a typical three-level job. The final total is given at the end of the job, and is usually the total of all the major totals.
4. Rather than have an addition line for each level of total on each record, only *one* total field is accumulated for that level. Just before it is printed and reset, it is transferred, by adding it into the sum for the next higher level.
5. Should you wish output for each control group to be on a separate page, you would need to use the L-indicator to initiate the printing and skipping at the change in the control field. Should you only need headings on the top of each page or when a page is full, you may use **1P** and **OF** in an *or* condition. If those headings are from a heading card, however, you must use the indicator that brought it in rather than the 1P indicator.
6. By putting **OR** on the line, spacing and skipping are handled as a unit, so if you want spacing different from the line above, give the skipping again also. If you want skipping different from the line above, give the spacing again also.
7. The detection of channel 12, during printing of detail lines, causes the OF indicator to be turned *on* after detail printing is complete; otherwise it is turned *off* then. The detection of channel 12 during printing of total lines, which occurs later in the program cycle, will cause the **OF** indicator to be turned *on following* total-time printing, if it is not already on because of detail line overflow detection. If, after total-time printing is completed, the OF indicator is *on* from either of the two printing times, and if the OF indicator is used on any lines in the file referring to the printer, overflow-time output will be done, with those OF lines specified as total lines being done *before* those given as detail lines.
8. The execution of the **RPG** object program before processing of the first input record. Fields are set to zeros or blanks, indicators for those fields and for 1P and L∅ are turned *on*, all others are turned *off*.
9. Because you may wish to use them for intricate control in the program. Certain indicators do *not* turn *on* and *off* automatically; you may cause them to go *on* at the detection of a certain condition, then you may have to turn them *off*, since otherwise they may stay *on* even after that condition is no longer present.
10. By having the header card turn *on* some indicator, which, when *off*, causes a halt. The *off* condition, set at run-in, will be present unless the header card changes it to *on*.

Calculations and output are specified in an **RPG** program at one of two distinctly different times: at *detail-time*, or at *total-time*. The circular logic chart, shown in Figure 14-1, and the RPG object program logic chart, in the Appendix, give the sequence of these operations. The heading and the detail lines specified by an **H** and **D**, respectively, in column 15 on the **OUT-PUT-FORMAT** form are both a part of detail-time output. Lines specified by a **T** are located in total-time output. Calculations using only the indicators in columns 9-11, 12-14, and 15-17, with columns 7 and 8 of the **CALCULATION** form left blank, are placed with the detail-time calculations; those, however, with indicators LØ, L1-L9, or LR given in columns 7 and 8, even though other indicators may also appear in columns 9-17, are placed with total-time calculations. Notice the distinctly different locations of detail-time and total-time on the **RPG** logic chart. Learning these in their properly *executed* sequence, rather than their *form-specified* sequence, is vital to becoming a successful **RPG** programmer.

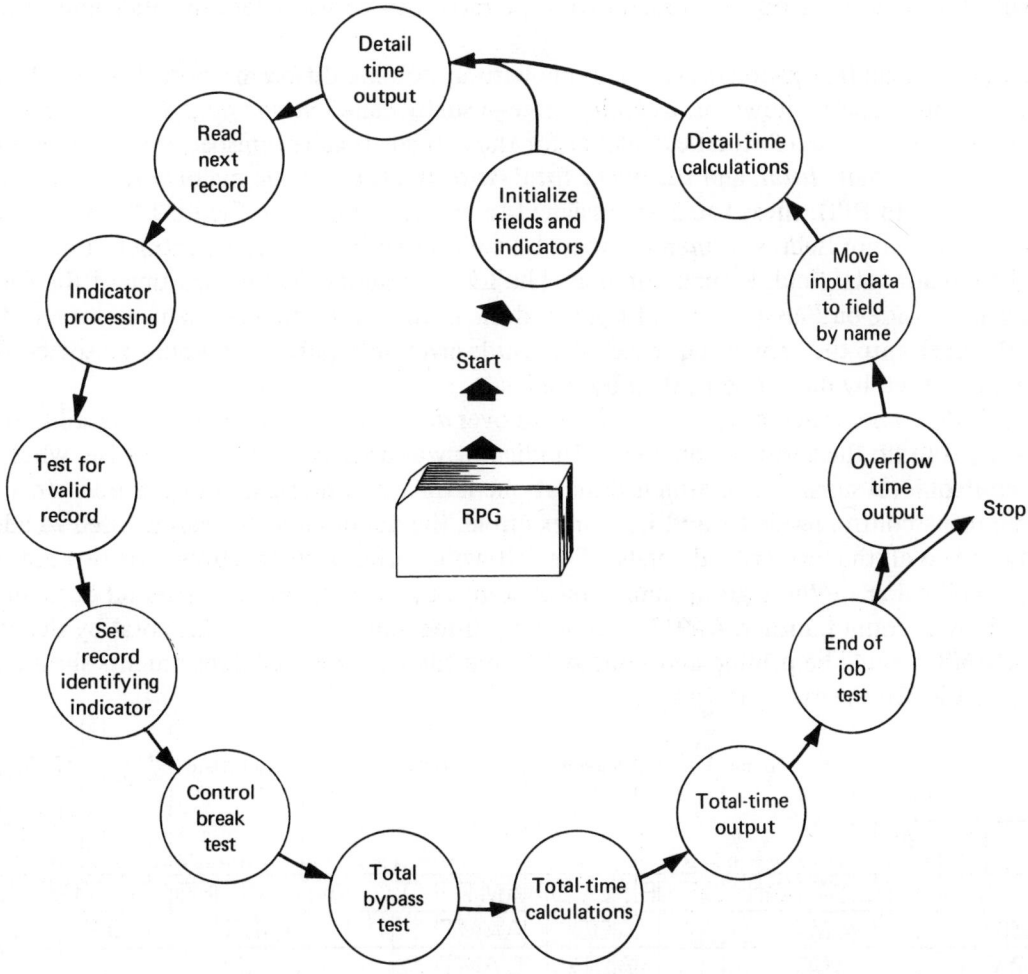

FIG. 14-1 Simplified RPG object program logic circle.

Control level indicators L1-L9 are designed to be used in recognizing control breaks. The LR indicator is designed to be used when the end-of-file card is detected. These indicators go *on* and *off* as conditions change in the program. Still another L-indicator, called L∅ or L-zero, is *on*, however, all the time; it can be used either at detail-time, or at total-time, operations even though no control break has occurred.

The L∅ indicator, when placed in columns 7 and 8 on any line of the CALCULATION form, causes it to be placed with the total-time calculations, rather than with the detail-time ones. It may then be used there to set on or off certain indicators, reset fields to zero, or transfer certain fields before printing. It can be used to perform total-time calculations on a card at a time when the *next* card indicator is already on, but the *previous* card fields are still available. Much of the intricate problem solving that can be done with the RPG programming system is based on use of the L∅ indicator.

When doing jobs with control groups, records *without* control group specification are permitted in the deck, such as the date header card. This type of card does *not* cause a control break; even though it is in the middle of a control group, it is handled without disturbing the comparisons that refer to the control fields. Since it is a noncontrol field, a comparison is not done, and L1 therefore remains *off*. It will stay *off* if the card following the noncontrol type is of the same control group as the card *before* it. The L∅ indicator, however, is *on*, and can be used with the indicator from the noncontrol type record to perform certain total-time operations.

You may recall that problems can be done with up to nine different control fields. Most routine business reports, however, use only three—usually called *minor field*, *intermediate field*, and *major field*. Each total calculated for those fields is called, respectively, the *minor total*, the *intermediate total*, and the *major total*, with the total of the major totals producing the *final total*. In RPG, these totals are assigned to levels, as shown in Figure 14-2, which has L1 assigned to minor field, salesman number; L2 to intermediate field, department number; and L3 to major total field, branch number. The LR corresponds to the printing of the final total. This "inside-out" assignment of fields is done in the same order as the necessary sorting to get the deck into the proper sequence. The cards given in Figure 14-2 would be sorted first by salesman, then by department, then by branch.

Recall that when calculating a sum of a field over *all* the cards in a deck, the detail indicator was used to do the addition, but the LR indicator was used to print it. Likewise, when doing control level sums, calculation is done at one level and printing at a higher one. In a problem using control levels L1 and L2, for example, the detail indicator can be used to add the amount to all the proper field totals. The following series of instructions, for *two* control levels, would calculate *three* group sums: by account, by department, and over all departments. The total by account number, **AAMT**, should be printed and reset at L1; the total by department, **DAMT**, should be printed and reset at L2; and the total over all departments should be printed at LR. In the example,

Form Ty	Control L₁		And		And		Factor 1	Operation	Factor 2	Result Field	Field Length	Decimal Positio	Half Adjust (H	Plus	Minus	Bl			
		Not		Not		Not								High 1>2	Low 1<2	E 1			
6	7 8	9	10 11	12 13 14	15 16 17	18 19 20 21 22 23 24 25 26 27	28 29 30 31	32 33 34 35 36 37 38 39 40 41 42	43 44 45 46 47 48	49 50 51	52	53	54 55	56 57	5
C	✱					DO ADDITION OF FIELD AMT		TO ALL NEEDED TOTALS								
C		∅1				AMT	ADD	AAMT	AAMT	82						
C		∅1				AMT	ADD	DAMT	DAMT	82						
C		∅1				AMT	ADD	FAMT	FAMT	82						
C																

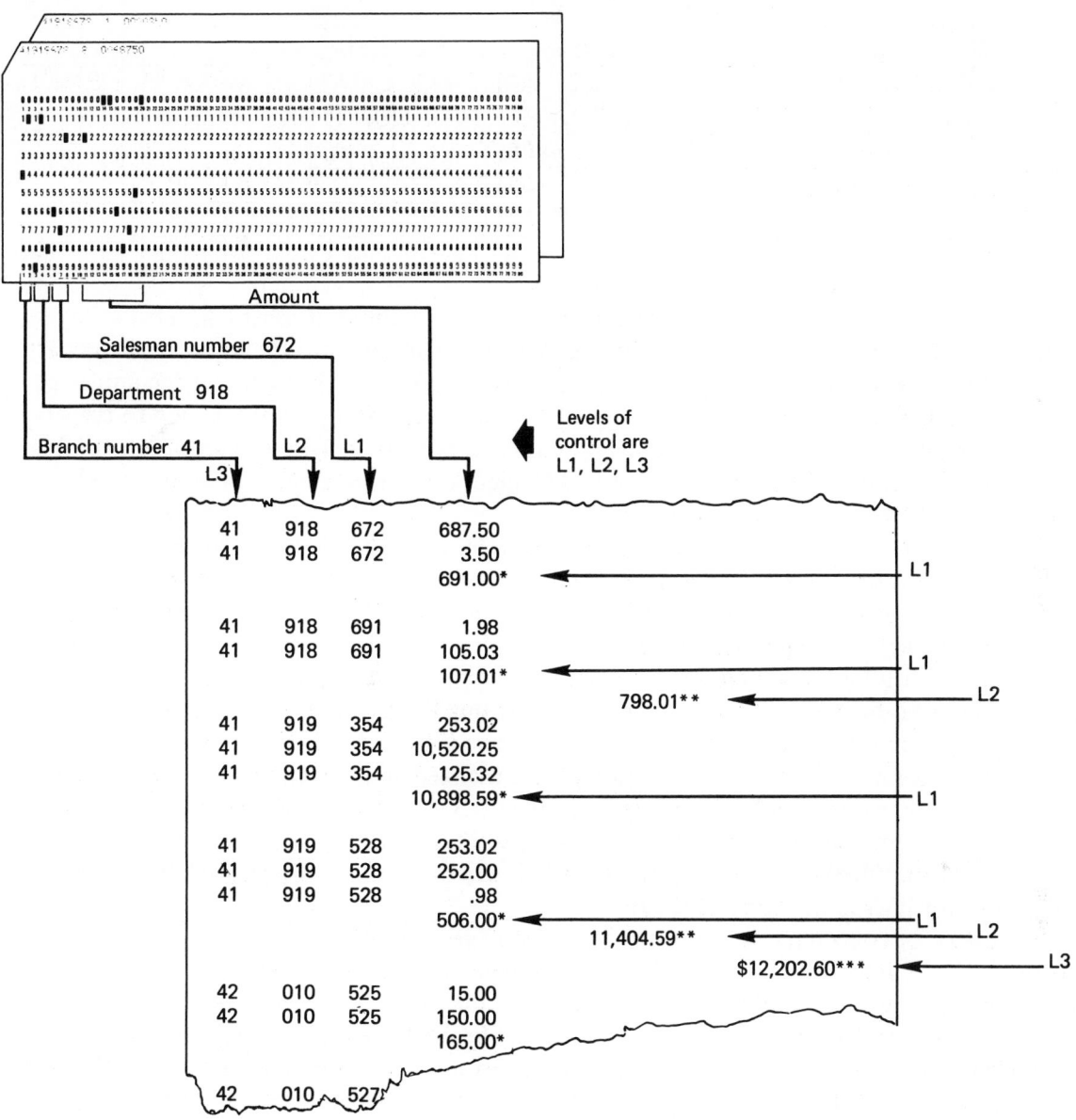

FIG. 14-2 Totals for three control levels.

each addition adds **AMT** to the proper total; notice that one more addition is required than the number of levels being handled by the job, and one more total—the one to be printed at LR—is also required.

The method of calculation using one addition for each total for each detail card is unnecessarily time consuming. A better way to calculate totals for several control levels is to use a *total-transfer* technique. The total by account number is accumulated by the instruction on the first line of coding, using the detail indicator. Before being printed, however, at indicator L1, its sum is *transferred* to the field for the total for the next *higher* level of control. In the example,

1	C	*	DO ADDITION OF FIELD AMT TO LOWEST GROUP LEVEL				
2	C	*	THEN USE TOTAL-TRANSFER AT CONTROL BREAKS				
3	C	01	AMT	ADD	AAMT	AAMT	82
4	C	L1	AAMT	ADD	DAMT	DAMT	82
5	C	L2	DAMT	ADD	FAMT	FAMT	82
6							

AAMT is the field that contains the total for the group by account number. At a break in account number, the total up to that point, **AAMT**, is transferred into the total for the department, **DAMT**. Notice that it is done not with a **MOVE** instruction, but with an accumulating **ADD** instruction, so that on successive account numbers, each group total is added to the sum of the entire group up to that point. Each time there is a break in a control group, its total is added into the total of the next higher level. The highest total, accumulated on one level lower, is printed at the LR indicator.

Note that one addition more than the number of levels in the job is still required, but that execution time is shortened since only *one* addition is done on each detail record, not several. By this method, calculations for each level are done only *once* for each group—and at one level lower than the level at which it is printed.

For a job with *two* control levels, such as an L1 total by account and an L2 total by department, *three* total-time output lines are needed, including the LR total for all departments. Skipping to a channel on the control tape may be done if these totals are needed on special places on the form. Each control total should be initialized *after* printing, *before* being used with the following group, either by being "blanked-after", or by having zeros put there immediately after the printing is done. Detail-time output, containing both headings and detail lines, usually specifies whatever skipping is needed, whether for a new page, or for positioning the printer for lines in the body of the report.

Headings for control levels can be programmed in several different ways. If no run-date is required, the 1P indicator, with the OF indicator in an *or* condition, may be used. If a run-date card is required, its indicator may be used instead of the 1P indicator. Whether a run-date is required or not, the control level indicator itself can be used. When deciding which of these methods to use, you need to know whether the report needs to be separated by control group, for distribution to different places. If so, it should be put on separate pages. The heading, using a date card indicator 99, given by

Line	Form Type	Filename	Type (H/D/T)	Stacker Select	Space Before	Space After	Skip Before	Skip After	Output Indicators And	And	Field Name	Zero Suppress (Z)	Blank After (B)	End Position in Output Record	Packed Field (P)
0 1	O	REPORT	H		3		01		99						
0 2	O		OR						OF						
0 3	O														
0 4	O														

should, in most cases, *not* be used, since skipping is then done only when a date card is detected, or after a form has been completely filled. The heading lines given by

	3 4 5	6	7 8 9 10 11 12 13 14	15 16 17	18	19 20	21 22	23	24 25	26	27 28	29	30 31	32 33 34 35 36 37	38	39	40 41 42 43	44	45 46 47 48 49 50 51 52 5
	0 1	o	REPORT	H		3Ø1			L1										
	0 2	o	OR						OFNL1										

however, cause skipping to a new page every time there is an **L1** control break, and will put each account group on a separate page. If indicators L1 and OF should both be *on* at the same time, the use of **L1 OR OF** to control the line would cause it to be printed twice! To prevent that, **NL1** with **OF** should be used in an *and* condition, on the same line, instead of the overflow indicator alone.

Overflow lines, for most **RPG** implementations, are not printed during the routine detail-time or total-time output, but are printed in a separate operation called *overflow-time* output. The **OF** indicator is associated with channel 12 on the forms control tape, or on IBM SYSTEM/3, with line 6Ø, or whatever line the **LINE COUNTER** form has specified. The OF indicator does not go *on* the instant a hole in channel 12, or the appropriate line, is detected. Even though the channel or line may be sensed during detail-time printing, all lines in that pass are completed before the OF indicator goes on; if it is *not* sensed during the pass, OF goes off. If, during the next total-time output, channel 12 is detected, if it was not already on, it then goes on, at the end of the total-time output. At that time, if it is *not* the end of the job, the OF indicator is tested. If the OF indicator is *on*, and if lines involving OF are given on the **OUTPUT-FORMAT** form for that file, the program branches into a special routine to do the overflow printing. OF total-time lines are done before OF detail-time lines, with whatever skipping and spacing is specified for them. Even after overflow-time output is complete, the OF indicator stays *on* to be used, if needed, in detail-time calculations. It is not reset until the completion of the detail-time output of the next cycle, and is reset at that time conditional to new detection of channel 12 or the specified overflow line.

If OF is *on* from detection of channel 12, but the OF indicator is not given on some output line for that file, then an automatic skip to a new page occurs, on most implementations. Since others do not have this automatic skipping to a new page, however, it is better to get in the habit of specifying the skip in your program and not relying on the **RPG** generator to do it for you.

Remember that any lines specified by an *or* condition without any spacing or skipping use that given on the previous line. If *either* spacing or skipping is given, *both* must be given, since if either one or the other is specified on a line, none of the previous line will be used. For example, the heading line given by

	3 4 5	6	7 8 9 10 11 12 13 14	15 16 17	18	19 20	21 22	23	24 25	26	27 28	29	30 31	32 33 34 35 36 37	38	39	40 41 42 43	44	45 46 47 48 49 50 51 5
	0 1	o		H		3Ø1			L1										
	0 2	o	OR	2					OFNL1										
	0 3	o																	
	0 4	o																	

will *not*, on the OF indicator, skip to channel 1 as specified on the previous line; since spacing is given, skipping must also be given if you want it to be done.

The execution of an object program prior to detail processing of the first card is called *run-in*. At this time, numeric fields are set to zero and all alphanumeric ones are set to blanks. Indicator 1P is turned *on*, and indicators Ø1-99 are turned *off*. The 1P indicator is designed specifically for the printing of headings that are to be printed only at run-in time, but never again. Since indicators Ø1-99 are *off* then, they can also be used, in a *not*-indicator condition, at run-in time. The line given by

	Form	Filename	Type (H/D/T)	Stacker Select	Before	After	Before	After	Not	And	Not	And	Not	Field Name	Zero Suppress	Blank After (B)	End Position in Output Record	Packed Field (P)	Constant
1	o	REPORT	H			3Ø1				N25									
2	o																1Ø		'ABC CO.'
3	o		H		2					1P									
4	o																26		'SINCE 1853'
5	o																		
6	o																		

will produce both lines of output before any detail cards are read. Afterwards, the 1P indicator automatically goes *off*. The other indicator, however, does not have *anything* done to it automatically, and unless you cause it to be turned *on*, the constant 'ABC CO.' will continue to print during every pass of detail-time output! The **SETON** instruction may be used to turn on indicator 25, causing the constant to be suppressed thereafter.

The **SETON** instruction, and its corresponding **SETOF**, is given in columns 28-32 of the **CALCULATION** form. Each time it is used it can apply to one, two, or three indicators in one instruction, with indicator numbers given in columns 54 and 55, 56 and 57, and 58 and 59, as needed. FACTOR 1, FACTOR 2, and RESULT FIELD should not be given. The **SETON** turns the indicators *on*, and the **SETOF** turns them *off*. Any indicator may be turned on or off, and it usually retains the setting given unless you change it. Indicator LØ, for example, is always on, as is indicator ØØ, which is available only on some implementations. Certain ones, however, such as the record-type indicators, L1-L9, LR, H1 or H2, and OF, are automatically turned on and off at certain times by the RPG program logic; caution against unnecessary use of them is recommended. If LR should be set *on*, for example, during total-time calculations, processing will terminate after LR output, with no restart possible. If H1 or H2 are set *on* and not set *off* again, processing is terminated at the end of the next detail-time output; restart, however, is possible. Note also that setting a control level indicator *on* does not set on all lower levels, as an automatic setting of them does.

Storage areas for control field comparisons are set to zeros at run-in time. If the control field of the first card is zero, or in some cases, blank, it will be the same as the value stored at run-in, and *no* control break will occur as it should. The **SETON** instruction can be used to turn on indicator L1, but an instruction to do this must be deactivated after execution, so that it does not *continue* to set L1 on, *every* time through the program. Any of the indicators Ø1-99 that are not to be used in the program elsewhere may be used. In the example given by

Form Ty	Control L	Not	And Not	And Not	Factor 1	Operation	Factor 2	Result Field	Field Length	Decimal Pc	Half Adju	Cc High 1 > 2
C	N25					SETON						L1
C												

an L1 control break is created even though one did not occur. Normal output of the first control group headings will then occur. To prevent L1 from being set on at *every* detail-time calculation, however, indicator 25 must be turned *on* so that the instruction will not be executed again. The detail-time calculation given by

Control	Not	And Not	And Not		Operation					De Hc	1 > 2 1 < 2
C	N25				SETON						L1 25
C											

will not only set L1 on, but will prevent L1 from being set on in that manner again since it also sets on 25! Notice that two of three possible indicators are turned on at a time in this example.

The instructions for turning indicators *on* and *off* can be used for data control. For example, it is possible to verify that the date card is in its header position in front of the data deck, and if it is not, then halt. Assuming that the date card has indicator $\emptyset$5, the instructions given by

Form Typ	Control L	Not	And Not	And Not	ractor 1	Operatic	Factc 2	esult Field	Length	Decima	Half A	Com High 1 > 2 1
C		$\emptyset$5				SETON						95
C	N95					SETON						H1

will cause the computer to stop if the run-date card is not present. Since indicator 95 is *off* at run-in time, unless a date card with indicator $\emptyset$5 comes in to turn it on again, indicator H1 will go *on*, causing the computer system to halt. Once set *on*, indicator 95 will stay on throughout the entire job unless reset by the programmer.

The OF and L$\emptyset$ indicators can be used to produce a report with totals given on each page. The total for each page can be transferred into the final total just before it is reset to zero. If only detail lines are being printed, the channel 12 punch will be detected during detail-time output, and the OF indicator turned on. When that occurs, an **L$\emptyset$** *and* **OF** instruction during the following total-time calculation may be used to transfer it. Printing occurs at the following overflow-time output, whether the line is type T or type D on the OUTPUT-FORMAT form. The page total, when transferred in this manner, may be blanked after printing in order to reset it *before* the next page. Recall that several implementations have the overflow routine done *before* the test for the last record indicator instead of *after*; see your reference manual to determine when it is done on your implementation.

PROBLEM DEFINITION: *Write a program called* **PAGETOT** *to list detail sales information, giving totals by the page, as well as at the end of the job. The amount of sales is given in columns 3Ø-33 of the input record; the information from column 1 through column 29 should also be printed as one field. The record identification code is a D in column 8Ø.*

The job has only one type of detail card; select indicator 5Ø to be turned on. The problem has no control fields. Columns 3Ø-33 are given the name **AMT**; they will be summed for each page as **PTOT**, and for the job as **FTOT**. The instruction given by

accomplishes the transfer of page total into final total every time a page is full. After the page total is printed, it must be reset. This can be done by using the "blank-after" feature on the OUTPUT-FORMAT form. On the last page of the report, the job could end before the page is entirely full, meaning that OF may not be on to cause the total-transfer. The additional instruction

can be used to accomplish this before printing the final total on indicator LR. The source program run-sheet and the output it produced are shown in Figure 14-3.

This technique for doing a page total can also be used on programs involving control levels. The transfer of page total by **LØ** *and* **OF**, however, must be made to the appropriate *group* total instead of to the *final* total. The transfer for the partial page at the end of each group, when OF may not have occurred, must also be done at the appropriate control level indicator. For a job with page totals that are to be printed both on OF and an L-indicator, you will print the page total *not only* at OF, but at control level breaks as well. Do not attempt to set *on* the OF indicator to force page total to print from the OF line already established! Use an **OR L1** line instead. Overflow output is done *after* regular total-time output, and, at a break, the page total, done by OF, would appear *below* the control level total. An **L1** *and* **OF**, when used in an *and* condition, would then appear *below* all other total-time L1 lines *not* involving OF, regardless of its order on the OUTPUT-FORMAT form. Note, also, from the RPG logic chart for DOS RPG in the Appendix, that an **LR** *and* **OF** output line would never print at all, since the LR causes termination of the job before overflow-time output is done. Some implementations, however, do have overflow-time output done *before* the test for the last record.

```
              H
              *      PAGE TOTALS FOR LISTING - - LITTLE
001           FINPUT   IP  F  80  80                      READ40 SYSROR
002           FOUTPUT   O  F 120 120      OF              PRINTERSYSLST
003           IINPUT   NS  50  80 CD
004           I                                       1  29 ALL
005           I                                          30 332AMT
006           C  50          AMT      ADD PTOT      PTOT   62
007           CLO OF         PTOT     ADD FTOT      FTOT   62
008           CLRNOF         PTOT     ADD FTOT      FTOT
009           OOUTPUT   H 301     1P
010           O                                   45 'LISTING WITH PAGE TOTALS'
011           O         H  2      1P
012           O        OR 201     OF
013           O                                   35 'CARD CONTENTS'
014           O                                   46 'AMOUNT'
015           O         D  2       50
016           O                        ALL        30
017           O                        AMT        45 ' 0. '
018           O         T  2      OFNLR
019           O        OR         LR
020           O                        PTOT     B 46 ' , 0. *'
021           O                        PAGE     Z 30
022           O                                   25 'PAGE'
023           O         T  3      LR
024           O                        FTOT       47 ' , 0. **'
025           O                                   25 'TOTAL FOR JOB'
```

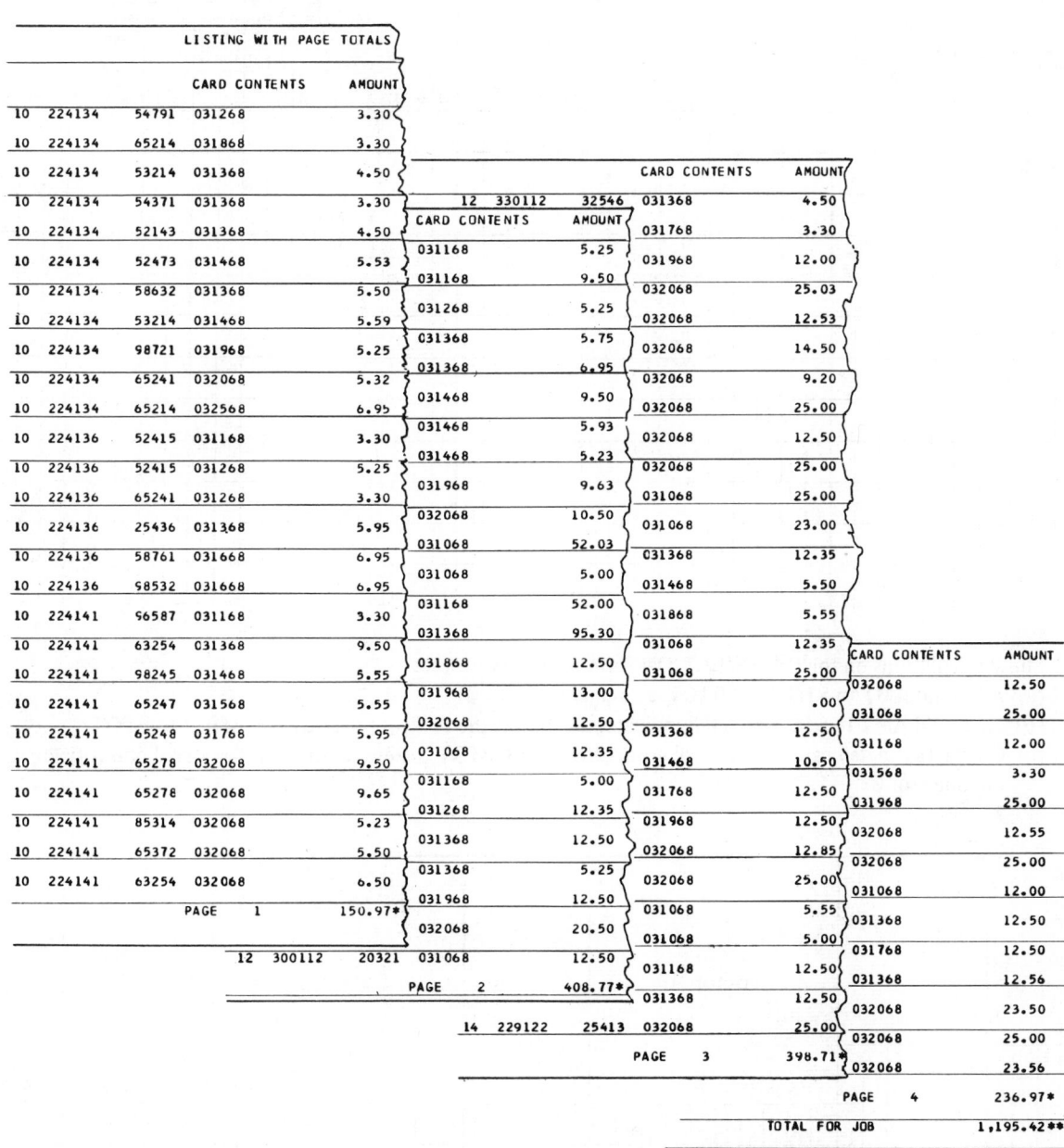

LISTING WITH PAGE TOTALS			
	CARD CONTENTS		AMOUNT
10 224134	54791	031268	3.30
10 224134	65214	031868	3.30
10 224134	53214	031368	4.50
10 224134	54371	031368	3.30
10 224134	52143	031368	4.50
10 224134	52473	031468	5.53
10 224134	58632	031368	5.50
10 224134	53214	031468	5.59
10 224134	98721	031968	5.25
10 224134	65241	032068	5.32
10 224134	65214	032568	6.95
10 224136	52415	031168	3.30
10 224136	52415	031268	5.25
10 224136	65241	031268	3.30
10 224136	25436	031368	5.95
10 224136	58761	031668	6.95
10 224136	98532	031668	6.95
10 224141	96587	031168	3.30
10 224141	63254	031368	9.50
10 224141	98245	031468	5.55
10 224141	65247	031568	5.55
10 224141	65248	031768	5.95
10 224141	65278	032068	9.50
10 224141	65278	032068	9.65
10 224141	85314	032068	5.23
10 224141	65372	032068	5.50
10 224141	63254	032068	6.50
PAGE 1			150.97*

FIG. 14-3 Program **PAGETOT** for page totals—IBM SYSTEM/36Ø, DOS.

EXERCISES

1. Use the **CALCULATION** form provided to do each of the following:
   (a) Set *on* indicator 17 at control break L1.
   (b) Set *off* indicator 99 when 95 is *on*.
   (c) Set *on* the 1P indicator when the header card, indicator 99, is *on*.
   (d) Set *on* the **1P** indicator during the processing of the first detail card of each L1 control group.
   (e) Set *on* indicator 29 at control break L1, then turn it *off* at the next detail-time calculation.

Line	Form Type	Control Level (L0-L9 LR)	Indicators And Not	And Not	And Not	Factor 1	Operation	Fa...	Decimal Positions	Half Adjust (H)	Plus	Minus	Zero or Blank	High 1>2	Low 1<2	Equal 1=2				
0 1 (a)	C																			
0 2	C																			
0 3 (b)	C																			
0 4	C																			
0 5 (c)	C																			
0 6	C																			
0 7 (d)	C																			
0 8	C																			
0 9 (e)	C																			
1 0	C																			
1 1	C																			
1 2	C																			

2. Show calculations on the **CALCULATION** form for each of these:
   (a) Add field **AMT** to **STOT** and **FTOT**, at detail indicator Ø1.
   (b) Add field **AMT** to **STOT** at detail indicator Ø1, but at the control break L1, transfer it to **FTOT**.
   (c) On the first detail card of a control group, initialize **GPTOT** to zero, then use it for a card-count field on indicator Ø1.

Line	Form Type	Control Level (L0-L9, LR)	Indicators And Not	And Not	And Not	Factor 1	Operation	Factor 2	Result Field	F L
0 1 (a)	C									
0 2	C									
0 3	C									

3	4	5	6	7	8	9	10	11	12	13	14	15	16	17	18	19	20	21	22	23	24	25	26	27	28	29	30	31	32	33	34	35	36	37	38	39	40	41	42	43	44	45	46	47	48	49
0	4	(b)	C																																											
0	5		C																																											
0	6		C																																											
0	7	(c)	C																																											
0	8		C																																											
0	9		C																																											
1	0		C																																											

3. Give specifications on the **OUTPUT-FORMAT** form provided, for each:

   (a) The heading 'EXETER CLEANERS' on every L1 control group or overflow, ending in print position 7∅, with each control group on a different page.

   (b) The heading 'J. K. MAGNIN'S FURRIER' on the first page only, ending in print position 50, and column headings for customer name, purchase date, and purchase value given on every page ending in print positions 2∅, 4∅, and 6∅, respectively.

   (c) The headings as shown on the printer spacing chart in Figure 3-6 for 'PIONEER SALES AND SERVICE', with both headings being placed on a new page every time the L1 control level on salesman name detects a new control group, or an overflow.

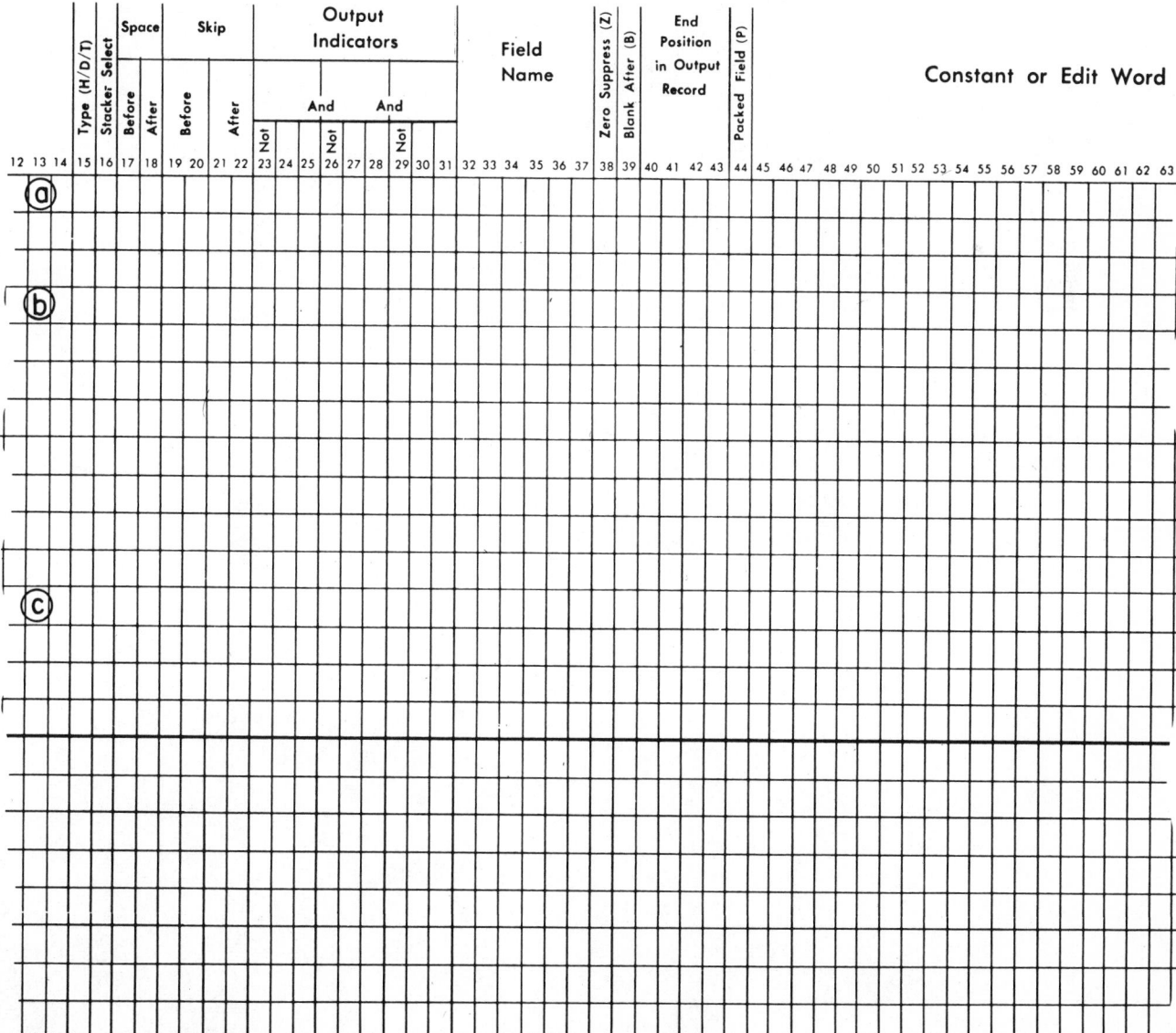

Lesson 15

A PRINTED REPORT WITH DETAIL AND GROUP LINES

You will learn to program either a detail-printed or a group-printed report.

The questions below summarize study of reports using control groups. If you have had previous experience with these types of reports, after answering the following questions, go on to the problems at the end of this section.

1. Compare a *group-printed* report to a *detail-printed* one.
2. How may a group-printed report be programmed?
3. What is meant by *group indication*?
4. How is group indication controlled by the programmer?
5. What is *output field selection* by indicator and how is it done?
6. What is the difference between *file-identification* line and *field-description* line on the OUTPUT-FORMAT form?
7. Why should the *off* condition of indicators $\emptyset$1-99 be used cautiously or with other *on* indicators on file-identification lines?
8. What is a *run-control header card* and how does it differ from a *job stream control card* or from a *run-date header card*?
9. Why is a run-control card sometimes called a programmed set-up switch?
10. How can you use the field-description line to reset the value of **PAGE** to start each new group with page $\emptyset\emptyset\emptyset$1?

ANSWERS

1. A *detail-printed report* includes a line for every transaction record, as well as group total lines, that may be required for the job. A *group-printed report*, however, does not give lines for each transaction, but only total lines, for some, perhaps all, control groups in the job.
2. By omitting specifications for all detail lines, or being sure that indicator conditions are not satisfied for those given so that no output will be produced.
3. Printing of certain information that is constant for the entire control group, only once on the *first* line of the group, and suppressing it on all other lines in that group.
4. By using an L-indicator at detail-time for field selection. It is *on* only for the card following the control break, and can be used for printing certain fields only at that time.
5. Selection of a field or constant to be printed by placing an indicator on the field-description line in columns 23-31. If the indicator condition is satisfied, the field or constant will print; otherwise, it will be suppressed.
6. *File-identification* gives specifications for one line or record to be output, and is identified by a valid character in column 15 of the **OUTPUT-FORMAT** specification form. Indicators given in columns 23-31 of that line refer to whether or not the entire line will be printed. *Field-description* allows the use of an indicator on a line with the field or constant, which, if the line is to be printed, controls whether or not that individual field or constant will be printed.
7. Because during run-in time, all fields are initialized to zero or blanks, and although indicators assigned to them will be turned *on*, those indicators from 01-99 that are not assigned will be *off* and can cause unwanted output from lines that are based only on an *off* condition.
8. It is a header card that changes the logic of the program to cause it to produce one of perhaps several alternate types of jobs. It is *not* the same as a job control card, which tells the operating system what you want to do during the run. Although it is placed in front of your data deck for the job just as a run-date card, it does not necessarily bring in any variable data as the date card does, and is used primarily to establish control over *what is to be done* during the program.
9. Because it sets up the program to do one of possibly several different jobs.
10. By placing an indicator on the line with the field named **PAGE** you do not control selection of it for output—it is always output when the file-condition line is satisfied. The indicator on the line with **PAGE** causes it to be *reset to zero* when that indicator condition is satisfied; 1 is automatically added to it before printing, resulting in resetting the printed value of **PAGE** to 0001.

Detail-printed reports list all or part of the information from each input record. Much of this information is exactly the same for a given control group. Control level fields, such as an account number or branch number, are the same for all the lines in that group and are repeated down the page through the entire group. If you were writing these columns by hand, you would probably write on just the first line and use ditto marks thereafter to show that they are the same as the previous line. To cause a field to be printed on the first line of a group, and to suppress it on all other lines of that group, is known as *group-indication*. Figure 15-1 shows a group-indicated report with three control levels.

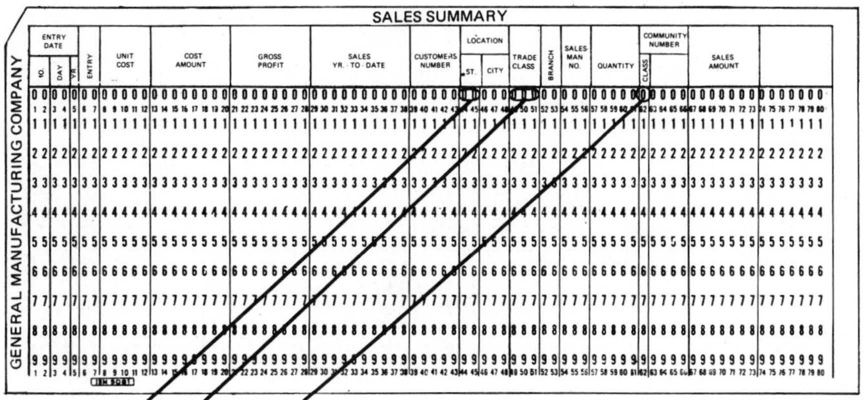

SALES BY STATE								
State	Trade Class	Comm Class	Sales Amount	Cost Amount	Gross Profit	Sales Amount by State	Cost Amount by State	Gross Profit by State
37	288	1	160.60	122.78	37.82			
			100.00	80.20	19.83			
			260.63*	202.98*	57.65*			
		2	527.58	411.37	116.21			
			527.58*	411.37*	116.21*			
			788.21*	614.35*	173.86*			
	300	1	96.04	73.89	22.15			
			292.95	225.45	67.50			
			388.99*	299.34*	89.65*			
			388.99*	299.34*	89.65*			
						1,177.20	913.69	263.51
40	686	1	217.81	117.52	43.29			
			327.50	255.95	71.55			

FIG. 15-1 Group-indicated report, three control levels. (Courtesy of International Business Machines Corporation.)

When preparing detail-printed reports, group indication is done by means of L-indicators at detail-time, to cause printing of the control field on the first card of the group and to suppress it at other times. The usual type of control on the OUTPUT-FORMAT specifications form is that of a *file-identification* line, or group of lines, which specifies the file to be used; whether the line is an H, D, or T type; what spacing or skipping to do; and by what indicator the line is to be controlled. The *field-description* line, however, allows the selection or suppression of an individual field within the line by additional use of indicators.

File-identification indicators determine whether or not a *line* is to be printed during execution of the job. If a line *is* to be printed, *field-selection* indicators determine which of the *fields* on the line are to be printed. Field selection is done by placing one, two, or three indicators in columns 23-25, 26-28, and 29-31 of the field-description line that contains the field name. When the indicator conditions given are all satisfied, the field will print, but if any one of the conditions is not satisfied, the field will *not* print. In the example,

Form Type	Filename	Type (H/D/T)	Stacker Select	Space Before	After	Skip Before	After	And Not (23)	(24 25)	And Not (26)	(27 28)	And Not (29)	(30 31)	Field Name	Zero Suppress (Z)	Blank After (B)	End Position in Output Record	Packed Field (P)	Constant
o	REPORT	D		1					98										
o														NAME			20		
o														ITEM			26		
o								N	25					AMTA			35		\ , Ø . '
o									35					AMTB			45		\ , Ø . '
o														AMTC			55		\ , Ø . '
o																			

the file-identification line specifies that the output is to occur when indicator 98 is *on*. The fields **NAME**, **ITEM**, and **AMTC** will print every time the line is to be printed. Field **AMTA**, however, will print only when indicator 25 is *off*, and field **AMTB**, only when indicator 35 is on.

An exception to field selection by indicator applies to any of the special fields named **PAGE**, **PAGE1**, . . ., **PAGE7**. When indicators are given along the side of **PAGE**, they do *not* condition whether or not it prints—they cause it to be reset to Ø *before* printing. In the example,

Form Type							And Not (23)	(24 25)	And Not (26)	(27 28)	And Not (29)	(30 31)	Field Name			End Position		Constant
o													DATE			40		\ / / '
o																60		'HEADING'
o												L1	PAGE			80		

PAGE is reset to Ø at every L1 control break, then has 1 added to it before it is printed. By use of indicators to reset **PAGE** in this manner, it can be used for line numbering within a page, or for page numbering within a control group. A field indication on output serves to control output either by selecting or suppressing. If the specified indicator condition is satisfied, the corresponding constant will be *selected* for printing; otherwise, it will be *suppressed*. In the example,

	Form	7–14	Type	Stacker Before	After	Before	After	Not / And	Not / And	Not	Name	Zero Sup / Blank At	Record (in Output)	Packed Fie	Constant
0 1	O		D	1				99							
0 2	O												3		'IBM'
0 3	O							85					10		'CREDIT'
0 4	O							N85					10		'DEBIT'
0 5	O														

the constant 'CREDIT' is selected if 85 is *on*, the constant 'DEBIT' is selected if 85 is *off*, and 'IBM' will be printed every time the line itself is printed, by indicator 99.

Field selection by indicator can be used to group-indicate a detail-printed report. Since the L-indicator is on only for the first card of each group, the field can be selected for printing only on the first card of each group. In the example,

Form Type	Filename	Type (H/D/T)	Stacker Select	Before	After	Before	After	Not / And	Not / And	Not	Field Name	Zero Suppress / Blank After	in Output Record	Packed Field	Constant
O		D	1 2					01							
O								L1			DEPT		8		
O											REF		20		
O											AMT		42	'	, 0 . '

the department number, **DEPT**, will print only in the first line of each group, and since L1 is *off* for all other lines in the group, it is completely suppressed on those lines.

PROBLEM DEFINITION: *A detail-printed list of expenses by account and by department should be made, with headings, on stock paper. Totals are needed by account, by department, and over the whole job. Account and department groups need not be printed on separate pages of the report, although page numbers should be placed on each page. No run-date header card will be used for this report. Input is given:*

Field Description	Field Name	Columns
Department number	**DEPT**	1-2
Account number	**ACCT**	5-1∅
Invoice number	**INV**	15-19
Transaction date	**TRDT**	22-27
Expense amount, 2 decimals	**AMT**	3∅-33

Cards are first sorted by date of transaction, so that the lines will be printed in the order of first occurrence. Next, they are sorted by account number, and then by department. L1 is assigned to account number, and L2 to department number. LR will be used to print the final total.

Indicator 1P is used to give the company name and column headings. The column headings and company name are repeated on overflow. Detail indicator ∅1 is used for addition of the field **AMT**, from each detail card, to the total by account number, **AAMT**. At an L1 break, that account sum total is transferred into department total; at an L2 break, the department total is transferred into the final total. The program, called **EXPDIST**, and a sample of its output are given in Figure 15-2.

A detail-printed report, with control fields, usually contains not only detail lines, but total lines as well. The total of all expenses for one account number, for example, is printed after the detail transactions for that account. It would often be helpful to the user of the report to have the individual transactions removed completely from the report, showing just the totals for the entire account. A report that has the total lines but that does not have the individual transaction lines is called a *group-printed* report. Figure 15-3 shows a report done in two ways— one in detail-print, the other in group-print.

To produce a group-printed report, the RPG programmer simply omits all detail lines from his specification sheets. If, on a given cycle through the RPG object program, there are no detail lines specified, then none are executed. Input of records and calculations, however, continues to be done in the same manner, progressing record by record through the file. When a control break occurs and the L-indicators go on, total lines are printed, producing a group-printed report. Should minor totals not be of interest, the report can produce intermediate, or possibly major ones, on certain control breaks and not on others. If a total by department rather than by account, is of interest, omit the specifications for the total line for account, putting one for department only. The processing will continue until all output lines are printed. Some programs may be designed for a complete job to be run without output until the last record indicator goes on, at which time totals over the whole job are produced.

The program for a detail-printed report can be modified to produce a group-printed report; not only must its detail line specifications be removed, but column headings, as well, for those fields no longer being printed. Rather than have two separate programs, however, it would be helpful to have a single program that, by some means of control, could produce either a detail-printed report or a group-printed one. One method of control is by use of a header card, placed at the front of the deck in much the same manner as a run-date card. It can be used to set indicators to suppress detail lines and their corresponding headings when a group report is requested.

Special information that is brought in to change the program in some manner, either in the way in which it operates, the number of times the job is done, or by an equation to be used in the program, is called a *run-control card*. It serves as a *switch* to control alternatives in the program. When the switch is set one way, the program carries out certain functions, but when the switch is changed, the program performs differently. The run-control card determines what type of report is to be produced during the run, by setting indicators that are used to select or suppress lines and fields for printing. This type of control card is *not* the same as the control card used to direct the activities of the operating system and job stream. This type controls only the alternatives possible *within* a given program, and is used to make one program produce different results from one run to another.

Several different codes could be used on a run-control header card. In the example,

Line	Form Type	Filename	Sequence	Number (1-N)	Option (O)	Resulting Indicator	Record Identification Codes 1 Position	Not (N)	C/Z/D	Character	Record Identification Codes 2 Position	Not (N)	C/Z/D	Character	Record Identification Codes 3 Position	Not (N)	C/Z/D	Character	Stacker Select	Packed (P)	Field Location From	To	Decimal Positions
3 4 5	6	7 8 9 10 11 12 13 14	15 16	17	18	19 20	21 22 23 24	25	26	27	28 29 30 31	32	33	34	35 36 37 38	39	40	41	42	43	44 45 46 47	48 49 50 51	52
0 1	I	CARDS	NS			91	02			CA														
0 2	I		OR			92	02			CB														
0 3	I		OR			93	02			CC														

```
                    H
        01 01   F* EXPENSE DISTRIBUTION LIST  ED01WC                      W.H.CATON       ED01WC
        01 02   F*                                                                        ED01WC
        01 03   F* TOTAL BY ACCOUNT NO., DEPT. TOTAL AND FINAL TOTAL                      ED01WC
        01 04   F*
        01 05   F* DETAIL CARDS SORT BY DEPT. NO. THEN BY ACCT. NO.                       ED01WC
        01 06   F*                                                                        ED01WC
001     01 07   FINPUT   IP  F  80  80         READ40 SYSRDR
002     01 08   FLIST    O   F 120 120     OF  PRINTERSYSLST
003     02 01   IINPUT   NS  01   80 CD                                                   ED01WC
004     02 02   I                                     1   20DEPT    L2                    ED01WC
005     02 03   I                                     5  10OACCT    L1                    ED01WC
006     02 04   I                                    15   19 INV                          ED01WC
007     02 05   I                                    22   27OTRDATE                       ED01WC
008     02 06   I                                    30   332AMT                          ED01WC
        03 01   C*                                                                        ED01WC
        03 02   C* CALC. AMT. TOTAL BY ACCT. NO. ON L1                                    ED01WC
        03 03   C* CALC. AMT. TOTAL BY DEPT. NO. ON L2                                    ED01WC
        03 04   C* CALC. FINAL TOTAL FOR LR LISTING                                       ED01WC
        03 05   C*                                                                        ED01WC
009     03 06   C   01         AMT      ADD AAMT      AAMT    52                           ED01WC
010     03 07   CL1            AAMT     ADD DAMT      DAMT    62                           ED01WC
011     03 08   CL2            DAMT     ADD FAMT      FAMT    72                           ED01WC
        04 03   O* LIST HEADINGS                                                          ED01WC
      S 04 02   O*                                                                        ED01WC
012     04 06   OLIST    H  201  1P                                                       ED01WC
013     04 06   O          OR      OF                                                     ED01WC
014   S 04      O                          55 'AUTOMATIC DISCOUNT'
015             O                          72 'DEPARTMENT STORE'
016     04 06   O       H  2     1P
017     04 07   O          OR      OF
018   S 04 04   O                          60 'EXPENSE DISTRIBUTION'                       ED01WC
019     04 05   O                          65 'LIST'                                       ED01WC
020     04 10   O                          92 'PAGE'                                       ED01WC
021     04 11   O                  PAGE Z  96                                             ED01WC
022     04 12   O       H  1     1P
023     04 13   O          OR      OF                                                     ED01WC
024     04 14   O                          23 'DEPT'                                       ED01WC
025     04 15   O                          33 'ACCOUNT'                                    ED01WC
026     04 16   O                          44 'INVOICE'                                    ED01WC
027     04 17   O                          55 'DATE'                                       ED01WC
028     04 18   O                          68 'AMOUNT'                                     ED01WC
029     04 19   O                          81 'TOTAL'                                      ED01WC
030     04 20   O                          96 'TOTAL'                                      ED01WC
031     05 01   O       H  3     1P
032     05 02   O          OR      OF                                                     ED01WC
033     05 03   O                          33 'GEN SUB'                                    ED01WC
034     05 04   O                          44 'NUMBER'                                     ED01WC
035   S         O                          58 'TRANSACTED'
036     05 05   O                          82 'ACCOUNT'                                    ED01WC
037     05 06   O                          96 'DEPT'                                       ED01WC
        05 07   O*                                                                        ED01WC
        05 08   O* LIST DETAILS NOW  PLEASE                                               ED01WC
        05 09   O*                                                                        ED01WC
```

```
038     05 10   O         D  1   01                                                       ED01WC
039     05 11   O                L2        DEPT  Z  22                                    ED01WC
040     05 12   O                L1        ACCT     33 '  &  '                            ED01WC
041     05 13   O                          INV      43                                    ED01WC
042     05 14   O                          TRDATE   56 '  /  /  '
043     05 15   O                          AMT      68 ' 0.  '
        05 16   O*                                                                        ED01WC
        05 17   O* LIST TOTALS          BY  DEPARTMENT                                    ED01WC
        05 18   O*                                                                        ED01WC
        05 19   O         T  1   L1                                                       ED01WC
044     05 20   O                          AAMT   B 81 ' 0.  '
045     06 01   O         T  1   L2        DAMT   B 99 ' , 0.  '
046     06 02   O                                                                         ED01WC
047     06 03   O*                                                                        ED01WC
        06 04   O* PRINT FINAL TOTAL IF ALL THAT OTHER JUNK IS OUT                        ED01WC
        06 05   O*                                                                        ED01WC
048     06 06   O         T  2   LR                                                       ED01WC
049     06 07   O                          78 'FINAL TOTAL'                               ED01WC
050     06 08   O                          FAMT   100 ' , 0.  *'
        06 09   O* THE END    TO                                                          ED01WC
```

AUTOMATIC DISCOUNT DEPARTMENT STORE

EXPENSE DISTRIBUTION LIST   PAGE 1

DEPT	ACCOUNT GEN SUB	INVOICE NUMBER	DATE TRANSACTED	AMOUNT	TOTAL ACCOUNT	TOTAL DEPT
10	224 134	54791	3/12/70	3.30		
		53214	3/13/70	4.50		
		54371	3/13/70	3.30		
		52143	3/13/70	4.50		
		58632	3/13/70	5.50		
		52473	3/14/70	5.53		
		53214	3/14/70	5.59		
		98632	3/16/70	6.95		
		65214	3/18/70	3.30		
		98721	3/19/70	5.25		
		652A1	3/20/70	5.32		
		65214	3/25/70	6.95		
					59.99	

AUTOMATIC DISCOUNT DEPARTMENT STORE

EXPENSE DISTRIBUTION LIST   PAGE 2

DEPT	ACCOUNT GEN SUB	INVOICE NUMBER	DATE TRANSACTED	AMOUNT	TOTAL ACCOUNT	TOTAL DEPT
		23511	3/10/70	12.00		
		52165	3/13/70	12.50		
		23517	3/17/70	12.50		
		21543	3/20/70	22.30		
					71.86	
						118.86

FINAL TOTAL   468.71*

FIG. 15-2 Program **EXPDIST** IBM SYSTEM/360, DOS.

215

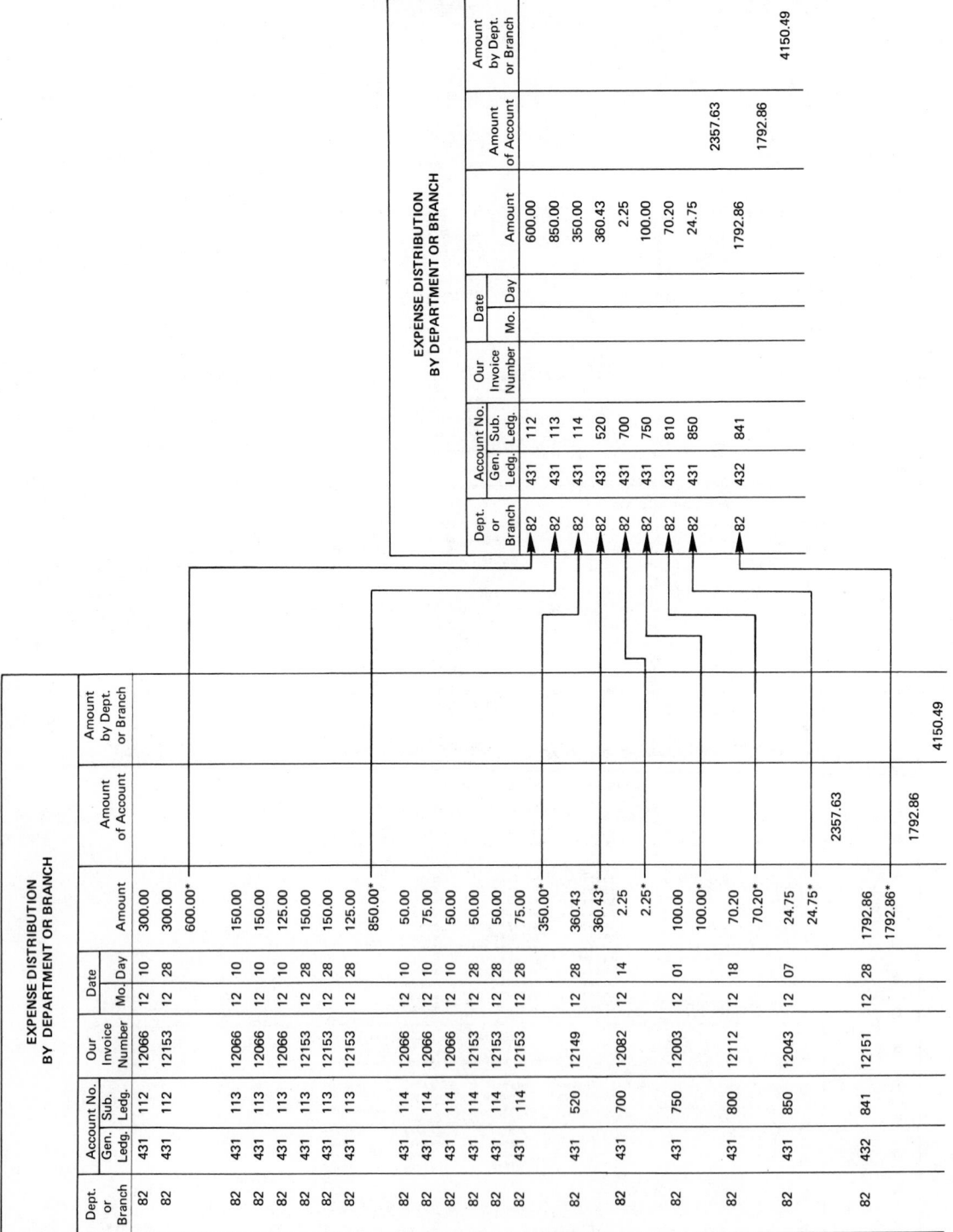

FIG. 15-3 Detail-printed and group-printed reports. (Courtesy of International Business Machines Corporation.)

the character A, B, or C turns on indicators 91, 92, or 93, respectively, and can be used for setting *other* indicators for program control. Remember that card-input-type indicators are turned *off* when another card type from the same file is read. Since indicators $\emptyset$1-99 are automatically *off* at run-in time, it is possible for them, when used in a *not* condition for suppression of lines, to cause printing of undesired information; caution and thorough checking of all output at run-in time is a necessity.

To have one program produce either a detail-printed or a group-printed report, a code must be devised for the run-control header card. The code could be a D in column 7 for the detail-printed report, and a G for the group-printed one, for example. It could, however, be an 8 for the detail-printed report, and *no card at all* for the group-printed one. The run-control card serves as a programmed *set-up switch* to determine which report type is to be produced.

In modifying **EXPDIST** for use of a programmed switch, a G in column 3 is used to mean a group-printed report, and a D in column 3 is used for a detail-printed one. Indicator 98 is used for detection of the G and indicator 99 for the D. Indicators 98 and 99 will then control printing of the heading lines, *instead* of the 1P indicator. Alternate output of fields by the 1P indicator is not possible because there is no way to modify that indicator at run-in time, before detail lines are printed.

Input specifications for the modification of program **EXPDIST** given by

	Form Type		Sequence	Number (1-N)	Option (O)	Resulting Indi	Position		Not (N)	C/Z/D	Character	Position		Not (N)	C/Z/D	Character	Position		Not (N)	C/Z/D	Character	Stacker Select	Packed (P)	From	To	Decimal Posi
0 1	I	INPUT		NS			98			03		CG														
0 2	I			OR			99			03		CD														
0 3	I																									

cause the coded character to turn on the appropriate indicator. No field descriptions need be given, since there are no fields to be read from the card. Indicators 98 and 99, however, may not be used to do field selection throughout the report, because they are card-type indicators and when another type of card comes in, they will go *off*. The indicator for the detail-printed report, 99, should be used to turn on another indicator, say, 95, which, once set, will stay on throughout the entire report to control certain line and field selections. The instruction given by

Control		And		And		Factor 1	Operation	Factor 2	Result Field	Field Length	Decimal P.	Half Adjus	Con High 1 > 2 1
	Not 99		Not		Not		SETON						95

will cause indicator 95 to be turned on; if it is not changed by the programmer, it will stay on for the whole job. It can therefore be used to signify a detail-printed report, with 95 used for printing of certain fields and column headings that are to be placed only on the detail-printed version.

To suppress the detail line completely on a group report, the file-indication given by

Line	Form Type	Filename	Type (H/D)	Stacker Sel.	Before	After	Before	After	And		And			Name	Zero Suppr	Blank After	Output Record	Packed F.
3 4 5	6	7 8 9 10 11 12 13 14	15	16	17	18	19 20	21 22	23	24 25	26	27 28	29 30 31	32 33 34 35 36 37	38	39	40 41 42 43	44	45 46 47 48 49 50 51 52
0 1	O		D	1					Ø1		95								
0 2																			

could be used. For the detail-printed report, 95 will be *on*; for a group-printed report, the entire line would be bypassed since 95 is off. If the entire line is suppressed, however, the department number and account number will not be printed as they should be. You will probably be able to find a way to print those headings that are needed. The program in Figure 15-2, after such modifications, can be used to print either a group-printed report or a detail-printed one, simply by putting the proper run-control header card in front of the data deck.

The technique of using a run-control card as a set-up switch can be used in many other applications. A program can be written to print and punch its output, with a run-control card specifying on each run whether to do both, do print only, or do punch only. A program can be written to do calculations by either of two formulas, with the code specifying, at execution time, which should be done. It is often used when one program should produce *similar*, but *slightly different*, output on different runs.

The IBM SYSTEM/36Ø, DOS, TOS, and the IBM SYSTEM/3 have special external indicators U1, U2, . . ., U8, which serve as set-up switches in much the same way. They are set by control cards that you put into the job stream before your program is executed; and once set, they cannot be changed during the processing of the program. They can be used to tell whether or not a certain file is to be used in the job, to control certain calculations to be done or not done, and to condition output lines. See the reference manual for more information on external indicators.

EXERCISES

1. Do field-description lines for each of these, using the OUTPUT-FORMAT form shown:
    (a) Show how to print the constant Ø.Ø25 or Ø.Ø45, depending on indicator 75's being on or off, respectively.
    (b) Show how to print the phrase 'OVER LIMIT' when indicator 15 is on.
    (c) Show how to print either the phrase 'O.K.' or 'NOT O.K.', depending on indicator 65's being on or off, respectively.
    (d) Show how to group-indicate employee number **EMPNUM**.
    (e) Show how to cause **PAGE** to be reset at the beginning of each control group.

Skip		Output Indicators						Field Name	Zero Suppress (Z)	Blank After (B)	End Position in Output Record	Packed Field (P)	Constant or Edit
Before	After		And		And								
		Not		Not		Not							
19 20	21 22	23 24 25	26 27 28	29 30 31	32 33 34 35 36 37	38	39	40 41 42 43	44	45 46 47 48 49 50 51 52 53 54 55 56 57 58 59 6
(a)										

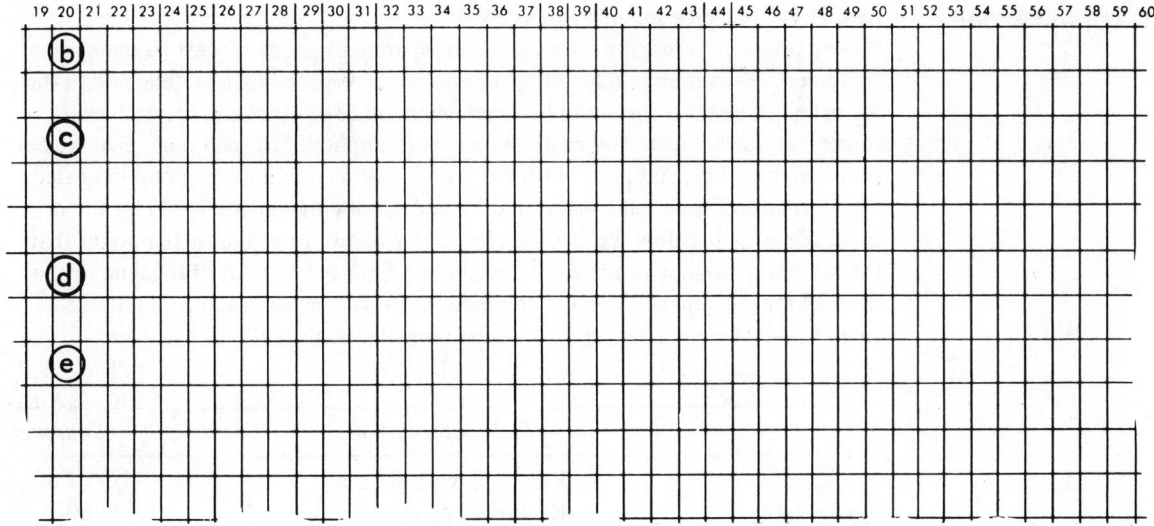

2. State whether or not each of the following, when used to control an output line, will cause printing of the line at run-in time. Assume that indicators 27 and 45 are record-identifying indicators. Assume an *and* relation if no other is given.

Example: **LØ 27** _____no_____   **LØ OR 27** _____yes_____

(a) **1P** _____   (b) **27** _____

(c) **45N27** _____   (d) **1P OR OF** _____

(e) **NOF** _____   (f) **1P OF** _____

(g) **L1** _____   (h) **N27N45** _____

(i) **27 45** _____   (j) **N1P** _____

Section 5

PROGRAMS TO WRITE

A. PROBLEM NAME: **TCHLST:** student lists for each teacher, with totals

Write a program to list course cards to provide each teacher with a list of the students they teach and the classes they are taking. Teacher name should be printed as a heading on that listing. At the control break, give the total number of students in that teacher's classes; at the end of the job, give the total number of teachers. Input records, sorted by teacher, are the same format as those from Project A, Sec. 1.

Field Information	Columns
Social security number	1-9
Student, last name	11-2Ø
Student, first name	21-3Ø
Course ID	31-4Ø
Course description	41-54
Teacher name	55-67
Credits for the course	79-8Ø

B. PROBLEM NAME: **ACCTINV:** invoice summary by account

Write a program to prepare statements, on separate pages, to request payment from customers. Each item purchased by a customer is recorded on one data card in the format given below. There will be a variable number of purchases for each customer; records are sorted by customer account number. For each item, give the description, quantity, and price, with the account number and name group indicated. Print the cost of each item, calculated by multiplying the quantity sold by the price each. Three lines below the last item for that account, print the total amount that the customer should pay for all the purchases. Give a final total of the amount due from all the customers. Give the company name as a major heading on all pages; give a run-date from a header card on the same line as the column headings.

	Field Information	*Columns*
Header card	Run-date, with slashes	1-8
	Record ID code: D	8Ø
Detail card	Account number	1-4
	Account name	5-2Ø
	Item description	21-3Ø
	Quantity sold	36-4Ø
	Price each, 2 decimals	47-5Ø
	Record ID code: *not* a D	8Ø

C. PROBLEM NAME: **DISCK:** discount by run-control card

The program should produce a report that lists amounts, discount applied, and amounts due. A discount of 10%, or no discount at all, should be applied, depending on whether the run-control card has a D or an N, respectively, in column 1. When *no* discount is applied, list discount amount as zero; calculate amount due as the entire amount. When a discount *is* applied, the discount amount is 10% of the amount given, and the amount due is the original amount minus the discount amount. At the end of the job, give a total of the amounts due, and specify whether or not a discount was applied to the run.

Sample output *with* a discount:

T AND M POWER COMPANY			
CLIENT NUMBER AND NAME	AMOUNT	DISCOUNT AMOUNT	AMOUNT DUE
1379 SPRUNG PAPER CO.	253.46	25.35	228.11
1398 COLD LAUNDRY CO.	152.97	15.3Ø	137.67

Field Information	*Columns*
Client number	1-4
Client name	5-24
Amount, 2 decimals	35-4Ø

D. PROBLEM NAME: **SLSLST:**   produce sales list by salesman, department, and branch
Write a program to produce a sales list, such as that shown in Figure 14-2, with totals given by salesman, then by department, then by branch. A final total should be given over all branches.

Field Information	Columns
Record ID code: ∅, 1, or 2	11
Branch number	1-2
Department number	3-5
Salesman number	6-8
Sales amount, 2 decimals	14-2∅

E. PROBLEM NAME: **EXPDISTK:**   group or detail expense distribution list
Write a revision of the program **EXPDIST** given in Figure 15-2 to be used with a run-control card, to produce either a detail-printed report or a group-printed one. The header card will contain either a G or a D, in column 3, to cause a group-print or detail-print, respectively.

SECTION 6

REPORTS WITH LOGICAL DECISIONS

Lesson 16

DECISIONS AND ALTERNATIVES

You will learn how to program tests and comparisons to cause the computer to recognize certain conditions and, when they arise, to perform alternate program steps.

The following questions summarize the lesson and are answered on the back of this page. If you have never done any type of programming before, be sure you fully understand this lesson and can answer all the questions before you go on to Lesson 17.

1. Describe how a decision is illustrated on a program flow chart.
2. Describe a decision table and tell how it is used.
3. Why is there less need for conventional program flow charts with RPG than with many other programming languages?
4. What types of decisions, of those that arise in business reports, can be handled by RPG by alternatives built into a computer program?
5. What is the difference between *field indicators* and *resulting indicators*?
6. What special problem does the assignment of a field indicator to the zero/blank condition bring about during run-in time and output of totals?
7. How can you determine whether the contents of a field are larger than a certain value?
8. Why is it sometimes advisable to avoid using the halt indicators?
9. Explain how alignment is done by RPG when using the **COMP** instruction.
10. When are the field indicators and resulting indicators reset?

ANSWERS

1. By a diamond-shaped decision box, with entrance at the top or side and up to three possible exits, often used for positive, negative, and zero alternatives.

2. Lists of conditions are given on the upper left, lists of alternatives on the lower left. Columns represent sets of conditions that are encountered and what is to be done when those conditions arise. Entries of Y and N for yes and no are used to designate the conditions; selection of alternatives is done by marking an X in the appropriate box. On some decision tables, certain responses may be written in the column where appropriate.

3. Because **RPG** follows the fixed-object-program logic given by the chart in the Appendix, leaving the programmer little control over the timing of input and output functions.

4. Those that can be based on an objective set of rules, for which conditions can be determined by tests and comparisons of fields and record types. Some examples are whether overtime work was done, whether enough social security deduction has been made, whether requirements for graduation have been met, and whether inventory is ready for reorder at this time.

5. *Field* indicators are assigned to *input fields* on data cards, to detect positive or negative, or zero or blank, in those fields. *Resulting* indicators may be assigned as input *record-identifying* indicators, as the *result* of high, low, or equal after a compare has been made, as the *result* of a test for zone, or as the *result* of a calculation.

6. On most implementations, indicators assigned to zero/blank are *on* during run-in time, reflecting the initialized zero/blank state of the fields. They are also turned *on* when "blank-after" is done on output. Spurious output may inadvertently occur at these times unless care is taken to use these indicators in an *and* condition with others that prevent it.

7. By using a compare instruction testing the field against that limit.

8. Because the entire computer system is brought to a halt, causing expensive loss of computer time.

9. The numeric comparisons are aligned by decimal points. Alphameric comparisons are aligned at the left end.

10. Field indicators are not reset until that appropriate record-type is again encountered and its fields are stored. Resetting of resulting indicators depends on the type: input, record-identifying, resulting indicators are reset to indicate the next record type that is brought into the computer; indicators assigned on the **CALCULATION** form are reset the next time that particular instruction is to be executed.

The information given on the various transaction records for a given job represents the many individual differences of people and situations. Recognizing them and determining what to do next in each case should be designed into a program that gives all alternatives and allows the proper one to be chosen by comparisons and tests. The run-control card, for example, was used to select proper output lines and constants for whichever variation of the program was needed for a particular job run. Another type of decision is that which is based on the individual data fields in each record, meaning that the decision can vary from one *record* to another, rather than from one *job* to another. For example, employee overtime calculations are necessary for some persons and not for others; a program must detect that overtime pay is needed for some persons and not for others; a program must detect that overtime pay is needed on one transaction card and calculate the pay accordingly, but on the next transaction, no overtime hours may have been worked at all and another method of calculating the pay would apply. Even within one individual's record, situations may arise that change the calculations from one run to another. During one pay period, for example, certain social security deductions may be required, but after deductions have been made up to a certain minimum amount, no more are required. The same computer program is used for all these various applications from one week to another; comparisons and testing of fields allow the computer to make the proper decision about what program steps are to be executed for a particular person's needs.

Other types of decisions that can be built into computer programs are checking to be sure that no paycheck larger than $500.00 is produced; checking to be sure that the working hours of an employee are not over 50 hours for each pay period; testing bond deductions to be sure that a person does not deduct more than he is making during a particular pay period; deciding whether or not the date of payment of a bill is within the minimum period to warrant a discount rate that may be applied; and deciding whether or not the conditions for graduation have been met as established by the college administration, and giving an appropriate message to that effect on the final grade report. These decisions may vary from one run to another, from one person's transactions to another, or according to one person's particular backlog of activity at a particular time. The program must contain all necessary alternatives; it is given the decision-making capability to choose the proper set to use for each condition as it arises.

Flow charts and decision tables are important tools in analyzing and documenting a particular decision that is to be designed into a program. The flow chart uses a *decision box*, the diamond-shaped figure used in Figure 16-1, to show comparisons and tests, after which one of several alternative paths of the program may be taken. The result of a calculation of the value of an input field may be tested for positive, negative, or zero; comparisons may be done and the result tested for high, low, or equal conditions. Flow charts have been used in data processing for illustrating program logic for quite a while. They are often placed onto special IBM FLOWCHARTING WORKSHEETS, also shown in Figure 16-1. These forms, available by order number X20-8021, have each rectangular position on the sheet identified by a letter and number. Each portion of the chart can be referred to by location, such as "the decision box in E3" or "the connector in D2." Flow charts giving the action of a particular program serve as documentation of that program, and are especially valuable when program revisions are required.

Decision tables, a fairly recent contribution to charting methods, are being used in some instances instead of the detailed flow chart to give a summary of the dispensation of the many con-

228   Lesson 16   Sec. 6

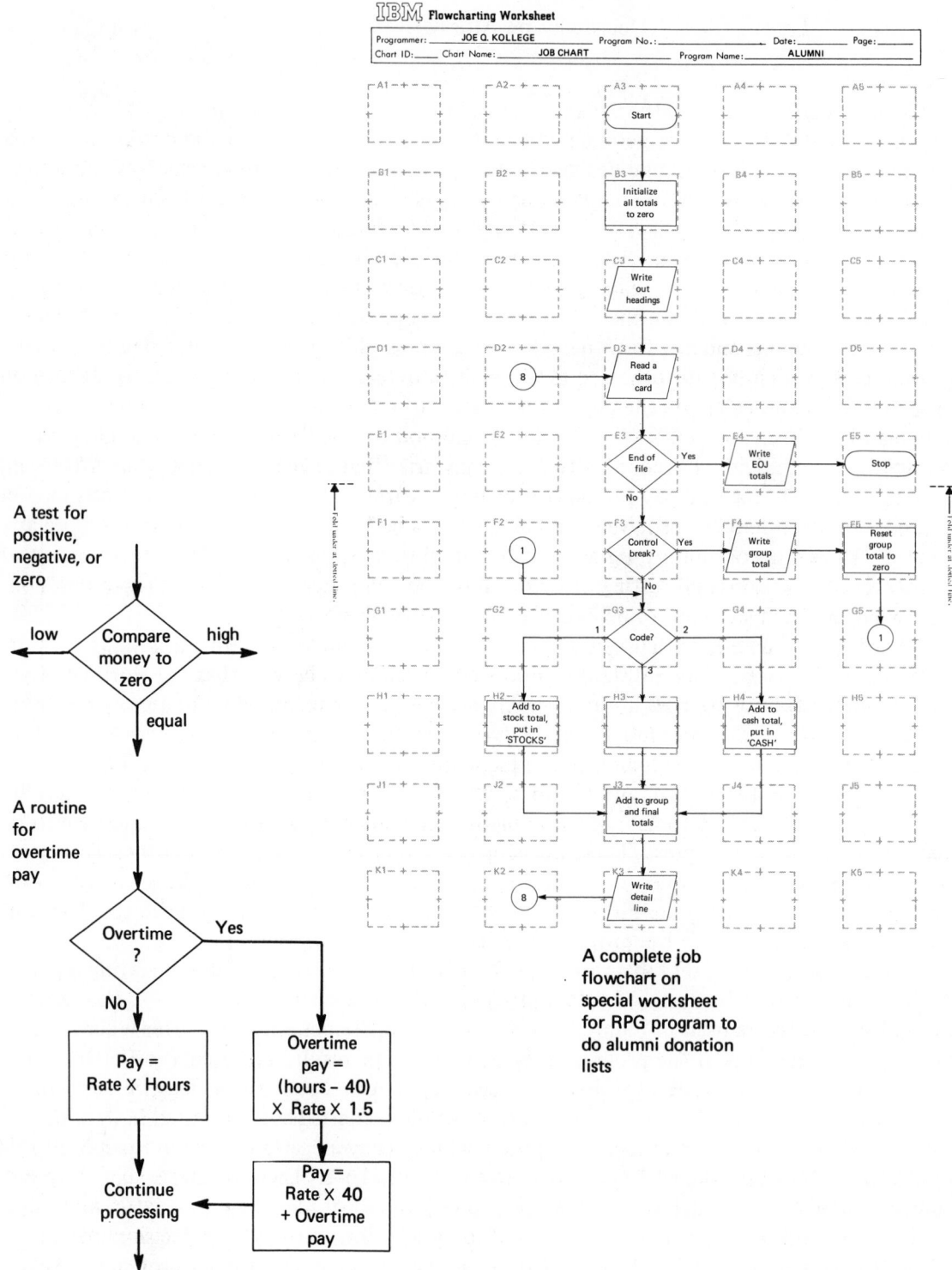

FIG. 16-1 Decisions and tests.

ditions that arise in the program. Since the **RPG** programming system has a fixed-program logic that controls input and output without the programmer's specifying when it is to be done, the conventional flow chart used with other programming languages is not always illustrative of what the programmer must code in **RPG**. Although a job flow chart in some instances should be made for documentation purposes, it is not always necessary on **RPG** programs. Analysis of many **RPG** programs is sometimes limited to the *types of records* possible, the *types of conditions* found in the records, the *calculations* for each condition, and the *output* requested for that condition. Decision tables serve this need, in some cases, quite as well as conventional flow charts, and are usually easier to make and to use.

A decision table has the basic format given in Figure 16-2. The conditions are given in the upper left. Each column in the table shows a certain set of these conditions that could arise in the program. Either a Y for yes or an N for no is given on conditions for which they are appropriate; those that do not apply are left blank. When more response is required, an entry is made in the table. The list of various actions that might be taken on those conditions is at the bottom left of the table. Actions taken for each particular column of conditions are marked with an X, or with an appropriate remark.

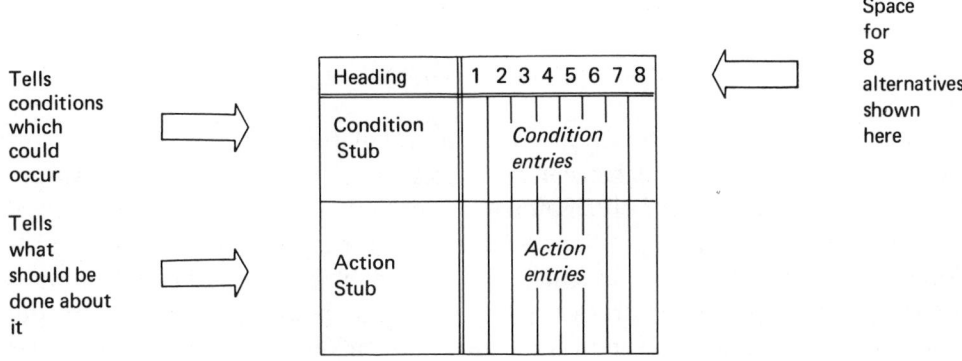

FIG. 16-2 Decision table format.

You will want to be able to document the decisions made in your programs by using one of these two methods—either program flow chart or decision table. A comparison between a segment of a flow chart and the corresponding decision table is given in Figure 16-3. It illustrates the decision by which a department store could determine whether or not a special courtesy call should be made to an "inactive" account. If the customer has a zero balance from the previous month, and has had no transactions—either payments or charges—for the last 6 months, then his name and address are put on a list for the call. This type of decision can either be built into an existing program, such as one that produces statements and updates old balances, or it can be done by a separate program, which may actually print a letter to be sent to the home address for that account.

On many decision tables and program flow charts, you will notice that some combinations of conditions cause the computer system to stop. Certain halt indicators are available in **RPG** to be set on by the programmer should these conditions arise. Some implementations offer two such indicators, H1 and H2; others offer nine, H1 through H9. The special **RPG** indicator, HØ, is set on and off internally in the **RPG** program when certain conditions arise. Unless the halt indicator is turned off by the programmer, it will cause the system to halt after the processing of the record that caused it. Should an appropriate action be taken by the operator at such a halt, processing can be continued. Find out, in your particular installation, how the

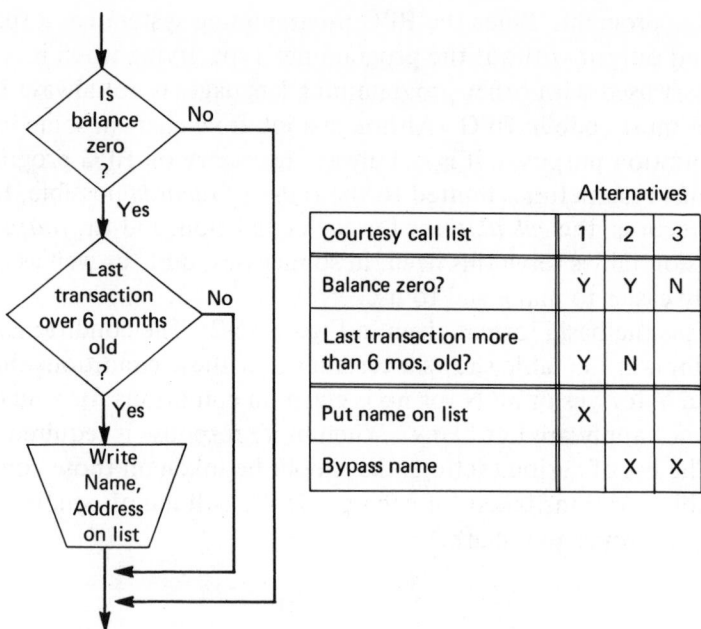

FIG. 16-3 Decision for courtesy call list.

management feels about such a system stop. In some installations, programs are not permitted to have system stops built into them, since even a short stop, during which the operator must decide what to do about it, can cost much money in computer time. Instead, these conditions may be used to produce certain output lines, such as an error message about that condition, so that later investigation may be done. In small job shops, however, and especially in open shops in which the programmer is running his own work, system stops are allowed to occur during a program; the operator/programmer can make proper adjustments at that time and continue with the job. It is important to remember that computer time is expensive and that your present or future employer will appreciate your concern about it!

Detection of positive or negative, and zero or blank values in numeric input fields is possible by assignment of *field indicators* on the INPUT form. Alphameric fields may be tested for blanks. Any of the indicators $\emptyset$1-99, as well as some of the others, may be specified in columns 65 and 66, 67 and 68, and 69 and 7$\emptyset$ alongside the proper field name, to determine whether the values of the fields are positive or negative, or zero or blank, respectively. In the example,

Record Identification Codes															Field Location				Field Name	Control Level (L1-L9)	Matching Fields or Chaining Fields	Field-Record Relation	Field Indicators			Sterling Sign Position
1				2					3				Stacker Select (P)	Packed (P)	From		To	Decimal Positions					Plus	Minus	Zero or Blank	
tion	Not (N)	C/Z/D	Character	Position	Not (N)	C/Z/D	Character	Position	Not (N)	C/Z/D	Character	Position														
23 24	25	26	27	28 29 30 31	32	33	34	35 36 37 38	39	40	41		42	43	44 45 46 47		48 49 50 51	52	53 54 55 56 57 58	59 60	61 62	63 64	65 66	67 68	69 70	71 72 73 74
															1		4		DEPT							
															5		8		REFNUM							
															11		2$\emptyset$2		BAL				65	75	85	
															25		3$\emptyset$2		MIN							

indicators 65, 75, and 85 are assigned to detect positive or negative, and zero or blank values in the field named **BAL**. If the assigned condition is met, the indicator is turned *on*; if not, it goes *off*. Unless reset by the programmer or changed by another part of the program, the indicator retains this setting until another card of *this particular record-type* is again read, and the field is again tested for setting. It is important to realize that the indicator assigned to a field is *not* set immediately after the record-type has come into the computer, but just *before* detail-time calculations are done, which occurs *after* total-time operations on the previous record-type. Should a calculation change the value of the field to which the indicator is assigned, the indicator will not change unless assigned again as a calculation-resulting indicator. When the "blank-after" feature is used to reset a field, and the field has a field indicator assigned to it in the zero/blank position, the indicator, on the IBM SYSTEM/36Ø, will turn *on* immediately after the field has been reset and will *not* necessarily be the same as the condition on the record-type that set it. The IBM 113Ø does not do this, but leaves the indicator at its former setting. Output lines or fields that are to be printed by use of a *field* indicator should, therefore, be printed in an *and* condition with other indicators, such as the record-type input resulting one, to prevent printing of undesirable information.

All three conditions that are possible—positive, negative, and zero/blank—need not be assigned an indicator number. If you wish to detect positive values only, then use an indicator in columns 65 and 66, leaving the other two conditions blank. An *on* indicator will denote positive; *off* will denote negative, blank, or zero. Any combination of conditions may be used, with the same or different indicators.

At run-in time, indicators Ø1-99 are set off, numeric fields are set to zero, and alphameric fields are set to blanks. Any indicators that have been assigned as zero/blank field indicators, however, are then turned *on* from that initialization, and are therefore *on* during the detail-time printing of the headings at the beginning of the job. Again, this does not hold on the IBM 113Ø, which sets field indicators off at the beginning of the job whether or not they are assigned as zero/blank field indicators. Output must be carefully checked for run-in errors caused by the *on* condition of indicators before the normal use of them. On the IBM SYSTEM/36Ø, the coding given by

3 4 5	Form 6	7 8 9 10 11 12 13 14	Type 15	Stacke 16	Before 17	After 18	Before 19 20	After 21 22	Not 23	And 24 25	Not 26	And 27 28	Not 29	30 31	32 33 34 35 36 37	Zero 38	Blank 39	40 41	42 43	Packe 44	45 46 47 48 49 50 51 52 53 54
0 1	O		D	2						5Ø											
0 2	O														DEPT			1 2			
0 3	O									83					DAYNUM			3Ø			
0 4	O								N	83					REFNUM			3Ø			
0 5	O														VAL			4 5	\ ,	Ø .	'
0 6	O																				

with indicator 5Ø assigned to test for zero in a field of the input record, will cause **DEPT** and **REFNUM** to print, as well as **VAL**. Since the field contents have not yet been stored, however, **DEPT** and **REFNUM** are blank and **VAL** is zero. The value of **VAL** will produce .ØØ on the output sheet. Be sure, during the debugging, to investigate any unusual printed matter appearing on the output report; it should be investigated and corrected before the program is released for use in production work.

Calculation resulting indicators may be used to test the contents of the RESULT FIELD on any of the arithmetic operations. Any indicator may be given in columns 54 and 55, 56 and 57, and 58 and 59 on the appropriate calculation line. After the execution of the arithmetic, the indicators will be set to reflect the positive, negative, and zero/blank condition of the final result of that calculation. Do note that the **MOVE** and **MOVEL** instructions are *not* arithmetic, and resulting indicators should not be used on them. In the example,

Control Level		And		And			Factor 1	Operation	Factor 2	Result Field	Field Length	Decimal Posit	Half Adjust	Plus 1>2 High	Minus 1<2 Low	or Blank 1=2 Equal
		Not		Not		Not								Compare		
6 7 8	9 10 11	12 13 14	15 16 17	18 19 20 21 22 23 24 25 26 27	28 29 30 31 32	33 34 35 36 37 38 39 40 41 42	43 44 45 46 47 48	49 50 51	52	53	54 55	56 57	58 59
C	10			NUM	SUB	1	NUM	40					15

the operation will be executed every time indicator 1∅ is on, and will subtract 1 from **NUM** each time, testing the value for zero. Indicator 15 will then turn *on*. In RPG, a positive or negative zero will, under most circumstances, turn on the *zero* indicator instead of an indicator representing its algebraic sign.

Resulting indicators ∅1-99, which are assigned to detect positive or negative results, are *off* at the beginning of program execution. Those assigned to zero or blank, however, go *on* to reflect the cleared condition of the field at run-in time, and are on immediately after the field has been cleared after a "blank-after" operation. Each time the specified instruction is executed, the indicator is changed to reflect the condition of the newly calculated field. When conditioned by an indicator, however, the instruction may not be executed during a given pass, in which case the indicator remains at its former setting. Calculation-resulting indicators of a special type, such as the L-indicators, are set on and off at predetermined times during the program execution; they should be used only with full understanding of their particular design.

Should data be punched with the sign position in the left-most, high-order position of the input field, instead of the customary right-most, low-order position, the **TESTZ** instruction can be used to determine what it is. The field to be tested must be read in alphameric mode. The **TESTZ** instruction is given under OPERATION in columns 28-32, and the name of the alphameric field is given in RESULT FIELD. Decimal places and half-adjust must not be given. In the example,

Indicators		And		And			Factor 1	Operation	Factor 2	Result Field	Field Length	Decimal Positions	Half. Adjust (H)	Plus High 1>2	Minus Low 1<2	Zero or Blank Equal 1=2
														Resulting Indicators		
														Compare		
9	10 11	Not 12 13 14	Not 15 16 17	18 19 20 21 22 23 24 25 26 27	28 29 30 31 32	33 34 35 36 37 38 39 40 41 42	43 44 45 46 47 48	49 50 51	52	53	54 55	56 57	58 59
					TESTZ		INAMT				30	40	50

the high-order, left most zone position of the field **INAMT** is tested; should a 12 zone be detected there, indicator 3∅ will go *on*, and 4∅ and 5∅ will go *off*. Should an 11 zone be there, indicator 4∅ will go on, and 3∅ and 5∅ will go *off*. Should neither of those zones be there, indicator 5∅ will go on, and 3∅ and 4∅ will go off. All three indicator positions need not be used—only one is necessary. You may use it to detect only one type of zone by using the indicator in its off condition to mean one zone, and in its on condition, to mean the other. Indicators assigned to the "no-zone" position, under zero/blank, must also be used with care, since they reflect the run-in condition and the "blank-after" condition in the same manner as other resulting indicators. They are usually used for output in an *and* relation with other indicators to prevent undesired output at those times.

Do keep in mind that the **TESTZ** is *not* designed for use on numeric data that has been properly punched with its sign in the low-order position of the field. It is used on much of the unit-record work being converted to computer operation, in which the sign is already punched in the high-order position. It is useful, however, in detecting the zone position of any alphameric character, since the **MOVE** instruction can be used to isolate any character to put it into a "high-order" position.

Certain other move-zone instructions are available in **RPG** to manipulate sign conditions. They provide for moving a zone from its position in one field to the same or different position in another field. These operations, **MHHZO**, **MHLZO**, **MLHZO**, and **MLLZO**, are not of vital use at this time; you are referred to the **RPG** reference manual for your equipment for more information about them.

For comparisons of fields to certain specific values, or for comparison of one field to another, the compare instruction **COMP** is used. Should a field need to be tested for an upper limit value, say, $500.00, field indicators and resulting indicators alone, which test for positive, negative, or zero/blank, are not adequate. The compare instruction does not place anything into a RESULT FIELD as arithmetic instructions do, but simply sets the indicator after the comparison is made. The operation code **COMP** is given in columns 28-32 of the CALCULATION form. FACTOR 1 and FACTOR 2 give the fields or constants that are to be compared. Columns 54 and 55, 56 and 57, and 58 and 59 are used to assign up to three indicators for conditions high, low, and equal, respectively. The same indicator may be assigned to one or more of the possibilities. Indicators are cleared at the beginning of the comparison and are set according to the following chart.

	FACTOR 1 is greater than FACTOR 2		HIGH	
If	FACTOR 1 is less than FACTOR 2	then	LOW	goes on.
	FACTOR 1 is equal to FACTOR 2		EQUAL	

They remain at that setting until the programmer changes them, or until the instruction is again executed.

FACTOR 1 and FACTOR 2 on a comparison may be both alphameric or both numeric, and either fields or constants. Field names that are used must have been previously defined, either by being brought into the computer as input, or by being named as a RESULT FIELD in a former calculation. Numeric fields should be compared only to other numeric fields and constants; alphameric fields should be compared only to other alphameric fields or constants. Constants must therefore be in a form recognizable by the computer as either numeric or alphameric mode. This is done by putting all alphameric constants inside single quotation marks. Any valid EBCDIC character may be used in an alphameric constant, except that, should a quotation mark itself be needed, two must be given. Numeric constants are not enclosed by quotation marks; they follow the rules as given for constants in calculations. They may consist of the digits 0-9, with possibly a plus or minus sign in their extreme left-most position. They may have a decimal point, but should have no commas or other special characters. In the example,

And		And		Factor 1	Operation	Factor 2	Result Field	Field Length	Decimal P.	Half Adju	Compare High 1 > 2	Low 1 < 2	Equal 1 = 2
10	11 Not 12	13 14	Not 15 16	17	18 19 20 21 22 23 24 25 26 27	28 29 30 31 32	33 34 35 36 37 38 39 40 41 42	43 44 45 46 47 48	49 50 51	52	53	54 55	56 57	58 59 6
				AMT		COMP	500.00					1 2		

indicator 12 will go *on* if the **AMT** field is more than $500.00, but will stay *off* if it is either equal to $500.00 or less than $500.00. In the example,

And		And		Factor 1	Operation	Factor 2	Result Field	Dec	Half	High 1 > 2	Low 1 < 2	Equal 1 = 2
10	11 Not 12	13 14	Not 15 16	17 18 19 20 21 22 23 24 25 26 27	28 29 30 31 32	33 34 35 36 37 38 39 40 41 42	43 44 45 46 47 48	49 50 51 52	53	54, 55	56 57	58 59 60
				AMT	COMP	MIN				1 5		

indicator 15 will go *on* if the **AMT** field is smaller than the **MIN** field; otherwise, it will go *off*. Numeric fields are aligned by decimal point before the comparison is done. In the example,

Not		Not		Not	Factor 1	Operation	Factor 2	Result Field	Dec	Half	High 1 > 2	Low 1 < 2	Equal 1 = 2
9 10	11	12 13	14	15 16 17	18 19 20 21 22 23 24 25 26 27	28 29 30 31 32	33 34 35 36 37 38 39 40 41 42	43 44 45 46 47 48	49 50 51 52	53	54 55	56 57	58 59 60
					INTER	COMP	50				Ø8	Ø8	

indicator Ø8 will go *on* if the **INTER** value is less than or equal to $50.00 even though the constant does not have a decimal point given. Even though fields may have different lengths and different numbers of decimal positions, extra zeros are padded on each end of both fields, if necessary, to keep the two values the same length and aligned at the decimal point. Numeric comparisons are done algebraically, as are other calculations, with proper positive or negative signs developed as needed. In the example,

And		And		Factor 1	Operation	Factor 2	Result Field	Dec	Half	High 1 > 2	Low 1 < 2	Equal 1 = 2
Not 10	11 Not 12	13 14	Not 15 16	17 18 19 20 21 22 23 24 25 26 27	28 29 30 31 32	33 34 35 36 37 38 39 40 41 42	43 44 45 46 47 48	49 50 51 52	53	54 55	56 57	58 59 60
				EARNED	COMP	-32.75				1 3		

indicator 13 will go on if the value of **EARNED** is less than −32.75. Assuming that the negative sign represents a credit, a credit of $45.00 would turn *on* the indicator. A credit of $15.00, however, would turn it *off*.

Alphameric fields are compared to one another by use of the "collating sequence" of the machine, which, on the IBM 36Ø, places blanks before letters and letters A, B, C, . . ., Z before numbers. Should one field be shorter than the other, the shorter one is assumed to contain blanks in enough additional positions to make them the same length. In the example,

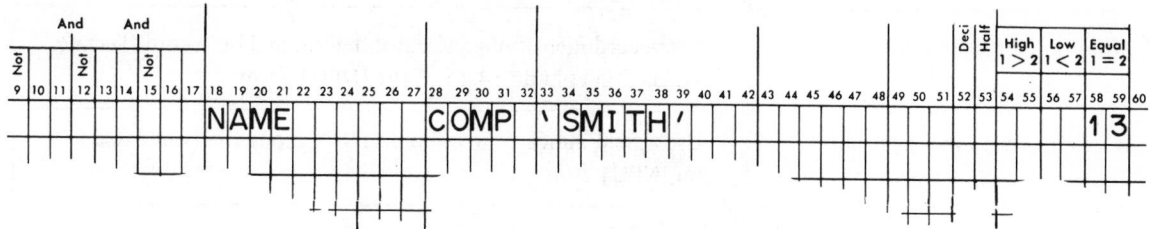

indicator 13 goes *on* if the **NAME** field contains the name 'SMITH'. The shorter field is padded with blanks at the right to make the first two fields the same length. Should the field contain 'SMITH, J. C.' or 'T. J. SMITH, JR.', however, the indicator would *not* be turned on. Alphameric comparisons are made character by character from the left end of the field; variations of a name, even though intended to be the same, would not be considered the same by RPG. Most comparisons on a name field are done, for that reason, on separate fields, one containing last name, and another containing initials, requiring several tests.

The purpose of the compare operation is to set indicators to denote high, low, or equal conditions when testing one field against another, or when testing one field against a specific constant. The indicators are usually used to control calculations and output results. The calculation of a discount, which depends on whether the amount of a sale is $100.00 or over, can be done as shown:

And	And									Length	Deci	Half	High 1 > 2	Low 1 < 2	Equal 1 = 2
02		SALES		COMP	100.00									60	60
02	60	SALES		MULT	0.05			DISC							
02	N60	SALES		MULT	0.01			DISC							

which causes indicator 60 to go on or off to control the proper selection of the necessary calculation. A discount of 5%, or .05, is to be applied to sales of $100.00 or over; a discount of 1%, or .01, is used for all other sales amounts. For an individual record, one of the lines will be used in calculating **DISC**, but not both; the proper one is selected by indicator 60.

Decisions made by the computer are based upon a set of objective rules, provided by people, and administered to data by tests within a computer program. Instructions for every possible alternative as a result of the test must be programmed. Computer decisions of this type then consist of selecting and using the proper set of instructions based upon indicators set as a result of comparisons and tests. Figure 16-4 summarizes the different assignments that indicators can have in programming of alternatives and decisions. It is recommended that indicators from 01 to 99 be used for these assignments, rather than special ones, such as the L-indicators. Indicators with special purposes are set and reset at specific times in the RPG object program appropriate to their purpose.

To Determine This	Do This
What type of record is in	Use record-identifying indicator determined by record ID code, assigned in column 14-15 of the INPUT form
If a field being input is blank	Use a field indicator in columns 69-70 along the field name on INPUT form
If a field being input is positive, negative, or zero	Use a field indicator in columns 65-66, 67-68, or 69-70, of the INPUT form, respectively
If an alphameric field has a zone position in its high-order position	Use the TESTZ instruction with an assigned resulting indicator given in columns 54-55, 56-57, or 58-59, for 12 zone, 11 zone, or no zone, respectively, on the same line of the CALCULATION form
If a field is above, below, or equal to some constant	Use the COMP instruction and assign indicators to high, low, or equal in columns 54-55, 56-57, or 58-59, respectively, on the line of the instruction on the CALCULATION form
If a calculation results in positive, negative, or zero	Use a calculation resulting indicator on the CALCULATION form in columns 54-55, 56-57, or 58-59 on the line containing the calculation.

FIG. 16-4   RPG indicators as decision tools.

Data control can be programmed by using decisions. For example, when sorting is used to get data records into sequence by some key or control field, it is reassuring to know that the sequence is correct. The compare instruction can be used to write a program to check the sequence in a deck of cards—to be sure that it is in either increasing or decreasing order. It can also be used to ensure that only *one* card of each type is present, should only one of each type be needed. The flow chart in Figure 16-5 illustrates a method to check the sequence, as well as to detect duplicate values in the control field in the deck. Each control field value is moved to a **HOLD** area and saved for comparison against the control field from the next card. For a key field in *increasing* order, each one coming in should be *larger* than the last. If any are *smaller than* the last, an out-of-sequence condition message should be given before processing continues. If any control field is *equal* to that on the last card, then a duplicate has been detected! Sequence checking of data records is a vital part of data control and should be done if the records are to be used in production work.

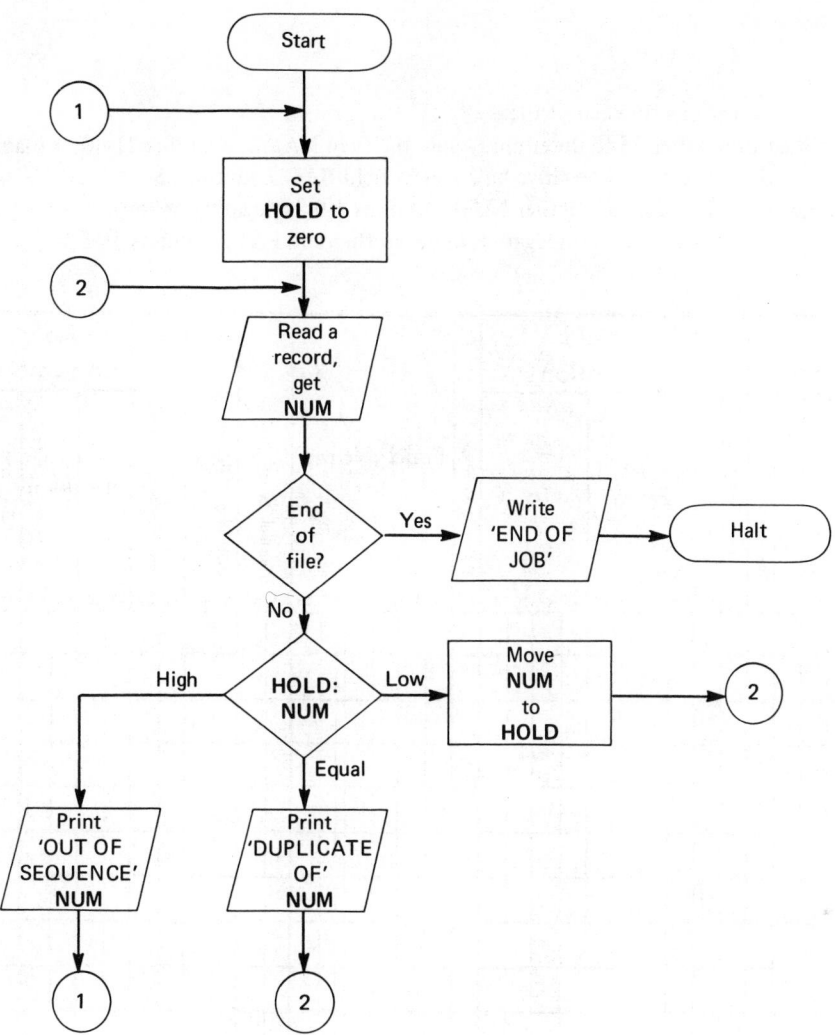

FIG. 16-5 Logic for a sequence checking program.

EXERCISES

1. Write INPUT specifications for each of these:
    (a) Assign indicator number 75 to determine when the field **NAME**, columns 21-4∅, is blank.
    (b) Assign indicator 15 to detect negative balances in field **BAL**, columns 25-3∅.
    (c) Assign indicator 27 to detect whether **NUM**, columns 5-9, is negative or zero.
    (d) Assign indicator 31 to detect nonnegative values in the field **PAY**, columns 46-5∅.

Codes							Field Location		Decimal Positions	Field Name	Control Level (L1-L9)	Matching Fields or Chaining Fields	Field-Record Relation	Field Indicators			Sterling Sign Position
Position			Not (N)	C/Z/D	Character	Stacker Select	Packed (P)	From	To						Plus	Minus	Zero or Blank	
35 36 37 38	39	40	41	42	43		44 45 46 47	48 49 50 51	52	53 54 55 56 57 58	59 60	61 62	63 64	65 66	67 68	69 70	71 72 73 74
(a)																	
(b)																	
(c)																	
(d)																	

2. Write **CALCULATION** specifications for each of these:
   (a) To determine whether the result of the calculation **N – 1** is zero.
   (b) To set the value of **RATE** to Ø.Ø5 if **NUM** is positive.
   (c) If **AMT** is more than $1000.00, add 1 to **CAT**, otherwise do not add 1 to it.
   (d) If **N** is nonzero, divide it into the value of **SUM** to get **AVE**.
   (e) If the value of **BAL** is between $100.00 and $500.00, calculate service charge **CHG** as 3% of **BAL**; if it is $100.00 or below, use 2%; and if $500.00 or over, use 5%.

3. Assume that A = $20.00, B = -7.50 and C = $10.25, and state each indicator that is on and each that is off as a result of each instruction:

	Factor 1	Operation	Factor 2	Result Field	Field Length	Decimal Position	Half Adjust (H)	Plus/High 1>2	Minus/Low 1<2	Zero or Blank/Equal 1=2
(a)	A	COMP	2.0					75		80
(b)	2.75	COMP	B							73
(c)	B	ADD	C	D				15		
(d)		Z-ADD	C	D				12		
(e)		Z-ADD	B	D					14	74
(f)	B	MULT	B	D				68		
(g)	C	DIV	2	D				18		
(h)	-7.50	COMP	B							12
(i)	B	COMP	-10.20					18	18	
(j)		Z-SUB	B	B				17		

Indicators

	Set On	Set Off
(a)		
(b)		
(c)		
(d)		
(e)		
(f)		
(g)		
(h)		
(i)		
(j)		

Lesson 17

MULTIPLE-RECORD INPUT

You will learn how to use field-record relation and record identification codes for defining more than one record type in a data file.

The questions that follow are answered on the back of this page. If you have had data processing experience, study the lesson until you can answer the questions correctly, then go on to Lesson 18.

1. What is meant by *multiple-record input*?
2. Why is the MULTIPLE-RECORD LAYOUT form helpful?
3. What is a record-identifying resulting indicator and how is it assigned?
4. When one record-identifying resulting indicator is on, in what state normally are the others?
5. Why are record types that occur most frequently listed first?
6. How can a record with only one of several possible identification codes be specified so that any of the codes will turn on the indicator?
7. How can you cause cards with invalid record ID codes to be bypassed during the processing, yet be separated from the deck for later examination?
8. What are the three types of record ID tests that can be used for ID codes?
9. When should you use field-record relation rather than write each record's fields out separately?
10. What are some special RPG features that depend on your particular input/output hardware?

ANSWERS

1. More than one type of record is to be brought in as input. Each one should have a unique code so that it can be recognized by type. The format of fields on the different records may have some common fields, but need not be alike at all.
2. So that fields for the various records can be drawn on the same form for you to see at the same time.
3. The indicator specified in columns 19 and 2∅ on the INPUT form, which will turn *on* when that type of card is brought in. It is selected from the indicators ∅1-99, and usually refers to a unique record identification code.
4. The other record-identifying resulting indicators are off, unless the programmer has used one of them for another purpose and it is on from another cause.
5. Because as each card is read, it is tested against the different record ID codes in the order listed on the INPUT form; when the most frequent record types are listed first, they will be located faster, which will cause execution time of the program to be less.
6. By use of an *or* condition. **OR** should be placed in columns 14 and 15 of the line following the first record identification line; the alternate record ID codes should be listed on the **OR** line, with the same, or different, indicator given in columns 19 and 2∅.
7. By using a line with alphabetic letters in columns 14 and 15, listed last on the INPUT form, with no record identification code given. Stacker select may be given in column 42 if hardware for it is available.
8. Character test, digit test, and zone test.
9. When half or more of the fields are in common among the multiple-record types.
10. Stacker select and combined input/output files.

Some problems require more than one type of data card. When statements are to be prepared for accounts receivable, for example, one type of record could be a payment, one could be a return, and still another could be a new charge. On an inventory problem, one type could be a receipt of a new order, another could be an issuance for a sale, and still another could be an adjustment. A run-date header card itself is actually a second record type when used along with a deck of one-record-type cards. A MULTIPLE-CARD LAYOUT form, such as those shown in Figure 17-1, is used for multiple-card input, to show visually what fields are used on each type, to align fields common to all records, and to show record ID codes. One of those shown illustrates the card formats for a job requiring three types of cards: one for hourly employees, one for monthly salaried employees, and one for incentive workers who are paid by the number of items that they make. Another shows a master accounts record, which is three punch cards long.

In doing a multiple-record job, the computer must have some way of distinguishing each record type. A record identification code is prepared by considering all record types in the job; each record type is assigned a unique code, which is a character or group of characters, or a digit or zone within some particular character. In RPG, this record ID code is detected and used to set indicators to perform certain job tasks. Assignments for record ID codes for the payroll job in Figure 17-1 are in column 1, and are 7, 8, and 9, respectively, for setting on indicators 7Ø, 8Ø, and 9Ø.

Up to three record ID codes can be tested on one coding line, in an *and* condition, by using POSITION's 1, 2, or 3 in columns 21-24, 28-34, or 35-41. They can be tested either as a character, as a numeric digit portion of a character, or as the zone portion of a character, as specified under CHARACTER of the INPUT specification form by a C, D, or Z, respectively. POSITION gives the column number of the data card in which the code will be found. When the NOT(N) column is blank, the test is to be for the *presence* of the code; when it contains N, for *not*, it specifies that the test is to be for the *absence* of the code.

Testing for a *character* causes the entire 8-bit EBCDIC-coded column to be tested, whereas the *digit* test refers only to digit punches, ignoring zones, and the *zone* test refers to a zone punch, ignoring digit punches. Record ID codes for digit and zone tests, therefore, need not be unique, since several characters have the same zone and several characters have the same numeric digit. Should the record ID test be specified as the zone of the letter A, for example, as given by

Line	Form Type	Filename	Sequence	Number (1-N)	Option (O)	Resulting Indicator	Record Identification Codes 1 Position	Not (N)	C/Z/D	Character	Record Identification Codes 2 Position	Not (N)	C/Z/D	Character	Record Identification Codes 3 Position	Not (N)	C/Z/D	Character	Stacker Select	Packed (P)	Field Location From	To	Decimal Positions	Fiel
3 4 5	6	7 8 9 10 11 12 13 14	15 16	17	18	19 20	21 22 23 24	25	26	27	28 29 30 31	32	33	34	35 36 37 38	39	40	41	42	43	44 45 46 47	48 49 50 51	52	53 54
0 1	I	CARDS	NS	1	2		2Ø		Z	A														
0 2	I																							

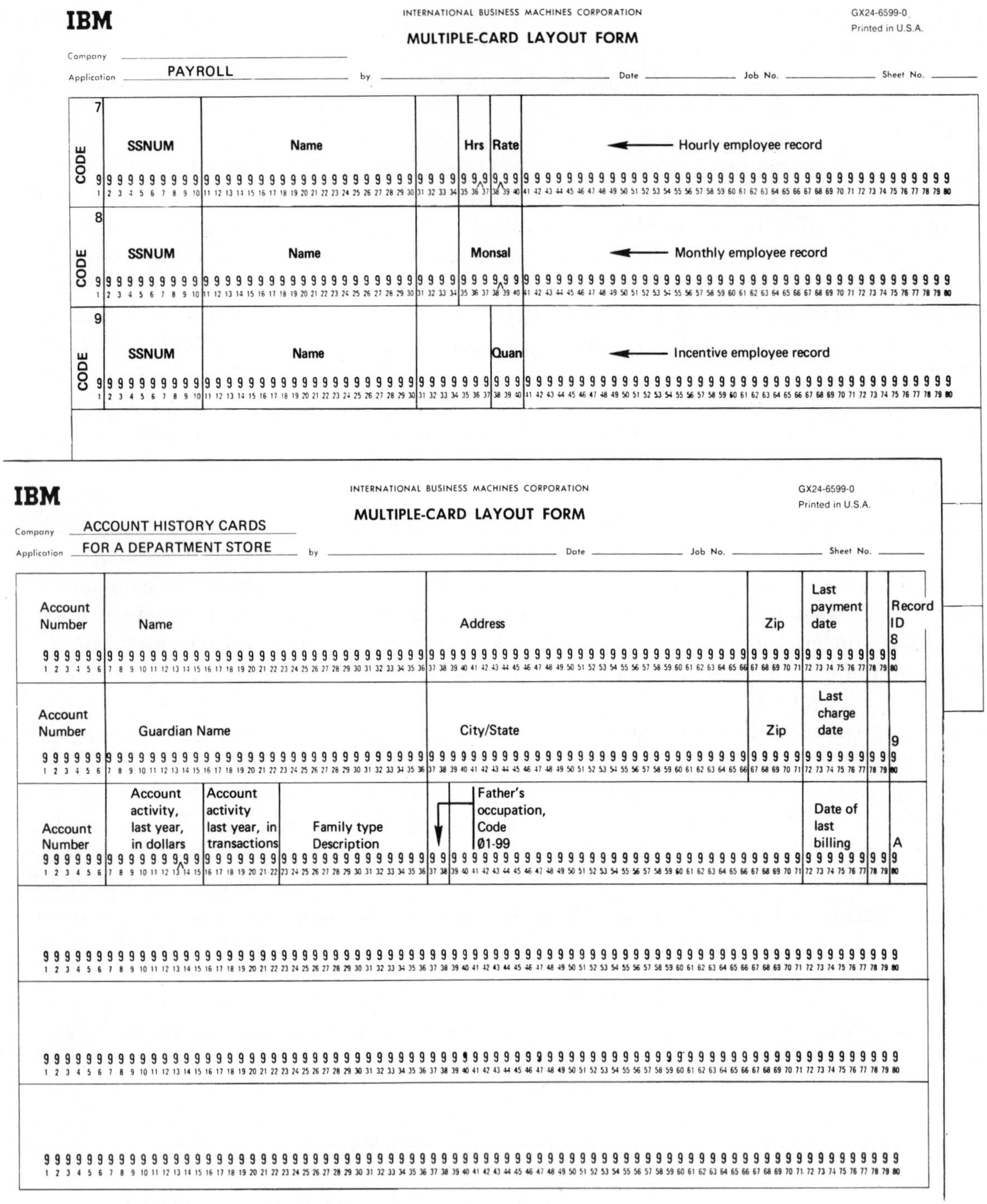

IBM

INTERNATIONAL BUSINESS MACHINES CORPORATION

MULTIPLE-CARD LAYOUT FORM

GX24-6599-0
Printed in U.S.A.

Company _____

Application ___ PAYROLL ___ by _____ Date _____ Job No. _____ Sheet No. _____

IBM

INTERNATIONAL BUSINESS MACHINES CORPORATION

MULTIPLE-CARD LAYOUT FORM

GX24-6599-0
Printed in U.S.A.

Company ___ ACCOUNT HISTORY CARDS ___

Application ___ FOR A DEPARTMENT STORE ___ by _____ Date _____ Job No. _____ Sheet No. _____

FIG. 17-1 MULTIPLE-CARD LAYOUT forms.

a positive identification would be made, turning on indicator 12, for any of the letters A-I in
column 2∅ of the data card, or ∅ or &, since each has the same zone punch. Should the record
ID test be specified as the digit of the number 2, for example, the letters K, B, or S would all
give a positive identification, since that is their digit portion. You should be cautious when

using zone and digit record ID tests for record identification codes since some implementations handle it differently from others.

One particular record identification that was often used on unit-record equipment deserves special comment. It was called an "X-punch" and was used often on multiple-record jobs to denote one record type, while *not* an X, the "NX-punch," often denoted the other. This X-punch is *not* the letter X but an 11 zone punch. When using data prepared in this manner, the record identification code given by

Line	Form Type	Filename	Sequence	Number (1-N)	Option (O)	Resulting Indic	Position	Not (N)	C/Z/D	Character	Position	Not (N)	C/Z/D	Character	Position	Not (N)	C/Z/D	Character	Stacker Select	Packed (P)	From	To	Decimal P.
0 1	I		NS	1 2			35		Z	-														

can be used to detect it, given here as being in column 35 and turning on indicator 12. The NX-punch can be detected either by the X-punch indicator being off, or by using N for that test on the coding form. The 12 punch was, at that time, likewise known as a Y-punch, but was not so commonly used for multiple-record identification.

Records are allowed to have several record ID codes. They may be required in certain combinations to denote a certain type of job. By using an *and* condition, with the letters **AND** given in columns 14, 15, and 16, one record may be tested for more than the three codes possible on one line of specification. In the example,

Line	Form Type	Filename	Sequence	Number (1-N)	Option (O)	Resulting Indica	Position	Not (N)	C/Z/D	Character	Position	Not (N)	C/Z/D	Character	Position	Not (N)	C/Z/D	Character	Stacker Select	Packed (P)	From	To	Decimal Positions
0 1	I	CARDS	NS	1 3			01		C	0	02		C	2	03		C	1					
0 2	I	AND					04		C	5	05		C	4									
0 3	I																						

the number 02154 in columns 1-5 is the record identification code! Of perhaps more importance is the use of the *or* condition, which allows a record to have *alternate* codes, only one of which is required to be detected in order to turn on the indicator. If, for example, either a P in column 7 or a zone 11 punch in column 15 were permitted to indicate a payments card, the input given by

Line	Form Type	Filename	Sequence	Number (1-)	Option (O)	Resulting In	Position	Not (N)	C/Z/D	Character	Position	Not (N)	C/Z/D	Character	Position	Not (N)	C/Z/D	Character	Stacker Sel	Packed (P)	From	To	Decimal P.
0 1	I	CARDS	NS	1 0			7		C	P													
0 2	I	OR					15		Z	-													
0 3	I																						

would turn on indicator 1Ø. On each **OR** line, different indicators can also be assigned to each of the different conditions, if needed. Notice that **OR** is not directly aligned under sequence, but is one position to the left.

    An input specification that could be used for the **MULTIPLE-CARD LAYOUT** form shown in Figure 17-1 is given by

Form	Filename	Seq	Num	Opti	Resu	Position	Not	C/Z	Char		From	To	De	Field Name
I	PAYCD	NS			70		Ø1		C7					
I											2	1Ø		SSNUM
I											11	3Ø		NAME
I											35	371		HRS
I											38	4Ø2		RATE
I		NS			8Ø		Ø1		C8					
I											2	1Ø		SSNUM
I											11	3Ø		NAME
I											35	4Ø2		MONSAL
I		NS			9Ø		Ø1		C9					
I											2	1Ø		SSNUM
I											11	3Ø		NAME
I											38	4ØØ		QUAN

which turns on indicators 7Ø, 8Ø, and 9Ø, depending on the record ID code. Fields that are common to more than one record are listed in every record where they apply. Since record types are tested in the order given, those that are expected to occur most frequently in the job should be listed first for better **RPG** efficiency.

    When several record types are used, many of the fields may be common to all the records. A shorter way to define the fields can be used, and *should* be used when half or more of the fields are common. Columns 63 and 64 of the INPUT form, called FIELD-RECORD RELATION, will be used to permit several record types to be defined together and will usually prevent the listing of common fields more than once.

    Field-record relation uses an **OR** line to give the record ID codes and indicators for all record types except the first, which uses the regular alphabetic letters under SEQUENCE. In the example,

Filename	Sequence	Number (1-N)	Option (O)	Resulting Indicator	Position	Not (N)	C/Z/D	Character	C/Z/D	Character	Stacker Select	Packed (P)	From	To	Decimal Positions	Field Name	Control Level (L1-L)	Matching Fields or Chaining Fields	Field-Record Relation
PAYCD	NS			70		Ø1		C7											
	OR			8Ø		Ø1		C8											
	OR			9Ø		Ø1		C9											
													2	1Ø		SSNUM			
													11	3Ø		NAME			
													35	371		HRS			7Ø
													38	4Ø2		RATE			7Ø
													35	4Ø2		MONSAL			8Ø
													38	4ØØ		QUAN			9Ø

7, 8, and 9 codes are used to turn on indicators 7∅, 8∅, and 9∅, respectively. Field descriptions follow, with those that are common listed *first*, and those that belong to a specific card type *next*. Along the side of each field, FIELD-RECORD RELATION in columns 63 and 64 gives the indicator number for the record to which this field belongs. Records in common are listed only once, with FIELD-RECORD RELATION for each one remaining blank. Remember that only one record is in use at a given time during execution, so while one record-type resulting indicator is *on*, the others are *off*. Storage areas used for the fields that are common to all records are filled, in turn, by whichever record is present in memory at the time.

Columns for field-record relation may be used, on the IBM SYSTEM/36∅, DOS/TOS, and on the IBM SYSTEM/3, to assign special external indicators U1, U2, . . ., U8. These are set either on or off by certain job control cards *before* the job is begun, and may not be changed during the run. When a U-indicator is assigned to a field on the INPUT specifications form, the field is processed if the indicator is *on*, but not processed if it is *off*. The U-indicators may be used to establish a set-up switch or data fields, to control calculations, to condition a file description, or to control output.

Two different types of charge accounts will be used to illustrate variations of field-record relation in multiple-record input. A *30-day charge* account is one for which the balance is to be completely paid at the end of 30 days; a revolving charge account is one that permits a portion of the balance to be paid in 30 days, but calculated interest is charged on the unpaid remainder. In doing a job with these two types of accounts in one file, the amount field for both types may be called by the same name, say, **AMT**, and may even be placed in the same columns of their respective records. In the example,

Sequence	Number (1-N)	Option (O)	Resulting Indi	Position	Not (N)	C/Z/D	Character	Position	Not (N)	C/Z/D	Character	Position	Not (N)	C/Z/D	Character	Stacker Select	Packed (P)	From	To	Decimal Posi
ACCTCD	NS			∅2		8∅	C8													
	OR			∅3		8∅	C9													
																		1	5	ACCT
																		6	1∅2	AMT

an 8 in column 8∅ means one type of account and a 9 means the other, but the amount field is called by the same name and comes from the same columns. Should the fields be in different columns, another set of specifications

	For			Seq	Nu	Op	Res				Ne	C/	Chr		Ste	Po					Co	M O	Fi
01	I	ACCTCD	NS		∅2		8∅	C8															
02	I		OR		∅3		8∅	C9															
03	I																1	5	ACCT			
04	I																6	1∅2	AMT			∅2
05	I																16	2∅2	AMT			∅3
06	I																					

may be written, using FIELD-RECORD RELATION. They specify that the **AMT** field in columns 6-1∅ belongs to the record-type identified by indicator ∅2 but that the other, in columns 16-2∅, belongs to the record type identified by indicator ∅3. Since the two record types are *not* in memory at the same time, they are permitted to use the same field name, which also saves core storage. Should the fields be of different lengths, however, or have different decimal places, they would require different names, such as **AMT3Ø** and **AMTREV**, for the 3Ø-day type and revolving type, respectively.

When multiple-record types of input are used in a program, it is often helpful to *stacker-select* them by type as they go through the card reader. This capability to separate an input deck into two or more decks during processing is available on some, but not all, card reading devices. Stacker selection, when available, is often for two pockets: the normal stacker pocket ordinarily used, and the nonnormal stacker pocket, used to separate cards from the main deck. Column 42 of the INPUT form is used to specify stacker selection for record types. By putting 1 there, or by leaving it blank, you will cause that card type to fall into its normal place, but by putting 2 there, you will cause that card type to be placed into the *nonnormal* select stacker. Some installations have a shop standard that recommends stacker selection of all run-date header cards. Others recommend that a record description be placed in the program so that all invalid card types throughout the deck will be bypassed, as given by

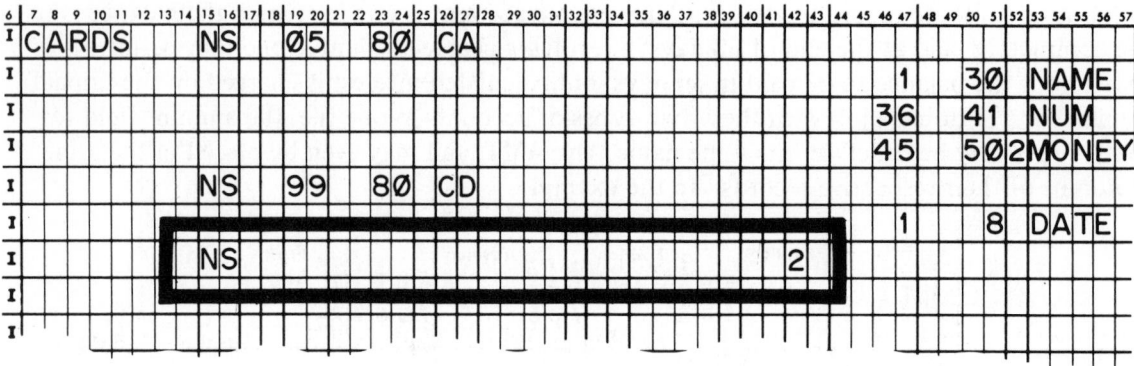

which prevents the system from halting due to invalid card types, and causes the offending cards to be stacker selected for later examination.

On different input/output hardware, different stacker-select capability is possible. Many devices can stacker-select punched-card output. The IBM 1442 with read-punch feature can even stacker-select *input* cards by use of the *output* stacker-select feature, by permitting the input file to be defined as a *combined* file instead of an input one. Combined-file capability allows one file to be used for both input and output, with punching possible either in a blank portion of the input card, or in blank cards that have been interspersed throughout the deck. Program design, however, based on a major use of these types of hardware differences, causes more machine dependence. Before investing much time in programming for special features not commonly available on most equipment, be sure that you will have continued access to that particular configuration for a time sufficient to make it worthwhile. Much time can be spent in reprogramming and redesigning problems that have stacker-select and combined file features in them, but that the new equipment cannot use.

One type of job that may use multiple-record input is a department store accounts receivable application. A *payment* card may have the same card design as a *charge* card, and may need a record identification code to denote the difference and to cause the program to do *subtraction* from the balance, rather than *addition*. Figure 17-2 illustrates how this might be done.

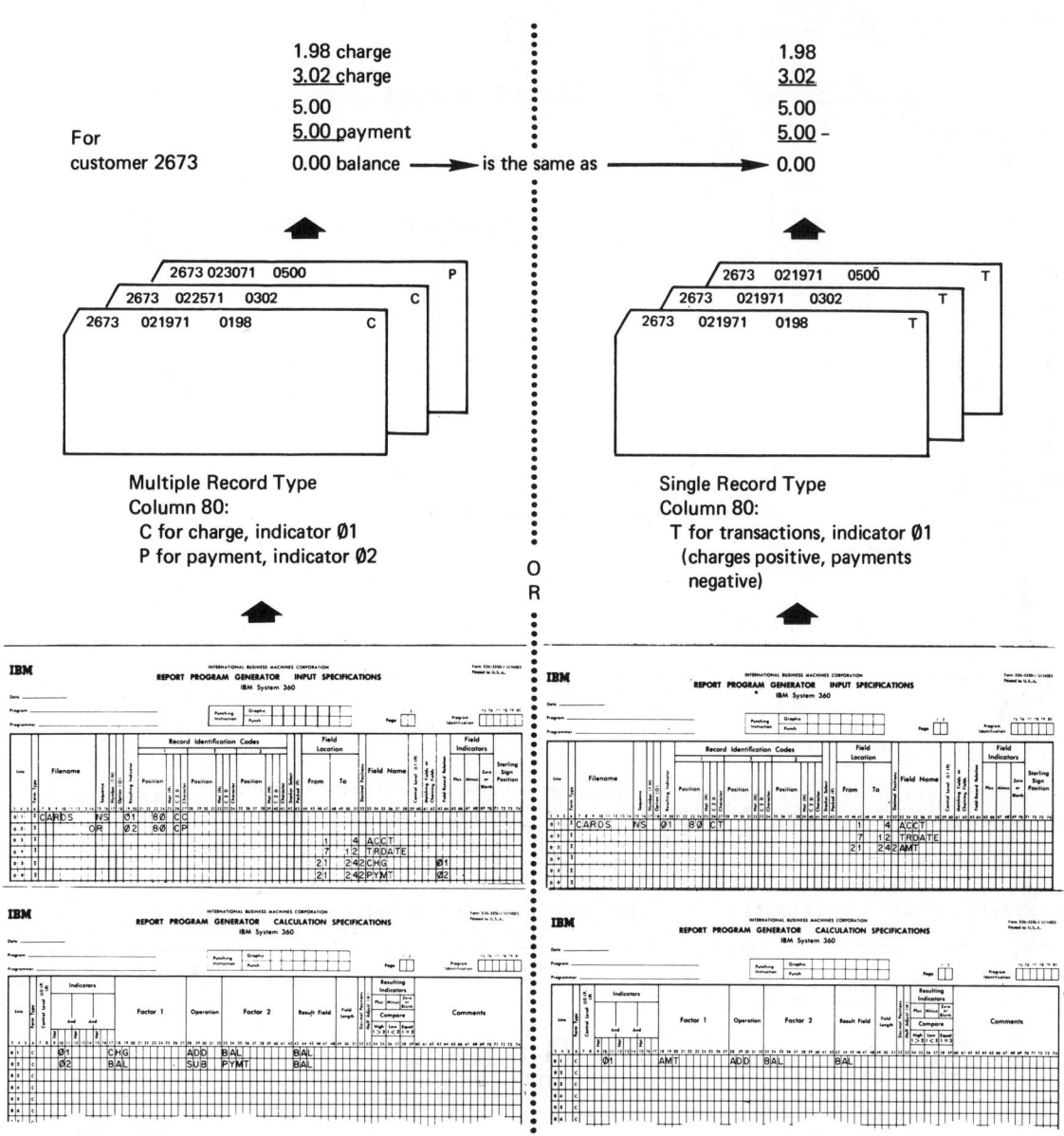

FIG. 17-2 Accounts receivable—multiple-record or single-record input.

Other accounts receivable systems may handle payments in exactly the same manner as charges, except that the payment amount is punched as *negative*, causing it to be handled as a *credit* throughout the program.

Another job using multiple-record header cards is that of sending form letters to customers or clients. In Figure 17-3, one layout shows such a form letter, on five message cards, each one with record ID, from 1 to 5. The return address card has an H in column 1. These cards are read and stored, then written out on an envelope for each addressee. Carbon stripping permits the name and address to print on the envelope face but prevents the message from printing there. The cover sheet containing the message will be removed and the presealed envelope sent to the addressee with the enclosed message unseen and untouched.

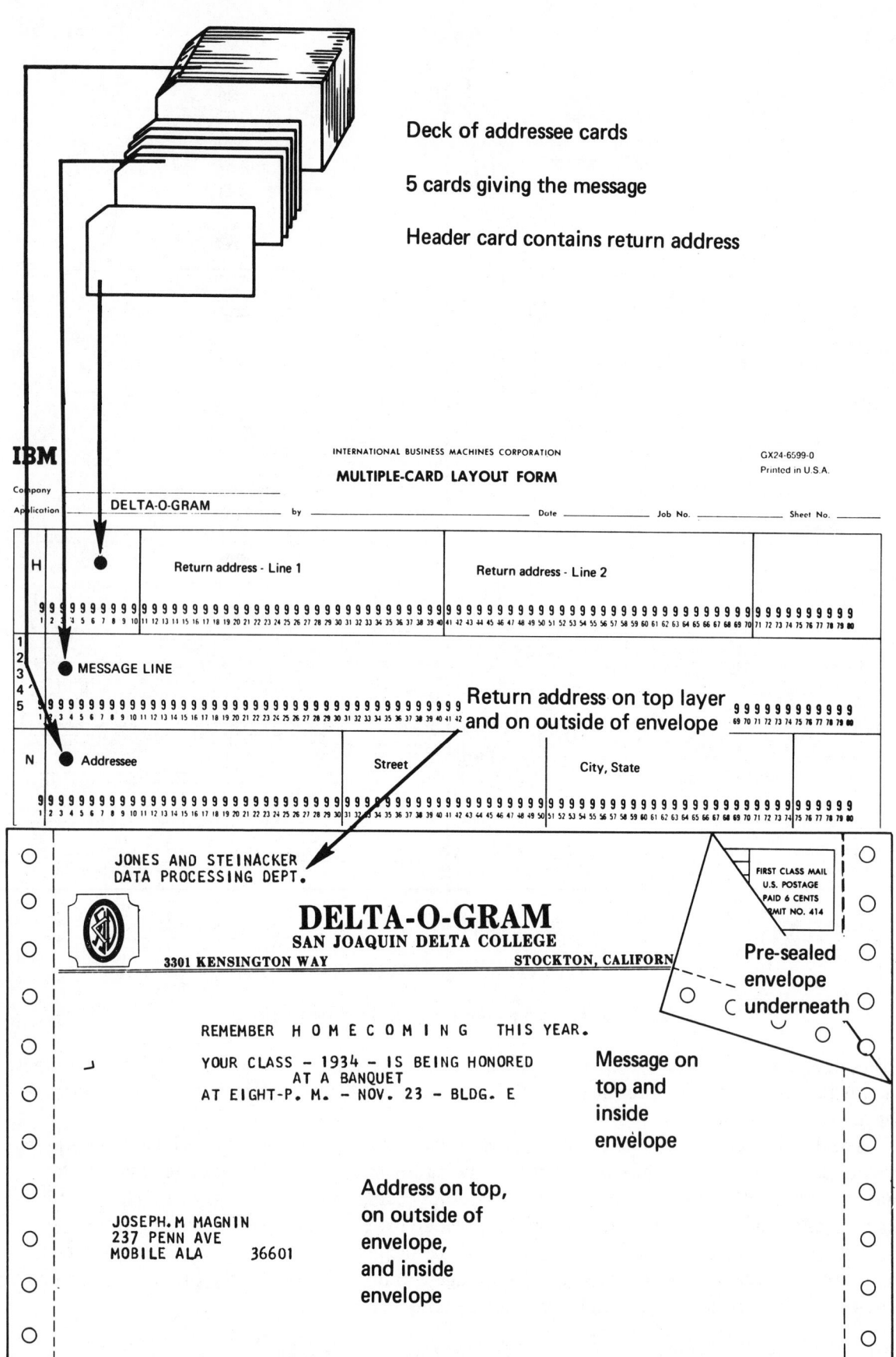

FIG. 17-3 Form letter using multiple records. (Form courtesy of UARCO, Inc.)

EXERCISES

1. Write INPUT specifications for the multirecord layout given for the account history cards in Figure 17-1.

Form Type	Filename	Sequence	Number (1-N)	Option (O)	Resulting Indicator	Position	Not (N)	C/Z/D	Character	Stacker Select	Packed (P)	From	To	Decimal Positions	Field Name	Control Level (L1-L9)	Matching Fields or Chaining Fields	Field-Record Relation	Plus
I																			
I																			
I																			
I																			
I																			
I																			
I																			
I																			
I																			
I																			
I																			
I																			
I																			
I																			
I																			

2. Write INPUT specifications for:
   (a) three cards that are punched with alphameric information from columns 2-8∅, to be stored as **HOLD1**, **HOLD2**, and **HOLD3**, respectively, and that have a 12 zone, 11 zone, and ∅ zone, respectively, in column 1.
   (b) the fields as given, turning on indicator 11, 12, or 13, depending on the value in column 8∅, which should be 7, 8, and 9, respectively. Allow all other cards to be bypassed.

Field Information	Columns
Name	1-3∅
Number	35-4∅
Amount, 2 decimals	46-5∅

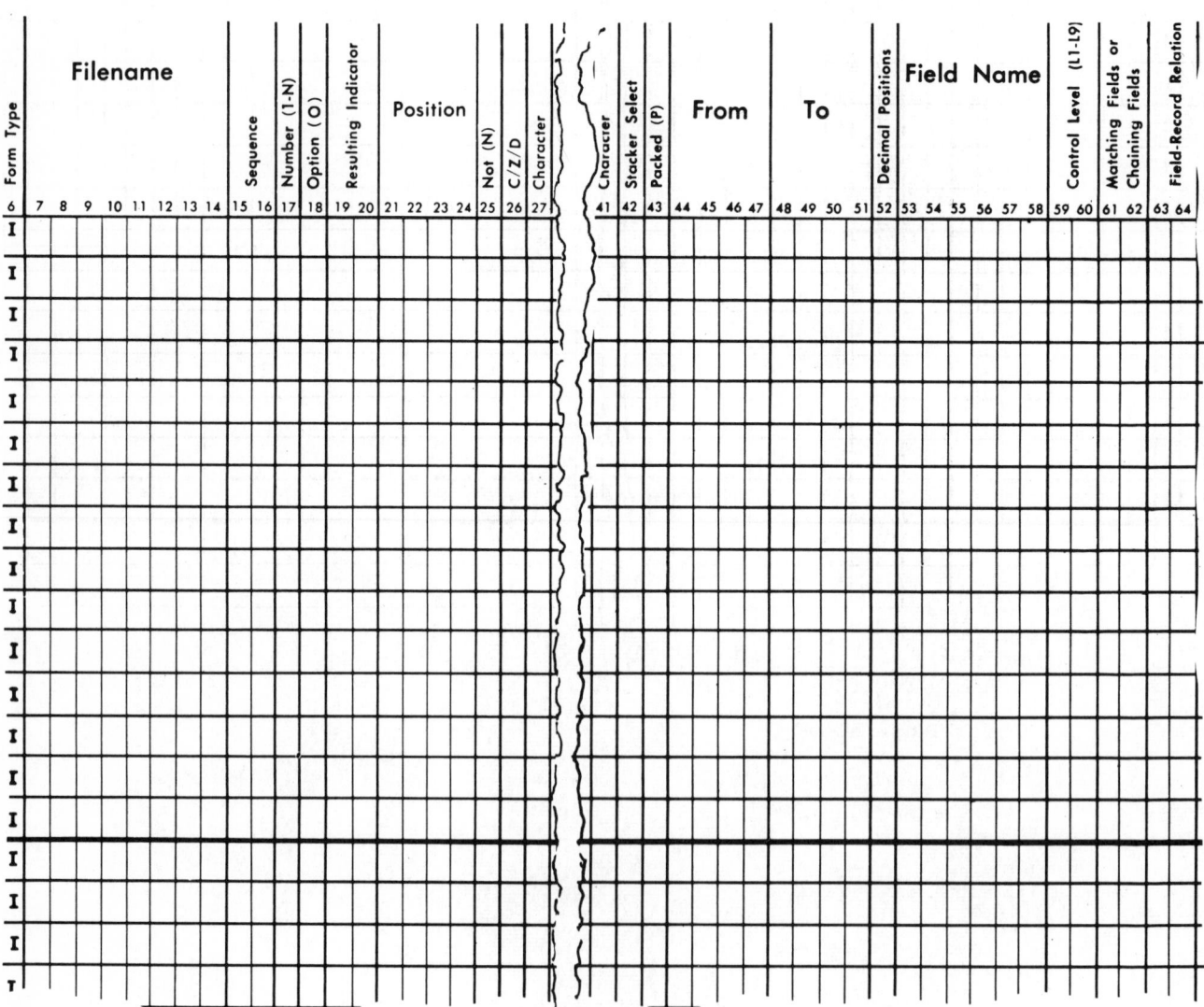

Lesson 18

A PRINTED REPORT WITH DECISIONS

You will learn how a report involving multiple-record types and decisions is written and debugged in RPG.

The questions below summarize material on comparisons, tests, and multiple records. After you have studied the lesson and understand the debugging of the program named **ACCTSUM**, answer the following questions and then go on to the programs to write at the end of this section.

1. What type of indicator is set as a result of comparisons and calculations?
2. What type of indicator is used to determine whether a field is positive, negative, or zero?
3. What is the purpose of the RPG INDICATOR SUMMARY form?
4. How does a decision table or flow chart aid in the writing of an intricate RPG program?
5. How can you determine whether you need to use a **MOVE** or a **Z-ADD** instruction for getting information from one place to another in the program?
6. What distinguishes a numeric constant from an alphameric one in FACTOR 2 of the **MOVE** or **MOVEL** instruction?
7. For what purpose can the **MOVE** be used that takes *advantage* of the fact that it does not clear the excess positions in the receiving field?
8. How do you determine whether or not an indicator must be set *off* after its use?

ANSWERS

1. A *resulting* indicator, set as a result of calculations or comparison. The card-type indicator set when a card comes in is also known as a resulting indicator, but as an *input*, record-identifying, resulting one.
2. A *field* indicator, *not* a resulting indicator.
3. To help the programmer summarize the indicators in the program and the purpose of each. Each line of the summary is punched with **F** in column 6 and ***** in column 7, and is placed onto the front of the source deck.
4. By assisting in the analysis of what the job is supposed to do. Flaws or incomplete information may, however, become apparent in a decision table as the job progresses; the programmer must get answers from the appropriate personnel and add them to the decision table as needed.
5. If you wish to move alphameric information, the **MOVE** or **MOVEL** must be used. If you wish to initialize a numeric field longer than 10 digits with a constant zero, the **Z-ADD** must be used. For some things, either one may be used. The **MOVE** should be used with exactly the right length and decimal places, since it does not clear the receiving field, whereas the **Z-ADD** both completely clears the receiving field of the previous value and aligns the decimal place.
6. A numeric constant should not have quotation marks around it; the alphameric constant *must* have them. Since the numeric constant may be moved to an alphameric field, and vice versa, decimal places in the RESULT FIELD cannot be used to determine mode of the constant.
7. By using it to break one long record into several short fields, or by using it to form several short fields into one long record.
8. By whether or not it is reset automatically next time through the program cycle, and whether or not it will do any damage when left *on*.

Lesson 18   A Printed Report with Decisions

Calculations for different record types are controlled by indicators. They may be set by *record-identifying indicators* representing the different record types, by *field indicators* assigned to positive, negative, or zero/blank conditions, or by *resulting indicators* set by a calculation or a comparison. When all the conditions given on a calculation line are satisfied, it will be executed; otherwise, it will be bypassed. All calculation lines for a given record type are usually placed together on the form. This not only makes it easier to find them, but is more efficient for RPG generation. Lines on the form are executed in the order of their occurrence when indicator conditions are satisfied.

In a program involving alternatives based on the contents of certain fields, several indicators may be necessary. For example, a *field* indicator may be assigned to check for an unpaid balance of zero; a *calculation* resulting indicator may be assigned to check for a new balance of zero. Each record-type will have its own record-identifying indicator, and there may also be an indicator for a run-date header card. A special form, shown in Figure 18-1, may be used for an indicator summary when several indicators are used. The lines on the form are prepared so that each one may be punched, with an F in column 6 and an asterisk in column 7, to be placed with the FILE DESCRIPTION form source cards at the front of the source deck.

Many jobs with decisions based on contents of fields use the **MOVE** or **MOVEL** instruction to cause contents of one field to be replaced by another. For example, when calculating a running balance, which is constantly changing by having charges and payments affect it, the starting amount is the unpaid balance from the previous period. By moving the unpaid balance into a new field to be used for the running balance, its own value will be unchanged; it can then be used for output on the total line at the end of that account group. In other cases, it is necessary to use the **MOVE** or **MOVEL** instruction to place certain constants into a field—perhaps, for example, a 5% discount for one type of record, and a 1% discount for another. Alphameric constants may sometimes be needed. The word 'DEBIT' or the word 'CREDIT', for example, can be moved into a field called **REMARK**, to be printed later.

Moving of one field to another is done by using FACTOR 2 as the sending field, and RESULT FIELD as the receiving field. The **MOVE** instruction causes information from the sending field to be moved, character by character, to the receiving field, starting at the *right* end. Transmission of characters is terminated when the end of either of the fields is reached. Should a longer field be sent to a shorter field, all the sending field does *not* get moved, since the receiving field does not have enough positions to hold it. Should a shorter field be moved to a longer one, however, the excess positions in the receiving field remain as they were *before* the instruction was executed. The **MOVEL** instruction performs the same function as the **MOVE**, except that transmission is from the *left* end of the fields, not the right. In the example,

255

IBM System/360 Report Program Generator Indicator Summary

Date MARCH ,--

Program ACCT SUM

Programmer CJC CLASS

Punching Instruction	Graphic				
	Punch				

Page [ ][ ]   Program Identification [ ][ ][ ][ ][ ]

Circle Indicators Used:

01	02	03	04	05	06	07	08	09	⑩	11	⑫	⑬	⑭	15	16	17	18	19	20
21	22	23	24	25	26	27	28	29	30	31	32	33	34	35	36	37	38	39	40
41	42	43	44	45	46	47	48	49	50	51	52	53	54	55	56	57	58	59	60
61	62	63	64	65	66	67	68	69	70	71	72	73	74	75	76	77	78	79	⑧⓪
81	82	83	84	85	86	87	88	89	⑨⓪	91	92	93	94	95	96	97	98	99	OF
L0	L1	L2	L3	L4	L5	L6	L7	L8	L9	Ⓛⓡ	M1	M2	M3	H1	H2	C1	C2	C3	OV

Line	Form Type	Input Resulting	Calc. Resulting	Field	Matching & Chaining	Ctrl. Break & Halt	Function of Indicators
0 1	F *	I	C	F	M	L	FUNCTION OF INDICATORS
0 2	F *						
0 3	F *	8Ø					THIRTY-DAY TYPE ACCOUNT
0 4	F *	9Ø					REVOLVING TYPE ACCOUNT
0 5	F *						
0 6	F *		1Ø				NEW BALANCE - $100.00 OR OVER -
0 7	F *		N1Ø				NEW BALANCE - LESS THAN $100.00
0 8	F *						
0 9	F *			12			ZERO UNPAID BALANCE FROM LAST RUN PERIOD
1 0	F *			13			ZERO CURRENT CHARGES
1 1	F *			14			POSITIVE UNPAID BALANCE FROM LAST RUN PERIOD -
1 2	F *						
1 3	F *					LR	FINAL TOTAL OF AMOUNTS DUE
1 4	F *						
1 5	F *						OTHERS MAY LATER BE ADDED
	F *						
	F *						
	F *						
	F *						
	F *						

FIG. 18-1 RPG INDICATOR SUMMARY.

the value of **OLDBAL** is moved to **RUNBAL**; **OLDBAL** is still available for printing at any time.

When moving constants into a field, they are given in FACTOR 2. Alphameric constants, or literals, are distinguished by being enclosed within two single quotation symbols. Since these take 2 of the 1Ø positions allowed in FACTOR 2, the size of the alphameric *constant* is limited to 8 characters, even though alphameric *fields* may be 256 characters long. In the example,

Line	Form Type	Control Lev		Not	And	Not	And	Not	Factor 1	Operation	Factor 2	Result Field	Field Length	Decimal Pos	Half Adjust
0 1	C									MOVE	'OVERDUE'	NOTE	7		
0 2	C														
0 3	C														

the word 'OVERDUE' is placed into the field named **NOTE**. Should a word or phrase be needed that is longer than 8 characters, it may be placed, piece by piece, into as many fields as needed, later to be printed in adjacent positions. Many constants, however, are placed onto the **OUTPUT-FORMAT** form as constants, *not* as fields, for selection by a field-selection indicator.

Numeric literals must be formed by the same rules as given for calculation. Digits 0-9 are permitted, with a plus or minus sign in the left-most position. They may *not* have special characters such as the comma or dollar sign, but a decimal point *is* permitted. They must be left-justified within the boundaries of FACTOR 2, which is 10 positions long. The important thing to remember is that the **MOVE** instruction does *not* do any decimal alignment. In the example,

01 C		MOVE 1268	OUT 42
02 C			

the value of out will be 12.68 even though no decimal point was given, since the length and decimal places are specified by those assigned to the RESULT FIELD. Keep in mind, too, that a shorter length moved into a longer one does *not* completely destroy what was formerly in the RESULT FIELD. In the example,

01 C		MOVE 15.08	KAT 62
02 C			

should the previous value of **KAT** have been 1001.26, the value after the **MOVE** will be 1015.08, since only the 4 digits 15.08 are moved, the left-most 2 digits remaining the same. It is recommended that exact lengths be used on all **MOVE** instructions to prevent error. It is recommended, too, that the instruction **Z-ADD** be used instead of the **MOVE** when a numeric constant is to be moved. It first clears the RESULT FIELD to zero, then adds in the constant. Since it is an arithmetic calculation, decimal alignment is done, so that in the example given by

01 C		Z-ADD10	OUT 62
02 C			
03 C			

the value of **OUT** is completely cleared of its former value, after which the value 10.00 is placed there. With the **Z-ADD** instruction, you need not worry about high-order leftover digits from a former value in that field!

The feature of the **MOVE** and the **MOVEL** that permits excess positions in the receiving field to remain unchanged can be used to advantage in forming new fields from several old ones. A **MOVE** places characters from the right, while the **MOVEL** places them from the left, so that the instructions given by

01 C		MOVE CARD1	NEWREC160
02 C		MOVELCARD2	NEWREC
03 C			

form a new field, named **NEWREC**, which receives perhaps 8∅ characters from **CARD1** and 8∅ more from **CARD2**, forming a 16∅-character record. The reverse can also be used to split a long record into individual fields by using the **MOVE** and **MOVEL** with a RESULT FIELD of the exact length needed, so that other fields in the sending record will not be transferred.

Moving of information can also be done from one mode-type to another. Should you find it necessary to transfer numeric to alphameric, or vice versa, it is possible. Should you simply need one field defined in both modes, however, it is far simpler to define the field *twice* on the input card, once in alphameric mode, by one name, and next in numeric mode, by another. To move alphameric fields to numeric, or numeric to alphameric, a full understanding of the sign position as it is stored in memory for your implementation is recommended. Consult the reference manual should a need arise for this in your programming requirements.

PROBLEM DEFINITION: *A department store expects its regular charge account customers to pay their bills every 3∅ days. For larger purchases, a time payment plan, called a revolving charge, may be obtained. Under that plan, a customer may pay only a part of the bill every 3∅ days, but must pay 1.5% interest charges on the unpaid balance each month.*

A summary of the amount due on each account is needed. Unless the unpaid balance and current charges are both zero, give the following information for each account: account number and the type of account; previous unpaid balance; current charges; interest charge, if any; new balance; and amount due. A total of all amounts due is needed at the end of the report.

Field Description	Field Name	Columns
Account number	**ACCT**	6-1∅
Account name	**NAME**	21-4∅
Unpaid balance, 2 decimals	**BAL**	46-5∅
Current charges, 2 decimals	**AMT**	56-6∅
Identification code: 8 for 3∅-day 9 for revolving		1

A summary of the provided information is presented in the decision table in Figure 18-2. Each column gives a set of conditions and the actions that should be taken for that set. The 3∅-day charge customers who have an unpaid balance should have the word 'OVERDUE' printed on the line giving their account information. The new balance for that type of account is obtained by adding charges to the old balance; the amount due is the entire new balance. For the revolving account customers, however, a 1.5% interest rate is to be assessed on unpaid balances. Interest and current charges should be added to the unpaid balance to get the new balance. The amount due is based on new balance; if the new balance is $100.00 or over, it is $25.00; otherwise, it is $10.00.

Indicators 8∅ and 9∅ will be assigned as record-identifying indicators, for the 3∅-day and revolving accounts, respectively. Field indicators 12 and 13 will be used to detect when the unpaid balance and the current charges, respectively, are zero. Indicator 14 will be used to detect a positive unpaid balance so that the message 'OVERDUE' may be printed on the 3∅-day accounts. Indicator 1∅ will be assigned as a calculation resulting indicator to detect new balance amounts of $100.00 or over on revolving accounts. These indicators are given on the RPG IN-DICATOR SUMMARY form, as shown in Figure 18-1; each line could be punched and placed at the beginning of the source program for reference. As a need for other indicators arises, they may be added to the summary sheet for documentation.

Account Summary	1	2	3	4	5	6	7	8
C O N D I T I O N S								
Type ?		Revolving			Thirty-Day			
Balance and charges zero?	Y	N	N	Y	N	N		
Balance positive?		Y	Y		Y	N		
New balance $100 or more?		Y	N					
A C T I O N S								
Print selection-type		'REVOLVING'			'THIRTY-DAY'			
Print 'OVERDUE'					X			
Calculate interest at 1.5% balance		X	X					
Print interest		X	X					
New balance is balance + charges					X	X		
New balance is charges + balance + interest		X	X					
Amount due is		$25.00	$10.00		New Balance	New Balance		
Bypass Output	X			X				

FIG. 18-2 Decision table for use with program development of ACCTSUM.

Since all the fields are present on all the record types, all fields are *common*, so the INPUT coding given by

Line	Form Type	Filename	Sequence	Number (1-N)	Option (O)	Resulting Indicat	Position	Not (N)	C/Z/D	Character	P⟨ ⟩om	To	Decimal Position	Field Name	Control Level (L	Matching Fields Chaining Fields	Field-Record Rek	Plus	Minus	Zero or Blank
0 1	Ø I	CARDS		N S			8 0		Ø 5	C 8										
0 2	I		O R				9 0		Ø 5	C 9										
0 3	I										1	5		A C C T						
0 4	I										6	3 0		N A M E						
0 5	I										4 6	5 0 2		B A L				1 4	1 2	
0 6	I										5 6	6 0 2		A M T					1 3	
0 7	I																			
0 8	I																			

may therefore be used. When unpaid balance and current charges are both zero, the entire detail line should be suppressed. Indicators 12 and 13 can be used, when both *on*, to turn on indicator 15. Should indicator 15 be *off*, it means that one or the other of the fields is not zero, and so a detail line should be printed. It is easier to use the extra indicator 15 to serve as one *off* condition, representing both 12 and 13 *on*, rather than to write specifications lines that say "either 12 *off* or 13 *off*, or both *off*", on an OUTPUT-FORMAT form. The extra indicator, however, must be set *off* after each use, because it is not reset by the reading of each new record type as 12, 13, and 14 are.

Notice that indicator 14, representing a positive unpaid balance, selects the word 'OVERDUE' for output. It must be used in an *and* relation with the indicator for the 3∅-day account, or it would be printed on the positive unpaid balances for both account types. Note that the **AMT** field could have been given *two* names instead of one, based on a field-record relationship, as given by

Form Type		Sequence	Number	Option	Resulting In	Position	Not (N)	C/Z/D	Character	Position	From	To	Decimal	Control	Matching/Chaining	Field-Re	blank
I	* ALTERNATE INPUT DESCRIPTION FOR ACCTSUM PROGRAM															
I	*															
I	* USING TWO FIELD NAMES, NOT ONE, REQUIRING MORE CORE STORAGE															
I	*															
I	CARDS	NS			80	01		C8									
I		OR			90	01		C9									
I										1	5	ACCT					
I										6	30	NAME					
I										46	502	BAL			14	12	
I										56	602	AMT3∅	80			13	
I										56	602	AMTREV	90			13	

which would then be used on appropriate calculations and output throughout the program.

Figure 18-3 shows a trial run for the program, called **ACCTSUM**, on the IBM SYSTEM/36∅, DOS. From the list of **NOTE**'s down the side of the source listing, many diagnostic errors are apparent. To see how interrelated one RPG specification is to all the others, examine **NOTE ∅25** and then try to discover just how many of the other errors given are caused by it. You will see that it is caused because **SYSRDR** is punched in columns 46-51, rather than columns 47-52! **CARDS** is therefore not stored as a valid file name, and so all input specifications that refer to **CARDS** are thought to be in error by the RPG programming system.

Mixed among errors due to the mispunching of **SYSRDR** are some valid diagnostics. **REPORT** is not acceptable as a file name since an **I**, and not an **F**, appears in column 6. **NOTE 192** is caused by that, as is **NOTE 179**. **NOTE 212** and **NOTE 214** indicate that invalid fields and indicators are being used, but after examination, it is found that all fields are satisfactory; they are thought to be in error because of the file name **REPORT**. The run had such serious errors that execution was impossible and the job was cancelled.

After corrections to the two FILE DESCRIPTION cards, another run produces the report in Figure 18-4, with answers! Before becoming overjoyed, however, examine the answers. You will notice that a person who owes $0.95 is being asked to pay $10.00! Although the decision table did not prepare us to anticipate a new balance less than $10.00, it can and does happen, and most assuredly the customer should pay only the amount he *owes*, even if it is less than $10.00. You will also notice that revolving accounts are not being held responsible for their old balances, but only for the interest and the new charges! That is an error—the decision table states that they must be charged for the balance from a previous period! One more addition instruction is needed for that. Note also that interest is being calculated on a *credit* balance, as a negative charge, which is therefore making it to the customer's *advantage* to overpay! That, too, though not specifically mentioned on the decision table, is not what the problem intended to do. You can see that the debugging of execution errors must be very carefully done.

Figure 18-5 (p. 265) shows a final version of the program **ACCTSUM**. Notice that another comparison has been added, to determine whether the revolving new balance is less than $10.00. Notice that field indicator 14, originally used to determine positive balances for the 3Ø-day old balances, can also be used for detecting positive balances for the revolving account as well, and so when 14 is off, no interest is charged. Interest is set to zero for those accounts; if this were *not* done, the value from a previous account would be printed! An additional **ADD** instruction causes revolving accounts to be held responsible for balances as well as for interest and new charges.

```
// JOB ACCSUM JOYCE LITTLE  000                13.16.35
// OPTION LIST,NODECK,LINK
// EXEC RPG

DOS/360*RPG*CL 3-5              ACCSUM            06/22/70        PAGE 0001

          H
          F* ACCOUNT SUMMARY WITH MULTIPLE RECORDS
          FCARDS  IP  F  80  80              READ40SYSRDR
                                                              NOTE 025
                                                              NOTE 201
                                                              NOTE 203
          IREPORT  O  F 120 120      OF      PRINTERSYSLST
                                                              NOTE 111
          ICARDS   NS  80  05 C8                              NOTE 111
          I        OR  90  05 C9                              NOTE 115
          I                         0  10 ACCT                NOTE 130
          I                        21  40 NAME                NOTE 130
          I                        46  50 2BAL      14 12     NOTE 130
          I                        56  60 2AMT         13     NOTE 130
                                                              NOTE 077
          C* THIRTY-DAY TYPE
001       C   80    BAL     ADD  AMT    AMTDUE 62
002       C   80            MOVE AMTDUE NEWBAL 62
          C* REVOLVING TYPE
003       C   90    BAL     MULT .015   INT    52H
004       C   90    INT     ADD  AMT    NEWBAL
005       C   90    NEWBAL  COMP 100.00             10 10
006       C   90 10         MOVE 0025.00 AMTDUE
007       C   90N10         MOVE 0010.00 AMTDUE
          C* BOTH TYPES
008       C          AMTDUE ADD  TOTDUE TOTDUE 72
009       C                 SETOF              15
010       C   12 13         SETON              15
011       OREPORT H  301    1P
012       O        OR       OF                      NOTE 192
013       O                          83 'PAGE'
014       O                 PAGE Z   80
015       O                          41 'ACCOUNT'
016       O                          37 'SUMMARY'
017       O        H  2     1P
018       O        OR       OF                      NOTE 192
019       O                          18 'ACCOUNT AND TYPE'
020       O                          28 'BALANCE'
021       O                          54 'CHARGES'
022       O                          71 'AMOUNT OWED'
023       O                          90 'AMOUNT DUE'
024       O        D  1     80N15                   NOTE 192
025       O        OR       90N15                   NOTE 192
          O                 ACCT     5

DOS/360*RPG*CL 3-5              ACCSUM            06/22/70        PAGE 0002
                                                              NOTE 179
026       O                 BAL      23 ' 0. &CR'
027       O              90 INT      35 ' 0. '           NOTE 192
028       O              90          45 'INTEREST'       NOTE 192
029       O                 AMT      58 ' 0. &CR'
030       O                 NEWBAL   71 ' . 0. &CR'
031       O                 AMTDUE   67 ' . 0. &CR'
032       O              14 80       44 'OVERDUE'        NOTE 192
                                                         NOTE 192
033       O              90          15 'REVOLVING'      NOTE 192
034       O              80          16 'THIRTY-DAY'     NOTE 192
035       O        T 31 LR
036       O                          63 'TOTAL AMOUNT DUE'
037       O                 TOTDUE   89 ' . 0. &CR**'
```

FIG. 18-3 Diagnostic errors—program ACCTSUM.

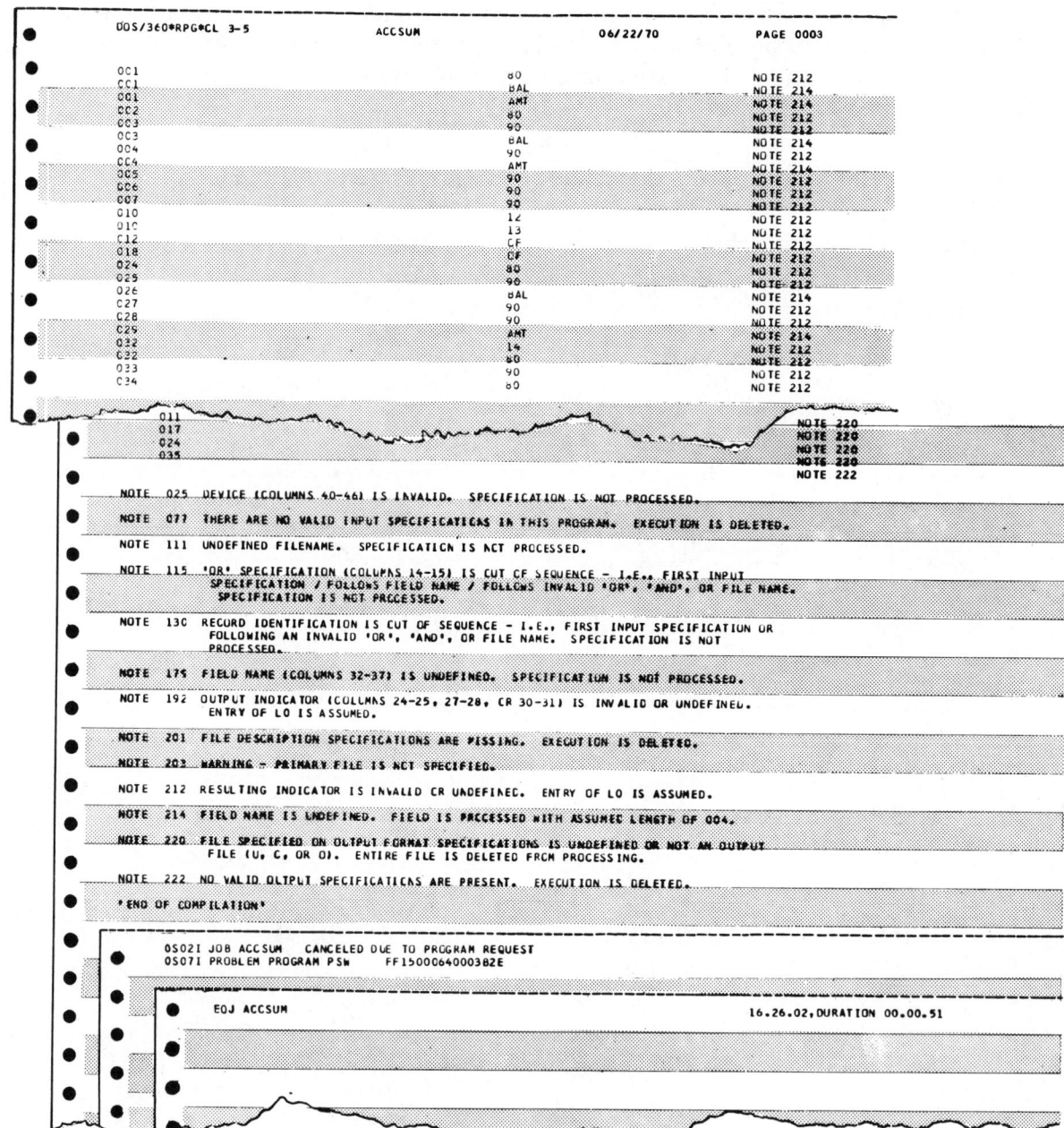

DOS/360*RPG*CL 3-5   ACCSUM   06/22/70   PAGE 0003

OC1	80	NOTE 212
CC1	BAL	NOTE 214
CC1	AMT	NOTE 214
CC2	80	NOTE 212
CC3	90	NOTE 212
OC3	BAL	NOTE 214
004	90	NOTE 212
CC4	AMT	NOTE 214
CC5	90	NOTE 212
GC6	90	NOTE 212
CC7	90	NOTE 212
O10	12	NOTE 212
O1C	13	NOTE 212
C12	CF	NOTE 212
O18	OF	NOTE 212
O24	80	NOTE 212
O25	90	NOTE 212
O26	BAL	NOTE 214
C27	90	NOTE 212
C28	90	NOTE 212
C29	AMT	NOTE 214
O32	14	NOTE 212
C32	80	NOTE 212
O33	90	NOTE 212
C34	80	NOTE 212

O11	NOTE 220
O17	NOTE 220
O24	NOTE 220
O35	NOTE 220
	NOTE 222

NOTE   025   DEVICE (COLUMNS 40-46) IS INVALID.   SPECIFICATION IS NOT PROCESSED.

NOTE   077   THERE ARE NO VALID INPUT SPECIFICATIONS IN THIS PROGRAM.   EXECUTION IS DELETED.

NOTE   111   UNDEFINED FILENAME.   SPECIFICATION IS NOT PROCESSED.

NOTE   115   'OR' SPECIFICATION (COLUMNS 14-15) IS OUT OF SEQUENCE - I.E., FIRST INPUT
             SPECIFICATION / FOLLOWS FIELD NAME / FOLLOWS INVALID 'OR', 'AND', OR FILE NAME.
             SPECIFICATION IS NOT PROCESSED.

NOTE   130   RECORD IDENTIFICATION IS OUT OF SEQUENCE - I.E., FIRST INPUT SPECIFICATION OR
             FOLLOWING AN INVALID 'OR', 'AND', OR FILE NAME.   SPECIFICATION IS NOT
             PROCESSED.

NOTE   175   FIELD NAME (COLUMNS 32-37) IS UNDEFINED.   SPECIFICATION IS NOT PROCESSED.

NOTE   192   OUTPUT INDICATOR (COLUMNS 24-25, 27-28, OR 30-31) IS INVALID OR UNDEFINED.
             ENTRY OF LO IS ASSUMED.

NOTE   201   FILE DESCRIPTION SPECIFICATIONS ARE MISSING.   EXECUTION IS DELETED.

NOTE   203   WARNING - PRIMARY FILE IS NOT SPECIFIED.

NOTE   212   RESULTING INDICATOR IS INVALID OR UNDEFINED.   ENTRY OF LO IS ASSUMED.

NOTE   214   FIELD NAME IS UNDEFINED.   FIELD IS PROCESSED WITH ASSUMED LENGTH OF 004.

NOTE   220   FILE SPECIFIED ON OUTPUT FORMAT SPECIFICATIONS IS UNDEFINED OR NOT AN OUTPUT
             FILE (U, C, OR O).   ENTIRE FILE IS DELETED FROM PROCESSING.

NOTE   222   NO VALID OUTPUT SPECIFICATIONS ARE PRESENT.   EXECUTION IS DELETED.

END OF COMPILATION

0S02I JOB ACCSUM   CANCELED DUE TO PROGRAM REQUEST
0S07I PROBLEM PROGRAM PSW   FF15000640003B2E

     EOJ ACCSUM   16.26.02,DURATION 00.00.51

FIG. 18-3—*Cont.*

FIG. 18-4 Execution errors–program ACCTSUM.

From these examples in debugging, you can see what a tiresome but crucial job it is. You must be sure to debug your programs thoroughly, for both diagnostic and execution errors. The IBM SYSTEM/3 has a special instruction to help you with execution debugging, called ***DEBUG**. By putting a 1 in column 15 of the **RPG CONTROL CARD**, this instruction, when given on the **CALCULATION** form, enables you to obtain a list of indicators that are *on* at that time during the calculations, and also permits you to dump the contents of whatever field you specify as the **RESULT FIELD** on the ***DEBUG** instruction. Without this instruction, other implementations often make it necessary to put in additional output lines to print partial answers to let you determine where errors are and then remove them later. A concern about detail, a knack for seeing cause and effect, perhaps a love of puzzles and mazes, but above all, patience and persistence under stress are all valuable traits often found in good programmers. They are often put to test during debugging.

EXERCISES

1. Write **MOVE** instructions to do each of these:
   (a) Set **SUM**, 5 digits long, to zero.
   (b) Put –75.27 into **RETURN**.
   (c) Put the word **'OVERDRAWN'** into field **REMARK**, length 9 characters.
   (d) Put the value for 5% into **RATE**, length 4, 3 decimals.
   (e) Put 4-digit **ACCT** field and 5-digit **EMPNUM** field into one long 9-digit field named **KEY**.
   (f) Separate the 15-character field **ALPHA** into 3 fields of 5 digits each, named **FLDA**, **FLDB**, and **FLDC**.

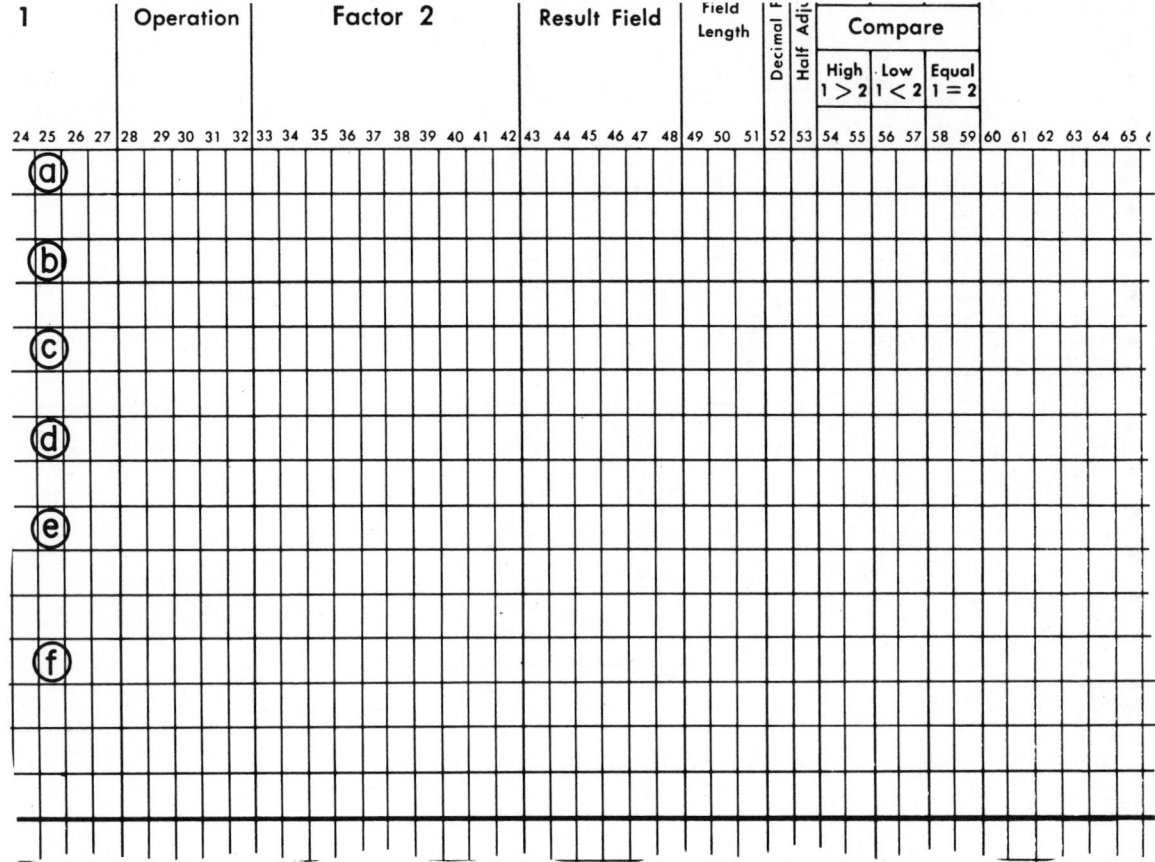

1				Operation					Factor 2										Result Field						Field Length			Decimal F	Half Adj	Compare						
																														High 1 > 2		Low 1 < 2		Equal 1 = 2		
24	25	26	27	28	29	30	31	32	33	34	35	36	37	38	39	40	41	42	43	44	45	46	47	48	49	50	51	52	53	54	55	56	57	58	59	60 61 62 63 64 65

(a)

(b)

(c)

(d)

(e)

(f)

2. Assume the report shown is a test run from debugging **ACCTSUM** discussed in the text. State what corrections are needed to clear its errors. _____

```
                    A C C O U N T   S U M M A R Y                        PAGE      1


  ACCOUNT AND TYPE    BALANCE                    CHARGES      AMOUNT OWED      AMOUNT DUE

  22540  THIRTY-DAY      .00                       25.50          25.50           25.50
  23456  THIRTY-DAY   200.00           OVERDUE      12.53         212.53          212.53
  23480  THIRTY-DAY   100.00           OVERDUE      25.30         125.30          125.30
  23560  THIRTY-DAY   100.00           OVERDUE     423.89         523.89          523.89
  31234  REVOLVING     12.53 CR                     12.53            .00           10.00
  34231  REVOLVING    321.50           INTEREST    4.82  321.50    647.82          25.00
  34235  REVOLVING       .00                       321.50         321.50           25.00
  34238  THIRTY-DAY    15.00           OVERDUE     218.50         233.50          233.50
  53240  REVOLVING    500.00           INTEREST    7.50  745.21  1,252.71          25.00
  54120  THIRTY-DAY      .00                       541.27         541.27          541.27
  62153  REVOLVING    335.50 CR                    335.50            .00           10.00
  62532  THIRTY-DAY    15.32           OVERDUE      15.32 CR         .00             .00
  64216  THIRTY-DAY    52.05           OVERDUE      12.89          64.94           64.94
  64365  THIRTY-DAY   123.58           OVERDUE     123.58         247.16          247.16
  64589  REVOLVING       .00                       300.00         300.00           25.00
  65270  THIRTY-DAY   100.00           OVERDUE     542.18         642.18          642.18
   ̄02  THIRTY-DAY   123.85           OVERDUE     123.85 CR         .00            .0
     ̄ TY-DAY       300.00           OVERDUE     310.22 CR      10.22 CR          1.
              15 52                   OVERDUE      15.50          31.02
                                                   25.00          25 00
```

3. What does the program **ACCTSUM** in Figure 18-5, do to handle this: On a revolving-charge-type account, a person sends the payment in full for the previous balance. What happens to the interest? Is he still sent a bill for the interest on that amount? Should he be or not? _____

_____

```
DOS/360*RPG*CL 3-3              ACCTSUM              10/14/69        PAGE 0001

        H
        F* ACCOUNT SUMMARY WITH MULTIPLE RECORDS
001     FCARDS  IP  F  80  80          READ40 SYSRDR
002     FREPORT  O  F 120 120    OF    PRINTERSYSLST
003     ICARDS    NS  80  05 C8
004     I      OR      90  05 C9
005     I                              6   10 ACCT
006     I                             21   40 NAME
007     I                             46  502BAL      14  12
008     I                             56  602AMT          13
        C* THIRTY-DAY TYPE
009     C   80      BAL      ADD  AMT     AMTDUE   62
010     C   80               MOVE AMTDUE  NEWBAL   62
        C* REVOLVING TYPE
011     C   90 14   BAL      MULT 0.015   INT      52H
012     C   90N14            Z-ADD0       INT
013     C   90      BAL      ADD  INT     TEMP     62
014     C   90      TEMP     ADD  AMT     NEWBAL
015     C   90      NEWBAL   COMP 100.00           10  10
016     C   90N10   NEWBAL   COMP 10.00            11  11
017     C   90N10 11         MOVE 0010.00  AMTDUE
018     C   90N10N11         MOVE NEWBAL   AMTDUE
019     C   90 10            MOVE 0025.00  AMTDUE
        C* BOTH TYPES
020     C           AMTDUE   ADD  TOTDUE   TOTDUE  72
021     C                    SETOF                 15
022     C   12 13            SETON                 15
023     OREPORT  H  301   1P
024     O       OR        OF
025     O                            80 'PAGE'
026     O                    PAGE Z  86
027     O                            41 'A C C O U N T'
028     O                            57 'S U M M A R Y'
029     O        H  2   1P
030     O       OR        OF
031     O                            18 'ACCOUNT AND TYPE'
032     O                            28 'BALANCE'
033     O                            54 'CHARGES'
034     O                            71 'AMOUNT OWED'
035     O                            86 'AMOUNT DUE'
036     O        D  1   80N15
037     O       OR        90N15
038     O                    ACCT     5
039     O                    BAL     28 '  0.  &CR'
040     O                90 14       37 'INTEREST'
041     O                90 14 INT   44 '  0. '
042     O                    AMT     56 '  0.  &CR'
043     O                    NEWBAL  71 ' ,  0.  &CR'
044     O                    AMTDUE  87 ' ,  0.  &CR'
045     O                14 80       36 'OVERDUE'
046     O                90          15 'REVOLVING'
047     O                80          16 'THIRTY-DAY'
048     O        T 31   LR
049     O                            69 'TOTAL AMOUNT DUE'
```

```
DOS/360*RPG*CL 3-3              ACCTSUM              10/14/69        PAGE 0002

050     O                    TOTDUE  89 '  0.  &CR**'
```

```
              A C C O U N T   S U M M A R Y            PAGE 0001

      ACCOUNT AND TYPE  BALANCE              CHARGES    AMOUNT OWED    AMOUNT DUE
      22540 THIRTY-DAY      .00              25.50         25.50         25.50
      23456 THIRTY-DAY   200.00  OVERDUE     12.53        212.53        212.53
      23480 THIRTY-DAY   100.00  OVERDUE     25.30        125.30        125.30
      23560 THIRTY-DAY   100.00  OVERDUE    423.89        523.89        523.89
      31234 REVOLVING     12.53 CR           12.53           .00           .00
      34231 REVOLVING    321.50  INTEREST 4.82 321.50     647.82         25.00
      34235 REVOLVING       .00              321.50        321.50         25.00
      34238 THIRTY-DAY    15.00  OVERDUE    218.50        233.50        233.50
      53240 REVOLVING    500.00  INTEREST 7.50 745.21    1,252.71        25.00
      54120 THIRTY-DAY      .00              541.27        541.27        541.27
      62153 REVOLVING    335.50 CR          335.50           .00           .00
      62532 THIRTY-DAY    15.32  OVERDUE     15.32 CR         .00           .00
      64216 THIRTY-DAY    52.05  OVERDUE     12.89         64.94         64.94
      64365 THIRTY-DAY   123.58  OVERDUE    123.58        247.16        247.16
      64589 REVOLVING       .00              300.00        300.00         25.00
      65270 THIRTY-DAY   100.00  OVERDUE    542.18        642.18        642.18
      67502 THIRTY-DAY   123.85  OVERDUE    123.85 CR         .00           .00
      67512 THIRTY-DAY   300.00  OVERDUE    310.22 CR      10.22 CR      10.22 CR
      67561 THIRTY-DAY    15.52  OVERDUE     15.50         31.02         31.02
      67562 THIRTY-DAY      .00               25.00         25.00         25.00
      67564 THIRTY-DAY      .00               12.05         12.05         12.05
      67652 REVOLVING       .00                .95           .95           .95
      67862 THIRTY-DAY    12.00 CR            12.00           .00           .00
      82356 REVOLVING    185.25  INTEREST 2.78 185.25      373.28         25.00
      82534 REVOLVING     10.00  INTEREST  .15   .05        10.20         10.00
      93415 THIRTY-DAY      .50  OVERDUE       .50          1.00          1.00
      93567 THIRTY-DAY   185.00  OVERDUE    230.56        415.56        415.56
      93862 REVOLVING      1.55  INTEREST  .02   .05         1.62          1.62
      93865 REVOLVING       .00                .05           .05           .05
      94683 REVOLVING     12.50  INTEREST  .19  12.53       25.22         10.00
      98356 REVOLVING     12.50  INTEREST  .19   .45        13.14         10.00
      98567 REVOLVING       .00               23.50         23.50         10.00


                                 TOTAL AMOUNT DUE    3,258.30   **
```

FIG. 18-5 Corrections to program ACCTSUM.

Section 6

PROGRAMS TO WRITE

A. PROBLEM NAME: **FULLPART**: full-time or part-time pay, with totals

Write a program to calculate **PAY** by multiplying the number of hours worked by the rate of pay per hour. Print **PAY** under the appropriate column and add to the proper full-time or part-time total. A sample output is shown.

```
                              PAY FOR WEEK


  EMPLOYEE            EMPLOYEE           HOURS     RATE      FULL TIME      PART TIME
   NUMBER               NAME            WORKED    OF PAY       PAY            PAY
    1087        PEGGY STANDISH            10       1.98                      19.80


    5126        MARY HILTON               22       1.60                      35.20


    3401        SYNDIE ELLIOT             40       2.44       97.60


    5289        JIM CARR                  36       2.20       79.20


    2116        TONY CUVI                 18       1.80                      32.40
```

Field Information	Column
Employee number	4-7
Employee name	9-28
Hours worked, ∅ decimals	38-39
Rate of pay, per hour, 2 decimals	42-44
Record ID code: part-time 1	6∅
full-time 6	

B. PROBLEM NAME: **ALUMNI**: donation lists with year totals

Card records, giving the amount donated by certain alumni, are sorted by year of graduation. Each record is coded as either cash, stocks, or bonds. Print a report as shown, giving amount and type of donation of each person, a total for each year represented, and an end-of-job total for each type of donation and the total of all types. A flow chart is given in Figure 16-1. Input records are the same as those in Problem C, Section 3, and Problem A, Section 4.

Field Information	Columns
Year of graduation	1-4
Name	11-3∅
Zip code of residence	36-4∅
Amount of donation, 2 decimals	65-7∅
Record ID code: 1 cash	72
2 stocks	
3 bonds	

```
                                ALUMNI
                            CONTRIBUTION
                                 LISTS


        CLASS              NAME              ZIP      INCOME TYPE        INCOME


        1945         ELSIE  MOORE           01232       STOCKS      $     125.25
                     SUSAN  MCLAUGHLIN      21207        CASH             125.75
                     TWIGGY  JONES          01525        BONDS            200.00
                     HAL  PRINCE            34521       STOCKS          5,000.00
                     JUDY  BEELER           02158        CASH             100.00
                     ALICE  STAUFFER        92453       STOCKS            125.00
                     PEGGY  LINZ            02165        CASH             500.00
                     JOSEPH  SMITHYE        85324        CASH             400.00
                     LUIS  GOLDEN           75235       STOCKS             55.21
                     LAURA  BISON           25235        BONDS            500.00
                     JIMMY  CARLIN          09532       STOCKS            432.52
                     KUREY  TILLERY         04322        CASH             253.25
                     SANCHEZ    SMITH       32586        CASH           5,000.00
                     HOLLY  GOLIGHTLY       99523        BONDS            100.75
                     SMITH ,   RAY          54255       STOCKS          4,244.51

                          1945  TOTAL  OF  15  DONORS  GAVE       $17,162.24*


        1948         JONES,  RAY            21209        CASH          $1,276.80
                     SMITH                  81307        BONDS            500.00
                     LANGLEY                21813        CASH              25.50

                          1948  TOTAL  OF   3  DONORS  GAVE       $ 1,802.30*


        1952         JOHNSON,  BARBARA      72185        CASH      $     500.00
                     ANDERSON,  JANIE       72135                       500.05
                     CARROLL  BEADER        72135
                     JONES,  L
                     SMITH,  L
```

C. PROBLEM NAME: **MAILNOTE:** message to be mailed

The program should print a lettergram five lines long, with a return address and name and address of addressee, as shown in Figure 17-3. The multiple-record layout there describes the fields on each record type. Assume that each run uses one return address, to be brought in as a header card, one set of five cards providing the message, and any number of addressee cards.

D. PROBLEM NAME: **SEQCK:** sequence check a card deck

Write a program to check and print the sequence of a key field, in columns 1-9, of a given card deck, by the logic illustrated in Figure 16-5. All values in the key field should be assumed to be positive and numeric.

SECTION 7

REPORTS WITH MERGED MASTER AND DETAIL CARDS

Lesson 19

MERGING INTO SEQUENCED GROUPS

You will learn how to use input data that have multiple-record types, in certain order and quantity, within each control group.

The questions below summarize the contents of this lesson and are answered on the back of this page. If you have previous programming or panel wiring experience with multiple record-types sequenced within a group, use the lesson only to assist you in answering questions 5-9 before going on to Lesson 20.

1. What does it mean for records in a data file to be *sequenced within a group*?
2. What is the difference in purpose of a *master* record from that of a *detail* record?
3. How can you get separate master and detail decks merged into one file?
4. What are *inactive masters* and *invalid details* and why are they often selected from the merged deck?
5. Explain the purpose of using *numeric* entries on the INPUT form under SEQUENCE in columns 15 and 16, instead of *alphabetic* ones, such as NS or AA.
6. How do you decide whether 1 or N goes in column 17 of the INPUT form?
7. How can you specify that a record type is *optional*, perhaps not even present in its expected place?
8. Give some of the limitations of sequence control checking and what happens when errors are detected during execution.
9. When both sequenced record-types and nonsequenced record-types are to be used in the same program, in what order are they listed on the INPUT specifications?
10. How can you use the M-indicators to sequence-check the records in a single file?

ANSWERS

1. That within a given control group, such as account number 1654, several different types of records are permitted, such as a master card, a payment card, a charge card, and a return card, with the types in some particular order, such as the master first, followed by payments, if any, followed by charges, if any, then followed by returns.

2. The master record contains information that is relatively permanent and unchanging, or accumulated information to be updated during each periodic use; the detail record represents transactions occurring that affect the master record or need to use the master information in some way, and are of interest only for a short time.

3. By using the IBM $\emptyset$85 or $\emptyset$88 collator; by using a computer, a merge utility program, and the data on magnetic tape; in an emergency, by using the IBM $\emptyset$82 or $\emptyset$83 sorter; or, in a *real* emergency, by hand.

4. *Inactive masters* are those for which no details are present, which may happen when you do not use your paid-up charge account at a department store during a given month; *invalid details* are those for which no master is present, usually caused by a mispunched detail card or by the presence of a new account that has not yet been placed on the master file.

5. Numeric entries, starting with $\emptyset$1 but using any numbers in increasing order thereafter, to identify the sequence of multiple records and to cause RPG to check for those particular records, in the required order, in the input data file. Alphabetic letters imply that the records are entirely optional in the deck, possibly occurring anywhere.

6. By determining whether exactly one of that record is to be present, or whether several are possible there. For exactly one, use **1**; should *one or more* be possible, put **N** there.

7. Use either **1** or **N** in column 17, whichever is appropriate, then put **O** in column 18 to denote *optional*, possibly even none.

8. Sequence control checking does *not* confirm that the control group for the records is correct, so that record-type may be present, but with a wrong control group number. If all record-types in the group are optional, the control checking accomplishes nothing. When an error in sequence or number is detected, the system should stop. Should an invalid record identification code be in the deck, however, it is possible, depending upon the specifications, for infinite looping to occur, caused by that record-type never being found.

9. The nonsequenced types, characterized by alphabetic letters under SEQUENCE, should be listed first.

10. By assigning M1, M2, . . . on the INPUT form, to the key fields, respectively, and putting **A** or **D** on the FILE DESCRIPTION form, for ascending or descending order, respectively.

The word *sequence* implies a sort of order. A file is said to be in *alphabetic* sequence when the values in its key field are in alphabetic order, and in *numeric* sequence when the key field is in numeric order. The file may be either in ascending or descending sequence. When these key fields are used as control fields with control levels assigned, however, their order is not considered; no automatic checking of the sequence is done by RPG on the control fields. Control breaks are caused by a *change* in the control field, whether the change is from low to high or vice-versa. Each control group is made up of all cards for one particular value of the control field that are *together*, such as those consecutive cards that refer to account number 9928. Should a card referring to account number 9927 be out of sequence in the middle of account number 9928, RPG would treat that as perhaps *three* control groups, producing a report for 9928, then one for the isolated 9927, then another for the 9928's which follow! Control breaks are caused by the occurrence of a *different* control value, even though it may not be in its proper sequence. RPG can provide a useful service in its ability to sequence-check one or more key fields within a sequenced file.

M-indicators M1, M2, M3, on up to M9 where available, are called *matching field* indicators because their main purpose is to control the matching of fields from different files, to be of interest later. They may be used now to sequence-check a single file, however, with up to three key fields on some implementations, and up to nine on others. When only one key field is to be checked, it is assigned a matching field indicator by putting **M1** in columns 61 and 62 under MATCHING FIELDS OR CHAINING FIELDS on the INPUT form; column 18 of the FILE DESCRIPTION form must specify by either **A** or **D** whether the sequence is ascending or descending order, respectively. Alphabetic order from A to Z should be assigned an ascending sequence; actually the term *alphameric order* is more appropriate, for, should characters other than those in the alphabet appear in the key field, they will in this case be sequence-checked according to the collating sequence of the machine. If the key field is not in proper sequence, a halt indicator goes on, which, if not set off by the program, causes termination of processing at the end of the record that is out of sequence.

Sequence-checking can also be done on a control field of a single file by assigning both a control level indicator and a matching field indicator to the field. When matching field indicators are assigned to more than one key field on a record in a file, however, they must be assigned in order—M1 first, then M2, and so on. Those fields which are assigned are compared, *together*, in a special matching field holding area, with the M1 field in the low-order position, and the others placed successively to the left.

Recall that a *sequenced file* is one for which the records within the file are in order by some key field. When there are several cards for each value of the key field and a control break is needed on each value, the key field becomes a control field, forming control groups. Within each control group, however, there may be another type of data arrangement to which the word sequence applies—that of multiple-record types within the group. This type of sequence is called *record-type sequence within a group*, or, often, *sequenced groups*. Among the records for one account number could be, for example, exactly one master card, several charge cards, several payment cards and perhaps a return card. One job might require that a group for each employee number contain exactly one master card and exactly one pay-request card; another job might require exactly one master card and any number of detail cards, perhaps none. *Multiple-record input* refers to having several different record-types in an input file. When

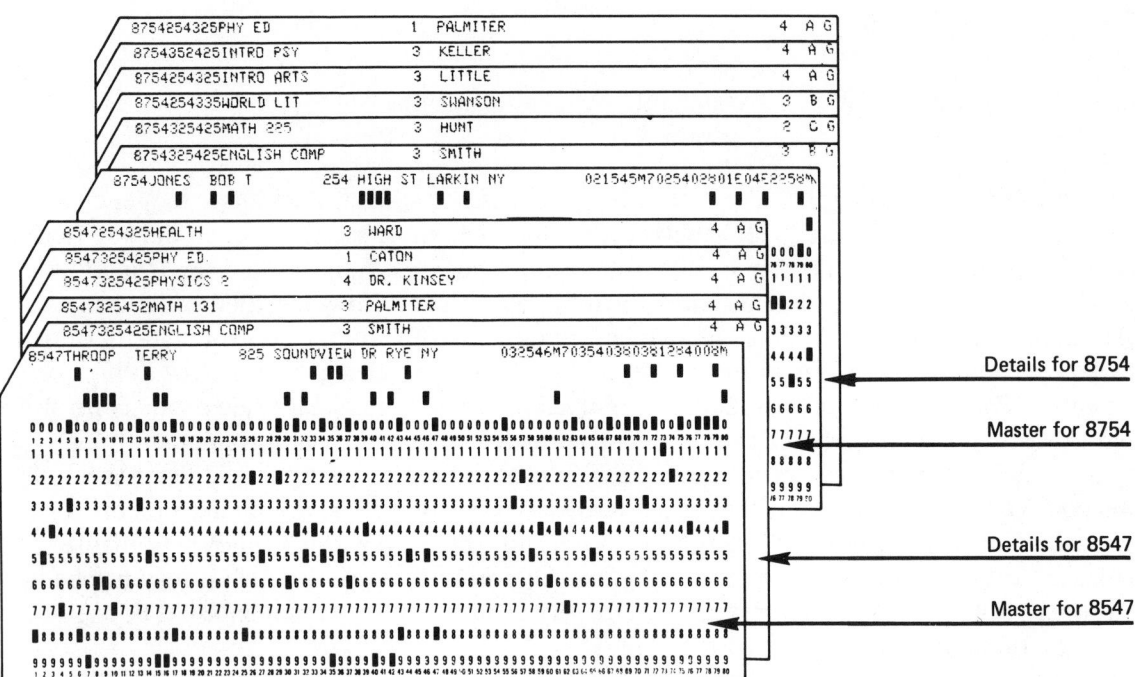

FIG. 19-1 Merged deck—masters and details.

those record types are within a given control group, in a particular order, with a particular quantity of each, then you need to use RPG coding for record-type sequencing within a group.

One of the most common jobs that uses multiple-record types within a control group is one based on a merged master/detail deck, as shown in Figure 19-1. The master record for a particular control field value is followed by all the detail cards for that same number. The master card, called *primary*, usually contains information that is relatively unchanging for some time, such as a name, address, and cumulative data up to the time it was made. The detail card, called *secondary*, usually contains information that is only of temporary interest—needed perhaps until a report can be made or an invoice sent. Some jobs require that exactly one detail card be used with each master; others allow several. In a payroll application, a detail card may request a paycheck to be made, but the name and address of the payee will usually come from the master card for that person. In a billing application, there will probably be several transactions, perhaps all of the same record type, affecting each master account. Inventory applications are likely to require several different records, usually sorted into an item number control group. Following each *master card* for item description may be a *receipt* card, a *return* card, a *customer order* card, an *adjustment* card, and a *back order* card! In all these applications, it is necessary that all records for one control group be *together* for processing. It is also necessary that each record-type be in proper order and quantity to be used in preparing the report. Some of the record-types may be *required*; others may be *optional*. Some record-types should have *exactly one* card present and no more; others may have *several* cards present. The record-type sequence is used to specify what records in a group must be present, and of those, how many of each type.

Record ID codes allow identification of each record when several record-types are in the deck. Records are usually listed on the INPUT specifications in the order of their most frequent occurrence. Those that may occur randomly at any time within the deck are given an alphabetic two-letter combination, such as **NS** or **AA**—in fact, any combination except **ND** and **R$\emptyset$**, used on **AND** and **OR** lines. Alphabetic letters, placed under SEQUENCE, in columns 15 and 16, automatically identify the records as *optional* and allow them to appear anywhere in the deck.

　　Record-type sequencing requires that columns 15 and 16, under SEQUENCE, be *numeric*. Consecutive record-types within a group are usually assigned numbers ∅1, then ∅2, then ∅3, and so on, in consecutive order. Although ∅1 is required as the first record-type, any other numbers in increasing order may be assigned as the others. For each record type, column 17, under NUMBER, may contain either **N**, which means that *one or more* of the type is expected, or **1**, which means that *exactly one* of that type is expected. An **O** is permitted in column 18 to specify the record-type as *optional*, meaning possibly *none*. In the example,

Form Type	Filename	Sequence	Number (1-N)	Option (O)	Resulting Indicat	Position	Not (N)	C/Z/D	Character	Not (N)	C/Z/D	Character	Position	Not (N)	C/Z/D	Character	Stacker Select	Packed (P)	From	To	Decimal Positio	Field Name	Control Level
I	CARDS	01	1		01	80		C	D														
I																			11	30		NAME	
I																			31	50		STRE	
I																			51	70		CITYS	
I																			1	9		NUM	
I		02	N		02	80		C	E														
I																			1	9		NBR	
I																			15	20	2	AMT	
T																							

two types of records are present, in sequence within the group. There is to be exactly one of the first card type, with a D in column 8∅. The next card type is recognized by an E in column 8∅; at least one must be present, but more than one is possible. Indicators ∅1 and ∅2 were arbitrarily selected. In the example,

	Form Ty	Filename	Sequence	Number	Option	Resulting	Not (N)	C/Z/D	Character	Not (N)	C/Z/D	Character	Not (N)	C/Z/D	Character	Stacker	Packed	From	To	
1	I	INPUT	01	1		90	07		C	A											
2	I																		1	5	
3	I																		6	20	
4	I																		21	28	RE
5	I																		29	30	SHI
6	I																		41	49	FLM
7	I																		51	70	THAD
8	I		02	1		91	07		C	B											
9	I																		1	5	THNU
0	I																		8	8	CLRN
1	I		03	1		92	07		C	C											
2	I																		1	9	FLV
3	T																		11	30	FI
																			33	40	2F

exactly three cards, in order, are required for each control group—one with an A in column 7, then one with a B, then one with a C. Should the second record-type be completely optional, then the example given by

3	4	5	Form Ty 6	7	8	9	10	11	12	13	14	Sequence 15	16	Number 17	Option (18	Resulting 19	20	21	22	23	24	Not (N) 25	C/Z/D 26	Characte 27	28	29	30	31	Not (N) 32	C/Z/D 33	Characte 34	35	36	37	38	Not (N) 39	C/Z/D 40	Characte 41	Stacker 42	Packed (43	44	45	46	47	48	49	50	51	Decimal 52	53
0	1		I									Ø2		N	Ø	9	1				Ø	7			CB																												
0	2		I																																																	

may be used. If records are out of sequence within a group, or if a required record-type is missing, an error stop will occur.

Not all sequence errors within a group will be caught! Since the control field is not compared to that on the *other* records in the group unless a control level indicator is used, the wrong control field could be present without being detected as an error. When a group consists of only a single card type, no checking in a group is possible, since the card represents the whole group! If all the record-types given are optional, checking is likewise ineffective. On some implementations the last group in the file is not checked for completeness, and the entire job could be ended without a line being printed for that last set! And, since sequence-type records are *not* checked from the *top* of the list each time, but are checked against whichever type is supposed to be *next*, it is conceivable that when an invalid record-type occurs, a particular checking routine could be continuously repeated, going from the bottom of the list to the top, infinitely, in a loop. Record-type sequence is therefore not to be used in place of careful preparation and sequencing of data. It serves only to *assist* in the control of data, causing a stop on any of the sequence errors that it is able to find.

Even though several record-types may be listed for sequencing within a group, only *one* of the types is brought into the computer at a time, and so only one of the record-identifying indicators is on at a time. The information from *all* the records in the group is sometimes required to be in the computer before an output line is produced. This means that the fields from one of the earlier record-types must be held, and must still be available at the time it is needed for printing. Names of any fields that are to be held to be printed later must be *unique*—not repeated on any of the other record-types in the group. Should the *same* field name be used for two records in a group, the field from the second card would cause the information from the field on the first one to be destroyed! When the last card of the group is in, its indicator may be used to control the printing of the output lines for the entire group.

Many jobs use sequenced multiple-record groups for input. Some may require that one of the records be *master* information, such as name and address. As is the case with the classified advertisement billing form shown in Figure 19-2, these may not already be on file, so they must be punched when needed. The billing card, telling whom to bill and where, is the first card—like a *master*. The second card, giving details about when the ad was placed, the rate per day, and the type of ad that was run, serves as a *detail* card. The RPG program can specify that exactly one card of each type must be present; the output line would then be printed by the indicator turned on by the *second* of the two cards.

Nonsequence types of records may be used in the same job as sequence types. A run-date card, for example, may be used even though group sequencing is to be used. Since it is not a part of any group, however, it is given alphabetic letters under SEQUENCE and written at the top of the form, before any sequenced types. If one of the sequenced types is to be permitted in any of *several* places in the deck but not in others, it must be listed in *every* place where it is allowed to appear. You may, however, use the same indicator number in its different locations.

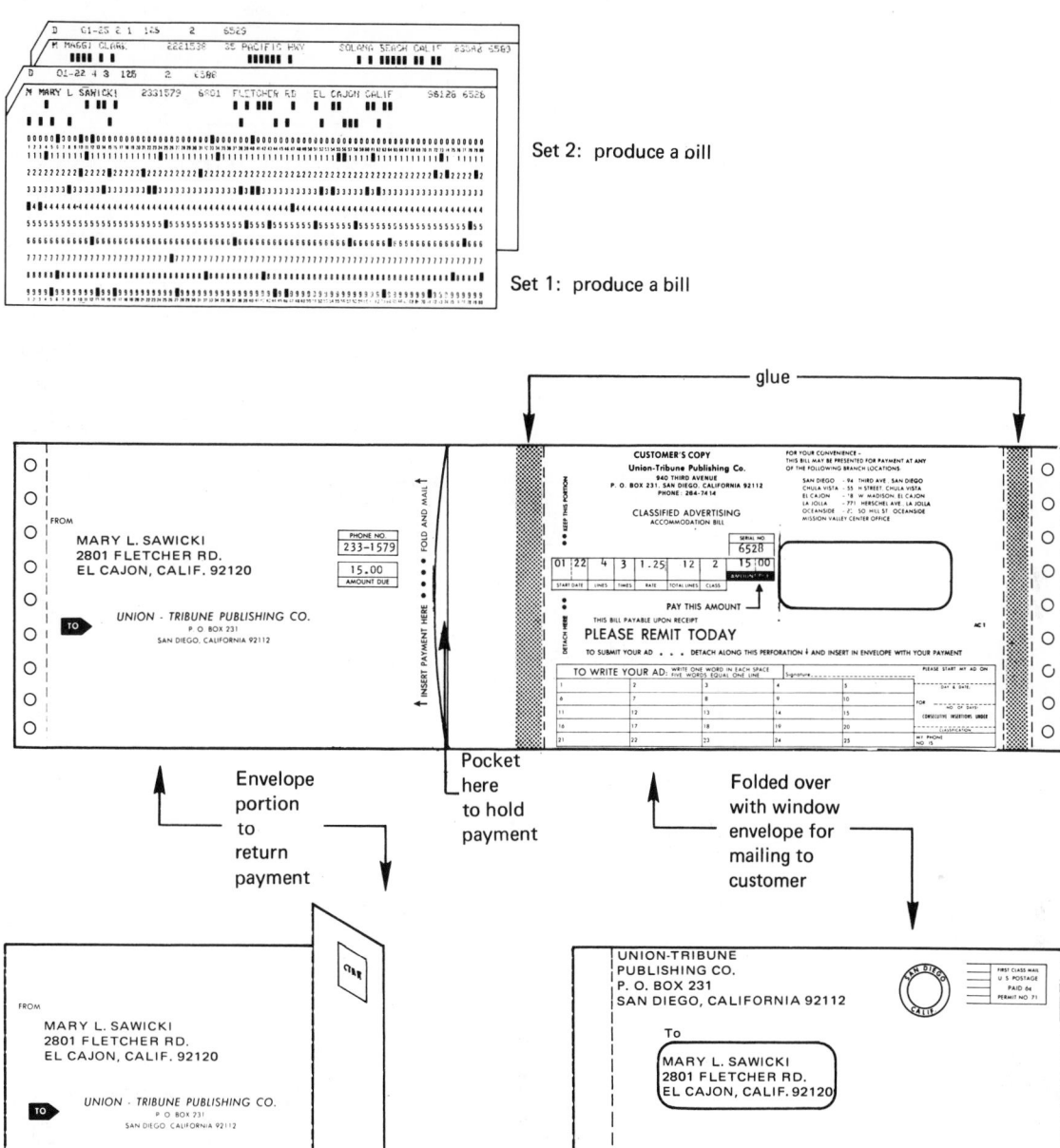

FIG. 19-2 Multiple record job—classified advertisement billing. (Courtesy of UARCO, Inc.)

A collator, such as the IBM Ø85 shown in Figure 19-3, is often used to merge two separate card decks into one. It is controlled by a wired set-up panel that is inserted into the machine. If more than two decks must be merged, more than one pass through the machine is required. There are two input hoppers—one called *primary* and one called *secondary*—but there are several output stackers, where cards are placed as they come out of the machine. Both decks should already be in sequence on the control field before being merged. Whichever deck contains the records belonging *in the front of* the sequenced group should be placed into the

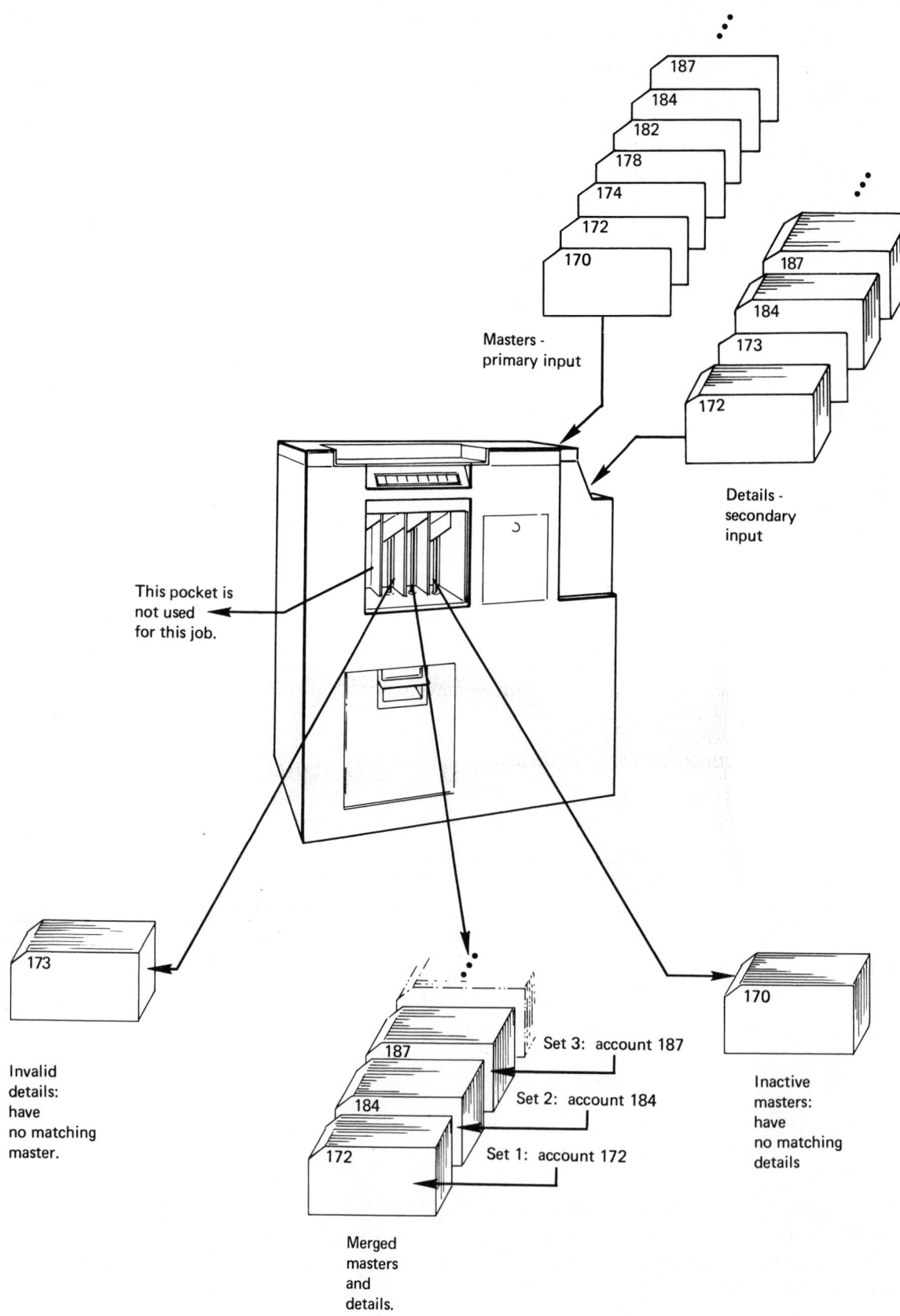

187
184
182
178
174
172
170

Masters -
primary input

187
184
173
172

Details -
secondary
input

This pocket is
not used
for this job.

173

Invalid
details:
have
no matching
master.

187
184
172

Set 3: account 187

Set 2: account 184

Set 1: account 172

Merged
masters
and
details.

170

Inactive
masters:
have
no matching
details

FIG. 19-3 Merging by collator—one master/multiple details.

278

primary hopper; the deck containing the records belonging *in the back of* the group should be placed into the secondary hopper. By appropriate wiring, a merged deck can be prepared in a variety of ways. It can place exactly one master and one detail in each group, called *merged and matched* records; it can allow one master but multiple secondaries to be in each group; or it can allow *any* number of *each* type to be present. It is possible to stack the *inactive masters*—those for which there are not any details—in the "selected primary" stacker. It is also possible to stack the *invalid details*—those secondaries for which no master is present—in the "selected secondary" stacker. The collator is still very much a part of those installations that use punch card data processing rather than magnetic tape or disk processing. It is used to merge cards into one continuous stream for processing, then to separate them back into different files after the job is done. Computer systems that have multiple-input card readers can enter the master file on one reader and the detail file on another, and therefore do not rely so greatly on the services of a collator. Those computer systems that have magnetic tape or disk capability use the computer itself for merging records together.

In some punch card installations, even the collator is not available. In that case, the IBM Ø82 or Ø83 sorter can be used to merge multiple-record decks. One restriction, however, when using these machines for merging, is that the control fields *must be in the same card columns* in all the respective record-types. The master deck is placed into the hopper *in front of* the detail deck, and numeric sorting is used, one pass on each column of the control field. The two decks will be merged as they are sorted, with the master records falling in front of the detail ones. It is not possible, however, to stacker-select the inactive masters or invalid detail records on these machines, nor is it possible to eliminate duplicate records in a group. This method is very slow compared to the collator, since it requires N passes for a control field with N columns, whereas the collator requires only one pass.

EXERCISES

1. Draw arrows as shown to illustrate which records of the two files given will be *merged*, which will be *inactive masters*, and which will be *invalid details*:

Inactive Masters	Masters	Merged	Details	Invalid Details
	27 → 27		27	
	32	27	27	
	35	27	32	
	36 → 32		34 → 34	
	39	32	35	
	42		35	
	43		39	
	44		39	
	48		39	
	51		44	
	54		44	
	57		51	
	62		54	
			58	
			60	
			62	
			62	

2. Write INPUT specifications for the following group sequence conditions, omitting field definitions:
   (a) Exactly one master, followed by exactly one detail.
   (b) Exactly one master, followed by at least one detail.
   (c) Exactly one master, followed by optional details.
   (d) Exactly one master, followed by exactly one detail, when used, or possibly none.

Line			Form Type	Filename								Sequence	Number (1-N)	Option (O)	Resulting Indicat	
3	4	5	6	7	8	9	10	11	12	13	14	15 16	17	18	19 20	2
0	1		I	(a) *masters*												
0	2		I													
0	3		I	(a) *details*												
0	4		I													
0	5		I	(b) *masters*												
0	6		I													
0	7		I	(b) *details*												

Line			Form Type	Filename								Sequence	Number (1-N)	Option (O)	Resulting Indicat	Position			
3	4	5	6	7	8	9	10	11	12	13	14	15 16	17	18	19 20	21	22	23	24
0	1		I	(c) *details*															
0	2		I																
0	3		I	(d) *masters*															
0	4		I																
0	5		I	(d) *details*															
0	6		I																

Lesson 20

PUNCH CARD OUTPUT

You will learn why punch card output may be needed and how to get it, with packed fields and stacker selection.

The questions below summarize the lesson on punch card output and are answered on the back of this page. Even though you have had former data processing experience, you may need to study the lesson to learn internal data format in the IBM SYSTEM/36∅. When you can correctly answer all the questions, go on to Lesson 21.

1. On what types of jobs might punch card output be needed?
2. Why does certain punch card output need to be edited and spaced completely as though for a printer?
3. What is a *summary card*?
4. When punching a new master file update card, using a merged master/detail input deck, at what output time should the card be punched and on what indicator?
5. How does stacker select vary from one card punch to another?
6. What kinds of records can be stacker selected on an output file that cannot be selected on an input file?
7. How do you find out what is on a card record that was punched on a computer system?
8. What is an *interpreter*?
9. In what internal data forms are RPG alphameric and numeric fields stored on the IBM SYSTEM/36∅?
10. In what way can you get the equivalent of more than 8∅ columns of information on a punch card?
11. What are some advantages in using packed-decimal form for numeric-field output?
12. How do you specify the *input* for numeric fields that were output in packed-decimal form from an RPG program?

ANSWERS

1. Master-file updating, summary totals by control groups, data collection of all types, and distribution of information.
2. Because it will be printed by an 8∅/8∅ list program.
3. A card that gives pertinent totals for a control group, without giving every detail transaction in the group.
4. During total-time output, on the control level indicator for that group.
5. Some machines have only one hopper for reading and punching and so stacker select is for combined files; some machines have separate read and punch hoppers, with two stacker pockets for each; one machine even has five pockets, with three accessible from each hopper.
6. Almost any kind. Whereas the input stacker select is restricted to selection by record-type, the output stacker has no such restriction, but can select whenever an indicator is *on*, making it possible to select certain results of calculations, select by field indicators, or select even on error conditions.
7. By using the interpret feature of the IBM ∅29, if available, to print the fields on the face of the card; by using the IBM 557 interpreter to do the same thing, but in bigger print, for fewer columns in one pass; by writing a computer program to list the deck, 8∅/8∅, on a printer; or, in a *real* emergency, by holding the card up and reading the holes!
8. A machine that can be used to read information on a card, and print it on the card face, in some manner.
9. Alphameric fields are stored in a zoned-decimal form, with the zone position of the card requiring 4 bits and the digit portion requiring 4, so that one character on the card is stored in one 8-bit byte with zone and digit portions. Numeric fields are stored in packed-decimal, which has 1 digit and a sign stored in the low-order byte, then 2 decimal digits in each byte to the left.
10. By using packed-decimal output for any numeric fields that are used only for later input back into the computer.
11. It uses fewer columns on the output card, and, therefore, on some punch devices, less time; it prevents the packing and unpacking conversions from being done, which saves processing time and core storage.
12. By placing a **P** in column 43 of the INPUT specifications form beside the name of the field, specifying the number of decimal digits the number should have after it is entered, and putting the column numbers that are *actually occupied* by the packed-decimal information on the input card, under FROM and TO.

Lesson 20   Punch Card Output

Several different input/output units may be attached to the IBM SYSTEM/36∅ for punch card output. Some of them have two hoppers, usually one for reading and one for punching, and some of them have only one, for both. A punch card file can therefore be an *input* file when it is an input hopper, an *output* file when it is an output hopper, or even a *combined* file when it is either, or both.

The IBM 254∅, the IBM 1442, and the IBM 252∅ are often found attached online to the IBM SYSTEM/36∅ computer for punching. The IBM 254∅ is perhaps the most common; its input and output hoppers are separate, allowing it to serve as two separate machines. It punches one entire card at a time in a row-wise manner, called *parallel*, at 3∅∅ cards per minute. Although it is usually found with one hopper exclusively as input and the other exclusively as output, an optional feature permits the punch hopper to be used as a limited read unit, permitting it to be used as a combined file as well. The IBM 1442, with only one pocket, comes in a variety of models; some can punch only, but others can both read and punch. It punches column-wise rather than row-wise, in a *serial* rather than parallel, manner; speeds vary from 91 to 265 cards per minute, depending on how many columns are being punched and their location on the card. The IBM 252∅, sometimes found on the Model 2∅ computer instead of the more common IBM 256∅ Multi-Function Card Machine, can be obtained either to read or punch or both.

Punch card output is defined in much the same manner as input—by defining fields, on records, in files. The FILE TYPE is given in column 15 on the FILE DESCRIPTION form as **O** for output only, or as **C** for combined. A name must be given for FILENAME; record format is **F** for fixed-length records; block and record lengths are 8∅. The device names for the IBM 1442, 254∅, and 252∅, in DOS/TOS RPG are **READ42**, **READ4∅**, and **READ2∅**, respectively, and not **PUNCH** as you might prefer! The symbolic device name, required only on some implementations, is more sensible, however—**SYSPCH**—for all three machines. After the punch card file has been defined, it is used in the same manner as any other type of file, except that since it is used for output, no spacing and skipping need be given.

One important use of punch cards is as an additional output file. When only one printer is attached to the computer system, only one report is usually produced at a time. Punch cards can be used for information that belongs in a second report, to be printed later, either by an 8∅/8∅ listing program, or by another RPG program. Lists of data exceptions, such as the names of all persons who are behind in installment payments, or the item number of those inventory items that are below a reorder point, can be obtained as by-products of a program. Punch card output is relatively slow; when you must consider the cost of computer execution time, you may find it an expensive means of output.

Master file updating is an important use of punch card output. Should magnetic tape or disk not be available, master files will probably be kept on punch cards. Each period the master file is merged with the detail cards affecting it, so that one file is created out of two or more. Reports are then produced, based on the merged information for each control group. At the control break at the end of each group, a new master card is punched, with some information duplicated from the old master, but with fields updated by the transactions affecting them during the period. The updated master cards, in turn, will be used during the following period to merge with the transactions for that period.

A *summary card* is often punched at the end of a control group, giving totals of the activity for that group. Sometimes decks are duplicated by punching; at other times certain records within a job will be punched for later use. Punch card output usually has record ID codes placed on each card so that, should several record-types be produced in one file, records can be easily distinguished from each other.

Output on punch cards is *normally* in the same punch card code as that which is used as input. The major difference between cards that are prepared on a keypunch machine and those that are punched by computer systems is that ordinarily there is *no* printing on those produced by the computer. This makes it difficult to scan the card to see what is on it or to tell what type of card it is. To read the information punched in the holes, you can place the deck into an IBM Ø29 keypunch machine with the optional interpret feature and, with the interpret switch *on*, print the card contents upon the face of the card. If this special feature is not on your keypunch, the IBM 557 interpreter, controlled by a wired panel and shown in Figure 20-1, can be used to read the information and print it onto the face of the card. The print made by these machines, however, is larger than that produced on the keypunch; each character does not fit directly over each column, but requires more space, so that only 6Ø positions can be printed across the face of the card during one pass through the machine. However, the row being printed upon can be changed by rotating a dial, so that the other 2Ø columns can be printed on *another* row of the card face, during a second pass through the machine. The IBM 548 interpreter can print either just above or just below row 12, but the IBM 557 can print on or between *all* rows, giving 25 different printing lines. Unit-record interpreters, however, do not recognize the entire IBM SYSTEM/36Ø character set, and will interpret some of the special characters in an unrecognizable manner. Punch cards produced by a computer system and interpreted are in many cases used for distribution or collection of data for jobs such as admissions, where class cards are taken to the instructor for entrance to the class; meter reading, by utility companies to collect information for billing; inventory status reports; and grading, using prepunched cards on which the teacher records the mark in the course.

Punch cards that are to be used in later 8Ø/8Ø listings should have fields placed conveniently apart when space permits. Numeric fields on the card should be edited or zero suppressed by the program. Any numeric fields that are *not* edited or zero suppressed will contain high-order zeros and low-order zones indicating the sign. The zone will cause the last digit of each field to be printed as its corresponding letter, if one exists. If numeric fields are expected to be negative, editing should be done to place the sign in a position either before or after the number, appropriate for 8Ø/8Ø printing.

Numeric fields being punched out merely for data storage, for later input to other programs, need not be zero suppressed, although it *may* safely be done if the fields are positive and nonzero. The negative and zero numeric fields, however, should *not* be zero suppressed, since they must be acceptable for future RPG input and because the use of **Z** for zero suppress will treat the field as a whole number and remove the zone position. Zone removal is therefore permitted for positive numbers, since they will still be considered positive *afterwards*, but it can cause mistakes if the number is negative, since the negative sign will be deleted from the card! And, if the number is zero, it will be made completely blank! If you have a job requiring special zone manipulations, consult your reference manual for the move-zone instructions, available in RPG but not discussed here.

Should certain numeric fields on a punch card output deck be needed only as input to a later RPG program, packing of them may be done on the IBM SYSTEM/36Ø. Punching numeric fields in a packed form permits 2 decimal digits to be placed into only one column of the output card, allowing the equivalent of more than 8Ø columns to be placed onto the card. It is

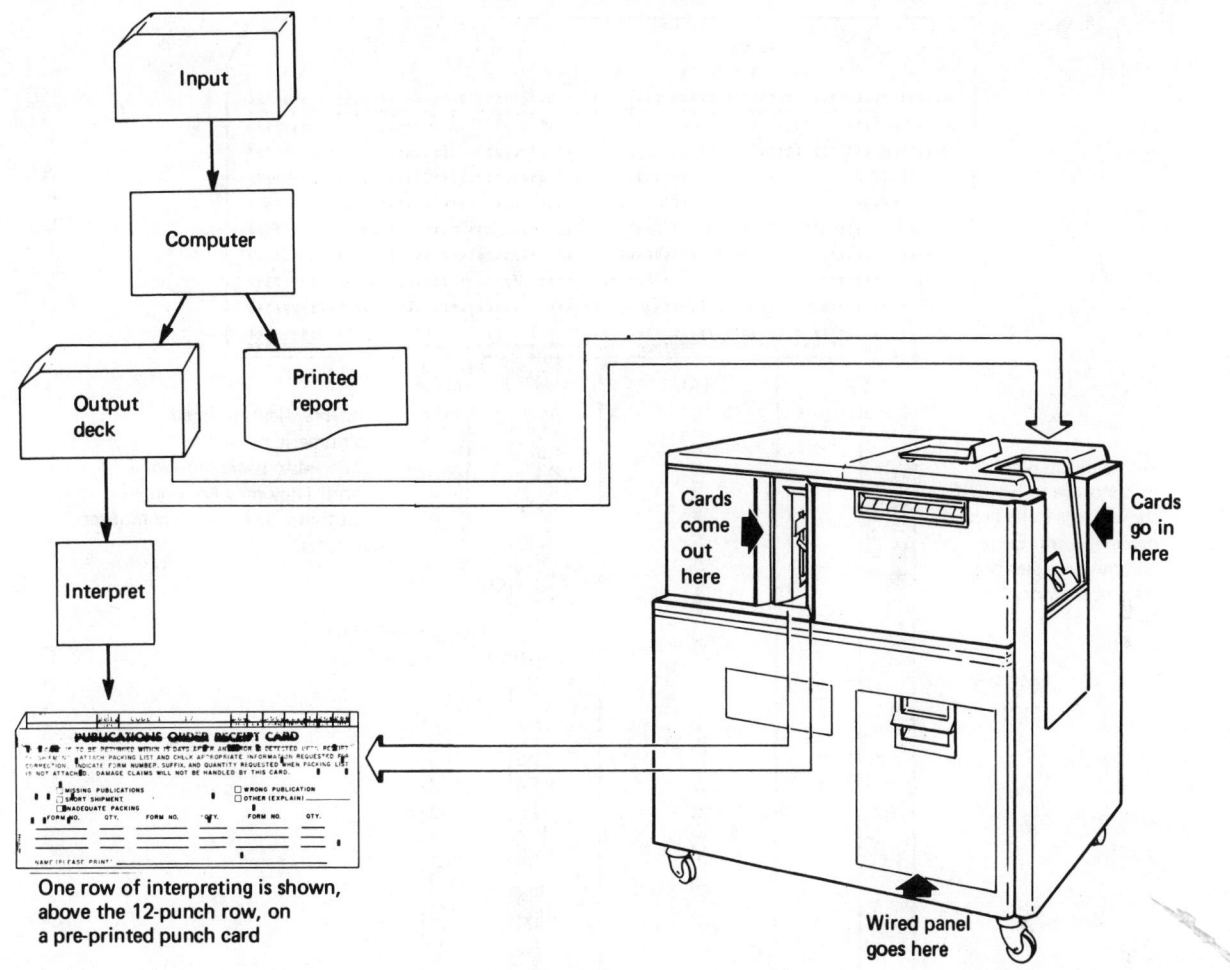

FIG. 20-1 IBM 557 interpreter.

done by putting **P** in column 16 of the **OUTPUT-FORMAT** form, beside the numeric field. The field must *not* be edited if it is packed. Each packed column will be multipunched in a pattern unique to the 2 digits stored there, acceptable as input in future **RPG** programs, but *not* acceptable for interpreting nor for printing in the normal manner.

It is important to know *exactly* how many columns of the output card will be needed for packing numeric fields of certain lengths. Since all numeric fields are stored in this packed mode internally, an understanding of its data form will help you to determine that.

When information is brought into the computer in **RPG**, the entire card is temporarily stored, with each column placed into 1 byte. The zone punch from the card, which must be either a 12, 11, Ø, or no zone at all, is stored in the left-most 4 bits, and the numeric digit punch, either a 1-9 or, in some cases, Ø, is placed in the right-most 4 bits. The binary patterns used, and their hexadecimal equivalent, are given in the Appendix. The zone portion of an alphabetic letter corresponds to hexadecimal C, D, or E, depending on which of the three letter sets it belongs to—A-I, J-R, or S-Z; the zone portion of numbers however, is a no-zone, and a hexadecimal F is stored for them at this time. The letter S, for example, is a Ø-2 punch in one column. It is stored in binary bits, but is usually shown, as in Figure 20-2, in its equivalent hexadecimal E2. The number 7, however, is represented by binary bits that are read as an F7 in hexadecimal.

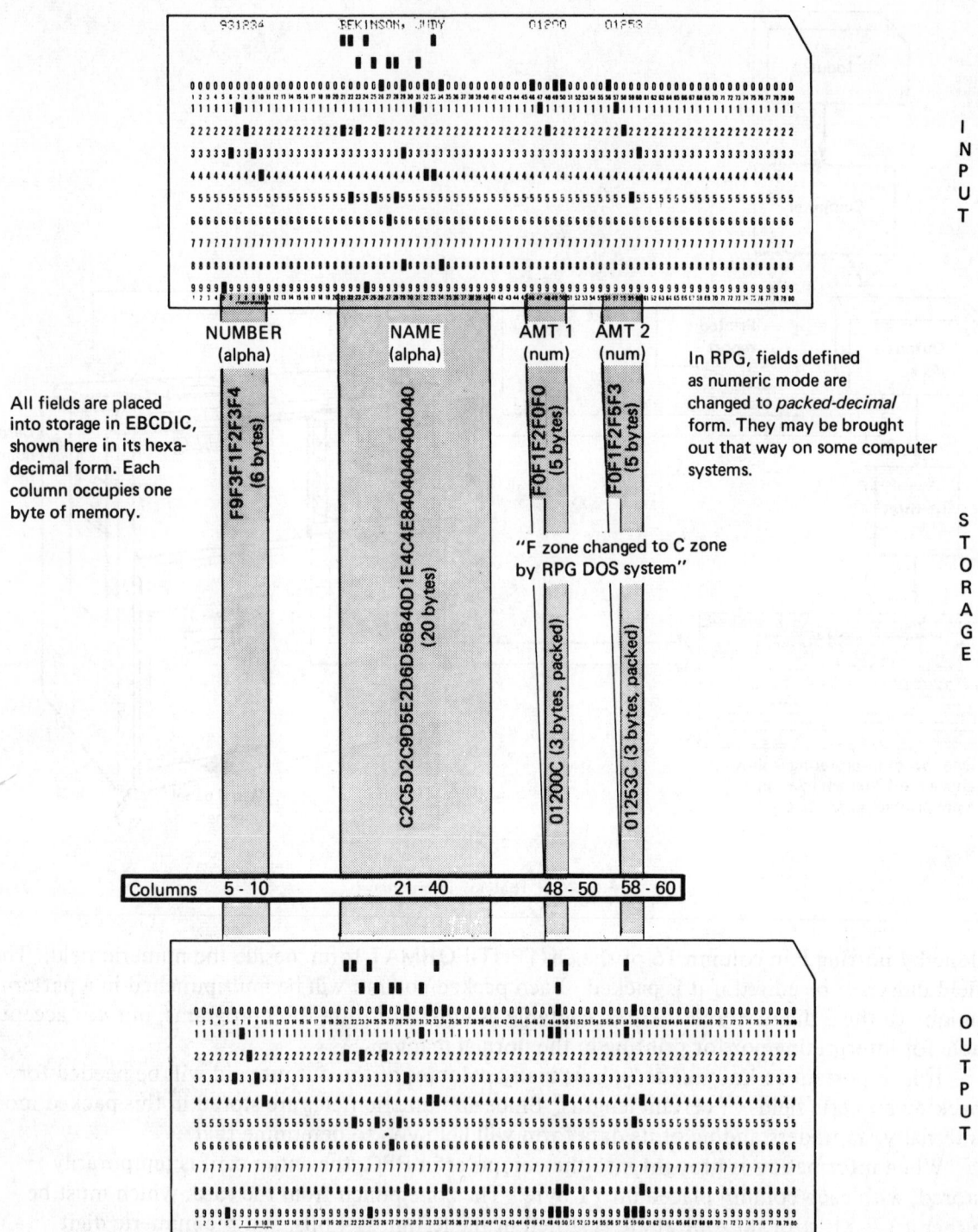

FIG. 20-2 Punching packed fields.

Just prior to detail-time calculations, all fields from the input area are moved to their appropriate name field areas. Even after being moved, alphameric fields remain in the internal mode, which uses 1 byte of memory for each column of the card, with the left-most nibble used as a *zone* portion, and the right-most nibble used as a *digit* portion. Numeric fields, however, unlike alphameric ones, are converted, as they are moved, into *packed-decimal* mode. *Packing* causes each of the numbers stored in the digit portion of the byte to be moved without any change. The units position digit is placed in the left-most nibble of the low-order byte of the packed-decimal form of the field; the other digits are placed, in pairs, in bytes to the left. The right-most nibble of the low-order byte is reserved for a sign. The zone portion belonging to the units position of the field is moved into these four bits. There it serves as the algebraic sign of the field—with the D zone, from an 11-punch hole, meaning negative, and with either the F zone, from a no-zone-punch, or the C zone, from a 12-punch hole, meaning positive. On the IBM SYSTEM/360, DOS, however, the F zone is automatically changed to a C zone, so that all positive numeric fields have the C zone and all negative ones have the D zone. At least one other implementation leaves the F zone unchanged unless the field is to be used in calculation. On most all implementations, the storage of the results of calculations, is also done by using the C zone for positive and the D zone for negative. For example, a numeric field given as 0000275 is eventually stored in packed-decimal mode as $0000275D$, occupying 4 bytes of storage, but when positive, would be stored as $0000275C$. Figure 20-2 gives an illustration of packing.

An easy rule to remember to determine the number of columns needed to hold a number in packed-decimal mode is: divide the length of the field by 2, drop any remainder, and then add 1. A numeric field of length 7 therefore requires 4 bytes of storage in packed form, and when punched out in that form, requires 4 columns. Should a field have length 6, however, 4 bytes will *still* be needed! One digit of the 6 is placed with the sign. The other 5 digits, when paired, make 2 more pairs with 1 left over, requiring that space for 3 pairs be used. Since a field boundary cannot fall on a half byte, the additional byte is required, holding not only the 1 digit necessary for the requested field length, but holding 1 additional digit as well. In summary, fields with an *odd* number of digits exactly fit into a certain number of bytes, but those with an even number actually use a packed form based on the *next larger odd length*. On some implementations, if calculations should cause that extra digit position to be needed, it will automatically be used! Its value can even be brought out when an edit word of sufficient size is given.

Using packed-decimal mode for output of numeric fields decreases the number of card columns necessary to hold the information, and by proper placement on the card, it can decrease punching time on a serial punch. When fields already in packed form are used as input to another RPG program, the conversion routine is avoided, thereby saving processing time during the execution of the program, and often saving storage by the elimination of the packing routine from the object program. To be properly read back into the computer by another RPG program, a packed field is indicated by a **P**, in column 43 of the INPUT form. Should a field name on *one* record-type be packed, that same field name may *not* be used on *another* record type, in any data form *other* than packed! On some implementations, packed-decimal fields should *not* be used for control fields. They should have decimal indication given, representing the number of decimal digits and *not* the number of packed columns the decimal digits might occupy. The FIELD LOCATION, both FROM and TO, however, must give the column numbers of the *occupied* columns, and *not* the equivalent of their decimal digit length. Since the maximum number of digits in a numeric field on most implementations is 15, the maximum number of columns that should be specified for packed input is 8, since that would hold 15 digits and a sign. A handy formula for converting N packed columns into the number of equivalent digits is given by $2N - 1$.

When doing multiple-file output, several of the fields may be needed for output on *both* output files. You must be careful *not* to use the "blank-after" too soon on those fields. If both the printer file and punch file require the same field for output, and if it must be reset before being used with the next control group, the **B** in column 39 for "blank-after" should be on the *last* of the field-description lines referring to that field. Output values of **PAGE** may also cause trouble when used on two output files. Each time **PAGE** is used, it is incremented by 1, so that if the line is written before the card is punched, 'PAGE 0007' may be on the report, but the card may contain 'PAGE 0008'! In DOS/TOS RPG, eight different field names for **PAGE** exist—**PAGE, PAGE1, PAGE2, . . ., PAGE7**—for use on up to eight different files. Up to eight different overflow indicators—OA, OB, . . . OG, and OV—are possible on that equipment.

The use of combined files and stacker select varies greatly according to the input/output hardware available on your system. The IBM 1442, Model N2, for example, has no stacker select at all, but the Model N1 has two pockets. Although two pockets are probably most common, the IBM 2540 has five, three available from each side, allowing the center one to be used for merging card decks, as illustrated in Figure 20-3.

When stacker select is used for separation of cards in the *input* deck, stacker-select codes for the pocket numbers are put in column 42 of the INPUT specification form, on the same line as the record identification. Records in an *or* relationship can be sorted into a different pocket from the other records being described. When stacker select is used for input cards that are also being punched, the file *must* be defined as a combined file; specifications for stacker select can then be given either on the INPUT form by record type or on the OUTPUT-FORMAT form by indicator. Input records can also be stacker selected on the OUTPUT-FORMAT form by defining them as a combined file, then specifying a "blank" punch to be placed into column 1 so that no punching is actually done at all. To designate stacker select on the OUTPUT-FORMAT form, column 16 is used to give the stacker codes for the pocket into which the record should be placed. If the position is left blank, the normal pocket, usually number 1, is used. See your reference manual for pocket numbers for your equipment.

Stacker selection on output during *detail-time* is done to cards containing fields from the input card presently in the computer. When it is done during *total-time*, even though the indicator for the detail card presently in the machine is *on*, the fields stored are from the *previous* detail card. Total-time output and stacker selection are often used when punching and selecting a summary card giving totals for the previous control group, or when punching a new master file update card for the previous group.

EXERCISES

1. Give the internal packed-decimal storage arrangement and number of bytes required for each of these numeric values, assuming an F for no-zone

               D for 11 zone, and

               C for 12 zone.

               Example: 012375 | 0012 37 5F | | 4 |

(a) 12743

(b) 012467 &

(c) 12405̄

(d) 214357

(e) 00013758̄0

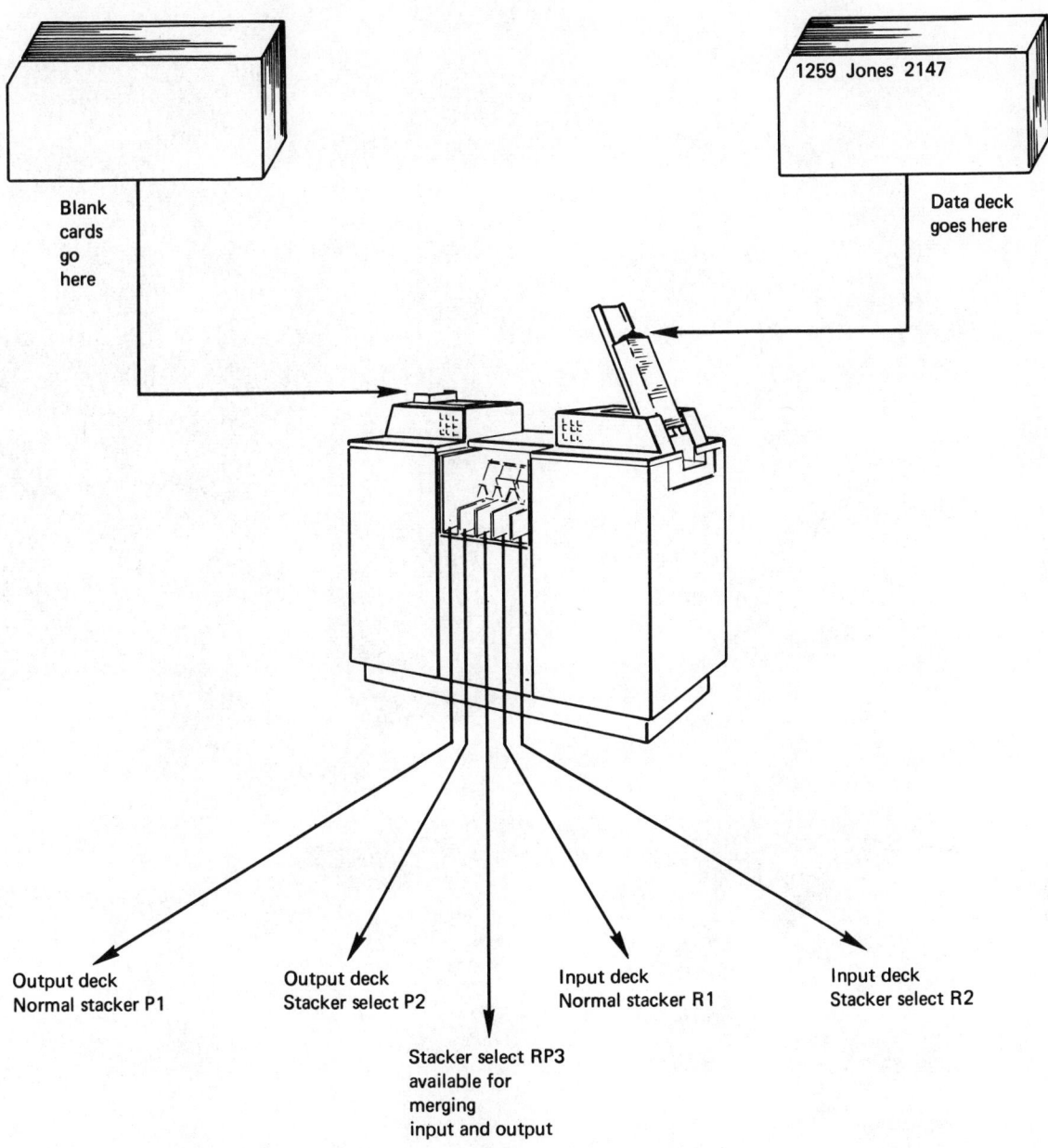

FIG. 20-3 Stacker select on the IBM 254∅ card read punch.

2. Give information in columns as requested below for numeric fields of lengths given:

	Bytes Needed for Internal Storage	*Columns Needed for Output in Packed-decimal*	*Decimal Indication*
Example: length 6, 2 decimals	3	3	2
(a) Length 7, 2 decimals			
(b) Length 12, 3 decimals			
(c) Length 3, 1 decimal			
(d) Length 6, ∅ decimals			

Lesson 21

A PRINTED REPORT WITH CARD FILE
UPDATING

You will learn to program a grade report file update job in RPG.

The questions given below are answered on the back of this page. They illustrate the concepts necessary for learning to program for file updating. When you have answered them correctly, and understand the program in this lesson, write and run the programs at the end of this section.

1. What is meant by *card file* updating?
2. Name some types of business problems that could use updating concepts.
3. How are master and detail cards arranged during card file updating?
4. On what indicator and during what time is the updated master punched in RPG?
5. How are carriage control tapes punched to position printing of the old master data, the new master data, and the transactions that cause the changes between?
6. What is a *sum of products*?
7. What is meant by *batched transactions*?
8. When programming for a preprinted form, why is it advisable to do as much testing as possible *without* putting the preprinted forms on the printer?

ANSWERS

1. File updating uses punch cards not only for the detail transactions, but also for the master record. Each period a new master card is punched, after updating the old one with the information given on the transactions.
2. Inventory, payroll, and billing.
3. Each deck sequential on some control field, then merged into one file.
4. On the control level indicator assigned to detect the change in control fields, at total-time.
5. By having a channel punch at the top of the report, where the old master information will be placed, another for the top line of the detail listing, and still another at the bottom of the report, where the summary information from the new master is placed.
6. A series of multiplications, summed over a certain group.
7. Those saved over a certain period of time for routine periodic updating.
8. Not only are forms too expensive to waste, but it is too time consuming to put on special forms during early testing of the program. After all answers are proved, the preprinted form is used in testing final alignment.

File updating is an important part of data processing. Many necessary and routine reports are produced from regularly punched cards, yet for many of them, no information from the cards is stored for later access by the computer system. Information may be retained from one period to the next, however, to be used either in periodic information retrieval, or to produce a report while the records themselves are being updated for future use.

Data files may be kept on any of several different types of external storage media. Internal memory, called *primary storage*, is expensive and usually limited; data files are not usually kept there permanently. Any of several *secondary storage* media may be used, such as punch cards, magnetic tapes, a disk or a drum. *Card* systems are less expensive, but much slower, and require much more handling than would the other types of storage. When updating is done on punch cards and when two input hoppers are *not* available on the card reader, a merged deck is formed, usually with a collator, to get all records for one student together before processing is begun.

Almost every business has inventory file updating; manufacturing companies have supplies on hand for their own production use, merchants have stock to sell, and schools have equipment to distribute and regulate. Inventory requires record-keeping from one period of activity to the next, and lends itself well to computerized file updating. Several types of data records may be involved; several types of reports may be needed. Each item in stock will have a master file record containing information such as description, how many are on hand, how many should be *kept* on hand, the usual reorder amount, the unit price of each, the vendor number of where more can be obtained, perhaps even the location of its storage within the company. Each time a sale is made, a check can be made of the current inventory, from a list, to determine whether an adequate supply is in stock. The sale itself can be recorded by punch card, requesting that stock on hand be lowered by the particular amount that was sold. Each time a new shipment of stock comes in, a notice of the addition may be recorded on a punch card. After allowing these transactions to be batched for a certain period, an updating computer run may be made, perhaps producing new master files, new inventory lists by department, sales record reports, shipping orders for new sales, updated location lists, and if necessary, purchase orders for all items currently below minimum order level.

One particular type of master file updating is of great concern on every college campus—grade reporting—concerning not only the current semester's work, but also that done over the student's entire college record. Each registration in each course may be recorded on one punch card, giving student name and number, course number and description, number of credits, meeting time and place, as well as teacher name and department. The sketch in Figure 21-1 illustrates how such a system might be organized. Course cards may even be available from other computer applications, such as registration. The cards are sorted into sequence by student number before being merged with the master file deck, producing a sequenced set for each student. During the grade report run, totals may be updated and a new master record produced for each student. The master record may contain student name and number, and perhaps a mailing address. Other information may also be kept, such as cumulative number of credits earned, since it is conceivable that credit will not be earned on all courses attempted.

One type of preprinted form currently in use for grade reports is shown in Figure 21-2. The heading information at the top of the form will usually be printed at the channel $\emptyset$1 punch on a special carriage control tape designed to fit the form, or on the IBM SYSTEM/3, at the line

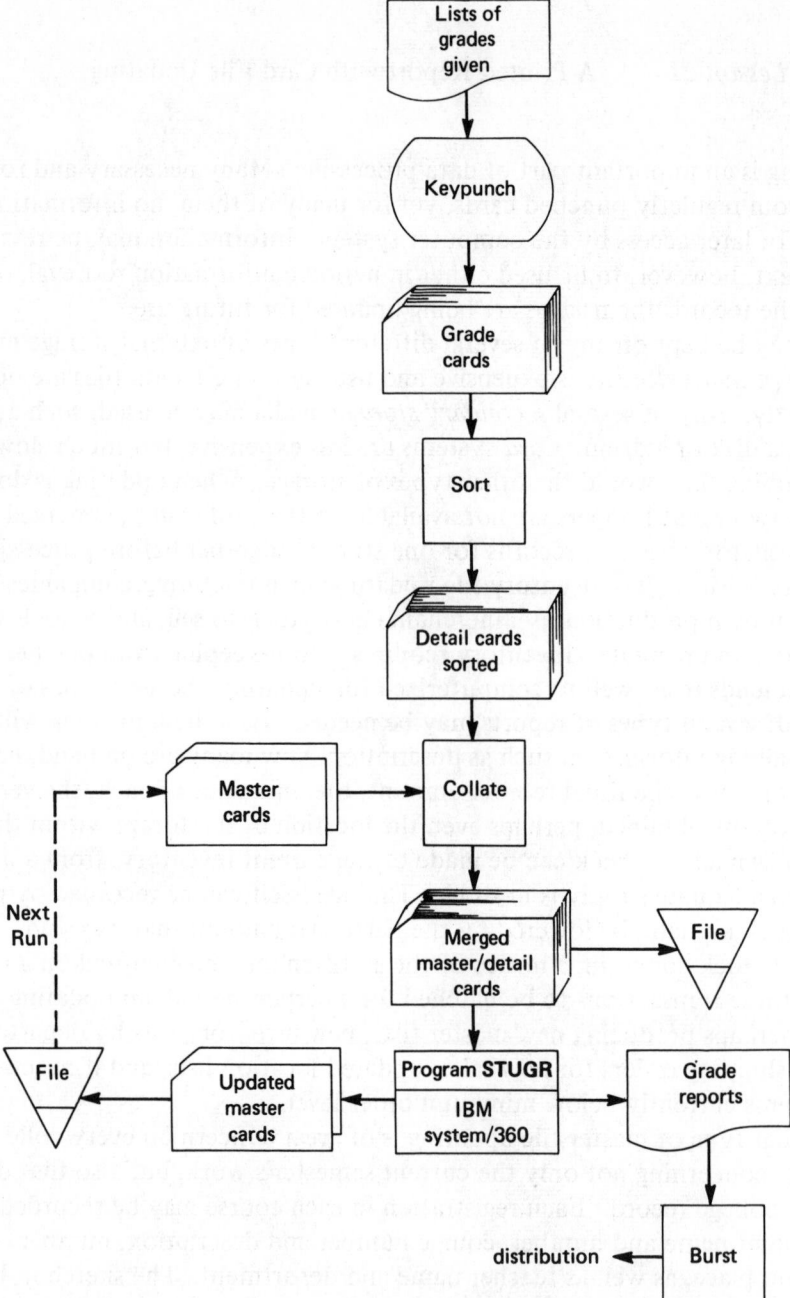

FIG. 21-1 Systems chart for card file updating—student grade report.

defined by RPG LINE COUNTER specifications to be at the top of the report form. Printing of the first body line may be controlled either by spacing a short distance from the heading, or, for longer distances, by skipping, *after* printing the last lines of the heading, to a channel punch or a line number. Since each student may be taking a different number of courses, the size of the body of the report may vary. A channel control punch must therefore be given for positioning the total line at the bottom of the form, since skipping, and *not* spacing, will be used to get there. Channel 12 will correspond to the last printing line of the *body* section, so that, should a student be taking more courses than will fit onto one form, an additional form may be used. Cumulative totals will then be given at the bottom of the last form used for that person.

Grade records in many colleges are based upon a *quality point average*, or QPA. Each course is worth a certain number of credits, and each credit can earn quality points based on the letter grade received in the course. In some schools, an A is worth 4 quality points, a B, 3, a C, 2, and a D, 1, with any other grade earning none. For example, an A in a three-credit course earns 4 × 3, or 12, quality points. The points earned for all courses during a given semester are added, and an average, based on the number of credits attempted that semester, is obtained. Figure 21-2 shows a sample grade report based on this method of calculation.

Notice that the pattern for calculations in this method of grade reporting is identical to that used in getting price extensions in purchasing, or in calculating hourly payroll with totals and averages by department. Each detail line requires one multiplication, after which the product is added to a total. A total of this type is therefore known as a *sum of products*, and is commonly encountered in data processing work. Averages for the entire group are obtained by dividing the sum of products by a total calculated for that group.

PROBLEM DEFINITION: *Write a program to produce grade reports on a preprinted form. Quality point averages should be calculated on a basis of the 4-3-2-1 point system. Total credits earned, total credits attempted, and QPA should be given, for each student, for the current semester as well as for the entire college record. The input file is a merged deck of master/detail cards, in ascending order by student number. Figure 21-3 shows input record descriptions, along with field descriptions and names for all data fields.*

When programming with a preprinted form, it is helpful to make a transparent overlay of it to use with the early test runs, rather than waste valuable forms and spend valuable computer time putting on and taking off the forms during the test runs. Some programmers even postpone all coding for skipping and spacing until they get reasonable output from a test run, in order to eliminate the need for changing the channel tape every time. Once the answers are correct, modifications are made for use with a carriage control tape. The result of that test run is examined by using the overlay; when it looks ready, a final test run is made using both the carriage control tape and the preprinted forms.

The FILE DESCRIPTION, INPUT, and CALCULATION specifications are given in Figure 21-4. FILE DESCRIPTION shows that three files are needed: *input* of merged master/detail card deck, *output* of printed report, and *output* of punched new master card. INPUT specifications define a header card, with an F in column 8Ø, to give the year and semester of the current run. It must be listed *first*, ahead of the sequenced group of data for each student. Each set consists of exactly one master, as specified by Ø1 1 on the INPUT form, and *at least one* detail, specified by Ø2 N on the next record. Sequence indication merely provides a check of the input records to ensure that at least one detail card is present for each master card, and that a master is *in front of* the details. It does *not* ensure that the control field of a detail card matches that from the previous master! A further check is done, as shown on line Ø25 of the CALCULATION form, to be sure that each course *does* belong with the previous master. Processing is either halted or continued on indicator Ø3, depending on the results of the comparison. For each valid course card, the grade code is multiplied by the number of credits, then the product is added into the sum **TOTQP** for that student. The field **CRHRS** is added into the sum of attempted credits, **TOTATT**. Should the student have a grade of D or better, as determined by the comparison done on line Ø28 of the calculations, the credit field **CRED** is added to total credits earned, **TOTCR**. Every time a new student number is detected on a master card, the L1 control break causes total-time calculations to occur. Total quality points for

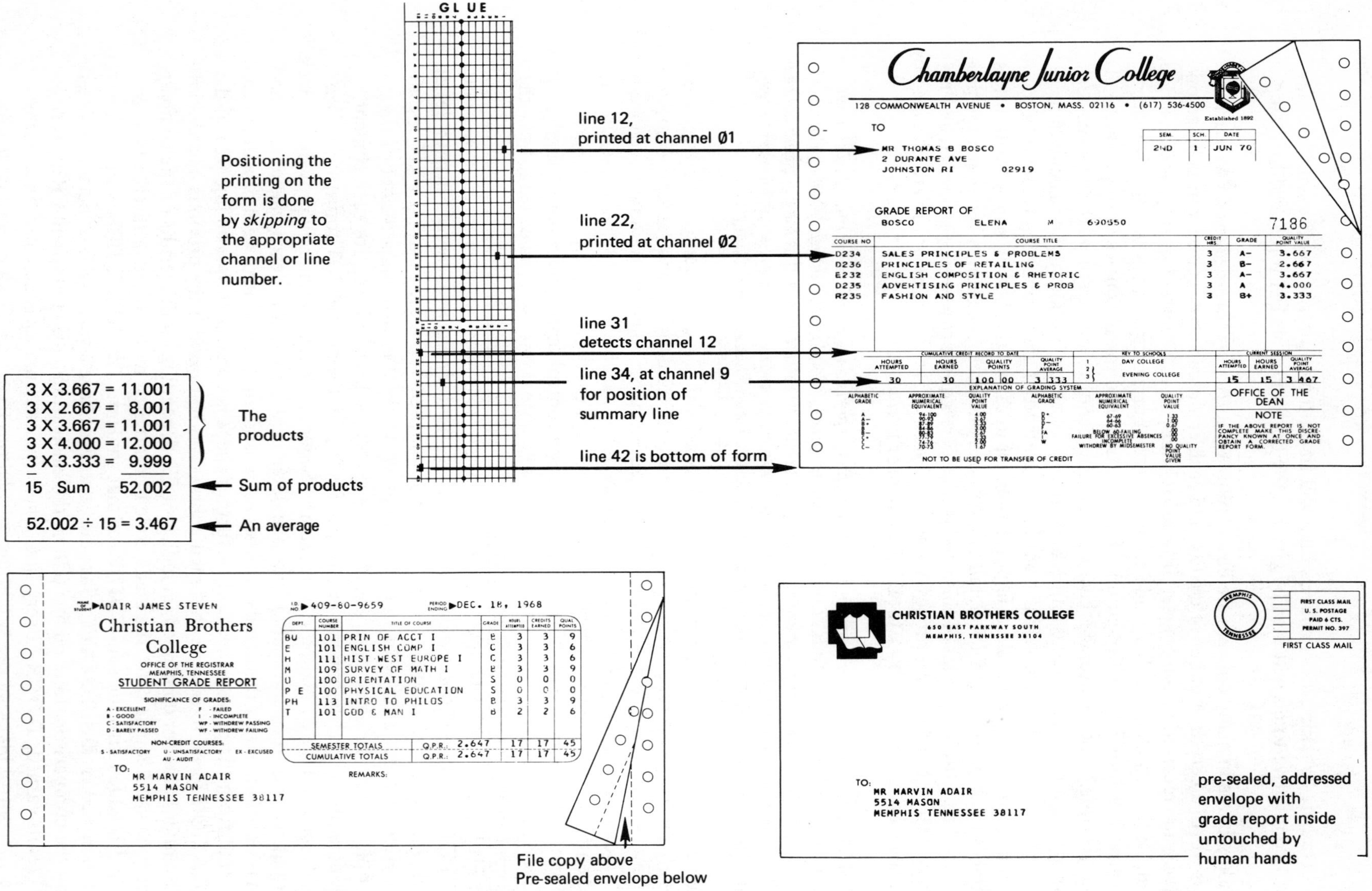

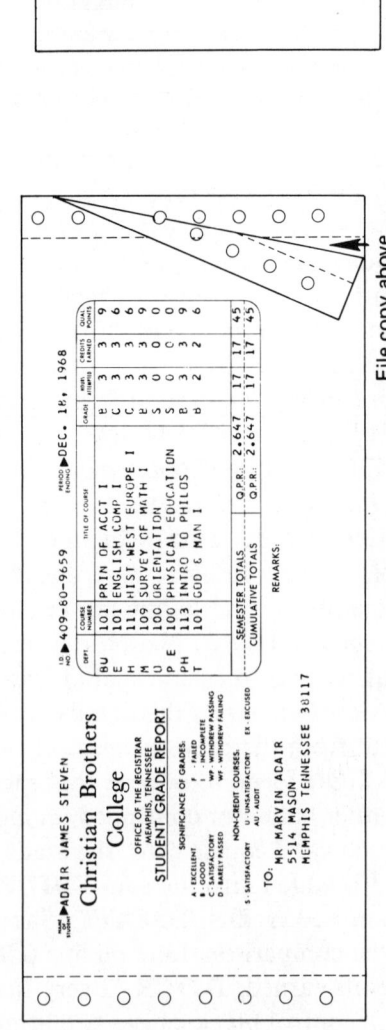

FIG. 21-2 Grade reporting with quality point average. (Courtesy of Haff Business Forms, Inc., and UARCO, Inc.)

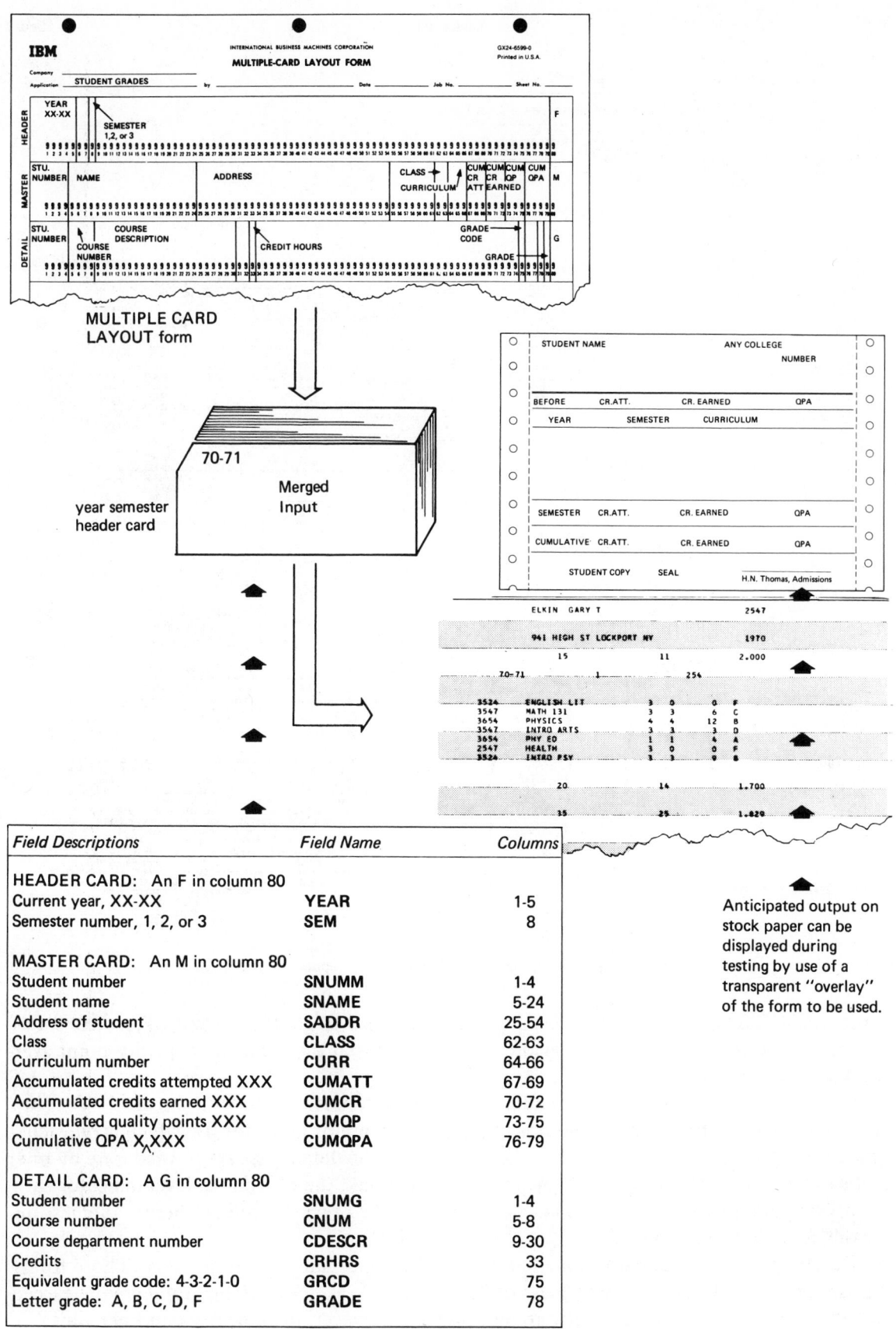

Field Descriptions	Field Name	Columns
HEADER CARD: An F in column 80		
Current year, XX-XX	**YEAR**	1-5
Semester number, 1, 2, or 3	**SEM**	8
MASTER CARD: An M in column 80		
Student number	**SNUMM**	1-4
Student name	**SNAME**	5-24
Address of student	**SADDR**	25-54
Class	**CLASS**	62-63
Curriculum number	**CURR**	64-66
Accumulated credits attempted XXX	**CUMATT**	67-69
Accumulated credits earned XXX	**CUMCR**	70-72
Accumulated quality points XXX	**CUMQP**	73-75
Cumulative QPA X.XXX	**CUMQPA**	76-79
DETAIL CARD: A G in column 80		
Student number	**SNUMG**	1-4
Course number	**CNUM**	5-8
Course department number	**CDESCR**	9-30
Credits	**CRHRS**	33
Equivalent grade code: 4-3-2-1-0	**GRCD**	75
Letter grade: A, B, C, D, F	**GRADE**	78

FIG. 21-3 Grade report problem setup.

297

```
DOS/360*RPG*CL 3-3              STUGR

        H
        F*   STUDENT GRADES WITH CUMULATIVES -    FOR LITTLE
        F*
        F*   MASTER CARDS    M  IN COLUMN 80
        F*     DETAIL CARDS  G  IN COLUMN 80
        F*   YEAR AND SEMESTER CARD  -  F IN COLUMN 80
001     FINPUT    IP  F  80  80          READ40 SYSRDR
002     FLIST      O  F 120 120          PRINTERSYSLST
003     FPUNCH     O  F  80  80          READ40 SYSPCH
```

```
        I*   YEAR SEMESTER HEADER CARD
004     IINPUT    NS  99  80 CF
005     I                                   1   5 YEAR
006     I                                   8   8 SEM
        I*    STUDENT MASTER CARD
007     I         011 01  80 CM
008     I                                   1  40SNUMM L1
009     I                                   5  24 SNAME
010     I                                  25  54 SADDR
011     I                                  62  63 CLASS
012     I                                  64  66 CURR
013     I                                  67  690CUMATT
014     I                                  70  720CUMCR
015     I                                  73  750CUMQP
016     I                                  76  793CUMQPA
        I*   GRADE CARDS
        I*
017     I         02N 02  80 CG
018     I                                   1  40SNUMG
019     I                                   5   8 CNUM
020     I                                  11  30 COESCR
021     I                                  33  330CRHRS
022     I                                  75  750GRCD
023     I                                  78  78 GRADE
        I*   INPUT DESCRIPTIONS COMPLETED
```

Calculations:

	CR.	GRCODE	Q.P.
Math:	3	4	12
Arts:	3	3	9
Eng:	3	2	6
PhyEd:	1	4	4
Speech:	3	3	9
TOT. CR.	13		40 TOT. Q.P.

40 ÷ 13 = 3.077

done for each card

done at L1 for each person

```
        C*
024     C                    SETOF                     03
        C*
        C*   COMPARE STUDENT NUMBERS  YOU BETCHUM   RED RIDER
025     C   02  SNUMM    COMP SNUMG               H1H103
026     C   03  CRHRS    ADD  TOTATT   TOTATT 20
027     C   03           MOVE CRHRS    CROUT  20
        C*   TURN ON  INDICATOR 04 FOR HIGH  OR EQUAL
028     C   03  GRCD    COMP 1                04  04
029     C   03 04        Z-ADDCRHRS    CRED   20
030     C   03N04        Z-ADD00       CRED
        C*   GET TOTAL CREDITS
031     C   03 04 CRED   ADD  TOTCR    TOTCR  20
        C*   ADD TO TOTAL QUALITY POINTS  -  DON'T GOOF NOW
032     C   03  CRED     MULT GRCD     QP     20
033     C   03  QP       ADD  TOTQP    TOTQP  20
        C* * THAT'S ALL UNTIL THE BREAK - OK -
        C*   AT L1 BREAK BETWEEN STUDENTS,  DO THESE TOO
034     CL1 TOTQP    DIV  TOTATT   QPA    43H
035     CL1 TOTQP    ADD  CUMQP    CUMQP
036     CL1 TOTATT   ADD  CUMATT   CUMATT
037     CL1 TOTCR    ADD  CUMCR    CUMCR
038     CL1 CUMQP    DIV  CUMATT   CUMQPA    H
        C*   SINCE TOTQP IS NOT PRINTED AND CANNOT BE BLANKED BY
        C*   USE OF BLANK AFTER,  MOVE ZEROES INTO IT
039     CL1          MOVE 00       TOTQP  20
```

FIG. 21-4 File description, input, calculations—grade report problem **STUGR**.

that student, **TOTQP**, is divided by total credits attempted to get the current **QPA**. The totals are then added to those from the previous college work, and the cumulative quality point average, **CUMQPA**, is calculated.

The OUTPUT-FORMAT coding and a sample grade report are shown in Figure 21-5. The heading lines at the beginning of the report are done by use of indicator Ø1, which is *on* each time a new master card is brought into the computer. The detail lines are printed, one by one, as they come in, using indicator Ø2. At each control break, the L1 control level indicator turns on, printing the totals at the bottom of each form for the previous student, before the heading for the next student is printed.

Resetting of certain totals is done to ensure accuracy of later control groups. Those totals that are printed out may be reset by use of "blank-after"—as, for example, total credits earned and attempted. Any total fields that are not printed, however, must be reset another way.

Total quality points, for example, may be reset by a **MOVE** that puts zeros into the field, either at total-time calculation, immediately after the field has been used to calculate **QPA**, or at the following detail-time, prior to its use with the next group. Initialization is not needed for all fields, such as **QPA** calculated anew for each student, and the cumulative totals brought in on the master card for each student. Those values will destroy the previous ones as they are placed into position by field name.

Throughout the program, indicators are used other than record-identifying ones. A warning message occurs during generation to say that indicator 99 is unreferenced, to bring to your attention the fact that, although it is assigned, it is never used. Since the information on the year/semester header card, which turned on indicator 99, is stored and later printed with the master card information, it is not necessary to use indicator 99 again, so the warning can be ignored.

Each indicator in use should be carefully examined to see whether it could cause calculations or output at unwarranted times. Indicator Ø3, for example, turns *on* each time a detail card matches its previous master, and controls the processing of that detail card. When the next detail card comes in, indicator Ø3, although at first still on from the previous card, will be reset by the execution of the comparison instruction. When a master card comes in, however, indicator Ø3 will *not* be reset by the comparison, because it is conditioned by a detail card and will not be executed for the master card! It will remain at its former setting during the processing of the master card, and will cause errors to occur. It must therefore be turned *off* after its use.

Indicator Ø4, also used on a comparison, is reset to reflect the grade condition D or better on each detail card. While a master card is in, however, it will retain its former setting; you must be certain that it causes no problem elsewhere in the program by its being on or off. After examination, it is found that it causes no other calculation or output to occur and need not be set off.

```
0*
0*    PREPARE OUTPUT LISTINGS FOR GRADE REPORT
0*
040  OLIST   D  301  01
041  0                        SNAME    63
042  0                        SNUMM  Z  87
043  0         D  2   01
044  0                        SADDR    73
045  0
046  0                        CLASS    87 '19'
047  0         D  2   01
048  0                        CUMATT   50 ' 0 '
049  0                        CUMCR    69 ' 0 '
050  0                        CUMQPA   87 '0.   '
051  0         D  3   01
052  0                        YEAR     42
053  0                        SEM      56
054  0                        CURR     75
055  0         D  1   03
056  0                        CNUM     37
057  0                        CDE SCR  62
058  0                        CROUT    66 '0 '
059  0                        CRED     70 '0 '
060  0                        QP       78 '0 '
061  0                        GRADE    82
062  0         T  21  L1
063  0                        TOTATT B 50 '0 '
064  0                        TOTCR  B 69 '0 '
065  0                        QPA      87 '0.   '
066  0         T  21  L1
067  0                        CUMATT   50 ' 0 '
068  0                        CUMCR    69 ' 0 '
069  0                        CUMQPA   87 '0.   '
070  OPUNCH    T      L1
071  0                        SNUMM    4
072  0                        SNAME    24
073  0                        SADDR    54
074  0                        CLASS    63
075  0                        CURR     66
076  0                        CUMATT   69
077  0                        CUMCR    72
078  0                        CUMQP    75
079  0                        CUMQPA   79
080  0                                 80 'M'
0*
0*    THE  END   AT  LAST
```

```
STUDENT NAME                          ANY COLLEGE
CATON WILLIAM H                       NUMBER 1234
101 POUND ST LOCKPORT NY

BEFORE     CR.ATT. 57    CR. EARNED 57    QPA 3.151

YEAR       SEMESTER 1    CURRICULUM 157

6542    MATH 131         3   3    12   A
5245    INTRO. ARTS      3   3     9   B
3254    ENGLISH COMP     3   3     6   C
2543    PHY ED           1   1     4   A
5245    SPEECH           3   3     9   B

SEMESTER     CR.ATT. 13    CR. EARNED 13    QPA 3.077

CUMULATIVE   CR.ATT. 70    CR. EARNED 70    QPA 3.143

STUDENT COPY    SEAL          H.N. Thomas, Admissions
```

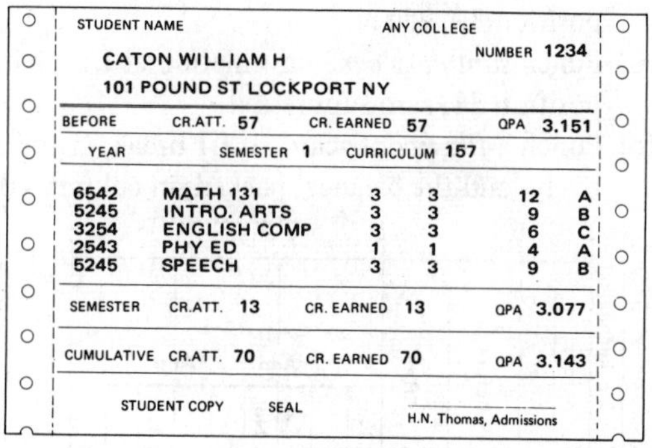

sketch of possible
form design

FIG. 21-5 Output specifications and output—grade report problem **STUGR**.

EXERCISES

1. Make a systems chart showing a job with input card deck of data, summary punching of control level totals, and the production of a report. Compare it to that for card file updating in Figure 21-1.

```
┌─────────────────────────────────────────────────────────────────────────┐
│                                                                           │
│                                                                           │
│                                                                           │
│                                                                           │
│                                                                           │
│                                                                           │
│                                                                           │
│                                                                           │
│                                                                           │
│                                                                           │
│                                                                           │
│                                                                           │
│                                                                           │
│                                                                           │
│                                                                           │
│                                                                           │
│                                                                           │
│                                                                           │
│                                                                           │
│                                                                           │
│                                                                           │
│                                                                           │
│                                                                           │
└─────────────────────────────────────────────────────────────────────────┘
```

2. Give **OUTPUT-FORMAT** specifications, omitting FILENAME, and assuming an amount field of length 6, 2 decimals.
   (a) Punch card output at detail indicator $\emptyset 1$, giving account number in position 8 and an amount in position 3$\emptyset$, edited.
   (b) Punch *summary card* information at L1, giving an account number in position 8, and an amount in position 3$\emptyset$, zero suppressed.
   (c) Punch a *file update* card, at L1 break, giving account number and name in positions 8 and 3$\emptyset$, respectively, and the balance, packed, in column 4$\emptyset$.

	Type (H/D/T)	Stacker Select	Before	After	Before	After	Not		And		Not		And	Not			Field Name						Zero Suppress (Z)	Blank After (B)	End Position in Output Record				Packed Field (P)					Constant					
2 13	14	15	16	17	18	19	20	21	22	23	24	25	26	27	28	29	30	31	32	33	34	35	36	37	38	39	40	41	42	43	44	45	46	47	48	49	50	51 52 53 54 55 5
(a)																																							

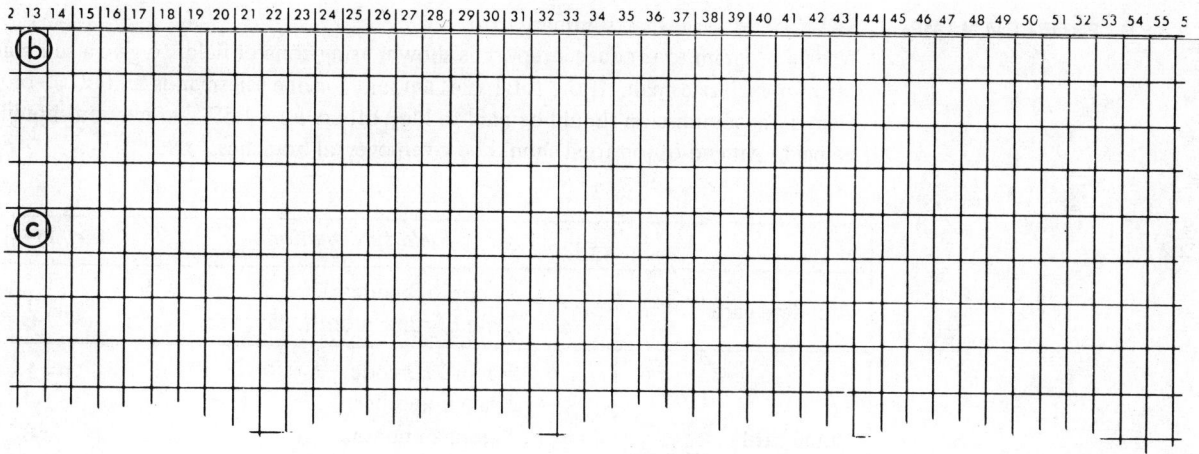

Section 7

PROGRAMS TO WRITE

A. PROBLEM NAME: **MULTRECD:**   classified ad billing with two record types

Write a program, based on the records shown, to prepare a bill similar to that in Figure 19-2. Assume that class 1 amount is calculated by the number of lines multiplied by the rate per line, that class 2 rate is charged over a weekend and should have an increase of $1.50 over the rate as calculated for class 1, and that class 3 is a special price for the rate given.

	Field Information	*Columns*
Card type 1	Record ID code: M	1
	Name	3-2Ø
	Telephone number	21-27
	Address	31-5Ø
	City, state	51-7Ø
	Zip code	71-75
	Serial number	77-8Ø
Card type 2	Record ID code: D	1
	Starting date: month, dash, year	6-1Ø
	Lines in the ad	12
	Times the ad ran	14
	Rate per line	17-2Ø
	Class: 1, 2, or 3	25
	Serial number	31-34

B. PROBLEM NAME: **SALESSUM:** salesman summary card

Write a program to produce a report as shown, using control fields to give a summary card for each salesman. If the total sales amount for one salesman is $5,000.00 or over, a 5% commission should be paid to him; otherwise a 1.5% commission should be paid. An end-of-job total should be given over all branches.

	Field Information	Columns
Run-date card	Record ID code: D Date of run: month, day, year	11 1-6
Detail card	Record ID code: ∅, 1, or 2 Branch number Salesman number Amount of sale, 2 decimals Invoice number of sale	11 1-2 6-8 14-20 26-30
Output summary card	Branch number Salesman number Sales total, edited Commission total, edited Run-date, edited	1-2 6-8 16-3∅ 36-5∅ 61-68

3/13/69		HONEST JOE CAR COMPANY			PAGE 1
BRANCH	SALESMAN	INVOICE NUMBER	SALES AMOUNT	COMMISSION RATE	COMMISSION
33	373	55550	$ 211.10	.015	$ 3.17
		88883	$ 33	.015	$ .00
		11220	$5,333.00	.050	$ 266.65
	373	SALESMAN TOTAL	$ 5,544.43		
	383	88830	$2,999.96	.015	$ 45.00
		66663	$2,777.30	.015	$ 41.66
	383	SALESMAN TOTAL	$ 5,777.26		
	393	54203	$3,654.73	.015	$ 54.82
		55203	$6,999.80	.050	$ 349.99
		88896	$8,999.69	.050	$ 449.98

C. PROBLEM NAME: **PKREC:** prepare packed master records

Write a program to prepare master records containing numeric information in packed form. Two punch cards containing alphameric and numeric information are used in making the new master record. List all fields from the new master so that proof-checking can be done.

	Field Information	Columns
Card 1 of group	Record ID code: 1	8
	Account number	1-6
	Balance, 2 decimals, credit possible	15-2∅
	Payment amount, 2 decimals	26-3∅
	Charge amount, 2 decimals	36-4∅
Card 2 of group	Record ID code: 2	8
	Name	11-3∅
	Street address	31-5∅
	City, state	51-7∅
	Zip code	71-75
Output master	Record ID code: P	8∅
	Account number, packed	1-4
	Name	5-24
	Street address	25-44
	City, state	45-64
	Zip code, packed	65-67
	Balance, packed	68-71
	Payments, packed	72-74
	Charges, packed	75-77

D. PROBLEM NAME: **INVUPD:** inventory update

Write a program to read inventory master balance-on-hand cards, followed by inventory receipt cards, followed by inventory issue cards, merged into control groups, each with exactly one master, but with any number of each type of detail. Print a report giving a major heading with run-date and page number, and with the columns heading line giving the beginning balance-on-hand for that item of inventory. Each detail card, whether a receipt or an issue, should be listed, with the number it represents placed under the appropriate column heading. At the control break for that item, give the total number of receipts, the total number of issues, and the remaining balance-on-hand for that item. An updated inventory master card, in the same format as the input master, should then be punched. Input records are described in the **MULTIPLE-CARD LAYOUT** form in Figure 2-7.

E. PROBLEM NAME: **LISTPCHK:** list or punch or both, by run-control card

Write a program to use a run-control card, punched with a P, L, or B in column 1, to cause it either to *punch* a duplicate deck, *list* the deck, or *both*, respectively. If the run-control card is missing, have the computer stop.

SECTION 8

REPORTS WITH TABLE INPUT, SEARCH, AND OUTPUT

Lesson 22

TABLE DESIGN AND STORAGE

You will learn what tables are, how they are used in programs, and how to design, punch, and give RPG specifications for them.

1. What is a *table*? How is it named?
2. What is meant by *table look-up*?
3. Compare an argument table to a function table.
4. Why is a table in RPG sometimes sorted into sequence before it is used, and specified either as ascending or descending?
5. How does RPG know that a line of the FILE DESCRIPTION specification is table input during execution, rather than a regular input data deck?
6. When alternating tables are used, how are the table data punched?
7. What is the difference between NUMBER OF TABLE ENTRIES PER TABLE and NUMBER OF TABLE ENTRIES PER RECORD on the FILE EXTENSION form?
8. When are table data placed into memory?
9. Where do you put the table cards in the job stream so that they will be properly loaded into storage?
10. Describe how tables might be designed for a job where mere *presence* on a table is all that must be determined; a job where a particular argument provides an associated description or name; and a job where a search argument must find the *range* of values into which it fits to provide an associated rate or amount.

ANSWERS

1. An array or column of data, of one particular type and purpose, that is stored in memory for access throughout the processing of the program. By a table name, six characters or less, starting with the letters TAB, on the FILE EXTENSION form.

2. The search that locates the table entry needed for a particular job.

3. The argument is usually the portion of a related table that is used for look-up; the function is usually the one that is referenced when its corresponding argument is *found* during a look-up. In RPG, however, any portion can be used as an argument and any portion can be used as a function.

4. Because table look-up may be done on either HIGH or LOW conditions, in which case the entries in the table must be in specified order.

5. Because there is a **T** in column ·16 following an **I** in column 15. An **E** is also entered in column 39, but this does not necessarily imply that the file is a table.

6. In pairs, with one entry of each table given and the table that is *first* described on the FILE EXTENSION form punched *first*. Many pairs can be placed on each card if specifications are so written.

7. The total number of entries in that portion of the table is given by NUMBER OF TABLE ENTRIES PER TABLE; NUMBER OF TABLE ENTRIES PER RECORD is the number of entries to be brought in on *each* table card until the NUMBER OF TABLE ENTRIES PER TABLE has been reached. When alternating related tables are used, the first refers to the *number of pairs in the entire file*, and the second, to the *number of pairs punched in each card*.

8. On some systems, such as the IBM SYSTEM/36∅, CPS, they must be loaded at *generation-time* and become a part of the object program. On the IBM 113∅ and the IBM SYSTEM/36∅, DOS, they are loaded at *execution-time* instead, just before the processing of the object program begins. On some systems, such as the IBM SYSTEM/3, you may select and use either of the two methods.

9. If tables are entered at execution time, they are put in the proper input device, as specified by the FROM FILENAME entry on the FILE EXTENSION form and its corresponding device as given on the FILE DESCRIPTION form. They should be *in front of* any data file also using that device.

10. Enter only the single table of arguments, and use an EQUAL indicator; enter a related table of arguments and functions, either alternately or separately; use the EQUAL indicator to find the appropriate argument, then use the function associated with it; select either the upper or lower value of the argument range and use it for the argument table, with indicators HIGH/EQUAL or LOW/EQUAL depending on the particular value of the associated function that is needed, with the table sorted by argument table and specified as either ascending or descending sequence on the FILE EXTENSION form.

RPG has the capability to read and store tabular information for it to be accessed by any record throughout the program. The entire table is entered into memory, and stored. Any item on it can be found by an instruction that does a table look-up. When the proper information is found, it can be used for calculations or output, or, on some systems, it can be modified and placed back into the table. Information used for look-up may be stored in sequence according to some key field, so that it can be accessed not only for an element that is exactly EQUAL to one of the items on the table, but for those that are LOW or HIGH when compared to it.

Tables can be used in a variety of ways, as shown in Figure 22-1. For example, the numbers of certain expired credit cards can be placed into memory, and every transaction that refers to any of them can be placed onto a special report. A list of license plate numbers of automobiles that are allowed in a certain parking area may be stored, with or without a table of names of owners. A table can contain the names of the months, with another giving corresponding month number, so that, for example, the month number of the date of hire for each employee can be converted to an actual month name before being printed onto a report. Tables, on some implementations, can be updated and retrieved after a run. They can be used to update accounts, with look-up being done by account number. Probably the most common use of tables, however, is for sales tax, where look-up depends on the amount of sales that fits into a range on a table of amounts.

The method of loading tables in RPG varies on the different computer systems. On some systems, such as the IBM SYSTEM/3, you must decide whether or not you wish the tables to become a permanent part of the object program. When the contents of the table are fairly permanent, they should be made a part of the object program. This method, called *generation-time*, or *compile-time*, is the only method available on several of the card systems of the IBM SYSTEM/36∅, Model 2∅. One advantage of this method is that the table cards need not be handled every time a production run of the job is made, thus eliminating some of the chance for error. The one disadvantage, however, is that should you decide to change the contents of the table for a particular run, you would have to generate another object deck. Even though, as is possible on some systems, you should have the program *modify* the table contents, during the next loading of that object program they would be stored in their *original* form and not in their modified form.

When the tables are made a permanent part of the object program, they are *not* considered a file, but are internal constants. There is therefore no file name given to them on the FILE DESCRIPTION form. The tables are placed with the source deck for generation, with special control cards for separators, and when the object deck is complete, the tables are part of it.

When the contents of the table are more temporary in nature, you may prefer to use the method of *execution-time* loading. The tables do *not* become part of the object program; instead, the table contents are reentered each time the job is run. This method is permitted on the IBM SYSTEM/3, but on some systems, such as the IBM 113∅ and the IBM SYSTEM/36∅, DOS, this method *must* be used. The tables in this case are considered a file, more specifically, a *table file*, and as such have an entry on the FILE DESCRIPTION form, with a T in column 16 following the I in column 15. Table cards are placed in that input device assigned to the file, *in front of* any data cards that perhaps use that same device. Some systems require that a special sepa-

PLAYER	BATTING AVERAGE
FRANK ROBINSON	.308
BROOKS ROBINSON	.234
MICKEY MANTLE	.308
BABE RUTH	.342
AL KALINE	.304

Argument table and corresponding
function; answers the question,
"What is the batting average
for Mr. Ruth?"   .342

Search argument: BABE RUTH
Argument table: player names
Function table: player batting
                            averages

Argument table only;
answers the question,
"Is credit card number
20115 invalid?" yes

Search argument: 20115
Argument table: credit
               card numbers
Function table: none

XTA GAS CO. INVALID CREDIT CARDS
12347
13986
15896
20115
21674
23588
39112
54117
67182

Age at Enrollment	Monthly Premium Per Person
0-18	$2.50
19-39	$3.80
40-54	$4.80
55-64	$5.80
65-74	$6.80
75 and over	$9.10

Argument table and corresponding function;
answers the question, "What is the monthly
premium payment for a person 25 years old?" $3.80

Search argument: 25
Argument table: a range of age categories
Function table: monthly premium payments

FIG. 22-1 Tables often needed.

rator card be placed between the table file and any data file following it, but on the IBM SYSTEM/36∅, DOS, there are no separators of any kind—the table cards immediately precede the data cards, and are loaded before normal execution of the program begins.

Since tables entered during execution are entered as a file, they must have their own given file name, just as input and output files do. Each line of the FILE DESCRIPTION form used for table file description has the letter **T** in column 16 to mean a table file, and has the letter **F** given in column 39, denoting that further description of the file will be given on a line of the FILE EXTENSION form. File format, file name, block and record lengths, device, and symbolic device are used in the same manner as on regular input/output files. Since more than one table is permitted in a program, each table may be defined on a separate line of the FILE DESCRIPTION form, with order of stacking of the table cards determined by the order in which they are listed on the form. Should several tables be entered on the *same* input device, however, the same *line* on the FILE DESCRIPTION form, and therefore the same file name, may be used, and several lines of the FILE EXTENSION form may refer to that file name. Table data with the same file name are in this case stacked in the order as listed on the FILE EXTENSION form. Should a *regular* data file use the same input device as a table file, two different file names must be assigned to the same device, so that a **T** can be placed in column 16 for the table file. Tables are in that case placed *in front of* the regular data deck on that device for execution.

The most common method of table design has two types of related information presented, in pairs, in an *alternating* form. One table is called the *argument* and the other, the *function*. The argument is the one used to look up information, such as instructor number, as shown in Figure 22-2. The function is the information, such as the instructor name, that the program needs to find, and that is located by its correspondence to the argument. Each argument with its corresponding function is, for convenience, called a *set*. Even though two columns of information may be considered *two single tables*, they are, when punched in alternating pairs, often considered *one* table file, with only one file name necessary. Each argument table and function table must have a name, up to six characters long, beginning with the letters **TAB**. Note that the file name need not begin with **TAB**, but the table name must. Table entries may be in

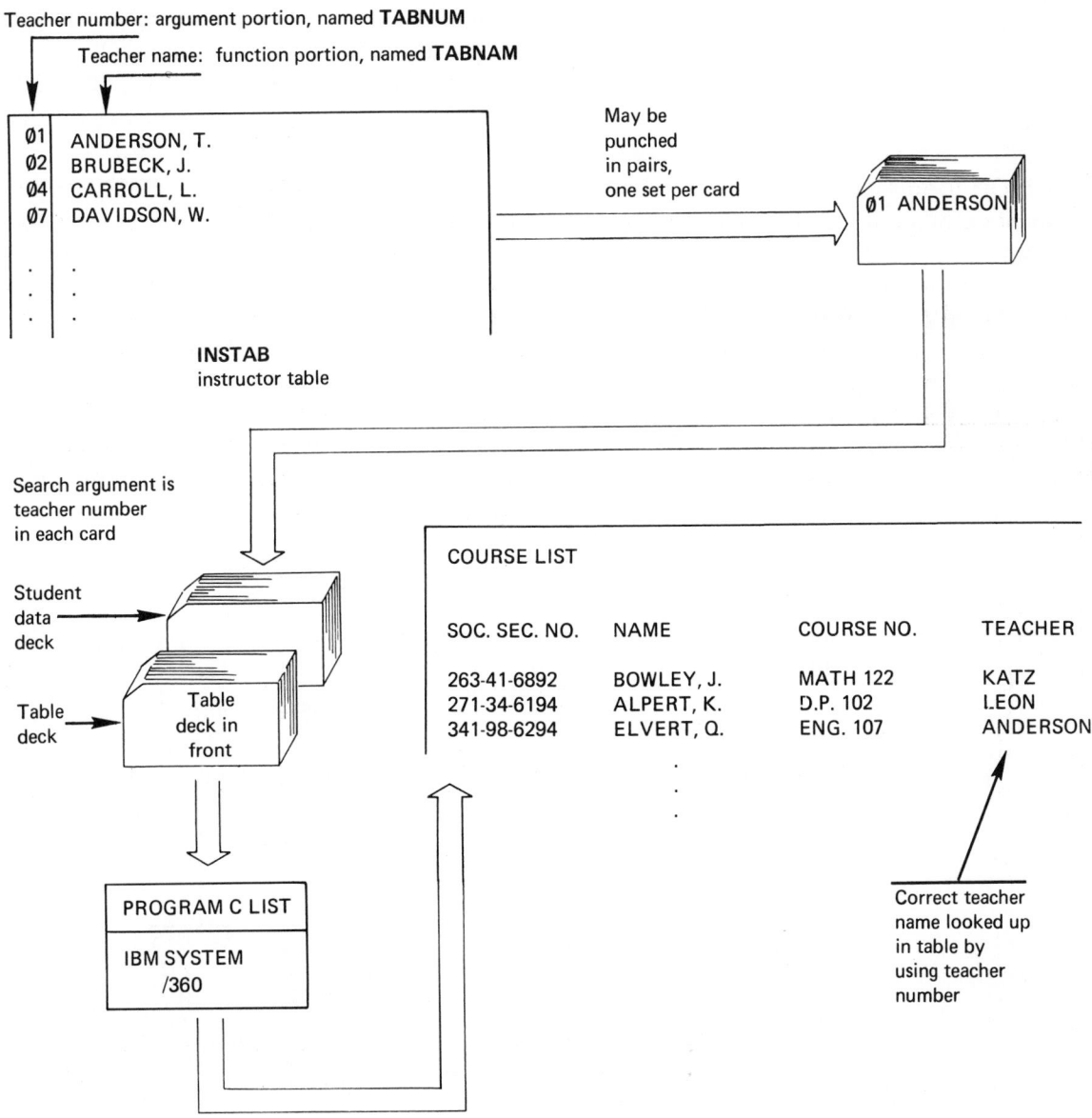

FIG. 22-2 Table preparation for use with EQUAL condition.

either numeric or alphameric mode, with numeric entries on most machines up to 15 digits, and alphameric ones up to 256 characters, but all entries in a single table must be the same length and mode, and must have the same number of decimal positions. The table file in Figure 22-2 is named **INSTAB**, for instructor table; it contains an argument portion, called **TABNUM**, that is 2 digits long, and a function portion, called **TABNAM**, that is 20 characters long.

After the table is stored in memory, it can be accessed by a search argument, either a field from an individual data card, or a constant—for example, look for instructor number 1∅. The program can specify an indicator under EQUAL so that the search argument is compared to every number in the argument table, if necessary, until it either finds the number *equal* to it, or signals that it cannot be found. Table look-up can be done not only for a number EQUAL to the search argument, but also for one higher or lower, by using indicators for HIGH or LOW, respectively. Should a look-up require table access just below, or just above, the one you have, the table must be *in order* and sequence must be specified, as either ascending or descending.

The FILE EXTENSION form is used to describe in detail how the table entries are punched. Comments may be placed in columns 58-74 of each line. The **E** in column 6 identifies the form type. When tables are entered during execution-time, FROM FILENAME, columns 11-18, gives the name of the file being used, in exactly the same way it is given on the FILE DESCRIP-TION form. When tables are entered at generation-time, however, there is *no* file name on the FILE DESCRIPTION form and therefore the FROM FILENAME field on the FILE EX-TENSION form should be left blank. Each line of the FILE EXTENSION has enough space for description of a related table with alternating format—the first portion of the set described in columns 27-45, and the next, in columns 46-57. If the argument is punched *in front of* the function in the paired sets, the argument should be given *first* on the FILE EXTENSION form line. The function, however, could instead be punched *first* in the paired set as long as it is also written first on the form. Punching of the table data begins in column 1 of each card; no space is allowed between the argument and function parts of the table. The NUMBER OF TABLE ENTRIES PER TABLE is the number of *pairs* in the *table* and is given in columns 36-39; the NUMBER OF TABLE ENTRIES PER RECORD is the number of pairs punched onto each *card* and is given in columns 33-35. All other entries pertain to the particular table they describe with name, length, decimal places, packing, and sequencing all specified for each table. The specifications given by

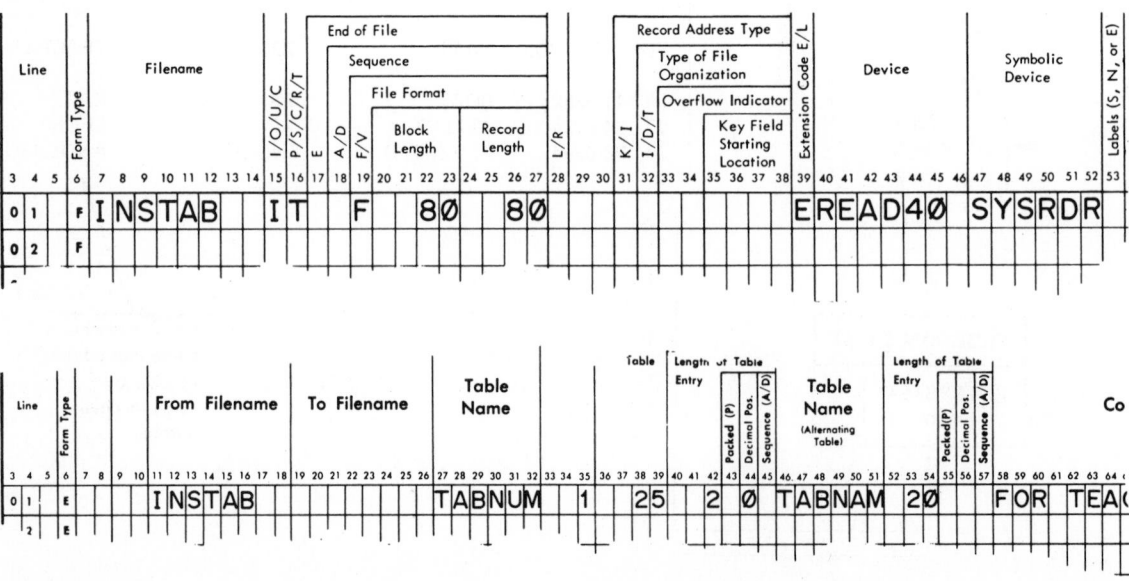

describes the table sketched in Figure 22-2. It has one set per record for 25 records. Teacher number is 2 digits long, in numeric mode, and teacher name is 20 alphameric characters long.

Tables may be punched with *more* than one set per card. All table cards, however, must have exactly the *same* number of sets on *each* card, except possibly the last, which may have fewer. A table entry may *not* be split onto two cards. The line given by

Form Type			From Filename	To Filename	Table Name			Entry	Packed (P)	Decimal Pos.	Sequence (A/D)	Table Name (Alternating Table)	Entry Packed (P)
5	6	7 8	9 10	11 12 13 14 15 16 17 18	19 20 21 22 23 24 25 26	27 28 29 30 31 32	33 34 35	36 37 38 39	40 41 42	43	44	45	46 47 48 49 50 51	52 53 54	55
E			MONTHS		TABNUM		7	1 2		2			ØATABNAM		9
E														

describes a table file named **MONTHS**, with a 2-digit numeric argument field named **TABNUM**, and a 9-character month field named **TABNAM**, punched with 7 sets per card, 12 sets for the entire table, in alternating fashion, with the number in ascending sequence. Related tables need not be entered in alternating form, but may be entered in *single* form. Either a table of arguments or a table of functions may be separately entered; one may immediately follow the other by having all of one table come in, then all of the other. In each of these cases, a separate line of the FILE EXTENSION form is used to describe each table. Even though the arguments and functions are separately entered, table look-up is done in exactly the same manner as for alternating tables, with a look-up on one yielding the corresponding value of the other. The order of the reading of the table data files is usually determined by the order given on the FILE DESCRIPTION form. Should the tables be input from the same device by the same file name, however, the order is determined by the order on the FILE EXTENSION form.

Should only an argument table be needed, without a corresponding function table, it is called a *single table*. It must have one specification line on the FILE EXTENSION form, but it uses only those fields between columns 27 and 45 to describe the table, leaving columns 46-57 blank. For some tasks, a single table is all that is needed. For example, the presence of an employee number on a table serves as verification that the person is indeed an employee; no reference material or name is required. The specification given by

Line			Form Type			From Filename	To Filename	Table Name			Entry	Packed (P)	Decimal Pos.	Sequence (A/D)	Table Name (Alternating Table)	Entry
3	4	5	6	7 8	9 10	11 12 13 14 15 16 17 18	19 20 21 22 23 24 25 26	27 28 29 30 31 32	33 34 35	36 37 38 39	40 41 42	43	44	45	46 47 48 49 50 51	52 53
0	1		E			INTABLE		TABSSA		8	1 1 5			9 Ø		
0	2		E													
0	"		.													

defines such a table, giving 9-digit employee numbers, punched eight on a card, for 115 employees. Since look-up will be done in this case on an EQUAL condition, an entry under SEQUENCE is not needed. The single table also requires a file name if table storage is done at execution-time.

Tables as those used for look-up of sales tax or discount rates often have a *range* of values in the argument table, not just a single number. Should the amount of sale be *between* the two values, the corresponding function amount should be used; if not, the search continues to the next item in the table. A table should not be entered with both ends of the range punched as arguments. Analysis will reveal that only one is needed, and that it alone need be punched, with the function, for the table look-up to be properly performed. In most cases, the *upper* range can be used, as, for example, that shown in Figure 22-3. The search argument can be compared to each table argument entry until a "position" is found where it would sequentially fit between two entries on the table. The amount $1.15, for example, would fit between two entries on the table. The LOW-condition indicator will give you the function for the entry *below* the "position," and the HIGH one will give you the one *above*. Since using the HIGH indicator would give you the proper sales tax to use when the search argument falls between argument table values, and since the EQUAL indicator would give you the proper tax to use when the search argument exactly fits one of the argument table values, you should, if you punch the high end of the range table, use indicators HIGH and EQUAL to perform the look-up. Notice that the high end of the last range of values on the table is punched as an entry of all nines, making all search arguments not fitting earlier categories fit the last one. Should you decide instead to punch the *low* end of the range of values in the argument table, you would use the LOW and EQUAL indicators to perform the look-up properly. Remember that when tables are to be accessed with either the HIGH or the LOW indicator, SEQUENCE must be given on the FILE EXTENSION form.

Sometimes more than one field is needed in a function table. Since each look-up can access

DISCOUNT TABLE

- Argument -	Function
AMOUNT OF SALE	DISCOUNT RATE
0- 24	.01
25- 49	.02
50- 74	.03
75- 99	.04
100-124	.05
125-149	.06
150-199	.07
200 and over	.10

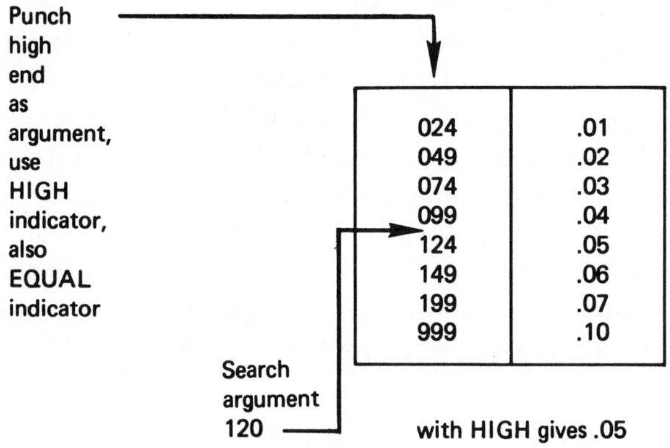

Punch high end as argument, use HIGH indicator, also EQUAL indicator

024	.01
049	.02
074	.03
099	.04
124	.05
149	.06
199	.07
999	.10

Search argument 120

with HIGH gives .05

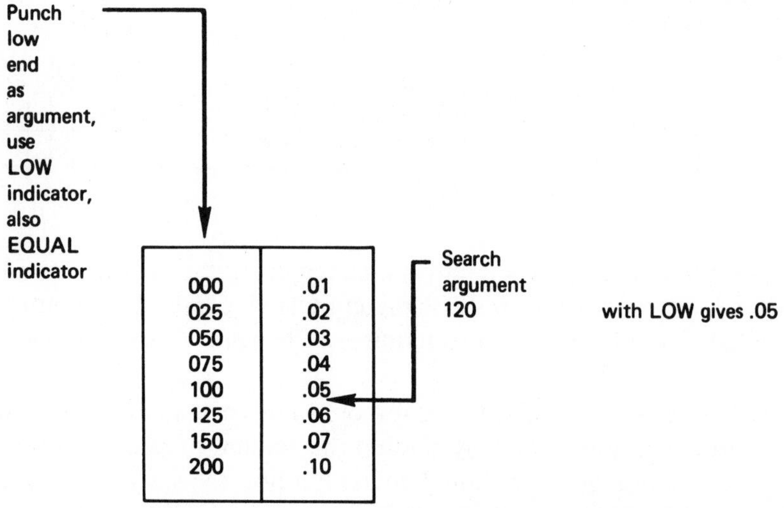

Punch low end as argument, use LOW indicator, also EQUAL indicator

000	.01
025	.02
050	.03
075	.04
100	.05
125	.06
150	.07
200	.10

Search argument 120

with LOW gives .05

FIG. 22-3 Table look-up preparation for use with HIGH/EQUAL or LOW/EQUAL conditions.

only *one* function table entry, only one entry can be stored there. However, it is possible to put several fields together into one entry for the purpose of defining the table. For example, in a table of inventory items stored as **TABNUM**, both the 20-character description of that inventory item and a 5-digit number giving the quantity on hand for that item could be stored as **TABINV**, 25 characters long. Then, when accessed by a look-up, the function entry can be separated into its two distinct pieces by use of the **MOVE** and **MOVEL** instructions.

EXERCISES

1. Give FILE DESCRIPTION and FILE EXTENSION specifications for each of these in the space provided below:

   (a) An alternating argument and function table, punched one set per card, to be read in by an IBM 254Ø card reader, with argument in columns 1-5, Ø decimals, and function columns 6-2Ø, alphameric. Assume that there are 1ØØ sets in the entire table, and that the argument is in increasing sequence. Use file name **ACCTNAME**.

   (b) A single argument, giving license plate numbers of employees, in a 1Ø-character field, to be read in on the IBM 25Ø1 card reader; 2ØØØ elements in the table, punched 8 elements per card; make up your own file name.

   (c) A single-argument table, to be followed by a single-function table, both from the IBM 254Ø card reader, but with the same file name; Assume 15Ø elements in each table, with argument 3 digits long, Ø decimals, punched 25 per card, and function 12 digits long, 2 decimals, punched 6 per card.

   (d) An alternating argument and function table, with argument 3 digits, Ø decimals, the function 8 characters long; punched in three pairs per card record, with 1ØØ pairs in the entire table; brought in on the IBM 25Ø1 card reader.

   (e) An alternating function and argument table, with the function 3 digits long, 3 decimals, and the argument 2Ø characters long; punched with 3 sets per card, 25 sets in the entire table; brought in on the IBM 254Ø.

Line	Form Type	Filename	I/O/U/C	P/S/C/R/T	E	A/D	F/V	Block Length	Record Length	L/R	Mode of Processing	K/I	I/D/T	Overflow Indicator / Key Field Starting Location	Extension Code E/L	Device	Symbolic Device	Labels (S, N, or E)
3 4 5	6	7 8 9 10 11 12 13 14	15	16 17	18	19	20 21 22 23	24 25 26 27	28	29 30	31	32 33 34	35 36 37 38	39	40 41 42 43 44 45 46	47 48 49 50 51 52	53
0 1 (a)	F																	
0 2	F																	
0 3 (b)	F																	
0 4	F																	
0 5 (c)	F																	
0 6	F																	
0 7 (d)	F																	
0 8	F																	
0 9 (e)	F																	
1 0	F																	
1 1	F																	
1 2	F																	

Sequence of the Chaining File						Number of Table Entries Per Record										
Number of the Chaining Field							Number of Table Entries									
						Per Table	Length of Table Entry						Length of Table Entry			
From Filename		To Filename		Table Name				Packed (P)	Decimal Pos.	Sequence (A/D)	Table Name (Alternating Table)			Packed(P)	Decimal Pos.	Sequence (A/D)
9 10	11 12 13 14 15 16 17 18	19 20 21 22 23 24 25 26	27 28 29 30 31 32	33 34 35	36 37 38 39	40 41 42	43	44	45	46 47 48 49 50 51	52 53 54	55	56	57	58
(a)															
(b)															
(c)															
(d)															
(e)															

2. Give instructions for keypunching the table shown in Figure 22-3 which has argument 3 digits long and function 2 digits long, for each of the following conditions:

Example: alternating, five sets per card

First set: columns 1-5, with sales amount in columns 1-3, discount rate in columns 4-5. Next four sets:

columns 6-25 on that card; on next card, put three other sets, using columns 1-15.

(a) Alternating, two sets per card.

_____

_____

(b) As two single tables, argument table, then function table, one entry per card.

_____

_____

(c) Alternating, eight sets per card.

_____

_____

(d) As two single tables, function first, then argument next, two entries per card.

(e) As two single tables, argument table first, then function table, five entries per card.

---

3. Design an alternating table to be used for storage of the description of each item in inventory, such as item number 1658, 'CLAW HAMMERS'. Assume that the item number is 4 digits long, and that the description could be up to 20 characters. Give FILE DESCRIPTION and FILE EXTENSION specifications as well as keypunching instructions.

	Form Type	Filename	I/O/U/C	P/S/C/R/T	E	A/D	F/V	Block Length	Record Length	L/R	K/I	I/D/T	Key Field Starting Location	Extension Code E/L	Device	Symbolic Device	Labels (S, N, or E)
1	F																
2	F																
3	F																
4	F																

Number of the Chaining Field / From Filename	To Filename	Table Name	Number of Table Entries Per Record	Number of Table Entries Per Table	Length of Table Entry	Packed (P)	Decimal Pos.	Sequence (A/D)	Table Name (Alternating Table)	Length of Table Entry	Packed (P)	Decimal Pos.	Sequence (A/D)

Lesson 23

TABLE SEARCH

You will learn how to use the table look-up instruction in RPG.

The questions below are answered on the back of this page. Should you already have had programming experience with table look-up, be sure you can correctly answer all the questions before going on to Lesson 24.

1. What instruction is used in RPG to do table look-up?
2. What is a *search argument*?
3. How must a search argument and a table argument be similar?
4. Give the purpose of FACTOR 1, FACTOR 2, and RESULT FACTOR in the **LOKUP** instruction.
5. How do indicators control the results of a table look-up?
6. When an unsequenced table is accessed by a search argument on an EQUAL condition, what terminates the search?
7. When an alphameric table is searched, how is order determined on numeric, alphabetic and special characters?
8. After a successful table look-up has been done, what name can be used to access the value in the function table that corresponds to the search argument?
9. When a table look-up indicator assigned to HIGH is *on*, what is the relationship between the search argument and the selected table argument?
10. What does an assignment of one indicator to both HIGH and EQUAL accomplish?

ANSWERS

1. **LOKUP.**
2. The literal or field that is to be looked up on the argument table.
3. They must be the same mode and length. No alignment is made for decimal places.
4. FACTOR 1 specifies the search argument; FACTOR 2 specifies the name of the argument table to be searched; RESULT FACTOR specifies the name of the function table from which an element corresponding to the "found" argument is to be taken.
5. By indicating that the element searched for is EQUAL, HIGH, or LOW, when compared to the search argument. HIGH/EQUAL and LOW/EQUAL are valid combinations to use.
6. Either an element on the table will be found *equal* to the search argument, in which case the indicator goes *on*, and the search is terminated, or the entire table is searched without success, at which time the indicator is set *off*, and the search is terminated.
7. By a collating sequence, which gives order to the coding of all characters. It considers blanks lower than letters, letters in order A, B, C, . . . , Z, letters lower than numbers, but special characters in various places in between.
8. The same name as that assigned to the function portion of the table.
9. The associated table argument selected will be the one *just higher than* the search argument, so that FACTOR 1 is less than FACTOR 2.
10. It causes a search for either one, with EQUAL having precedence. Should an equal condition be found, the EQUAL indicator goes on, and the corresponding function is used. Should an equal condition *not* be present the element just higher than the search argument, if present, will be used, and the HIGH indicator will go on. If only a LOW condition exists, then both indicators will be *off*.

Lesson 23   Table Search

After tables are designed and prepared, they are stored in the computer. The information on *any* of the tables can be accessed by the table look-up instruction to set indicators on or off; a corresponding entry from *any* other table may be obtained as a result of the look-up. The indicator setting may be used for control of calculations or output; the table entries found by the look-up are available for calculations, output, or, in some systems, modification.

Table look-up is done by use of a *search argument*—the number or name that you want to find on the table. For example, it may be the *number* of the teacher whose name you need, the *account number* of an unpaid balance you wish to use in calculation, or an *amount of sales* for which you need to know the proper tax. It is placed under FACTOR 1 on the **CALCULATION** form and may be either a literal, such as **1.15** or **'BOND'**, or a field name, such as **ACCT** or **NAME**. The instruction **LOKUP** is placed under OPERATION. The name of the table to be searched is given as FACTOR 2. One or two, *but not three*, indicators may be assigned to control the search routine. The search argument and the table to be searched must be the same mode and length. Should the number of decimal places be different, however, the search is done anyway, but without alignment. Look-ups are done algebraically on numeric fields. For alphameric fields, comparisons are based on the collating sequence of the machine, given in the reference manuals for your equipment. Usually the collating sequence considers the letter A lower than B, B lower than C, etc. through the alphabet. Blanks are lower than A, numbers are higher than Z, and the special characters, with a few exceptions, are higher than the numbers.

Should you wish to find the search argument in its *exact* form on the table, an indicator must be assigned to EQUAL. Should the search result in a "*find*," sometimes called a *hit*, the indicator will be turned *on*. The table need not be in sequence; its entire contents will be searched, and if the search argument is *not* found, the indicator will remain off. For maximum efficiency, arguments most frequently accessed with an EQUAL condition may be placed at the beginning of the table. A search is performed with a **LOKUP** instruction, as given by

	And		And				Factor 1		Operation	Factor 2		Result Field	Field Length	Decimal Position	Half Adjust (H)	Plus High 1 > 2	Minus Low 1 < 2	Zero or Blank Equal 1 = 2
?	10 11	Not 12 13	14	Not 15 16	Not 17	18 19 20 21 22 23 24 25 26 27	28 29 30 31 32	33 34 35 36 37 38 39 40 41 42	43 44 45 46 47 48	49 50 51	52	53	54 55	56 57	58 59 60
						NUMEMP	LOKUP	TABNUM						1 5

The employee number, **NUMEMP**, when found in the table **TABNUM**, turns on indicator 15; if it is *not* found on the table, the indicator will be *off*. The indicator setting may be used to condition calculations for that employee.

The **LOKUP** instruction is also used to locate the element on a function table corresponding to the argument. THE RESULT FIELD gives the name of the function table, and should a "*find*" occur, the value in the corresponding position of that table will be moved into a field *by that same name*. In the example,

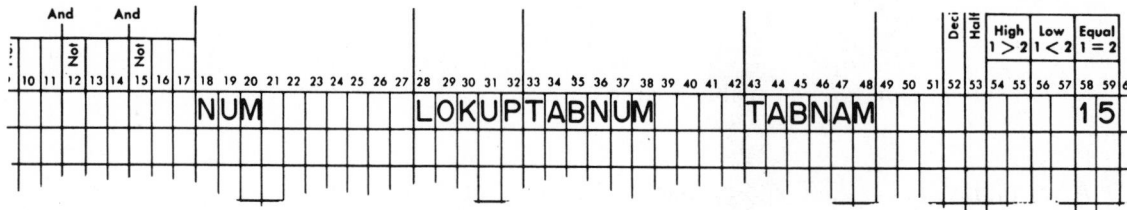

	And		And																				Deci	Hold	High 1 > 2	Low 1 < 2	Equal 1 = 2	
10	11	Not 12 13	14	Not 15 16	17	18 19 20 21 22 23 24 25 26 27	28 29 30 31 32	33 34 35 36 37 38 39 40 41 42	43 44 45 46 47 48	49 50 51	52 53	54 55	56 57	58 59 6														
		NUM				LOKUPTABNUM		TABNAM						15														

when the teacher number **NUM** is found, the corresponding element of the table **TABNAM** is brought from the table and placed into a field named **TABNAM**, to be available for output or, on some implementations, for modification. When **TABNAM** is used as output, it may even be reset by "blank-after" on the OUTPUT-FORMAT form, should you so desire. It may be *modified* on some systems; this is done by a **MOVE** or calculation instruction, which uses it as a RESULT FIELD and places it back into the table from whence it came. Otherwise it remains available until another table look-up results in a "find," which brings another value into it.

PROBLEM DEFINITION: *Write a program named* **TABMON** *to prepare a listing giving information about each employee for a company, including his date of hire, by month name instead of month number. Should an invalid number be given for the month, print an appropriate message by indicator selection. Edit the other information concerning the employee as needed for easy reading of the list. Description of the input job stream and the input data card is given in Figure 23-1.*

FILE DESCRIPTION and FILE EXTENSION forms define the table as a related table, punched in alternating form, and entered during execution-time. The month number field is 2 numeric digits, with $\emptyset$ decimals, specified in ascending order. The names of the months are each nine alphameric characters long. There are one table pair, or set, punched per card and 12 sets in the entire table. The search argument for each employee date of hire is **MNUM**, from columns 75 and 76 of the input card. Should the table look-up be unsuccessful, indicator 15 will go *off*, and the word 'INVALID' will be printed where the month name should be. Notice that this program need *not* have the month number stored in sequenced order as it does, since the EQUAL indicator is being used and not the HIGH or LOW indicators. Notice also that the overflow indicator is not **OF** as is used generally, but **OA**, one of the additional overflow indicators available on multiple-file output systems. You will also see that when indicator **OA** is used for overflow, it must be specified in that way on the FILE DESCRIPTION form.

On sequenced tables, an individual indicator may be assigned to EQUAL, to HIGH, or to LOW. Two indicators may be assigned *together* to HIGH/EQUAL, or to LOW/EQUAL. On some implementations, the *same* indicator may be assigned to HIGH and EQUAL; when that is not permitted or needed, two *different* indicators are assigned. Should either the HIGH or the LOW conditions be assigned, however, the argument table *must* be specified as sequenced, either in ascending or descending order. *No verification of the sequence is made when table cards are entered.* When an EQUAL indicator is assigned, the first item on the table that matches it turns on the indicator, even though there may be several duplicate items on the table. When only the HIGH or LOW indicators are assigned, the search argument cannot indicate an EQUAL condition, even though one may exist! The HIGH and LOW should not *both* be used on one look-up. When using either a HIGH or a LOW indicator, the table is assumed to be in sequence, and the search argument is "positioned" according to where it fits into that sequence, as shown in Figure 23-2. Elements 1.5 and 2.$\emptyset$ will be the first-encountered *fit* for numeric search argument **1.6**, for example, and the name '**BOND**' will be "positioned" between '**BATES**' and '**BUNDY**' in a alphameric table look-up. The LOW indicator will cause the entry *lower than* the search argument to be selected, such as 1.5 or '**BATES**', but should the HIGH indicator be given, it will cause the entry *higher than* the search argument to

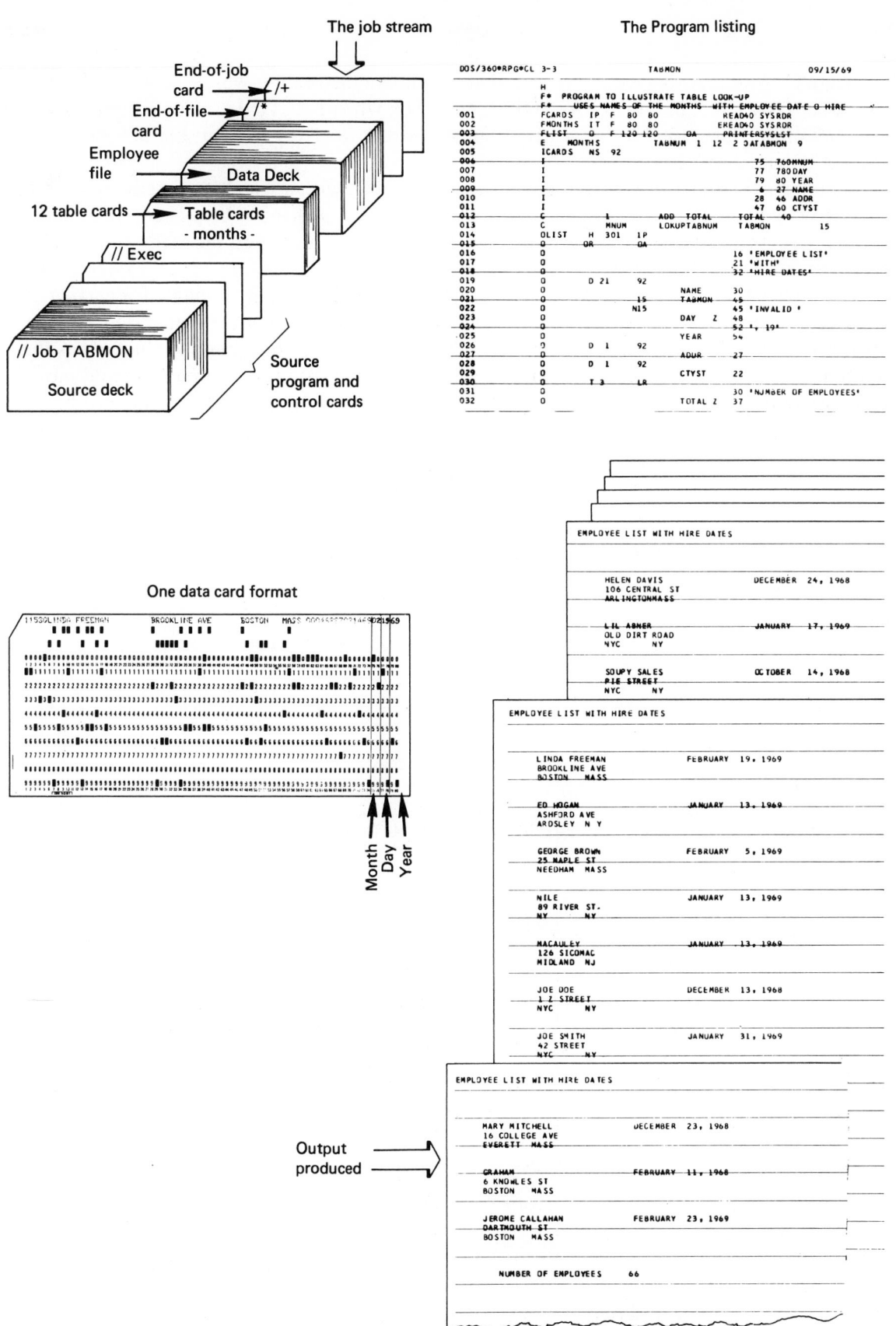

FIG. 23-1 Table look-up of month names—program **TABMON**—IBM SYSTEM/36Ø, DOS.

be selected. Note that this is *not* the way that a compare instruction works—which is HIGH when FACTOR 1 is higher than FACTOR 2, and LOW when FACTOR 1 is lower than FACTOR 2. Think of the "position" of the search argument rather than any relationship between FACTOR 1 and FACTOR 2.

Should there be identical entries in the argument table, with a search argument equal to that entry, a LOW indicator causes the entry just *below the first* of them to be picked, since that is below where its position is assumed to be. A HIGH indicator, however, picks the entry just above the *last* of the duplicates.

The table given in Figure 23-3 gives the production ranges and pay amounts for certain employees who are paid by the number of items they produce. The table is analyzed and the upper range of each pay group is entered into an argument table, with the pay amounts as the function table. The last range specified, however, is to pay $0.75 for *each* piece should more than 25Ø items be made, which is not the same as the other table entries. It should not be

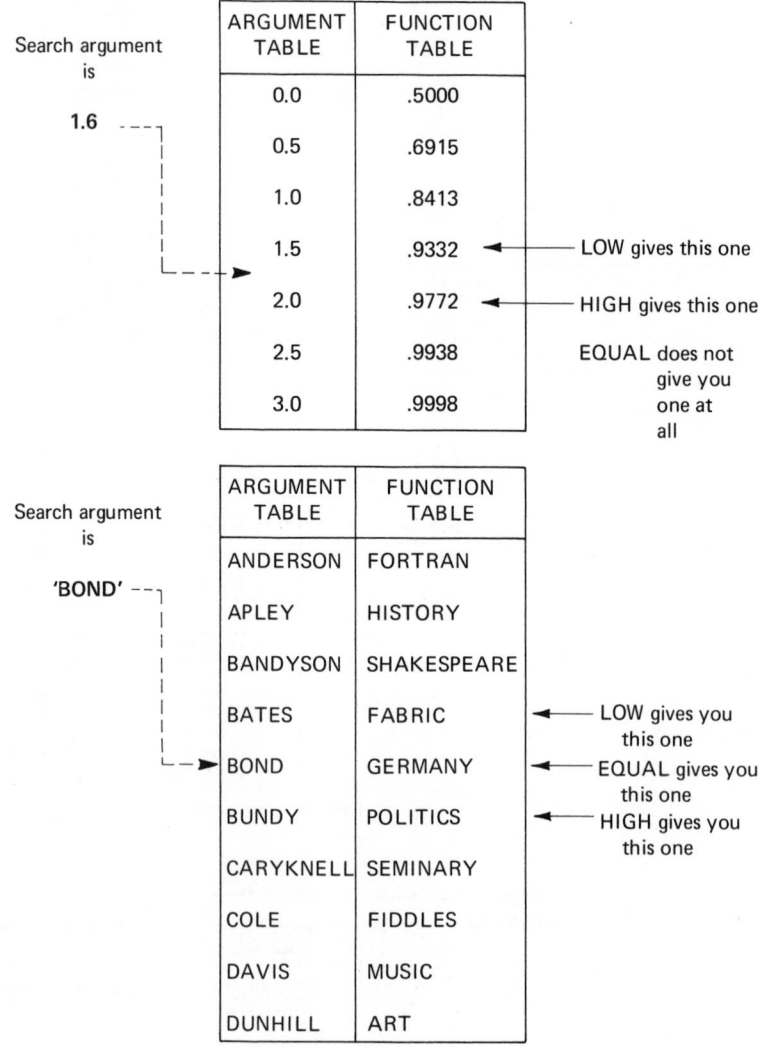

FIG. 23-2 Table look-up positioning for use of HIGH, LOW, or EQUAL indicators.

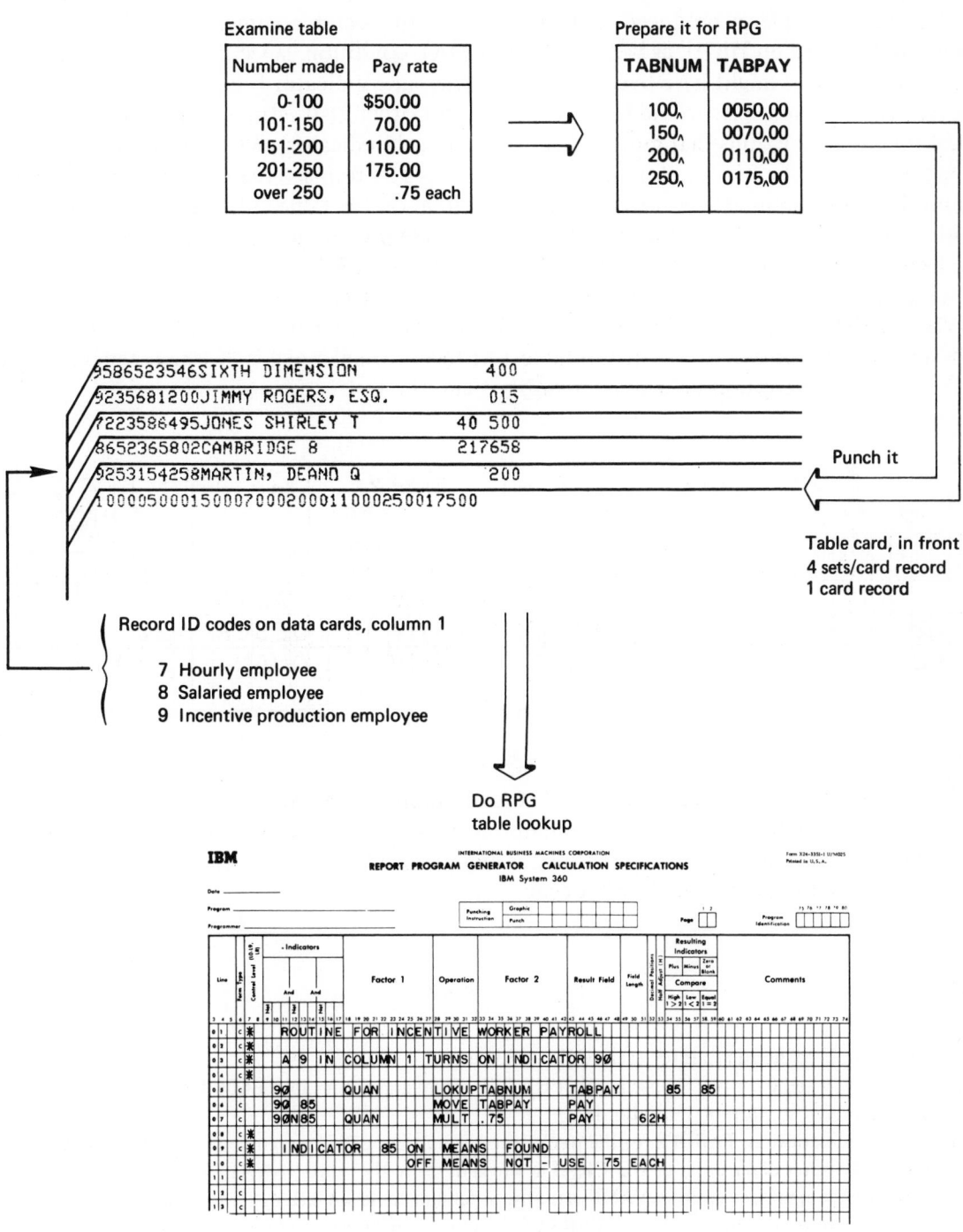

FIG. 23-3 Table preparation and look-up for pay based on number of items produced.

placed on the table at all, since only when the table look-up for the number of pieces is *unsuccessful* will $0.75 each be used for calculating the pay. The table data are punched and placed into the position shown in the job stream.

The number of pieces produced, **QUAN**, is used as the search argument in the table look-up of **TABNUM**, based on HIGH, as well as on an EQUAL condition, since it is possible that *exactly* that number might have been produced. The same indicator is used for HIGH and for EQUAL; two different ones could have been used, but other instructions would then be required for the calculations that must follow, one for each indicator. When the proper entry in the table is found, the indicator causes the next instruction to place the proper value into **PAY**. Should the search argument be *larger than* the last item on the table, alternate calculations will be done, controlled by the indicator 85 being *off*. Table preparation and the appropriate instructions are given on the CALCULATION form in Figure 23-3.

When it is necessary for the function portion of a table to contain more than one field, the **MOVE** and **MOVEL** instructions are used to separate them, after the look-up, into distinct fields appropriate for use. If a function table **TABINV**, for example, is 25 characters long, and contains both a description field and a quantity field, the instructions given by

Not		And / Not	And / Not	Factor 1	Operation	Factor 2	Result Field	Field Length	Decimal Pos	Half Adjust	Compare High 1>2	Low 1<2	Equal 1=2
				ITEM	LOKUP	TABNUM	TABINV						1 2
	1 2				MOVEL	TABINV	DESCR	2Ø					
	1 2				MOVE	TABINV	QUAN	5Ø					

would, when the item number given by **ITEM** is found in **TABNUM**, move the left-most 20 characters to a field named **DESCR**. The right-most 5 characters would be moved to a field named **QUAN**, and since an alphameric field is being moved into a numeric one, conversion from alphameric to numeric mode will occur.

EXERCISES

1. Write table look-up instructions for each of the following:
   (a) Determine whether or not license number HA-2754 is on argument table **TABCAR**, length 7, alphameric mode; if so, turn on indicator 48.
   (b) Find the description, **TABDES**, of the item stored as number 2765 in argument table **TABNUM**; move the 2Ø-character description to **DESCR**; if not found, move the word 'INVALID' to **DESCR**.
   (c) If the search argument given in **NAME** is on the argument table **TABPLY**, get the corresponding batting average for that player from **TABAVE**, length 3, 3 decimals, and move it to **AVE**.
   (d) For the table argument **TABVAL** just bigger than the search argument **VAL**, add the corresponding function **TABOVR**, length 6, 2 decimals, to **TAX**.
   (e) If the search argument **AMT** is less than or equal to the value in **TABAMT**, move the corresponding **TABRAT**, length 6, 2 decimals, to **TAX**.

Form Type	Control Level (L0-L9, LR)	Indicators						Factor 1	Operation	Factor 2	Result Field	Field Length	Decimal Positions	Half Adjust (H)	Resulting Indicators		
				And		And									Plus	Minus	Zero or Blank
			Not		Not		Not								Compare		
															High 1 > 2	Low 1 < 2	Equal 1 = 2
6	7 8	9	10 11	12	13 14	15	16 17	18 19 20 21 22 23 24 25 26 27	28 29 30 31 32	33 34 35 36 37 38 39 40 41 42	43 44 45 46 47 48	49 50 51	52	53	54 55	56 57	58 59 60
C	(a)																
C																	
C	(b)																
C																	
C																	
C																	
C	(c)																
C																	
C																	
C	(d)																
C																	
C																	
C	(e)																
C																	
C																	
C																	
C																	
C																	
C																	
C																	

2. Write FILE DESCRIPTION and FILE EXTENSION specifications for the table described in Figure 23-3, using the IBM 254∅ as an input device, and the file name **RTABLE**.

Line		Form Type	Filename	I/O/U/C	P/S/C/R/T	End of File	File Type — File Designation — Sequence — File Format				Mode of Processing — Record Address Type — Length of Key Field or of Record Address Field	L/R	K/I	I/D/T	Type of File Organization — Overflow Indicator — Key Field Starting Location	Extension Code E/L	Device	Symbolic Device	Labels (S, N, or E)
						E	A/D	F/V	Block Length	Record Length									
3	4 5	6	7 8 9 10 11 12 13 14	15	16	17	18	19	20 21 22 23	24 25 26 27	28	29 30	31	32	33 34 35 36 37 38	39	40 41 42 43 44 45 46	47 48 49 50 51 52	53
0 1		F																	
0 2		F																	
0 3		F																	
0 4		F																	
0 5		F																	

equence of the Chaining File							Number of Table Entries Per Record														
umber of the Chaining Field								Number of Table Entries													
								Per Table		Length of Table								Length of Table			
From Filename		To Filename		Table Name						Entry		Packed (P)	Decimal Pos.	Sequence (A/D)	Table Name (Alternating Table)			Entry		Packed(P)	Decimal Pos.	Sequence (A/D)
10	11 12 13 14 15 16 17 18	19 20 21 22 23 24 25 26	27 28 29 30 31 32	33 34 35	36 37 38 39	40 41 42	43	44	45	46 47 48 49 50 51	52 53 54	55	56	57

Lesson 24

TABLE MODIFICATION AND OUTPUT

You will learn how changes can be made to tables and how to get them out of the computer system.

The following questions are answered on the back of this page. If you can do updated tables on your equipment, study the lesson and answer all the questions before writing the programs at the end of this section.

1. How can one value of a table be replaced by another during the processing of a job?
2. What specifications must be used to cause the automatic output of a table?
3. When does the output table come out?
4. What format and mode will the output table have?
5. If the printer is used for table output at table output time, what special consideration must the program make for it?
6. Tell how to get a table printed, in edited form, into a report during program processing, rather than at the table output time.
7. How can you locate a vacant entry on the argument table in order to use it for a new value?
8. What are some jobs that could use table modification?

ANSWERS

1. By using the name of the table as a RESULT FACTOR in a **MOVE** or a calculation, immediately after a **LOKUP** instruction has located the element that you wish to replace.

2. A file name must be given under TO FILENAME on FILE EXTENSION specifications, and the file name must be defined as an output file on the FILE DESCRIPTION form. All other specifications are the same as those required for the input of the table.

3. After all processing for the job is completed.

4. Exactly the same as the input table.

5. The program should contain a skip to channel Ø1 after the report is completed, so that the table will not be printed on the last page of the report.

6. By using a counter to access an argument table made up of numbers Ø1, Ø2, Ø3, etc., for look-up, in a loop, so that every line will be accessed and printed out.

7. By setting a field to zero and using it as a search argument, or by using a literal zero, or blank, as a search argument, depending on the mode of the argument table.

8. Frequency distributions, unpaid balance by accounts, on-hand inventory lists, valid credit cards, etc.

Tables stored for table look-up may, on some implementations, such as the IBM SYSTEM/ 360, TOS/DOS, and the IBM SYSTEM/3, be modified during the execution of a program, and may be brought out of the computer. Tables that are output in this manner are always in the same mode and arrangement by which they were entered, since the same FILE EXTENSION specifications form line is used for both input and output. The output device will automatically bring out the tables when processing for the job is complete.

A table may be used to maintain totals for certain categories of data accumulating throughout the run. It may be used for storage of totals, with incrementing done when certain types of activity are encountered. Balance records for accounts may be kept in a table, updated during the production run, and punched out, to be used as later input in much the same manner as a master record.

Tables are output through a file specified on the FILE DESCRIPTION form, which identifies the device and symbolic device to be used for output. The file name is given, and an **O** in column 15, but column 16 should be blank, since no special indication need be made that the file is to be used by a table. File format and block and record lengths are used as for regular data output. Column 39 should be blank—the FILE EXTENSION reference, **E**, is required for table *input* files, but *not* for *output* ones. A separate file name for tables is *not* required; one already assigned to another data file may be used. Even though an output file name is required for table output, *no* other special coding is given on the OUTPUT-FORMAT form at all; the table format is the same as was described for input, and since table output is atuomatic, it is *not* controlled by specifications on that form. If the printer is to be used for output at the end of the job, you must be sure that your program causes a skip to a new page *after* your report is complete, or the tables will be printed on the last page of your report! The file name selected for table output is given on the FILE EXTENSION form, under TO FILENAME, in columns 19-26. That device may be used for normal file output as well, since table output occurs *last*, after all other output is completed.

A table entry is accessible for use or modification only when it has been referenced by a table look-up instruction. At the completion of a look-up, entries located by the search of the argument table, on both the argument table and the function table, are available. They may be used by giving the field name of the respective table, either for output or as a factor in calculations. Should they be used as a RESULT FACTOR, however, the value is placed back into the table, destroying the previous value there. This feature of changing a value on the table allows *table modification.*

Several different methods of modification are possible. In the example given by

Indicators							Factor 1	Operation	Factor 2	Result Field	Field Length	Decimal Positions	Half Adjust (H)	Indicators			
	And		And											Plus	Minus	Zero or Blank	
Not		Not		Not										Compare			
9	10 11	12 13	14	15 16	17	18 19 20 21 22 23 24 25 26 27	28 29 30 31 32	33 34 35 36 37 38 39 40 41 42	43 44 45 46 47 48	49 50 51	52	53	High 1 > 2 54 55	Low 1 < 2 56 57	Equal 1 = 2 58 59	60
						NAME	LOKUP	TABNAM	TABDTE							1 2	
	1 2						MOVE	NEWDTE	TABDTE								

the value of the function is replaced by the field **NEWDTE**. In the example given by

Not	And Not	And Not	Factor 1	Operation	Factor 2	Result Field	Deci Half	High 1 > 2	Low 1 < 2	Equal 1 = 2
			NUM	LOKUP	TABACCT	TABAMT				15
15			AMT	ADD	TABAMT	TABAMT				

accumulation of the field **AMT** is placed back into **TABAMT** after each table look-up. The function value may even be cleared of its former value, as given by

Not	And Not	And Not	Factor 1	Operation	Factor 2	Result Field	Deci Half	High 1 > 2	Low 1 < 2	Equal 1 = 2
			ACCT	LOKUP	TABACC	TABBAL				75
75				Z-ADD00		TABBAL				

which places zeros in the balance field for that account. Should the value of the balance be needed for printing the detail or total line associated with that account, however, it has been reset *too soon* and will be zero upon the output sheet! Should you wish to print the table value on the report, the use of "blank-after" can be used instead to clear the table *after* normal printing has occurred.

Although *two* table entries cannot be obtained from *one* use of the look-up, *two* successive look-ups may be used to accomplish that. Should the table entries *just below* the search argument and *just above* it be needed for an output line, one look-up should be done with the HIGH indicator to get the corresponding higher table entry. It must then be moved into a temporary holding area, such as **TEMP**, for storage, while the next table look-up, with the LOW indicator, is done. Both the entries are then available for use, one under the name **TEMP**, and the other under the regular function table name.

The length and modes of the entries on the table may not be changed; they must remain as described on the FILE EXTENSION form. Neither can the total number of entries on the table be increased or decreased. By entering a table *purposely* containing dummy data entries of zeros or blanks, new categories that occur may be placed onto the table, giving the effect of increasing the number of values on the table; on the IBM SYSTEM/3, this type of table is called a *short* table. Values may also be deleted from the table, giving the *effect* of decreasing the table size. Dummy data in numeric mode should be punched with zeros; alphameric dummy data may be blanks. All dummy table data must be included in the count of the NUMBER OF RECORDS PER TABLE, which is given on the FILE EXTENSION form. The series of instructions given by

Not	And Not	And Not	Factor 1	Operation	Factor 2	Result Field	Field Length	Decimal Po Half Adjus	High 1 > 2	Low 1 < 2	Equal 1 = 2
				Z-ADD00		NUM	40				
			NUM	LOKUP	TABNUM	TABFCN					30
30				MOVE	NEWNUM	TABNUM					
30				MOVE	NEWFCN	TABFCN					

will locate the first "empty" position in the argument table; the new values of both argument and function are then entered in the table there.

It is possible to form an array of table data from information available in the detail deck of a job, or from that presented in other tables. Employee numbers of all persons who requested bond deductions, for example, may be placed onto a table for later listing. Employees on each shift might be counted, and totals for each type later printed. Counting the number of each type of response to a question or a survey, or the number of people in a certain category, can produce a frequency distribution in a table, which can then be punched out. The table must be defined, however, as an *input* table, and zero or blank fields must be entered for it into numeric or alphameric fields, respectively. The new table is created by modification to the dummy input table.

PROBLEM DEFINITION: *Write a program to count the numbers of people in certain age categories, keeping the total in an appropriate function table. Data for the survey are punched as shown in Figure 24-1.*

The **AGE** field, in columns 9 and 10, is the search argument and is looked up on the argument table so that a 1 can be added to the proper group for this particular person. Two different indicators are in this case assigned to HIGH and EQUAL. The value of **AGE** will be positioned on the argument list, selecting the table item equal to it, if one is present, but otherwise, selecting the one just higher. On some implementations, the same indicator may be used both for HIGH and for EQUAL.

The **FILE DESCRIPTION** lines, given on the run sheets in Figure 24-2, show the input table file **INTABLE** and the table of data assigned to the same device. The table data are therefore placed *in front of* the regular data. The **FILE EXTENSION** line, with an **E** in column 6, specifies an alternating table, punched with the argument first and the function next. **TABAGE** is 2 digits long, numeric, and **TABNUM** is 4 digits long, numeric. Each pair is punched onto one card; six cards are needed for the entire table.

The listing shown in Figure 24-2 was produced by the program; it gives meaningful phrases or words on the report instead of coded data. The **COMP** instruction is used to select which of two alternative words should be printed. Should more than two alternatives be necessary, a table could be used for that look-up as well. At the detection of end-of-file, the last record indicator goes on, and the total number of cards is printed. The updated table then comes out automatically. The punched cards, interpreted on an IBM $\emptyset$29 keypunch, are shown in Figure 24-1.

Since any table in memory can be accessed by a look-up from any other table, one argument table can be used for look-up on several different function tables. Should data from a survey, for example, require several tables to be stored, only one argument table need be entered for them. It could contain question number, or the counting numbers from 1 to the largest number on the table. By the use of such an argument table, the entire table contents can be put in a printed report, with table information edited into readable form. A counter could serve as a search argument, and when incremented by 1 each time, using loop techniques not yet introduced, every table value can be found by look-up, thereby making it accessible for output. It is even conceivable that, through tricky looping, a new table entry may be inserted in *its proper sequence* in a table, moving everything below it down one entry farther to provide the necessary space. With the use of a counter as an argument, even an *entire deck of cards* can be stored into a table, then later accessed by looping, permitting reuse of the entire deck.

A counter used as search argument could also cause a complete search of a table, to find the smallest positive entry on the function table, and its entry number. The look-up would be counter controlled, in a loop, so that every element on the table would be examined. Each one

Table as defined by:

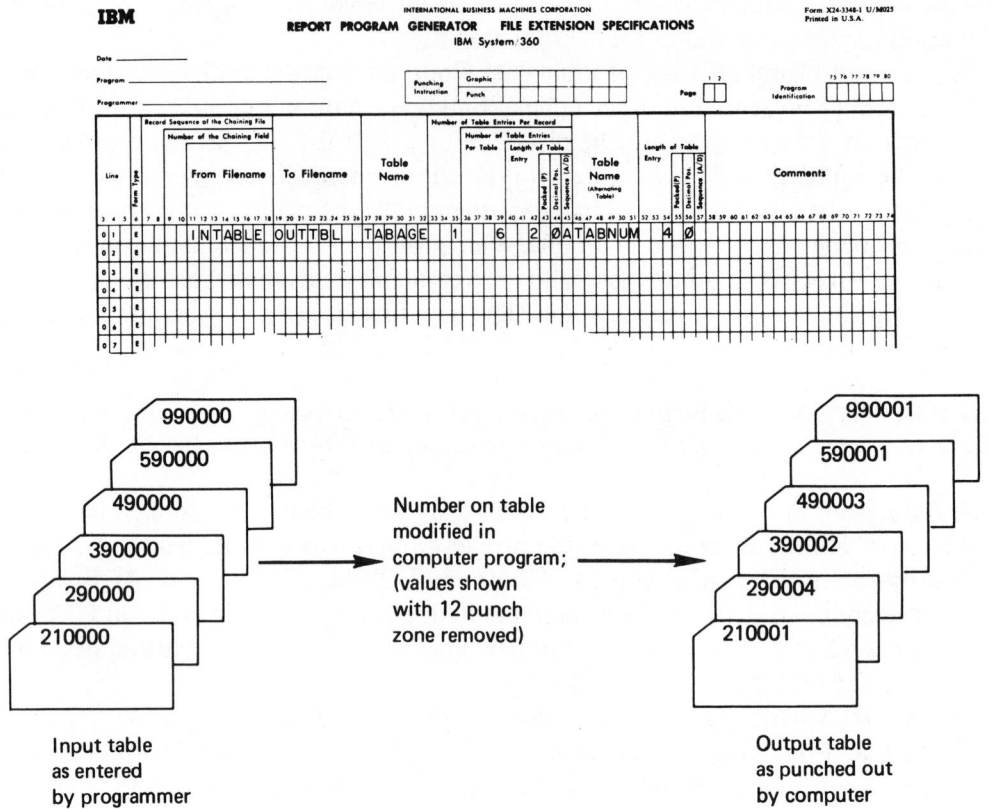

as calculated by

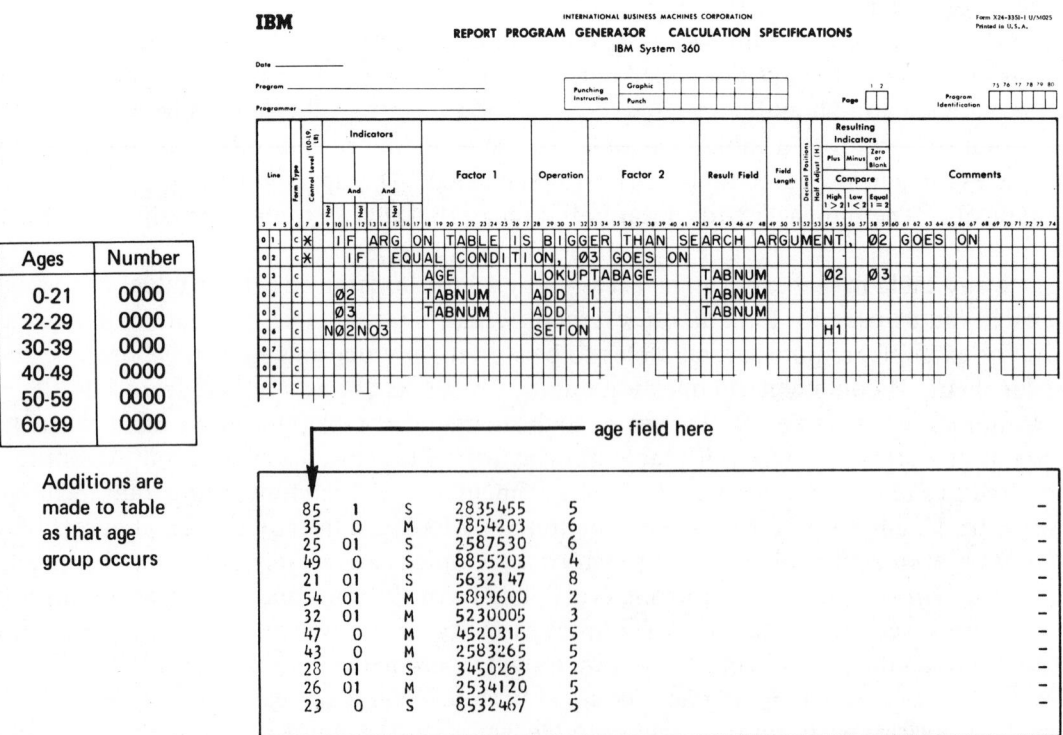

FIG. 24-1 Updating a table for a frequency distribution.

334

```
                        H
                        F*       TESTS USE OF A TABLE FOR FREQUENCY COUNTS
001                     FINPUT   IP  F  80  80             READ40 SYSRDR
002                     FINTABLE IT  F  80  80             EREAD40 SYSRDR
003                     FOUTTBL  O   F  80  80             READ40 SYSPCH
004                     FLIST    O   F 120 120             PRINTERSYSLST
005                     E     INTABLE OUTTBL  TABAGE 1   6  2 0ATABNUM  4 0
006                     IINPUT    NS  01   80 C-
007                     I                                      9   100AGE
008                     I                                     14   140SEX
009                     I                                     19   19 MCODE
010                     I                                     24   302INCOME
011                     I                                     35   35 CARS
                        C*  IF ARG ON TABLE IS BIGGER THAN SEARCH ARGUMENT, 02 GOES ON
                        C*  IF EQUAL CONDITION, 03 GOES ON
012       04 01  C              AGE       LOKUPTABAGE  TABNUM    02 03
013       04 02  C     02       TABNUM    ADD  1       TABNUM
014       04 021 C     03       TABNUM    ADD  1       TABNUM
015       04 022 C     N02N03             SETON                    H1
016       04 03  C              TOTAL     ADD  0001    TOTAL   40
017       04 04  C              SEX       COMP 1                      04
018       04 05  C              MCODE     COMP 'S'                       07
                        S
                        C* INDICATOR 04 ON MEANS FEMALE , OFF MEANS   MALE
                        C* INDICATOR 07 MEANS SINGLE ,  OFF MEANS MARRIED
019       05 01  OLIST    H  201     1P
020       05 02  O        OR         OF
021       05 03  O                                55 'SURVEY REPORT'
022       05 04  O        H  3       1P
023       05 05  O        OR         OF
024       05 06  O                                10 'AGE'
025       05 07  O                                23 'SEX'
026       05 08  O                                45 'MARITAL CODE'
027       05 09  O                                65 'ANNUAL INCOME'
028       05 10  O                                90 'NUMBER OF AUTOMOBILES'
029       05 11  O        D  1       01
030       05 13  O                        AGE  Z   9
031       05 14  O                   04           25 'FEMALE'
032       05 15  O                   N04          23 'MALE'
033       05 16  O                   07           42 'MARRIED'
034       05 17  O                   N07          42 'SINGLE '
035       06 01  O                        INCOME  62 '$ , 0. '
036       06 02  O                        CARS    75
037       06 06  O        T  3       LR
038       06 07  O                                31 'TOTAL NUMBER OF CARDS'
039       06 08  O                                41 'PROCESSED'
040       06 09  O                        TOTAL Z 47
```

```
                               SURVEY REPORT


          AGE       SEX      MARITAL CODE    ANNUAL INCOME    NUMBER OF AUTOMOBILES


          85      FEMALE      MARRIED        $28,354.55       5
          35      MALE        SINGLE         $78,542.03       6
          25      FEMALE      MARRIED        $25,875.30       6
          49      MALE        MARRIED        $88,552.03       4
          21      FEMALE      MARRIED        $56,321.47       8
          54      FEMALE      SINGLE         $59,996.00       2
          32      FEMALE      SINGLE         $52,300.05       3
          47      MALE        SINGLE         $45,203.15       5
          43      MALE        SINGLE         $25,832.65       5
          28      FEMALE      MARRIED        $34,502.63       2
          26      FEMALE      SINGLE         $25,341.20       5
          23      MALE        MARRIED        $85,324.67       5


       TOTAL NUMBER OF CARDS PROCESSED     12
```

Printed output report

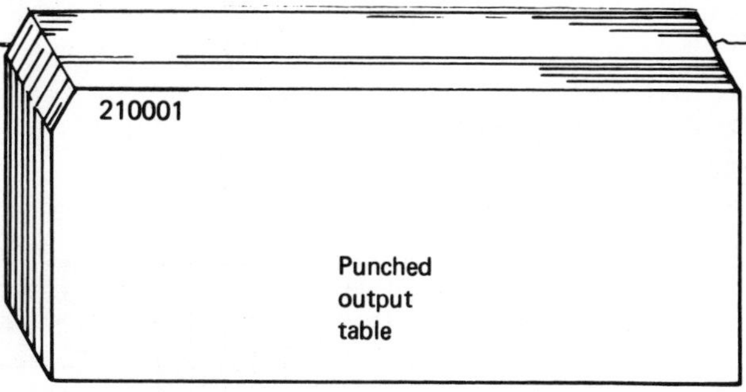

210001

Punched output table

FIG. 24-2 Program **FREQTBL**—IBM SYSTEM/36Ø, DOS.

found is compared to the smallest one found *that far*, with the first one compared to zero. Should any item be found *smaller* than the *previous* one held as the smallest, a *swap* should be made—putting the "new" smallest one into the hold area. At the end of one pass through the table, the smallest element on the table will be available. By repetition of this method, a limited sort can be done. As each smallest number is found, it is moved to another table, as the first element there, then the second, and so on. It is then eliminated from the first table, so that future searches for the smallest number no longer get the same "smallest" one. By this method, a *sequenced* table can be brought out at the end of the job.

EXERCISES

1. Give FILE DESCRIPTION and FILE EXTENSION specifications for each input and output of modified tables in the following:

   (a) File updated master information, for 250 accounts, given by account number in columns 1-5 and account balance in columns 6-12, 2 decimals, punched five sets per card, in alternating arrangement, brought in from the IBM 2540 and punched out on the same device.

   (b) Frequency distribution of the number of orders placed with each vendor during a purchase order listing run, given by vendor number in columns 1-5 and number of orders placed in columns 6-10, 0 decimals, punched in alternating pairs, one set per card, for 100 cards; read in on the IBM 2501, punched out on the IBM 1442.

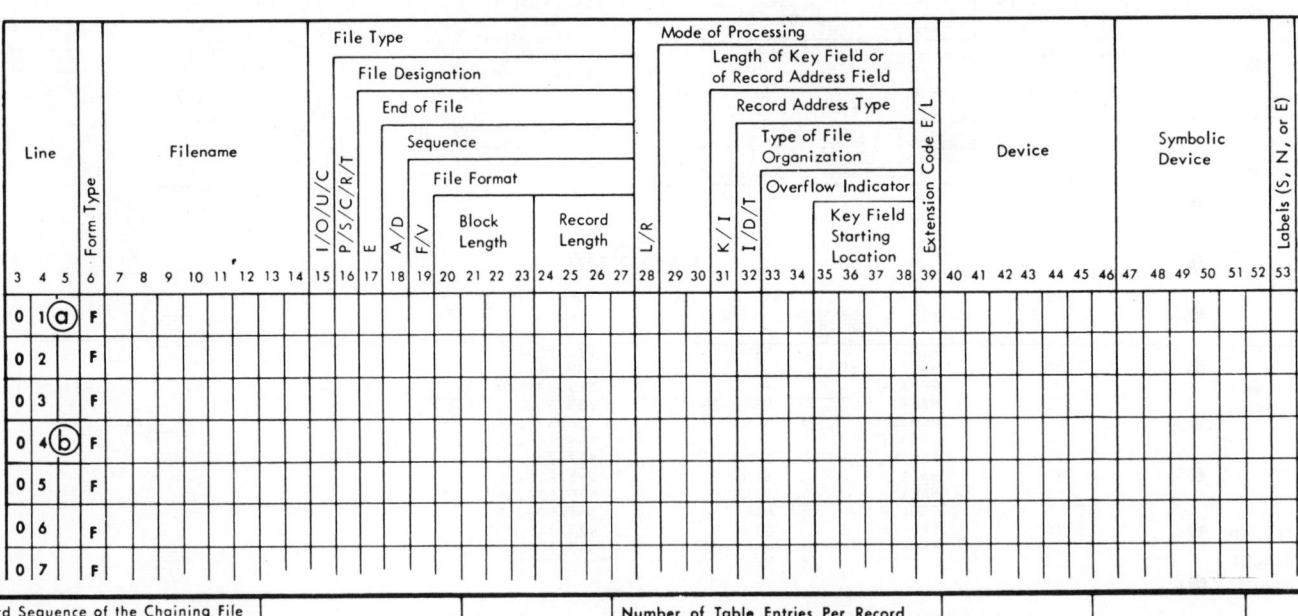

2. Write **CALCULATION** specifications to perform each of the following:
   (a) Look up the account number given by alphameric search argument **REFNUM** in the argument table **TABREF**, and replace both the 5-character argument and the 20-character account name **TABNAM** with blanks.
   (b) Look up the first argument that is zero in argument table **TABARG**, and put the 15-character field **NAME** into the corresponding function **TABFCN**. Put the field named **NUM**, 5 digits long, into the argument table.

Form Type	Control Level	And		And			Factor 1	Operation	Factor 2	Result Field	Field Length	Decimal Positions	Half Adjust (H)	Plus High 1 > 2	Minus Low 1 < 2	Zero or Blank Equal 1 = 2
6	7 8	Not 9 10 11	12 13 14	Not 15 16 17	18 19 20 21 22 23 24 25 26 27	28 29 30 31 32	33 34 35 36 37 38 39 40 41 42	43 44 45 46 47 48	49 50 51	52 53	54 55	56 57	58 59 60
C	(a)										
C											
C											
C											
C											
C											
C											
C											
C	(b)										
C											
C											
C											
C											
C											

Section 8

PROGRAMS TO WRITE

A. PROBLEM NAME: **CARSPOT:** check auto registration by table

Write a program to list employees, checking to see that each person has registered his automobile with the company by receiving a sticker. All cars with stickers have their license tag identifications given in an argument table, length 15 characters, punched four per card, for five cards. Print a report as shown on page 338.

Field Information	Columns
Record ID code: M	1
Employee number	2-7
Employee name	8-3∅
Telephone extension number	5∅-52
Automobile license tag	54-68

A U T O R E N T A L C O .		
NAME	AUTO REGISTRATION	TELEPHONE
KURTZ, W	OK	217
LYONS, J.	NONE	217
MAINS, L.	NONE	3Ø4
MAZER, W.	OK	356

B. PROBLEM NAME: **EMPDSCT:**   sales discount summary for employees

Write a program to calculate total amounts due company employees, who are given discounts on all purchases for the month, based on their monthly total:

AMOUNT OF SALES	DISCOUNT
$0.00-25.00	1%
25.01-50.00	3%
50.01-100.00	5%
100.01-500.00	1Ø%
over $500.00	15%

Detail cards itemize each purchase and are sorted by employee number in ascending order. Produce a group-printed report giving a summary line of purchases, amount of discount, and amount due for each employee. Totals should be given at the end of the job for purchases, discounts, and amounts due.

Field Information	Columns
Employee number	1-4
Employee name	5-24
Amount of sales, 2 decimals	35-4Ø

C. PROGRAM NAME: **PAYCALC:**   to calculate pay by three methods

Write a program to prepare a payroll for three types of workers, as described in Figure 23-3. Hourly pay is calculated by multiplying the number of hours worked by the rate of pay per hour; assume that no overtime rates are paid. Salaried pay is calculated by dividing the monthly salary by 4 1/3. Incentive pay is by table look-up if the number of items made is given on the table; otherwise, pay $0.75 for each item made. The input records are defined in Figure 17-1. Produce a report listing each employee name and number and his correct pay amount underneath appropriate column headings.

D. PROGRAM NAME: **MSTUPDT:**   master balance update by table

Write a program to summarize purchase order costs by department. Calculate cost on each detail card by multiplying quantity ordered by price each; accumulate the sum over the entire department, then print a summary line for that department. On each detail card, the vendor number should be found by table look-up in the master vendor table. The balance amount found on the table, for that vendor, should be updated by the amount of the cost of the item being ordered. If the vendor number is missing, give an appropriate comment. At the end-of-job, give a total of the costs over all departments, and retrieve the updated master vendor table.

	Field Information	Columns
Master vendor table, alternating type, six sets per record, for five records	Vendor number Previous balance, 2 decimals, signed Sets 2-6 occupy columns 13-72, in same form	1-5 6-12 } Set 1
Detail transactions on cards, sorted by department number	Department number Purchase order number Vendor number Item description Quantity ordered Price each, 2 decimals Transaction date: month, day, year	1-2 3-1∅ 11-15 16-35 38-4∅ 45-5∅ 61-66

SECTION 9

REPORTS WITH MAGNETIC TAPE

Lesson 25

MAGNETIC TAPE CONCEPTS

You will learn basic principles of magnetic tape data processing and how to make a tape file in RPG.

The questions below are answered on the back of this page. If you have had experience in programming with data files on magnetic tape and can answer the following questions, go on to Lesson 26.

1. What is the difference between *sequential* and *random* storage of data?
2. What are some ways to get source data onto a reel of magnetic tape?
3. Give the relationship between characters, fields, records, and blocks.
4. What is the difference between a *logical* record and a *physical* record? How do you select the size of each?
5. What are some of the recording modes used on magnetic tape?
6. What is meant by *tape density*, in bpi? by *tape speed*, in ips?
7. What is meant by *data transfer rate*, in bps? How is it calculated?
8. Distinguish between *internal* and *external labels* on magnetic tape.
9. What instructions should be given to the computer operator by the programmer, and how?
10. When using magnetic tape for data input or output, what should be used on the FILE DESCRIPTION form for DEVICE? for SYMBOLIC DEVICE?

ANSWERS

1. Data stored sequentially is in order according to some key field; to get to a particular record, all those in front of it must be searched. Data stored randomly is not in any particular order; each record is found by its address, without searching through all records that might have a lower value in the key field.
2. Use the keypunch machine to put the record of information onto one or more cards, then write a program to transfer each record onto a tape; or get a data recorder, which allows direct keying onto a tape reel.
3. Groups of characters make up fields, groups of fields make up records, and groups of records make up blocks.
4. A *logical* record is one complete set of information concerning one unit or one transaction, wherein a *physical* record is the same as a block, perhaps consisting of several logical records. The size of the logical record is determined by how much information you must have in each record to get the particular job done. The size of the physical record must be small enough to fit into available computer storage along with the program it is used with, but should be as large as possible to minimize the number of times the tape unit must be accessed.
5. *EBCDIC*, pronounced E-by-dick or Ib-sy-dick, standing for Extended Binary Coded Decimal Interchange Code, usually stored in a nine-track pattern on tape, used on 8-bit byte computers or 16-bit binary word-type computers; *BCD*, pronounced in letters, standing for Binary Coded Decimal, stored on seven-track tape, used on 6-bit character-type computers; and *binary*, which requires several frames on the tape to be used together to represent a pure binary number or word, usually stored on seven-track tape, most often used on binary word-type computers; or in 8-bit *USASCII-8*, from the 7-bit *USASCII*, USA Standard Code for Information Interchange, which can be stored in a nine-track tape pattern on magnetic tape.
6. The number of characters, or bytes, in 1 in. of tape, in bytes per inch; the rate at which tape can be moved past the read/write heads, in inches per second.
7. The rate at which data can be transferred from tape to memory, in bytes per second; by multiplying tape density and tape speed.
8. External labels are those that are on the *outside* of the reel to identify the reel; internal ones are recorded on the tape itself so that the program can verify that the correct reel is being used.
9. Whether or not to put on a tape ring to permit writing on the tape; whether or not to save the tape reel after the run; which tape reel to use for the run, and which unit to put it on; and sometimes what density or mode is to be used. Usually given on a job submittal form and on remarks in the job control stream, which print on the console typewriter.
10. **TAPE**; one of the available system numbers between $\emptyset\emptyset\emptyset$ and 255, given as **SYSXXX**, where **XXX** is the number of the one you are to use. An *assign card* is used in the control stream to identify the system number with an available physical unit number.

Magnetic tape is one of the most common means of input and output on medium-size computer systems. It is often available on IBM 36Ø, DOS, but always on TPS and TOS. A reel of this tape can be mounted on a unit on-line to the computer system or can be kept on shelves off-line in storage. Information on a tape must be placed into the memory before processing of the data can be done. The preservation of data off-line, for storage, is said to be *external* or secondary storage, as compared to the computer memory, which is called *internal* or primary storage. The tape is used for recording on only one side, and is rewound after each use so that the front end of the tape is always accessible. Tape usually comes on a continuous roll of 24ØØ ft, and is 1/2 in. wide, on a circular reel about 10.5 in. in diameter. Each reel has a plastic case, with snap lock; the tape should always be kept in the case when not on the tape unit. To mount magnetic tape onto the unit, the reel is fastened in the *file reel* position, threaded through the read/write head assembly, then wrapped around the *take-up reel*, as shown in Figure 25-1. After the read-write head assembly has been locked into place and the unit activated, it can be used for recording data on the tape anywhere between the *beginning-of-tape* marker, called the *load point*, and the *end-of-tape* marker. Both these points are identified by a visible metallic strip called a *reflective marker*. The load point identifies the starting point of the usable tape, and prevents the tape from running off the reel while being rewound. The load point is about 10 ft from the beginning of the tape; the end-of-tape point is about that same distance from the end of the tape.

Data are recorded on the tape in magnetized spots, called *bits*, placed across a frame of the tape in certain channel positions. The channels, running lengthwise along the tape, are called *tracks*, with identification given to each track in the manner shown in Figure 25-2. Each frame corresponds to a card column and can be coded either as a character, a byte, or part of a binary word, depending on the type of computer and the recording mode used to make the tape. Most tape is recorded in either seven- or nine-track patterns. It can be stored in character mode, 6-bit BCD with a bit for parity checking making the seventh track, in byte mode, 8-bit EDBCIC or USASCII-8 with a bit for parity checking making the ninth track, or in other forms of pure binary, used mostly on binary word-type machinery. The IBM SYSTEM/36Ø, which can have any of several different models of tape unit attached to it, ordinarily stores data on nine-track tape, in EBCDIC. Each frame can contain either one alphameric character, 2 numeric packed-decimal digits, or any valid EBCDIC-coded combination. Since a byte usually contains one character, the terms byte and character are often used synonomously when referring to a track of an EBCDIC tape. It is not usually necessary that a programmer know the bit patterns of code on magnetic tape, but it is important to know that several different types exist and are not completely compatible with each other.

Recall that on punch cards, groups of adjacent columns are called fields, and the collection of fields is called a record. The group of records placed together on tape by one operation of the tape unit is called a *block*. Each block is followed by a blank portion of tape called a *gap*. Since a block was known for a long time as a tape record, the gap became known as an interrecord gap, or IRG. A recent trend, however, is to call it an *interblock gap*, since that more accurately describes its position following each block.

A punch card is a fixed-length, 8Ø-column record and cannot be any longer than that. Tape, however, is continuous, and record size on tape is not necessarily restricted to 8Ø columns in length. It may be smaller, or larger, than 8Ø. If all the records within a given task are the *same*

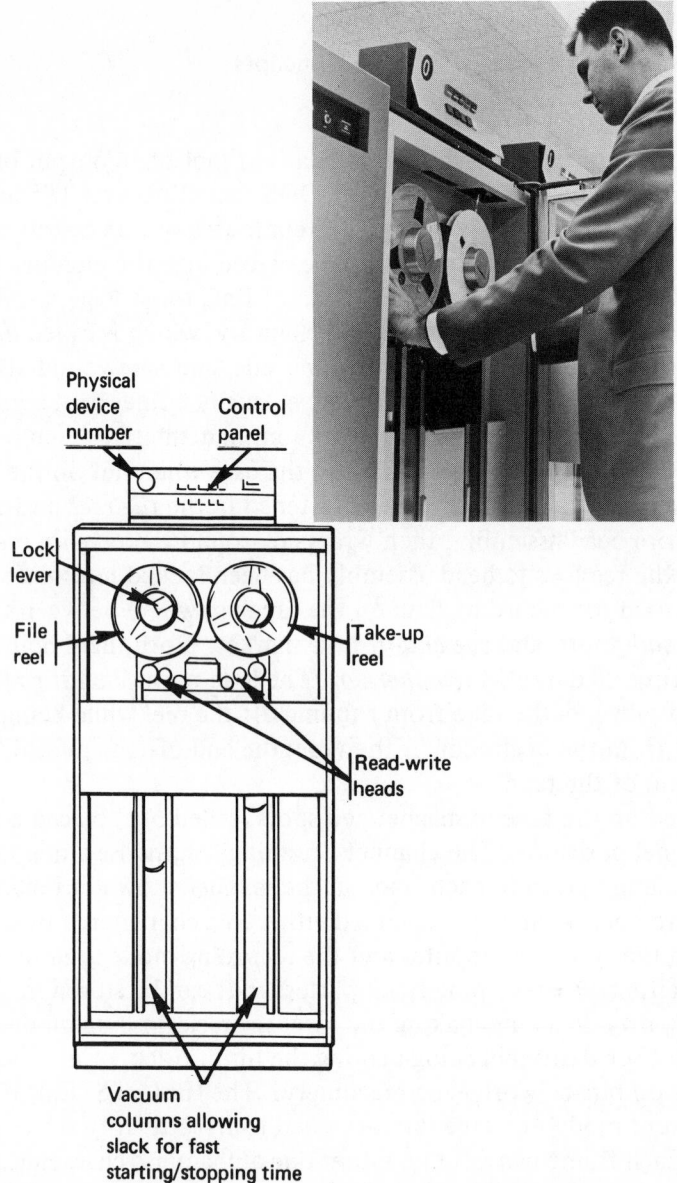

Physical
device
number

Control
panel

Lock
lever

File
reel

Take-up
reel

Read-write
heads

Vacuum
columns allowing
slack for fast
starting/stopping time

FIG. 25-1 IBM 24Ø1 magnetic tape unit. (Courtesy of International Business Machines Corporation.)

length, however, they are said to be *fixed-length* records, no matter what that fixed length may be. Since record sizes for different records within the same job may vary, it is possible to have them specified as *variable length* instead of fixed. Each record may be a different length, requiring that an extra field be stored in front of the record to give the record length. Likewise, when a block contains a variable number of variable-length records, each block contains an extra field to specify how many records are stored on that block. Although these extra fields do require space that fixed-length records do not require, the use of variable-length records is definitely an advantage when the range of record sizes within a given task is large. For example, if most of the records for a job are of length 1ØØ characters, but a few are of length 3ØØ, it is far better to use variable-length records and blocks than to use a fixed length of size 3ØØ for all records. The letter **V** is placed into column 19 of the FILE DESCRIPTION form to specify

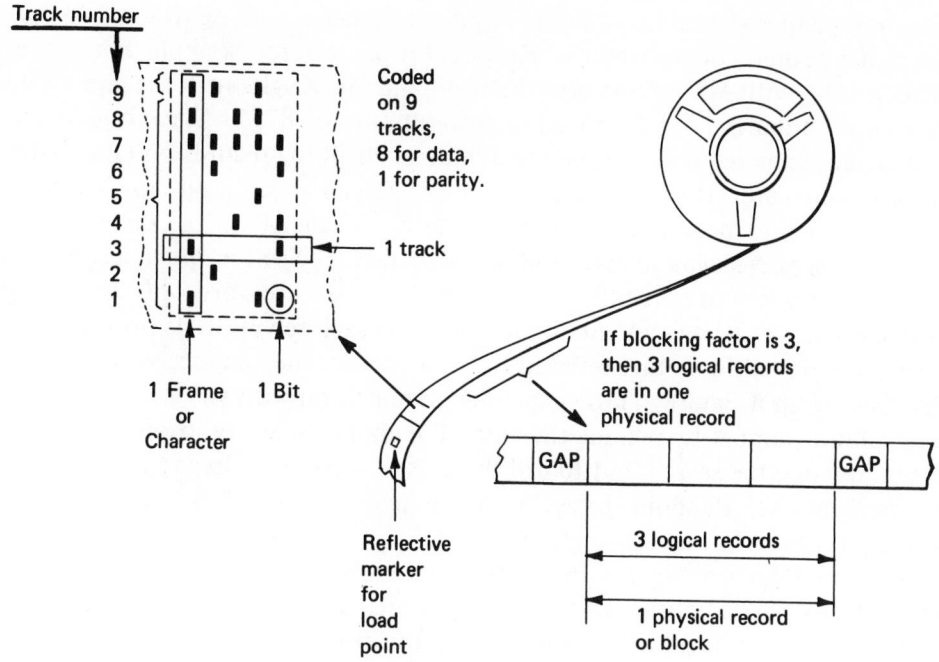

Track number

9
8   Coded
7   on 9
6   tracks,
5   8 for data,
4   1 for parity.
3
2   ← 1 track
1

1 Frame   1 Bit
or
Character

Reflective
marker
for
load
point

If blocking factor is 3,
then 3 logical records
are in one
physical record

GAP   GAP

3 logical records

1 physical record
or block

FIG. 25-2 Data on magnetic tape.

variable-length fields and records. Record and block lengths then specify the size of the biggest record and block that you expect to use.

The number of records in each block is called the *blocking factor*. When it is 1, the records are said to be *unblocked*. For fixed-length records, block length can be calculated by multiplying the length of each record by the blocking factor. A blocking factor of 25, for example, used on records of 1ØØ characters each, would require that 25ØØ characters be brought into the memory! You can see that a small computer memory might restrict your selection of block size to some reasonable minimum! Other restrictions concerning maximum block size depend on what tape device you are using; consult your reference manual for maximum sizes for your configuration. The larger the block size, however, the more information is placed into memory with one access of the tape unit, and therefore the execution time will decrease and the job will be finished faster.

A special character, called a *tape mark*, is placed onto the tape following the last recorded block. It serves as an end-of-file condition, known as *EOF*, so that when the tape is used as input, its detection is a signal that all data are processed. At the time that the tape is made, the tape mark is automatically placed at the end of the recorded information on the tape by the use of the end-of-file card at the back of your data deck.

Generally, one record at a time is processed in a program. For each record, there is usually some type of requested output, after which the program is repeated for the next record. Each record is therefore called a *logical record*. A set of logical records grouped together is called a *physical record*, and is exactly the same thing as a block! The programmer controls the logical record—what fields are used from it, and what should be done with them in the program. Although the programmer must supply the length specification for the physical record, control of it is not his responsibility. When a block is brought in, records from it are used one by one. When all the logical records currently in memory have been processed by a given program, the computer system will automatically bring in another one, without any action on the part of the programmer.

Records on tape files should be stored in sequential order according to some *key field*. This key may be either numeric or alphameric. Records for payroll, for example, may be recorded either alphabetically, with Mr. Adams near the front and Mr. Zeigler near the end, or numerically, with account number 1756 far ahead of account number 8732. The sequential nature of storage on magnetic tape requires that you search through all the records on tape that are in front of the one you want. If you are looking for Mr. Ziegler's record on tape in alphabetic sequence, a lot of time may be used in finding it. Another means of storage, called *random*, offers a faster means of access. Magnetic disks and drums, called *DASD*, for *direct access storage device*, permit either random or sequential storage. Random storage of records does not place them in any particular order as sequential does, but puts each record in its own special place with its *address* preserved for future reference. Each one can then be located by using its address, or by looking up its address, rather than by searching through all the records for it. To look up a telephone number by reading the entire telephone directory, from the beginning, is an example of a sequential search, but to call the person when you already know his telephone number is a random one. Random storage is more expensive, but offers the faster access necessary for many types of information retrieval.

Data density on tape is defined as the number of characters or bytes per inch that can be written on the tape. Several different densities are available commercially on some tape units, with those capable of handling higher density being the more expensive. A density of 800 bytes per inch, called 800 bpi, is fairly standard. On some tape units, density can be changed by operator setting of a switch on the tape unit.

As a means of comparing tape to cards, an equivalent number of 80 column cards can be determined for tape. Since each character or byte corresponds to one column of a punch card, an 80-column card occupies about 1/10 in. of space when recorded at 800 bpi. On most nine-track tapes, the gap between blocks is about 6/10 in. wide. That size gap would hold the equivalent of six cards! Since each block is followed by a gap, it is possible for a reel of tape to be mostly blank space and very little information! Assuming that 80 column cards are to be placed onto tape in card image form, unblocked at 800 bpi, each card will take 1/10 in., making each record occupy 7/10 in. of tape. On a 2400-ft reel, there are approximately 41,142 lengths of 7/10 in. each, so as many as 41,000 cards, about 20 boxes, could be put onto a reel. Although that seems like a lot, the tape actually has six times more blank spaces than data! Assuming instead a blocking factor of 20, the 20 records in the block would require 2.0 in. and the gap 6/10 in., making a block occupy 2.60 in. Approximately 11,000 blocks could be placed onto the reel, which is equivalent to more than 200,000 cards, or about 100 boxes! You can see that magnetic tape will occupy much less space than its equivalent number of punch cards.

Tape speed is specified in *ips*, the number of inches per second that pass under the read/write head on the tape unit. On most tape units, data are recorded only when the tape is moving at full operating speed. The rapid speed of the tape during read/write operations requires that very fast starts and stops occur. To allow the tape to be jerked rapidly without breaking, a loop of the tape remains suspended in a vacuum column on each side of the read/write mechanism. The start and stop action does cause some tape space to be left, forming the *interblock gap*. *Data transfer rate*, in bps, bytes per second, can be calculated from tape density and tape speed. For 800 bpi at 112.5 ips, a data rate of 90,000 bps can be attained. Data transfer rates for various models of the IBM 2401 tape unit, shown in Figure 25-1, can range from 20,000 to 180,000 bps.

Data recorded on tape can be used over and over indefinitely, since reading a tape does not destroy its magnetization. When data on a tape are no longer needed, the reel is put aside to be reused; data already on it are destroyed as new data are placed there. Tapes that are not permanently assigned to a job can be used as *scratch* tapes to hold temporary output from programs, somewhat in the same manner as scratch paper is used in doing hand calculations. Scratch tapes are often called *work tapes* and for TOS, are required during the generation process.

Since data are destroyed when writing occurs on a tape, it can be accidentally ruined by being written on. In an effort to prevent inadvertent destruction in this manner, a *file protection ring* is used. This plastic ring is manually inserted in the back of every reel before any writing can be done on that reel. When the ring is *not* on the reel, writing is *not* allowed to occur; reading, however, can be done whether a ring is used or not. When preparing a data tape, the programmer must specify to the operator that a ring is to be used. He must also specify that the ring should be removed after the tape is made, so that no more writing on it can occur. Remember the phrase: *Ring, write; no ring, no write.*

Another accident involving tape is using the *wrong* reel for a computer run. Since the data cannot be seen, the only way to determine the correct reel is to read the handwritten label on the outside of the reel cover and on the reel. This *external label*, shown in Figure 25-3, usually includes job name, recording mode, density, and a tape number. The number is usually assigned at the time the tape is prepared and supplied to the programmer by a *tape save* card. All future references to the tape should use that number.

Just as the external label is used by the operator to select the proper reel for the job to be done, an *internal label* may be used by the program to ensure that the correct reel is being used. Certain information about the reel is recorded on the tape, in the portion between the load point and the first data record; another portion is placed at the end of the recorded data. This information, the internal label, usually contains such things as job name, date of last usage, number of records on the reel, and expiration date. The computer can be instructed to do label checking in several different ways in RPG. Column 53 on the FILE DESCRIPTION form is used to indicate which of these options you would like. An **S** there implies that labels that are standard for that equipment will be used and checking of the labels should be done. A blank in that column means that no labels are to be either written or checked. If labels are to be used that are *different* from the standard for that manufacturer, either an **E** or an **N** may be used. An **E** means that a standard for the installation is to be used; an **N** means a nonstandard label is to be used; in either case, the checking is done by a previously written assembler subroutine, identified by the program name given in columns 54-59. Some implementations permit an **M** in column 53, meaning more than one reel of unlabeled tape is to be used. Unless you are in an installation with a large tape library where some danger exists in using the wrong reels you may, as a beginner, omit internal labels from your tape jobs unless your installation rules otherwise. Column 53 may therefore be left blank.

Some positioning of tape can be done in RPG. The programmer can specify control codes in column 7∅ of the FILE DESCRIPTION form on the line for the tape file. An **N** there indicates *no* rewinding of the tape, either before the tape is used or after the job is complete. A **U** there, which is what you get by default on most RPG systems when you leave the column blank, unloads the tape after the job is complete. The RPG as implemented for DOS, IBM SYSTEM/ 36∅, does provide many more tape-positioning options, including an **R** for rewinding the tape to its load point both before and after the job. See your RPG specifications manual for more information.

PROBLEM DEFINITION: *Make a tape from punch card records, 8∅ columns each, with blocking factor 1∅, and no internal labels. The punched input records should each be handled as one field of 8∅ columns. Output is two files: a printed list of the contents of the tape, and the tape. A tape ring must be used when making the tape. Make an appropriate operator message.*

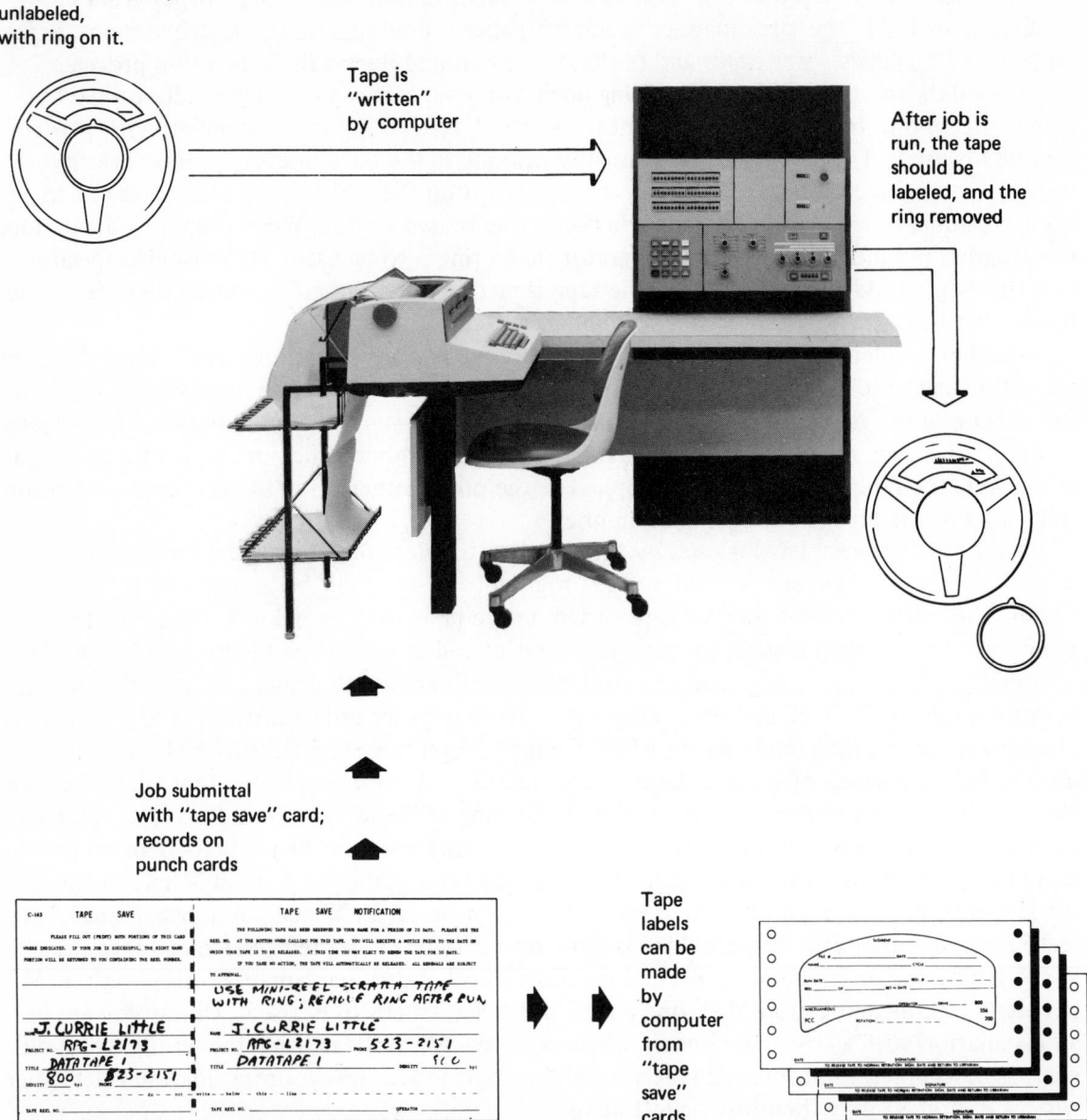

FIG. 25-3 Creating tape records. (Courtesy of Moore Business Forms, Inc.) and International Business Machines Corporation.)

Figure 25-4 shows a systems sketch for the job, a copy of the source program **MKTPE** as run on the IBM SYSTEM/36Ø, DOS, and the listing of the tape contents. Notice that the first page indicator is used to cause a skip to channel Ø1 on the printer. **N1P** is used to condition the value of **CARD** so that it is printed only *after* cards have been read in. If all reference to 1P is removed, no carriage return will be done and the contents of the tape will be printed on the same page as the // **EXEC** control card, rather than on a separate page. Double spacing of the tape listing is done *before* printing, not after; note that the report is actually triple spaced, since, unless you specify, this implementation does an automatic single space *after* printing.

On the FILE DESCRIPTION form, the device name is **TAPE**. The symbolic device is a sys-

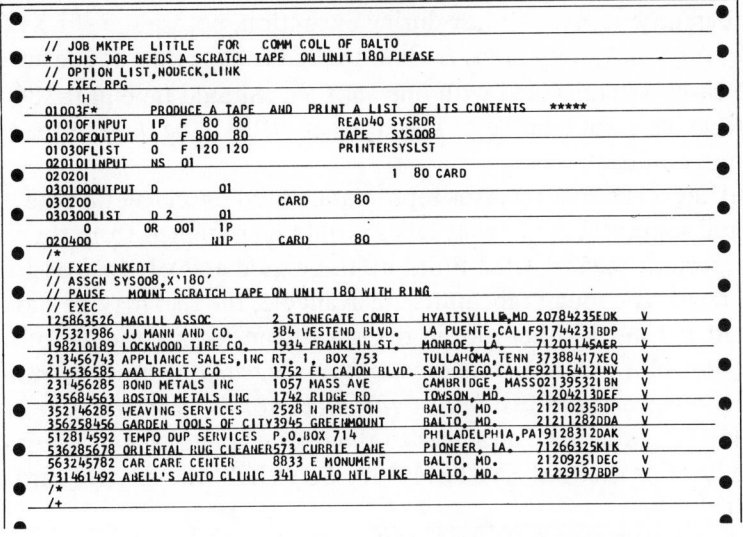

80/80 listing of stacked deck,
including control cards

listing of tape contents

Systems chart

Input data deck

PROGRAM MKTPE

IBM SYSTEM/360

Tape reel

Printed copy of tape contents

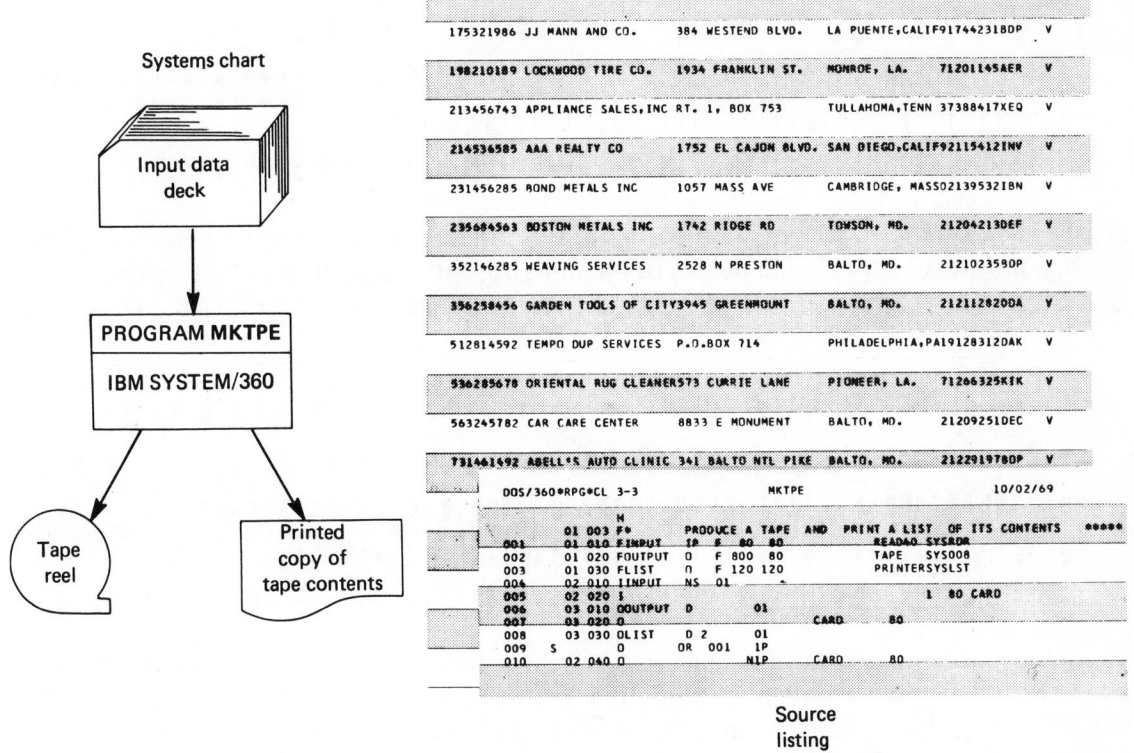

Source listing

FIG. 25-4 Program **MKTPE** to make a tape—IBM SYSTEM/36∅, DOS.

tem number from ∅∅1 to 255. In some installations, standard assignments are established for all personnel to use; you may use the one assigned, such as **SYS∅∅2**, for example, which could be routinely assigned to physical tape unit number 183. However, you may select an unassigned system number and assign it yourself with a special control card called an *assign card*. The program **MKTPE** uses **SYS0Ø8** and an assign card given by // **ASSGN SYS0Ø8, X'18Ø'**, which specifies that tape unit 18Ø should be used as **SYS0Ø8**. This card need not appear during generation of the object program, but *must* appear during execution, before the // **EXEC** control card. This method of assigning system numbers to a particular tape unit at execution-time allows tape units to be easily interchanged with one another. Should tape unit 18Ø be *down*, in need of service, an assign card can be used to specify that 181 will be used instead, without any changes in the program itself.

When submitting a job that involves input data stored on magnetic tape, it is customary to specify, on the job submittal card, what tapes should be obtained from the tape library before the run. It is important to state what units are to be used and whether or not a ring should be put on the tape reels. If enough tape units are available, the reel may be mounted and the unit made ready ahead of time; if other jobs in the job stream require the use of that unit, however, that will not be possible; *if all available tape units are needed for the generation process, the tape must not be mounted until just before the execution is indicated.* Special control cards are used in the job stream to give messages to the operator and to halt the system until the tape can be made ready. For the IBM SYSTEM/36Ø, TOS/DOS, the control card given by

```
/* PUT SCRATCH TAPE ON UNIT 180, PLEASE, WITH RING
```
(punched card)

is called a *remarks card*; the message on this card is printed on the console typewriter, telling the operator that a tape should be placed on unit 18Ø, with a ring on it so that writing can be done; it does *not*, however, cause the computer system to halt. The control card given by

```
// PAUSE  PUT SCRATCH TAPE ON UNIT 180, WITH RING — SAVE AFTER RUN
```
(punched card)

not only gives a message but also causes the system to halt so that tape mounting can be done, after which the operator initiates a continuation of the job when mounting is complete. Although any number of *remarks cards* may precede the *pause card*, keep in mind that the typewriter is a slow output medium, and that much computer time will be consumed by lengthy operator messages. It is customary to restrict tape-mounting messages to one remarks card and one pause card, given just before the card that initiates execution. Tape-unmounting messages are given in the same way, but are placed just after the end-of-file card that follows the data deck. See your installation manager for instructions concerning operator messages on your computer system.

By using a key recorder machine, often called a magnetic encoder or inscriber, information can be keyed directly onto a tape in somewhat the same manner that data are keypunched onto cards. These machines, such as the IBM Ø5Ø shown in Figure 25-5, can record any keyed information onto the tape, can display recorded information from the tape, and can also be used as a verifier to check the keyed data. Data recorders, however, are relatively expensive; cards, along with a program such as **MKTPE**, are still used in many installations to get source information placed onto tape.

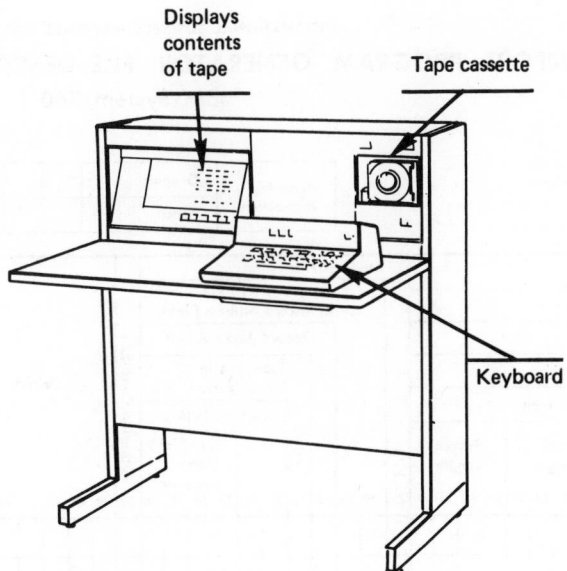

FIG. 25-5 IBM Ø5Ø magnetic data inscriber.

EXERCISES

1. How much core storage would one *block* of tape require for the following:

   (a) Fixed-length records, blocking factor 8, record size 1ØØØ characters? _____

   (b) Fixed-length records, unblocked, record size 1ØØØ characters? _____

2. At a density of 8ØØ bpi and with an interblock gap of .6 in., approximately how many feet of magnetic tape would 1Ø,ØØØ records, each 1ØØ characters long, need for each of these:

   (a) Unblocked records? _____

   (b) Blocking factor 1Ø? _____

   (c) Blocking factor 2Ø? _____

3. Give **FILE DESCRIPTION** specifications for each:
   (a) Tape input of a detail file, using **SYSØØ8**, blocking factor 1Ø, records 25 characters each; card output on an IBM 1442.
   (b) Tape output of summary totals, using **SYS155**, unblocked 2Ø-character records; card input on the IBM 25Ø1.
   (c) Input of a master tape file and a detail card file; the inventory tape records are fixed-length, 1ØØ characters in each record, blocking factor 5, on **SYS111**; cards on the IBM 25Ø1; output on the printer.
   (d) Tape input on **SYS24Ø** with block length 2ØØ, blocking factor 8; printer output.

IBM

INTERNATIONAL BUSINESS MACHINES CORPORATION

REPORT PROGRAM GENERATOR FILE DESCRIPTION SPECIFICATIC

IBM System/360

Date ______________

Program ______________

Programmer ______________

Punching Instruction	Graphic							
	Punch							

Line (3 4 5)	Form Type (6)	Filename (7 8 9 10 11 12 13 14)	File Type I/O/U/C (15)	File Designation P/S/C/R/T (16)	End of File E (17)	Sequence A/D (18)	File Format F/V (19)	Block Length (20 21 22 23)	Record Length (24 25 26 27)	L/R (28)	Mode of Processing; Length of Key Field or of Record Address Field (29 30)	Record Address Type K/I (31)	Type of File Organization I/D/T (32)	Overflow Indicator (33 34)	Key Field Starting Location (35 36 37 38)	Extension Code E/L (39)	Device (40 41 42 43 44 45 46)	Symbolic Device (47 48 49 50 51 52)	Labels (S, N, or E) (53)	54 55
0 1 ⓐ	F																			
0 2	F																			
0 3	F																			
0 4 ⓑ	F																			
0 5	F																			
0 6	F																			
0 7 ⓒ	F																			
0 8	F																			
0 9	F																			
1 0	F																			
1 1 ⓓ	F																			
1 2	F																			
1 3	F																			
1 4	F																			
1 5	F																			

Lesson 26

MULTIPLE-FILE INPUT—CARDS AND TAPE

You will learn how to use matching records in RPG *to access information from two different sequential input files.*

The questions below summarize multiple-file input and are answered on the back of this page. If you have never used multiple files in RPG, study the lesson and answer the questions before going on to Lesson 27.

1. What is meant by *multiple-file input*?
2. How can you cause the card file to control the LR indicator even though the tape file still has unprocessed records on it?
3. Which of the files should be marked **P** for primary?
4. What is the purpose of using matching fields indication?
5. How does the computer know which field or fields you are going to be *matching* on?
6. Assuming that the primary file has indicator Ø1 and the secondary file has indicator Ø2, give the various possibilities of matching and nonmatching conditions, and what indicators signal them.
7. After a *match* has been found between primary and secondary file records, which file is processed next? If they do *not* match, which record is processed next?
8. What is meant by *multiple primaries*? *multiple secondaries*?
9. When a record with *no matching* specified, such as a date header card, is detected in one of the input files, what happens to the matching record indicator?
10. At what point in the RPG object program logic chart does the MR indicator turn *on* or *off*?

ANSWERS

1. More than one input file is used in the job.
2. By putting an **E**, for end-of-file detection, in column 17 of the FILE DESCRIPTION form on the line describing the card file.
3. The one that should be brought in first.
4. To cause the records from the several input files to be properly merged into one continuous stream of input records, as though in one file.
5. By your placing the appropriate matching field assignment, such as **M1**, **M2**, etc., into columns 61 and 62 of the INPUT specifications form for that field.
6. **MR** and Ø1 is a matching primary record; **MR** and Ø2 is a matching secondary record; **NMR** and Ø1 means an unmatched primary record, and **NMR** and Ø2 means an unmatched secondary record.
7. The primary. All of the records in the primary file that match the secondary record are processed, one by one, *before* the secondary file feeds. Then all the records in the secondary file that match the *last* matched primary record are processed. When the two records do *not* match, the record to be processed next depends on whether the specified sequence for the key fields of the two files is *ascending* or *descending*. For key fields specified in ascending order, the record with the *lowest* key field is processed next, then another record from that file feeds in; for key fields specified in descending order, the record with the *highest* key field is processed, then a record from that file feeds in.
8. More than one primary record is present for one particular value of the key field; more than one secondary record is present for one particular value of the key field.
9. It goes *off* while that record is processed, then is reset to its former value.
10. After total-time output, but before detail-time calculations.

Since data on magnetic tape are more compact and can be accessed much faster than data on punch cards, magnetic tape is often used instead of cards for input on jobs requiring large volumes of data. Punch cards can easily be transferred to tape, in any kind of order. A utility program can be used to sort the records on the tape into order by some key field, producing another tape. The sorted tape is then used as input to any other program. A comparison of a tape sort and a mechanical sort done on a sorter is shown in the systems chart in Figure 26-1.

When the entire data file for a job is on tape, a run-date card can, on most computer systems, be put into the read hopper and read before the data from the tape enters the system. Even though there is only one card in the reader, it is considered a *file*. If more than one input file is being used, even in this manner, the program is then a *multiple-file input* job.

An end-of-file control card or mark should be present in *each* of the input files. Since there is more than one file, the first one to become empty detects the end-of-file condition before the other one does. This detection is noted, but ordinarily *it is not until all input files have reached this condition that the LR record goes on*. In many instances, the EOF in a particular

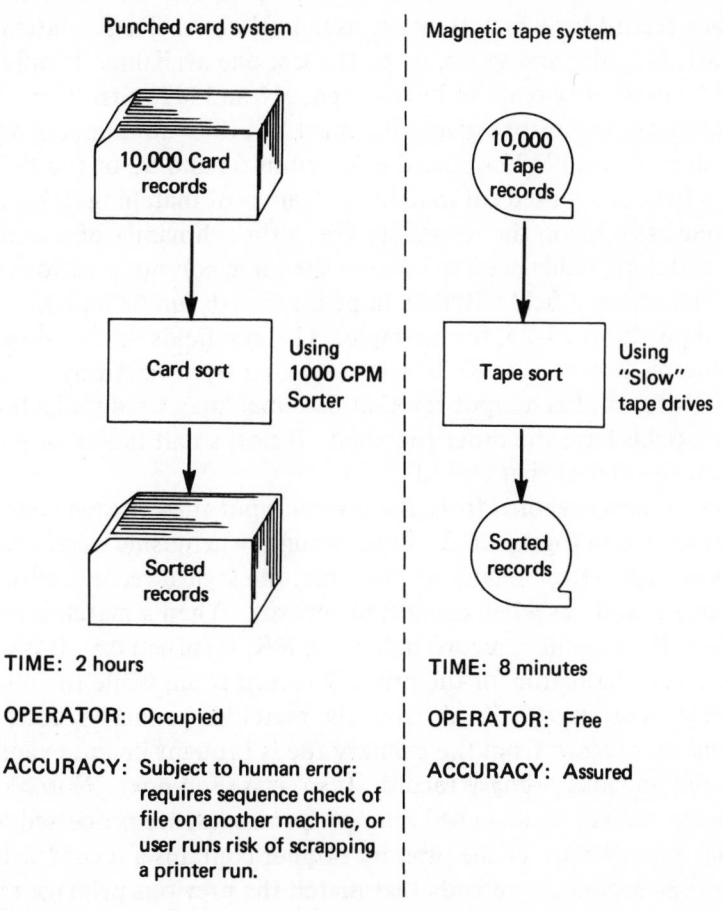

FIG. 26-1 Comparison of card and tape sorting. (© 1968, Sperry Rand Corp.
Reproduced by permission of UNIVAC Division, Sperry Rand Corp.)

one of the input files should be used to turn on the LR indicator, with the other files having no effect on LR at all. You may specify that *one* particular file turn on the LR indicator by putting an **E** in column 17 of the FILE DESCRIPTION form on the line for that file. The LR indicator will then go *on* when all the records from that file are processed. The **E** can be placed on more than one file; the LR indicator will then go on when *all* the files so marked have reached the EOF condition. The use of **E** for this purpose will perhaps vary with each particular job, since some multiple-file jobs will be completed when the cards run out and others, when the tape runs out.

Each input file must be specified as either **P** for primary or **S** for secondary. The file that is to be read first should be the primary, and is usually written first on the FILE DESCRIPTION form; all others are marked **S** for secondary. The key field on each file must be identified as either ascending or descending, by putting either an **A** or a **D**, respectively, in column 18 of the FILE DESCRIPTION form. The files used on multiple input can either be on card decks in separate read hoppers, on two tape units, or on a mixture of units. The RPG fixed-program logic uses *matching fields indication* to cause records to be read and merged by a key field into one continuous stream as they enter the computer system; the *matching record indicator*, MR, goes on or off to indicate to the programmer when the records from the two files contain the same value in the matching fields that have been so indicated.

In some implementations, up to three fields can be assigned matching field indication on each record of a multiple file; in others, up to nine can be used. The same *number* of fields must be used in each record for which they are used in the job. These matching field indications are given as M1, M2, M3, and so on, up to the last one available. If only one is to be assigned, M1 must be used; if two are to be assigned, M1 and M2 must be used. The fields used for matching field indication, for one given file, must be either all numeric, or all alphameric. The indication, such as M1 and M2, is placed in columns 61 and 62 of the INPUT specifications form, alongside the field being used for matching. Names of matching fields on the primary file need not be the same as those on the secondary file, although names of a similar nature are advised. Neither do matching fields need to occupy the same column positions within their individual records. The primary field **CDNUM** in positions 1-6 can be matched with the secondary field **TPNUM** in positions 21-26, for example. The key fields of the file must *both* be either ascending or descending, however, marked with an **A** or a **D**, respectively, in column 18 on the FILE DESCRIPTION form. Each input file that uses matching field indication is checked to be sure that the key fields have the order specified. If not, a halt indicator goes on and processing terminates at the end of that record.

Matching serves to merge records from the several input files into one continuous stream of input records, as shown in Figure 26-2. Even though, when using magnetic tape, an *entire block* of records is brought into memory at one time, the logical records within the block are handled *one* at a time exactly as when using card records. When a match is found between two fields in the two files, the matching record indicator, MR, is turned *on*. It is on *at the same time* that the record-type indicator for the primary record is on, while the record-type indicator for the secondary record is *off*. Fields from the matching primary record are available at that time. Next, another record from the primary file is brought in and examined to see if it is the same key as the previous primary record. If so, it is used next. Note that primary records with the same value in the key field, called *multiple primaries*, are processed *before* the first secondary with that key. Whenever the primary hopper contains a record with a different key, it is held back, while all secondary records that match the previous primary record are processed. If more than one secondary record has the same key field value, then multiple secondaries are said to exist. At this time, the primary indicator is *off*, but the matching record indicator MR and the record-type indicator for the secondary record are both on. The fields on

Primary File		Secondary File	
Matching Field In The Record	Processed	Matching Field In The Record	Processed
001	1st.	001	3rd.
001	2nd.	001	4th.
002	5th.	002	6th.
004	9th.	003	7th.
004	10th.	003	8th.
006	12th.	005	11th.

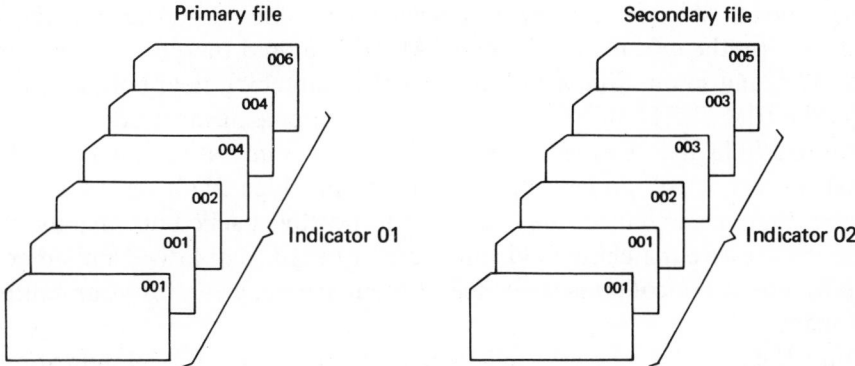

FIG. 26-2 Order of processing with matching records. (Reproduced by permission from *IBM SYSTEM/360 Disk and Tape Operating Systems, RPG Specifications.* © 1966 by International Business Machines Corporation.)

the secondary record and the previous matching primary are available for printing lines on the report. Secondaries with the same key as the previous primary are processed, one by one, until a secondary record is found that does *not* match the previous primary. At that time, a record from the file that has the lower key field is processed if *ascending* order is specified, but the one from the file with the higher key field is processed if *descending* order is given. It is important to remember that if multiple primaries occur, the machine will use all of them before using the secondaries, with fields from the last primary still available to use when the secondaries are being processed. Assuming that the primary record uses indicator Ø1 and the secondary record uses Ø2, a summary of the conditions can be given:

MR Ø1   Primary record now being processed, matches the secondary, which is next.

MR Ø2   Secondary record now being processed, matches the previous primary.

NMR Ø1   Primary record now being processed, does *not* match the secondary, which is next.

NMR Ø2   Secondary record now being processed, does *not* match the previous primary.

If a record within a file has no matching field indication, such as a header card, it is processed as soon as it is brought in, with MR *off*, after which the MR indicator will be reset to its previous setting.

Multiple-file input records often use the concept of a master file and a detail file. For example, master information for inventory can be input from tape, with detail information about current orders or issues input from cards. One record from each file is read; matching inventory numbers signal that two records with identical keys have been found in the data stream; a report line may be printed based on information from the processing of those records. Another multiple-file problem might require that a master file and a detail file be merged and output onto another magnetic tape file. Still another job could be to search a tape file, listing everybody under 3Ø years of age, for example! You will find that in most master file/detail file applications, such as accounts receivable for a department store, there is only *one* master record for each account, not several. Several transactions may affect that master record, however. They are collected in batches and saved for a periodic processing run.

Each file, for which matching fields have been specified, uses a special *matching field hold area*, in which all matching fields for that file are handled *together as one field*. The lowest-order matching indication, M1, is placed on the *right*, low-order end of the hold area, with the higher ones, such as M2, M3, and the others when available, placed successively on the left, with the highest one on the *left*, high-order end. All M1's should therefore be the same length, as should all M2's, and so on. The length of the entire matching field hold area is usually restricted; in the IBM SYSTEM/36Ø, DOS/TOS, for example, it must not exceed 256 characters. In addition to a hold area reserved for each file, one *save area* is reserved to hold the key of the record that was previously processed, no matter from which file it was taken. It is important to remember that numeric fields are converted to positive packed-decimal mode after they are brought in, so negative matching field values are not used as negative; alphameric fields are compared by use of the collating sequence of the machine, given for your equipment in your reference manual.

Matching field indication works independently from control level indication, although in some instances the same field will be used for control level as for matching. Some matching field jobs will not have any control levels used at all; others may have several. When used in the same job, matching field indication should be assigned to fields in the same order as the control levels are assigned. For example, fields marked L1, L2, and L3 should be given matching indication M1, M2, and M3 so that comparisons in the hold area will be properly aligned; should control level L1 not influence matching, however, M1 and M2 could be assigned to L2 and L3, with the *order* the same for proper alignment within the hold area. Keep in mind that matching is used to select *which* record to process next, but control levels are used to determine *whether the record that was selected* represents a break in the key field for those records. The MR indicator is not turned on or off until after total-time operations, so that totals for an entire group of matching records can be used for control level totals before being set for the next record.

When using an input file from tape, it is often helpful to be able to access a header card in the card reader. The file for the header card must be marked **P** for primary so that it will be brought in first. You will, on most implementations, receive a warning message during the generation process, telling you that a multiple-file job is being done without matching fields indicated. These messages can be ignored and the program executed anyway. On other implementations, you are not permitted to access a header card from the card reader in this manner.

PROBLEM DEFINITION: *A master tape file of names and addresses of vendors who sell products and services to a firm is available on a tape reel. Certain of these vendors are to be paid for their services for this month. A deck of cards contains the vendor number for each one who should be paid, and the amount that he should receive. Prepare a program, named* **CKCNTRL**, *to produce a check control list, giving the information as it will look on the preprinted check form when the actual checks are produced. A systems chart is given in Figure 26-3. It shows that a discrepancy card should be made for any card for which a master record cannot be found, giving perhaps the account number and the amount to be paid. End-of-job totals should be the amount to be paid, the number of checks to be made, and the number of discrepancies found.*

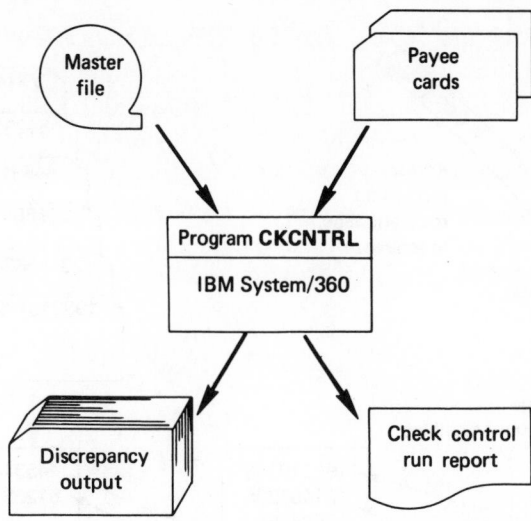

FIG. 26-3 Systems chart—program **CKCNTRL**.

	Field Information	*Columns*
Run-date header card	Record ID code: D Date	8∅ 1-8
Master records, on tape	Record ID code: V Employee number Employee name Street and address City and state Zip code Division number Department number	80 1-9 11-3∅ 31-5∅ 51-65 66-7∅ 71-73 74-76
Detail records, on cards	Record ID code: P Employee number Amount of payment	8∅ 1-9 45-5∅

Presumably many of the names and addresses on the master file will not be needed for this job. Purchases and services may not have been obtained from all the vendors during the period; only those that are active will match a secondary record. Unmatched ones, detected by **NMR** and **01**, will be bypassed on this job. Each secondary record, however, should match a record on the primary file, and if it does not, something is wrong. Perhaps the master record for that vendor is not yet on the tape, or perhaps the vendor number was mispunched. Whatever the reason, this error, detected by **NMR** and **02**, should be brought to someone's attention, so a discrepancy card is to be punched. The punch card file **PUNCH** is established for this type of error detection. The total number of discrepancy cards punched will be printed after the check control run is complete. Figure 26-4 summarizes these conditions and shows sample data used to test the program.

The complete program is shown in Figure 26-5, with sample output. The master file should be marked **P** for primary and the card file, **S** for secondary. Since the job will be complete when the detail card file is exhausted, put an **E** in column 17 of the **FILE DESCRIPTION** form

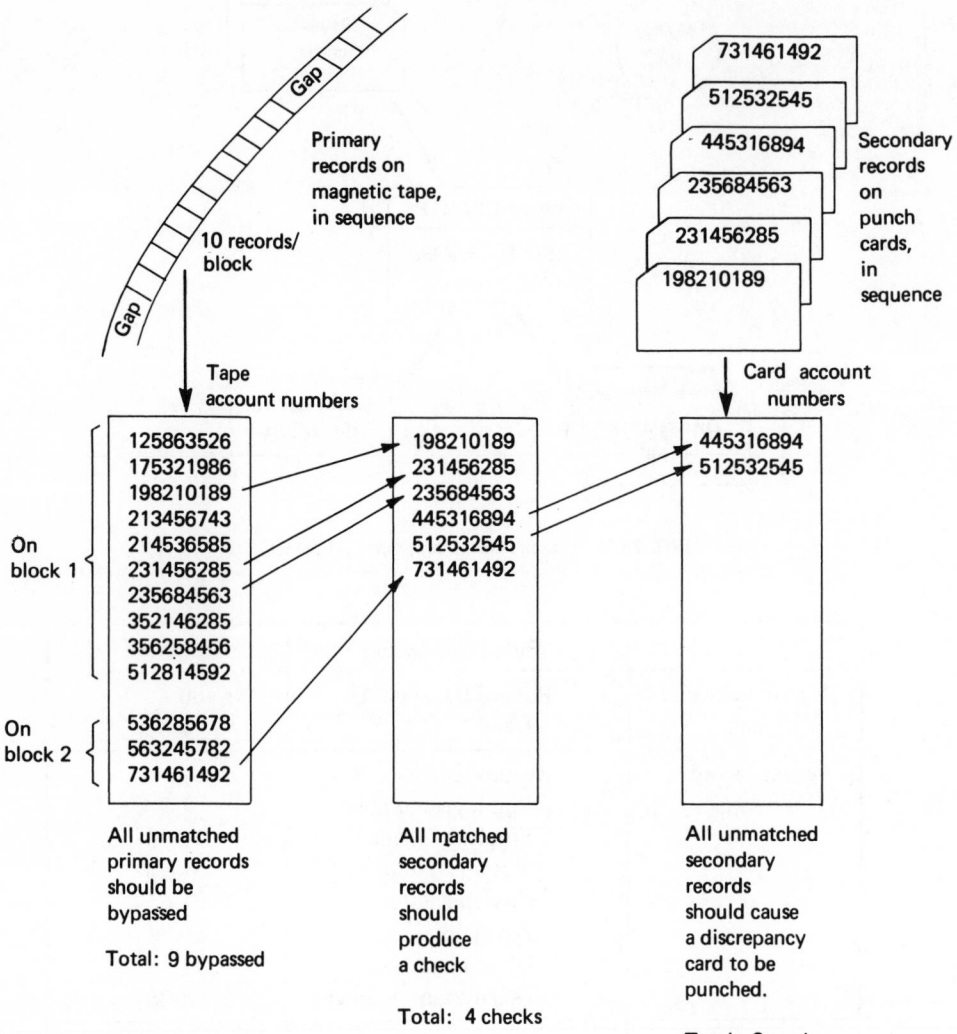

FIG. 26-4 Matching records in program **CKCNTRL**.

to turn on the LR indicator when that hopper detects the end-of-file card. Mark both files with
A for ascending matching file fields in column 18 of the FILE DESCRIPTION form. An **M1**
is placed alongside the field named **NUM** both in the primary and secondary file. Indicator Ø1
is chosen for the primary file record and indicator Ø2, for the secondary.

This program represents the type of payroll application that accesses a master tape file but
does not update it. It can be used for a control run to permit data totals to be checked before
a final run is made on preprinted check forms. Skipping to proper channels on the carriage control tape will be given in the program when the run is made on special forms.

Run sheets from program generation

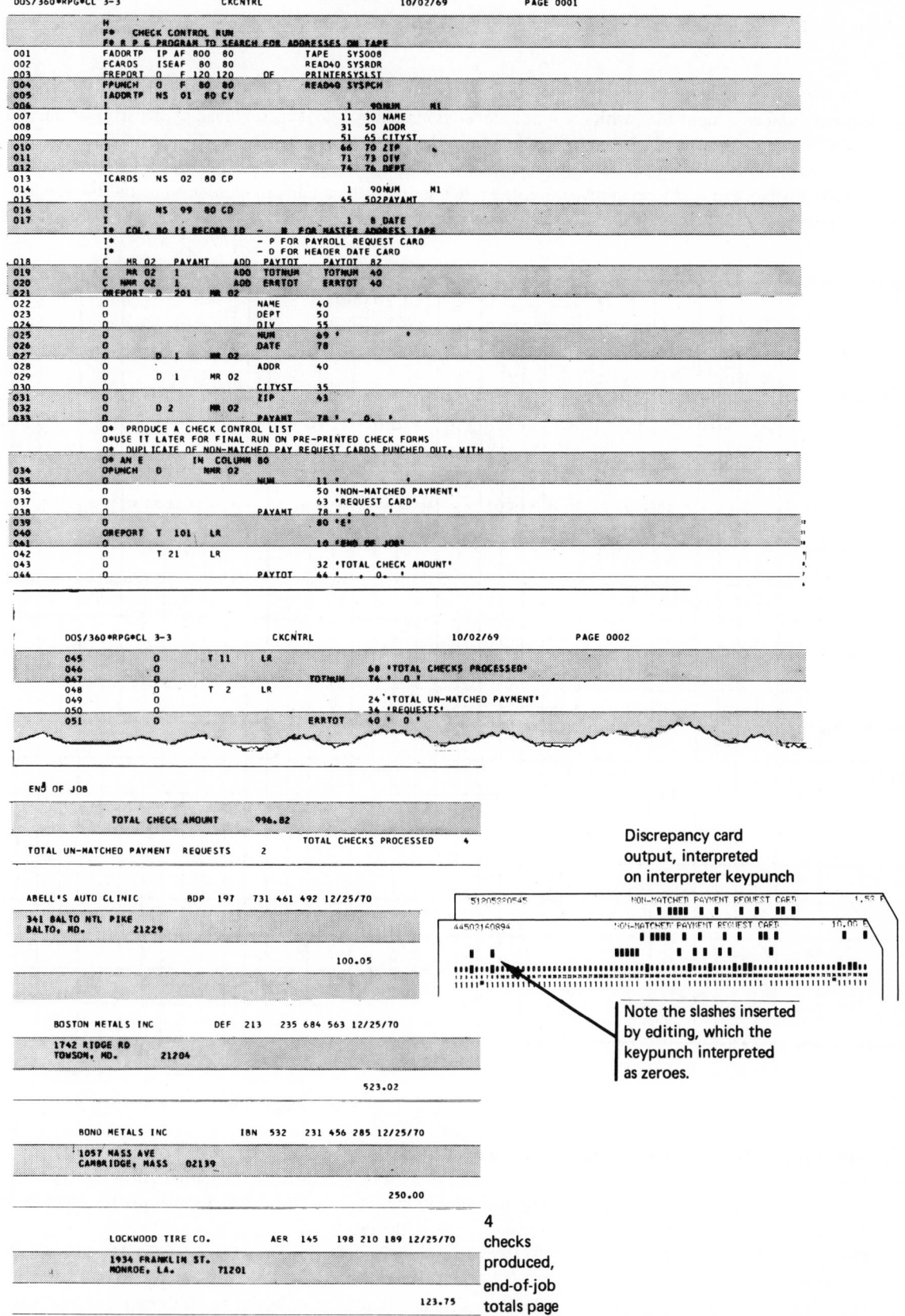

FIG. 26-5 Program **CKCNTRL**–IBM SYSTEM/360, DOS.

EXERCISES

1. Give INPUT specifications for each of the following, omitting FIELD LOCATION and RECORD ID codes:
   (a) Tape and card input files, with account number as matching field; control break by department number on the cards, name and address to be taken from the master tape record.
   (b) Item number on one tape file to be matched to another; one tape contains the item description and on-hand balance of that item in inventory; the other contains the minimum reorder point and the vendor name and address where more of that item can be ordered.

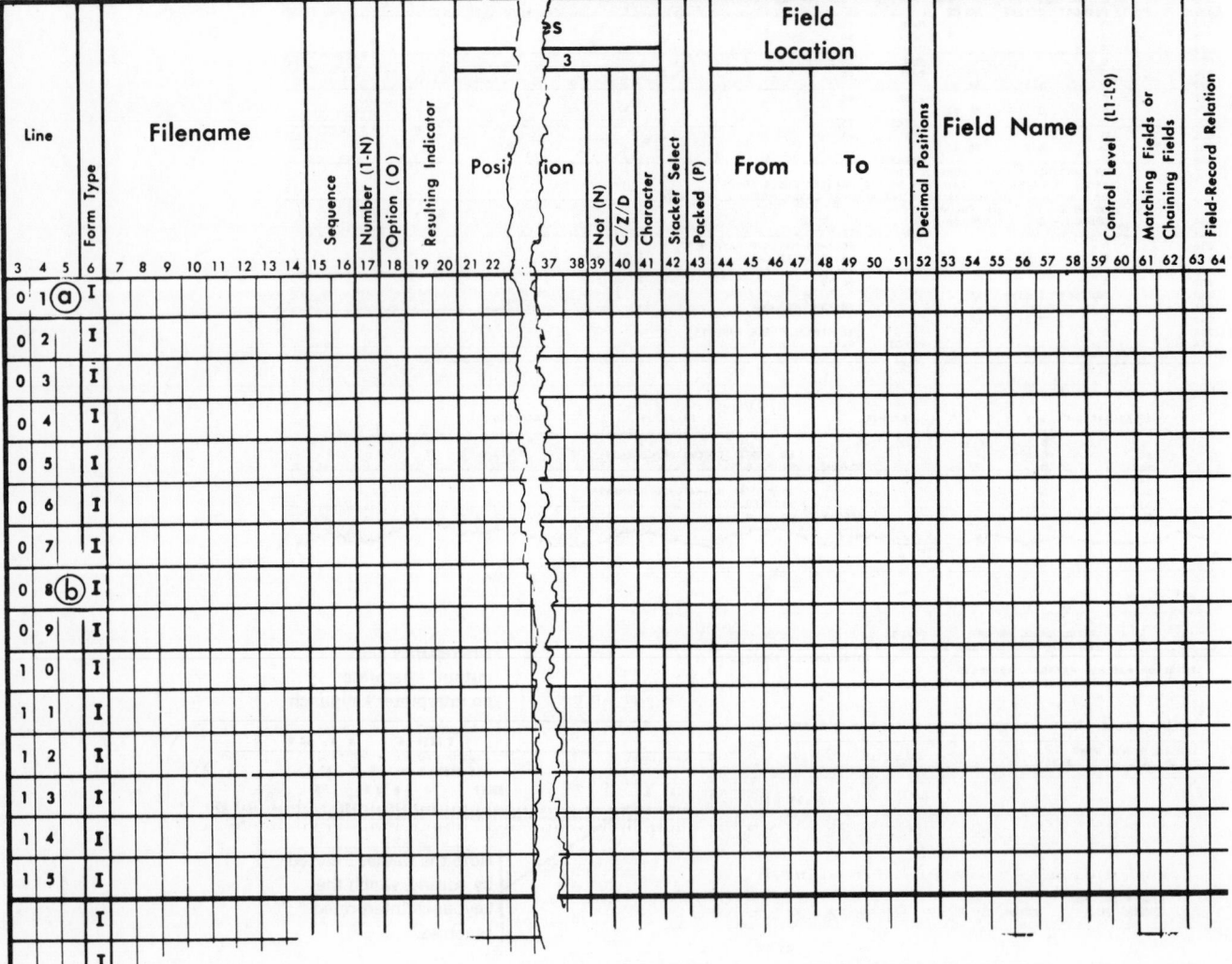

2. Give FILE DESCRIPTION specifications for the following:
   (a) Tape output of a table, further defined on the FILE EXTENSION form, to contain the numbers of the employees who have not yet paid their insurance premiums; blocking factor 1∅, records 1∅ characters each, on unit SYS∅∅8, with rewind of the tape after the job.
   (b) Tape input of a master file from SYS21∅, with end-of-file to turn on the LR indicator, block size 5∅∅, record size 1∅∅.
   (c) Tape input of a table giving the number of orders placed with each vendor so far during this fiscal year, on SYS∅∅7, unblocked, 1∅ columns in each record, with no rewind of the tape after the job.

Line	Form Type	Filename	I/O/U/C	P/S/C/R/T	E (End of File)	A/D (Sequence)	F/V (File Format)	Block Length	Record Length	L/R	Mode of Processing	K/I	I/D/T	Type of File Organization	Key Field Starting Location / Overflow Indicator	Extension Code E/L	Device	Symbolic Device	Labels (S, N, or E)
3 4 5	6	7 8 9 10 11 12 13 14	15	16	17	18	19	20 21 22 23	24 25 26 27	28	29 30	31	32	33 34	35 36 37 38	39	40 41 42 43 44 45 46	47 48 49 50 51 52	53
0 1 (a)	F																		
0 2	F																		
0 3 (b)	F																		
0 4	F																		
0 5 (c)	F																		
0 6	F																		
0 7	F																		
0 .																			

3. Give the order of processing of the records given as multiple-input file data, giving the indicator conditions that are satisfied at the time the record is processed. Assume that indicator 51 is for the primary file record, indicator 99 for the date card in the secondary file, and indicator 52 for the detail record in the secondary file. Assume that no **E** is marked for end-of-file detection.

Records in Primary File		Records in Secondary File		As Processed		
M2	*M1*	*M2*	*M1*	File Card		Indicators
Ø5	Ø7	Date		1. S Date		NMR 99
Ø5	Ø9	Ø5	Ø9	2. P Ø5 Ø7		NMR 51
Ø5	11	Ø5	11	3. P Ø5 Ø9		MR 51
Ø5	11	Ø5	11	4.		
Ø5	38	Ø5	19	5.		
Ø7	15	Date		6.		
Ø7	23	Ø7	15	7.		
Ø8	Ø1	Ø7	15	8.		
Ø8	15	Ø7	23	9.		
Ø8	33	Ø8	Ø1	10.		
/*		/*		11.		
				12.		
				13.		
				14.		
				15.		
				16.		
				17.		
				18.		
				19.		
				20.		

Lesson 27

A PRINTED REPORT WITH TAPE FILE MAINTENANCE

You will learn how file maintenance and updating is done with magnetic tape master files.

The questions that follow are answered on the back of this page. If you have already had experience with programming for file maintenance with another computer language, answer questions 7, 8, and 9 and then attempt the programs at the end of this section.

1. What is meant by *file maintenance*?
2. What is meant by *file updating*?
3. What is a *batching period*?
4. Explain the meaning of the *grandfather method of tape cycling*.
5. What should the systems chart show for file maintenance and updating jobs?
6. What is a *change report*?
7. When *additions* are made to an employee file of master records, what indicators are used to represent the situation during the program?
8. When *deletions* are made in an employee file of master records, what indicators are used to represent the situation during the program?
9. How may *changes* to the master file records that are already present be accomplished?
10. Compare card file maintenance with that done using magnetic tape.

ANSWERS

1. Periodic renewal of a file of information, to add new records into their proper places in sequence, delete other records, and make necessary changes to some of those records that remain on the file.
2. Periodic updating of a master file by posting certain transactions to the account that they affect, or by making changes in the balances or totals appropriate to those transactions.
3. The length of time you collect those transactions before doing a computer run. For file maintenance of an employee file, it may be once each month, or once a year depending on the purpose of the file; for file updating on an application such as accounts receivable billing, it may be done just before bills are prepared.
4. An old master tape is used with transactions to form a new tape master on another reel. The new tape master, called the *son*, is kept until the end of the next batching period, when it becomes the *father*, and with the transactions, produces another son, making the older master the *grandfather*. The master file from each run is preserved for a certain period of time; should any errors be found or a file accidentally destroyed, a new run could recover the situation by making another.
5. Each input file and how it is obtained, and each output file and what happens to it after the run.
6. A list of the additions, deletions, or changes that have been put in to make a new master file of records.
7. A valid *addition* record should have a control field that is not already on the master file, so it must use the **NMR** indicator, along with the indicator that means an addition. If it does not have that indicator, yet has **NMR**, assume that it is an invalid detail card.
8. A valid *deletion* record should have a control field that matches one already on the master file, so use the **MR** indicator, and the indicator for a deletion, since records for changes will also match a record on the master file.
9. A valid *change* record should have a control field that matches one already on the master file, so use **MR** and an indicator for a change record to cause it to replace the master record already on the file with the new one.
10. When file maintenance is done with cards, the cards to be deleted or added may be located and replaced by hand or with a collator if available. When done on tape, however, the grandfather method of cycling on tape is used, to preserve the old file while using it to make a new one with the modifications on it.

Lesson 27   A Printed Report with Tape File Maintenance

File maintenance refers to keeping a file of information current by either adding new records to it as needed, deleting old ones as needed, or making changes to those that remain in the file. Changes of this nature will continually occur—an employee file of names and addresses will be affected by events such as women employees getting married and changing their names, changes in the number of deductions a person is allowed for income tax purposes, employees buying new homes and changing addresses, or employees leaving the company and others replacing them. Record-keeping of this nature must be handled in a reliable and routine manner by careful job design based on use of the computer system.

File updating is a term often used to mean the same thing as maintenance; it has in the past, however, meant rather to keep a file of information *current* by posting or recording changes in the *fields* of the records in the files due to current *transactions*, and not necessarily adding new records or removing old ones. The term updating usually implies that the transactions, which affect the totals or balances from a previous run, will be used with the old totals or balances, to make new ones to be retained in another file. The charges made by a customer at a department store, for example, affect the balance from the previous month's billing. When preparing a statement, the charges, payments, and returns are used with the old balance in calculating a new balance; this new balance is placed onto a new file to be used the following period in the same manner.

The practice of holding transactions for a period of time until they can be processed in a group, according to some prearranged schedule, is called *batch processing*. In certain billing operations, statements are run once each month, with all charges, payments, and returns saved until that time. In other installations with a larger volume, statements are prepared perhaps three times each month, each time with accounts being done for only a portion of the entire customer file. Selection of those to be run at each of the batching periods may be based on last name or on account number. Billing that is separated into several different periods in this manner is called *cycle billing*, since several cycles are required before billing is completed for the entire file. In file maintenance, batches of requests for additions, deletions, or changes to the master file are usually saved to be run at one time—perhaps monthly, perhaps more often, depending on the volume. File maintenance for small volumes could be done with regular billing operations, but the program would indeed be much more difficult to write and would take more time to be executed.

Records permanently maintained in a file are usually referred to as *master* records. Names and addresses of subscribers to a magazine, records from the inventory of automobile parts, or the balance of payments remaining on the purchase of an automobile, are all examples of master files. Records that are not of such a permanent nature, that perhaps are of interest for only a short time, are called transactions, or *detail* records. They might be individual charges at a department store, the grade a student made in a particular class, or the issuance of an item from inventory storage at the warehouse.

When files are kept on punch cards, the master card can be located manually and the card pulled out. After updated cards are punched and sorted, they are merged into the old file, usually on a collator, such as the IBM Ø85. Where magnetic files are used, however, the record is not visible, and changes must be made either by computer processing or by a key recorder machine.

369

A typical file maintenance job has master file records on tape and detail file changes on cards. The master file is kept in sequential order, according to some key field in the record, such as numerically by account number or alphabetically by name. Since processing ordinarily brings one record at a time into the computer, the records in the detail file must be sorted into the same order as the records on the master file, so that both files are in the same arrangement. Matching field indicators will be used to locate the record on the master file that corresponds to the detail record. You may observe, however, that the *additions* to be made to the file during file maintenance are characterized by *not* having a matching field on the master file.

In designing a system either for maintaining a file or for updating it, the possibility of destroying records from a previous run must be considered. If some catastrophe should befall the run, as sometimes happens, you must be able to reconstruct the file from old records and transactions. For that reason, the *grandfather method* of cycling on magnetic tape, as shown in Figure 27-1, is often used. Each time a run is made, the old master tape is used to create a new master tape, rather than itself being changed. Each new master is considered the son of the father that created it. The old master is kept until the son itself becomes a father, making it a grandfather. After a time on the shelf, the grandfather may be released, allowing it to be used for some other purpose. A systems chart for a file maintenance or updating job should give the dispensation of each file that it uses. If an old file is to be shelved, a special shape for filing is used. If the file is to be used in a later run, a dotted line shows which position in the following cycle it should take. The systems chart should give a complete picture of what is to be done.

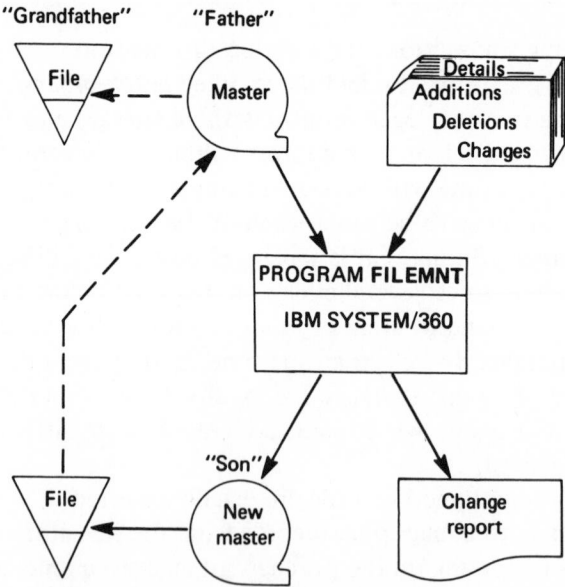

FIG. 27-1 File maintenance systems chart.

When a master file is to be used with a detail file, the master is generally called *primary*, since it is to be read first, and the detail is called *secondary*. On many jobs there will be exactly one primary record for each secondary record; on others there may be only one primary record, but several secondaries, with the same control field. It is possible to have several primaries with that same control field, but for most applications, *multiple primaries* are not allowed. It is not likely that an item in inventory will have two "on-hand" cards, nor is it likely that you would have two different accounts open with one store. It is likely, however, that you make several purchases or payments during each period, and so *multiple secondaries* are quite common. By the use of the grandfather method of tape cycling, each file maintenance or updating run starts with an *old master* file and some transactions, and produces a *new master* file. During a file maintenance run, the additions, deletions, and changes are usually printed in a *change report*; unusual activity of any type can be detected during this run and can be listed in an *exception report*. During a file updating run, however, such as accounts payable or accounts receivable, a *production report* is usually produced, such as statements that must be prepared or checks written. Although it is possible to do both these types of run in one pass through the computer, it is more common for maintenance to produce a new file and a change report, which is then thoroughly checked before statements are produced or checks written based on the new file.

To illustrate file maintenance wherein a change report is written, a file of master student records at a college will be used. The file requires maintenance at the beginning of each semester in order to remove former students, to add entering students, and to change the records for some of the returning students. Figure 27-2 shows some of the alternatives that could occur on such a file maintenance job. There should be a record identification code to represent whether an *addition*, a *deletion*, or a *change* is requested. The matching record indicator can be used to aid in determining which of these is being done.

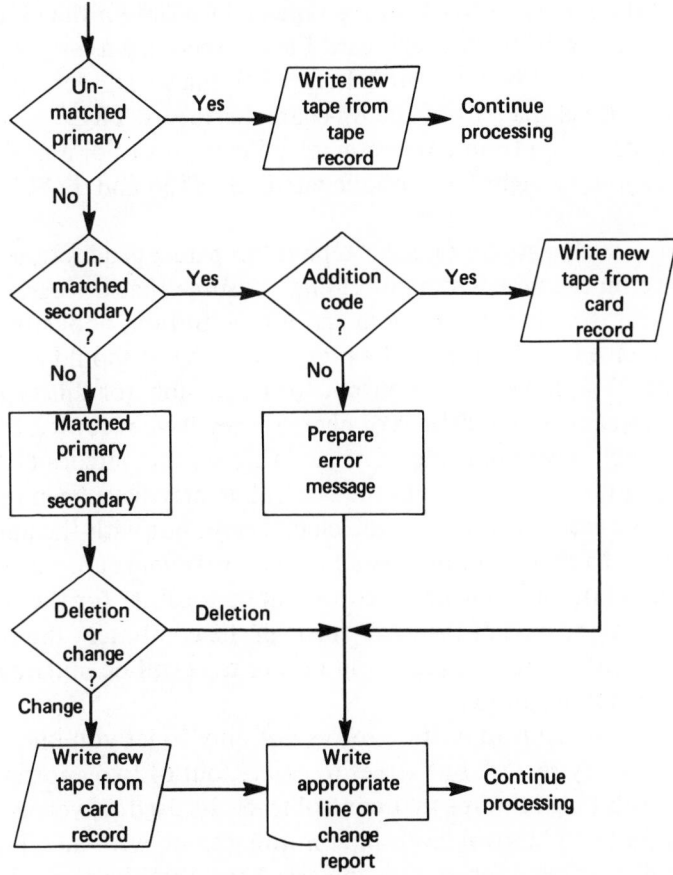

FIG. 27-2 Alternatives in file maintenance.

PROBLEM DEFINITION: *Write a program that will accept a master tape file of student records and make changes in the records as determined by a card deck of changes. Deletions and additions will not be done in this same program at this time. The master file is in 80-character records, 800 characters in a block. The records are stored in ascending order by social security number. The record to be changed is punched exactly as it is to be placed on the magnetic tape file, with information that is not being changed also punched; the card record should then be placed onto the new master file instead of the old record found on the tape master. The card deck is sorted in ascending order by social security number. Produce a change report, giving both the old record and the new one that replaced it. Should an invalid detail record be detected, give notice about it on the change report.*

The flow chart given in Figure 27-2 illustrates the logic needed for a program that would handle changes, additions, and deletions. This problem is defined to do changes only, not additions and deletions; therefore, you need follow only the part that refers to changes. The following conditions could arise: *a matched primary and secondary*, representing a record that should be changed—place the card record onto the new master tape instead of the one from the old master tape; *an unmatched primary*, representing an old master tape record that needs no changes—place the old master tape record onto the new master; *an unmatched secondary*, representing a request for a change to an old master tape record that is *not* found on the old master file—give a message about that on the change report, so that investigation can be made.

The program to accomplish this type of file maintenance, as run on the IBM SYSTEM/360, DOS, is shown in Figure 27-3. There are two input files—the tape and the cards—and two output files—the tape and the report. **TNUM** on the tape and **CNUM** on the card are assigned M1 matching fields indication; both the tape and card file are specified as ascending sequence on the **FILE DESCRIPTION** form. Notice that columns 1-9, the social security number, are multiply defined, since they are also a part of the 80-character record **TREC** and **CREC**. Records going onto the new master come from either a matched card record or a nonmatched tape record. Control cards should assign the symbolic names **SYS008** and **SYS009** to tape units 180 and 181, respectively.

A job that might use such a student master tape to prepare a production report and to update the master balance on the tape is student billing. Assume that the parents of students are billed several times a year, for charges for room and board, tuition, bookstore, laundry, and so on. If any previous balance is unpaid from the previous billing, it should also be included in the current bill. Figure 27-4 shows sample output forms possible for this type of job. Each department on campus prepares source listings of charges they have recorded for students; from these source listings, punch cards are made. The cards are sent in batches to the data processing department. Meanwhile, payments from the last billing may have been received, so a payment card is prepared in a manner similar to the charge card, but with the amount field negative, representing a *credit* to that account. Detail cards for students are sorted into sequence by student number so that all of one student's records will be together for the run. Two things will be accomplished with one pass of the cards through the computer—the statements will be made to send to the student's parent, and the old master tape will be updated to reflect the new balance at the end of the billing period.

Recall that the matching fields indication serves not only to let you know when the primary record matches the secondary record, but serves to create, out of two entering files, one. Since file updating for student billing requires that control levels be used as well as matching records, it is essential to remember that control levels have nothing to do with matching the records from the two files. It does often happen, as is the case here, that the same field is used for matching as for control level! Control break must be detected in the file updating job for student billing so that one student's record can be completed, with total line and output tape record, before going on to do the heading for the next statement.

these records on a tape

125863526	KROLL, EDMOND	2 STONEGATE COURT	RENTON, WASH.	98055235EDK M
175321986	ALVERSON, JUDY	384 WESTEND BLVD.	HURON, KANSAS	67112254AES M
198210189	DAVIDOFF, HERMAN	1934 FRANKLIN ST.	MONROE, LA.	71201145AER M
213456743	BERNARD, CHARLES	RT. 1, BOX 753	SHREVEPORT, LA.	71109417XEQ M
214536585	THOMPSON, RALPH	1752 EL CAJON BLVD.	SAN DIEGO, CALIF.	92104412INV M
231456285	GERVICK, CLIFTON	1057 MASS AVE.	CAMBRIDGE, MASS.	02139532IBN M
235684563	PATTERSON, MICHAEL	1742 RIDGE RD.	TOWSON, MD.	21204213DEF M
352146285	GRADEN, BEN	2528 N. PRESTON	BALTO, MD.	21210235BDP M
356258456	MYERBERG, CLAUD	3945 GREENMOUNT	BALTO, MD.	21213282DDA M
512814592	JOHNSON, AMY	P.O.BOX 714	OGDENSBURG, NY	13669312DAR M
536285678	HANNA, PRESTON	573 CURRIE LANE	PIONEER, LA.	71266325KIR M
563245782	SCHOTZ, SIGMOND	8833 E. MONUMENT	BALTO, MD.	21211251DEC M
731461492	EVERS, EMMELINE	341 BALTO NTL PIKE	BALTO, MD.	21229197BDP M

put through this program with records for changes

produce these updated records on a new tape

and this report

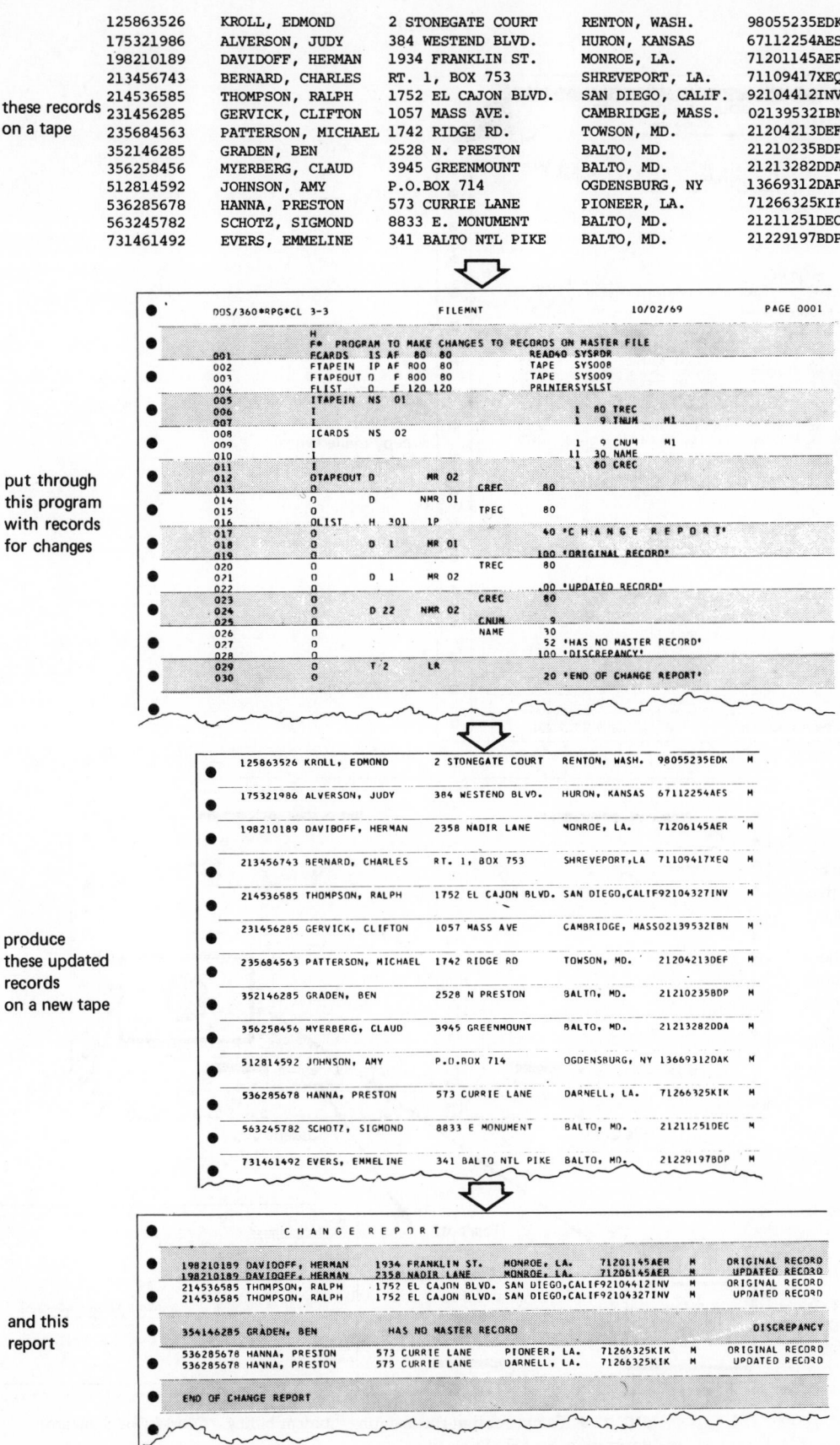

FIG. 27-3 Program **FILEMNT** for changes—IBM SYSTEM/36Ø, DOS.

373

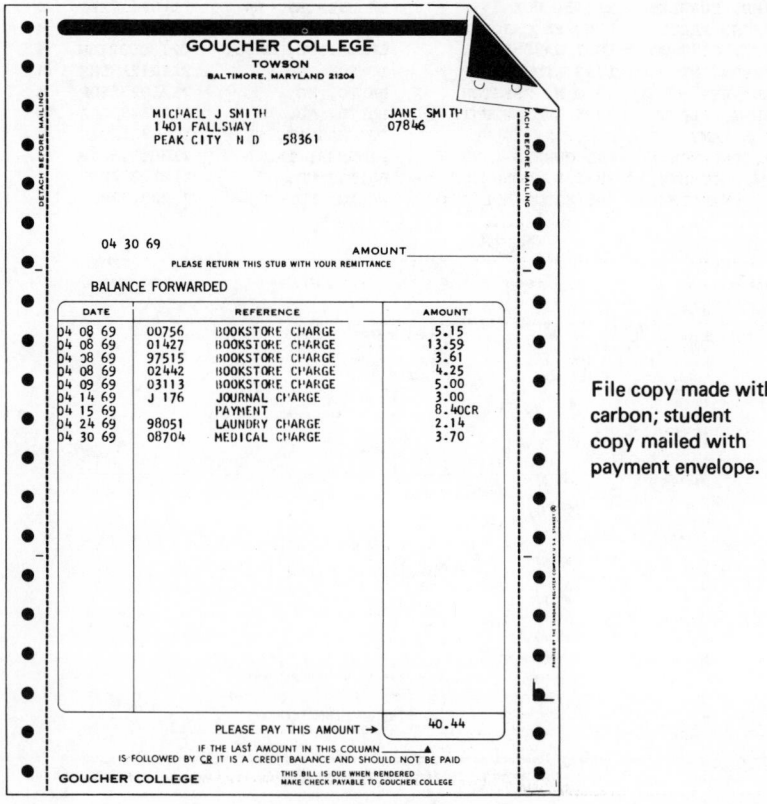

File copy made with
carbon; student
copy mailed with
payment envelope.

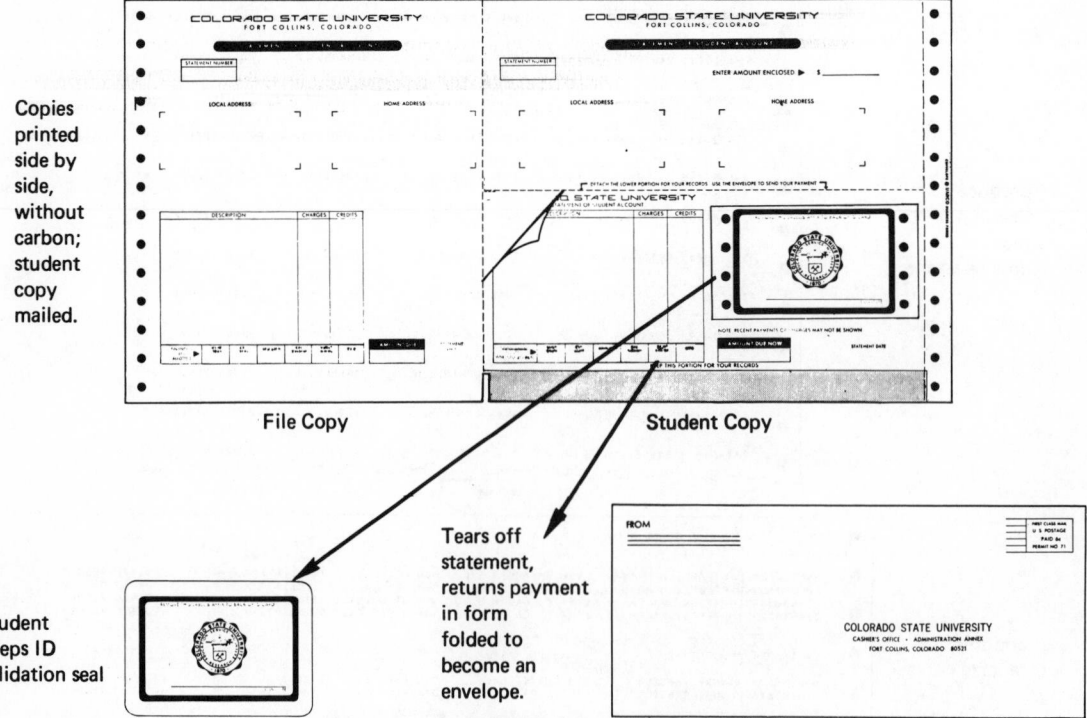

Copies
printed
side by
side,
without
carbon;
student
copy
mailed.

File Copy   Student Copy

Tears off
statement,
returns payment
in form
folded to
become an
envelope.

Student
keeps ID
validation seal

FIG. 27-4 Sample output-file updating—student billing. (Courtesy of Standard
Register Co., and UARCO, Inc.)

File updating of this type can be done with two card files when equipment permits, with two tape files, or with a tape and a card file; all these are considered multiple-file jobs, since more than one file is entering the computer. When done with a single file of merged master/ detail records, however, the job is *not* considered a multiple-file job; therefore, matching record indicators are not used. Figure 27-5 shows a comparison between a file update using a merged deck of master/detail cards and that of a multiple-file tape and card update job. In both dia-

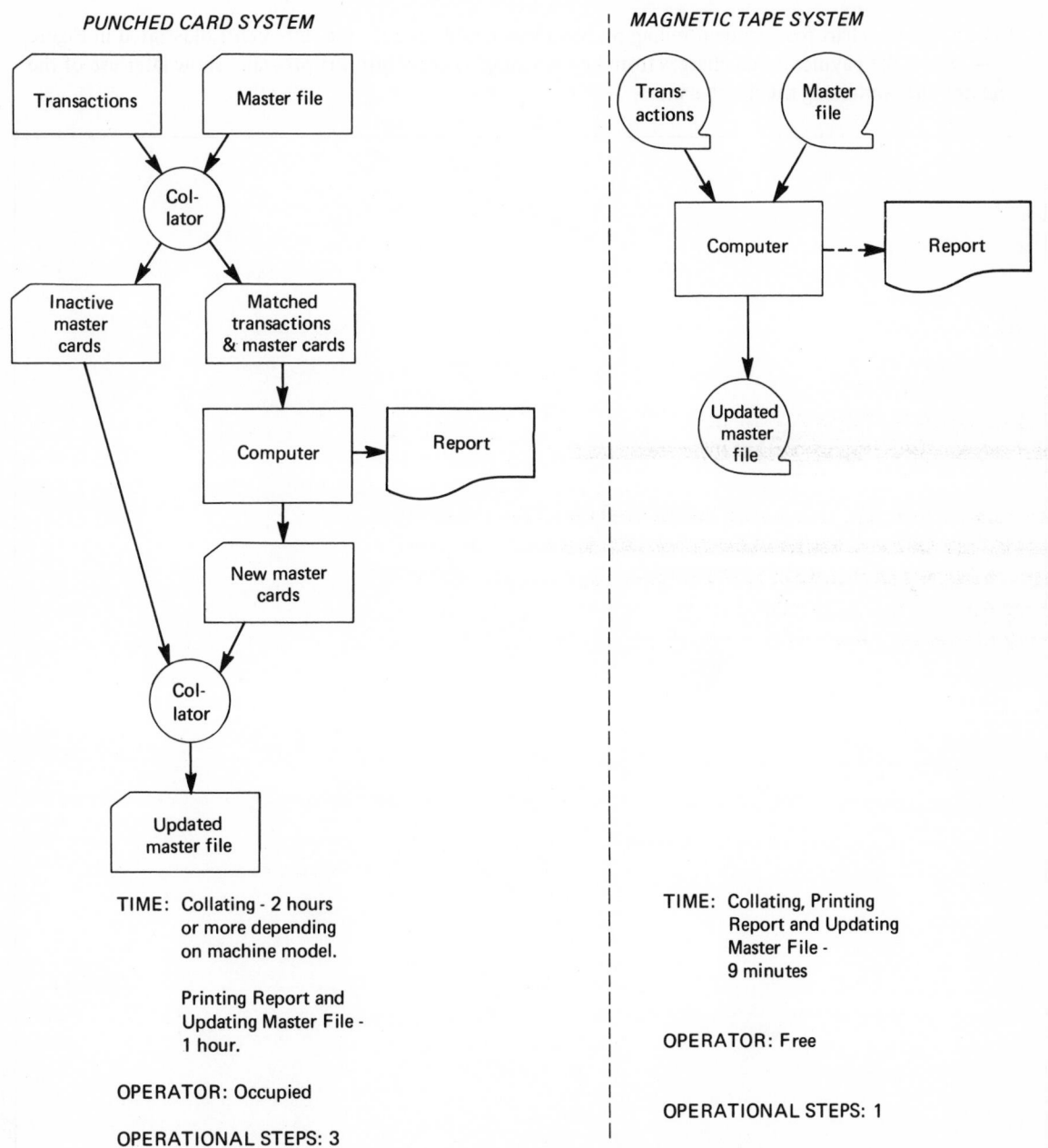

FIG. 27-5   Report generation and file updating—tape file versus card file. (© 1968, Sperry Rand Corp. Reproduced by permission of UNIVAC Division, Sperry Rand Corp.)

grams, it is assumed that the transaction file is about 8ØØØ records, representing about 5ØØØ different items, and that the master file is about 5Ø,ØØØ records. You will note that not only does the tape system do the complete run in approximately 9 minutes as compared to 2 hours, but it permits less handling of records, which may eliminate many costly errors.

EXERCISES

1. Make a systems chart for a student billing problem that could produce the statements illustrated in Figure 27-4. Show the payments and charges from keypunching to entry into the program; show later use of the updated file containing the new balances.

2. Write **CALCULATIONS** specifications for each, assuming the master record to use indicator 51 and the detail record to use indicator 52.

    (a) Each inactive master account should be checked to ensure that its master balance is zero. If so, turn on indicator 15; otherwise, turn it off.

    (b) The account number of each invalid detail record that does not match the master record is to be checked against a table **TABNUM** to see whether it is present there; if so, turn on indicator 29, if not, turn it off.

    (c) Each detail record that matches the master record must be checked to be sure that the number of days before delivery, given by **NDEL** on the detail record, is more than the number of days needed for delivery, given by **NSHP** on the master record. If so, turn on indicator 21; if not, turn it off.

    (d) Each detail record is an inventory issue card, containing the number for the item that is to be subtracted from the number-on-hand given by the master record for that item. If there is enough on hand, subtract the requested number from the number-on-hand and turn on indicator 99. If exactly $\emptyset$ of that item is left after the subtraction, turn on indicator 75. If there is not enough left on hand to do the subtraction, do not do it, but turn off indicators 99 and 75.

Line	Form Type	Control Level (L0-L9, LR)	Indicators And Not	And Not	And Not	Factor 1	Operation	Factor 2	Result Field	Field Length	Decimal Positions	Half Adjust (H)	Resulting Indicators Plus High 1>2	Minus Low 1<2	Zero or Blank Equal 1=2
0 1	C	(a)													
0 2	C														
0 3	C	(b)													
0 4	C														
0 5	C														
0 6	C														
0 7	C	(c)													
0 8	C														
0 9	C														
1 0	C	(d)													
1 1	C														
1 2	C														
1 3	C														
1 4	C														
1 5	C														
	C														
	C														
	C														
	C														
	C														

Section 9

PROGRAMS TO WRITE

A. PROGRAM NAME: **SHPLBLS**: print shipping labels
Write a program to make four shipping labels for each specified customer, using
adhesive labels, four-up across the form. The customer numbers are given in a deck
of cards, one number per card; each one should be matched to its proper record on
the master tape to get the correct name and address information for the labels.

	Field Information	*Columns*
On cards	Customer account number Record identification code: S	1-6 8Ø
On tape	Account number Account name Street address City and state Zip code	1-6 11-3Ø 31-5Ø 51-7Ø 71-75

B. PROGRAM NAME: **MERGE**: create a merged master/detail file from tape and cards
Write a program to read records from a master tape file and from a detail card file,
and merge them into one tape output file. Use social security number from columns
1-9 on both input files as the key field, with columns 1-8Ø of each record handled as
a unit. Should any invalid detail records be encountered, they should not be placed
onto the output tape, but should be listed onto a discrepancy report on the printer,
with appropriate headings. Make a systems chart for the job.

C. PROBLEM NAME: **BNDREQ**: test bond requests against master records
A bond deduction plan is contemplated. Each employee who has requested that
a certain number of bonds be deducted from his paycheck must have his records
examined to see whether that amount can be deducted from his check, leaving
what he considers the minimum check amount acceptable to him. Write a program
to access the master tape records, get his hourly rate of pay and number of hours
worked weekly, and calculate the paycheck amount *before* and *after* bond deduction. If the amount after deduction is equal to or more than his minimum check
amount, then his deduction will be approved; if not, it will be denied. Prepare a
report with appropriate headings, giving employee number and name, paycheck
amount *before* deduction, amount of deduction, paycheck amount *after* deduction,
minimum amount, and whether or not the deduction is accepted or denied.

	Field Information	*Columns*
On cards	Employee number Bond deduction code: Ø-9; $18.75 each Minimum check amount, 2 decimals	1-4 11 15-2Ø
On tape	Employee number Employee name Rate of pay per hour Regular hours per week Record ID code: 6	4-7 9-28 42-44 38-39 6

D. PROBLEM NAME: **TAPESCH:** search for certain zip codes

A letter is to be sent to every account customer who lives in a certain zip code area, with continuous-form envelopes to be used for mailing. Every record on tape that has that zip code should be used to make an address for an envelope. Either put the zip code search argument into a punch card to be read through the card reader, or use it as a constant in your program. Assume sequence is by social security number.

	Field Information	Columns
On tape	Account number	1-6
	Account name	11-3∅
	Street address	31-5∅
	City and state	51-7∅
	Zip code	71-75
	Month of last transaction	77-78

E. PROBLEM NAME: **ACCTTRDT:** search for inactive accounts

Write a program to list the names and addresses of all accounts that have not had transactions during the last six monthly billing periods. The number of the month of their last transaction is contained on the tape record, which is in ascending order by account number. The month number should be compared to the month number of the date of this run, taken either from a run-date card or from **UDATE**, or given as a constant in the program. At the end of the job, give the total number of names on the list. Use tape records as given for Problem D above.

F. PROBLEM NAME: **ADDROP:** file maintenance with additions and deletions

Make a systems chart and write a program that will read a master tape and a detail file of additions and deletions to be made to the file; make a new file reflecting those changes, giving a change report. Assume that both files are in ascending order, by student number, in columns 1-9. Let the addition card contain an A in column 8∅ but change to an M as it is placed onto the new tape. Let the deletion card contain a D in column 8∅. Use record size 8∅, block size 8∅∅, and no labels.

G. PROBLEM NAME: **STUBILL:** student billing from master tape, detail cards

Write a program to prepare statements to send to the parents of students, as shown in Figure 27-4. Each file is in ascending sequence by student social security number; there are perhaps several detail cards for each student. Totals of all charges, credits, old balances, and new balances should be given at the end of the job.

	Field Information	Columns
On tape	Social security number	1-9
	Student name	11-25
	Parent name	26-45
	Parent street address	46-55
	City, state	56-65
	Zip code	66-7∅
	Old balance, 2 decimals	75-8∅
On cards	Social security number	1-9
	Description of transaction	11-3∅
	Reference number for transaction	31-36
	Transaction date, to be edited	41-46
	Amount of this transaction, 2 decimals, negative for a payment or credit, positive for a charge	56-6∅

SECTION 10

REPORTS WITH BRANCHING

Lesson 28

BRANCHES AND LOOPS

You will learn how to use branching to control program steps and to form loops for repetitive calculations.

The questions below summarize branching techniques. If you have not had experience with branching in other programming languages, study the lesson thoroughly before attempting to answer the following questions.

1. What does *branching* mean?
2. What is the difference between an *unconditional* and a *conditional* branch?
3. What RPG instruction is used to cause a branch to occur?
4. How is the *destination* of a branch instruction identified?
5. Why is a **TAG** often needed at the bottom of all detail-time instructions?
6. What is the difference in purpose of *branching forward* from that of *branching back*?
7. What is a *loop*?
8. How does the programmer control the *termination* of a loop?
9. What is meant by *iteration*?
10. What kinds of problems can be done in RPG with looping that could not be done without it?

383

ANSWERS

1. Causing deviations from the normal sequential execution of the instructions by telling the computer to go elsewhere for its next instruction.

2. An unconditional branch is one that is *always* executed, such as a **GOTO**, which has no indicators conditioning it. A conditional branch is not always executed since it *depends* on something, such as conditioning indicators.

3. The **GOTO** instruction, which goes under OPERATION; FACTOR 2 specifies the place where control should go next.

4. By the *name*, as given in the **GOTO**, in FACTOR 1, and **TAG** under OPERATION, both placed on the line above the instruction that should be done when the branch occurs.

5. Because for some record types, certain calculations should perhaps be bypassed. The **TAG** can be used as the destination for the **GOTO** instruction causing the bypass.

6. Branching forward is used to select the set of specific program instructions that are to be done, based on field conditions or record-type. Branching *backward* allows repetition of program steps already executed, to form a loop.

7. The instructions that are repeated by a *branch backward* to a point in the program already executed. The repetition of these instructions is usually controlled by a counter or by one of the fields being calculated in the loop.

8. By testing a counter for a certain value, and changing the indicator to cause the loop to terminate; or by examining fields within the loop to cause the loop to terminate.

9. Finding an answer by a looping technique, which converges to the required answer by successive passes through the loop.

10. Compound interest, exponentials, square roots, sums and products of sequences, infinite series, and factorials.

Lesson 28   Branches and Loops

Programs involving tests and comparisons may require quite a few indicators to control the calculations and output. Although the RPG INDICATOR SUMMARY form does help you to keep track of those in use, an extremely complicated program may be difficult to follow logically, and can become completely unbearable when attempting to put modifications into it. To help relieve the complications that arise when using many indicators, *branching* is often used to direct the execution of the calculations in the program. Branching not only causes the program to use less core storage, but also makes it more readable, which is especially helpful later when changes to it are requested. Since branching is controlled by indicators, it may be based on such things as record-type, field contents, or control breaks. Calculations in RPG are ordinarily examined in sequence, with conditions for each one tested to see whether or not it should be executed. Branching can be used to break the sequence, causing routines unique to certain conditions to be executed *only* on those conditions, and bypassed otherwise. It can be used to cause alternate calculations to be done at certain points in the program, with the main calculation queue reentered at a later point. Instructions already executed can even be repeated, causing a *loop*. A branch is *conditional* when it sends control to one place at one time, but to a different place, perhaps, at another. If a branch always occurs to the same place each time, it is *unconditional*.

To tell the computer to branch out of its normal sequence of calculations, the **GOTO** instruction is used; to identify the place to which branching should go, the **TAG** is used. The **GOTO** and **TAG** are used together to create different logical paths through the calculations given on the CALCULATION specifications form.

The **GOTO** is placed under OPERATION in columns 28-32 of the CALCULATION form. FACTOR 2 is used to tell where to go to next, by name. The name, known as a *label* or *tag*, is assigned to a set of instructions, usually elsewhere in the program. The name must start with an alphabetic letter and be six characters or less in length. The name of a routine for handling a new master card might be, for example, **NEWMAS**, for new master, or **MSTRTN**, for master routine. The instruction given by

Line	Form Type	Control Level (L0-L9, LR)	Indicators And Not	And Not	And Not	Factor 1	Operation	Factor 2	Result Field	Field Length	Decimal Positions	Half Adjust (H)
3 4 5	6	7 8	9 10 11	12 13 14	15 16 17	18 19 20 21 22 23 24 25 26 27	28 29 30 31 32	33 34 35 36 37 38 39 40 41 42	43 44 45 46 47 48	49 50 51	52 53
0 1	C		Ø7				GOTO	REGPAY				

causes, when indicator Ø7 is *on*, branching to a set of instructions named **REGPAY**. The place to which the branch should occur is given a tag line for identification by putting the name under FACTOR 1, and the word **TAG** under OPERATION. The line given by

	For	Con	And Not	And Not	And Not						Deci	Half
3 4 5	6	7 8	9 10 11	12 13 14	15 16 17	18 19 20 21 22 23 24 25 26 27	28 29 30 31 32	33 34 35 36 37 38 39 40 41 42	43 44 45 46 47 48	49 50 51	52 53	
0 1	C					REGPAY	TAG					
0 2	C											
0 3	C											

385

identifies the lines that follow as a routine named **REGPAY**. **TAG** serves only to identify the *position* of the following instruction; it does not itself generate any action during execution of the program. If the tag is needed in total-time calculations, control level must be given in columns 7 and 8 of the line. Should those columns be left blank, the tag will be placed with detail-time calculations. On a **TAG** operation line, columns 9-17 should not contain indicator numbers. Some implementations will allow them to be there, but should you attempt to branch to the instruction and those indicators are *not* satisfied, it may be impossible to complete the branch, leaving the program in an internal loop exasperatingly difficult to debug.

The selection of calculations may be based on the contents of fields, since field indicators or resulting indicators may be used to condition the **GOTO** instruction. Figure 28-1 illustrates one method of calculating payroll in which overtime hours require that additional calculations be done. Should the number of hours worked be more than 4∅, overtime pay for all hours over 4∅ will be earned at 1 1/2 times the regular pay rate. Should the field be 4∅ hours or less, the overtime routine is bypassed by a branch to **JUMP**. Note that both types of cards go through the regular pay routine tagged by **JUMP**. Should the overtime routine be done, however, the **JUMP** routine calculates regular pay only for *4∅* hours, rather than for the original amount of time, and adds it to the previously calculated overtime pay.

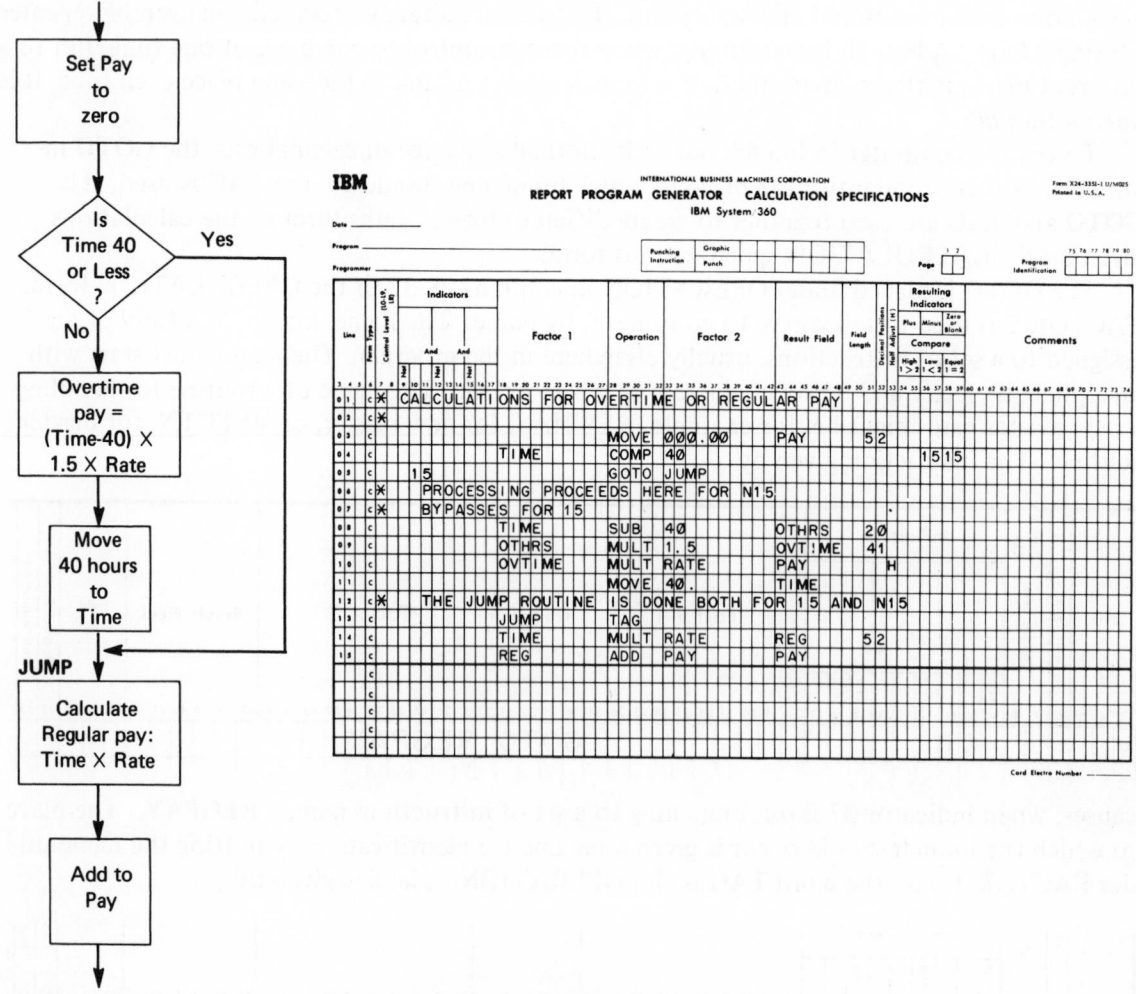

FIG. 28-1 Branching to bypass.

Should two completely different sets of instructions be needed for two conditions, a branch will prevent the calculations of *both* routines, allowing only *one* of them to be executed. A **TAG** identifies the first line of each set. Should the first of the routines be executed, the following one must be jumped. A **TAG** may be given as the last calculation line on the form, and used as a place to go when jumping over other routines. Branching can be made to the last line, usually called **END** or **LAST**, to bypass all other calculations on the page. Processing then continues with the next logical routine in the RPG object program cycle.

Figure 28-2 shows, on a flow chart segment, two completely different paths of calculations. If the **AMT** field is bigger than $500.00, the routine for **HIGH** is done; otherwise the routine **NOTHI**, for not high, is done. The **HIGH** routine uses as discount 10% of the first $500.00 of **AMT**, which is $50.00, plus 3% of all over $500.00; **NOTHI** uses a flat 7% of **AMT** as the discount amount. The **GOTO** and **TAG** shown on the CALCULATION specification form cause branching to the proper place. Notice that the tag **END** is at the bottom of all other calculations. The **GOTO END** immediately ahead of it is *not* necessary, since **END** is the next line, but the unconditional **GOTO END** on line 1ØØ *is* necessary, to prevent the **HIGH** routine from also doing the **NOTHI** one immediately after. Line Ø3Ø, giving the branch to **HIGH**, could also be omitted, since it is next; control will go there anyway if indicator 12 is *on*.

When several types of records are used in a program, each record-type indicator may be used for branching to a routine unique for that record. Assume that a payroll job requires three different kinds of calculations, one for each of three different types of records—hourly, salary, and production types. Three indicators may be assigned to the three records, such as 7Ø, 8Ø, and 9Ø, respectively. Figure 28-3 shows a flow chart segment and gives branching instructions to send each card type to the proper calculation set. Calculations for hourly employees are shown *without* the possibility for overtime; if overtime is to be included, another branch within that section must be used. Calculation for the pay for salaried employees is done by dividing the monthly salary of each by 4 1/3. Production employees are paid in amounts according to the number of pieces that they produce, by a table look-up method, which is not shown. Notice that after each routine a **GOTO END** causes execution to jump over all other routines. Notice also that a safeguard is built in to halt the system if none of the proper indicators is *on*.

All the branching performed has been to a point *forward* in the list of calculations. Repeating instructions that have *already* been executed can be done, however, by the use of a **GOTO** that refers to an instruction in a line *above* it. As the instructions are repeated, the **GOTO** is *again* reached, causing the instructions to be repeated, again and again, in a *loop*. Should a loop be repeated without any means of exit, it is said to be an *infinite loop*, and will cause the computer never to reach a completion of the job being done. Some way to control exits on loops must be used, such as counting the number of repetitions and making an exit from the loop when a certain number of times has been completed. Processing may continue *forward* then, rather than back. The appropriate **GOTO**, *conditional* on the number of times through the loop, is used.

Calculations of powers of numbers, such as $(1.Ø3)^{15}$, is needed in business on many kinds of financial reports. When the exponent is a whole number, repeated multiplication may be used to calculate powers. When the exponent is large, however, listing the multiplication instructions, one by one, on the CALCULATION form, may take a long time and produce a source program too big to handle! A loop may instead be used to cause *one* multiplication instruction to be executed over and over.

To calculate X^4 in a loop, the multiplication of $X \times X \times X \times X \times X$ is needed. Assume that **X** and **N** are on a data card. Figure 28-4 shows a flow chart and the calculations for X^N, based

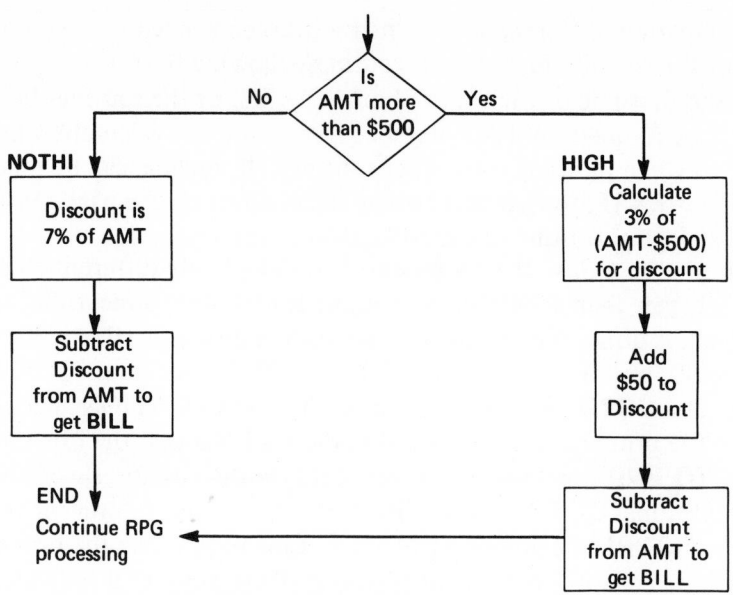

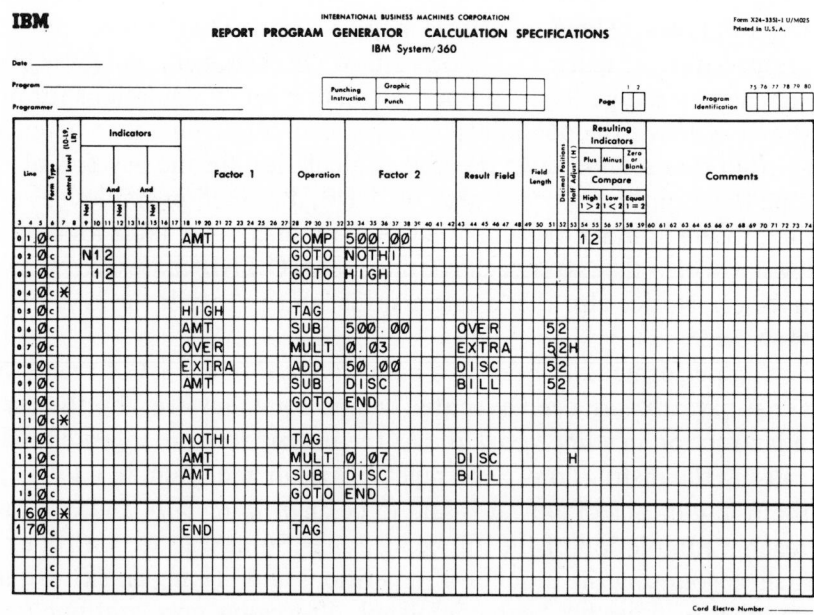

FIG. 28-2 Branching—two alternative paths.

on the use of a product field, **PROD**, which holds the result after each multiplication. Notice that it is initialized to 1, *not* to $\emptyset$, since that would cause the answer to be $\emptyset$ regardless of how many times through the loop it went! The value of **X** from the input data card, is multiplied by **PROD**, and placed back into **PROD**. After each such multiplication, a higher power of **X** is obtained in **PROD**. A counter is used to count each multiplication. When it reaches the predetermined value, it should *stop* the looping process. When it is equal to 4, since X^4 is needed, indicator $1\emptyset$ goes *on*, causing the branch instruction to be bypassed. Processing continues with the next calculation, if one is given, or proceeds to the next logical routine in the RPG object program cycle.

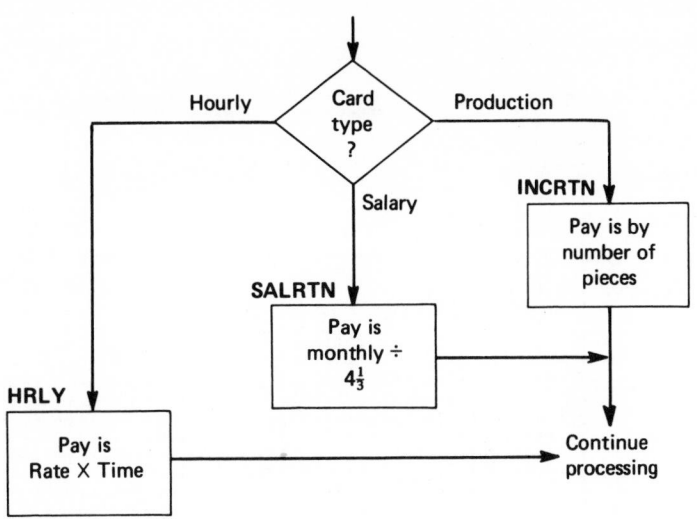

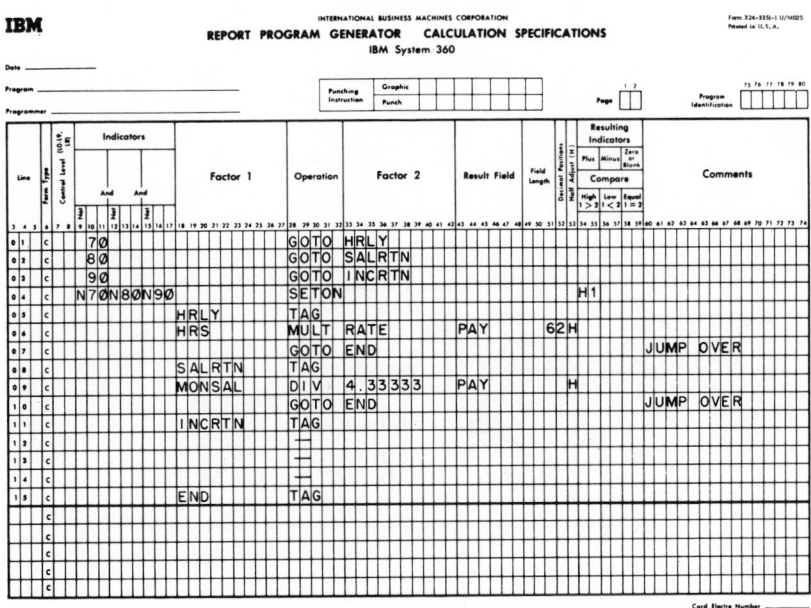

FIG. 28-3 Branching—three alternative paths.

The multiplication of **X** is done with *one* **X** at a time, *not* two. Should an effort be made to multiply two at a time, in a manner such as

```
Set PROD
to 1,
COUNT
to zero
   │
   ▼
Multiply
X by
PROD
   │
   ▼
Add 1
to
COUNT
   │
   ▼
 Is
COUNT ─── No ──┐
 = 4           │
  ?            │
   │ Yes       │
   ▼           │
Continue
processing
```

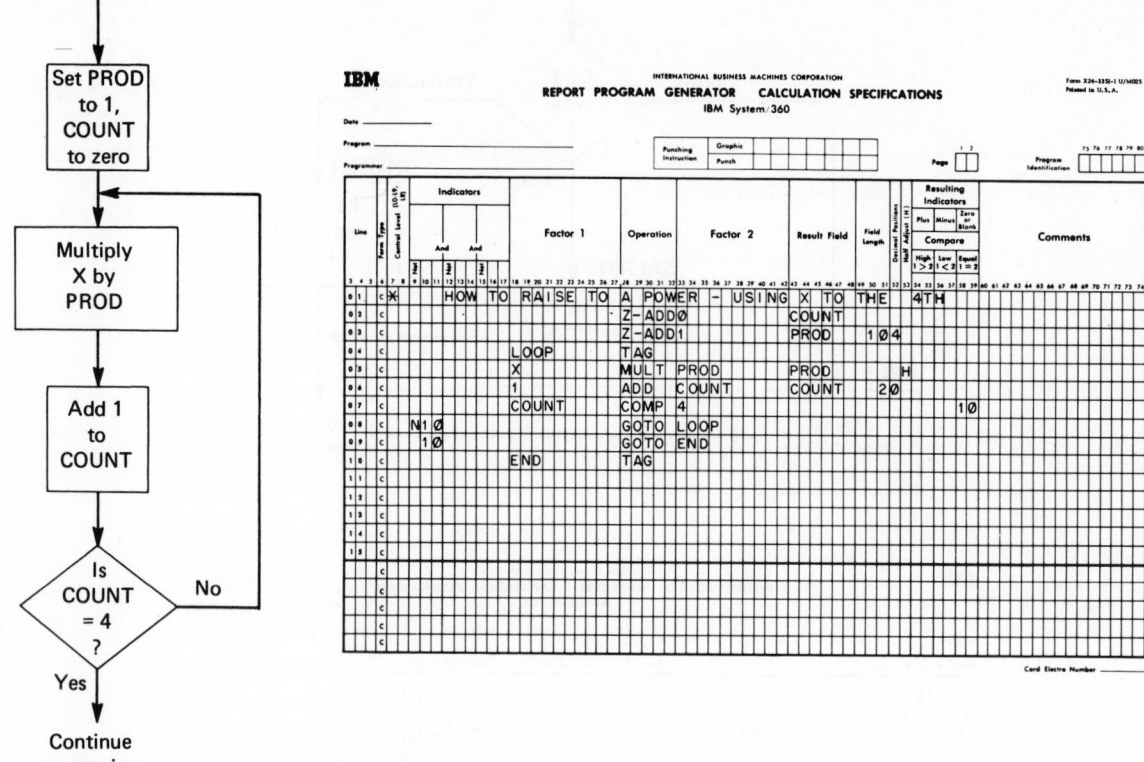

SAMPLE CALCULATION OF X⁴

let X be 1.03:

COUNT	X	PROD=1	
1	1.03	1.0300	
2	1.03	1.0609	
3	1.03	1.092727	rounded 1.0927
4	1.03	1.125487	rounded 1.1255

FIG. 28-4 Branching for a loop.

the value of **PROD** will continually be X^2, no matter how many times through the loop it goes. The value of **PROD** must be made to *accumulate*; therefore, **PROD** must appear in both the RESULT FACTOR and one of the other FACTOR's as well.

Looping techniques can be used to form sums or products of certain sequences. The sum of the odd numbers from 1 to 113, for example, may be calculated in a loop as given by

Form Type	Control Level	And		And			Factor 1	Operation	Factor 2	Result Field	Field Length	Decimal Posit	Half Adjust	Plus Min Com
C								Z-ADD1		K	30			
C								Z-ADD0		SUM	40			
C							AGAIN	TAG						
C							K	ADD	SUM	SUM				
C							K	ADD	2	K				
C							K	COMP	113					25
C	N25							GOTO	AGAIN					

The counter **K** varies by the amount of the numbers in the sequence, in this case, 2, and each time it is added to the previous value of **SUM**.

The number of times through a loop can be controlled not only by a counter, but by some field involved in the calculations. An approximation for a square root can be found by a looping method that is controlled by the number of decimal places needed in the answer. This method of calculation, called *iteration*, causes the answer to be improved by each pass through the loop, until the degree of accuracy that you want is obtained. For example, when two successive answers for the square root of 2 are found to be 1.414 and 1.413, within .$\emptyset\emptyset$5 of each other, the indicator can cause the loop to terminate.

With the aid of looping techniques, sums and products of sequences, compound interest, square roots, factorials, infinite series, and exponentials can all be calculated, extending the power of RPG to enable it to do some of the more mathematical business applications.

EXERCISES

1. Use the CALCULATION form provided to write specifications for these:
   (a) If **BAL** is bigger than $5000.00, go to **LIMIT**; otherwise, go to **OK**.
   (b) If field indicator $\emptyset$7 is *on*, go to **NOGO**, bypassing the instructions that follow.
   (c) If the value of **MONEY** is between $100.00 and $500.00, go to **GOOD**; otherwise go to **NOGOOD**.
   (d) If the value of **K** is 1$\emptyset$, go to **DONE**; otherwise, branch back to **START**.
   (e) If the amount of **BAL** is less than $100.00, but is positive, then charge 1.5% interest as a service charge; otherwise, charge 1.5% of all up to $100.00 and 2% of all over that amount; charge none if **BAL** is negative or zero.

Date _____

Program _____

Programmer _____

Punching Instruction	Graphic						
	Punch						

Page [1 | 2]

Line	Form Type	Control Level (L0-L9, LR)	Indicators And	Not	And	Not	And	Not	Factor 1	Operation	Factor 2	Result Field	Field Length	Decimal Positions	Half Adjust (H)	Plus	Minus	Zero or Blank
0 1	C	(a)																
0 2	C																	
0 3	C																	
0 4	C	(b)																
0 5	C																	
0 6	C	(c)																
0 7	C																	
0 8	C																	
0 9	C																	
1 0	C	(d)																
1 1	C																	
1 2	C																	

3 4 5	6	7 8	9 10 11	12 13 14	15 16 17	18 19 20	21 22 23	24 25 26 27	28	29 30 31	32	33 34	35 36 37	38 39	40 41	42	43 44 45	46 47	48	49 50	51	52	53	54 55	56 57	58 59
1 3	C	ⓔ																									
1 4	C																										
1 5	C																										
	C																										
	C																										
	C																										
	C																										
	C																										

2. What will be calculated as the value of NUM in the example given by the following CALCULATION form?

_____

	FIN	R	FOUT	DIFF	ABS(DIFF)	R + FOUT	$\frac{1}{2}$(R + FOUT)
Pass 1	2.0	2.0	1.0	1.0	1.0	3.0	1.5
Pass 2	2.0	1.5					
Pass 3	2.0						
Pass 4							
Pass 5							
Pass 6							

Lesson 29

BRANCHING FOR LOGIC CHANGE

You will learn to do exception-output either by a branch into total-time or by exception lines.

The following questions are answered on the back of this page. If you have experience in data processing, you may still need to study the chapter before answering the questions about RPG logic changes. When you understand the answers to all the questions, go on to Lesson 30.

1. What is meant by RPG *fixed-program logic*?
2. What logic changes are possible in RPG fixed-program logic?
3. What is meant by *exception-output*?
4. On what types of jobs might *identical* repetitive output be needed?
5. For what purpose might a repetitive output, where each line is based on the previous one, be used?
6. What is meant by a *branch into total-time*?
7. What decisions and actions of RPG are repeated during a branch into total-time?
8. What specifications in the program are given to cause the branch into total-time?
9. Under what conditions is the total-time operation bypassed completely?
10. Describe the different techniques for one-to-one, one-to-many, and many-to-one relation of input to output.

ANSWERS

1. The sequence of decisions and resulting actions taken in the RPG object program, illustrated by the RPG object program logic chart. The programmer has no control over most of the actions on that chart.
2. The programmer may specify a branch from detail-time calculations to total-time calculations, and on some implementations, the reverse.
3. Output specified by an **E** in column 15 of the OUTPUT-FORMAT form, which is executed on the instruction **EXCPT**, listed either with detail-time or total-time calculations. This type of output can be done by using branching into total time, but when done by that method, the lines are not labeled **E** for exception, but **T** for total, lines.
4. Production of identical mailing labels, stickers for putting on folders, and duplicating many of one input card.
5. Construction of tables for depreciation, sales tax, discount rates, or any formula, or partial answers to powers of numbers, terms in an infinite series, and sequence numbering of punch cards.
6. A change in logic to cause the total-time calculations and all program steps after to be repeated from a certain point.
7. Part, or all, of total-time calculations, total-time output, test for last record, overflow output, setting of matching record indicator, and moving of data fields.
8. A **GOTO** with the name of a label as FACTOR 2, given in detail-time calculations; and a **TAG** for that label given in total-time calculations.
9. During the first pass at the beginning of the program; before any specified control break actually occurs; when a branch from total-time into detail-time is specified; and anytime the conditions on total-time calculations are not satisfied, or line conditions on total-time output are not met.
10. One-to-one is the basic data processing cycle—input, calculation, output—that is normal for RPG. Many-to-one, used in *group printing*, can be accomplished by omitting all detail-time output lines. One-to-many, used to produce repetitive output, can be accomplished by a branch to total-time.

RPG has a fixed-program-logic cycle, which generally is in effect to control the execution of all object programs. Unlike other programming languages such as COBOL and FORTRAN, RPG does not allow the programmer to control the timing of the reading of input data. Output records, although under programmer control by the use of indicators, are output by RPG at fixed times in the cycle, normally either at detail-time or at total-time, but, when necessary, at overflow-time. A deviation from this fixed-program-logic cycle, called *exception output*, can be done to prepare certain types of reports which cannot be accomplished with the basic data processing cycle. It is important to understand the basic fixed-program-logic cycle before attempting to use exception output.

The complete logic chart for RPG TOS/DOS, given in the Appendix and in the reference manual, shows the sequence of decisions and events that occur within the RPG object program. The basic flow of the cycle is shown in simplified form in Figure 29-1. As you can see from these two charts, detail and heading output is done *before* any cards are read in. Afterwards, the basic cycle is performed repeatedly—read a record, process it, print a line—until the end-of-file condition is detected. The total-time processing loop, bypassed completely the first time through the program and before the first of specified control breaks, is called into action at other times by the presence of a satisfied L-indicator on calculations, or by total-time output lines that have conditions satisfied. Overflow output is done only when needed, and is completely bypassed when no overflow indicators are specified on output lines. Notice that overflow-time output, if any, is done on this implementation *after* total-time output is completed, with the total-time overflow lines done *before* detail-time overflow lines.

The basic data processing cycle—*input, processing, output*—is done by the fixed-program-logic, but in a different order—*output, input, processing.* This accomplishes the same result, yet allows the output portion to be used to produce headings at the beginning of a report, before the input portion is reached. After input comes processing, followed by output. The basic data processing cycle usually causes each detail record to produce one detail output line.

It is quite normal in RPG for the output portion of the cycle to be suppressed under certain conditions. In a program that is to produce a *group-printed* report, for example, no detail lines are specified at all. Output is done only at the control break, giving group totals calculated over a group of cards. This application of the cycle has *many* records brought in for *one* output line, in contrast to the more common *one-to-one* relationship.

Many jobs to be done by the computer require the reverse—*one* data record producing *many* output lines. The fields from one card, for example, can be separated so that they appear on different lines of the report. Many times, however, the same line or group of lines needs to be produced many times; in other cases, each line must vary somewhat from the previous one by a further calculation. This type of output, called *exception output*, represents a change in the object program logic normally executed by RPG. In RPG II and on implementations which have the RPG "extensions", special output lines, coded with an E in column 15 of the OUTPUT-FORMAT form, will be printed out during calculation time by the instruction **EXCPT**. After the printing is done, control is automatically returned to the calculation line following the **EXCPT**. The **EXCPT** instruction may be conditioned by indicators, and may appear either in total-time or in detail-time calculations. Should **EXCPT** be in a loop, repetitive output of identical or similar nature can occur as often as the loop permits. Consult

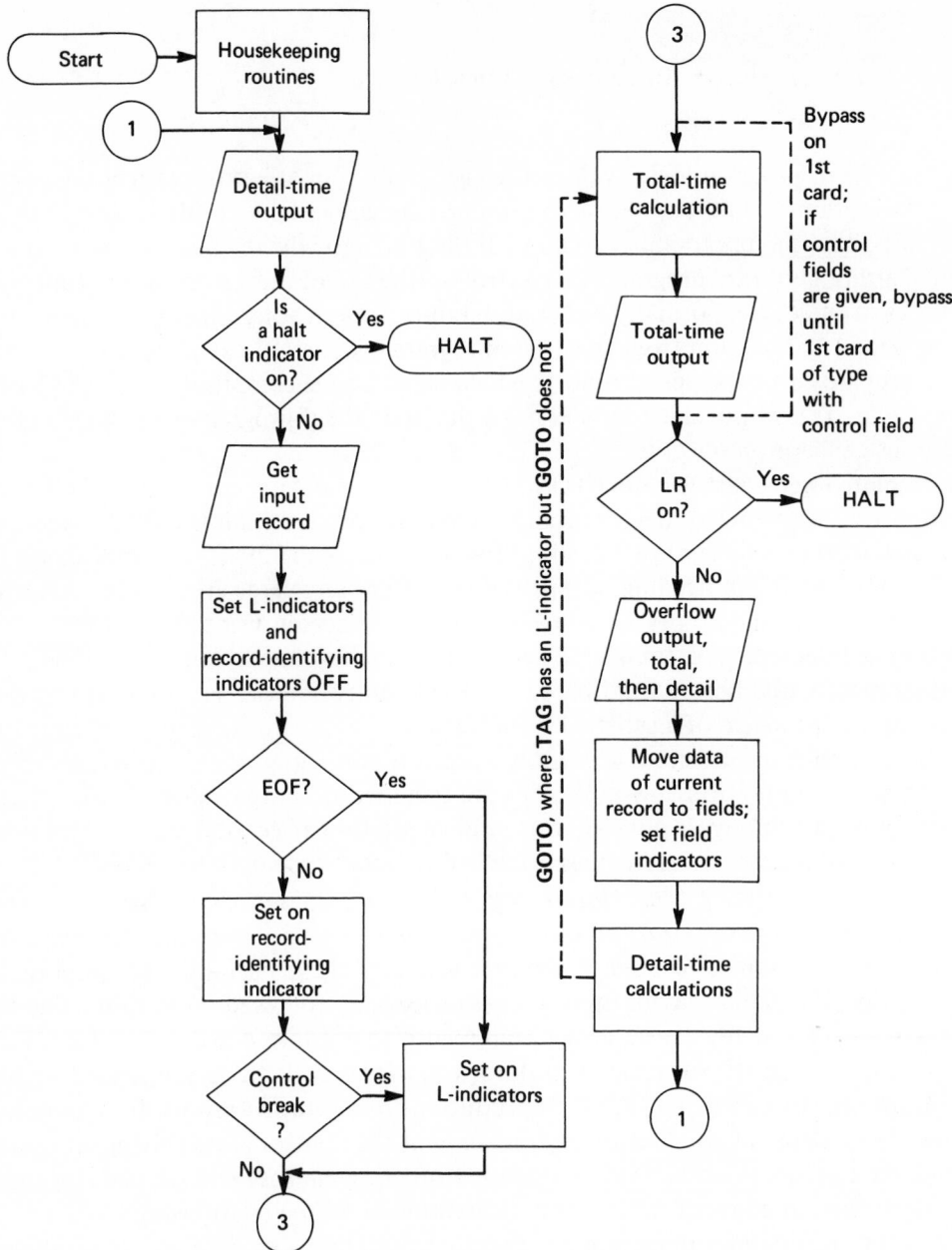

FIG. 29-1 RPG object program logic showing branch from detail-time to total-time.

the reference manual for your computer system, or the Appendix, to determine whether or not you will be able to use this feature.

When exception lines are not permitted on a particular implementation, the programmer can accomplish the same result by causing a branch from detail-time calculations to total-time calculations, called a *branch into total-time*. A **GOTO** in detail-time calculations may give the name of a label that has its **TAG** in total-time, as given by L∅ or any other L-indicator in columns 7 and 8 on the CALCULATIONS specifications form. This causes an immediate branch *backward* in the program cycle, with corresponding repetition of instructions which have conditions that are satisfied. As shown by the dotted flow line on the logic chart in Figure 29-1, several

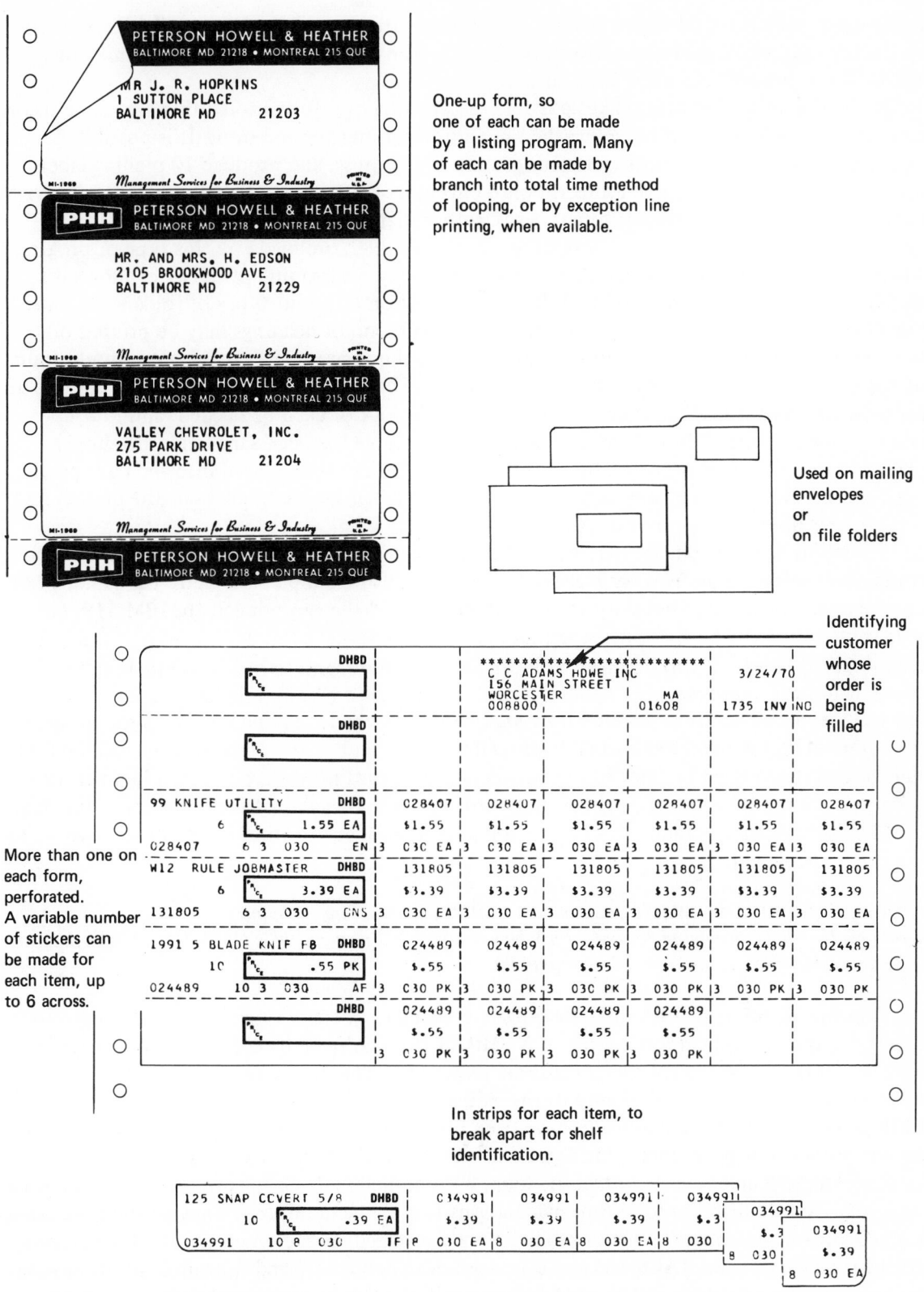

One-up form, so
one of each can be made
by a listing program. Many
of each can be made by
branch into total time method
of looping, or by exception line
printing, when available.

Used on mailing
envelopes
or
on file folders

Identifying
customer
whose
order is
being
filled

More than one on
each form,
perforated.
A variable number
of stickers can
be made for
each item, up
to 6 across.

In strips for each item, to
break apart for shelf
identification.

FIG. 29-2 Label-making with RPG and pressure-sensitive forms. (Courtesy of
Standard Register Co., and Warren Business Forms. (John P. Warren).)

things are repeated: total-time calculations, starting with the one that has the **TAG** specified by the branch; total-time output; overflow output, if any; test for last record; and moving of input data to proper field name locations.

Branching into total-time makes possible the printing of information either from one record or a set of records, without rereading the same information over and over. It is possible, for example, to read one data card, containing name and address, and produce 1∅ mailing labels just alike. These may be placed directly onto envelopes for mailing. Labels may be made with name and address taken from different cards, rather than from one. Many of the different types of adhesive labels, such as those shown in Figure 29-2, are made by this type of program when several of one kind of label are needed. The sticky reverse side of the label allows it to be placed on boxes as a shipping label, for example, or on different types of folders for filing purposes. Preprinted information may be already on them, or headings may be printed on them by the computer. Labels with *one* frame in a column are said to be *one-up*; should four of them be side by side, they are said to be *four-up*. The type of program necessary for one-up forms is different from that done on four-up. Should four of each be needed, and *four-up* labels be used, a branch into total-time is not needed, since the necessary fields are simply placed in four different print positions to form the first line, then placed into the next print positions for the next line, and so on. Should *one-up* labels be used, however, the branch into total-time is used to make four of each.

Branching for logic change may be used to duplicate one card several times. Much of the course card information used for registration in a class, for example, is exactly the same; 3∅ of one type may be needed, but only 15 of another. Should the reproducer, the IBM 519, be used, much time will be spent because that machine, given one card, duplicates one and given two, duplicates two. From that four you can get four more, and so on! It is much more efficient to have a *program* that takes one card, and makes a certain number—perhaps 5∅ one time, and 12∅ another. Exactly *how many* are to be made may be built into the program as a numeric literal, but a more flexible program would result if the number were specified on a *run-control card* placed in front of the data deck. This card must have a record identification code to distinguish it from the regular data cards; some knowledge of the contents of the data card being duplicated is required so that a unique record identification code can be assigned to the run-control card.

PROBLEM DEFINITION: *Write a program named DUP∅1 to duplicate any number of each data card. A header card, with a C in column 8∅, will specify how many should be made, in columns 1-3. Assume that the cards in the data deck do not have a C in column 8∅.*

Run-sheets in Figure 29-3 show the program **DUP∅1**. A letter C in column 8∅ is used to detect the run-control card; the value of **NUMBER** is taken from its columns 1-3; it specifies how *many* of each of the following cards are requested. The data card, recognized by the *absence* of the letter C in column 8∅, turns indicator ∅1 on. The counter named **NUM** keeps track of how many of the duplicates have been made. The counter is incremented as processing proceeds through the total-time loop, until it reaches the number given by **NUMBER**. Indicators 99 and 98 are used to control the loop, with branching back to total-time occuring when 99 is *on*. Even though the total-time calculations follow the detail-time ones on the CALCU-LATION form, their relative positions are actually reversed, as shown on the RPG object program logic chart. Since **BACK** has an L∅ indication in columns 7 and 8, control reverts to that point. Since no total-time instructions follow the **TAG**, total-time output is done next, at which time the duplication of the card is done. When indicator 98 goes *on*, the instruction **GOTO END** is executed and the loop terminates, after which another card is brought in.

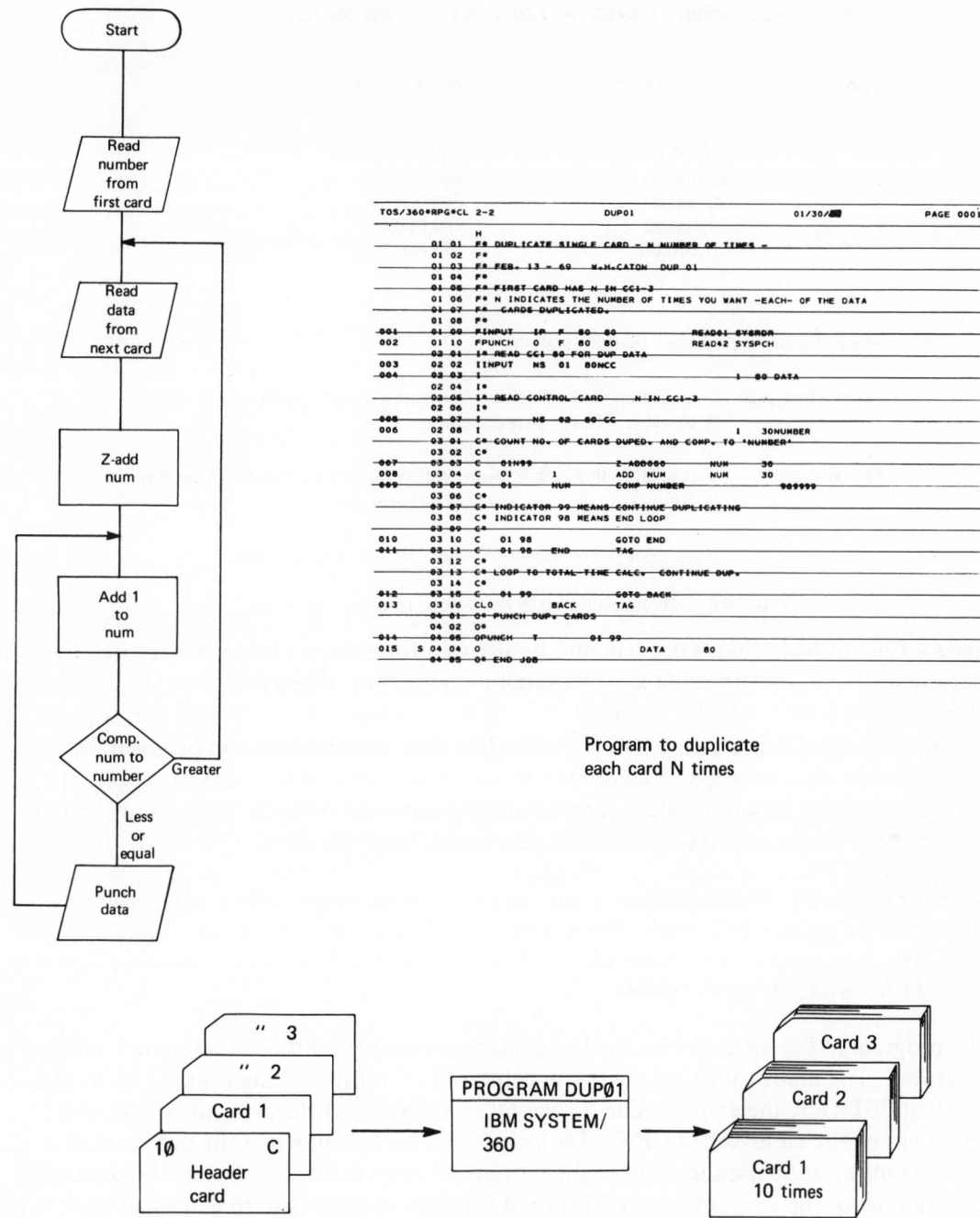

Program to duplicate
each card N times

FIG. 29-3   Looping by a branch into total-time–program DUPØ1.

Should a new value for **NUMBER** be brought in at any point in the data deck, the duplication will be changed to that number of times. The instruction **Z-ADD**, which initializes **NUM**, is done whenever indicator 99 is *off*, which is the case after a given loop is complete. Cards requiring variable numbers of copies may then be preceded by the appropriate **NUMBER** card, producing perhaps 3Ø of one kind and 12Ø of another.

Repetitive printing, where each line is *not* exactly the same as the previous one, but is based somehow upon it, may also be done by this method. A single data card can give information to

LIFE = 5   ACC. DEPR. CONST. = 1.00 COST = 1,000,000.00

YEAR	DEPRECIATION	BOOK VALUE
1	200,000.00	800,000.00
2	160,000.00	640,000.00
3	128,000.00	512,000.00
4	102,400.00	409,600.00
5	81,920.00	327,680.00

where calculations are done by the equations:

For the first year: Depreciation = (Acceleration Constant x Cost) ÷ Useful life
Book value = Cost – Depreciation

For later years: Depreciation this year = (Acceleration Constant x Previous Year Book
Value) ÷ Useful life

Book value = Previous book value – Depreciation this year

FIG. 29-4 Depreciation table in RPG—done from one input card.

designate a type of table that is needed, and by use of a formula, each line may represent another evaluation of that formula at some small increment of difference from the previous line. On a depreciation table, for example, the value of an item, and its useful life, is given; the amount of annual depreciation and the value left after depreciation can be given for each of the years of its estimated life. Figure 29-4 shows such a table, which was produced in RPG. Other tables may give function values for small increments of a formula, terms of an infinite series, successive integer powers, or discount rate tables, among others.

PROBLEM DEFINITION: *Write a program to generate a table giving centigrade temperatures and the corresponding Fahrenheit for each, by formula. One input data card gives a starting centigrade value, for the first line of the table, in columns 1-5, the ending value of the table in columns 6-10, and the amount of increment in columns 13-15. Each field has 2 decimals.*

The program in Figure 29-5 uses the branch into total-time method to prepare a table of temperatures. The input card gives values, in centigrade, for the starting value to be on the table, called **CSTART**, the ending value on the table, **CEND**, and the amount of increment between lines of the table, called **CINC**. Indicator 99 is turned *on* when the data card is detected. It may *not* be used to control the looping. Since certain things must be done only at the beginning of the loop, indicator 99 is used for that, so indicator 98 is instead used to go *on* and *off* to determine when the looping is complete. Remember that *all* the instructions in detail-time will be repeated after total-time output; you must be sure that indicators are set on and off as necessary to prevent certain things from being redone after a pass through total-time. The loop, labeled as **TABLOUT**, is in total-time, as you can see by the LØ in columns 7 and 8.
    Since the incrementing of C is done *before* C is printed, it is moved to the field named **COUT** for safekeeping until being printed, because when C is not yet to the value of **CEND**, it is incremented to prepare for the next pass. Output of the table line is done with indicator 98; when it is off, the table is complete. A total-time heading using indicator 98 would print before each line! Indicator 97 is used instead to print the heading at total-time; it is turned *on* at each new data card, but turned off during the detail-time calculations *following* its use to print the headings. Since the table could be longer than one page, the OF indicator specifies that the

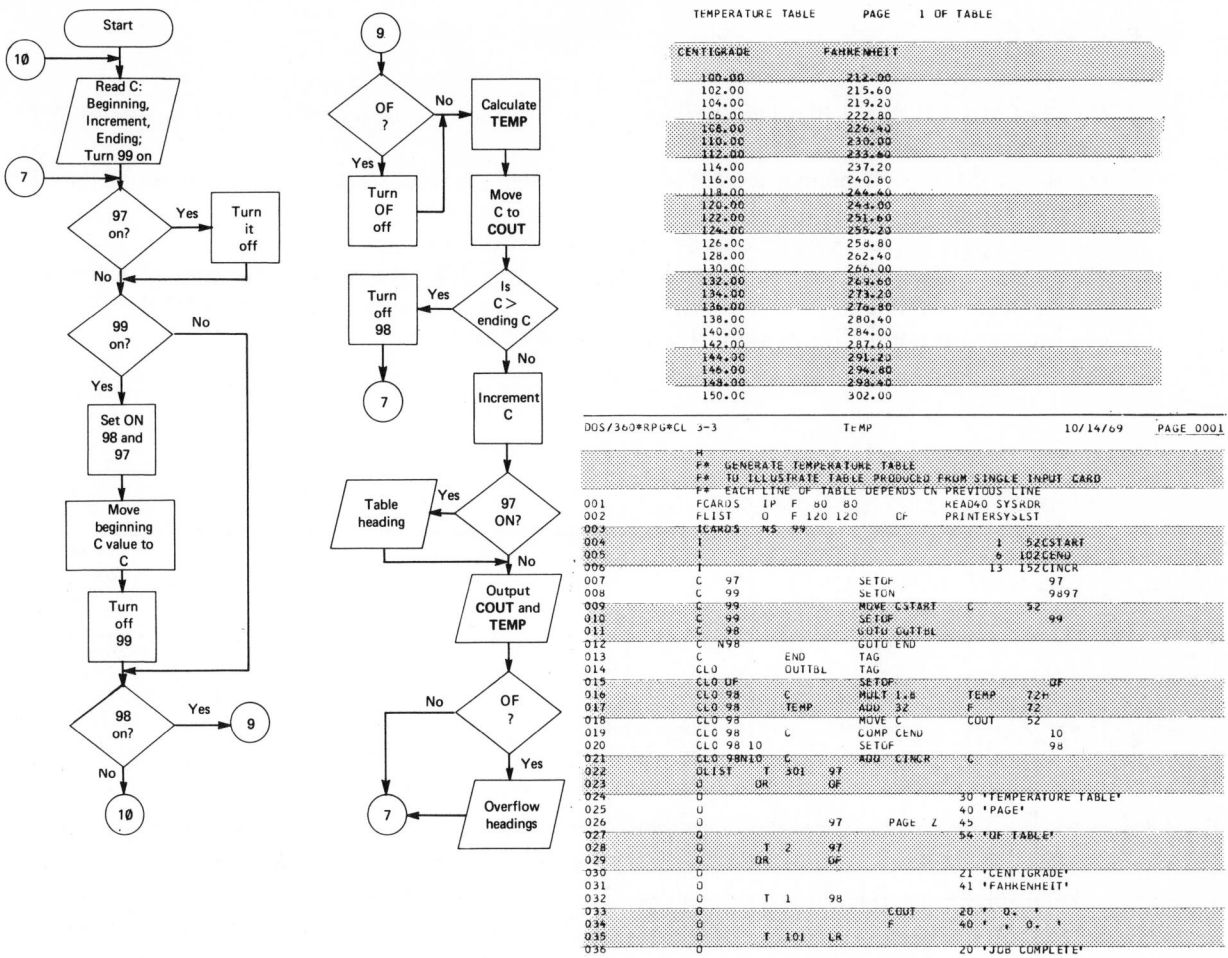

FIG. 29-5 Program **TEMP**—using branch into total-time. IBM SYSTEM/36Ø, Model 3Ø.

headings should be repeated on each page. It is turned off after it is used. Page numbers will be given on each page of the table; the field **PAGE** is *reset* by indicator 97, given alongside the field name, for individual table page numbering, starting with page 1 at each new table.

Although the program that does the temperature table has calculations *both* in detail-time and in total-time, it is far better that you restrict calculations to detail-time, and use the total-time only to contain the **TAG** used for logic change. By that arrangement, all incrementing, testing, and moving is done *after* a line has been printed, so that many of the steps necessary in the temperature table, for example, will not be necessary in every program of this type. Remember, however, that the total-time operations are *bypassed* during the first pass of the program; detail-time calculations may therefore be used for initialization of counters as usual, then a branch can change the logic to go *back* to the total-time specifications.

The branch into total-time method can also be used, at the detection of certain conditions and the setting *on* of the LR indicator, to cause a premature end of a job, by branching back to total-time to reach the end-of-file test without reading another card. The branch in the *opposite* direction, from total-time to detail-time, although possible in some implementations, such as the IBM SYSTEM/36Ø, CPS, is apparently not as useful. It is a branch *ahead* in the program cycle, causing the card currently in memory to be bypassed along with other things. It would however, allow RPG user-written subroutines in detail-time calculations to be accessed from total-time, as well as from detail-time, so that they need not be stored twice.

EXERCISES

1. Give CALCULATION specifications for each of these situations, where branch into total-time or **EXCPT** must be used.

   (a) Read a value for X, multiply it by 1, print it, then multiply it by 3, print it, and so on, for all the odd numbers from 1 to 99.

   (b) Read in a card, call it **CARD**, list it five times, then repeat with the next card.

   (c) Read in a value for N, print it, subtract 1 to get N − 1, multiply it by N, print the product, subtract 1 from N − 1 giving N − 2, multiply it by the previous product, print it, and repeat until the value becomes equal to 1. This is called N factorial, symbolized N!

Line	Form Type	Control Level (L0-L9, LR)	Indicators							Factor 1	Operation	Factor 2	Result Field	Field Length	Decimal Positions	Half Adjust (H)	Resulting Indicators		
					And		And										Plus	Minus	Zero or Blank
			Not		Not		Not										High 1>2	Low 1<2	Equal 1=2
																	Compare		
3 4 5	6	7 8	9	10 11	12	13 14	15	16 17	18 ... 27	28 29 30 31 32	33 ... 42	43 ... 48	49 50 51	52	53	54 55	56 57	58 59 60 61
0 1 (a)	C																		
0 2	C																		
0 3	C																		
0 4	C																		
0 5	C																		
0 6	C																		
0 7	C																		
0 8	C																		
0 9 (b)	C																		
1 0	C																		
1 1	C																		
1 2	C																		
1 3	C																		
1 4	C																		
1 5	C																		
	C																		
(c)	C																		
	C																		
	C																		
	C																		
	C																		
	C																		
	C																		
	C																		

2. Given on a punch card the value of an item as $5000.00 and its useful life as 5 years, calculate values by hand to form a depreciation table, using the same method as shown in the table in Figure 29-4.

Year	Depreciation	Book Value
1		
2		
3		
4		
5		

3. Write a loop, on the CALCULATION and OUTPUT FORMAT forms provided, to look up *every* argument in the table **TABK**, which is numbered from 1 to 5∅, by ones, with 2 digits, and ∅ decimals. Branch into total time, or use **EXCPT**, to get the corresponding function **TABAMT** and print it, 1∅ digits, 2 decimal places, edited, onto a report. Repeat until all 5∅ items on the table have been printed.

Line	Form Type	Control Level (L0-L9, LR)	Indicators And Not	Indicators And Not	Indicators And Not	Factor 1	Operation	Factor 2	Result Field	Field Length	Decimal Positions	Half Adjust (H)	Plus	Minus	Zero or Blank	High 1>2	Low 1<2	Equal 1=2
0 1	C																	
0 2	C																	
0 3	C																	
0 4	C																	
0 5	C																	
0 6	C																	
0 7	C																	
0 8	C																	
0 9	C																	
1 0	C																	
1 1	C																	
1 2	C																	
1 3	C																	
1 4	C																	
1 5	C																	
	C																	
	C																	
	C																	
	C																	
	C																	

Line			Form Type	Filename									Type (H/D/T)	Stacker Select	Space		Skip			Output Indicators									Field Name						Zero Suppress (Z)	Blank After (B)	End Position in Output Record				Packed Field (P)	Constant or Edit Word																								
															Before	After	Before		After		And			And																																										
																					Not			Not			Not																																							
3	4	5	6	7	8	9	10	11	12	13	14	15	16	17	18	19	20	21	22	23	24	25	26	27	28	29	30	31	32	33	34	35	36	37	38	39	40	41	42	43	44	45	46	47	48	49	50	51	52	53	54	55	56	57	58	59	60	61	62	63	64	65	66	67	68
0	1		O																																																													
0	2		O																																																													
0	3		O																																																													
0	4		O																																																													
0	5		O																																																													
0	6		O																																																													
0	7		O																																																													
0	8		O																																																													
0			O																																																									1				

Lesson 30

RPG SUBROUTINES

You will learn why RPG *subroutines are needed and how to write linkage for them.*

The following questions summarize the important points of this lesson and are answered on the back of this page. Should you already have experience with programming of subroutines, study the lesson and be sure you can answer the questions before attempting the problems at the end of this section.

1. What is a *subroutine*?
2. Contrast the *open* subroutine to the *closed* one.
3. What are *dummy* variables?
4. What is meant by subroutine *linkage*?
5. What prevents a closed subroutine from being executed inadvertently by the main sequence of instructions "falling into" it?
6. What instructions cause the closed subroutine to be executed when needed?
7. What instructions are used to accomplish a return from the subroutine to the proper place in the main program?
8. What *special* capability for RPG subroutines in RPG is available in the "extensions" and in RPG II?
9. How should RPG subroutines written in RPG be documented for later reference?
10. What is the purpose of the **EXIT** instruction?

ANSWERS

1. A set of programmed instructions necessary to direct the computer to perform a certain procedure usually used as a portion of another program.
2. An *open* subroutine is one that is directly inserted into the sequence of instructions right where it is needed; a *closed* one is placed in the program only once and executed by branching out of sequence and back.
3. *Dummy* variables are those used to identify variables and to specify what should be done with them, as in a subroutine. The actual field names used in the main program will contain the values of the variables, and the values are placed into the dummy field before a closed subroutine is executed.
4. The instruction set necessary to provide for getting back and forth between the main program and a closed subroutine.
5. A **GOTO** should be directly above it, and a **TAG** directly below, causing a branch around it to occur.
6. By an unconditional branch to the tag, which identifies its instructions. This is accomplished in the main program by a **GOTO** with a name, with a corresponding **TAG** for that name as the first line of the subroutine.
7. A conditional branch, which is dependent on indicator settings established before the subroutine is executed. This can be accomplished by several **GOTO** instructions conditioned by indicators.
8. Closed subroutines called by **EXSR**, coded with **SR** in columns 7 and 8 of the CALCULATION specification form, preceded by **BEGSR** and followed by **ENDSR**.
9. By listing the subroutine name and all field names and indicators used explaining linkage works, and stating what the subroutine is supposed to do.
10. To allow access to separately compiled assembler language subroutines.

A subroutine is a set of instructions that does some particular task usually subordinate to the major task of the program. Just as you might ask for the square root of 1∅ in the middle of a calculation, you might want the square root routine placed into a program where it is needed. A subroutine can cause the path of execution of the program to be altered by branching out of sequence to the subroutine and back, or it may be put into the sequential path in every place it is needed. The subroutine that is inserted into its proper place in as many places as needed is called an *open* subroutine; one that is placed in the program once and accessed by branching is called *closed*.

An *argument* is the value that is put *into* the subroutine, such as the number whose square root you take, or the variable name assigned to that value. A subroutine may have *no* arguments, as, for example, one that generates a random number to be used in probability, or may have *many*, such as one that receives an array and sorts it. The word *function*, which is often used to denote what the subroutine does, is also used to mean the answer obtained by it, such as the number 8 for the square root of 64. There are usually one or more function values obtained by a subroutine. Remember that the *arguments* are the values of the fields you put *into* the subroutine, and the *functions* are the values of the fields you get *out* of them.

A subroutine may be used *once* in a program or many times. When used once, it is usually an open subroutine. The same field name may, in this case, be used for both the argument name in the main program and the argument name in the subroutine. Should you need the value of P^R, P to the R power, for positive whole numbers of R, the repeated multiplication routine may be used, and the subroutine may be written with variable names **P** and **R**. An open subroutine, used *once* in the program to calculate P^R, is shown in Figure 30-1. Notice that the loop named **LOOP** is executed **R** times, after which indicator ∅1 goes *off* to denote the completion of the loop and of the subroutine. The operations **GOTO NEXT** and **NEXT TAG** are shown for illustrative purposes to identify the end of the subroutine; execution would fall through to there next, even though they were not present. The **GOTO POWER** and the **POWER TAG** show the entrance to the subroutine and may also be omitted, since an open subroutine is next in sequence, anyway.

When a subroutine is needed *more than once* in the program, use of an open one requires that the same basic set of instructions be *repeated*, but with some variation, in each place where needed. Figure 30-2 shows the subroutine inserted in *two* places in the same program. Notice that the variable names are different; the first one uses **P**, **R**, and **SAVE1**, while the second one uses **Q**, **S**, and **SAVE2**. The variable names must be different, but either a different indicator or the same one may be used to denote the completion of the routine. Should the same one be used, however, its previous setting would be replaced by that obtained as a result of the comparison in each routine so that once used, it need not be turned *off* before being used again. Tag names, however, *must* be different, since the tag serves to identify the *location* of a set of instructions and two different locations are intended. **LOOP1** and **LOOP2** are used in the two usages of the subroutine, respectively. **POWER1** and **POWER2**, and **NEXT1** and **NEXT2** are tags whose names must also differ in the two usages. They are shown, however, only for identification of the respective beginning and end of each subroutine, and may be omitted since the subroutines are in proper sequence and no actual branching to get to them is required.

The *closed* subroutine makes it possible for only *one* set of the subroutine instructions to

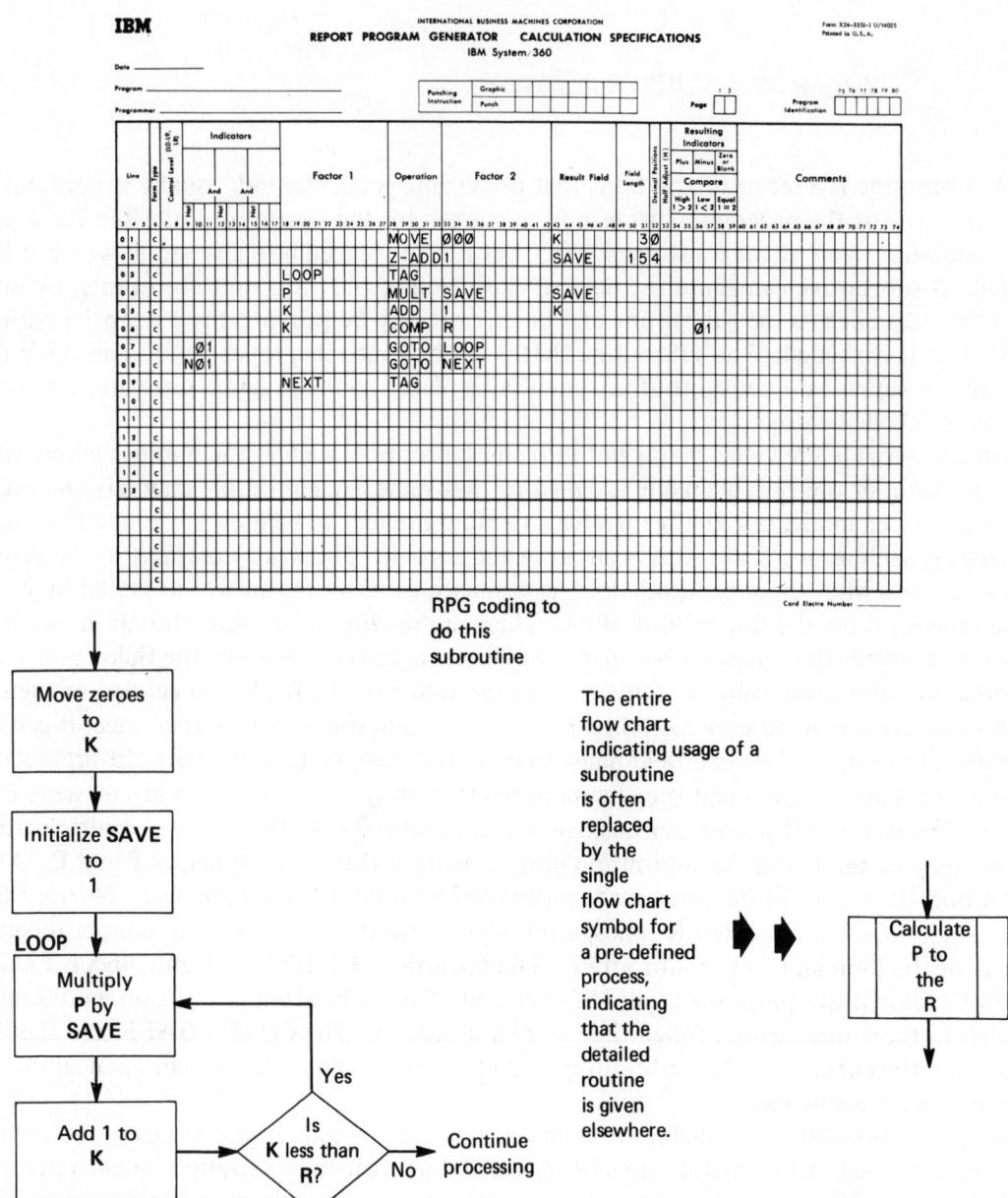

FIG. 30-1 Open subroutine—as used once in a program to calculate P to the R power.

be placed into the program, instead of many. No matter how many times the subroutine will be used in the program, the one set will usually suffice, since it will be accessed by branching out of sequence to it. *Dummy* variables names must be used, however, since it generally will on one instance calculate with a different argument from another. Before the subroutine is used, the appropriate argument must be placed into the dummy variable field. A **POWER** subroutine written for the calculation of X^M, where **X** and **M** are dummy variables, could be used to calculate P^R, by placing **P** and **R** into **X** and **M**, respectively, before branching to the subroutine. The function result will be available by whatever field name is used in the subroutine. Since any subsequent use of the routine will destroy its value, the function result should either be used immediately by that name in the main program, or else moved to another field for storage.

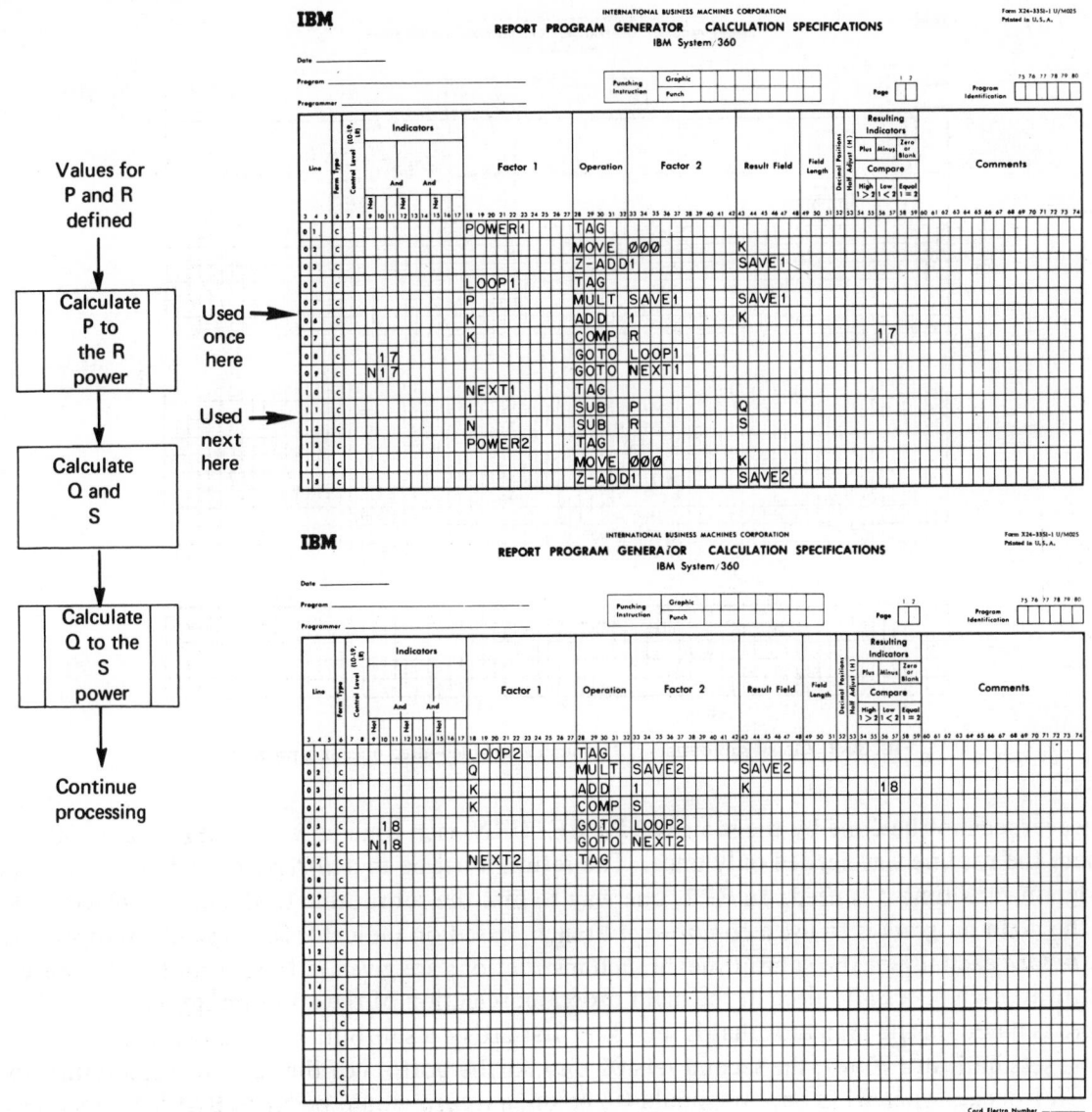

FIG. 30-2 Open subroutine—as used twice in a program to calculate P to the R power.

The instructions for a closed subroutine are usually placed *after* all other detail instructions. Figure 30-3 shows a closed subroutine named **POWER**, which is used once to calculate P^R, by substituting arguments **P** and **R** for **X** and **M**, respectively. The calculation of **Y** will be completed by the time the **GOTO RETURN** is encountered. Note that **RETURN** is a tag on the *instruction that follows the branch* to the subroutine. After completion of the subroutine, the instructions following **RETURN** cause the value of **Y** to be put into **SAVE** for later use in the program. Note also the **GOTO END** just above the subroutine **POWER**. This unconditional branch prevents regular calculations from "falling through" into the **POWER** subroutine, instead going to the label marked **END TAG** at the bottom of all detail-time calculations.

Instructions that accomplish getting back and forth from the closed subroutine are called *linkage*. Getting *to* the subroutine is done by an unconditional branch instruction that causes its execution to be next. No matter how many times the closed subroutine is accessed, the branch instruction to go there is the same for each usage. Getting *back* from the subroutine,

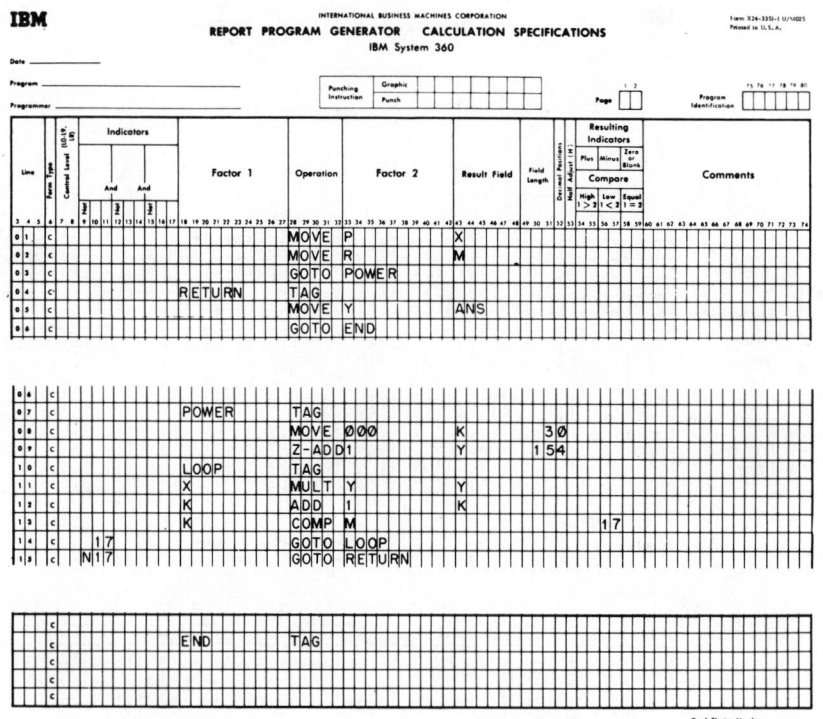

FIG. 30-3 Closed subroutine—with dummy variables—used once in a program.

however, cannot be done by the same **GOTO RETURN** each time, as was used in Figure 30-3, where the routine was needed only once. The return must be to a *different* location in the main program each time it is used. In RPG, one way to link the subroutine to the proper place back in the main program is to use a *conditional* branch, based on indicator settings. An indicator is set *before* each use of the subroutine; branch instructions are given in the subroutine to cause return to each necessary place in the main program; selection of the appropriate one for each usage is based on the indicator that is set. The first use of a subroutine, as shown in Figure 30-4, sets indicator Ø1 *on*; the second sets Ø2 *on*. At the bottom of the subroutine, a return to **BACK1** occurs when Ø1 is *on*, but should Ø2 be on, a return would occur to **BACK2**. Each use of the subroutine can have a different indicator and a branch instruction that is executed only when that indicator is *on*. Care must be taken, however, to be sure that indicators set on by a previous use of the subroutine do not cause error in the linkage. Once an indicator is turned on by the **SETON** instruction as shown in Figure 30-4, *it stays on until turned off,* so either turn it *off,* or arrange the **GOTO** instructions in such a way that the most recent return is encountered first in the linkage instructions.

The use of dummy variables in subroutines makes it possible for duplicated decks of those used often to be kept on hand. Documentation about what they do should be recorded before time filled with concern about other programs causes forgetfulness. It is important to write down the name, length, and mode of all dummy argument fields, and the name, length, and mode of all results, so that the programmer will be able to access the subroutine properly and return from it without studying it in detail. To write linkage, the number of returns and which indicators they use must be known. Any field names or indicators used in the calculations of the subroutine should be specified so that the main program can be written without use of them. Subroutine packages that are often kept are those for square root, raising to a power, and table

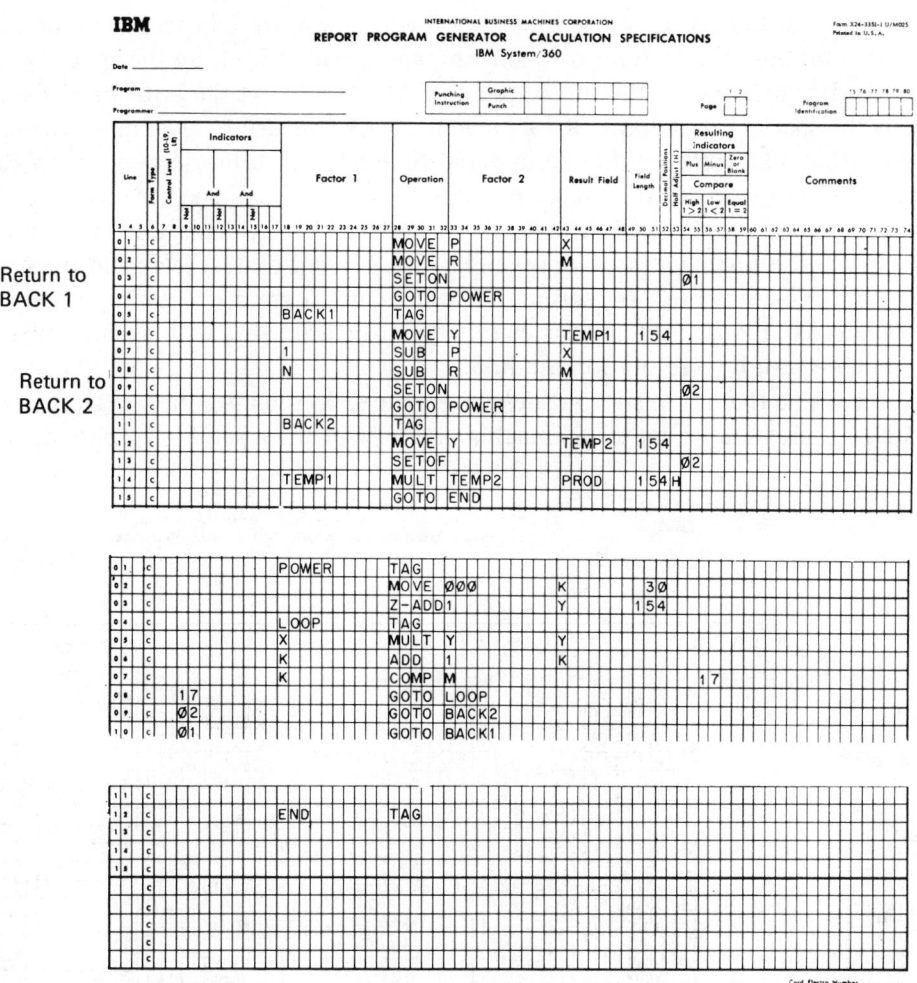

FIG. 30-4 Closed subroutine, with two programmed returns.

search for the smallest or largest number. Of interest in special business statistics applications are those for logarithmic and trigonometric functions, factorials, and random number generation.

A closed subroutine is placed in whichever calculation time it is needed, should it be needed there alone. When it is needed in both detail-time and in total-time, however, in the same program, it may be required on some implementations to be in *both*, causing you to need *two* decks of the subroutine, one with LØ in columns 7 and 8 and one with blanks there. This is caused by the fact that, in some implementations, branches are not always permitted back and forth between detail-time and total-time to gain access to the subroutine. When branches in both directions are permitted, as is the case with IBM SYSTEM/36Ø, Model 2Ø CPS, a subroutine in one place can be accessed from the other; care must be taken to get to the subroutine and immediately back after it is completed, so that execution does not "fall through" to cause errors in the sequence of RPG object program logiç.

Some implementations with the RPG "extensions", such as the IBM SYSTEM/36Ø, Model 2Ø, DPS, and the IBM 113Ø, and RPG II on the IBM SYSTEM/3, offer a special facility for closed internal subroutines, which eliminates any concern about where to put them. Instructions in this type of closed subroutine contain **SR** in columns 7 and 8, normally used for control level, on the CALCULATION specifications form. Subroutine instructions are placed *behind* all other total-time calculations on the form, and are identified by the special operation **BEGSR**, used with the name of the subroutine as FACTOR 1. At the bottom of the closed subroutine is the special operation **ENDSR**, which causes a return to the main program. This type of subroutine is accessible either from detail-time or from total-time by use of the operation **EXSR**, giving the name of the subroutine in FACTOR 2. Linkage for return to the proper place in the main program, either to total-time or to detail-time calculations, is automatic; you need not worry about setting indicators on and off to control that. Fields and indicators used within the subroutine, however, are common to the main program, so dummy names should continue to be used. Figure 30-5 illustrates this type of subroutine with calculations necessary to obtain a square root by an iteration method.

RPG also permits the use of subroutines programmed in the assembly language. The instruction **EXIT** causes branching to the machine address of the assembler program. The name

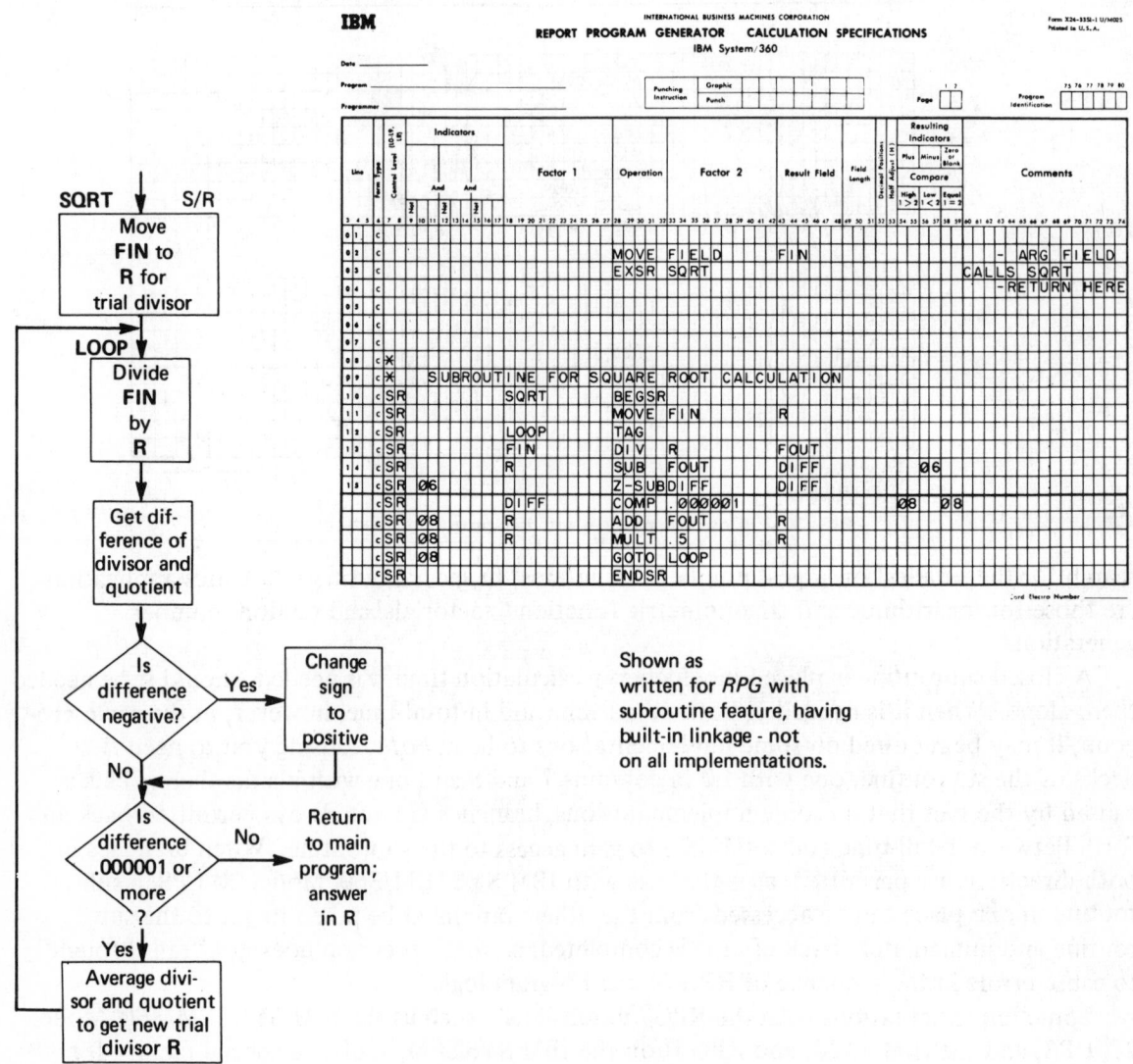

FIG. 30-5 Square root subroutine using iteration.

of the routine should be given in FACTOR 2 of the **EXIT** instruction, and must be the same as the name of the corresponding **START** instruction in assembler language program. Linkage for the proper return to the RPG main program is controlled by registers. Each data field and indicator used by the subroutine must be identified by a specification known as **RLABL**. In some implementations, the specification **ULABL** is used to identify fields and indicators brought *back* from the subroutine. Programs written in RPG using assembler language subroutines give full capability of the computer system, doing in that language many of the things not easily done in RPG. An RPG-to-assembler program offers easy access to assembler instructions for doing calculations and data manipulation without requiring that the entire instruction set be mastered.

On some implementations the **RLABL** operation may be used to establish field names that may later be used for initializing other fields to zeros or blanks. Since all fields are set to zero or blank at run-in time, these fields are available throughout the program, should long records of blanks or zeros be needed.

EXERCISES

1. Write a closed subroutine for each of the following:

   (a) Calculate the value of **N**!, defined as in Lesson 29, Exercise 1, part c, but by multiplying $1 \times 2 \times 3 \ldots \times \mathbf{N}$ in that order, storing the result in **PROD**. Write enough linkage for it to be used as many as three times within a program, returning to **OUT1**, **OUT2**, and **OUT3** with indicators $\emptyset 1$, $\emptyset 2$, and $\emptyset 3$, respectively. Assume that the value of **N** is length 4, $\emptyset$ decimals.

Line	Form Type	Control Level (L)	Not		Not	And	Not	And	Factor 1	Operation	Factor 2	Result Field	Field Length	Decimal Position	Half Adjust (H)	Plus High 1>2	Minus Low 1<2	Zero or Blank Equal 1=2
0 1 (a)	C																	
0 2	C																	
0 3	C																	
0 4	C																	
0 5	C																	
0 6	C																	
0 7	C																	
0 8	C																	
0 9	C																	
1 0	C																	
1 1	C																	
1 2	C																	
1 3	C																	

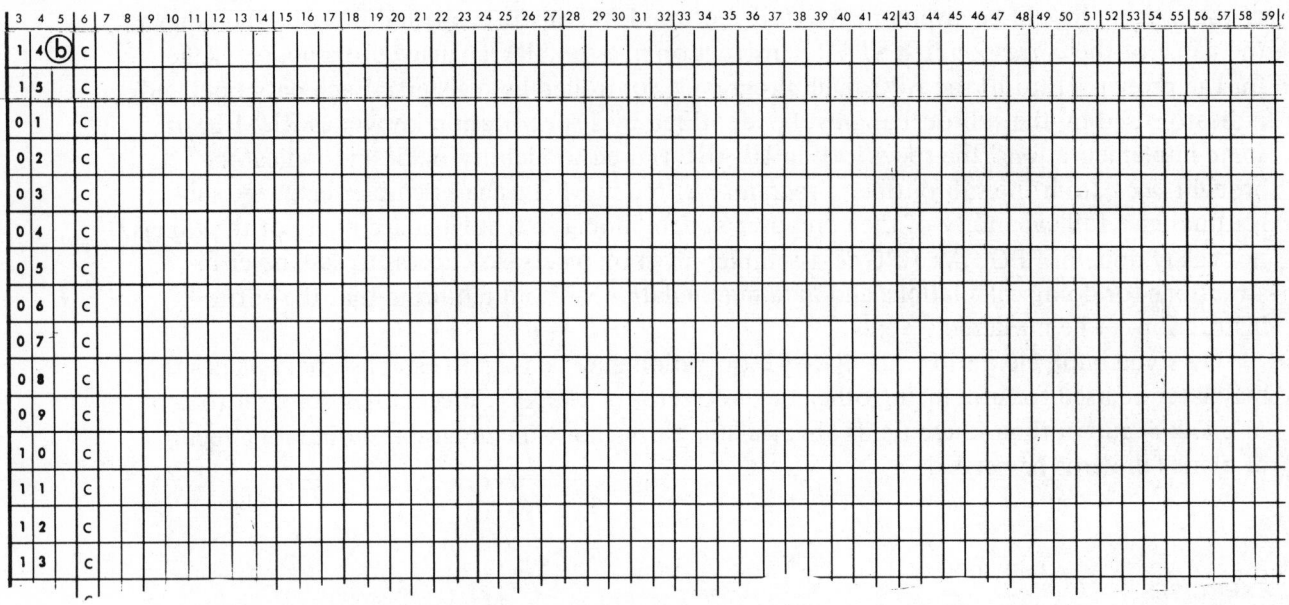

(b) Calculate service charge based on **VAL**. If the value of **VAL** is strictly between $0.00 and $100.00, it should be 1.5%; if **VAL** is $100.00 or over, it should be 2%; if **VAL** is zero or negative, it should be 0%. Write linkage with indicators Ø1 and Ø2 to allow return to tag locations **DETOUT** and **TOTOUT**, respectively, returning the value of **SERCHG** to the main program.

2. Write a closed subroutine to determine whether the value of integer field **NUM** is even or odd, returning the value of **K** as Ø if it is even, and as 1 if it is odd. Assume that **NUM** is 6 digits long, Ø decimals. Assume that your implementation has the subroutine feature, and use the **BEGSR** and **ENDSR** instruction.

IBM

INTERNATIONAL BUSINESS MACHINES CORPORATION

REPORT PROGRAM GENERATOR   CALCULATION SPECIFICATIONS
IBM System/360

Date _____

Program _____

Programmer _____

Punching Instruction — Graphic / Punch

Page ☐☐

Line	Form Type	Control Level (L0-L9, LR)	Indicators And Not / And Not / Not	Factor 1	Operation	Factor 2	Result Field	Field Length	Decimal Positions	Half Adjust (H)	Resulting Indicators — Plus	Minus	Zero or Blank — Compare — High 1>2	Low 1<2	Equal 1=2
01	C														
02	C														
03	C														
04	C														
05	C														
06	C														
07	C														
08	C														
09	C														
10	C														

3. Using $\sqrt{2}$ as a test case, do calculations by iterations as done by the square root subroutine in the program shown in Figure 30-5, recording values you get for each pass through the loop, until the answer is obtained.

	FIN	R	FOUT	DIFF	ABS(DIFF)	R + FOUT	$\frac{1}{2}$(R + FOUT)
Pass 1	2.∅	2.∅	1.∅	1.∅	1.∅	3.∅	1.5
Pass 2	2.∅	1.5					
Pass 3	2.∅						
Pass 4							
Pass 5							

Section 10

PROGRAMS TO WRITE

A. PROBLEM NAME: **INVSUM**:   summarize inventory
Write a program to give the quantity-on-hand for each item in inventory. The input deck is a merged deck with card formats as shown in Figure 2-7, with one master card followed by any number of receipt cards and issue cards. Use branching to handle each card type. Print one summary line for each item, giving item number, item description, quantity-on-hand *before* this run, total receipts and issues during this run, and *remaining* quantity-on-hand. Give appropriate headings on the report.

B. PROBLEM NAME: **COMPINT**:   amount earned by compound interest
Write a program to calculate the amount of return from an investment at compound interest, as given by the formula $A = P \cdot (1 + R)^T$, where

         P = principal invested
         R = annual interest rate, and
         T = number of years invested.

Use an open subroutine for **X** to the **N** power as given in the text for raising **1 + R** to the **T** power. Print account number, principal, rate, time, and amount of return under appropriate headings.

Field Information	*Columns*
Account number	1-2
Principal, 2 decimals	7-12
Rate, 2 decimals	17-19
Time, years	24-26

C. PROBLEM NAME: **ALTPAY:** to calculate payroll by three methods
Write a program to prepare a payroll for three types of workers, using branching to get to the appropriate instructions for each of the three types: hourly, salaried, and incentive. Hourly pay is calculated as rate of pay multiplied by number of hours worked, with all hours over 4Ø earning time-and-a-half pay. Salaried pay is calculated by dividing the monthly salary by 4 1/3. Incentive pay is by the table look-up method using the table shown in Figure 23-3. Produce a report giving all input information as well as the pay amount and the proper phrase—'HOURLY', 'SALARY', or 'INCENTIVE'—alongside the detail line. Give appropriate company name and column headings. Use input records from Figure 17-1, also used in Problem C, Section 8.

D. PROBLEM NAME: **LABELS:** make name and address labels
Write a program to use one-up label forms, printing four of each.
Option 1: Use a single-input data card, containing fields for name, address, city, state, and zip code; use exception line method or branch into total-time method.
Option 2: Use a set of three input data cards, containing the field for name on card 1, for address on card 2, and for city, state, and zip code on card 3. At detection of the third card type, turn on indicator L1 and use the branch into total-time method.

E. PROBLEM NAME: **DEPR:** produce a depreciation table
Write a program that uses the branch into total-time method to produce a depreciation table, such as the one shown in Figure 29-4. Depreciation and book value for each year can be found by the following formula:

$$DEPR_1 = (COST/LIFE) \times ACC$$
$$BOOK_1 = COST - DEPR_1$$
$$\cdots\cdots\cdots\cdots$$
$$DEPR_N = (BOOK_{N-1}/LIFE) \times ACC$$
$$BOOK_N = BOOK_{N-1} - DEPR_N$$

Field Information	*Columns*
Useful life of article	1-2
Acceleration constant, 2 decimals	4-6
Cost of the article, 2 decimals	11-20

F. PROBLEM NAME: **VENDNBR:** possible vendor number assignments
Write a program to find the number of vendor numbers possible using L columns, each of which may contain any of K different characters in each column. The formula is $K!/(K-L)!$. Use a closed subroutine for $N!$, to be used twice, once for $K!$ and once for $(K-L)!$

Example: Using five columns and digits 1-9 in any of them, without repetition, there are 15,12Ø different numbers possible, or 9!/4!.

Field Information	Columns
K: number of characters to be used	1-3
L: number of columns occupied	4-6

APPENDIX

EBCDIC CODING

Extended Binary-Coded-Decimal Interchange Code (EBCDIC)†

The 256-position table at the right, outlined by the heavy black lines, shows the graphic characters and control character representations for EBCDIC. The bit-position numbers, bit patterns, hexadecimal representations and card hole patterns for these and other possible EBCDIC characters are also shown.

To find the card hole patterns for most characters, partition the 256-position table into four blocks as follows:

Block 1: Zone punches at top of table; digit punches at left
Block 2: Zone punches at bottom of table; digit punches at left
Block 3: Zone punches at top of table; digit punches at right
Block 4: Zone punches at bottom of table; digit punches at right

Fifteen positions in the table are exceptions to the above arrangement. These positions are indicated by small numbers in the upper right corners of their boxes in the table. The card hole patterns for these positions are given at the bottom of the table. Bit-position numbers, bit patterns, and hexadecimal representations for these positions are found in the usual manner.

Control characters given are not needed when using RPG. They may be ignored. Some of the characters shown, such as the small letters of the alphabet, are not generally available. Many of these use an additional zone punch: the 9. These may also be ignored.

Of greatest benefit to know are those codes for alphabetic characters and the digits 0-9, given in block 1, and the array of special characters given in block 2. Some examples are:

	EBCDIC		Card Holes	
Character	*Binary*	*Hex*	*Zone*	*Numeric*
A	1100 0001	C1	12	1
R	1101 1001	D9	11	9
7	1111 0111	F7		7
$	0101 1011	5B	11	3-8
=	0111 1110	7E		6-8

†The first paragraph above and the EBCDIC chart opposite are reprinted by permission from *IBM SYSTEM/360, Principles of Operation.* © 1967 by International Business Machines Corporation.

Main Code Chart

		Bit Positions 0,1 →	00				01				10				11				
		Bit Positions 2,3 →	00	01	10	11	00	01	10	11	00	01	10	11	00	01	10	11	
		First Hexadecimal Digit →	0	1	2	3	4	5	6	7	8	9	A	B	C	D	E	F	
		Digit (9)	9	9	9	9	9	9	9	9									
		Zone Punches (12)	12				12	12		12	12	12		12	12				
		Digit Punches (11)		11				11	11	11		11	11	11		11			
		(0)			0		0		0	0	0		0	0			0		
Binary	**Hex**	**Punch**	**0**	**1**	**2**	**3**	**4**	**5**	**6**	**7**	**8**	**9**	**A**	**B**	**C**	**D**	**E**	**F**	**Punch**
0000	0	B-1	(1) NUL	(2)	(3) DS	(4)	(5) SP	(6) &	(7) –	(8)					(9)	(10)	(11)	(12) 0	8-1
0001	1	1			SOS				(13)		a	j			A	J	(14)	1	1
0010	2	2			FS						b	k	s		B	K	S	2	2
0011	3	3			TM						c	l	t		C	L	T	3	3
0100	4	4	PF	TES	BYP	PN					d	m	u		D	M	U	4	4
0101	5	5	HT	NL	LF	RS					e	n	v		E	N	V	5	5
0110	6	6	LC	BS	EOB	UC					f	o	w		F	O	W	6	6
0111	7	7	DEL	IL	PRE	EOT					g	p	x		G	P	X	7	7
1000	8	8									h	q	y		H	Q	Y	8	8
1001	9	8-1									i	r	z		I	R	Z	9	9
1010	A	8-2		CC	SM		¢	!	(15)	:									8-2
1011	B	8-3					.	$	'	#									8-3
1100	C	8-4					<	*	%	@									8-4
1101	D	8-5					(	)	_	'									8-5
1110	E	8-6					+	;	>	=									8-6
1111	F	8-7							¬	?	"								8-7
		(9)	9	9	9	9									9	9	9	9	
		(12)	12				12				12	12		12	12	12		12	Zone Punches
		(11)			11			11	11			11	11	11		11	11	11	
		(0)				0					0		0	0	0		0	0	

Card Hole Patterns

(1)	12-0-9-8-1	(5)	No Punches	(9)	12-0
(2)	12-11-9-8-1	(6)	12	(10)	11-0
(3)	11-0-9-8-1	(7)	11	(11)	0-8-2
(4)	12-11-0-9-8-1	(8)	12-11-0	(12)	0

(13)	0-1
(14)	11-0-9-1
(15)	12-11

Control Character Representations

NUL	Null		SOS	Start of Significance
PF	Punch Off		FS	Field Separator
HT	Horizontal Tab		BYP	Bypass
LC	Lower Case		LF	Line Feed
DEL	Delete		EOB	End of Block
TM	Trade Mark		PRE	Prefix
RES	Restore		SM	Set Mode
NL	New Line		PN	Punch On
BS	Backspace		RS	Reader Stop
IL	Idle		UC	Upper Case
CC	Cursor Control		EOT	End of Transmission
DS	Digit Select		SP	Space

Special Graphic Characters

¢	Cent Sign		–	Minus Sign, Hyphen
.	Period, Decimal Point		/	Slash
<	Less-than Sign		,	Comma
(	Left Parenthesis		%	Percent
+	Plus Sign		_	Underscore
|	Logical Or		>	Greater-than Sign
&	Ampersand		?	Question Mark
!	Exclamation Point		:	Colon
$	Dollar Sign		#	Number Sign
*	Asterisk		@	At Sign
)	Right Parenthesis		'	Prime, Apostrophe
;	Semicolon		=	Equal Sign
¬	Logical NOT		"	Quotation Mark

421

IBM Flowcharting Template, X20-8020-1. (Courtesy of International Business Machines Corporation.)

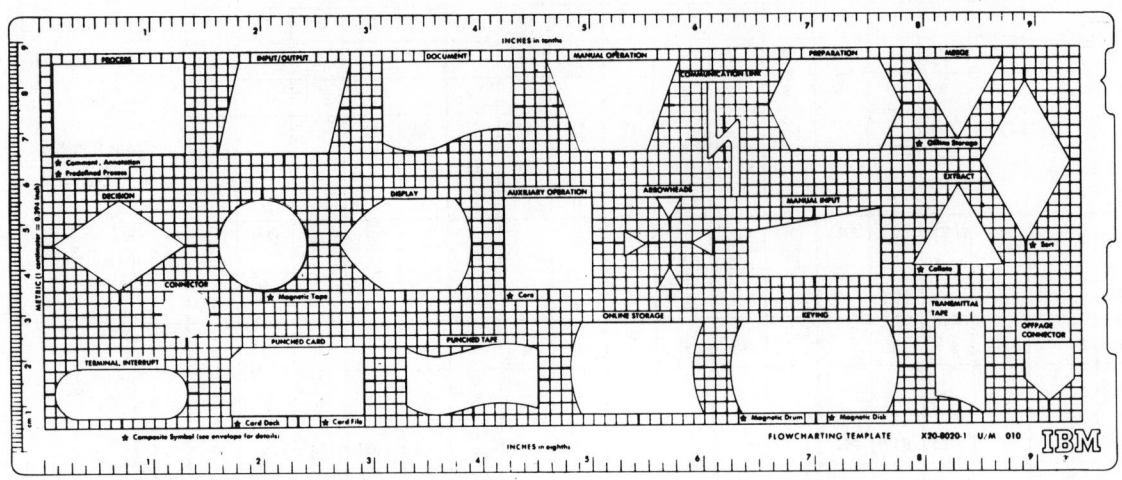

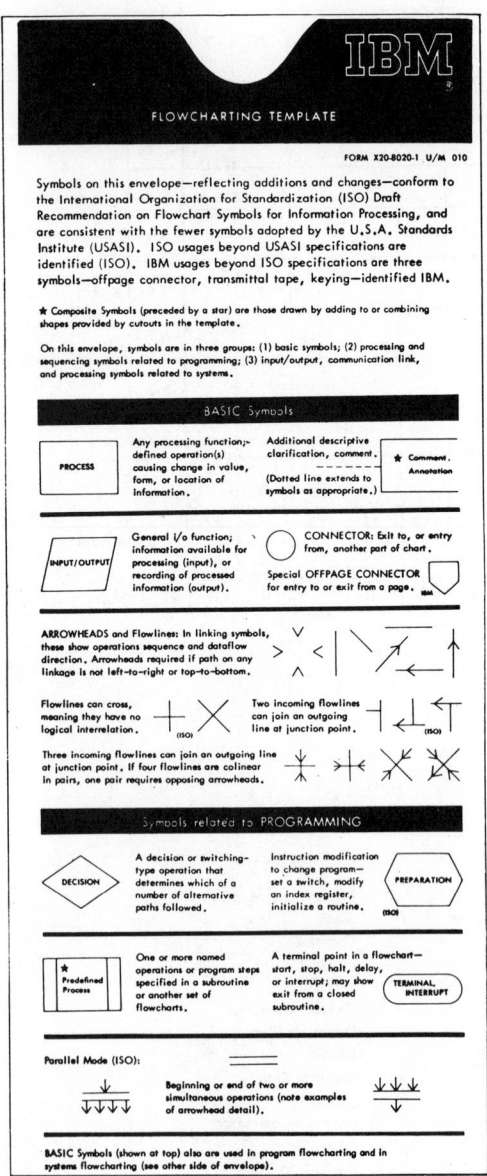

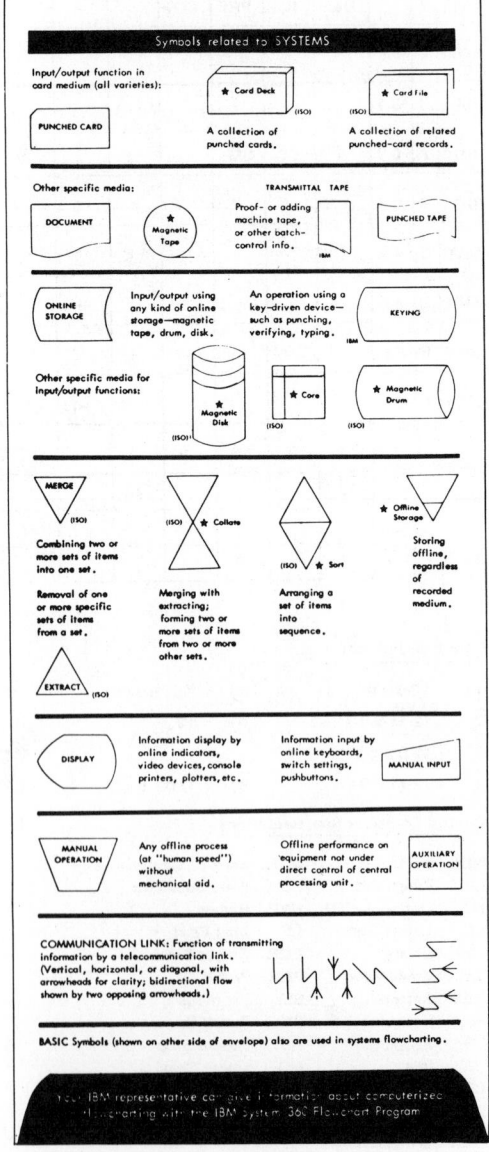

RPG Logic Flow for IBM SYSTEM/360 DOS/TOS RPG Object Program. (Reprinted by permission from *IBM SYSTEM/360 Disk and Tape Operating Systems, RPG Specifications.* © 1966 by International Business Machines Corporation.

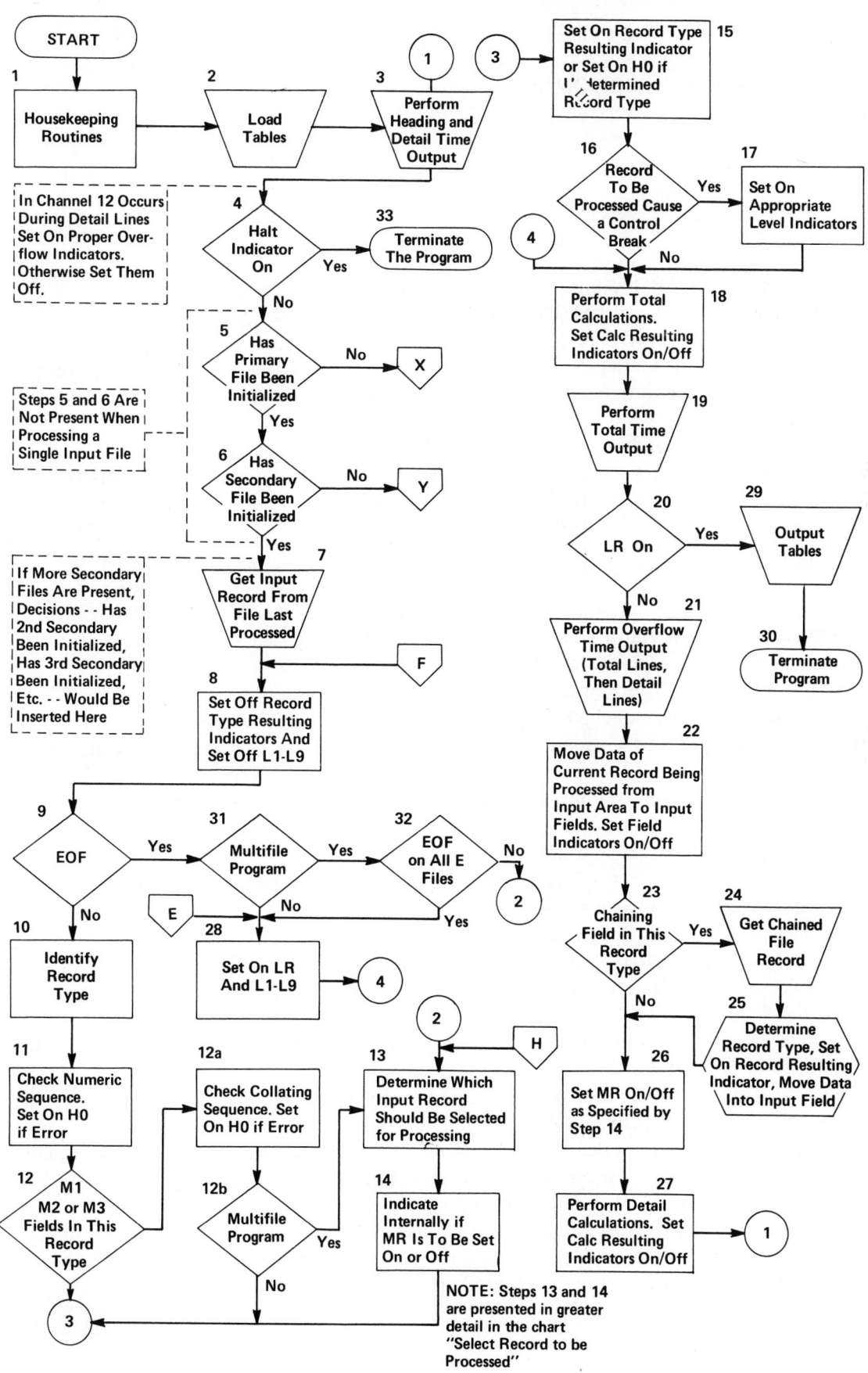

IBM 1130 RPG COMMENTS

1. RPG CONTROL CARD requires only an **H** in column 6.
2. FILE DESCRIPTION requires that record length be given, but not block length.
3. File names must begin with one of the 26 letters of the alphabet, and may be up to 8 characters long, but the first 5 characters of the name must be unique within that program.
4. Field names may be up to 6 characters long, and must begin with one of the 26 letters of the alphabet.
5. Symbolic device is not used; when disk is available, this field is used for another purpose.
6. Devices and their names:

IBM 2501 Card Reader	**READØ1**
IBM 1442 Card Reader/Punch	**READ42**
IBM 1442 Card Punch	**PUNCH42**
IBM 1403 Printer	**PRINTØ3**
IBM 1132 Printer	**PRINTER**
IBM 1130 Console keyboard	**CONSOLE**

7. Combined files are permitted only when using the IBM Card Reader/Punch.
8. Source deck cards are placed in order: **H, F, E, I, C, O.**
9. The LINE COUNTER form is never used.
10. When columns 1-5 are punched, they are sequence-checked; if they are out of sequence, they will be flagged on the source listing. Duplicate numbers on adjacent cards will not be flagged.
11. Length of numeric fields is limited to 14 digits; alphameric, 256 characters, except on tables, where it is 248.
12. Halt indicators H1-H9 are supported.
13. Alphabetic characters are the 26 letters of the alphabet; numeric characters are digits Ø-9; all others are special characters.
14. Packing of fields is not permitted on punch card output.
15. Indicators which are assigned to blank/zero are not initialized *on* when their fields are set to blank/zero at run-in time; neither are they set *on* after "blank-after" has been used to clear those fields.
16. An unlimited number of **PAGE** counters are available; use any field name beginning with **PAGE**, such as **PAGE1.**
17. **TESTZ** instruction can be used to test a field for either a 12 zone, an 11 zone, or any other zone, by using HIGH, LOW, and EQUAL indicators.
18. Zone tests for record ID code, comparisons, matching records, and control level tests, compare the zone portion of the stored EBCDIC configuration, and *not* the card zone, to that of the character you specify. Therefore a Z record ID test for the letter A would favorably compare to any of the other characters which had that same zone configuration in storage.
19. Use of a numeric field in calculation forces the hexadecimal F sign for the zone of positive results. D is always used for negative numbers.

20. Matching record indicators M1-M9 are supported.
21. RPG internal subroutines, using **SR** under CALCULATION LEVEL on the CALCULATION form, are available, with the corresponding **BEGSR, ENDSR, EXSR** statements.
22. External subroutines in the assembler language are permitted; **EXIT** and **RLABL** statements are used with them.
23. Offers a special external assembler subroutine named **INDX**, for indexing, to permit consecutive extraction of fields from a data record, or handling the N'th field within any data area.
24. Exception output lines are permitted. **OF** lines may not be specified to condition **E** lines, however.
25. Edit codes are available to use instead of certain edit words.
26. Does the overflow-time routine *before* the test for last record, not *after*. Both **OF** and **OV** indicators can be used by proper specification on the FILE DESCRIPTION form.
27. Edit words will permit an ampersand, &, to be used either in the status portion or expansion portion; it produces a blank when used in the status portion, but produces an ampersand when used in the expansion portion.
28. The console printer does not have a carriage control tape, and therefore skipping and overflow indication is not permitted on it.
29. The IBM 1132 printer does have a carriage control tape, but does not permit the use of channels 7, 8, 10, and 11.
30. Space before, or after, on the OUTPUT-FORMAT form permits entries of ∅, 1, 2, or 3.
31. Stacker select is operable if hardware for it is available on your equipment.

IBM SYSTEM/3 RPG COMMENTS

RPG for the System/3 is called RPG II; it is available in a card system and a disk system. It offers several extensions to the basic RPG language, several of which are mentioned here.

1. FILE DESCRIPTION form requires that record length be given, but not block length.
2. The multi-function card unit has two input pockets. One version of the printer has a dual carriage feature. The device names are: **MFCU1** and **MFCU2** for the input card reader; **PRINTER** for either the single printer or the left side of the dual printer; **PRINTR2** for the right side of the dual printer.
3. Numeric fields may be 15 digits long; alphameric fields may be up to 256 characters.
4. Tables may be put in either during generation or during execution.
5. **UDATE, UMON, UDAY, UYEAR** are all available.
6. External indicators U1-U8 and halt indicators H1-H9, are supported.
7. Stacker select is available both on input and output.
8. RPG internal closed subroutines, using **SR** under CONTROL LEVEL on the CALCU-LATION form, are permitted.
9. Overflow-time is done *before* the test for last record, not *after*. **OA, OB, . . . OG,** and **OV** are available for overflow indicators.
10. Exception output is permitted; the **OF** in overflow indicators cannot be used to condition **EXCPT** lines, however.
11. Space before, or after, may have ∅, 1, 2, or 3 used; blank means no spacing, unless *all* spacing is omitted, in which case, an automatic space *after* is done.
12. The printer does not require a carriage control tape, but instead is assumed to have the basic 60 line form, running from line 6 to 66. You may change this for other sizes by use of the LINE COUNTER specification form.
13. SKIP BEFORE, or AFTER, refers to line numbers and not to channel punches on a carriage control tape. Lines 01-99 are entered in exactly that way; lines 100-109 are entered as A∅-A9; lines 110-112 are entered as B∅-B2.
14. Matching fields indicators M1-M9 are supported; you are not permitted to use split matching fields, however.
15. Edit codes are permitted.
16. *File translation* can be used to translate any character to any other character.
17. *Arrays* are permitted, allowing indexing. They are defined on the FILE EXTENSION form, are available for input, calculations, and output. The instruction **XFOOT** is available for summing arrays.
18. The ***PLACE** instruction may be used to cause repetition of output several times on one line or card. This is especially useful where more than one image of the report is being printed at one time.

19. The ***DEBUG** instruction can be used to cause dumping of one field during execution, as well as to specify the condition of all indicators during that job.

20. The ***PRINT** instruction can be used to both print and punch information onto cards, with the option of printing the information over different columns from those where it is to be punched.

21. An **F** given under STACKER SELECT can be used to call the fetch overflow routine, to cause overflow-time output to occur before its usual time.

22. A **FORCE** instruction enables you to specify which record should be processed next, either from an I or C file, or perhaps from a special file exclusively for this purpose, a D, for demand, file.

23. The *look-ahead* feature is used to permit information to be obtained from records *following* the one being processed. This feature causes another record to be brought in just before detail-time calculations occur.

IBM SYSTEM/360 RPG COMMENTS

The many machine configurations of this computer system make it possible to use RPG in several different implementations. Among those available are BPS, CPS, DPS, and TPS, which means Basic, Card, Disk, and Tape Programming System, respectively; BOS, DOS, and TOS, which means Basic, Disk, and Tape Operating System, respectively; and OS, which means Operating System. The most noticeable difference in programming for these different systems is that done for the "small-scale" Model 20 with its IBM 2560 MFCM input as compared to that for the "medium- to large-scale" Models 25, 30, and up with separate input and output hoppers. For that reason, comparisons here will be concerned mostly with those differences, although others will alert you toward what to watch for when switching from one type of machine to another. By far the best of all the RPG reference manuals is that for CPS; it is replete with examples, and has an appendix section with many programming tips which can help a user on larger equipment to become aware of the many "tricks" that RPG can accomplish.

1. Source program cards are not always entered in the same order on the different systems. DOS/TOS uses the order H, F, E, I, C, and O; other systems use different orders.
2. The LINE COUNTER specification form is used only for specifying carriage control actions on reports which are to be temporarily stored on magnetic tape or disk, rather than being printed immediately.
3. Multiple-file input is possible on the Model 20 with the IBM 2560 MFCM Multi-Function Card Machine; it has two input hoppers and several stackers which allow many variations in stacker selection.
4. Interpretation of punch card output can be done when using the Model A1, IBM 2560 MFCM, on the Model 20.
5. CPS on the Model 20 permits the omission of several features on the FILE DESCRIPTION form that DOS/TOS requires, such as SYMBOLIC FILENAME, BLOCK LENGTH, and RECORD LENGTH; other implementations permit certain omissions when referring to cards, but do not permit them when referring to tape or disk.
6. CPS requires that primary files be listed *before* secondary files on the FILE DESCRIPTION form; DOS/TOS does not require any particular order.
7. CPS requires that control level assignments be listed *in order*, with the field assigned to L1 listed *before* the one assigned to L2, and so on; DOS/TOS has no such limitation.
8. In CPS, an output field in numeric mode, entered without a sign, need not be edited nor zero-suppressed as long as it has had no calculations done with it or on it; in DOS/TOS, however, all output fields in numeric mode must either be edited or zero-suppressed.
9. Although alphameric field lengths may be as long as 256 characters, alphameric comparisons are usually limited to 40 characters, and alphameric table look-up, to 80.

10. CPS does not permit the entry of tables at execution-time, but only at generation-time; DOS/TOS tables must be entered at execution-time; some RPG's permit a choice.

11. CPS does *not* do an automatic "single-space after" when the SPACE AFTER portion of the OUTPUT-FORMAT form is left blank; DOS/TOS does.

12. CPS and TOS both permit up to three matching record indicators; DOS permits nine.

13. CPS has only two overflow indicators, OF and OV; DOS/TOS has eight - OA, OB, OC, OD, OE, OF, OG, and OV.

14. DOS/TOS has an additional indicator, ∅∅, that is always *on*, for use on the OUTPUT-FORMAT form.

15. DOS/TOS has ten halt indicators, H1, H2, H3, up to H9, and H∅, which is used for automatic program termination upon detection of certain program errors; most other RPG's have only two, H1 and H2.

16. In DOS/TOS, the fixed-program-logic can be altered to branch from detail-time to total-time, but not vice-versa; CPS can branch both ways.

17. DOS permits the use of user date fields **UDATE, UDAY, UMONTH,** and **UYEAR**; TOS does not.

18. DOS permits use of external indicators U1, U2, up to U8; TOS does not.

19. Edit words in DOS/TOS may be longer than the defined field length of the field being edited; CPS requires that the edit word be designed to fit exactly.

20. The use of a minus sign as a dash or hyphen in the body of an edit word in DOS/TOS will cause a dash or a hyphen to print; in TPS, however, the $\bar{\emptyset}$ must be used in the body to obtain a printed hyphen, while in DOS it produces a printed ampersand!

21. DOS/TOS permits certain magnetic tape positioning which is not available in TPS.

22. DOS supports multi-volume, unlabeled tape files, on alternate reels in order to prevent delay in mounting additional tapes on the same unit; TOS does not.

23. The recently announced "extensions" of RPG for DPS offer several features of RPG II, only one of which is available on DOS/TOS. They are *user date* (available on DOS/TOS); *closed subroutines* within RPG; *edit codes* in addition to the **Z** presently available there; and *exception lines*, coded by an **E** on the OUTPUT-FORMAT form and used with the **EXCPT** instruction.

RCA SPECTRA 70 RPG COMMENTS

RPG is available for POS, the Primary Operating System; DOS, the Disc Operating System; TOS, the Tape Operating System; and TDOS, the Tape-Disc Operating System.

1. Numeric fields may be 15 digits long; alphameric fields, 256 characters long.
2. Line and page numbers must be present on all forms.
3. File format may not only be F or V, but G or W, respectively, for those cases where alternate areas for input are to be allocated.
4. Block and record lengths should be given.
5. Devices are:

PRINTER	printer
TAPE	magnetic tape
READER	card reader
PUNCH34	Model 234 Card Punch
PUNCH36	Model 236 Card Punch

6. Symbolic device names are **SYSIPT**, in all systems except POS; **SYSRDR** in POS; **SYSLST**, for printer or tape; **SYSOPT**, for punch card or tape; **SYS∅∅∅-SYS249**, for any other input or output, including tape and disc.
7. Halt indicators H1-H9 are supported.
8. **PAGE, PAGE1**, . . . are supported.
9. Overflow indicators **OA, OB**, . . . **OG**, and **OV** are supported.
10. A result field may be assigned with two different lengths on the CALCULATION form.
11. You may enter either ∅, 1, 2, or 3 for spacing before or after printing. However, if spacing *after* is omitted, one space will automatically be taken.
12. You may *not* skip to channels ∅9 or 12.
13. When indicators are assigned to detect blank/zero in a field, and that field is cleared by "blank-after", the indicators go *on*, immediately, for that field, to reflect that clearing, but the indicators assigned to plus/minus are not changed from their former setting.
14. Edit codes, exception lines, and internal **RPG** subroutines using **SR** in CONTROL LEVEL are not available.
15. The **Z** test, in the C/Z/D test for record identification code, tests for card zone 12, 11, zero zone, or none, rather than testing the 4 internal bits stored for the zone.

UNIVAC 9300 RPG COMMENTS

The 9000-series of computers have RPG systems in card, tape, and disk form. These remarks are based on the tape system.

1. FILE DESCRIPTION uses file format, record length, and block length for all tape files; they are permitted on card files, but are not required.
2. SYMBOLIC DEVICE is not used; instead, a logical device number is given there. On one system, 8 is for card reader; 9, for punch, and 10 for the printer.
3. *The order of entry of the source program cards is different:* H, R F, E, C, I, and O. When an invalid order is detected, the remainder of the source program is not used and generation is terminated.
4. Input files must be defined on the FILE DESCRIPTION form *before* output files.
5. When multiple input files are specified, at least one record type from each file must have a matching record field given. Up to 3 input files are permitted.
6. DEVICE NAME is given by:

CCPRI	1001 Card Controller, Primary
CCSEC	1001 Card Controller, Secondary
READER	card reader
PUNCH	column punch
CRP	column read/punch
ROWPNCH	row punch
RRP	row read/punch
PRINT63	Printer, 63 character set
PRINT16	Printer, 16 character set
TAPE	magnetic tape - 9 channel
TAPE7	magnetic tape - 7 channel

7. Several stacker select instructions are available to use on the CALCULATION form for stacker selection. Other routine stacker selection is possible when hardware permits.
8. When using indicators for both LOW/EQUAL or HIGH/EQUAL, you are not permitted to use the same indicator in both places, but must use two *different* indicators.
9. Indicators U1-U8 are *not* available; indicators H1, H2 are available.
10. Numeric fields may be up to 15 digits long; alphameric, 255 characters long.
11. Overflow-time output is *apparently* done both during detail-time output, and during total-time output, depending on the OF indicator. It is set *on* if the overflow channel has been detected during either total-time output or detail-time output, and remains on for the next detail-time cycle. After total-time output, the test for the last record is done *before* the test for overflow, rather than after.
12. It is possible to perform total-time operations *during run-in time,* using indicator LØ. You may use this technique to initialize fields to starting values or to turn on indicators before the job begins.

13. The **TESTZ** instruction is not available.
14. The move zone instructions are somewhat different. See the manual.
15. On a record ID test using Z, the characters & and – should be specified to test for a 12 zone, and an 11 zone, respectively, rather than any of the corresponding alphabetic letters with those zones.
16. Exception lines are not available; use branch into total-time method.
17. Edit words cannot be too long or too short, but *must* fit exactly.
18. An edit word may contain a floating dollar sign, but may *not* contain a fixed one. Use a separate alphameric literal to put a fixed dollar sign onto the report.
19. Interpreting onto the card face cannot be done.
20. The zero suppress stop digits are called "significance start characters".
21. When the "blank-after" feature is used, any zero/blank indicator assigned to that field does not get set *on* to reflect that clearing has been done.
22. SKIP BEFORE or AFTER must be changed from IBM conventions, because the carriage control tape is different, running from channel 07 to 01. The top of a new page is channel 07; overflow is detected by channel 01. Channels 02 through 06 are available for positioning the paper, but 08, 09, 10, 11, and 12 do not exist.
23. A constant may be defined in hexadecimal by using the character "X" preceding it; the constant must be enclosed in apostrophes.
24. The date field **D?TE** is available from the operating system and can be accessed by that name for output onto printed reports.
25. A repetition character, an * , can be used on the CALCULATION form or on OUTPUT-FORMAT form to cause conditioning indicators from the previous line to be used again.
26. Fields assigned as split control fields must be listed sequentially on the INPUT form.
27. SPACE BEFORE, or AFTER, permits 0, 1, or 2 to be entered. Using a 3, however, will not prevent generation; it will, however, produce only 2 lines during execution.

BIBLIOGRAPHY

A. ARTICLES

1. Daschler, Hannelore, "DPS RPG—Object Program Logic," *COMMON Proceedings*, April 16, 1969.

2. Friedberg, Lou, "RPG: The Coming of Age," *Datamation*, June 1967, pp. 29-31.

3. Leslie, Harry, "The RPG," *Datamation*, June 1967, pp. 26-28.

4. Ottman, Josef S., "Extensions to DPS-RPG," *COMMON Proceedings*, September 1969.

B. BOOKS

1. Cashman, Thomas J., and Fletcher, Dennis A., *IBM SYSTEM/360 RPG Programming*, Volume I and II, Anaheim, Calif.: Anaheim Publishing Co., 1967.

C. MANUFACTURER PUBLICATIONS

1. IBM STUDENT TEXT, *Introduction to IBM Data Processing Systems*, C20-1684

2. IBM SYSTEM/3:
   - C21-7502   *Card and Disk System, RPG II Fundamentals, Programmer's Guide*
   - C21-7504   *Disk System RPG II Reference Manual*
   - GC-21-7500 *Card System RPG II Reference Manual*

3. IBM SYSTEM/360:
   - A22-6810   *System Summary*
   - A22-6821   *Principles of Operation*
   - R29-0091,   *Programmed Instruction Course in RPG*
   - -0096,
   - -0097,
   - -0098

   Model 20:
   - C26-3600   *Card Programming Support RPG*
   - C24-9001   *Disk Programming Support RPG*
   - C33-6010   *Disk Programming Support, Extensions to the RPG, Planning Guide*

   Model 25, 30, and up:
   - A24-3510   *Functional Characteristics, Model 25*
   - C26-3570   *DOS/TOS RPG Specifications*

4. IBM 1130:   C21-5002   *IBM 1130 RPG Language*

5. IBM 407:   A24-1011   *Reference Manual, Accounting Machine*

6. RCA SPECTRA/70:   70-00-606 *RCA Information Systems, RPG Reference Manual, POS, DOS, TOS, TDOS*

7. UNIVAC 9200/9300: UP-7579   *RPG Reference Card*
                      UP-7620   *Tape and Disc RPG Programmers Reference*
                      UP-7588   *TIP's*
                      UP-7618   *Introduction to Magnetic Tape Processing*
                      UP-4149   *Introduction to RPG*
                      9200-21   *Rev. 1, Product Support Release for Conversion of 360-20 Card RPG*

INDEX